PRAXIS II® MATHEMATICS
Content Knowledge (0061/5061)

Mel H. Friedman, M.S.
Mathematics Instructor

Sandra Rush, M.A.
Mathematics Instructor

Research & Education Association

Research & Education Association
61 Ethel Road West
Piscataway, New Jersey 08854
E-mail: info@rea.com

PRAXIS II Mathematics Content Knowledge (0061/5061) with Online Practice Exams, 2nd Edition

Printed in the United States of America

Library of Congress Control Number 2012947437

ISBN-13: 978-0-7386-1052-8
ISBN-10: 0-7386-1052-6

The knowledge and competency framework upon which this book is based was created and implemented by Educational Testing Service (ETS®). ETS® is a registered trademark of Educational Testing Service. All other trademarks cited in this publication are the property of their respective owners.

Cover image: JGI/Blend Images/Getty Images

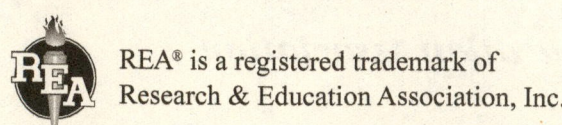

REA® is a registered trademark of
Research & Education Association, Inc.

About Our Editors

Mel H. Friedman, M.S., has a diversified background in mathematics and has developed test items for Educational Testing Service. His teaching experience is at both the high school and college levels.

Sandra Rush has a B.A. in mathematics from Temple University and an M.A. in ionospheric physics from UCLA. Her career has been focused on education, serving as a mathematics and physics instructor at the secondary school and college levels in Massachusetts and Colorado. Her interest in education has extended beyond the classroom to the publishing field, including writing and editing preparation manuals for standardized tests for all ages as well as one-on-one tutoring and coaching.

About Research & Education Association

Founded in 1959, Research & Education Association is dedicated to publishing the finest and most effective educational materials—including study guides and test preps—for students in middle school, high school, college, graduate school, and beyond.

Today, REA's wide-ranging catalog is a leading resource for teachers, students, and professionals. Visit *www.rea.com* to see a complete listing of all our titles.

Acknowledgments

In addition to our authors, we would like to thank REA's Larry B. Kling, Vice President, Editorial, for supervising development; Pam Weston, Publisher, for setting the quality standards for production integrity and managing the publication to completion; John Paul Cording, Vice President, Technology, for coordinating the design and development of the REA Study Center; Kathleen Casey, Senior Editor, for project management and editorial preflight review; Alice Leonard, Senior Editor, and Diane Goldschmidt, Managing Editor, for post-production quality assurance; Christine Saul, Senior Graphic Artist, for cover design; and Kathy Caratozzolo of Caragraphics for typesetting.

CONTENTS

CHAPTER 3
MEASUREMENT, GEOMETRY, AND TRIGONOMETRY   75

CHAPTER 4
FUNCTIONS AND CALCULUS
179

CHAPTER 5
DATA ANALYSIS, STATISTICS, AND PROBABILITY
261

CHAPTER 6
MATRIX ALGEBRA AND DISCRETE MATHEMATICS   377

CHAPTER

Introduction 1

Congratulations! By taking the PRAXIS II Mathematics Content Knowledge 0061/5061 test, you're on your way to a rewarding career as a mathematics teacher. Our book and the online tools that come with it, give you everything you need to succeed on this important exam, bringing you one step closer to being certified to teach. Our PRAXIS test prep package includes:

- A complete overview of the PRAXIS II Mathematics Content Knowledge test

- A comprehensive review of every content category tested

- Three full-length practice tests with online diagnostic tools to help you personalize your prep

There are many different ways to prepare for the PRAXIS II Mathematics Content Knowledge 0061/5061 test. What's best for you depends on how much time you have to study and how comfortable you are with the subject matter. To score your highest, you need a study system that can be customized to fit you: your schedule, your learning style, and your current level of knowledge. Let our experts help put you on the path to success and get you ready for the PRAXIS exam.

HOW TO USE THIS BOOK

About the Review

The review chapters in this book are designed to help you sharpen the basic skills you need to approach the PRAXIS II Mathematics Content Knowledge 0061/5061 test. This book contains a thorough review of the material tested in each of the content categories as detailed in the *Test-at-a-Glance* published by ETS.

Keep in mind that your schooling has taught you most of what you need to know to answer the questions on the test. The education classes you took should have provided you with the know-how to make important decisions about situations you will face as a teacher. Our review is designed to help you fit the information you have acquired into specific domain components. Studying your class notes and textbooks together with our review will give you an excellent foundation for passing the exam.

About the REA Study Center

The best way to personalize your study plan is to get feedback on what you know and what you don't know. At the online REA Study Center, we give you three full-length practice tests with detailed score reports that pinpoint your strengths and weaknesses.

Before you review with the book, go to the REA Study Center and take Practice Test 1 as a diagnostic test. Armed with your score reports, you can personalize your study plan. Review the parts of the book where you're weakest and focus your study on the areas where you need the most review.

After reviewing with the book, take Practice Tests 2 and 3 at the REA Study Center to ensure that you have mastered the material and are ready for test day.

If you are studying and don't have Internet access, you can take the printed tests in the book. These are the same practice tests offered at the REA Study Center, but without the added benefits of timed testing conditions and diagnostic score reports.

AN OVERVIEW OF THE TEST

What's on the Test?

The PRAXIS II Mathematics Content Knowledge exam is designed to assess the mathematical knowledge and competencies for a beginning secondary school teacher. The exam addresses five main content categories and five process categories.

The content categories were designed to measure the ability to integrate knowledge of mathematics and may involve more than one competency, as well as competencies from more than one content area.

In addition to content categories, the test contains process categories. Entry-level mathematics teachers must demonstrate that they have an understanding of the various ways in which math content knowledge is acquired and used. The process categories test and assess this ability, and one or more may be applied to any of the content topics in the test.

There are 50 multiple-choice questions on the PRAXIS Mathematics test, and each contains four response options, (A) through (D). You are given two hours to complete the test, so be aware of the amount of time you are spending on each question. Using the online practice tests will help you pace your time evenly, efficiently, and productively.

Test Structure: PRAXIS II Mathematics Content Knowledge		
Content Categories	Approximate Number of Questions	Percentage
I. Algebra and Number Theory	8	16%
II. Measurement	3	6%
Geometry	5	10%
Trigonometry	4	8%
III. Functions	8	16%
Calculus	6	12%
IV. Data Analysis and Statistics	5–6	10–12%
Probability	2–3	4–6%
V. Matrix Algebra	4–5	8–10%
Discrete Mathematics	3–4	6–8%
Process Categories		
Mathematical Problem Solving; Mathematical Reasoning and Proofs; Mathematical Connections; Mathematical Representation; Use of Technology.	Distributed across all content categories	

Format of the Test

The PRAXIS II Mathematics Content Knowledge 0061/5061 exam is offered in paper- and computer-based formats. The test is made up of multiple-choice questions which are designed to assess your knowledge of the domains and related skills mentioned previously and reviewed in this book. In general, the multiple-choice questions are intended to make you think logically. You are expected in most cases to demonstrate more than an ability to recall factual information; you may be asked to think critically about the information, analyze it, consider it carefully, compare it with knowledge you have, or make a judgment about it.

Answering the multiple-choice questions is straightforward. You must mark your choice on a separate answer sheet or, if you are taking the computer-based version of the test, directly below each test item. You should have plenty of time in which to complete the test, so speed is not important. However, be aware of the amount of time you are spending on each question; maintaining a steady pace when answering the questions will ensure that you complete the whole test.

When Should the Test be Taken?

Traditionally, teacher preparation programs determine when their candidates take the various tests required for teacher certification. These programs will also clear you to take the examinations and make final recommendations for certification to the certifying authority of your particular state. For those seeking certification right out of school, the test is generally taken just before graduation. If you are planning to become a teacher of secondary school mathematics you must take and pass this test.

The PRAXIS II Mathematics Content Knowledge 0061/5061 exam is administered six times a year at locations throughout the country. The usual testing day is Saturday, but the test may be taken on an alternate day if a conflict, such as a religious obligation, exists.

The PRAXIS Registration Bulletin offers detailed information about test dates and locations, as well as registration information and instructions on how to arrange testing accommodations for those with special needs. The registration bulletin is available at *www.ets.org/praxis/*.

Is There a Registration Fee?

Yes, you must pay a registration fee to take the PRAXIS Mathematics exam. If you are using the registration form, all fees must be paid in full by personal check, cashier's check, or money order. All payments must be made in U.S. dollars. Cash will not be accepted. If you are registering via the Internet or phone during the emergency registration period, payment must be made by VISA or MasterCard.

A Note About Graphing Calculators

Graphing calculators are required for the PRAXIS Mathematics test, so one should be used during your practice tests in this book. On test day, bring your graphing calculator to the testing site as one will not be provided. ETS states that the calculator should be able to:

1. produce a graph of a function within an arbitrary viewing window.

2. find the zeros of a function.

3. compute the derivative of a function numerically.

4. compute definite integrals numerically.

Calculator memories need not be cleared. No calculators with typewriter-type QWERTY keyboards and electronic writing pads are allowed. Please see the ETS website for further details on the types of calculating devices that are prohibited.

SCORING THE EXAM

Keep in mind that examinees are not penalized for wrong answers. A question answered correctly is worth one raw point, and your total raw score is the number of questions answered correctly on the full test. Passing scores vary from state to state, and test-takers should check with their state board of education for their state's requirements.

How many correctly answered questions equal a passing grade? According to ETS, there is no way to predict this. There are several editions of each test, and each edition contains different questions. The questions on one edition may be slightly more difficult (or easier) than those on another edition. To make all editions of a test comparable, the conversion tables adjust for difficulty among editions. There is no way to predict which edition of the test you will take.

When and Will I Receive My Score Report?

Test scores will be mailed approximately four weeks after test day to those who you designated to receive them. There is a fee for each additional score report requested.

6-WEEK STUDY PLAN

Although our study plan is designed to be used in the six weeks before the exam, it can be condensed or expanded to suit your schedule. Be sure to set aside enough time (at least two hours each day) to study. The more time you spend studying, the more prepared and confident you will be on the day of the test.

Week	Activity
1	At the REA Study Center, take Practice Test 1 as a diagnostic exam. Your detailed score report will identify topics where you need the most review.
2–3	Study the review chapters. Use your score reports from Practice Test 1 to focus your study. Useful study techniques include highlighting key terms and information, taking notes as you review the book's sections, and putting new terms and information on note cards to help retain the information.
4	Reread all your note cards, refresh your understanding of the exam's competencies and skills, review your college textbooks and class notes. This is also the time to consider any other supplementary materials that will help you study.
5	Condense your notes and findings. A structured list of important facts and concepts, based on your note cards and this book's content categories, will help you thoroughly review for the test. Review the answers and explanations for all missed questions.
6	Take Practice Test 2 at the REA Study Center to see how much your score has improved. If you still got a few questions wrong, go back to the review and study any topics you missed. Now take Practice Test 3 and see how much you have improved with this guide and the diagnostic feedback from the REA Study Center.

TEST-TAKING TIPS

Although you may not be familiar with tests like the PRAXIS Mathematics, this book will acquaint you with this type of exam and help alleviate your test-taking anxieties. Listed below are ways to help you become accustomed to this PRAXIS exam, some of which may be applied to other tests.

Tip 1. Become comfortable with the format of the test. When you are practicing, stay calm and pace yourself. After simulating the test only once, you will boost your chances of doing well, and you will be able to sit down for the actual PRAXIS II Mathematics Content Knowledge 0061/5061 with much more confidence.

Tip 2. Familiarize yourself with the directions on the test. This will not only save time but will also help you avoid anxiety (and the mistakes anxiety causes).

Tip 3. Read all of the possible answers. Just because you think you have found the correct response, do not automatically assume that it is the best answer. Read through each choice to be sure that you are not making a mistake by jumping to conclusions.

Tip 4. Use the process of elimination. Go through each answer choice and eliminate as many as possible. If you can eliminate two answer choices, you will give yourself a better chance of getting the item correct since there will only be two choices left from which to make your guess. Do not leave an answer blank; it is better to guess than to not answer a question on the PRAXIS as there is no additional penalty for wrong answers.

Tip 5. Place a question mark in your answer booklet next to answers you guessed, and re-check them later if you have time.

Tip 6. Work at a steady pace and avoid focusing on any one question too long. Taking the timed practice tests online at the REA Study Center will help you learn to budget your time.

Tip 7. If you are taking the paper-and-pencil exam, be sure that the answer circle you are marking corresponds to the number of the question in the test booklet. The test is graded automatically, and marking one answer in the wrong space can throw off your answer key and your score. Be careful to mark your answers in accurate sequence.

Tip 8. If you are taking the computer-based exam, be sure that your answer registers before you go to the next item. Look at the screen to see that your mouse-click causes the pointer to darken the proper oval. If your answer doesn't register, you won't get credit for that question.

THE DAY OF THE TEST

On the day of the test, make sure to dress comfortably so that you are not distracted by being too hot or too cold while taking the test. Plan to arrive at the test center early. This will allow you to collect your thoughts and relax, and will also spare you the anguish that comes with being late.

Check your PRAXIS II Mathematics Content Knowledge 0061/5061 registration information to find out what time to arrive at the testing center. Also, 24 hours before the test, return to your testing account and review your admission ticket for any changes. If there is a change, you will have to print out a new ticket.

Before you leave for the test center, make sure that you have your admission ticket and two forms of identification, one of which must contain a recent and recognizable photograph, your name, and your signature (e.g., a driver's license). All documents must be originals (no copies). You will not be admitted to the test center and you will forfeit your test fees if you do not have proper identification.

If you are taking the paper-based exam, you must bring several sharpened No. 2 pencils with erasers, as none will be provided at the test center. Don't forget your graphing calculator, but note that all dictionaries, textbooks, notebooks, briefcases, or packages will not be permitted. Do not bring cell phones, smart phones, PDAs, and other electronic or photographic devices into the test center. Drinking, smoking, and eating are prohibited.

Good luck on the PRAXIS II Mathematics Content Knowledge test!

Number Theory and Algebra

NUMBER THEORY

The Real Number System and Its Subsystems

The set of all real numbers has various components. These components are the set of all natural numbers, $\mathbb{N}$, the set of all whole numbers, W, the set of all integers, $\mathbb{Z}$, the set of all rational numbers, $\mathbb{Q}$, and the set of all irrational numbers, S. Then,

$\mathbb{N} = \{1, 2, 3, ...\}$, *natural numbers (NO 0) (+)*

$W = \{0, 1, 2, 3, ...\}$, *whole numbers (YES 0) (+)*

$\mathbb{Z} = \{..., -3, -2, -1, 0, 1, 2, 3, ...\}$, *integers (includes negative)*

$\mathbb{Q} = \left\{ \dfrac{a}{b} \mid a, b \in \mathbb{Z} \text{ and } b \neq 0 \right\}$; *rational numbers*

and $S = \{x \mid x$ is a nonterminating decimal number without a repeating pattern$\}$. *irrational*

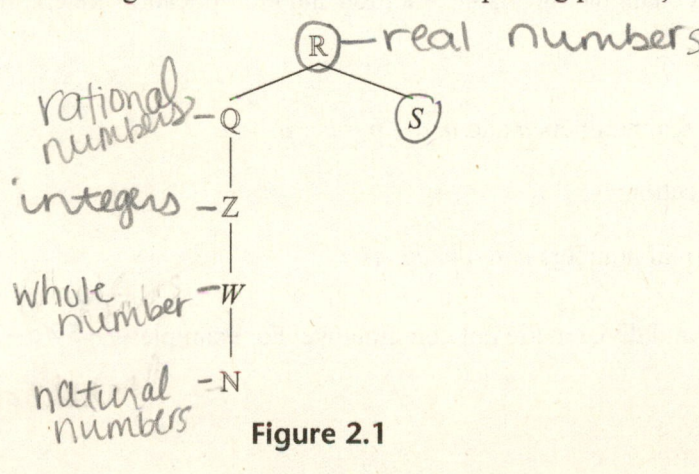

real numbers
rational numbers — Q
integers — Z
whole number — W
natural numbers — N

Figure 2.1

It is obvious that $\mathbb{N} \subseteq W, W \subseteq \mathbb{Z}$, and $\mathbb{Z} \subseteq \mathbb{Q}$, but a similar relationship does not hold between $\mathbb{Q}$ and S (see Figure 2.1). In fact, there are no numbers common to both sets. The elements of S cannot be expressed as simple fractions. More specifically, the decimal equivalents for elements of $\mathbb{Q}$ are

(1) terminating or

(2) nonterminating with a repeating block.

For example, $\frac{1}{2} = .5$ and $\frac{1}{3} = .\overline{3}$ are rational numbers and $\sqrt{2} = 1.414213...$ and π are irrational numbers.

All real numbers are normally represented by $\mathbb{R}$ and $\mathbb{R} = \mathbb{Q} \cup S$. This means that every real number is either rational or irrational. A nice way to visualize real numbers geometrically is that real numbers can be put in a one-to-one correspondence with the set of all points on a line.

Real Number Properties

The rules used in performing operations on real numbers are based on the following properties that are often taken for granted.

Closure Property

A set is **closed** under an operation if when the operation is performed on two members of the set, the result is also a member of the set. The real numbers are closed under addition and multiplication. For every real number a and b, $a + b$ and ab are real numbers. However, not every set is closed under all operations. For example, the whole numbers are not closed under subtraction. That is, $6 - 9 = -3$, and -3 is not a whole number.

Commutative Properties of Addition and Multiplication

An operation is **commutative** if the order of the numbers it is being performed on can be changed without changing the result. Addition and multiplication are commutative.

For addition:

For any real numbers a and b, $a + b = b + a$.

For multiplication:

For any real numbers a and b, $ab = ba$.

Subtraction and division are not commutative. For example: $7 - 5 \neq 5 - 7$ and $\frac{1}{2} \neq \frac{2}{1}$.

Associative Properties of Addition and Multiplication

As operation is **associative** if you can group the numbers it is being performed on in any way without changing the result. Addition and multiplication are associative.

For addition:

For any real numbers a, b, and c, $(a + b) + c = a + (b + c)$.

For multiplication:

For any real numbers a, b, and c, $(ab)c = a(bc)$.

Subtraction and division are not associative. For example: $(8 - 2) - 6 \neq 8 - (2 - 6)$ and $(10 \div 5) \div 2 \neq 10 \div (5 \div 2)$.

Distributive Property of Multiplication over Addition

The Distributive Property of Multiplication over Addition states multiplying a number by a sum is equal to the sum of the products of the number and each of the addends. Additionally, the Distributive Property allows you to pull a common factor out of a sum.

For any real numbers a, b and c, $a(b + c) = ab + ac$.

Identity Properties of Addition and Multiplication

When an operation is performed on a number and the identity of that operation, the number does not change. The additive identity is 0 because adding zero to a number does not change the number. The multiplicative identity is 1 because multiplying a number by 1 does not change the number.

For any real number a, $a + 0 = 0 + a = a$ and $a \times 1 = 1 \times a = a$.

Inverse Properties of Addition and Multiplication

The inverse of an operation 'undoes' the operation. Addition and subtraction are inverse operations as are multiplication and division. When an operation is performed on a number and its inverse under that operation, the result is the identity element of that operation. The additive inverse of any number is its opposite and the multiplicative inverse is its reciprocal.

For every real number a, there is a real number $-a$ such that $a + (-a) = 0$.

For every nonzero real number a, there is a real number a^{-1} such that $a \times a^{-1} = a^{-1} \times a = 1$.

EXAMPLE 1

Name the property illustrated by each equation.

a) $(a+2)+b=a+(2+b)$ *associative of add.*

✗ b) $7(a\times1)=7a$ *Identity prop. of mult.*

c) $a^2+2a=a(a+2)$ *distributive of mult. over addition*

d) $a^2+b^2=b^2+a^2$ *commutative of add.*

inverse? e) $a(b+-b)=a(0)$ *Identity Prop of add.*

✗ f) $(a+4)b=b(a+4)$ *Commutative prop. of mult.*

SOLUTION

a) The Associative Property of Addition is used because the parentheses indicate that the terms are grouped differently.

b) The Identity Property of Multiplication is used because the right side of the equation simplifies $a \times 1$ to a.

c) The Distributive Property of Multiplication over Addition is used because a common factor has been pulled out of a sum.

d) The Commutative Property of Addition is used because the sum is the same despite the order of the terms.

e) The Identity Property of Addition is used because the sum of b and its opposite is the additive identity, 0.

f) The Commutative Property of Multiplication is used because the product is the same despite the order of the expressions being multiplied.

Complex Numbers

Because the square of a real number cannot be negative, an equation like $x^2 = -1$ has no solution in the real numbers. The solution to this equation is an imaginary number. Imaginary numbers consist of all numbers of the form bi where b is a non-zero real number and i is the imaginary unit such that $i^2 = -1$. Obviously, imaginary numbers are not real numbers. They are part of the complex number system, denoted $\mathbb{C}$, which contains both real and imaginary numbers. The complex numbers consist of all sums $a + bi$, where a and b are real numbers. Every real number is a complex number because $a = a + 0i$. Therefore, the real numbers are a subset of the complex numbers ($\mathbb{R} \subseteq \mathbb{C}$) (See Figure 2.2).

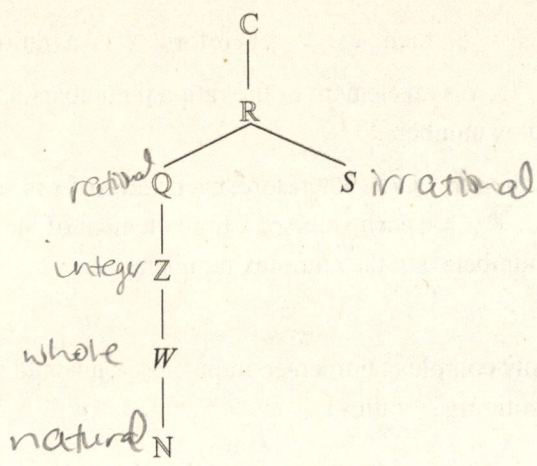

Figure 2.2

EXAMPLE 2

Identify the type of each number or set of numbers. List all other sets to which the number or set of numbers belong.

a) 0 *whole*

b) $.\overline{6}$ *rational*

c) $\sqrt{4}$ *natural number*

d) $5\pi - \pi$ *irrational*

e) $\{x \mid 6x + 1 = 8\}$ *rational*

f) $\{x \mid x^2 = 3\}$ *irrational*

SOLUTION

a) 0 is a whole number. Since $W \subseteq \mathbb{Z} \subseteq \mathbb{Q} \subseteq \mathbb{R} \subseteq \mathbb{C}$, 0 is an element of the whole numbers, the integers, the rational numbers, the real numbers and the complex numbers.

b) $.\overline{6}$ is a repeating decimal. Therefore, it is a rational number. Since $\mathbb{Q} \subseteq \mathbb{R} \subseteq \mathbb{C}$, $.\overline{6}$ is an element of the rational numbers, the real numbers and the complex numbers.

c) $\sqrt{4} = 2$. 2 is a natural number. Since $\mathbb{N} \subseteq W \subseteq \mathbb{Z} \subseteq \mathbb{Q} \subseteq \mathbb{R} \subseteq \mathbb{C}$, $\sqrt{4}$ is an element of the natural numbers, the whole numbers, the integers, the rational numbers, the real numbers, and the complex numbers.

d) $5\pi - \pi = 4\pi$. The number 4π is irrational. Since $S \subseteq \mathbb{R} \subseteq \mathbb{C}$, $5\pi - \pi$ is an element of the irrational numbers, the real numbers and the complex numbers.

e) If $6x + 1 = 8$, then $x = \dfrac{7}{6}$. Therefore, x is a rational number. Since $\mathbb{Q} \subseteq \mathbb{R} \subseteq \mathbb{C}$, x is an element of the rational numbers, the real numbers and the complex numbers.

f) If $x^2 = 3$, then $x = \pm\sqrt{3}$. Therefore, each value of x is an irrational number. Since $S \subseteq \mathbb{R} \subseteq \mathbb{C}$, each value of x is an element of the irrational numbers, the real numbers and the complex numbers.

To add, subtract, or multiply complex numbers, compute as you would with binomials (like $a + bx$) and then simplify by substituting i^2 with -1.

$$(a + bi) + (c + di) = (a + c) + (b + d)i$$

$$(a + bi) - (c + di) = (a - c) + (b - d)i$$

$$(a + bi)(c + di) = ac + adi + bci + bdi^2$$
$$= ac - bd + (ad + bc)i$$

EXAMPLE 3

Simplify $(3 + i)(2 + i)$.

$6 + 3i + 2i + i^2$

$6 + 5i - 1$

$5 + 5i$

SOLUTION

$(3 + i)(2 + i) = 3(2 + i) + i(2 + i)$
$= 6 + 3i + 2i + i^2$
$= 6 + (3 + 2)i + (-1)$
$= 5 + 5i$

Division of two complex numbers is usually accomplished with a special procedure that involves the conjugate of a complex number. The conjugate of $a + bi$ is denoted by

$$\overline{a + bi}, \text{ and } \overline{a + bi} = a - bi.$$

Also, $(a + bi)(a - bi) = a^2 + b^2$.

To divide a complex number by a complex number, multiply the numerator and denominator by the conjugate of the denominator. The usual procedure for division is illustrated below.

$$\frac{x + yi}{z + wi} = \frac{x + yi}{z + wi} \times \frac{z - wi}{z - wi}$$
$$= \frac{(xz + yw) + (-xw + yz)i}{z^2 + w^2}$$
$$= \frac{xz + yw}{z^2 + w^2} + \frac{-xw + yz}{z^2 + w^2}i$$

EXAMPLE 4

Simplify $\dfrac{15+5i}{1-2i}$.

SOLUTION

The conjugate of $1 - 2i$ is $1 + 2i$. Therefore, multiply the numerator and the denominator by $1 + 2i$.

$$\frac{15+5i}{1-2i} = \frac{15+5i}{1-2i} \cdot \frac{1+2i}{1+2i}$$

$$= \frac{15+30i+5i+10i^2}{1-4i^2}$$

$$= \frac{15+35i-10}{1+4}$$

$$= \frac{5+35i}{5}$$

$$= 1+7i$$

All the properties of real numbers described in the previous section carry over to complex numbers.

Factors, Multiples, and Primes

The product of any number and an integer is a **multiple** of that number. For example, 15 is a multiple of 3 because $3 \times 5 = 15$. The **least common multiple (lcm)** of two numbers is the smallest number that is a multiple of both numbers. The **factors** of a number are the positive numbers that divide the number with no remainder. For example, 3 is a factor of 15 because $15 \div 3 = 5$. The **greatest common factor (gcf)** of two or more numbers is the largest factor shared by the two numbers. A **prime** number is an integer greater than 1 that has no factors other than 1 and itself. A number that is not prime is called **composite**. The number 2 is the first prime number and the only even prime number since all other even numbers have 2 as a factor. The **prime factorization** of a number is the expression of the number as a product of its prime factors. To find the great common factor and/or least common multiple of two numbers, compare their prime factorizations. The greatest common factor is the product of the lowest power of each prime factor common to both numbers. The least common multiple is the product of the highest power of each of the prime factors.

EXAMPLE 5

Find the lcm and gcf of 2450 and 10,290.

SOLUTION

First, find the prime factorization of both numbers:

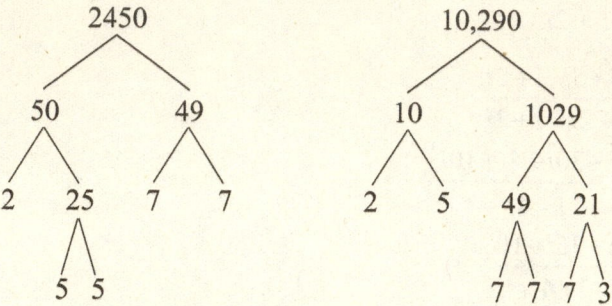

So, $2450 = 2 \times 5^2 \times 7^2$ and $10,290 = 2 \times 5 \times 7^3 \times 3$. The prime factors common to both are 2, 5 and 7, so the gcf of 2450 and 10,290 is $2 \times 5 \times 7^2 = 490$. To find the lcm, multiply the highest power of each of the prime factors: $2 \times 3 \times 5^2 \times 7^3 = 51,450$.

EXAMPLE 6

During track practice, Julia can run $\frac{1}{8}$ of a lap in 1 minute. Lilly can run $\frac{1}{6}$ of a lap in 1 minute and Larissa can run $\frac{1}{3}$ of a lap in 1 minute. Assuming they start together, how many minutes will it take for them to complete a lap together?

SOLUTION

Julia finishes 1 lap every 8 minutes. Lilly finishes 1 lap every 6 minutes and Larissa finishes 1 lap every 3 minutes. The first time the girls finish a lap together is the lcm of 8, 6 and 3. Therefore, it will take 24 minutes for them to complete a lap together.

EXAMPLE 7

The area of a rectangular garden is 36 square meters. List all possible whole-number dimensions of the garden.

SOLUTION

Since area is the product of length and width, the whole number dimensions of the garden are the factors of 36. They are: 1 m $\times$ 36 m, 2 m $\times$ 18 m, 3 m $\times$ 12 m, 4 m $\times$ 9 m, and 6 m $\times$ 6 m.

EXAMPLE 17

An integer z is the product of four unique prime numbers each greater than 2. How many factors does z have that are greater than 2?

SOLUTION

Let l, m, n and p be unique prime numbers greater than 2 such that $z = l \times m \times n \times p$. Then each of the following are factors of z:

$$1, l, m, n, p, z, lm, ln, lp, mn, mp, np, lmn, lmp, lnp, \text{ and } mnp$$

There are sixteen total factors and only the factor 1 is less than 2. Therefore, fifteen factors of z are greater than 2.

Odd and Even Numbers

An **even** number is an integer that is divisible by 2. An **odd** number is an integer that is not divisible by 2.

The following table summarizes the results of the addition/subtraction and multiplication of even and odd numbers.

1st Number	Operation	2nd Number	=	Result	Example
even	$\pm$	even	=	even	$4 - 2 = 2$
odd	$\pm$	odd	=	even	$3 + 9 = 12$
even	$\pm$	odd	=	odd	$19 - 4 = 15$
even	$\times$	even	=	even	$2 \times 10 = 20$
odd	$\times$	odd	=	odd	$5 \times 7 = 35$
even	$\times$	odd	=	even	$4 \times 7 = 28$

The following table summarizes the result of raising positives and negatives to even and odd powers.

Base	Power	=	Result	Example
positive	even	=	positive	$3^2 = 9$
positive	odd	=	positive	$2^3 = 8$
negative	even	=	positive	$(-3)^2 = -3 \times -3 = 9$
negative	odd	=	negative	$(-2)^3 = -2 \times -2 \times -2 = -8$

EXAMPLE 9

Suppose a and b are odd prime numbers and c is an even number.

Determine if each statement is sometimes, always or never true.

a) $a + b$ is prime

b) c^b is positive

c) $ab - c$ is odd

SOLUTION

a)   Numbers a and b are both odd and the sum of two odd numbers is even. The only even prime number is 2. However, the sum cannot be 2 because the smallest odd prime number is 3. Therefore, $a + b$ is never prime. This statement is <u>never</u> true.

b)   A positive number raised to an odd power is positive but a negative number raised to an odd power is negative. The number c can be either positive or negative. Therefore, c^b is sometimes positive. This statement is <u>sometimes</u> true.

c)   The product of two odd numbers is odd. So, ab is odd. The difference of an odd number and an even number is odd. Therefore, $ab - c$ is always odd. This statement is <u>always</u> true.

Ratio, Proportion, Variation, and Mean

Ration and Proportion

The **ratio** of two numbers x and y, written $x:y$, is the fraction $\dfrac{x}{y}$, where $y \neq 0$. A **proportion** is an equality of two ratios. The laws of proportion are listed below:

If $\dfrac{a}{b} = \dfrac{c}{d}$, then:

(A) $ad = bc$

(B) $\dfrac{b}{a} = \dfrac{d}{c}$

(C) $\dfrac{a}{c} = \dfrac{b}{d}$

(D) $\dfrac{a+b}{b} = \dfrac{c+d}{d}$

(E) $\dfrac{a-b}{b} = \dfrac{c-d}{d}$

Given a proportion $a{:}b = c{:}d$, then a and d are called the extremes, b and c are called the means, and d is called the fourth proportional to a, b, and c.

EXAMPLE 10

If $\dfrac{a}{b} = \dfrac{c}{d}$, $a + b = 60$, $c = 3$, and $d = 2$, find b.

SOLUTION

We are given $\dfrac{a}{b} = \dfrac{c}{d}$, so we know that

$$\dfrac{a+b}{b} = \dfrac{c+d}{d}$$

Replacing $(a + b)$ by 60, c by 3, and d by 2, we obtain

$$\dfrac{60}{b} = \dfrac{3+2}{2}$$
$$\dfrac{60}{b} = \dfrac{5}{2}$$

Cross multiplying, $5b = 120$

$$b = 24.$$

EXAMPLE 11

A chemist is preparing a chemical solution. She needs to add 3 parts sodium and 2 parts zinc to a flask of chlorine. If she has already placed 300 grams of sodium into the flask, how much zinc must she now add?

SOLUTION

With any word problem, your first step is to define your variable.

Let x = the number of grams of zinc that must be added to the solution.

The ratio given is $\dfrac{\text{sodium}}{\text{zinc}} = \dfrac{3}{2}$. Use the information given, the ratio and the variable to create a proportion.

$$\dfrac{3}{2} = \dfrac{300}{x}$$

Solve the proportion to find the solution.

$$\frac{3}{2} = \frac{300}{x}$$
$$3x = 600$$
$$x = 200$$

So 200 grams of zinc need to be added to the solution.

EXAMPLE 12

A baker is making a new recipe for chocolate chip cookies. He decides that for every 6 cups of flour, he needs to add 1 cup of sugar. He puts 30 cups of flour and 2 cups of sugar into the batter. How much more sugar does he need?

SOLUTION

Define your variable.

$$\frac{6}{1} = \frac{30}{x+2} \qquad 6x+12 = 30$$
$$6x = 18$$
$$x = 3$$

Let x = the number of additional cups of sugar needed.

The ratio given is $\dfrac{\text{flour}}{\text{sugar}} = \dfrac{6}{1}$. Use the information given, the ratio and the variable to create a proportion. The baker has already added 2 cups of sugar, so the total amount of sugar needed for 30 cups of flour is $x + 2$.

$$\frac{6}{1} = \frac{30}{x+2}$$

Solve the proportion to find the solution.

$$\frac{6}{1} = \frac{30}{x+2}$$
$$30 = 6x + 12$$
$$18 = 6x$$
$$3 = x$$

So 3 additional cups of sugar are needed.

Variation

If y is **directly proportional** to x, then $y = kx$, where k is the constant of proportionality or the constant of variation. If y **varies inversely** as x, then $y = \dfrac{k}{x}$.

EXAMPLE 13

If y varies inversely as the cube of x, and $y = 7$ when $x = 2$, express y as a function of x.

$$7 = \frac{K}{2}$$

SOLUTION

The relationship "y varies inversely with respect to x" is expressed as,

$$y = \frac{k}{x}$$

The inverse variation is now with respect to the cube of x, x^3, and we have,

$$y = \frac{k}{x^3}$$

To express y as a function of x, use the given values of x and y to find k.

Since $y = 7$ and $x = 2$ must satisfy this relation, we replace x and y by these values,

$$7 = \frac{k}{2^3} = \frac{k}{8}$$

and we find $k = 7 \times 8 = 56$. Substitution of this value of k in the general relation gives

$$y = \frac{56}{x^3}$$

We may now, in addition, find the value of y corresponding to any value of x. If we had the added requirement to find the value of y when $x = 1.2$, $x = 1.2$ would be substituted in the function to give

$$y = \frac{56}{(1.2)^3} = \frac{56}{1.728} \approx 32.41$$

Other expressions in use are "is proportional to" for "varies directly," and "is inversely proportional to" for "varies inversely."

varies inversely   directly proportional

EXAMPLE 14

If y varies directly with respect to x, and $y = 3$ when $x = -2$, find y when $x = 8$.

SOLUTION

If y varies directly as x, then y is equal to some constant k times x; that is, $y = kx$ where k is a constant. We can now say $y_1 = kx_1$ and $y_2 = kx_2$ or $\frac{y_1}{x_1} = k$, $\frac{y_2}{x_2} = k$, which implies $\dfrac{y_1}{x_1} = \dfrac{y_2}{x_2}$ which is a proportion. We use the proportion $\dfrac{y_1}{x_1} = \dfrac{y_2}{x_2}$. Thus

$\dfrac{3}{-2} = \dfrac{y_2}{8}$. Now solve for y_2:

$$8\left(\dfrac{3}{-2}\right) = 8\left(\dfrac{y_2}{8}\right)$$

$$-12 = y_2$$

When $x = 8$, $y = -12$.

Exponents

Mathematics problems often contain exponents. Exponential notation is an abbreviated way to show repeated multiplication. When repeated multiplication is indicated, the number is said to be raised to a power. In the expression $a^n = b$, a represents the base, n is the exponent or power that tells the number of times the base is a factor to be multiplied by itself, and b is the product of the multiplication. In the expression 2^3, 2 is the base and 3 is the exponent. This means that 2 is multiplied by itself 3 times ($2 \times 2 \times 2$), and the product is 8.

An exponent may be either positive or negative. A negative exponent is defined as follows: If $n > 0$, then $a^{-n} = \dfrac{1}{a^n}$, provided that $a \neq 0$. Thus, $3^{-2} = \dfrac{1}{3^2} = \dfrac{1}{9}$.

An exponent of 0 gives a result of 1, as long as the base is not equal to 0:

$$a^0 = 1, a \neq 0.$$

An exponent may also be a fraction. If m and n are positive integers, $a^{\frac{m}{n}} = \sqrt[n]{a^m}$. Here, the numerator remains as the exponent of a, and the denominator tells what root to take.

fraction power
Numerater = power
denominator = root

EXAMPLE 15

What is the value of $8^{\frac{2}{3}}$?

SOLUTION

$8^{\frac{2}{3}} = \sqrt[3]{8^2} = \sqrt[3]{64} = 4$

$\sqrt[3]{8^2}$
$= \sqrt[3]{64}$
$= 4$

EXAMPLE 16

What is the value of $\left(\dfrac{1}{16}\right)^{\frac{3}{2}}$?

SOLUTION

$$\left(\frac{1}{16}\right)^{\frac{3}{2}} = \left(\sqrt{\frac{1}{16}}\right)^3 = \left(\frac{1}{4}\right)^3 = \frac{1}{64}.$$

If the exponent is negative, we can still evaluate the expression.

EXAMPLE 17

What is the value of 7^{-3}?

SOLUTION

$$7^{-3} = \frac{1}{7^3} = \frac{1}{343}$$

EXAMPLE 18

What is the value of $(8)^{-\frac{1}{3}}$?   *move to denominator first*

SOLUTION

$$(8)^{-\frac{1}{3}} = \frac{1}{(8)^{\frac{1}{3}}} = \frac{1}{\sqrt[3]{8}} = \frac{1}{2}.$$

If the base is negative, be extra careful in evaluating the expression, especially with regard to the sign of the answer.

EXAMPLE 19

What is the value of $(-2)^{-4}$?

SOLUTION

$$(-2)^{-4} = \frac{1}{(-2)^4} = \frac{1}{16}.$$

$\dfrac{1}{(-2)^4}$

EXAMPLE 20

What is the value of $\left(-\dfrac{1}{9}\right)^{-3}$?

SOLUTION

$$\left(-\frac{1}{9}\right)^{-3} = \frac{1}{\left(-\dfrac{1}{9}\right)^{3}} = \frac{1}{-\dfrac{1}{729}} = -729.$$

There are several rules related to simplifying numbers with exponents.

1. $a^m \times a^n = a^{m+n}$

2. $(a^m)^n = a^{mn}$ *product rule*

3. $\dfrac{a^m}{a^n} = a^{m-n}$ *quotient rule*

4. $(ab)^m = a^m b^m$

5. $\left(\dfrac{a}{b}\right)^n = \dfrac{a^n}{b^n}$, if $b \neq 0$.

EXAMPLE 21

What is the value of $2^2 \times 2^3$? 2^5 *(add powers)*
   $= 32$

SOLUTION

$2^2 \times 2^3 = 2^{2+3} = 2^5 = 32$.

EXAMPLE 22

What is the simplified expression for $(y^3)^4$?

y^{12}

SOLUTION

$(y^3)^4 = y^{3 \times 4} = y^{12}$

EXAMPLE 23

What is the value of $\dfrac{2^7}{2^3}$? $2^4 = 16$

SOLUTION

$\dfrac{2^7}{2^3} = 2^{7-3} = 2^4 = 16$.

EXAMPLE 24

What is the simplified expression for $(2x)^3$? $2^3 x^3 = 8x^3$

SOLUTION

$(2x)^3 = 2^3 x^3 = 8x^3$.

EXAMPLE 25

What is the value of $\left(\dfrac{2}{3}\right)^3$? $\dfrac{2^3}{3^3} = \dfrac{8}{27}$

SOLUTION

$\left(\dfrac{2}{3}\right)^3 = \dfrac{2^3}{3^3} = \dfrac{8}{27}$.

Radical Expressions

The inverse operation of squaring is taking the square root. Every positive real number has two real-number square roots. The square roots of 9 are $\pm\sqrt{9} = \pm 3$. The symbol $\sqrt{}$ is called the **radical sign**. It represents the nonnegative square root. There are also 4th roots, 5th roots, 6th roots, etc. The symbol $\sqrt[k]{a}$ is used to represent the **kth root of a**. The variable a is called the **radicand**. The number k is called the **index**. When no index is given it is assumed to be 2, the square root. An expression written with a radical sign is called a **radical expression.**

Likewise, the square roots of -4 are $\pm\sqrt{-4}$. The imaginary number i is used to represent $\sqrt{-1}$. So, the square roots of -4 are $\pm\sqrt{-4}$, $\pm\sqrt{4 \cdot -1}$, $\pm 2\sqrt{-1}$, $\pm 2i$.

The signs of a and k impact the evaluation of $\sqrt[k]{a}$.

a	k	$\sqrt[k]{a}$	Example
Positive	Even	Positive	$\sqrt{4} = 2$
	Odd	Positive	$\sqrt[3]{8} = 2$
Negative	Even	Imaginary	$\sqrt{-4} = 2i$
	Odd	Negative	$\sqrt[3]{-8} = -2$
Zero	Even	Zero	$\sqrt{0} = 0$
	Odd	Zero	$\sqrt[3]{0} = 0$

When operating arithmetically on radical expressions, the radical behaves as if it were a variable.

Multiplying and Simplifying

The radicand is not always a perfect square. However, there may be a perfect square amongst its factors. To simplify the expression, factor the argument and "take out" anything that is a perfect square. This also hold true for roots higher than two. That is, the multiplication of a root is the root of the multiplication.

$$\sqrt[k]{ab} = \sqrt[k]{a} \cdot \sqrt[k]{b}$$

EXAMPLE 26

Simplify $\sqrt{75}$.

SOLUTION

$$\sqrt{75} = \sqrt{25 \cdot 3} = \sqrt{25} \cdot \sqrt{3} = 5\sqrt{3}$$

The rule above can also be applied to the multiplication of radical expressions. The product of the kth roots of two numbers is the kth root of the product of the numbers.

EXAMPLE 27

$$\sqrt[3]{2} \cdot \sqrt[3]{15} =$$

SOLUTION

$$\sqrt[3]{2} \cdot \sqrt[3]{15} = \sqrt[3]{2 \cdot 15} = \sqrt[3]{30}$$

EXAMPLE 28

Multiply and simplify: $5\sqrt[3]{12} \cdot 7\sqrt[3]{10}$.

SOLUTION

$$5\sqrt[3]{12} \cdot 7\sqrt[3]{10} =$$
$$5 \cdot 7\sqrt[3]{12 \cdot 10} =$$
$$35\sqrt[3]{(3 \cdot 2^2) \cdot (2 \cdot 5)} =$$
$$35\sqrt[3]{2^3 \cdot 3 \cdot 5} =$$
$$35 \cdot 2\sqrt[3]{3 \cdot 5} =$$
$$70\sqrt[3]{15}$$

$5 \cdot 7 \sqrt[3]{12 \cdot 10}$

$35 \sqrt[3]{(2^2 \cdot 3) \cdot (2 \cdot 5)}$

$35 \sqrt[3]{2^3 \cdot 3 \cdot 5}$

$35(2)\sqrt[3]{3 \cdot 5}$

$70 \sqrt[3]{15}$

To multiply radical expressions with more than one term, use the same procedures as used for multiplying polynomials.

EXAMPLE 29

Expand $(5\sqrt{3}+\sqrt{2})(6\sqrt{3}-4\sqrt{2})$.

[handwritten: FOIL]

[handwritten:
$90-20\sqrt{6}+6\sqrt{6}-4(2)$
$90-14\sqrt{6}-8$
$82-14\sqrt{6}$ *]*

SOLUTION

$(5\sqrt{3}+\sqrt{2})(6\sqrt{3}-4\sqrt{2})$

$=5\sqrt{3}\cdot6\sqrt{3}-5\sqrt{3}\cdot4\sqrt{2}+\sqrt{2}\cdot6\sqrt{3}-\sqrt{2}\cdot4\sqrt{2}$

$=30(\sqrt{3})^2-20\sqrt{6}+6\sqrt{6}-4\left(\sqrt{2}\right)^2$

$=30\cdot3-14\sqrt{6}-4\cdot2$

$=90-14\sqrt{6}-8$

$=82-14\sqrt{6}$

Addition/Subtraction of Radical Expressions

In algebra, we add and subtract by collecting like terms. That is:

$5x^2+8x^2=(5+8)x^2=13x^2$

$3y^3-17y^3=(3-17)y^3=-14y^3$

Similarly, we find the sum or difference of radical expressions by collecting terms that have the same index and radicand. Sometimes, we need to simplify the radical expression in order to have like terms.

EXAMPLE 30

$\sqrt{27}+5\sqrt{12}-\sqrt{3}$

[handwritten:
$\sqrt{9\cdot3}+5\sqrt{3\cdot4}-\sqrt{3}$
$3\sqrt{3}+10\sqrt{3}-\sqrt{3}$
$12\sqrt{3}$ *]*

SOLUTION

First, simplify each of the terms:

$\sqrt{27}+5\sqrt{12}-\sqrt{3}=\sqrt{9\cdot3}+5\sqrt{4\cdot3}-\sqrt{3}$

$=3\sqrt{3}+10\sqrt{3}-\sqrt{3}$

Then, collect like radical terms:

$=(3+10-1)\sqrt{3}$

$=12\sqrt{3}$

Division of Radical Expressions

To divide radical expressions with the same index, divide the radicands. That is,

$$\frac{\sqrt[k]{a}}{\sqrt[k]{b}} = \sqrt[k]{\frac{a}{b}}$$

EXAMPLE 31

Divide and simplify $\dfrac{\sqrt[3]{40}}{\sqrt[3]{5}}$. $= \sqrt[3]{8}$

$= 2$

SOLUTION

$$\frac{\sqrt[3]{40}}{\sqrt[3]{5}} = \sqrt[3]{\frac{40}{5}}$$

$$= \sqrt[3]{8}$$

$$= 2$$

Similarly, the kth root of a quotient is equal to the quotient of the kth root of the numerator and the kth root of the denominator.

EXAMPLE 32

Simplify $\sqrt{\dfrac{16}{25}}$. $\dfrac{4}{5}$

SOLUTION

$$\sqrt{\frac{16}{25}} = \frac{\sqrt{16}}{\sqrt{25}}$$

$$= \frac{4}{5}$$

In order to ensure consistency in solutions, results are expressed without radicals in the denominator. This is called **rationalizing the denominators**. To rationalize a denominator, multiply by the form of 1 needed to make the denominator a perfect power.

EXAMPLE 33

Rationalize the denominator of $\sqrt[3]{\dfrac{x}{4a}}$. $\dfrac{\sqrt[3]{x}}{\sqrt[3]{4a}} \cdot \dfrac{\sqrt[3]{2a^2}}{\sqrt[3]{2a^2}} = \dfrac{\sqrt[3]{2a^2 x}}{\sqrt[3]{8a^3}} = \dfrac{\sqrt[3]{2a^2 x}}{2a}$

SOLUTION

First, convert the expression to the quotient of cube roots.

$$\sqrt[3]{\frac{x}{4a}} = \frac{\sqrt[3]{x}}{\sqrt[3]{4a}}$$

Find a form of 1 that makes the denominator a perfect cube. Since the radicand in the denominator is $4a = 2 \cdot 2 \cdot a$, we need another 2 and two more *a*s to make a perfect cube. So, multiply by $\dfrac{\sqrt[3]{2a^2}}{\sqrt[3]{2a^2}}$.

$$\sqrt[3]{\frac{x}{4a}} = \frac{\sqrt[3]{x}}{\sqrt[3]{4a}} \cdot \frac{\sqrt[3]{2a^2}}{\sqrt[3]{2a^2}}$$

$$= \frac{\sqrt[3]{2a^2 x}}{\sqrt[3]{8a^3}}$$

$$= \frac{\sqrt[3]{2a^2 x}}{2a}$$

When the denominator is a binomial containing a radical expression, the form of 1 used to rationalize is called the **conjugate**. The rational terms of conjugates are the same but the radical terms have opposite signs. Multiplying conjugates is a form of the difference of perfect squares. It allows the middle term of the binomial expansion to cancel out and the last term to be a rational number. That is, the conjugate of $a+\sqrt{b}$ is $a-\sqrt{b}$ and $(a+\sqrt{b})(a-\sqrt{b}) = a^2 - b$.

EXAMPLE 34

Rationalize $\dfrac{3}{2-\sqrt{5}} \cdot \dfrac{(2+\sqrt{5})}{(2+\sqrt{5})} \quad \dfrac{6+3\sqrt{5}}{4+2\sqrt{5}-2\sqrt{5}-5} = \dfrac{6+3\sqrt{5}}{-1} = -6-3\sqrt{5}$

SOLUTION

The conjugate of $2-\sqrt{5}$ is $2+\sqrt{5}$. Multiply $\dfrac{3}{2-\sqrt{5}}$ by $\dfrac{2+\sqrt{5}}{2+\sqrt{5}}$.

$$\frac{3}{2-\sqrt{5}} = \frac{3}{2-\sqrt{5}} \cdot \frac{2+\sqrt{5}}{2+\sqrt{5}}$$

$$= \frac{6+3\sqrt{5}}{2^2 - (\sqrt{5})^2}$$

$$= \frac{6+3\sqrt{5}}{4-5}$$

$$= -6-3\sqrt{5}$$

MEAN, MEDIAN, AND MODE

Several measures can be used to describe a set of data. The **mean** of a set of numbers is simply the average of the numbers, which is a fairly good measure of the center of the data. It is computed by adding all of the numbers and dividing that sum by how many numbers are in the set. For example, if the salaries of nine employees are

$$\$250, \$300, \$500, \$425, \$250, \$300, \$400, \$300, \$200$$

the mean of the salaries is computed as:

$$\text{Mean wage} = \frac{250+300+500+425+250+300+400+300+200}{9} = \frac{2925}{9} = \$325$$

The **median** is the middle number of a set of data. To find the median, the numbers should be put in order (highest to lowest or lowest to highest); the median is then the middle number. If there are an even number of data points, the median is the average of the middle two. For the salary data above, we first have to order the numbers (write every number, even if it is a repeat):

$$\$200, \$250, \$250, \$300, \$300, \$300, \$400, \$400, \$425$$

So the median of this data set is the middle number, $300.

Both the mean and the median describe a set of data, and in this case, where the salaries are similar, the two measure are close, $325 and $300, and they describe the data rather well.

Let's next look at a similar data set, except now we are going to include the salary of the manager, who earns $1050. The mean now becomes

$$\text{Mean wage} = \frac{250+300+400+425+250+300+400+300+200+1050}{10} = \frac{3875}{10} = \$387.50$$

And the median can be found by ordering the data, so we have

$$\$200, \$250, \$250, \$300, \$300, \$300, \$400, \$400, \$425, \$1050$$

The median is the average of the two middle numbers, $300 and $300, so it is $300.

In this case, the mean and the median are not so close in value ($387.50 versus $300). We can see from the ordered set that most people earned similar salaries except for the manager. The addition of the large number $1050 has moved the mean toward larger numbers, but it has left the median the same. This situation occurs when a data point is quite different from the rest of the data. Whereas in a set of data that are fairly symmetric, the mean or median are good measures of the center of the data, in asymmetric data with an outlying value, the median is a better measure of the center of the data because it is affected little or not at all by the outlier.

Depending on the importance given to individual data points, a "weight" can be assigned to the data. Weighted means are discussed in Chapter 5.

A third descriptor of a set of data is the **mode, which is simply the data value that appears most frequently**. In both sets of data above, it is the value $300. This is not a measure of the center of the data, as the mean or median are, but simply a description of the data.

A data set can have more than one mode, since the mode is just the value mentioned the most, and there can be two or more values mentioned the same number of times. Also, there can be no mode if all values are mentioned only once.

EXAMPLE 35

For the data set 1, 2, 3, 4, 5, 6, 7, 8, 9, compute the mean, median, and mode.

SOLUTION

The mean is $\dfrac{1+2+3+4+5+6+7+8+9}{9} = \dfrac{45}{9} = 5$.

The median is 5, and there is no mode.

EXAMPLE 36

Now consider the same data set as in Example 35, but add the number 1,000. What are the mean, median, and mode now?

SOLUTION

The mean is $\dfrac{1+2+3+4+5+6+7+8+9+1000}{10} = \dfrac{1045}{10} = 104.5$.

The median is the average of 5 and 6, or 5.5. There is still no mode. Notice the extreme difference that the addition of the obvious outlier of 1000 makes in the values of the mean and median.

EXAMPLE 37

Find the mean, median, and mode for the data set 2, 5, 3, 7, 8, 5, 5, 1, 6, 7.

SOLUTION

The mean is $\dfrac{(2+5+3+7+8+5+5+1+6+7)}{10} = \dfrac{49}{10} = 4.9$. The ten numbers, arranged in order, are 1, 2, 3, 5, 5, 5, 6, 7, 7, 8. Then the median can be found by locating the two middle numbers, which are the fifth and sixth numbers. Since both these positions are held by the number 5, this means that 5 is the median. We notice that 5 occurs three times, which is more frequently than any other number. Thus, the mode is 5.

Use the following scenario for Examples 38–40.

A sample of eight people were given a certain brand of sleeping pills to test its effectiveness. They were asked to track the number of hours of sleep they had for a week without the pills, and then the number of hours of sleep they had for a week while taking the pills.

Participant	1	2	3	4	5	6	7	8
Before pills	30	32	28	35	40	30	36	25
After pills	35	40	40	35	34	46	50	40

EXAMPLE 38

What was the mean weekly sleep time of this group before taking the pills? After taking the pills? Do the pills appear to have made a difference?

SOLUTION

The mean sleep time before the pills was $\frac{30+32+28+35+40+30+36+25}{8} = \frac{256}{8} = 32$ hours

The mean sleep time after the pills was $\frac{35+40+40+35+34+46+50+40}{8} = \frac{320}{8} = 40$ hours

There does appear to be a difference.

EXAMPLE 39

What was the median weekly sleep time of this group before taking the pills? After taking the pills? Do the pills appear to have made a difference?

SOLUTION

The median sleep time before the pills was (ordered data: 25, 28, 30, 30, 32, 35, 36, 40) 31 hours.

The median sleep time after the pills was (ordered data: 34, 35, 35, 40, 40, 40, 46, 50) 40 hours.

There does appear to be a difference.

EXAMPLE 40

Did the pills make a positive difference to all of the participants?

SOLUTION

No, they made no difference to Participant 4 and in fact made a negative difference to Participant 5.

Chapter 5 explains how to determine whether a difference is actually statistically significant.

ALGEBRA

Solving Linear Equations

Linear equations with one variable can be put into the form $ax + b = 0$, where a and b are constants, and $a \neq 0$. To solve a linear equation means to transform it into the form $x = \dfrac{-b}{a}$. To solve any algebraic equation, first simplify each side of the equation, combine like terms, and follow the order of operations. Then, you may need to add, subtract, multiply, or divide the same number and/or variable from each side of the equation. If an equation has a variable on both sides of the equal sign, it is convenient to group similar terms on the same side of the equal sign. While the process really involves adding, subtracting, multiplying, or dividing a value or a variable from each side of the equation, many students learn to solve equations by "moving" terms to opposite sides of the equal sign in order to have similar terms on the same side. In that case, be sure to change the sign of any terms that "move across" the equal sign.

EXAMPLE 41

Solve for x: $9x - 4 = 5x + 8$. $4x = 12$
$x = 3$

SOLUTION

First, move the $5x$ to the left side of the equation and change its sign. This results in $9x - 5x - 4 = 8$. Then, move the -4 to the right side of the equation and change its sign. Now the equation reads as $9x - 5x = 8 + 4$. Combining like terms, we get $4x = 12$. Thus, the answer is $x = \dfrac{12}{4} = 3$.

Sometimes a linear equation appears in fractional form. In these problems, first eliminate the fractions by using cross-multiplication, and then solve the equation as usual.

EXAMPLE 42

Solve for n: $\dfrac{2n-4}{3} = \dfrac{n-1}{6}$.

$12n - 24 = 3n - 3$
$9n = 21$
$n = \dfrac{7}{3}$

SOLUTION

By using cross-multiplication, we get $6(2n - 4) = 3(n - 1)$. This is equivalent to $12n - 24 = 3n - 3$. Next, move like terms to the same side of the equal sign, changing the signs of the terms you move, then solve for the variable. Then we get $12n - 3n = 24 - 3$, followed by $9n = 21$. Thus, the answer is $\frac{21}{9} = \frac{7}{3}$.

Occasionally, there may be radicals in the equation. In these problems, it is necessary to square both sides to eliminate the radical before solving. Since it is possible to get extraneous solutions in this type of equation, it is very important to check all answers.

EXAMPLE 43

Solve for x: $\sqrt{3x+1} = 5$.

SOLUTION

The first step is to square both sides of the equation. Then $(\sqrt{3x+1})^2 = 5^2$, which becomes $3x + 1 = 25$. Then $3x = 24$, and thus $x = 8$.

Note that the answer of 8 does check out in the original equation.

EXAMPLE 44

Solve for x: $\sqrt{1 - 3x} + 3 = 1$.

SOLUTION

First, subtract 3 from each side to get $\sqrt{1 - 3x} = -2$. By squaring both sides, the equation will read $1 - 3x = 4$. Then $-3x = 3$, so $x = -1$. But wait! We need to check this answer. By substituting -1 for x, the expression under the square root sign has a value of $1 - (3)(-1) = 4$. However, $\sqrt{4} + 3 = 2 + 3 \quad 1$. Therefore, the answer of -1 is extraneous. This means that there is no solution.

<u>Reminder:</u> Even though $(-2)^2 = 2^2 = 4$, the symbol $\sqrt{4}$ <u>always</u> means 2. Similarly, the symbol $-\sqrt{4}$ means -2.

Linear Inequalities with One Variable

An **inequality** is a statement where the value of one quantity or expression is greater than ($>$), less than ($<$), greater than or equal to ($\geq$), less than or equal to ($\leq$), or not equal to ($\neq$) that of another. The solution of a given inequality in one variable x consists of all values of x for which the inequality is true.

The properties used to solve equations are also true of inequalities with one exception:

When multiplying or dividing each side of an inequality by a negative number, the inequality symbol must be reversed for the inequality to remain true.

EXAMPLE 45

Solve the inequality: $-2x + 5 > 9$.

[handwritten: $-2x > 4$ $x < -2$ $\{x \mid x < -2\}$]

SOLUTION

Add –5 to both sides:

$-2x + 5 + (-5) > 9 + (-5)$

Additive inverse property:

$-2x + 0 > 9 + (-5)$

Additive identity property:

$-2x > 9 + (-5)$

Combine like terms:

$-2x > 4$

Multiply both sides by $-\dfrac{1}{2}$ and change the direction of the inequality when multiplying/dividing by a negative:

$-\dfrac{1}{2}(-2x) < -\dfrac{1}{2}(4)$

$x < -2$

The solution set is $\{x \mid x < -2\}$ (that is all x, such that x is less than –2).

The graph of an inequality in one variable is represented by either a ray or a line segment on the real number line. The endpoint is not a solution if the variable is strictly less than or greater than a particular value.

EXAMPLE 46

Graph $x < 5$.

SOLUTION

The number 5 is not included in the solution set so 5 is marked with an open circle. Shading to the left of 5 indicates that the solutions are all numbers less than 5.

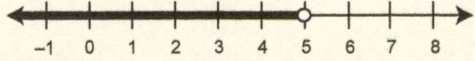

EXAMPLE 47

Provide an inequality that describes the graph below.

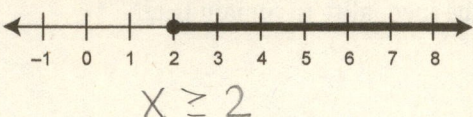

$$x \geq 2$$

SOLUTION

Because the graph is shaded to the right of 2, the solution to the inequality must include all numbers greater than 2. The solid dot at 2 indicates that 2 must also be included as a solution to the inequality. Using the variable x, the inequality $x \geq 2$ describes the given graph.

EXAMPLE 48

Graph $2 \leq x < 5$.

SOLUTION

The number 2 is included in the solution set so 2 is marked with a closed circle. The number 5 is not included in the solution set so 5 is marked with an open circle. Shading between 2 and 5 indicates that the solutions are all numbers greater than or equal to 2 but less than 5.

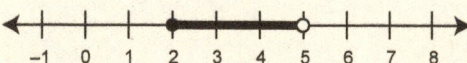

Absolute Value

Equations

The absolute value of a number is its distance from zero. Since distance is a nonnegative measure, absolute value is always positive (or zero). That is, $|4| = 4$ and $|-4| = 4$.

The absolute value of a, $|a|$, is defined as

$|a| = a$ when $a > 0$,

$|a| = -a$ when $a < 0$,

$|a| = 0$ when $a = 0$.

When the definition of absolute value is applied to an equation, the quantity within the absolute-value symbol is considered to have two values. This value can be either positive or negative before the absolute value is taken. As a result, each absolute-value equation actually contains two separate equations.

When evaluating equations containing absolute values, proceed as follows:

EXAMPLE 49

Solve $|3x - 2| = 7$.

SOLUTION

The value of $(3x - 2)$ may be positive or negative. However, taking the absolute value of $(3x - 2)$ makes it positive. To acknowledge that $(3x - 2)$ may be positive or negative when you evaluate the absolute value, you must split the equation into two cases.

Case 1: $(3x - 2)$ is positive	Case 2: $(3x - 2)$ is negative
If $(3x - 2) > 0$ then $$\|3x - 2\| = 3x - 2$$ Solving the equation: $$3x - 2 = 7$$ $$3x = 9$$ $$x = 3$$	If $(3x - 2) < 0$ then you must change the sign to make it positive, so $$\|3x - 2\| = -(3x - 2)$$ Solving the equation: $$-(3x - 2) = 7$$ $$3x - 2 = -7$$ $$3x = -5$$ $$x = -\frac{5}{3}$$

The solution set to $|3x - 2| = 7$ is $\{x \,|\, x = -\frac{5}{3}, 3\}$.

Substituting these solutions into the equation is a way to verify they are correct:

$$|3(-\frac{5}{3}) - 2| = |-5 - 2| = |-7| = 7$$

$$|3(3) - 2| = |9 - 2| = 7$$

To solve any equation involving absolute value, isolate the absolute-value expression and then split the equation into two possible cases.

EXAMPLE 50

Solve $2|x + 4| + 1 = 21$.

[handwritten: $2|x+4| = 20$
$|x+4| = 10$
$x+4=10 \qquad x+4=-10$
$x=6 \qquad x=-14$]

SOLUTION

First, isolate the absolute-value expression:

$$2|x + 4| + 1 = 21$$

$$2|x + 4| = 20$$

$$|x + 4| = 10$$

Next, evaluate the absolute value by splitting the equation into two cases:

$$(x + 4) = 10 \qquad \text{or} \qquad -(x + 4) = 10$$

$$x = 6 \qquad\qquad\qquad x + 4 = -10$$

$$x = -14$$

The solution set to $2|x + 4| + 1 = 21$ is $\{x \mid x = -14, 6\}$.

Inequalities

There are two forms of absolute-value inequalities: one with less than/less than or equal to and the other with greater than/greater than or equal to.

Form	$|x| < 5$ *and*	$|x| > 5$ *or*
Translation	What are the real numbers x whose distance from zero is less than 5 units?	What are the real numbers x whose distance from zero is greater than 5 units?
Graph		
Solution	$x > -5$ and $x < 5$ which is written as $-5 < x < 5$	$x < -5$ or $x > 5$

The process used to solve an absolute-value inequality is similar to that used to solve an absolute-value equation. First, isolate the absolute-value expression. As with equations, the absolute-value expression can be either positive or negative. Therefore, two cases must be used to solve the inequality.

EXAMPLE 51

Solve $|5x + 3| \leq 48$.

Handwritten annotations:
$5x + 3 \leq 48 \qquad 5x + 3 \geq -48$
$5x \leq 45 \qquad\qquad 5x \geq -51$
$x \leq 9 \qquad\qquad x \geq -\frac{51}{5}$
$\qquad\qquad\qquad x \geq -10\frac{1}{5}$

SOLUTION

less thand *and*

Case 1: $(5x + 3)$ is positive	Case 2: $(5x + 3)$ is negative
If $(5x + 3)$ is positive, then $|5x + 3| = 5x + 3$ Solving the inequality: $5x + 3 \leq 48$ $5x \leq 45$ $x \leq 9$	If $(5x + 3)$ is negative then you must change the sign to make it positive, so $|5x + 3| = -(5x + 3)$ Solving the inequality: $-(5x+3) \leq 48$ $(5x + 3) \geq -48$ Remember to change the sign when multiplying/dividing by a negative $5x \geq -51$ $x \geq -10\dfrac{1}{5}$

The solution set to $|5x + 3| \leq 48$ is therefore $\{x|\, x \geq -10\frac{1}{5}$ and $x \leq 9\}$ which is written $\{x|\,-10\frac{1}{5} \leq x \leq 9\}$.

EXAMPLE 52

Solve $9|2x - 1| - 6 > 39$.

Handwritten annotations:
$9|2x - 1| > 45$
$|2x - 1| > 5$
$2x - 1 > 5 \qquad 2x - 1 < -5$
$2x > 6 \qquad\quad 2x < -4$
$x > 3 \qquad\quad x < -2$

SOLUTION

First, isolate the absolute-value expression:

$9|2x - 1| - 6 > 39$ *greater than* *or*

$9|2x - 1| > 45$

$|2x - 1| > 5$

Next, evaluate the absolute value by splitting the inequality into two cases:

$(2x - 1) > 5 \qquad$ or $\qquad -(2x - 1) > 5$

$2x > 6 \qquad\qquad\qquad 2x - 1 < -5$

$x > 3 \qquad\qquad\qquad\quad 2x < -4$

$\qquad\qquad\qquad\qquad\quad x < -2$

The solution set to $9|2x - 1| - 6 > 39$ is $\{x|x < -2$ or $x > 3\}$.

Linear Equations with Two Variables

An equation whose graph is a line is called a **linear equation**. The standard form of a linear equation with two variables, x and y, is $Ax + By = C$, where A and B are not both equal to zero; A, B, and C are integers whose greatest common factor is 1; and A is nonnegative. Linear equations can be described by their *slope, y-intercept* and/or *x-intercept*.

The **slope** of a line describes its steepness. Slope is a rate of change. It is the ratio of the vertical change to the horizontal change between any two points on the line. The slope of the line containing two points (x_1, y_1) and (x_2, y_2) is given by:

$$\text{slope} = \frac{\text{vertical change}}{\text{horizontal change}} = \frac{\text{rise}}{\text{run}} = \frac{y_2 - y_1}{x_2 - x_1} \qquad \frac{\Delta y}{\Delta x}$$

For $y = 2x + 1$, the slope is (see Figure 2.3):

$$\text{slope} = \frac{\text{up } 2}{\text{right } 1} = \frac{2}{1} = 2$$

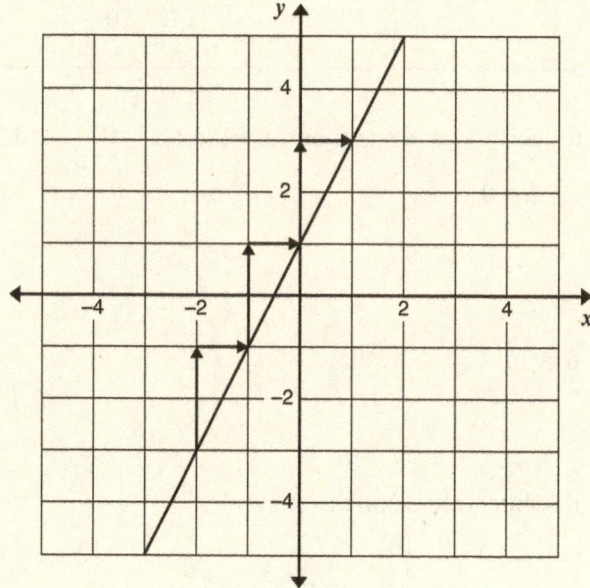

Figure 2.3

Horizontal lines, such as $y = 3$, have a slope of zero (Figure 2.4), and the slope of vertical lines, such as $x = -2$, is undefined (Figure 2.5).

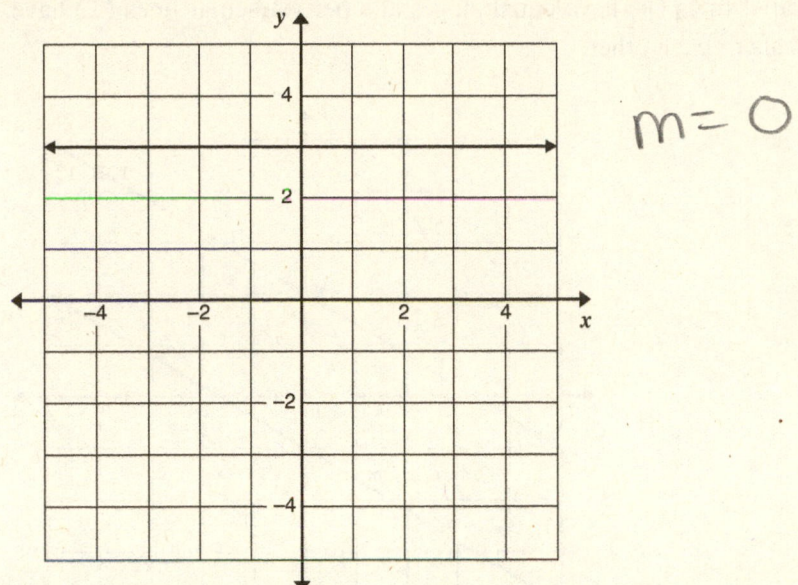

$m = 0$

Figure 2.4

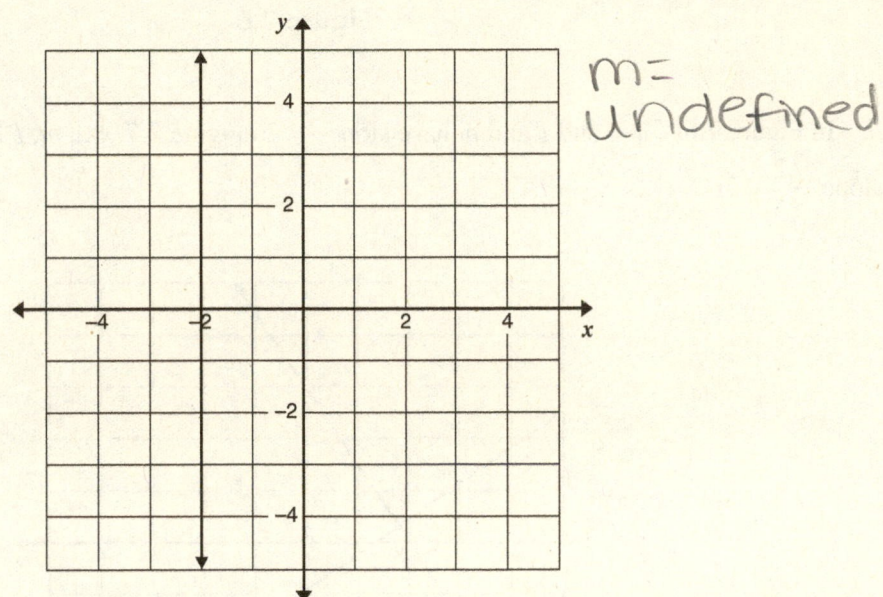

$m =$ undefined

Figure 2.5

Parallel lines (∥) have equal slopes and perpendicular lines (⊥) have slopes that are negative reciprocals of each other.

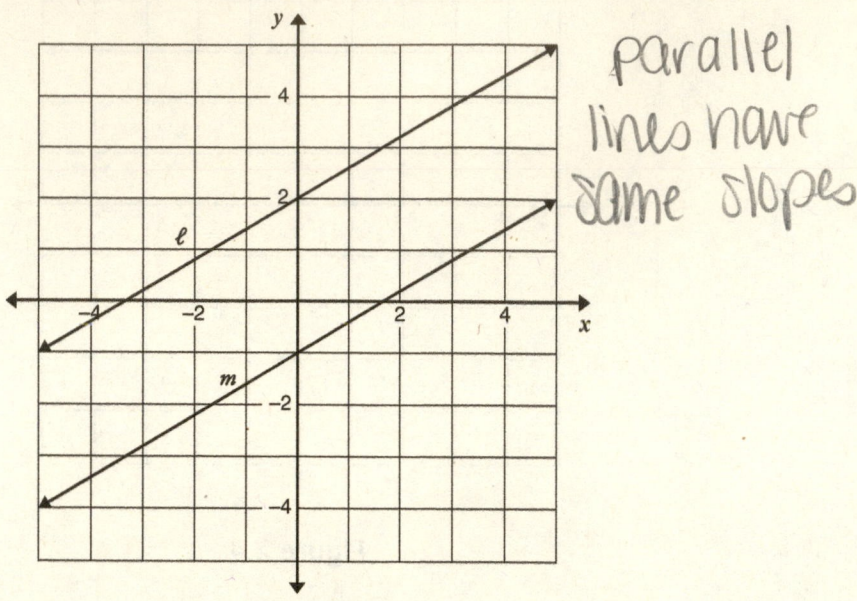

parallel lines have same slopes

Figure 2.6

In Figure 2.6, $\ell \parallel m$ and ℓ and m have slope $\frac{3}{5}$. In Figure 2.7, $\ell \perp m$, ℓ has slope $\frac{3}{2}$, and m has slope $-\frac{2}{3}$.

perpendicular lines have negative reciprocal slopes

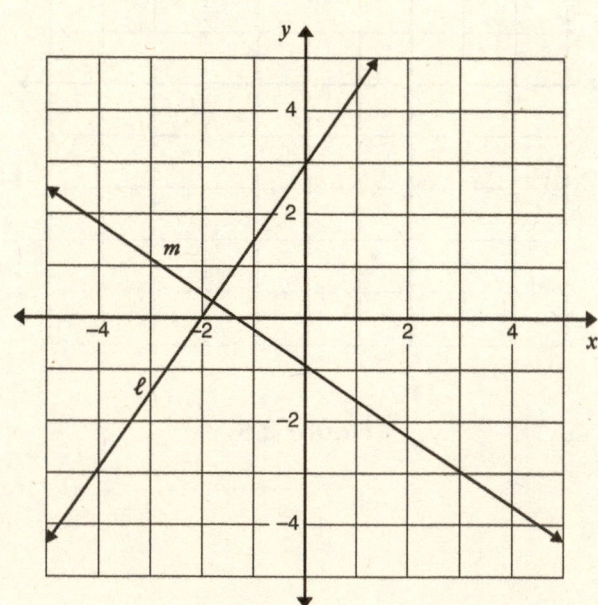

Figure 2.7

The **y-intercept** is the point at which the graph intersects the y-axis. The **x-intercept** is the point at which the graph intercepts the x-axis (Figure 2.8). Since the value of x on the y-axis is always 0, the y-intercept is the y-value of the equation when the x-value is 0. Similarly, the x-intercept is the x-value of the equation when the y-value is 0.

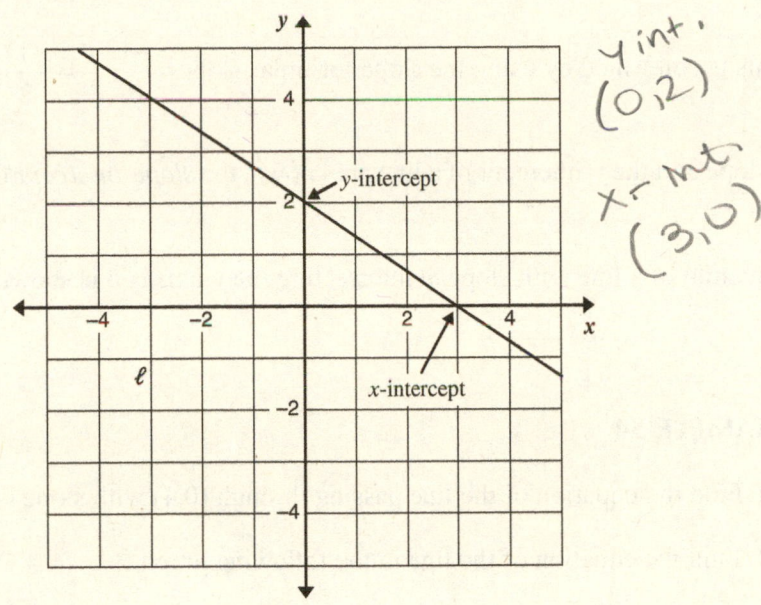

y int.
(0,2)

x-int.
(3,0)

Figure 2.8

EXAMPLE 53

Identify the slope, x-intercept and y-intercept of the following graph.

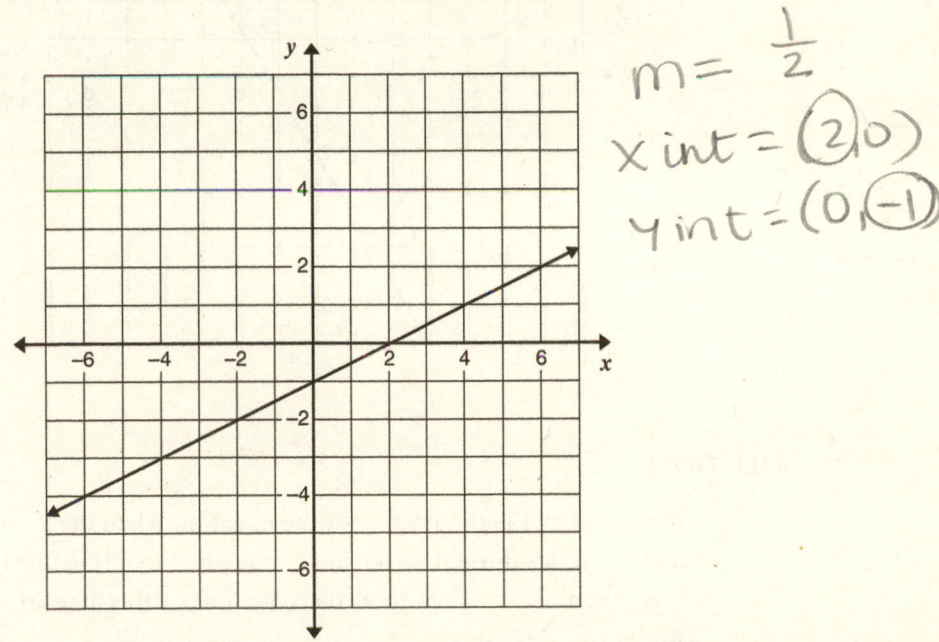

$m = \frac{1}{2}$

x int = (2,0)

y int = (0,-1)

SOLUTION

The line crosses the y-axis at the point $(0,-1)$, so the y-intercept is -1. It crosses the x-axis at $(2,0)$ so the x-intercept is 2. From $(0,-1)$ to $(2,0)$, the vertical change is up 1 unit and the horizontal change is to the right 2 units. Therefore, the slope is $\dfrac{1}{2}$.

This is confirmed by using the slope formula: $\text{slope} = \dfrac{-1-0}{0-2} = \dfrac{-1}{-2} = \dfrac{1}{2}$.

If the slope and the y-intercept of a line are known, the *slope-intercept* form can be used to find its equation.

The equation of a line with slope m intersecting the y-axis is b is shown by:

$$y = mx + b$$

EXAMPLE 54

(a) Find the equation of the line passing through $(0,4)$ with slope -5.

(b) Find the equation of the line in the following graph.

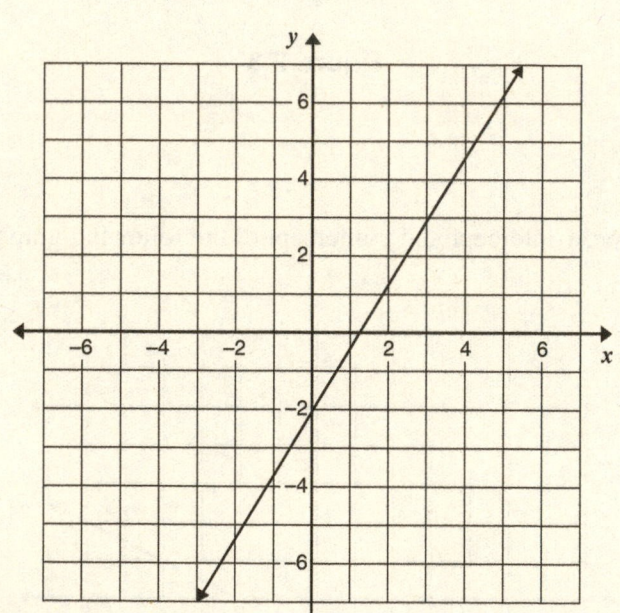

$y_1 - 4 = -5(x_1 - 0)$

$y_1 - 4 = -5x$

$\boxed{y = -5x + 4}$

SOLUTION

(a) The y-intercept is the y-value of the equation when the x-value is 0. Since this line passes through $(0,4)$, the y-intercept, b, of this line is 4. The slope, m, is given as -5. Therefore, the equation of this line in slope-intercept form is $y = -5x + 4$.

(b)   The line crosses the y-axis at the point $(0,-2)$, so the y-intercept, b, is -2. The line also passes through the point $(3,3)$. Using the slope formula with $(0,-2)$ and $(3,3)$, $m = \dfrac{-2-3}{0-3} = \dfrac{5}{3}$. Therefore, the equation of this line in slope-intercept form is $y = \dfrac{5}{3}x - 2$.

If the slope and one point of a line are known, the *point-slope* form can be used to find its equation.

The equation of a line with slope m passing through a point $Q(x_0, y_0)$ is of the form:

$$y - y_0 = m(x - x_0)$$

If two points on a line are known, the slope formula can be used to find the value of m and then either point can be used in the point-slope form to find its equation.

EXAMPLE 55

Find the slope, the y-intercept, and the x-intercept of the equation $2x - 3y - 18 = 0$.

SOLUTION

Solving the equation for y will put it into slope-intercept form.

$$2x - 3y - 18 = 0$$
$$2x - 3y = 18$$
$$-3y = -2x + 18$$
$$y = \frac{2}{3}x - 6$$

The value of m, the slope, is $\dfrac{2}{3}$. The value of b, the y-intercept, is -6.

Verify the y-intercept is correct by substituting 0 for x and solving for y.

$$2x - 3y - 18 = 0$$
$$2(0) - 3(y) - 18 = 0$$
$$-3y - 18 = 0$$
$$-3y = 18$$
$$y = -6$$

yint x=0
xint. y=0

To find the *x*-intercept, substitute 0 for *y* and solve for *x*.

$$2x - 3y - 18 = 0$$

$$2x - 3(0) - 18 = 0$$

$$2x - 18 = 0$$

$$2x = 18$$

$$x = 9$$

The *x*-intercept is 9.

EXAMPLE 56

(a) Find the equation of the line passing through (2, 5) with slope 3.

(b) Suppose a line passes through the *y*-axis at (0, *b*). How can we write the equation if the point-slope form is used?

SOLUTION

(a) In point-slope form, let $x_1 = 2$, $y_1 = 5$, $m = 3$.

The point-slope form of a line is:

$$y - y_1 = m(x - x_1)$$

$$y - 5 = 3(x - 2)$$

$$y - 5 = 3x - 6$$

$$y = 3x - 1$$

(b) $y - b = m(x - 0)$

$$y = mx + b.$$

Notice that this is the slope-intercept form for the equation of a line.

EXAMPLE 57

Find the equation for the line passing through (6, 5) and (4, –3).

$$\frac{-3-5}{4-6} = \frac{-8}{-2} = 4$$

SOLUTION

First, find the slope of the line by using the slope formula:

$$\text{Slope} = \frac{-3-5}{4-6} = \frac{-8}{-2} = 4$$

$$y - 5 = 4(x - 6)$$

$$y - 5 = 4x - 24$$

$$y = 4x - 19$$

Next, substitute the slope and either point into point-slope form to find the equation:

$$y - y_1 = m(x - x_1)$$
$$y - 5 = 4(x - 6)$$
$$y - 5 = 4x - 24$$
$$y = 4x - 19$$

or

$$y - (-3) = 4(x-4)$$
$$y + 3 = 4x - 16$$
$$y = 4x - 19$$

That is, both points result in the same answer.

EXAMPLE 58

Construct the graph of the function defined by $y = 3x - 9$.

SOLUTION

This linear equation is in the slope-intercept form, $y = mx + b$.

A line can be determined by two points. Let us choose the intercepts. The x-intercept lies on the x-axis and the y-intercept is on the y-axis.

We can find the y-intercept by assigning 0 to x in the given equation and then find the x-intercept by assigning 0 to y. It is helpful to have a third point. We can find a third point by assigning 4 to x and solving for y. Thus, we get the following table of corresponding numbers:

x	$y = 3x - 9$	y
0	$y = 3(0) - 9$	-9
3	$0 = 3x - 9, x = \dfrac{9}{3} = 3$	0
4	$y = 3(4) - 9$	3

The three points are $(0, -9)$, $(3, 0)$, and $(4, 3)$. Draw a line through them as in the figure below.

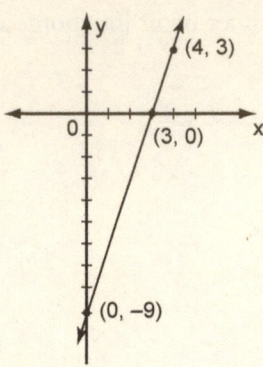

EXAMPLE 59

Graph the function defined by $3x - 4y = 12$.

SOLUTION

Solve for y:

$$3x - 4y = 12$$
$$-4y = 12 - 3x$$
$$y = -3 + \frac{3}{4}x$$
$$y = \frac{3}{4}x - 3$$

The graph of this function is a line since it is of the form $y = mx + b$. The y-intercept crosses (intersects) the y-axis at the point $(0, -3)$ since for $x = 0$, $y = b = -3$. The x-intercept crosses (intersects) the x-axis at the point $(4, 0)$ since for $y = 0$, $3x - 4(0) = 12$, or $3x = 12$, $x = 4$.

These two points, $(0, -3)$ and $(4, 0)$, are sufficient to determine the graph (see figure below). A third point, $(8, 3)$, satisfying the equation of the function is plotted as a partial check of the intercepts. Note that the slope of the line is $m = \frac{3}{4}$. This means that y increases three units as x increases four units anywhere along the line.

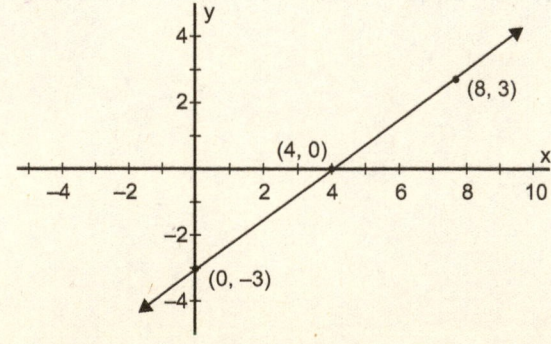

Linear Inequalities with Two Variables

Graphing two-variable linear inequalities is similar to graphing a single variable inequality on a number line. To graph single variable inequalities on the number line, points are plotted and the inequality is represented by shading. When graphing two variable inequalities, a linear equation is graphed and the inequality is represented by shading. Just as the endpoints were not included for strictly less than or strictly greater than single variable inequalities, the line is not included for strictly less than or strictly greater than two variable inequalities. To indicate the line is not included, a dashed line is used in the graph. To determine which direction to shade, test a point not on the line. If the point satisfies the inequality, then shade the region of the graph that includes the point. If it does not satisfy the inequality, then shade the region of the graph that does not include the point.

EXAMPLE 60

Graph the solution to $2x - 3y < -12$.

$-3y < -2x - 12$

SOLUTION

Shade above $y \textcircled{>} \frac{2}{3}x + 4$

First, graph the line $2x - 3y = -12$ with a dashed line to represent the strict inequality.

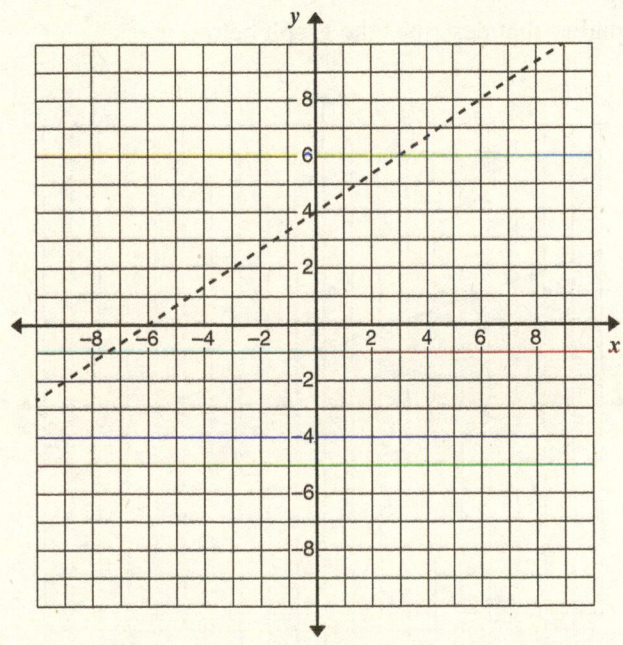

Next, test the point $(0,0)$ in $2x - 3y < -12$ since it is not on the line:

$$2(0) - 3(0) < -12$$

$$0 - 0 < -12$$

$$0 < -12 \quad \text{NOT TRUE}$$

if does not work shade where 0,0 is NOT

Shade the region of the graph that does NOT include the point $(0,0)$.

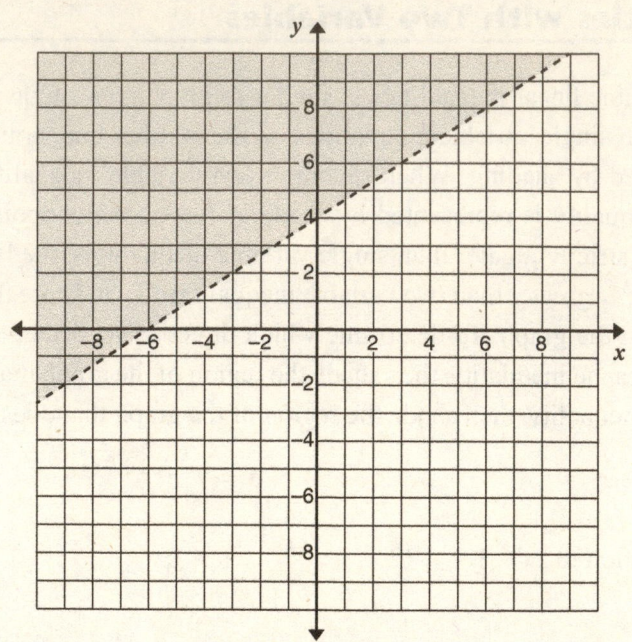

EXAMPLE 61

Provide an inequality that describes the graph below.

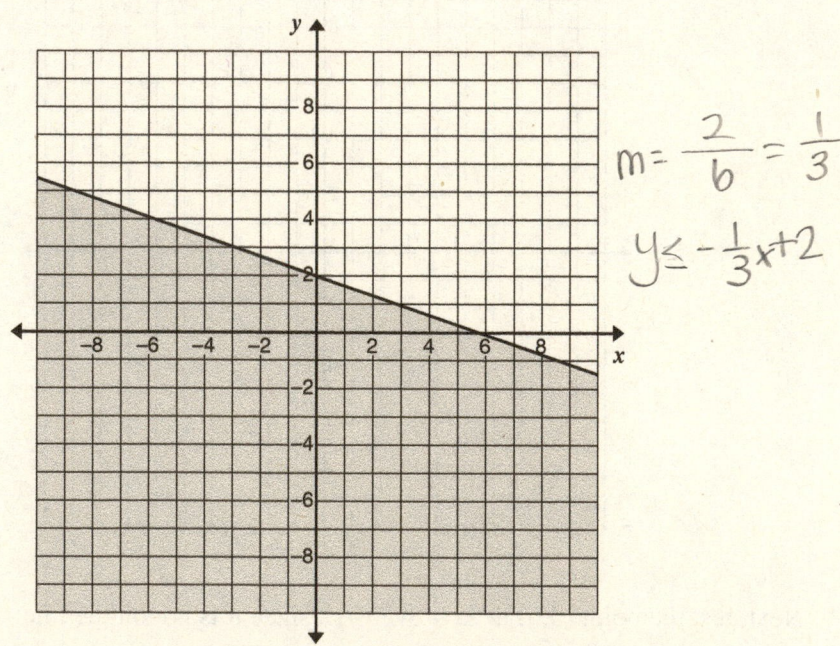

$m = \dfrac{2}{6} = \dfrac{1}{3}$

$y \leq -\dfrac{1}{3}x + 2$

SOLUTION

The line has a y-intercept, b, of 2 and a slope, m, of $-\dfrac{1}{3}$. Thus, the equation of the line in slope-intercept form is $y = -\dfrac{1}{3}x + 2$. The solid line indicates that the points on the line are included in the solution to the inequality. The shading indicates that the solutions are all values less than or equal to the line. Therefore, $y \leq -\frac{1}{3}x + 2$ describes the graph.

Systems of Linear Equations

A **system of equations** is a set of two or more equations with the same set of unknowns. The solution to a system of equations is a solution that satisfies each equation in the set.

Every system of equations falls into one of the following categories:

Type of Equations	Description of Lines	Example Equation	Graph (sketch the graph of the lines)	Solution
Consistent	Intersecting *1 Solution*	$x + y = 6$ $-3x + y = 2$		Intersect at the solution to the system of equations (point (1,5))
Inconsistent	Parallel lines *no Solution*	$-2x + 3y = -3$ $-2x + 3y = 12$		Since there are no intersection points, there is no solution to an inconsistent system of equations.
Dependent	The same line (coincident lines) *infinite Solutions*	$-2x + y = 1$ $-4x + 2y = 2$		Since these lines intersect at an infinite number of points, dependent systems have an infinite number of solutions.

There are several ways to solve systems of linear equations with two variables.

Method 1: **Addition or subtraction** *Elimination*—If necessary, multiply the equations by numbers that will make the coefficients of one unknown in the resulting equations numerically equal. If the signs of equal coefficients are the same, subtract the equation; otherwise, add.

The result is one equation with one unknown; we solve it and substitute the value into the other equations to find the unknown that we first eliminated.

Method 2: **Substitution**—Find the value of one unknown in terms of the other. Substitute this value in the other equation and solve.

Method 3: **Graph**—Graph both equations. The point of intersection of the drawn lines is a simultaneous solution for the equations, and its coordinates correspond to the answer that would be found analytically.

EXAMPLE 62

Find the point of intersection of the graphs of the equations:

$$5x + 4y = 16$$
$$(3x - 2y = 14)2$$

(handwritten):
$$5x + 4y = 16$$
$$6x - 4y = 28$$
$$11x = 44$$
$$x = 4$$

$$3(4) - 2y = 14$$
$$12 - 2y = 14$$
$$-2y = 2$$
$$y = -1$$

$$(4, -1)$$

SOLUTION

The point of intersection is the solution to the system of equations. To find the solution, multiply the second equation by 2. Add the two equations to eliminate the variable y.

$$5x + 4y = 16$$
$$6x - 4y = 28$$

$$11x = 44$$

Solve for x to obtain $x = 4$. Substitute this into $5x + 4y = 16$ to get $y = -1$. The solution to this system of equations is $(4, -1)$.

To check that $(4, -1)$ satisfies both equations, substitute this point into both equations.

(handwritten): check

$$5x + 4y = 16 \qquad\qquad 3x - 2y = 14$$

$$5(4) + 4(-1) = 16 \qquad\qquad 3(4) - 2(-1) = 14$$

$$20 - 4 = 16 \qquad\qquad 12 + 2 = 14$$

$$16 = 16 \qquad\qquad 14 = 14$$

These coordinates satisfy both equations, and hence are the coordinates of the point of intersection of the two lines.

EXAMPLE 63

Solve the equations $2x + 3y = 6$ and $4x + 6y = 7$ simultaneously.

SOLUTION

We have two equations and two unknowns,

$$2x + 3y = 6 \tag{1}$$

and

$$4x + 6y = 7 \tag{2}$$

There are several methods to solve this problem. We have chosen to multiply each equation by a different number so that when the two equations are added, one of the variables drops out. Thus,

Multiply equation (1) by 2:	$4x + 6y = 12$	(3)
Multiply equation (2) by -1:	$\underline{-4x - 6y = -7}$	(4)
Add equations (3) and (4):	$0 = 5$	

We obtain a peculiar result!

Actually, what we have shown in this case is that if there were a simultaneous solution to the given equations, then 0 would equal 5. But the conclusion is impossible; therefore, there can be no simultaneous solution to these two equations, hence no point satisfying both.

The lines which are the graphs of these equations must be parallel if they never intersect, but not identical, which can be seen from the graph of these equations (see the figure).

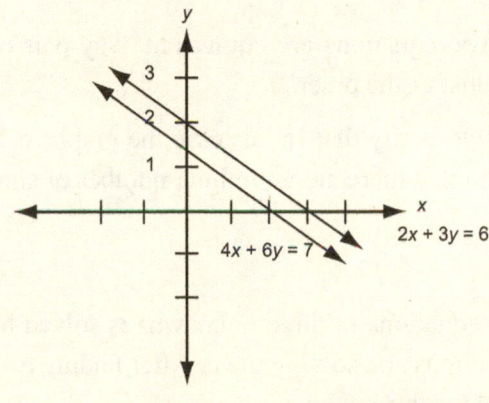

EXAMPLE 64

Solve the equations $2x + 3y = 6$ and $y = -\left(\dfrac{2x}{3}\right) + 2$ simultaneously.

We have two equations and two unknowns.

$$2x + 3y = 6 \qquad\qquad\qquad (1)$$

and

$$y = -\left(\frac{2x}{3}\right) + 2 \qquad\qquad\qquad (2)$$

plug in for Y in 1st equation

SOLUTION

There are several methods of solution for this problem. Since equation (2) already gives us an expression for y, we use the method of substitution.

Substitute $-\left(\dfrac{2x}{3}\right) + 2$ for y in the first equation:

$$2x + 3\left(-\frac{2x}{3} + 2\right) = 6$$

Distribute: $2x - 2x + 6 = 6$

$$6 = 6 \quad \textit{infinite solutions}$$

Actually, our work shows that no matter what real number x is, if y is determined by the second equation, then the first equation will always be satisfied.

The reason for this peculiarity may be seen if we take a closer look at the equation $y = -\left(\dfrac{2x}{3}\right) + 2$. It is equivalent to $3y = -2x + 6$, or $2x + 3y = 6$.

In other words, the two equations are equivalent. Any pair of values of x and y which satisfies one satisfies the other.

It is hardly necessary to verify that in this case the graphs of the given equations are identical lines, and that there are an infinite number of simultaneous solutions to these equations.

A system of three linear equations in three unknowns is solved by eliminating one unknown from any two of the three equations and solving them. After finding two unknowns, substitute them in any of the equations to find the third unknown.

EXAMPLE 65

Solve the system

$$2x + 3y - 4z = -8 \qquad (1)$$

$$x + y - 2z = -5 \qquad (2)$$

$$7x - 2y + 5z = 4 \qquad (3)$$

SOLUTION

We cannot eliminate any variable from two pairs of equations by a single multiplication. However, both x and z may be eliminated from equations (1) and (2) by multiplying equation (2) by -2. So we have

$$2x + 3y - 4z = -8 \qquad (1)$$

$$-2x - 2y + 4z = 10 \qquad (4)$$

By addition, we have $y = 2$. Although we may now eliminate either x or z from another pair of equations, we can more conveniently substitute $y = 2$ in equations (2) and (3) to get two equations in two variables. Thus, making the substitution $y = 2$ in equations (2) and (3), we have

$$x - 2z = -7 \qquad (5)$$

$$7x + 5z = 8 \qquad (6)$$

Multiply equation (5) by 5 and multiply equation (6) by 2. Then add the two new equations. Then $x = -1$. Substitute x in either equation (5) or (6) to find z.

The solution of the system is $x = -1$, $y = 2$, and $z = 3$. Check by substitution.

Systems of equations can be used to model real-world situations. To do so, define the unknowns as variables. Then, use the information given to create the same number of equations as there are unknowns. The solution to the system of equations provides the values of the unknowns.

EXAMPLE 66

Matt, Mike and Nick buy lunch at a concession stand. Matt buys 1 lemonade, 1 hotdog and 1 hamburger for $6. Mike buys 2 lemonades, 1 hotdog and 2 hamburgers for $10. Nick buys 2 lemonades and 3 hamburgers for $11. Find the cost of one lemonade, one hotdog and one hamburger.

SOLUTION

There are three unknowns in this scenario. Assign a variable to each unknown:

Let x = the cost of one lemonade

Let y = the cost of one hotdog

Let z = the cost of one hamburger

Use the information given to create three equations to model the scenario. Since Matt buys 1 lemonade, 1 hotdog and 1 hamburger for \$6, $x + y + z = 6$. Since Mike buys 2 lemonades, 1 hotdog and 2 hamburgers for \$10, $2x + y + 2z = 10$. Since Nick buys 2 lemonades and 3 hamburgers for \$11, $2x + 3z = 11$. Thus, the system of equations is:

$$\begin{cases} x + y + z = 6 & (1) \\ 2x + y + 2z = 10 & (2) \\ 2x + 3z = 11 & (3) \end{cases}$$

Equation (3) has only two variables, x and z, so use equations (1) and (2) to eliminate the y variable. The difference of equation (1) and equation (2) is equation (4):

$$\begin{array}{ll} x + y + z = 6 & (1) \\ -(2x + y + 2z = 10) & (2) \end{array} \rightarrow \begin{array}{ll} x + y + z = 6 & (1) \\ -2x - y - 2z = -10 & (2) \\ \hline -x - z = -4 & (4) \end{array}$$

Now, equations (3) and (4) create a system in two variables which can be solved using the addition/subtraction method:

$$2x + 3z = 11 \quad (3)$$

$$-x - z = -4 \quad (4)$$

Multiply equation (4) by 2 to eliminate the x variable:

$$2x + 3z = 11$$

$$-2x - 2z = -8$$

$$z = 3$$

Substituting z into equation (3), we find x:

$$2x + 3(3) = 11$$

$$2x + 9 = 11$$

$$x = 1$$

Substituting x and z into equation (1), we find y:

$$1 + y + 3 = 6$$

$$y + 4 = 6$$

$$y = 2$$

The solution to the system of equations is $x = 1$, $y = 2$, and $z = 3$. This means the cost of one lemonade is \$1, the cost of one hotdog is \$2 and the cost of one hamburger is \$3.

Systems of Inequalities

A system of inequalities is a set of two or more inequalities with a same set of unknowns. The solution to a system of inequalities satisfies all the inequalities simultaneously. To solve a system of inequalities, graph each of the inequalities on the same axes and find their intersection.

EXAMPLE 67

Solve the following system of inequalities:

$$2x + y > 3$$

$$3x - 2y \geq 8.$$

SOLUTION

Graph of $2x + y > 3$:

[handwritten notes:]
$>, <$ dotted line
$\geq, \leq$ solid line

$>, \geq$ above line
$<, \leq$ below line

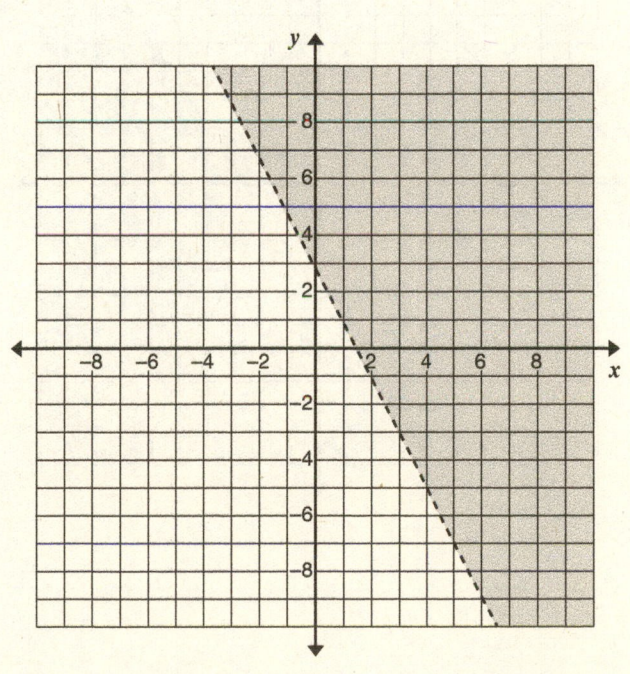

Graph of $3x - 2y \geq 8$:

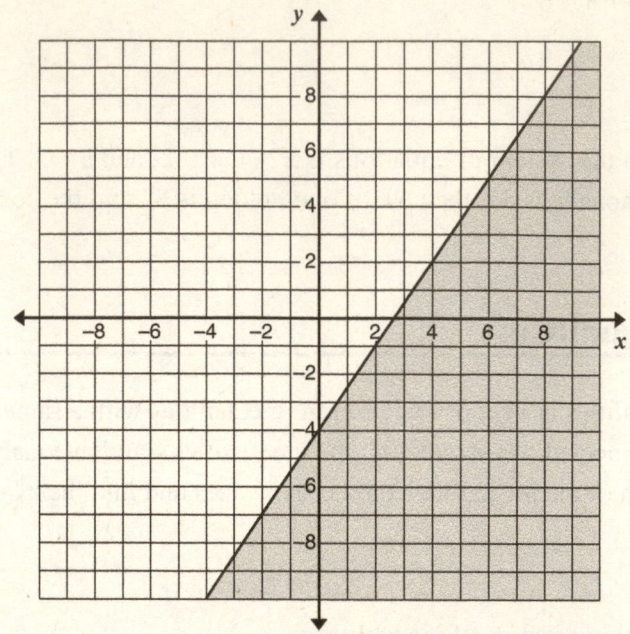

The intersection of the individual graphs is the graph of the system. Thus, the solution to this system is the set of ordered pairs in the overlapping region:

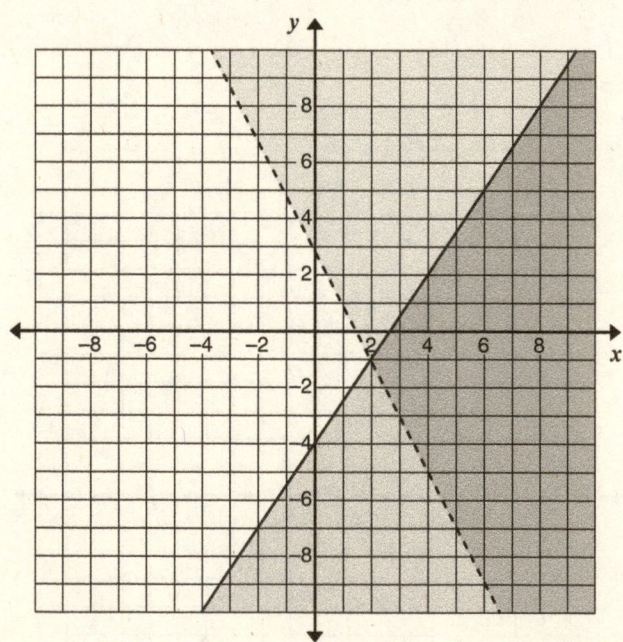

Polynomials

A **polynomial in** x is an expression of the form

$$a_n x^n + a_{n-1} x^{n-1} + \dots a_1 x + a_0$$

where n is a nonnegative integer and the coefficients $a_0, a_1, \dots, a_n$ are real numbers. Polynomials are often referred to with the notation $P(x)$.

The following expressions are polynomials:

$$-8x^9 \tag{1}$$

$$3x^6 + 5x^3 \tag{2}$$

$$-5x^5 + 2x^3 - x \tag{3}$$

$$-2x^3 + x^2 + 5x + 10 \tag{4}$$

Expression (1) is a **monomial** because it has only one term. Expression (2) is a **binomial** because it has two terms. Expression (3) is a **trinomial** because it has three terms. Any polynomial with four of more terms, like expression (4), is simply called a polynomial.

Addition of Polynomials

Addition of polynomials is achieved by combining like terms. Like terms differ only in their numerical coefficients.

EXAMPLE 68

If $P(x) = x^2 - 3x + 5$ and $Q(x) = 4x^2 + 6x - 3$, find $P(x) + Q(x)$.

SOLUTION

$P(x) + Q(x) = (x^2 - 3x + 5) + (4x^2 + 6x - 3)$

By using the commutative and associative laws, we can rewrite $P(x) + Q(x)$ as:

$P(x) + Q(x) = (x^2 + 4x^2) + (-3x + 6x) + (5 - 3)$

Using the distributive law, $ab + ac = a(b + c)$ yields:

$P(x) + Q(x) = (1 + 4)x^2 + (-3 + 6)x + (5 - 3)$

$= 5x^2 + 3x + 2$

Subtraction of Two Polynomials

Subtraction of two polynomials is achieved by first changing the sign of all terms in the expression that are being subtracted and then adding this result to the other expression.

EXAMPLE 69

If $P(x) = 5x^2 + 4y^2 + 3z^2$ and $Q(x) = 4xy + 7y^2 - 3z^2 + 1$, find $P(x) - Q(x)$.

SOLUTION

$$\begin{aligned}
P(x) - Q(x) &= (5x^2 + 4y^2 + 3z^2) - (4xy + 7y^2 - 3z^2 + 1) \\
&= 5x^2 + 4y^2 + 3z^2 - 4xy - 7y^2 + 3z^2 - 1 \\
&= 5x^2 + (4y^2 - 7y^2) + (3z^2 + 3z^2) - 4xy - 1 \\
&= 5x^2 - 3y^2 + 6z^2 - 4xy - 1
\end{aligned}$$

Multiplication of Polynomials

Multiplication of a polynomial by a polynomial is achieved by multiplying each of the terms of one polynomial by each of the terms of the other polynomial and combining the result.

EXAMPLE 70

If $P(x) = 5y + z + 1$ and $Q(x) = y^2 + 2y$, find $P(x) \cdot Q(x)$.

SOLUTION

$$\begin{aligned}
P(x) \cdot Q(x) &= (5y + z + 1)(y^2 + 2y) \\
&= (5y)(y^2) + (5y)(2y) + (z)(y^2) + (z)(2y) + (1)(y^2) + (1)(2y) \\
&= 5y^3 + 10y^2 + y^2z + 2yz + y^2 + 2y \\
&= 5y^3 + 11y^2 + y^2z + 2yz + 2y
\end{aligned}$$

Division of Polynomials

Division of a polynomial by polynomial is achieved by following the given procedure, called long division.

Step 1: The terms of both the polynomials are arranged in order of ascending or descending powers of one variable.

Step 2: The first term of the dividend is divided by the first term of the divisor which gives the first term of the quotient.

Step 3: This first term of the quotient is multiplied by the entire divisor and the result is subtracted from the dividend.

Step 4: Using the remainder obtained from Step 3 as the new dividend, Steps 2 and 3 are repeated until the remainder is zero or the degree of the remainder is less than the degree of the divisor.

Step 5: The result is written as follows:

$$\frac{\text{dividend}}{\text{divisor}} = \text{quotient} + \frac{\text{remainder}}{\text{divisor}},$$

$$\text{divisor} \neq 0$$

[handwritten: long division showing]

$$x+1\overline{)2x^2+x+6} \quad \frac{2x-1}{}$$
$$\ominus\ 2x^2+2x$$
$$\overline{-x+6}$$
$$\ominus\ -x-1$$
$$\overline{7}$$

[handwritten: put remainder over divisor]

EXAMPLE 71

$$\frac{2x^2+x+6}{x+1}$$

SOLUTION

$$(x+1)\overline{)2x^2+x+6} \quad \frac{2x-1}{}$$
$$\underline{-(2x^2+2x)}$$
$$-x+6$$
$$\underline{-(-x-1)}$$
$$7$$

[handwritten: $= 2x-1+\dfrac{7}{x+1}$]

The result is $(2x^2+x+6) \div (x+1) = 2x-1+\dfrac{7}{x+1}$

Rational Expressions

The quotient of two polynomials is a **rational expression**. That is, it is a polynomial fraction. Any operation performed on fractions can be performed on rational expressions. However, special attention must be paid to the variables in the denominator. Since division by zero causes the fraction to be undefined, the domain must be restricted to ensure that the values of the variables in the denominator do not cause division by zero.

EXAMPLE 72

Find the domain of $\dfrac{x+2}{x^2-x-12}$.

[handwritten: $\dfrac{x+2}{(x-4)(x+3)}$ $x-4=0$ $x+3=0$ $x=4$ $x=-3$]

SOLUTION

First factor the denominator: $x^2 - x - 12 = (x+3)(x-4)$.

Set the denominator equal to zero and solve:

$$(x+3)(x-4)=0$$
$$x+3=0 \qquad x-4=0$$
$$x=-3 \qquad x=4$$

[handwritten: domain is all real numbers except $x = -3, 4$]

So, when $x = -3$ or $x = 4$ the denominator is 0.

Therefore, the domain is all real numbers except $x = -3, 4$.

Fractions like $\dfrac{2}{6}$ can be simplified by removing the factor of two from the numerator and denominator. That is, $\dfrac{2}{6} = \dfrac{\cancel{2}}{\cancel{2} \cdot 3} = \dfrac{1}{3}$ because $\dfrac{2}{2} = 1$.

The same procedure is used to simplify rational expressions. Factor the numerator and denominator and remove any common factors. However, in doing this you may eliminate some of the domain restrictions of the original problem. To avoid this, always find the domain restrictions before simplifying. The solution must restrict values that are not excluded from the domain of the simplified expression.

EXAMPLE 73

Simplify $\dfrac{x+1}{2x^2 - 3x - 5}$.

$$\frac{x+1}{2x^2-3x-5} = \frac{x+1}{(2x-5)(x+1)}$$

SOLUTION

Factor the denominator: $2x^2 - 3x - 5 = (x+1)(2x-5)$.

Find the domain restrictions:

$$(x+1)(2x-5) = 0$$

$$x = -1 \qquad x = \frac{5}{2}$$

domain: all real numbers except $\dfrac{5}{2}$ and -1

The domain is all real numbers except $x = -1, \dfrac{5}{2}$.

Cancel all factors common to the numerator and denominator.

$$\frac{\cancel{(x+1)}}{\cancel{(x+1)}(2x-5)} \quad \text{because} \quad \frac{(x+1)}{(x+1)} = 1$$

$$\frac{1}{2x-5}$$

$$x \neq -1, \frac{5}{2}$$

So, $\dfrac{x+1}{2x^2 - 3x - 5} = \dfrac{1}{2x-5}$.

$x \neq \dfrac{5}{2}$ based on the denominator of this expression. However, x can equal -1 in this simplified expression. Still, since $x \neq -1$ in the original problem, we must exclude it in the simplified solution.

$$\frac{x+1}{2x^2 - 3x - 5} = \frac{1}{2x-5} \text{ where } x \neq -1, \frac{5}{2}.$$

Multiplication and division of rational functions is analogous to the multiplication and division of fractions. When multiplying fractions, it is generally easier to simplify first before multiplying. For example:

$$\frac{8}{45}\cdot\frac{27}{2}=\frac{8}{\cancel{45}^{5}}\cdot\frac{\cancel{27}^{3}}{2}=\frac{\cancel{8}^{4}}{\cancel{45}^{5}}\cdot\frac{\cancel{27}^{3}}{\cancel{2}^{1}}=\frac{4\cdot3}{5\cdot1}=\frac{12}{5}.$$

This process (simplifying before multiplying) is also used when multiplying rational expressions.

EXAMPLE 74

Multiply and simplify $\dfrac{2x^2+9x+10}{x^2-3x}\cdot\dfrac{x-3}{x+2}$.

[handwritten:] $=\dfrac{(2x+5)(x+2)}{x(x-3)}\cdot\dfrac{x-3}{x+2}$

$\dfrac{2x+5}{x}$

where $x\neq0,3,-2$

SOLUTION

Factor the numerators and denominators:

$$\frac{2x^2+9x+10}{x^2-3x}\cdot\frac{x-3}{x+2}$$
$$=\frac{(2x+5)(x+2)}{x(x-3)}\cdot\frac{x-3}{x+2}$$

Find the domain restrictions

$$x(x-3)=0 \qquad x+2=0$$
$$x=0,3 \qquad\quad x=-2$$

Simplify by canceling any factors common to the numerators and denominators:

$$\frac{(2x+5)\cancel{(x+2)}}{x(x-3)}\cdot\frac{x-3}{\cancel{x+2}} \quad\text{because}\quad \frac{x+2}{x+2}=1$$

and

$$\frac{(2x+5)\cancel{(x+2)}}{x\cancel{(x-3)}}\cdot\frac{\cancel{x-3}}{\cancel{x+2}} \quad\text{because}\quad \frac{x-3}{x-3}=1$$

So, $\dfrac{2x^2+9x+10}{x^2-3x}\cdot\dfrac{x-3}{x+2}=\dfrac{2x+5}{x}$ where $x\neq0,3,-2$.

Just as with division of fractions, rational expressions are divided by multiplying the first expression by the reciprocal of the second.

EXAMPLE 75

Divide and simplify $\dfrac{-a-1}{a-1} \div \dfrac{a+1}{a^3-1}$.

$$\dfrac{-(a+1)}{a-1} \cdot \dfrac{(a-1)(a^2+a+1)}{a+1}$$

$$-a^2 - a - 1$$

$$\text{where } a \neq 1, -1$$

SOLUTION

Rewrite as a multiplication problem:

$$\frac{-a-1}{a-1} \cdot \frac{a^3-1}{a+1}$$

Factor the numerators. Note: to cancel the $(a + 1)$ from the denominator, factor -1 from $(-a - 1)$.

$$\frac{-(a+1)}{a-1} \cdot \frac{(a-1)(a^2+a+1)}{a+1}$$

Find the domain restrictions

$$a-1=0 \qquad a+1=0$$
$$a=1 \qquad a=-1$$

Simplify by canceling any factors common to the numerators and denominators:

$$\frac{-\cancel{(a+1)}}{a-1} \cdot \frac{(a-1)(a^2+a+1)}{\cancel{a+1}} \quad \text{because} \quad \frac{a+1}{a+1}=1$$

and

$$\frac{-\cancel{(a+1)}}{\cancel{a-1}} \cdot \frac{\cancel{(a-1)}(a^2+a+1)}{\cancel{a+1}} \quad \text{because} \quad \frac{a-1}{a-1}=1$$

So, $\dfrac{-a-1}{a-1} \div \dfrac{a+1}{a^3-1} = -(a^2+a+1)$

$$= -a^2 - a - 1 \text{ where } a \neq -1, 1$$

Addition and subtraction of rational expressions, like their fraction counterparts, require finding the least common denominator. The least common denominator of rational expressions is the least common multiple (lcm) of the denominators. To find the lcm, factor each denominator and identify the greatest number of times each factor occurs in any of the factorizations. The lcm is their product.

EXAMPLE 76

$$\frac{12}{x^3 - 2x^2 + x} - \frac{10}{x^4 - x^3}$$

[handwritten annotations:] $x(x^2-2x+1)$ $x^3(x-1)$ $x(x-1)(x-1)$

SOLUTION

Factor the denominators and find the lcm.

$$x^3 - 2x^2 + x = x(x^2 - 2x + 1) = x(x-1)^2$$

$$x^4 - x^3 = x^3(x-1)$$

The lcm is $x^3(x-1)^2$. *[handwritten:]* lcm: $x^3(x-1)^2$

Next, convert each of the rational expressions to an expression with denominator $x^3(x-1)^2$.

$$\frac{12}{x(x-1)^2} \cdot \frac{x^2}{x^2} = \frac{12x^2}{x^3(x-1)^2}$$

$$\frac{10}{x^3(x-1)} \cdot \frac{x-1}{x-1} = \frac{10x-10}{x^3(x-1)^2}$$

Finally, subtract the numerators by distributing the negative to each term of the second numerator.

$$\frac{12x^2}{x^3(x-1)^2} - \frac{10x-10}{x^3(x-1)^2} = \frac{12x^2 - 10x + 10}{x^3(x-1)^2}$$

Solving Quadratic Equations

Let a, b, and c be real numbers. An equation in the form $ax^2 + bx + c = 0$, with $a \neq 0$, is called a **quadratic equation in x**. There are three basic methods in solving this type of equation.

If $b = 0$, the easiest method is to simply isolate x and take the square root of each side of the equation.

EXAMPLE 77

Solve for x: $4x^2 - 3 = 17$.

SOLUTION

Add 3 to each side to get $4x^2 = 20$. Now divide by 4 to get $x^2 = 5$. By taking the square root of each side, the two answers are $x = \sqrt{5}$ or $x = -\sqrt{5}$.

Sometimes, the given equation can be factored. Recall that if a product of two (or more) quantities is zero, then at least one of these quantities must equal zero. This is commonly known as the product rule for zero.

EXAMPLE 78

Solve for x: $2x^2 + x - 2 = 1$.

SOLUTION

First, subtract 1 from both sides so that the equation has all nonzero terms on one side. Then $2x^2 + x - 3 = 0$. We can factor the left side so that $(2x + 3)(x - 1) = 0$.

Now, either $2x + 3 = 0$ or $x - 1 = 0$. The two answers are $x = -\dfrac{3}{2}$ or $x = 1$.

even
non-factorable ones

A third approach, which actually works for *all* quadratic equations, is the quadratic formula.

The solution to $ax^2 + bx + c = 0$ is always given by $x = \dfrac{-b \pm \sqrt{b^2 - 4ac}}{2a}$.

(Note that this equation represents *two* answers, namely $\dfrac{-b + \sqrt{b^2 - 4ac}}{2a}$ and $\dfrac{-b - \sqrt{b^2 - 4ac}}{2a}$.)

EXAMPLE 79

Solve for x: $2x^2 + 9x + 5 = 0$

SOLUTION

We identify $a = 2$, $b = 9$, and $c = 5$. Then

$$x = \frac{-9 \pm \sqrt{9^2 - 4(2)(5)}}{2(2)} = \frac{-9 \pm \sqrt{81 - 40}}{4} = \frac{-9 \pm \sqrt{41}}{4}.$$

Note that if we wish to approximate the two answers, we could write $\sqrt{41} \approx 6.4$. Then

$$\frac{-9 + \sqrt{41}}{4} \approx \frac{-9 + 6.4}{4} = -0.65. \text{ Similarly, } \frac{-9 - \sqrt{41}}{4} \approx \frac{-9 - 6.4}{4} = -3.85.$$

EXAMPLE 80

Solve for x: $x^2 - 4x + 5 = 0$

SOLUTION

The expression $x^2 - 4x + 5$ cannot be factored. Therefore, the equation $x^2 + 4x + 5 = 0$ must be solved by using the quadratic formula, where $a = 1$, $b = -4$ and $c = 5$.

$$x = \frac{-b \pm \sqrt{b^2 - 4ac}}{2a}$$

$$= \frac{-(-4) \pm \sqrt{(-4)^2 - 4(1)(5)}}{2(1)}$$

$$= \frac{4 \pm \sqrt{16 - 20}}{2}$$

$$= \frac{4 \pm \sqrt{-4}}{2}$$

$$= \frac{4 \pm 2i}{2}$$

$$= 2 \pm i$$

We can also check the answers for Examples 44 and 45 by using the quadratic formula.

In Example 44, we write the equation as $4x^2 - 20 = 0$. Note that $b = 0$. Then

$$x = \frac{-0 \pm \sqrt{0^2 - (4)(4)(-20)}}{(2)(4)} = \frac{\pm\sqrt{320}}{8}$$

$$= \frac{\pm(\sqrt{64})(\sqrt{5})}{8} = \pm\sqrt{5}.$$

This matches our answer to Example 44.

The Discriminant of a Quadratic Equation

The answers to any quadratic equation are commonly referred to as **roots**. Not all quadratic equations have two real roots. Consider the equation $x^2 - 6x + 9 = 0$. By factoring, we have $(x - 3)(x - 3) = 0$. Thus, the only root is 3.

By contrast, consider the equation $x^2 - 4x + 9 = 0$. Using the quadratic formula, the roots are $\frac{-(-4) \pm \sqrt{(-4)^2 - (4)(1)(9)}}{2(1)} = \frac{4 \pm \sqrt{16 - 36}}{2} = \frac{4 \pm \sqrt{-20}}{2}$.

However, $\sqrt{-20}$ is not a real number. Thus, this equation has no real roots.

The number of real roots of any quadratic equation is determined by the value of $b^2 - 4ac$, which is called the **discriminant**. If $b^2 - 4ac < 0$, there are no real roots.

If $b^2 - 4ac = 0$, there is one real root. If $b^2 - 4ac > 0$, there are two real roots.

Furthermore, if $b^2 - 4ac$ is a perfect square, then both roots are rational.

EXAMPLE 81

How many real roots are there for the equation $10x^2 - x - 2 = 0$?

SOLUTION

$a = 10, b = -1$ and $c = -2$. Then $b^2 - 4ac = (\ 1)^2 - 4(10)(-2) = 1 + 80 = 81 > 0$.
Therefore, there are two real roots. (Both are rational, since 81 is a perfect square.)

EXAMPLE 82

The equation $3x^2 - 11x + k = 0$ has exactly one real root. What is the value of k?

$$b^2 - 4ac = 0 \qquad\qquad 121 = 12k$$
$$(-11)^2 - 4(3)(k) = 0 \qquad k = \frac{121}{12}$$
$$121 - 12k = 0$$

SOLUTION

We must have $b^2 - 4ac = 0$. By substitution, $(\ 11)^2 - 4(3)(k) = 0$. This equation
simplifies to $121 - 12k = 0$, so $k = \dfrac{121}{12}$.

Rational Equations

A **rational equation** is an equation that contains one or more rational expressions. One method
used for solving rational equations is to clear fractions by multiplying both sides by the LCM of
the denominators. However, multiplying both sides of an equation by an expression containing a
variable may result in an equation with solutions that are not valid for the original equation. For this
reason, always check all solutions in the original equation.

$$(x^2 - 4) = (x-2)(x+2)$$

EXAMPLE 83

Solve $\dfrac{8}{x^2-4} = \dfrac{x}{x+2}$.

$$(x^2-4)\frac{8}{x^2-4} = \frac{x}{x+2}(x^2-4)$$
$$8 = x(x-2)$$
$$8 = x^2 - 2x$$
$$0 = x^2 - 2x - 8$$
$$(x-4)(x+2)$$

SOLUTION

The lcm of the denominators is $x^2 - 4$.

Multiply both sides of the equation by $x^2 - 4$ and simplify.

$$x = 4, -2$$

$$(x^2 - 4)\frac{8}{x^2-4} = \frac{x}{x+2}(x^2 - 4)$$

$$8 = \frac{x}{x+2} \cdot \frac{(x-2)(x+2)}{1}$$

$$8 = x(x-2)$$

Solve the equation:

$8 = x(x-2)$

$8 = x^2 - 2x$

$0 = x^2 - 2x - 8$

$0 = (x-4)(x+2)$

$x = 4, -2$

Check the solution in the original equation:

For 4:

Check

$\dfrac{8}{x^2-4} = \dfrac{x}{x+2}$

$\dfrac{8}{4^2-4} \overset{?}{=} \dfrac{4}{4+2}$

$\dfrac{8}{12} \overset{?}{=} \dfrac{4}{6}$

$\dfrac{2}{3} = \dfrac{2}{3}$

So 4 is a solution.

For –2:

*So at x = 4
it is undefined*

$\dfrac{8}{x^2-4} = \dfrac{x}{x+2}$

$\dfrac{8}{(-2)^2-4} \overset{?}{=} \dfrac{-2}{-2+2}$

$\dfrac{8}{0} \overset{?}{=} \dfrac{-2}{0}$

undefined

So –2 is not a solution because it results in undefined expressions.

Dimensions

One Dimension

A line has one dimension, meaning it has only length—no width, no height. The real-number line is one-dimensional with its center on 0, positive values to the right, and negative values to the left (Figure 2.9). The distance from a point x on the line to 0 is measured as $|x-0|$.

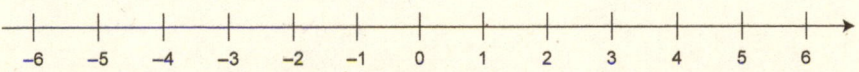

Figure 2.9

Two Dimensions

The two spatial dimensions are length and width. A two-dimensional surface is called a plane. A typical example is a piece of paper, if you think of it as having no height. Two-dimensional figures are, for example, rectangles, polygons, and circles.

If we intersect a horizontal real-number line with a vertical one so that they cross at their centers at right angles (at a point called the origin), we have Cartesian coordinates, and they form a two-dimensional plane with four quadrants, numbered I, II, III, and IV, as shown in Figure 2.10.

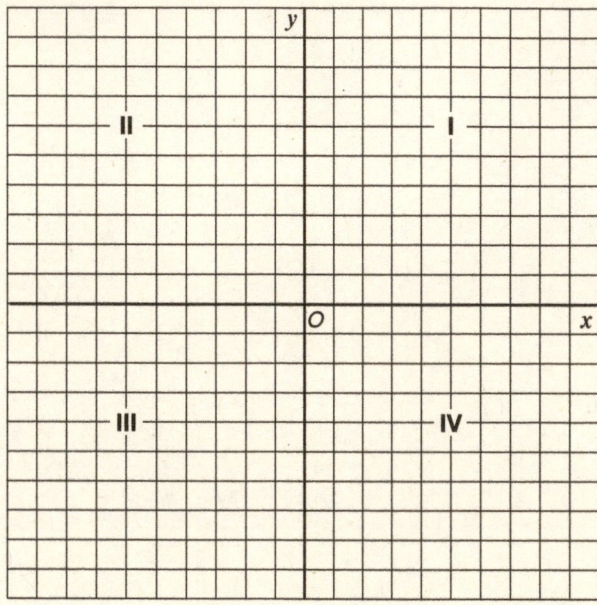

Figure 2.10

Any point in the plane has two coordinates, which are written as an ordered pair. Each ordered pair is associated with only one point on a graph. The first coordinate is the horizontal component of the distance from the point to the origin, and the second coordinate is the vertical component of the distance from the point to the origin. The Cartesian coordinate plane is sometimes called the xy-plane because the coordinates usually are given in terms of x (horizontal) and y (vertical). Thus, the point (3, 4) has an x value of 3 and a y value of 4, and the distance from this point to the origin is actually the hypotenuse of a right triangle, as shown in Figure 2.11.

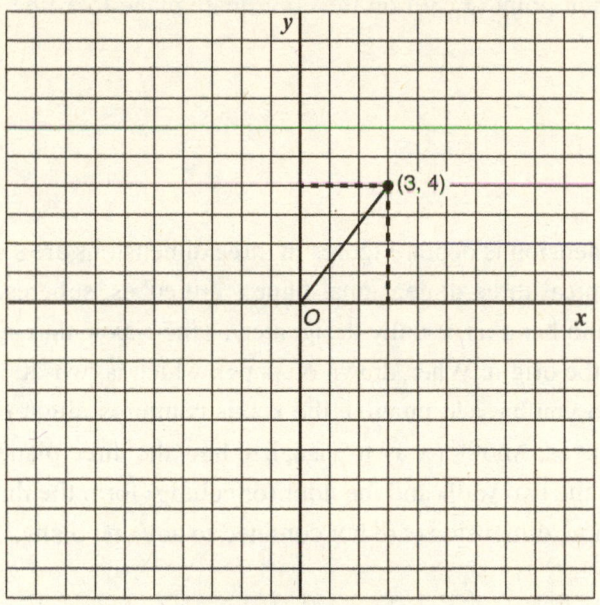

Figure 2.11

The distance between two points (x_1, y_1) and (x_2, y_2) in the coordinate plane (see Figure 2.12) is given by the formula

$$d = \sqrt{(x_1 - x_2)^2 + (y_1 - y_2)^2}$$

distance formula (distance

$$d = \sqrt{(x_1 - x_2)^2 + (y_1 - y_2)^2}$$

b/t 2 points)

and the midpoint between these points has the coordinates

$$\left(\frac{x_1 + x_2}{2}, \frac{y_1 + y_2}{2} \right).$$

midpoint

$$\left(\frac{x_1 + x_2}{2}, \frac{y_1 + y_2}{2} \right)$$

(midpoint between 2 points)

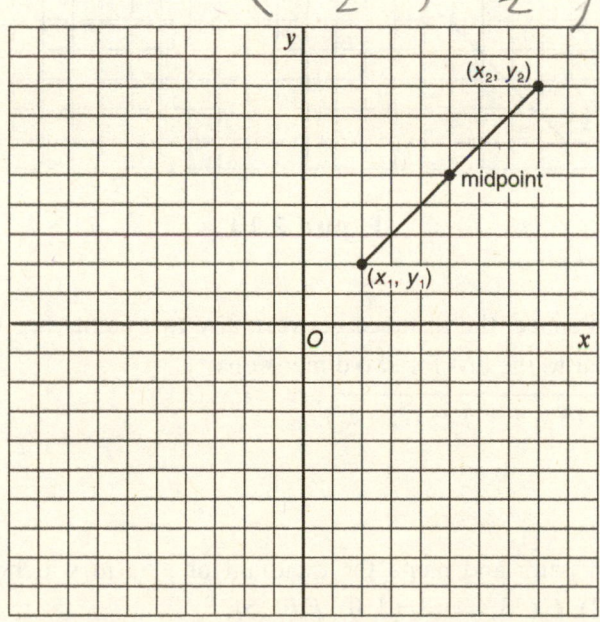

Figure 2.12

distance from pt to line

The distance from any point (x_1, y_1) on the coordinate plane to a line given by $ax + by + c$ is

$$d = \frac{|ax_1 + by_2 + c|}{\sqrt{a^2 + b^2}}.$$

$d = \dfrac{|ax_1 + by_2 + c|}{\sqrt{a^2 + b^2}}$

Three Dimensions

The third spatial dimension is depth. Figures in three dimensions are said to have depth as well as height and width. Typical three-dimensional figures are cubes, spheres, prisms, and cylinders. The third dimension is another axis, usually designated as the z-axis, that meets both the x-axis and y-axis at right angles at the origin. When drawn on paper, which is two-dimensional, the three axes look like Figure 2.13, so you have to imagine the x-axis coming straight out of the paper and not at an angle to the other axes. Another way to visualize how the three planes meet is to look at the corner of a room, where the two walls and the floor (or ceiling) form the three planes and the joints are the axes. Points in three dimensions are not confined to any one plane.

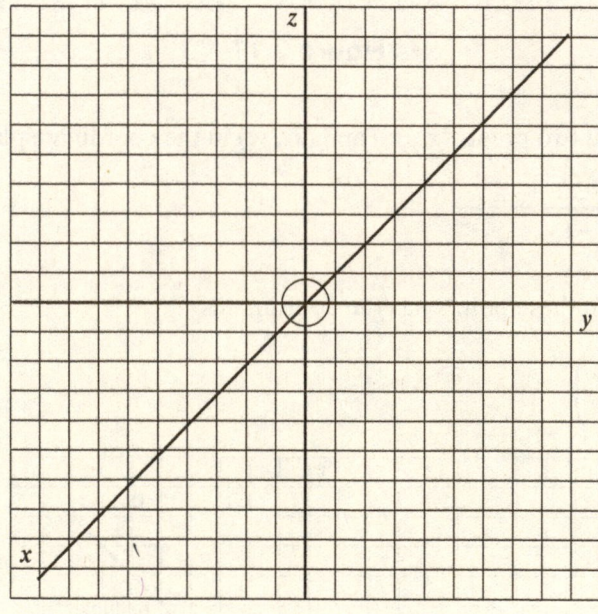

Figure 2.13

In three-dimensional space, the distance between any two points (x_1, y_1, z_1) and (x_2, y_2, z_2) is given by a formula similar to the one for two dimensions:

$$d = \sqrt{(x_1 - x_2)^2 + (y_1 - y_2)^2 + (z_1 - z_2)^2}$$

EXAMPLE 84

Plot the ordered pairs and name the quadrant or axis in which the point lies:
$A\ (2, 3)$, $B\ (-1, 2)$, $C\ (-3, -4)$, $D\ (2, 0)$, $E\ (0, 5)$.

SOLUTION

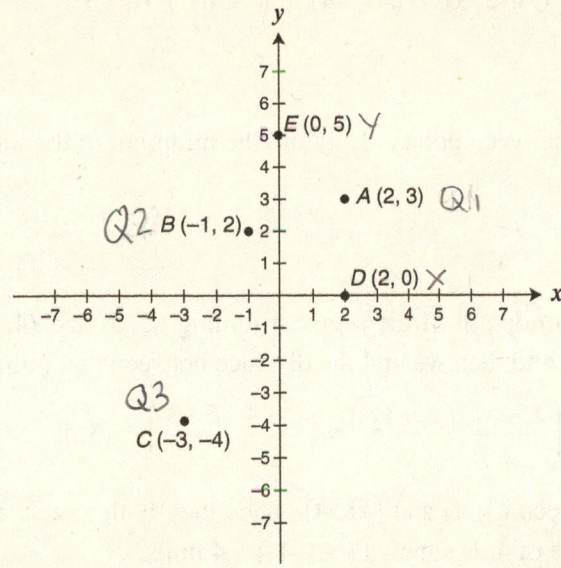

A (2, 3) lies in Quadrant I.

B (−1, 2) lies in Quadrant II.

C (−3, −4) lies in Quadrant III.

D (2, 0) lies in on the *x*-axis.

E (0, 5) lies on the *y*-axis.

EXAMPLE 85

Find the ordered pairs of the labeled points in the following figure.

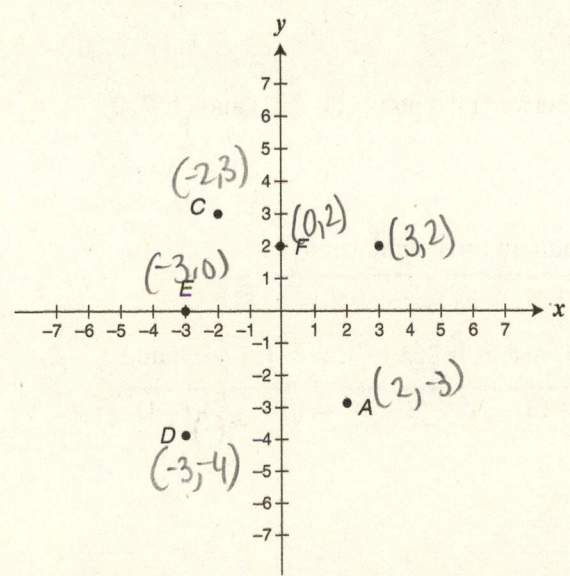

SOLUTION

A (2, –3); B (3, 2); C (–2, 3); D (–3, –4); E (–3, 0); F (0, 2).

EXAMPLE 86

Find the distance between point (–1, 4) and the midpoint of the line segment joining (2, 5) and (4, 3).

SOLUTION $\left(\dfrac{2+4}{2}, \dfrac{5+3}{2}\right) = (3, 4)$ $d = \sqrt{(-1-3)^2 + (4-4)^2}$ $= \sqrt{(-4)^2 + 0^2}$ $= \sqrt{16} = 4$

First, we find the midpoint of the segment joining (2, 5) and (4, 3) by using the midpoint formula, and then we find the distance between that point and (–1, 4).

For the midpoint: $\left(\dfrac{x_1 + x_2}{2}, \dfrac{y_1 + y_2}{2}\right) = \left(\dfrac{2+4}{2}, \dfrac{5+3}{2}\right) = (3, 4)$

The distance between (3, 4) and (–1, 4), since they both have a 1, 4), since they both have a y-value of 4, is simply $(3 - (-1)) = 4$ units.

EXAMPLE 87

Find x and y if (3, 5) is the midpoint of points (x, y) and (–4, 6).

SOLUTION $\left(\dfrac{x+(-4)}{2}, \dfrac{y+6}{2}\right)$

The midpoint formula gives: $(3, 5) = \left(\dfrac{x+(-4)}{2}, \dfrac{y+6}{2}\right)$, which gives us $3 = \dfrac{x-4}{2}$ and $5 = \dfrac{y+6}{2}$.

$\dfrac{x-4}{2} = 3$ $x - 4 = 6$ $x = 10$

$\dfrac{y+6}{2} = 5$ $y + 6 = 10$ $y = 4$

Then $x = 6 + 4 = 10$ and $y = 10 - 6 == 4$, so the point is (10, 4).

(10, 4)

EXAMPLE 88

Find the distance between the points (1, 2, 3) and (1, 3, 2).

SOLUTION

$\sqrt{(1-1)^2 + (2-3)^2 + (3-2)^2}$

$\sqrt{0 + 1^2 + 1^2}$

$= \sqrt{2}$

The distance formula in three dimensions is

$d = \sqrt{(x_1 - x_2)^2 + (y_1 - y_2)^2 + (z_1 - z_2)^2}$

For these points, $x_1 = 1$; $y_1 = 2$; $z_1 = 3$; $x_2 = 1$; $y_2 = 3$; and $z_2 = 2$.

So $d = \sqrt{(1-1)^2 + (3-2)^2 + (2-3)^2} = \sqrt{0 + 1^2 + (-1)^2} = \sqrt{2}$.

CHAPTER 3

Measurement, Geometry, and Trigonometry

MEASUREMENT

Measurement Units

The two most common systems of measurement are the English system (also called customary units) and the metric system. The English system includes units such as inches, pounds, and quarts, whereas the corresponding units in the metric system would be centimeters, kilograms, and liters. Of the two systems, the metric system is considered the more logical because conversions involve powers of 10.

Length is a measurement of distance. Examples would be someone's height, the distance between two cities, and the dimensions of the floor of a room. If we are measuring relatively small distances, such as the width of a roll of tape or the length of a pen, then the appropriate units would be inches or centimeters. For longer distances, such as the length of a basketball court or the height of a building, the appropriate units would be feet, yards or meters. Finally, for much longer distances, such as the height of a mountain or the distance between two cities, we would resort to units such as miles or kilometers.

Mass is the measure of the amount of matter in an object. **Weight** is a similar measure that depends on gravity. On Earth, the mass and weight are just about equal; on the moon, however, while you would have the same mass as on Earth, you would weigh 1/6th of your Earth weight. Small objects such as a paper clip or rubber ball would be measured in ounces or grams. For larger objects, such as a person or a package to be mailed, the appropriate measurement would be pounds or kilograms. Objects such as an elephant or an automobile would be weighed in units of tons, or in the metric system, tonnes (1,000 kilograms).

Volume is a measurement of the amount of space within a three-dimensional object. Volume can be calculated in either liquid or solid form. As with length and weight, we would use different units for objects of noticeably different sizes in calculating volume. For example, the volume of a dose of one's medication could be measured in ounces or milliliters; the amount of soda in a bottle would be measured in pints, gallons or liters. To measure the capacity (another word for volume) of a large container, such as a swimming pool or boxcar, gallons, cubic feet or cubic meters would be used.

Sometimes we need to estimate a particular item with a reasonable level of accuracy. For example, suppose you are 5 feet 6 inches (5.5 feet) tall. You could estimate the length of a room by imagining yourself lying flat on the floor. Try to picture how many times your height could be duplicated from one end of the floor to the other. If you guess this number to be four, then the length of the room would be approximately $(4)(5.5) = 22$ feet. As another example, suppose a large sack of potatoes weighs 25 pounds. If the average weight of one potato is 6 ounces, we could estimate how many potatoes are in this sack. One method would be to change pounds to ounces. $((25)(16) = 400$ ounces). Then estimate the number of potatoes as $\frac{400}{6} \approx 67$.

Here are a few common measurements to use for estimation:

1. The thickness of a line drawn by a wooden pencil is about 1 millimeter.

2. The length of a sheet of paper is about 1 foot.

3. A nickel weighs about 5 grams; a paper clip weighs about 1 gram. A standard dictionary weighs about 1 kilogram.

4. A bathtub holds about 50 gallons of water.

5. The distance from the floor to a doorknob is about 1 yard, or 3 feet.

Conversion of Units

The metric system is based on powers of 10, so it is useful to know the following suffixes:

milli- = 1/1000   centi- = 1/100   kilo- = 1000

Therefore, for example,

1 kilometer = 1000 meters

1 meter = 100 centimeters = 1000 millimeters

1 centimeter = 10 millimeters

1 metric ton = 1000 kilograms

1 kilogram = 1000 grams

1 gram = 1000 milligrams

1 liter = 1000 milliliters

The English system dates back to the Anglo-Saxons and Romans. It is useful to know the following equivalences in use in the United States.

1 mile = 5280 feet   1 m = 5280 ft

1 yard = 3 feet   1 yd = 3 ft

1 foot = 12 inches   1 ft = 12 in

1 ton = 2000 pounds   1 t = 2000 lb

1 pound = 16 ounces   1 lb = 16 oz

1 gallon = 4 quarts   1 g = 4 q

1 quart = 2 pints   1 q = 2 p

1 pint = 2 cups   1 p = 2 c

1 cup = 16 tablespoons   1 c = 16 tbs

1 tablespoon = 3 teaspoons   1 tbs = 3 t

Conversion between the metric and English systems is not straightforward and usually must be looked up on charts. Some useful approximations are:

English System	Metric System
1 inch	2.5 cm
1 yard	0.9 meter
1 mile	1.6 km
2.2 pounds	1 kg
1 quart	0.9 liter

Unit Conversion

When solving problems that involve units, it is vital that they be consistent. Consequently, conversion of units is required, whether all the units are English, metric, or a combination of both these measurement systems.

Unit analysis involves canceling units and is based on the identity principle that multiplying a value by 1 doesn't change its value. The "1" used in unit analysis comes from conversion equivalences, such as those listed above. For example, some equivalences would be: $\frac{5280 \text{ feet}}{1 \text{ mile}} = 1$, $\frac{1 \text{ hour}}{60 \text{ minutes}} = 1$, $\frac{4 \text{ quarts}}{1 \text{ gallon}} = 1$, or $\frac{1 \text{ gallon}}{4 \text{ quarts}} = 1$. The important consideration in unit analysis is to use the correct conversion fraction, which should be chosen so that units cancel each other.

EXAMPLE 1

Six identical concrete bricks weigh a total of 15 kilograms. What is the weight, in pounds, of eight of these bricks?

SOLUTION

We can use a proportion to calculate the weight (x), in kilograms, of eight bricks. The proportion becomes $\frac{6}{8} = \frac{15}{x}$. The next step is to cross-multiply, which leads to $6x = (8)(15) = 120$. Then $x = \frac{120}{6} = 20$. However, we are not finished since the number 20 represents the weight of 8 bricks in kilograms. To convert this to pounds, $\frac{20 \text{ kilograms}}{1} \times \frac{2.2 \text{ pounds}}{1 \text{ kilogram}}$, which becomes $20 \times 2.2 = 44$ pounds. Thus, 8 bricks weigh 44 pounds. Note that we use the conversion fraction that has 2.2 pounds/1 kilogram (rather than 1 kilogram/2.2 pounds) so that the kilogram units will cancel.

EXAMPLE 2

A large vat contains 7,560 pints of liquid. How many vats should be ordered to hold 6,000 gallons of liquid?

SOLUTION

Change 7,560 pints to gallons by $\frac{7{,}560 \text{ pints}}{1} \times \frac{1 \text{ gallon}}{4 \text{ quarts}} \times \frac{1 \text{ quarts}}{2 \text{ pints}} = 945$ gallons. Finally, the number of vats needed to hold 6,000 gallons of liquid is $\frac{6{,}000}{945} \approx 6.35$. Since we can order only a whole number of vats, 6.35 must be rounded up to 7.

EXAMPLE 3

A car travels 50 miles per hour. How many feet does it travel in 3 hours?

SOLUTION

We must convert 50 miles to feet.

$$\frac{50 \text{ miles}}{1 \text{ hour}} \times \frac{5280 \text{ feet}}{1 \text{ mile}} = \frac{264,000 \text{ feet}}{\text{hour}}.$$

Thus, in 3 hours the car will travel $(264,000)(3) = 792,000$ feet.

Accuracy and Percent of Error

Measuring a particular object's length, weight, or volume involves some degree of error. The accuracy of a measurement refers to how true a measurement is, but the precision relates to the unit of measurement. So a measurement can actually be precise without being accurate.

Suppose, for example, that your cousin Mike is 5 feet $10\frac{3}{4}$ inches tall. If you were to use an unmarked yardstick to measure his height, your answer would be two yards—precise only in the sense that he is closer to two yards tall than three yards tall. Suppose now you used an unmarked ruler 1 foot in length; then you would say Mike is 6 feet tall. But if you used a tape measure calibrated in inches, you might measure his height to be 5 feet 11 inches—more precise and also more accurate. If the tape measure were calibrated in half inches, you might come up with 5 feet $10\frac{1}{2}$ inches, which is even more precise, but not accurate. The idea is that the smaller the measurement unit, the more precise you can be, and the closer to being accurate.

Measurements should therefore be reported along with a maximum possible error, which is half the measurement error. So for the example above, Mike's height would finally be reported to be 5 feet $10\frac{1}{2} \pm \frac{1}{4}$ inches.

As another example, suppose Charlene steps on her bathroom scale and her weight shows 122 pounds. Bathroom scales are normally accurate to the nearest pound. Suppose her weight is really 122.3 pounds. Charlene's weight from the scale should be read as 122 ± 0.5 pounds (the 0.5 pounds represents half the unit of measurement). This is sometimes stated as a range of 121.5 to 122.5, which represents the lower bound and upper bound, respectively, of the measurement. It is easy to see that if Charlene used a scale that measured to a unit of 0.1 pounds, her weight would be measured even more precisely (even accurately).

In each of these illustrations, there is a degree of error between the actual value and the value obtained from a measurement tool. The percentage of error is defined as 100% times the quotient of the absolute value of this difference in values and the actual value. In the example involving Charlene's weight, the percentage of error is $(100\%)\dfrac{|122-122.3|}{122.3} \approx 0.245\%$.

As a final example, suppose you had a highly precise scale for weighing light objects. On your scale, a spoonful of salt weighs 2.38 grams. You would report it as 2.38 ± 0.005 grams, or 2.375-2.385 grams. The lower bound is the smallest number that would round off to 2.38 to the nearest hundredth and the upper bound is the largest number that would round off to 2.38 to the nearest hundredth, which is 2.385. Note that the lower and upper bounds are written to one additional decimal place when compared to the given number.

Successive Approximation, Bounds, and Limits

To solve an equation by approximating the answer, we can use successive approximation. Essentially, it involves estimating the value of the unknown quantity by repeated comparison to a sequence of known quantities. Each comparison will give a new value for the unknown quantity that will be within a range of values (between a lower bound and an upper bound) and eventually reach a limit that is close to (or exactly) the correct value. Essentially, you start with an upper bound that is an overstatement of the value and a lower bound, which is an understatement of the value, and you successively increase the precision of the measurement based on these measurements as you get closer to the true value as a limiting value.

This concept is best understood by example. The theory of successive approximations involves calculus, but an interesting example of this theory (due to Newton) can be used to find the square root of a number.

Let's say we want to find the square root of 2, and we guess it is 1. The formula that Newton proposed for finding square roots is to use the equation (derived through calculus) $y_{n+1} = \dfrac{(y_n)^2 + x}{2y_n}$, where the y_n are our successive guesses and x is the number whose square root we want to find.

So for a first step, we get $\dfrac{1+2}{2(1)} = 1.5$

For the next successive approximation, we use $y_2 = 1.5$: $y_3 = \dfrac{1.5^2 + 2}{2(1.5)} = 1.417$.

Again, another approximation give us: $y_4 = \dfrac{1.417^2 + 2}{2(1.417)} = 1.414$.

And again, $y_5 = \dfrac{1.414^2 + 2}{2(1.414)} = 1.414$.

When y_n repeats, we have found our answer, $\sqrt{2} = 1.414$

The **lower bound** for $\sqrt{2}$ was our initial guess of 1 since no other values of y_n were lower than 1.

The **upper bound** for $\sqrt{2}$ was 1.5 since no other values of y_n were higher than 1.5.

The limit is 1.414 since the sequence of numbers converges to 1.414 with each successive step.

GEOMETRY

Properties of Sides and Angles of Triangles

1. The **largest side** of a triangle is opposite the largest angle. The same situation exists for the smallest side and the smallest angle. Consider $\triangle ABC$, as shown in Figure 3.1.

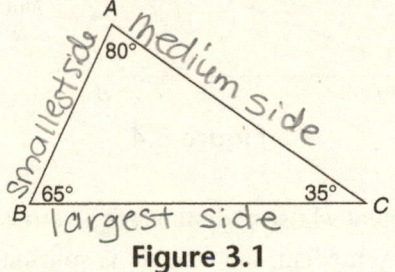

Figure 3.1

The correct inequality for the sides is $BC > AC > AB$.

2. The **sum of any two sides** of a triangle must exceed the length of the third side. This is known as the **Triangle Inequality**. Consider $\triangle DEF$, for which it is known that $DE = 6$ and $EF = 9$. Without seeing the actual triangle, we know that DF must satisfy the following inequality: $3 < DF < 15$.

3. A **midsegment** joins the midpoints of two sides of a triangle. It is parallel to and one-half the length of the third side. In Figure 3.2, we can conclude that $KL = 5$ and $\overline{KL} \parallel \overline{HJ}$.

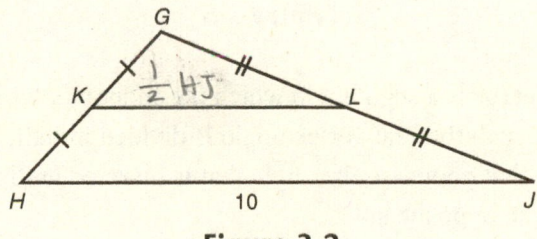

Figure 3.2

4. An **altitude** is a segment that originates at a vertex and is perpendicular to the opposite side of a triangle. In some cases, the opposite side must be extended. In particular, given an obtuse triangle, an altitude that is drawn from a vertex at which the angle measure is greater than 90° will meet the extension of the opposite side. Figures 3.3 and 3.4 show the appearance of altitudes in an acute triangle and in an obtuse triangle.

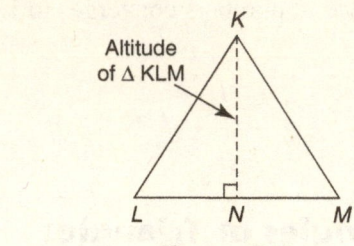

Figure 3.3

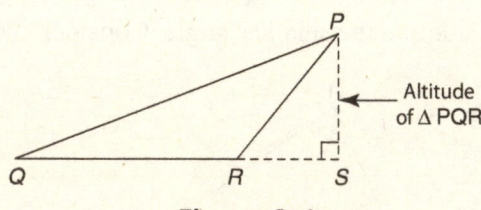

Figure 3.4

5. A **median** is a segment whose endpoints are a vertex and the midpoint of the opposite side. In drawing any median, the triangle is split into two smaller triangles of equal area. This results from the fact that the bases of these two smaller triangles are congruent and their altitudes are also congruent.

    In Figure 3.5, $\overline{MQ}$ is a median of $\triangle MNP$, and the areas of $\triangle MNQ$ and $\triangle MPQ$ are equal.

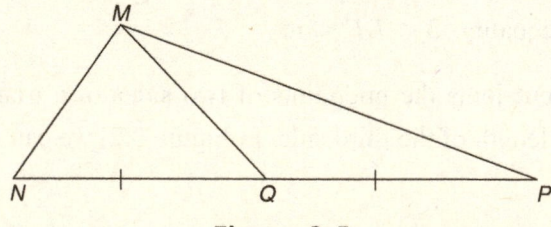

Figure 3.5

6. An **angle bisector** is a segment in which the endpoints are a vertex and a point on the opposite side such that the vertex angle is divided in half. In addition, the lengths of the two sides that comprise the angle that is bisected are in the same ratio as the two segments of the opposite side.

In Figure 3.6, $\overline{TV}$ is the angle bisector of $\angle UTW$. This implies that $\dfrac{TU}{TW} = \dfrac{UV}{VW}$.

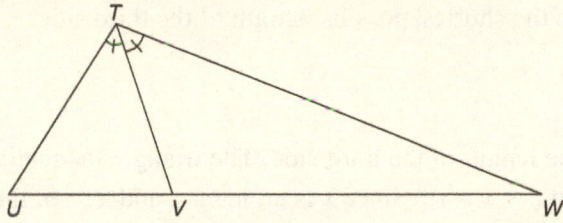

Figure 3.6

7. The **geometric mean** of any two numbers is the square root of their product. For example, given the numbers 4 and 9, the positive geometric mean is $\sqrt{(4)(9)} = \sqrt{36} = 6$.

    Another way to view this is as follows: If x is the geometric mean of 4 and 9, then $\dfrac{4}{x} = \dfrac{x}{9}$.

    In a right triangle, the length of the altitude drawn to the hypotenuse is the geometric mean between the two legs of the triangle.

    In Figure 3.7, $\overline{ZB}$ is the altitude drawn to the hypotenuse of right triangle AYZ. Then $\dfrac{YB}{ZB} = \dfrac{ZB}{AB}$.

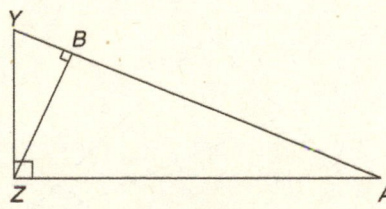

Figure 3.7

EXAMPLE 4

In $\triangle BCD$, $\angle B = 42°$ and $\angle C = 75°$. Which side is the largest?

SOLUTION

$\angle D = 180° - 42° - 75° = 63°$. Since the largest side lies opposite the largest angle, $\overline{BD}$ is the largest side.

EXAMPLE 5

All the sides of a triangle are integers. If two sides have lengths of 7 inches and 16 inches, what is the shortest possible length of the third side?

SOLUTION

Let x represent the length of the third side. The triangle inequality for the lengths of sides states that $7 + x > 16$. Since x is an integer and $x > 9$, the lowest value of x is 10 inches.

EXAMPLE 6

In $\triangle BCD$, $\overline{BE}$ is the median to $\overline{CD}$. If the area of $\triangle BCE$ is represented by $13 - x$, and the area of $\triangle BCD$ is represented by $x + 5$, what is the value of x?

SOLUTION

The area of $\triangle BCD$ must be twice the area of $\triangle BCE$. Then $x + 5 = 2(13 - x)$. This equation simplifies to $3x = 21$, so $x = 7$.

EXAMPLE 7

Consider $\triangle XYZ$, as shown below, in which $\overline{WZ}$ is the angle bisector of $\angle Z$.

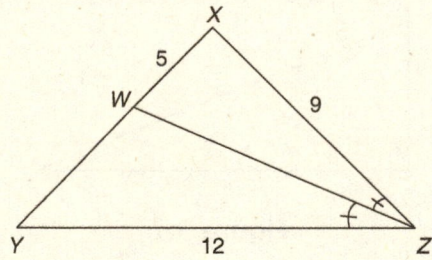

What is the value of WY?

SOLUTION

Since $\overline{WZ}$ is an angle bisector, we have the proportion $\dfrac{XZ}{YZ} = \dfrac{WX}{WY}$. Using x to represent WY and making all substitutions, we get $\dfrac{9}{12} = \dfrac{5}{x}$. Then $9x = 60$, so $x = 6.\overline{6}$.

$$\frac{5}{9} = \frac{x}{12}$$

$$60 = 9x$$

$$x = 6.\overline{6}$$

EXAMPLE 8

Consider right triangle *GHJ*, as shown below, in which $\overline{HK}$ is the altitude to the hypotenuse.

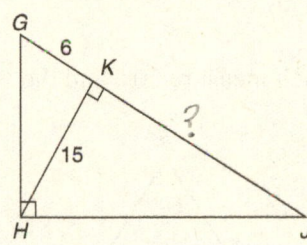

$$\frac{6}{15} = \frac{15}{x}$$

$$6x = 225$$

$$x = \frac{225}{6}$$

$$x = 37.5$$

What is the value of *JK*?

SOLUTION

Since $\overline{HK}$ is the altitude to the hypotenuse, *HK* is the geometric mean for *GK* and *JK*. Let *x* represent JK, so that $\frac{6}{15} = \frac{15}{x}$. Thus, $x = \frac{225}{6} = 37.5$.

EXAMPLE 9

$\angle B$ exceeds the measure of $\angle A$ by 30°. Find the measure of each angle in the triangle.

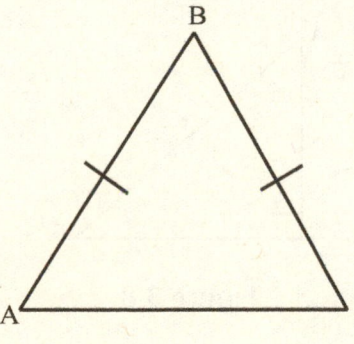

$$A = x$$
$$C = x$$
$$B = x + 30$$

$$x + x + x + 30 = 180$$
$$3x + 30 = 180$$
$$3x = 150$$
$$x = 50$$

$$A = 50°$$
$$C = 50°$$
$$B = 80°$$

SOLUTION

The triangle is isosceles with legs $\overline{AB} \cong \overline{BC}$. We know that the sum of the values of the angles of a triangle is 180°. In an isosceles triangle, the angles opposite the congruent sides (the base angles) are, themselves, congruent and of equal value.

Therefore,

(1)   Let *x* = the measure of each base angle.

(2)   Then *x* + 30 = the measure of the vertex angle.

We can solve for *x* algebraically by keeping in mind the sum of all the measures will be 180°.

$$x + x + (x + 30) = 180$$
$$3x + 30 = 180$$
$$3x = 150$$
$$x = 50$$

Therefore, the base angles each measure 50°, and the vertex angle measures 80°.

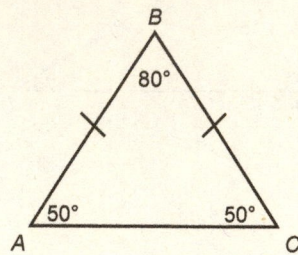

Right Triangles

The Pythagorean Theorem

The sum of the squares of the lengths of the legs of a right triangle is equal to the square of the length of its hypotenuse (Figure 3.8).

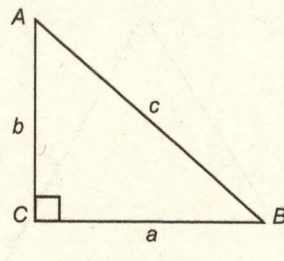

$$a^2 + b^2 = c^2$$

Figure 3.8

EXAMPLE 10

Using the Pythagorean Theorem, calculate a in the figure below.

$$4^2 + a^2 = 7^2$$
$$16 + a^2 = 49$$
$$a^2 = 33$$
$$a = \sqrt{33}$$

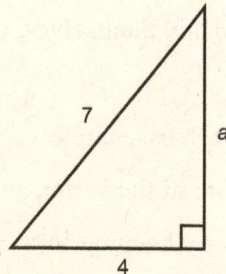

SOLUTION

1. Write the Pythagorean Theorem.

    $a^2 + b^2 = c^2$

2. Substitute the values of b and c into the equation.

    $a^2 + (4)^2 = 7^2$

3. Simplify the equation.

    $a^2 + 16 = 49$

4. Subtract 16 from both sides and rewrite the equation.

    $a^2 = 33$

5. Solve for x.

    $a = \sqrt{33}$

Pythagorean triples are sets of whole numbers that satisfy the Pythagorean Theorem. The most common Pythagorean triples are:

3,4,5 $\quad 3^2 + 4^2 = 5^2 \Rightarrow 9 + 16 = 25 \Rightarrow 25 = 25$

5,12,13 $\quad 5^2 + 12^2 = 13^2 \Rightarrow 25 + 144 = 169 \Rightarrow 169 = 169$

8,15,17 $\quad 8^2 + 15^2 = 17^2 \Rightarrow 64 + 225 = 289 \Rightarrow 289 = 289$

The converse of the Pythagorean Theorem is also true. It states that if the sum of the squares of the lengths of two sides of a triangle are equal to the third, then the triangle is a right triangle. In fact, it can be generalized to classify both acute and obtuse triangles also.

Type of Triangle	Relationship Between the Sides
Right	$c^2 = a^2 + b^2$
Acute	$c^2 < a^2 + b^2$
Obtuse	$c^2 > a^2 + b^2$

EXAMPLE 11

Determine if the given side lengths form a triangle. If they do, determine if the triangle is right, acute or obtuse:

a) 9, 40, 41 *Triangle exists* *49 > 41* *81 > 9* *50 > 40* *41² ? 40² + 9²* *1681 = 1600 + 81 (1681)*

b) 7, 8, 15 *7 + 8 = 15* *15 ≯ 15*

c) 5, 7, 10 *12 > 10* *15 > 7* *17 > 5*

5² + 7² ? 10²

SOLUTION

25 + 49 < 100

74 < 100 *Obtuse*

The Triangle Inequality can be used to determine if the given lengths form a triangle. The Triangle Inequality states that the sum of the length of any two sides of a triangle is greater than the third side. Then the converse of the Pythagorean Theorem can be applied to classify the triangle as right, acute or obtuse.

a) $9+40=49$ $49 > 41$

$9+41=50$ $50 > 40$

$40+41=81$ $81 > 9$

A triangle exists.

$41^2 \leq 9^2 + 40^2$

$1681 \leq 81 + 1600$

$1681 = 1681$

It is a right triangle.

b) $7+8=15$ $15 \ngtr 15$

This is not a triangle.

c) $5+7=12$ $12 > 10$

$5+10=15$ $15 > 7$

$7+10=17$ $17 > 5$

A triangle exists.

$10^2 \, ? \, 5^2 + 7^2$

$100 \, ? \, 25 + 49$

$100 > 74$

It is an obtuse triangle.

30°-60°-90° Triangles

Drawing an altitude in an equilateral triangle forms two triangles (Figure 3.9).

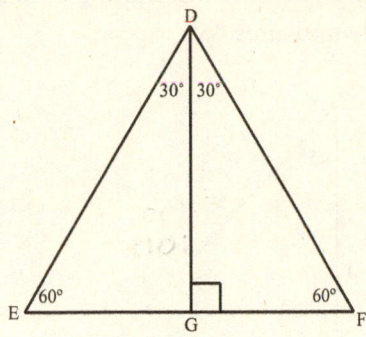

Figure 3.9

If the length of each of the sides of the equilateral triangle is $2x$, then $EG = GF = x$ because the altitude to the base on an isosceles (or equilateral) triangle is also the median to the base.

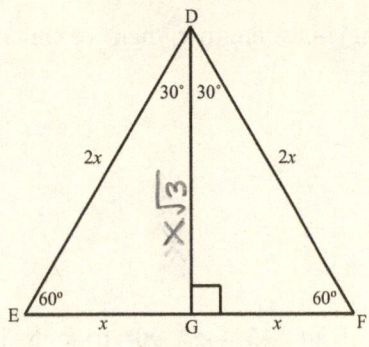

Figure 3.10

Apply the Pythagorean Theorem to Figure 3.10 to find DG:

$$DG^2 + x^2 = (2x)^2$$
$$DG^2 + x^2 = 4x^2$$
$$DG^2 = 3x^2$$
$$DG = x\sqrt{3}$$

Thus, the ratio of the sides of any **30°-60°-90°** triangle is $x : x\sqrt{3} : 2x$, which reduces to $1 : \sqrt{3} : 2$.

45°—45°—90° Triangles

In an isosceles right triangle, the vertex angle is 90°. Since the base angles of an isosceles triangle are congruent and the sum of the measures of the angles of a triangle is 180°, each of the base angles of an isosceles right triangle measures 45°.

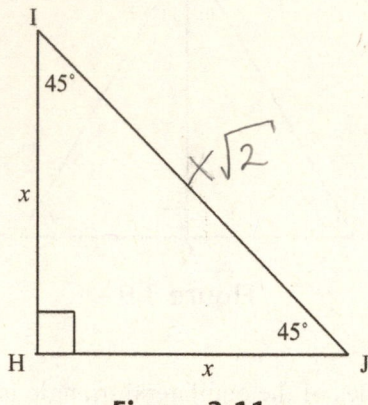

Figure 3.11

If each of the legs of the triangle has length x, then we can apply the Pythagorean Theorem to Figure 3.11 to find the hypotenuse.

$$x^2 + x^2 = IJ^2$$
$$2x^2 = IJ^2$$
$$x\sqrt{2} = IJ$$

Thus, the ratio of the sides of any 45°–45°–90° triangle is $x : x : x\sqrt{2}$, which reduces to $1:1:\sqrt{2}$.

Theorems Concerning Congruent and Similar Triangles

Congruent Triangles

We will now investigate the requirements for two triangles to be exactly the same size. Two triangles are **congruent** if each of the three sides and angles of one triangle are equal in measure to each of the three sides and angles of a second triangle. The symbol for "congruent" is "≅". By stating that $\triangle ABC \cong \triangle DEF$, we are confirming that: $\overline{AB} \cong \overline{DE}$, $\overline{AC} \cong \overline{DF}$, $\overline{BC} \cong \overline{EF}$, $\angle A \cong \angle D$, $\angle B \cong \angle E$, and $\angle C \cong \angle F$.

The order of the sets of congruencies must match the order in which the letters are presented for the triangles. Other congruencies are possible, but not required. For example, if we can determine that $AB = AC$, then it must be true that $DE = DF$. *Two triangles can be proved congruent with just a minimum of three sets of congruencies.*

Demonstrating that *all* corresponding angles and sides are congruent can be quite a lengthy process. However, there are five 'shortcut' theorems used to prove triangles are congruent.

Name	Postulate	Diagram
SSS	If there exists a correspondence between the vertices of two triangles such that three sides of one triangle are congruent to the corresponding sides of the other triangle, the two triangles are congruent.	
SAS	If there exists a correspondence between the vertices of two triangles such that two sides and an included angle of one triangle are congruent to the corresponding parts of the other triangle, the two triangles are congruent.	
ASA	If there exists a correspondence between the vertices of two triangles such that two angles and an included side of one triangle are congruent to the corresponding parts of the other triangle, the two triangles are congruent.	
AAS	If there exists a correspondence between the vertices of two triangles such that two angles and a non-included side of one triangle are congruent to the corresponding parts of the other triangle, the two triangles are congruent.	
HL	If there exists a correspondence between the vertices of two right triangles such that the hypotenuse and one leg of one triangle are congruent to the corresponding parts of the other triangle, the two triangles are congruent.	

CAUTION

It is important to recognize why certain combinations of congruencies between the parts of triangles do <u>not</u> imply that the triangles are congruent. We'll label these as fallacies. The figures below illustrate that the triangles are not congruent.

1. **Side-Side-Angle Fallacy (SSA)**—Figure 3.13 *does not work*

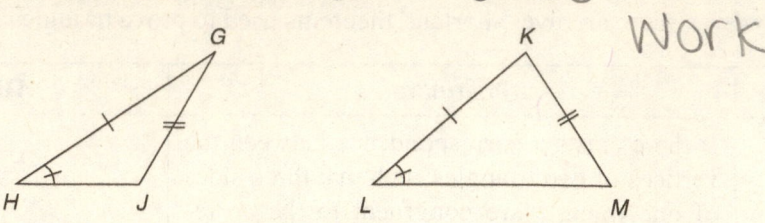

Figure 3.13

For this example, $\overline{GH} \cong \overline{KL}$, $\overline{GJ} \cong \overline{KM}$, and $\angle H \cong \angle L$. However, the triangles are not congruent.

2. **Angle-Angle-Angle Fallacy (AAA)**—Figure 3.14

does not work

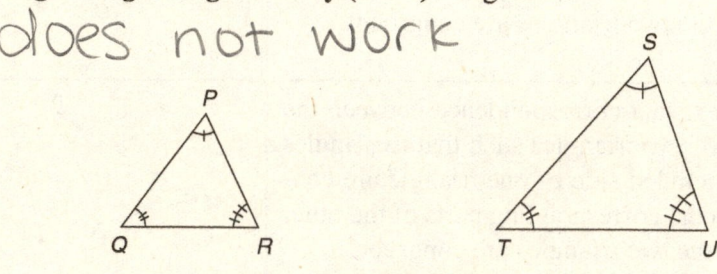

Figure 3.14

For this example, $\angle P \cong \angle S$, $\angle Q \cong \angle T$, and $\angle R \cong \angle U$. Although the triangles are not congruent, there is a relationship that does exist. This relationship will be discussed in our next topic.

CAUTION

Be certain that <u>corresponding</u> sides and angles match up when identifying a congruence between two triangles. Consider the two triangles shown in Figure 3.15.

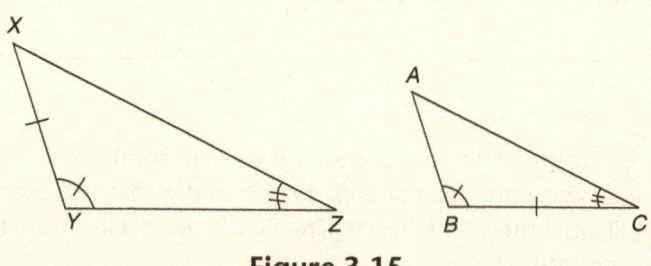

Figure 3.15

Even though $\angle Y \cong \angle B$ and $\angle Z \cong \angle C$, the corresponding sides of $\overline{YZ}$ and $\overline{BC}$ are not congruent. The fact that we also have $\overline{XY} \cong \overline{BC}$ is not sufficient to establish a congruence between these two triangles.

Similar Triangles

Similar: ~

As we look back at Figure 3.14 in which all three pairs of angles are congruent, we can make an assertion about these triangles. Two triangles are **similar** if the corresponding pairs of angles are congruent. Technically, we just need two pairs of congruent angles; the third pair must then be congruent because the sum of the angles of any triangle is 180°. The symbol for similarity between any two geometric figures is "~". Thus, using Figure 3.14, we can write $\triangle PQR \sim \triangle STU$.

There is also a strong relationship concerning the sides of similar triangles, namely that the ratio of any two corresponding sides must be constant. This means that in Figure 3.14, $\dfrac{PQ}{ST} = \dfrac{PR}{SU} = \dfrac{QR}{TU}$. Furthermore, the ratio of corresponding medians, altitudes, midsegments, and angle bisectors of similar triangles must be the same as the ratio of any two corresponding sides. Let's consider Figure 3.16, which is a re-creation of Figure 3.14, plus the altitudes $\overline{RB}$ and $\overline{UC}$.

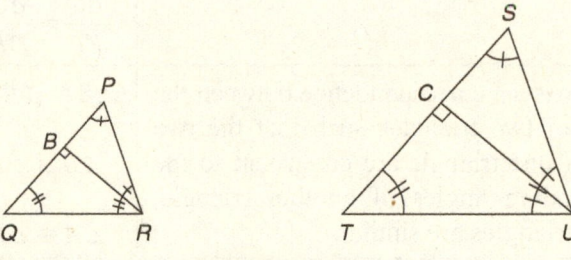

Figure 3.16

We can now state that the ratio of RB to UC must be equal to the ratio of any two corresponding sides. Thus, $\dfrac{PQ}{ST} = \dfrac{PR}{SU} = \dfrac{QR}{TU} = \dfrac{RB}{UC}$. A similar argument can be made for any pair of corresponding medians, midsegments, or angle bisectors.

There are three 'shortcut' theorems used to prove triangles are similar (refer to Figure 3.17).

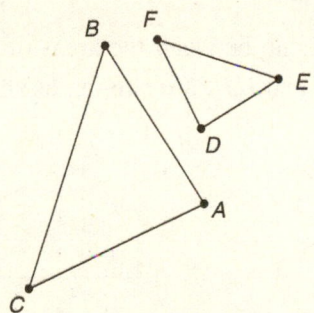

Figure 3.17

Used to Prove Triangles are Similar

Name	Theorem	Necessary Conditions to Prove $\triangle ABC \sim \triangle DEF$
SSS	If there exists a correspondence between the vertices of two triangles such that the ratios of the measures of the corresponding sides are equal, then the triangles are similar.	$\dfrac{AB}{DE} = \dfrac{BC}{EF} = \dfrac{AC}{DF}$
SAS	If there exists a correspondence between the vertices of two triangles such that the ratios of the measures of the two pairs of corresponding sides are equal and the corresponding included angles are congruent, then the triangles are similar.	$\dfrac{AB}{DE} = \dfrac{BC}{EF}$ and $\angle B \cong \angle E$ or $\dfrac{AB}{DE} = \dfrac{AC}{DF}$ and $\angle A \cong \angle D$ or $\dfrac{BC}{EF} = \dfrac{AC}{DF}$ and $\angle C \cong \angle F$
AA	If there exists a correspondence between the vertices of two triangles such that the two angles of one triangle are congruent to the corresponding angles of another triangle, then the triangles are similar.	$\angle B \cong \angle E$ and $\angle A \cong \angle D$ or $\angle B \cong \angle E$ and $\angle C \cong \angle F$ or $\angle A \cong \angle D$ and $\angle C \cong \angle F$

Relationships between Perimeters and Areas of Similar Triangles

We know that any two congruent triangles ought to have the same perimeter and the same area. *The ratio of the perimeters of similar triangles is the same as the ratio of any two corresponding sides.* Suppose the first triangle has sides of lengths 4, 7, and 9. The second triangle has lengths of 8, 14, and 18. Their perimeters are 20 and 40, respectively. Notice that the ratio of a pair of corresponding sides is 1 : 2, and so is the ratio of the perimeters.

In order to establish the relationship between the areas of two similar triangles, let's consider Figure 3.18, in which triangles *DEF* and *HJK* are similar, as shown by the angle markings.

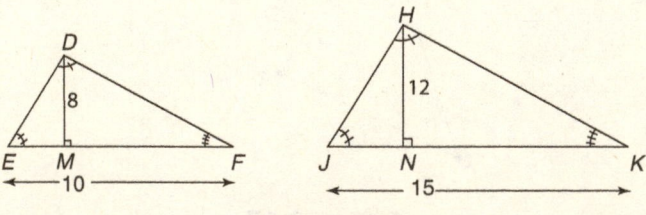

Figure 3.18

The ratio of corresponding sides is 10 : 15, which reduces to 2 : 3. Notice that the ratio of the altitudes $\overline{DM}$ and $\overline{HN}$ is also 2 : 3. The area of $\triangle DEF$ is $\left(\dfrac{1}{2}\right)(10)(8) = 40$, whereas the area of

$\triangle HJK$ is $\left(\dfrac{1}{2}\right)(15)(12) = 90$. So the ratio of the areas is 40 : 90, which reduces to 4 : 9. Even though 2 : 3 is not equal to 4 : 9, we do observe that $\left(\dfrac{2}{3}\right)^2 = \dfrac{4}{9}$.

> Although not formally proven, we conclude that the ratio of the areas of similar triangles is equal to the square of the ratio of the corresponding sides. This statement is reversible in the sense that the ratio of the sides is the square root of the ratio of the areas.

EXAMPLE 12

If $\triangle BCF \sim \triangle GLM$ and $\dfrac{BC}{GL} = \dfrac{3}{5}$, which other ratio has a value of $\dfrac{3}{5}$?

SOLUTION

There are many answers that would be correct. For examples, any two corresponding altitudes or corresponding angle bisectors would have the same ratio $\dfrac{3}{5}$. In terms of the sides of the two triangles, we could use ratio $\dfrac{CF}{LM}$.

EXAMPLE 13

Referring back to Example 12, suppose the perimeter of $\triangle BCF$ is 36. What is the perimeter of $\triangle GLM$?

SOLUTION

The perimeters are in the same ratio as a pair of corresponding sides. Letting x represent the perimeter of $\triangle GLM$, $\dfrac{3}{5} = \dfrac{36}{x}$. Thus, $x = 60$.

EXAMPLE 14

Referring back to Example 12, suppose the area of $\triangle GLM$ is 65. What is the area of $\triangle BCF$?

SOLUTION

The ratio of the area of $\triangle BCF$ to the area of $\triangle GLM$ is $\left(\dfrac{3}{5}\right)^2 = \dfrac{9}{25}$. Letting x represent the area of $\triangle BCF$, $\dfrac{9}{25} = \dfrac{x}{65}$. Thus, $x = 23.4$.

EXAMPLE 15

The ratio of the perimeter of Triangle I to the perimeter of Triangle II is $\frac{8}{3}$. The altitude to the base of Triangle I is five units more than twice the corresponding altitude to the base of Triangle II. How many units is the altitude to the base of Triangle I?

SOLUTION

The ratio of the altitudes matches the ratio of the perimeters. Let $2x + 5$ and x represent the corresponding altitudes of Triangles I and II, respectively. Then $\frac{8}{3} = \frac{2x + 5}{x}$, which simplifies to $8x = 6x + 15$, so $x = 7.5$. Thus, the corresponding altitude to the base of Triangle I is 20 units.

EXAMPLE 16

The ratio of the areas for two similar triangles is $\frac{4}{5}$. If the perimeter of the smaller triangle is 30 inches, what is the perimeter of the larger triangle to the nearest hundredth?

SOLUTION

The ratio of the perimeters is $\sqrt{\frac{4}{5}} = \frac{2}{\sqrt{5}}$. Let x represent the perimeter of the larger triangle. Then $\frac{2}{\sqrt{5}} = \frac{30}{x}$. Thus, $x = 15\sqrt{5} \approx 33.54$ inches.

Parallel Lines

Coplanar lines that do not intersect are called **parallel** (Figure 3.19).

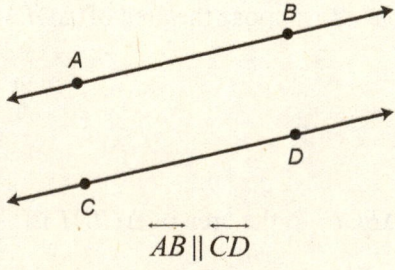

$$\overleftrightarrow{AB} \parallel \overleftrightarrow{CD}$$

Figure 3.19

A **transversal** is a line that intersects two or more coplanar lines. When two lines are cut by a transversal, eight angles are usually formed. **Interior** angles lie between the two lines. **Exterior** angles lie outside the two lines. Pairs of angles are given names to describe their location in relation to the lines.

In Figure 3.20, the transversal t intersects with lines a and b. Angles 3, 4, 5, and 6 are interior. Angles 1, 2, 7, and 8 are exterior.

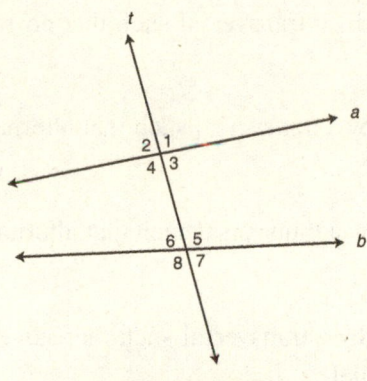

Figure 3.20

Two angles are corresponding angles if they occupy corresponding positions. The following pairs of angles are corresponding angles: $\angle 2$ and $\angle 6$, $\angle 4$ and $\angle 8$, $\angle 1$ and $\angle 5$, $\angle 3$ and $\angle 7$.

Two angles are alternate interior angles if they lie in the interior of a and b, on opposite sides of t and have different vertices. The following pairs of angles are alternate interior angles: $\angle 3$ and $\angle 6$, $\angle 4$ and $\angle 5$.

Two angles are alternate exterior angles if they lie in the exterior of a and b, on opposite sides of t and have different vertices. The following pairs of angles are alternate exterior angles: $\angle 1$ and $\angle 8$, $\angle 2$ and $\angle 7$.

Two angles are same side interior (or consecutive interior) if they lie in the interior of a and b and on the same side of t. The following pairs of angles are same-side interior angles: $\angle 3$ and $\angle 5$, $\angle 4$ and $\angle 6$.

Two angles are same-side exterior (or consecutive exterior) if they lie in the exterior of a and b and on same side of t. The following pairs of angles are same-side exterior angles: $\angle 1$ and $\angle 7$, $\angle 2$ and $\angle 8$.

The following theorems hold true when the lines cut by the transversal are parallel:

Theorem: When two parallel lines are cut by a transversal, corresponding angles are congruent.

Theorem: When two parallel lines are cut by a transversal, alternate interior angles are congruent.

Theorem: When two parallel lines are cut by a transversal, alternate exterior angles are congruent.

Theorem: When two parallel lines are cut by a transversal, same-side interior angles are supplementary.

Theorem: When two parallel lines are cut by a transversal, same-side exterior angles are supplementary.

The converse of each of these statements is also true. That is, each of the above relationships can also be used to prove lines are parallel.

Theorem: If two lines are cut by a transversal such that corresponding angles are congruent, the lines are parallel.

Theorem: If two lines are cut by a transversal such that alternate interior angles are congruent, the lines are parallel.

Theorem: If two lines are cut by a transversal such that alternate exterior angles are congruent, the lines are parallel.

Theorem: If two lines are cut by a transversal such that same-side interior angles are supplementary, the lines are parallel.

Theorem: If two lines are cut by a transversal such that same-side exterior angles are supplementary, the lines are parallel.

Quadrilaterals

A **quadrilateral** is a four-sided polygon.

A **kite** is a quadrilateral in which two distinct pairs of consecutive sides are congruent.

A **trapezoid** is a quadrilateral with exactly one pair of parallel sides (Figure 3.21).

- The parallel sides of a trapezoid are called bases. The non-parallel sides are called legs.

- The median of a trapezoid is the line joining the midpoints of the non-parallel sides.

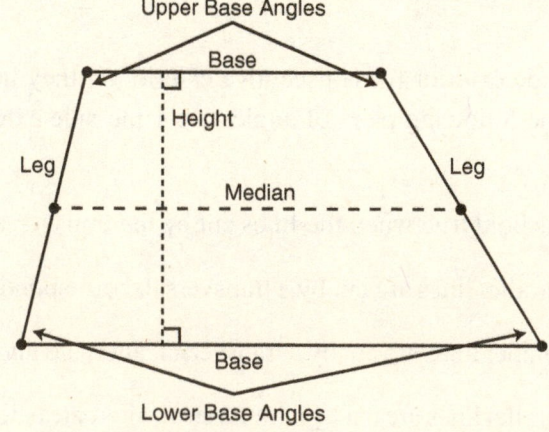

Figure 3.21

An **isosceles trapezoid** is a trapezoid in which the nonparallel sides are congruent.

A **parallelogram** is a quadrilateral in which both pairs of opposite sides are parallel.

A **rectangle** is a parallelogram in which at least one angle is right.

A **rhombus** is a parallelogram in which consecutive sides are congruent.

A **square** is a parallelogram that is both a rectangle and a rhombus.

all right angles & congruent sides

Diagonals of Quadrilaterals

Every quadrilateral has two diagonals. The properties of the diagonals for specific quadrilaterals are charted below.

Squares	The diagonals are congruent and are perpendicular bisectors of each other. They also bisect the angles from which they originate.	• congruent • perpendicular bisector • bisect angles
Rectangles	The diagonals are congruent and bisect each other, but they are not perpendicular to each other, nor do they bisect the angles from which they originate.	• congruent • bisect
Rhombi	The diagonals are perpendicular bisectors of each other. They also bisect the angles from which they originate. They are not congruent.	• perpendicular bisectors • bisect angles
Parallelograms	The diagonals bisect each other.	• bisect
Trapezoids	The diagonals show no special properties, except for isosceles trapezoids; in that case, the diagonals are congruent.	
Kites	The diagonals are perpendicular to each other. Only the longer diagonal bisects both the angles from which it originates and the short diagonal.	• perpendicular

Summary of Properties of Quadrilaterals

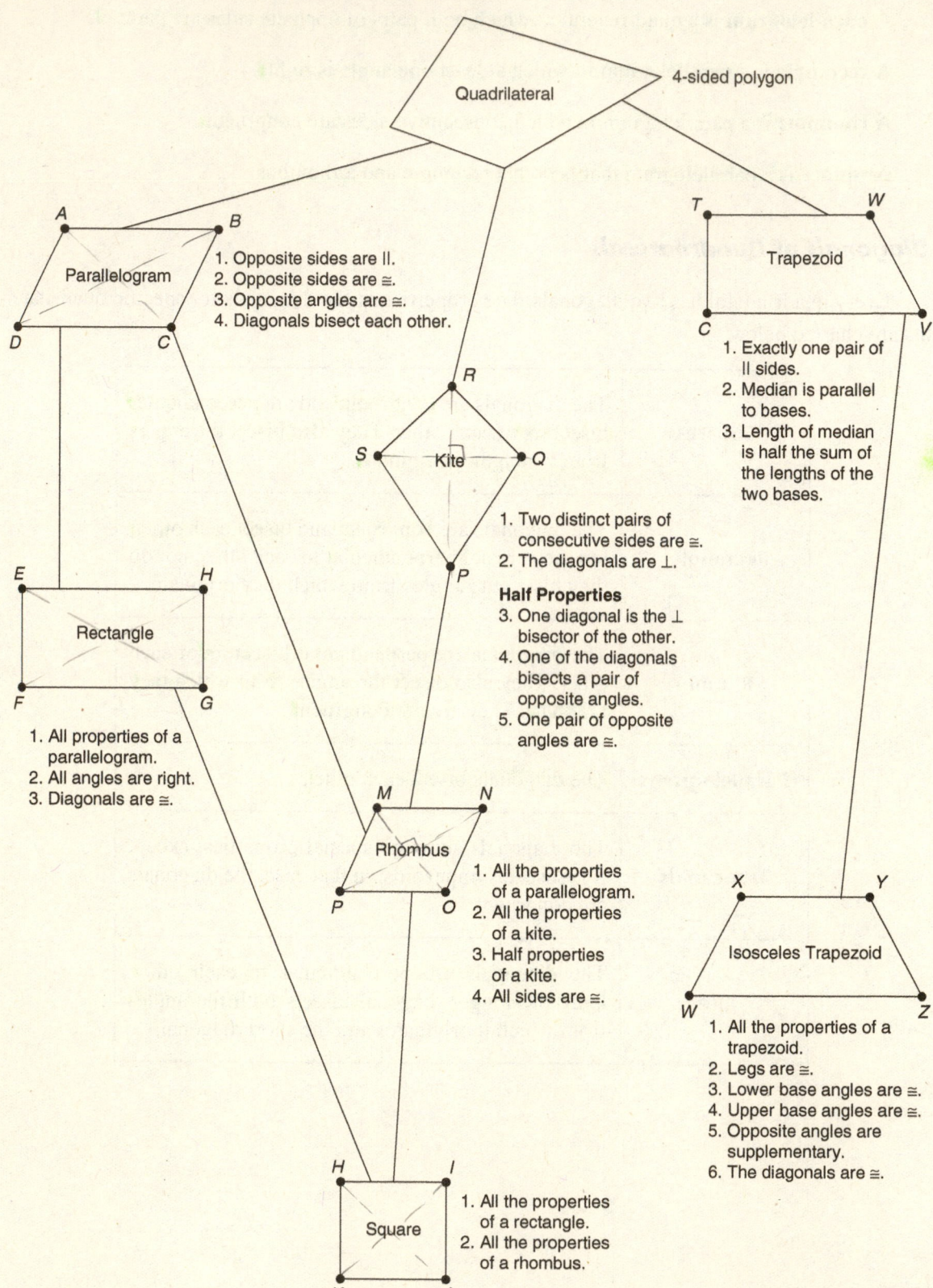

Quadrilateral — 4-sided polygon

Parallelogram
1. Opposite sides are ∥.
2. Opposite sides are ≅.
3. Opposite angles are ≅.
4. Diagonals bisect each other.

Trapezoid
1. Exactly one pair of ∥ sides.
2. Median is parallel to bases.
3. Length of median is half the sum of the lengths of the two bases.

Kite
1. Two distinct pairs of consecutive sides are ≅.
2. The diagonals are ⊥.

Half Properties
3. One diagonal is the ⊥ bisector of the other.
4. One of the diagonals bisects a pair of opposite angles.
5. One pair of opposite angles are ≅.

Rectangle
1. All properties of a parallelogram.
2. All angles are right.
3. Diagonals are ≅.

Rhombus
1. All the properties of a parallelogram.
2. All the properties of a kite.
3. Half properties of a kite.
4. All sides are ≅.

Isosceles Trapezoid
1. All the properties of a trapezoid.
2. Legs are ≅.
3. Lower base angles are ≅.
4. Upper base angles are ≅.
5. Opposite angles are supplementary.
6. The diagonals are ≅.

Square
1. All the properties of a rectangle.
2. All the properties of a rhombus.

EXAMPLE 17

ABCD is a parallelogram with $m\angle ACB = 18°$ and $m\angle CDA = 137°$. Find $m\angle CAB$.

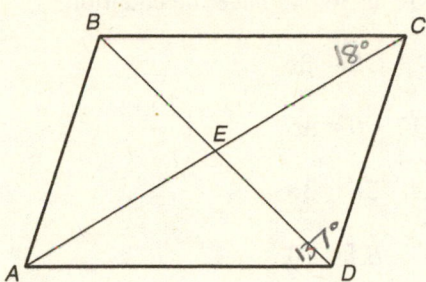

Consecutive angles add to 180°

SOLUTION

Opposite sides of a parallelogram are parallel. Since $\overline{BC} \parallel \overline{AD}$ and alternate interior angles are congruent, $m\angle CAD = 18°$. Since $\overline{CD} \parallel \overline{BA}$ and same-side interior angles are supplementary,

$$m\angle CDA + m\angle DAB = 180°$$
$$137° + m\angle DAB = 180°$$
$$m\angle DAB = 43°$$

Finally,
$$m\angle DAB = m\angle CAD + m\angle CAB$$
$$43° = 18° + m\angle CAB$$
$$25° = m\angle CAB$$

EXAMPLE 18

ABCD is an isosceles trapezoid with legs $\overline{BA}$ and $\overline{CD}$. $BC = 9$ and $BD = 17$. The perimeter of $\triangle ABC$ is 36, and the perimeter of *ABCD* is 50. Find *AD*.

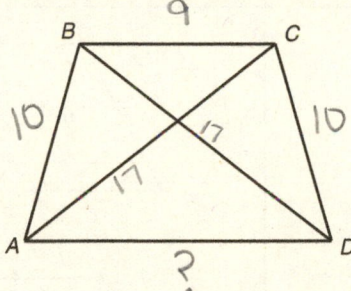

P = 50

perimeter
ABCD = 50
9 + 10 + 10 + AD = 50
29 + AD = 50
AD = 21

perimeter
△ABC = 36
17 + 9 + AB = 36
AB + 26 = 36
AB = 10

SOLUTION

The diagonals of an isosceles triangle are congruent, so $AC = BC = 17$. Since the perimeter of triangle ABC is 36, we have the equation:

$$BA + AC + CB = 36$$

$$BA + 17 + 9 = 36$$

$$BA + 26 = 36$$

$$BA = 10$$

Thus, since the legs of an isosceles trapezoid are congruent, $BA = CD = 10$. Since the perimeter of $ABCD$ is 50, we have the equation:

$$AB + BC + CD + AD = 50$$

$$10 + 9 + 10 + AD = 50$$

$$29 + AD = 50$$

$$AD = 21$$

Perimeters and Areas of Triangles and Quadrilaterals

The **perimeter** is the distance around a two-dimensional figure. The perimeter is measured in linear units, such as centimeters, inches, or miles. The perimeter of a polygon is found by summing the lengths of its sides.

The **area** of a two-dimensional figure is the amount of space inside its boundary. Area is measured in square units such as square meters, square feet and square kilometers. The formulas below can be used to find the areas of the indicated figures.

Name and Formula	Diagram
Parallelogram $A = bh$	
Square $A = s^2$	

Name and Formula	Diagram
Rectangle $A = lw$ bh	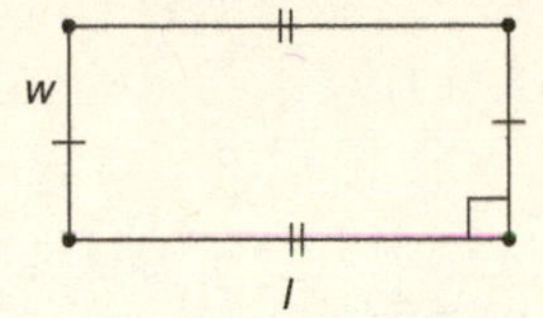
Triangle $A = \dfrac{1}{2}bh$	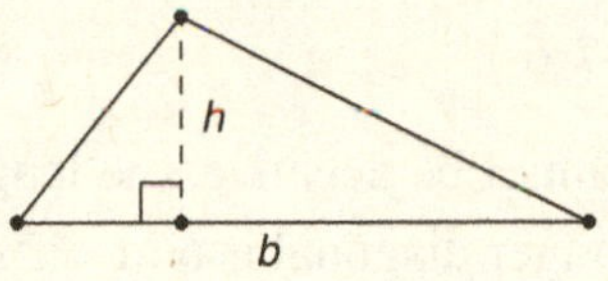
Kite $A = \dfrac{1}{2}d_1 d_2$	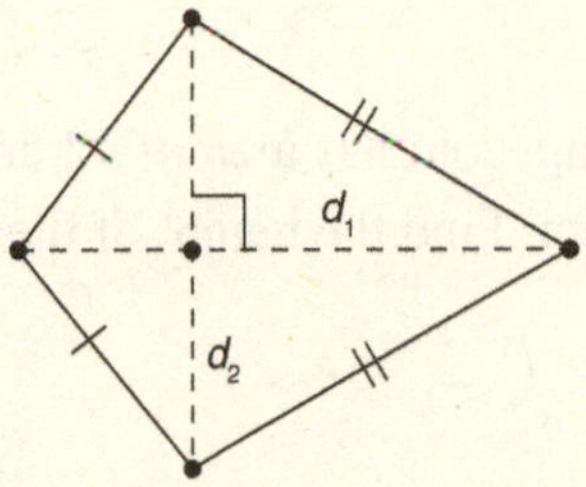
Rhombus $A = \dfrac{1}{2}d_1 d_2$ or $A = bh$	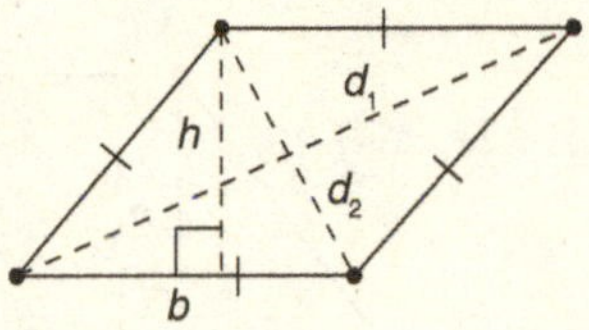
Trapezoid $A = \dfrac{1}{2}h(b_1 + b_2)$	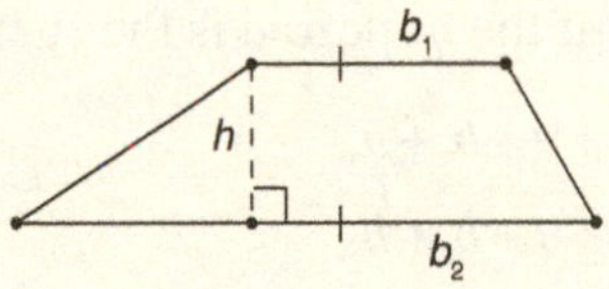

EXAMPLE 19

One diagonal of a kite is one meter larger than the other. If the area of the kite is 21 m², find length of each diagonal.

SOLUTION

Let d_1 the length of the shorter diagonal. Then, $d_2 = d_1 + 1$. Substitute these expressions and the given area into the area formula to find the length of each of the diagonals.

$$A = \frac{1}{2}d_1 d_2$$

$$21 = \frac{1}{2}x(x+1)$$

$$42 = x^2 + x$$

$$0 = x^2 + x - 42$$

$$0 = (x+7)(x-6)$$

$$x = -7, 6$$

[handwritten:] $\frac{1}{2}x(x+1)$

$21 = \frac{1}{2}x^2 + x$

$42 = x^2 + x$

$= x^2 + x - 42$

$= (x+7)(x-6)$

$x = -7, 6$

6 and 6+1

6 and 7

Since length cannot be negative, the length of the shorter diagonal is 6 m and the length of the longer diagonal is 6 m + 1 m = 7 m.

EXAMPLE 20

An isosceles trapezoid has area of 42 cm² and perimeter of 30 cm. The leg of the trapezoid is 9 cm. Find the height of the trapezoid.

SOLUTION

Begin by sketching a diagram with the given information.

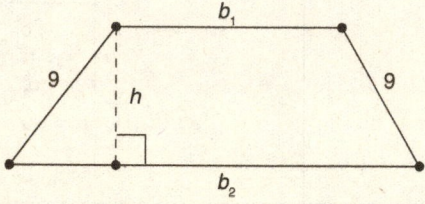

[handwritten:]

$30 = 9 + 9 + b_1 + b_2$

$30 = 18 + b_1 + b_2$

$12 = b_1 + b_2$

$A = \frac{1}{2}(b_1 + b_2)(h)$

$42 = \frac{1}{2}(12)(h)$

$42 = 6h$

$h = 7$

The perimeter of the trapezoid is the sum of the lengths of the sides.

$$P = 9 + 9 + b_1 + b_2$$

$$30 = 9 + 9 + b_1 + b_2$$

$$12 = b_1 + b_2$$

Substitute this information into the area formula to find the height.

$$A = \frac{1}{2}h(b_1 + b_2)$$

$$42 = \frac{1}{2}h(12)$$

$$42 = 6h$$

$$7 = h$$

The height of the trapezoid is 7 cm.

Congruent and Similar Quadrilaterals

The concepts of congruence and similarity that we explored for triangles are very close to the ones needed for quadrilaterals.

- Two quadrilaterals are congruent if each pair of angles and each pair of sides can be matched.

- Two quadrilaterals are similar if each pair of angles can be matched and each pair of corresponding sides are in the same ratio.

For similar quadrilaterals:

- The ratio of the corresponding diagonals and the ratio of the perimeters is the same as the ratio of corresponding sides.

- The ratio of corresponding altitudes is also the same as the ratio of the perimeters.

- The ratio of the areas is the square of the ratio of corresponding sides.

> Any two squares are automatically similar. This statement cannot be made regarding other quadrilaterals.

EXAMPLE 21

Rectangles TVAB and UXCD, shown below, are similar.

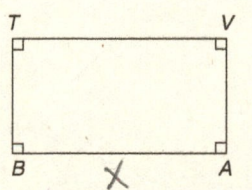
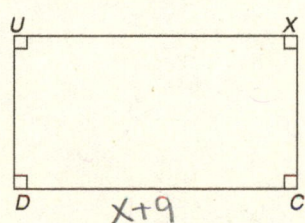

The ratio of the perimeter of *TVAB* to that of *UXCD* is $\frac{7}{10}$. If *CD* is 9 units larger than *AB*, what is the value of *CD*?

SOLUTION

Let x and $x + 9$ represent *AB* and *CD*, respectively. Then $\frac{7}{10} = \frac{x}{x + 9}$. Then $7x + 63 = 10x$, so $x = 21$. Thus, $CD = 30$ units.

EXAMPLE 22

Trapezoids *ACEG* and *JLNP*, shown below, are similar.

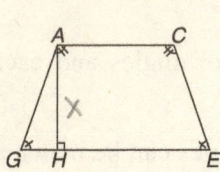 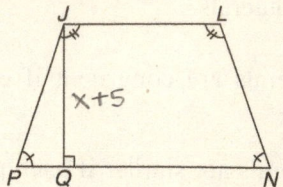

The area of *ACEG* is 64 and the area of *JLNP* is 110. If *JQ* is five units larger than *AH*, what is the value of *AH* (to the nearest hundredth)?

$$\frac{64}{110} \qquad \frac{8}{\sqrt{110}} = \frac{x}{x+5} \qquad 8x+40 = \sqrt{110}\,x$$

SOLUTION

The ratio of corresponding altitudes is $\sqrt{\dfrac{64}{110}} = \dfrac{8}{\sqrt{110}}$. Let *x* represent *AH* and

$x + 5$ represent *JQ*. Then $\dfrac{8}{\sqrt{110}} = \dfrac{x}{x+5}$. Since $\sqrt{110} \approx 10.49$, we have. $10.49x = 8x + 40$, $x \approx 16.06$. Thus, *AH* = 16.06 units.

EXAMPLE 23

Quadrilaterals *UWYZ* and *VABD* are similar, as shown below.

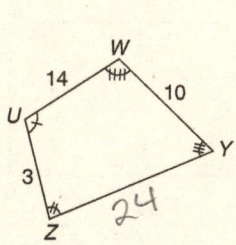 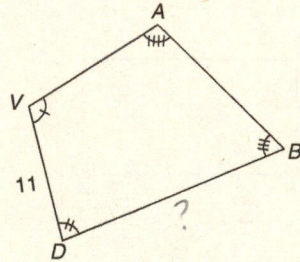

If the perimeter of *UWYZ* is 51, what is the value of *DB*?

SOLUTION

$ZY = 51 - 3 - 14 - 10 = 24$. Let *x* represent *DB*. Then $\dfrac{3}{11} = \dfrac{24}{x}$, so $x = 88$.

Thus, *DB* = 88.

$$\frac{3}{11} = \frac{24}{x}$$

$$3x = 264$$
$$x = 88$$

EXAMPLE 24

Consider the two similar rhombi shown below.

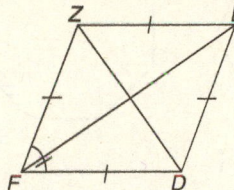 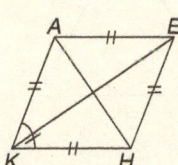

The area of *ZBDF* is 35 square inches larger than the area of *AEHK*. $\dfrac{FD}{KH} = \dfrac{4}{3}$.
What is the product of the diagonals in *ZBDF*?

SOLUTION

Let $x + 35$ and x represent the areas of *ZBDF* and *AEHK*, respectively. Then
$\dfrac{x+35}{x} = \left(\dfrac{4}{3}\right)^2 = \dfrac{16}{9}$, which leads to $16x = 9x + 315$. Then $x = 45$, so the area
of *ZBDF* is 80 square inches. The area of a rhombus is one half the product of its
diagonals. Thus, the product of the diagonals in *ZBDF* is 160 square inches.

Polygons

A **polygon** is a figure with the same number of sides as angles.

An **equilateral polygon** (Figure 3.22) is a polygon all of whose sides are of equal measure.

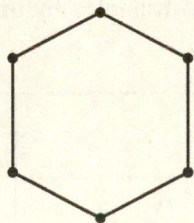

Figure 3.22

An **equiangular polygon** (Figure 3.23) is a polygon all of whose angles are of equal measure.

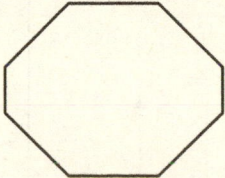

Figure 3.23

A **regular polygon** (Figure 3.24) is a polygon that is both equilateral and equiangular.

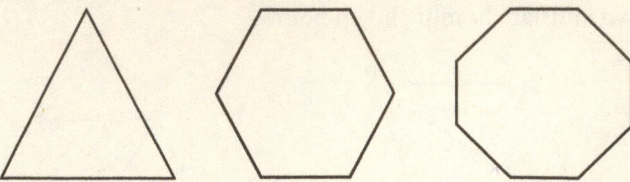

Figure 3.24

Number of sides	Name
3	Triangle
4	Quadrilateral
5	Pentagon
6	Hexagon
7	Heptagon
8	Octagon
9	Nonagon
10	Decagon
12	Dodecagon
15	Pentadecagon

Angles of a Polygon

Every polygon can be broken up into triangles by drawing the diagonals from one vertex as shown below:

	# of sides	# of triangles
	4	2
	5	3

	# of sides	# of triangles
	6	4
	7	5

So, if the number of sides of the polygon is n, then the number of triangles formed by drawing the diagonals from one vertex is $(n-2)$. Since the sum of the angles of a triangle is 180°, the sum of the interior angles of a polygon with n sides is $(n-2)180°$. *Sum of interior angles*

At each vertex of a polygon, there is a pair of interior and exterior angles that are supplementary. Thus, the sum of the interior and exterior angles of a polygon is $180n$.

$$\text{Sum of Exterior Angles} + \text{Sum of Interior Angles} = 180n$$
$$\text{Sum of Exterior Angles} = 180n - \text{Sum of Interior Angles}$$
$$= 180n - (n-2)180°$$
$$= 180n - 180n + 360°$$
$$= 360°$$

Therefore, the sum of the exterior angles of a polygon with n sides is 360°.

In an equiangular polygon, there are n congruent interior angles and n congruent exterior angles. Therefore, in an equiangular polygon, the measure of each exterior angle is $\dfrac{360°}{n}$. The measure of each interior angle of an equiangular polygon is $\dfrac{(n-2)180°}{n}$. Alternatively, because interior angles and exterior angles are supplementary, each interior angle of an equiangular polygon is $180° - \dfrac{360°}{n}$.

EXAMPLE 25

Find the measure of $\angle 1$ in the figure below.

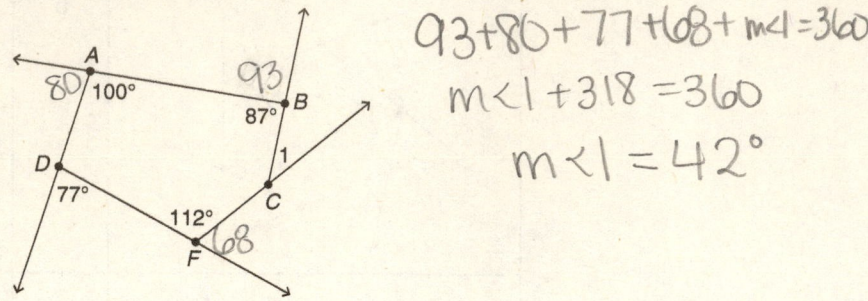

$93 + 80 + 77 + 68 + m\angle 1 = 360$

$m\angle 1 + 318 = 360$

$m\angle 1 = 42°$

SOLUTION

First, find the exterior angle at each of the vertices that it is not given by taking the supplement of the given interior angle:

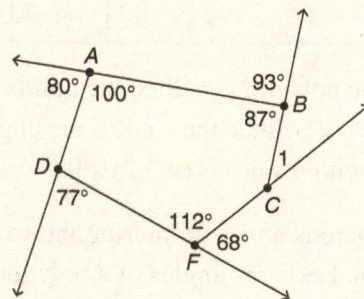

Create and solve an equation equating the sum of the exterior angles to 360°.

$$m\angle 1 + 93° + 80° + 77° + 68° = 360°$$

$$m\angle 1 + 318° = 360°$$

$$m\angle 1 = 42°$$

EXAMPLE 26

Each interior angle of a regular polygon contains 120°. How many sides does the polygon have?

SOLUTION

At each vertex of a polygon, we can draw an exterior angle that is supplementary to the interior angle, as shown in the diagram below.

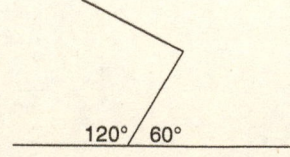

Since we are told that the interior angle measures 120°, we can deduce that the exterior angle measures 60°.

Each exterior angle of a regular polygon of n sides measures $\dfrac{360°}{n}$ degrees. We know that each exterior angle measures 60°, and, therefore, by setting $\dfrac{360°}{n}$ equal to 60°, we can determine the number of sides in the polygon. The calculation is as follows:

$$\frac{360°}{n} = 60°$$

$$60°n = 360°$$

$$n = 6$$

Exterior angles

$$\frac{360}{n} = 60$$
$$360 = 60n$$
$$n = 6$$

Therefore, the regular polygon, with interior angles of 120°, has six sides and is called a hexagon.

Congruent Polygons

Two polygons are **congruent** if

1. Their corresponding interior angles are congruent.

2. Their corresponding sides are congruent.

Congruent polygons have the same shape and size but may have different orientations (Figure 3.25).

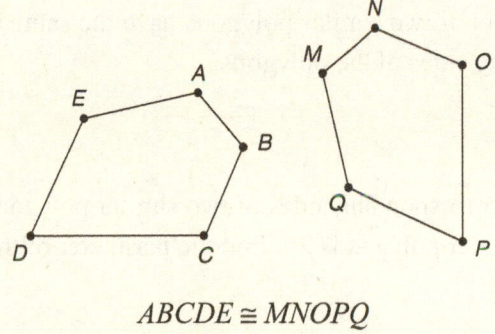

$$ABCDE \cong MNOPQ$$

Figure 3.25

Similarly, if two polygons are congruent then their corresponding angles and sides are congruent. For example, if pentagon *ABCDE* is congruent to pentagon *MNOPQ*, then $\angle A \cong \angle M$, $\angle B \cong \angle N$, $\angle C \cong \angle O$, $\angle D \cong \angle P$, $\angle E \cong \angle Q$.

Similar Polygons

Two polygons are **similar** if

1. The measures of their corresponding interior angles are congruent.

2. The ratios of the lengths of their corresponding sides are equal.

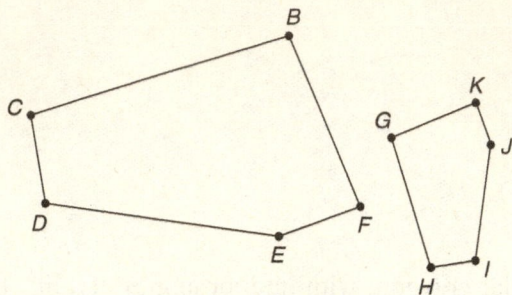

$$BCDEF \sim GHIJK$$

Figure 3.26

Similar polygons will have the same shape but may have different sizes and/or orientations, as shown in Figure 3.26.

The converse is also true. That is, if the corresponding angles of two polygons are congruent and their corresponding sides are proportional, then the polygons are similar.

Theorem: The ratio of the lengths of two corresponding diagonals of two similar polygons is equal to the ratio of the lengths of any two corresponding sides of the polygons.

Theorem: The perimeters of two similar polygons have the same ratio as the measures of any pair of corresponding sides of the polygons.

EXAMPLE 27

The lengths of two corresponding sides of two similar polygons are 4 and 7. If the perimeter of the smaller polygon is 20, find the perimeter of the larger polygon.

SOLUTION

We know, by theorem, that the perimeters of two similar polygons have the same ratio as the measures of any pair of corresponding sides. Let x be the perimeter of the larger polygon.

$$\text{Then } \frac{20}{x} = \frac{4}{7}$$
$$4x = 140$$
$$x = 35$$

Therefore, the perimeter of the larger polygon is 35.

Area of a Regular Polygon

The area of a regular polygon can be determined by using the **apothem** and the **perimeter** of the polygon. The apothem, a, of a regular polygon is the segment from the center of the polygon perpendicular to a side of the polygon. The radius, r, of a regular polygon is the segment joining the vertex with the center of a regular polygon.

(1) All radii of a regular polygon are congruent.

(2) All apothems of a regular polygon are congruent.

(3) An apothem of a regular polygon bisects the side to which its drawn.

(4) The radius of a regular polygon bisects the interior angle to which it is drawn.

The area of a regular polygon equals one-half the product of the length of the apothem and the perimeter of the polygon.

$$A = \frac{1}{2}aP$$

EXAMPLE 28

Find the area of a regular hexagon if one side has length 6.

SOLUTION

Create a right triangle by drawing an apothem and a radius. Since the apothem bisects the side to which it is drawn, the base of the right triangle has length 3.

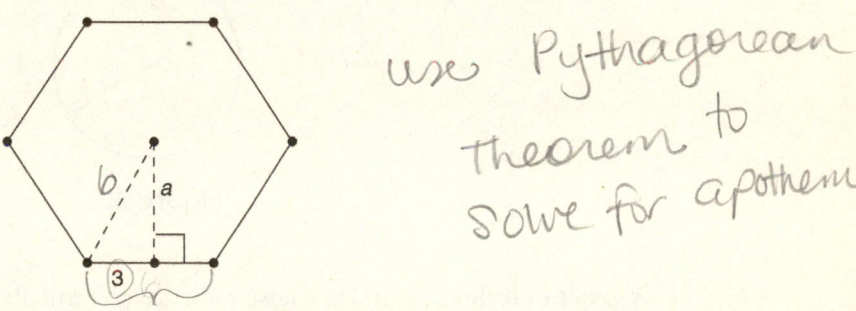

use Pythagorean theorem to solve for apothem

The interior angle of a regular hexagon is $180° - \dfrac{360°}{6} = 120°$. Since the radius bisects the interior angle, two 60° angles are formed. The triangle created by the apothem, radius and half the side length is a 30°–60°–90° triangle.

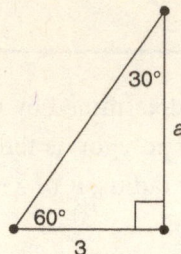

Since the side opposite 30° is 3, the apothem is $3\sqrt{3}$. The perimeter of the hexagon is $6 \times 6 = 36$. Substitute these values into the area formula to find the area of the hexagon:

$$A = \frac{1}{2}aP$$
$$= \frac{1}{2}(3\sqrt{3})36$$
$$= 54\sqrt{3} \text{ square units}.$$

Circles

Definitions

A **circle** is a set of points in the same plane equidistant from a fixed point, called its **center**. Circles are often named by their center point, such as circle O in Figure 3.27.

A **radius** of a circle is a line segment drawn from the center of the circle to any point on the circle (Figure 3.27).

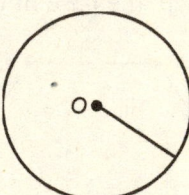

Figure 3.27

Congruent circles are circles whose radii are congruent.

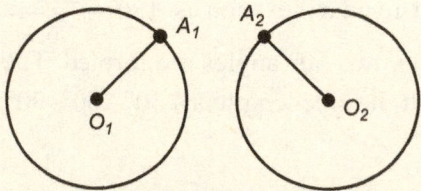

Figure 3.28

In Figure 3.28, if $O_1A_1 \cong O_2A_2$, then $O_1 \cong O_2$.

The measure of a semicircle is 180°.

A **circumscribed circle** is a circle passing through all the vertices of a polygon (Figure 3.29). The polygon is said to be **inscribed** in the circle.

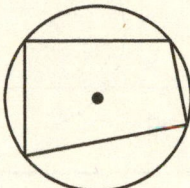

Figure 3.29

Circles that have the same center and unequal radii are called **concentric circles** (Figure 3.30).

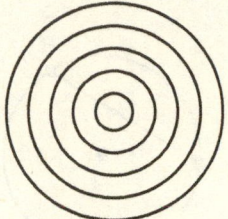

Figure 3.30

A line that has one and only one point of intersection with a circle is called a **tangent** to that circle, and their common point is called a **point of tangency.** In Figure 3.31, Q and P are each points of tangency.

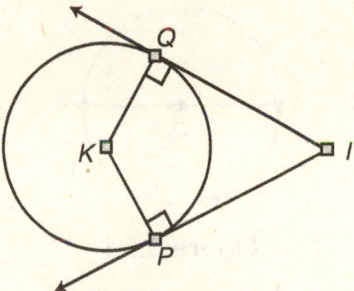

Figure 3.31

A tangent segment is the part of a tangent line that joins a point outside a circle for the point of tangency. Tangent segments from the same exterior point are equal. A tangent is perpendicular to the radius drawn to the point of tangency. In Figure 3.31, $\overline{IQ}$ and $\overline{IP}$ are tangent segments. Therefore, $\overline{IQ} \cong \overline{IP}$, $\overline{KQ} \perp \overline{IQ}$, and $\overline{KP} \perp \overline{IP}$.

A line that intersects a circle in two points is called a **secant.**

A secant segment is the part of a secant line that joins a point outside the circle to the farther intersection point of the secant and the circle. The **external part** of a secant segment is the part of a secant segment that joins the outside point to the nearer point of intersection. See Figure 3.32.

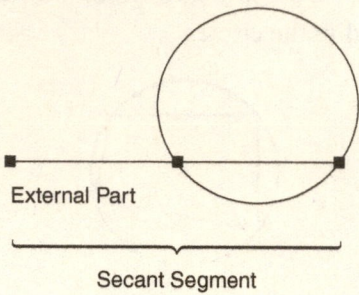

Figure 3.32

A line segment joining two points on a circle is called a **chord** of the circle (Figure 3.33).

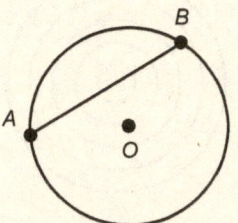

Figure 3.33

A chord that passes through the center of the circle is called a **diameter** of the circle. In Figure 3.34, $\overline{AB}$ is a diameter.

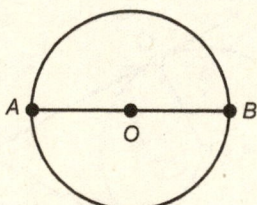

Figure 3.34

The line passing through the centers of two (or more) circles is called the **line of centers.**

Theorem: If a radius is perpendicular to a chord, then it bisects the chord.

Theorem: If a radius of a circle bisects a chord that is not the diameter, then it is perpendicular to that chord.

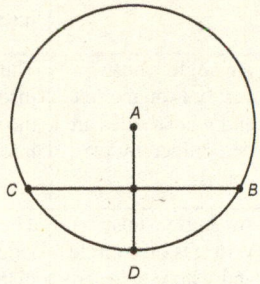

Figure 3.35

In Circle A (Figure 3.35), $\overline{AD} \perp \overline{CB}$ if and only if $\overline{AD}$ bisects $\overline{CB}$.

A portion of a circle is called an **arc** of the circle. A semicircle is an arc whose endpoints are the endpoints of a diameter. The measure of a semicircle is 180°. A minor arc is an arc whose measure is less than 180°. Minor arcs are named using the two endpoints. A major arc is an arc whose measure is greater than 180°. Major arcs are named using the endpoints and one point in between. See Figure 3.36.

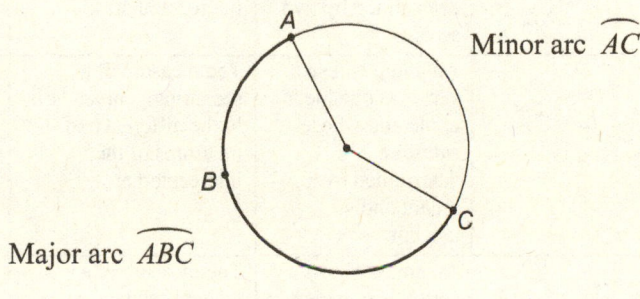

Figure 3.36

Angles in a Circle

Type of Angle	Illustration	Description	Theorem	Measure Formula Based on Illustration
Central Angle *arc & angle equal*		An angle whose vertex is at the center of the circle.	The measure of a central angle is equal to the measure of its intercepted arc.	$m\angle CAB = m\overset{\frown}{CB}$
Inscribed Angle *½ of arc measure*		An angle whose vertex is on a circle and whose sides are determined by two chords.	The measure of an inscribed angle is ½ the measure of its intercepted arc.	$m\angle CBD = \frac{1}{2}m\overset{\frown}{CD}$
Tangent-Chord Angle *½ of arc measure*		An angle whose vertex is on a circle and whose sides are determined by a tangent and a chord that intersect at the point of tangency.	The measure of a tangent-chord angle is ½ the measure of the intercepted arc.	$m\angle CBD = \frac{1}{2}m\overset{\frown}{CB}$
Chord-Chord Angle		An angle formed by two chords that intersect inside a circle but not at the center.	The measure of a chord-chord angle is ½ the sum of the measures of the intercepted arcs.	$m\angle ATB = m\angle CTD = \frac{1}{2}(m\overset{\frown}{CD} + m\overset{\frown}{AB})$
Secant-Secant Angle *½(arc-arc) measure*		An angle whose vertex is outside a circle and whose sides are determined by two secants.	The measure of a secant-secant angle is ½ the difference of the measures of the intercepted arcs.	$m\angle CBD = \frac{1}{2}(m\overset{\frown}{CD} - m\overset{\frown}{SE})$
Secant-Tangent Angle		An angle whose vertex is outside a circle and whose sides are determined by a secant and a tangent.	The measure of a secant-tangent angle is ½ the difference of the measures of the intercepted arcs.	$m\angle GFE = \frac{1}{2}(m\overset{\frown}{GE} - m\overset{\frown}{GH})$
Tangent-Tangent Angle		An angle whose vertex is outside a circle and whose sides are determined by two tangents.	The measure of a tangent-tangent angle is ½ the difference of the measures of the intercepted arcs, *or* The measure of a tangent-tangent angle is the supplement of the minor intercepted arc.	$m\angle CBD = \frac{1}{2}(m\overset{\frown}{CED} - m\overset{\frown}{CD})$ *or* $m\angle CBD = 180° - m\overset{\frown}{CD}$

EXAMPLE 29

Find the measure of $\overset{\frown}{GD}$ in the figure below.

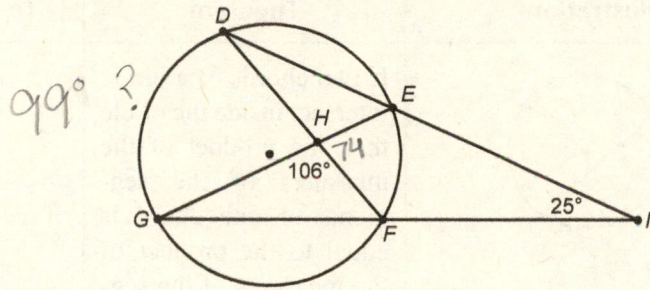

SOLUTION

Since they form a straight line, $\angle EHF$ is supplementary to $\angle GHF$ so $m\angle EHF =$ $180° - 106° = 74°$. Let $x = m\overset{\frown}{DG}$ and $y = m\overset{\frown}{EF}$. From the figure, $\angle EHF$ is a chord-chord angle with $\overset{\frown}{DG}$ and $\overset{\frown}{EF}$. So

$$74 = \frac{1}{2}(x + y)$$

Likewise, $\angle DIG$ is a secant-secant angle with intercepted arcs $\overset{\frown}{DG}$ and $\overset{\frown}{EF}$. So

$$25 = \frac{1}{2}(x - y)$$

Solve the system of equations for x to find the measure of $\overset{\frown}{GD}$.

$$74 = \frac{1}{2}(x + y) \rightarrow 148 = x + y$$
$$25 = \frac{1}{2}(x - y) \rightarrow \underline{50 = x - y}$$
$$198 = 2x$$

$$99 = x$$

The measure of $\overset{\frown}{GD}$ is 99°.

(handwritten) 99° ?

(handwritten)
$$74 = \frac{1}{2}(x+y) \Rightarrow \quad 48 = x+y$$
$$25 = \frac{1}{2}(x+y) \qquad 50 = x-y$$
$$198 = 2x$$
$$x = 99$$

Intersecting Segments of a Circle

Type of Intersection	Illustration	Theorem	Theorem Applied to Illustration
Chord-Chord		If two chords of a circle intersect inside the circle then the product of the measures of the segments of one chord is equal to the product of the measures of the segments of the other chord.	$CG \cdot GD = EG \cdot GF$
Tangent-Secant		If a tangent segment and a secant segment are drawn from an external point to a circle, then the square of the measure of the tangent segment is equal to the product of the measures of the entire secant segment and its external part.	$CD^2 = BD \cdot ED$
Secant-Secant		If two secant segments are drawn from an external point to a circle, then the product of the measures of one entire secant segment and its external part is equal to the product of the measures of the other entire secant segment and its external part.	$BD \cdot ED = FD \cdot CD$

EXAMPLE 30

Line segment $\overline{DE}$ is tangent to $\odot H$. Use the lengths given in the following figure to find BC.

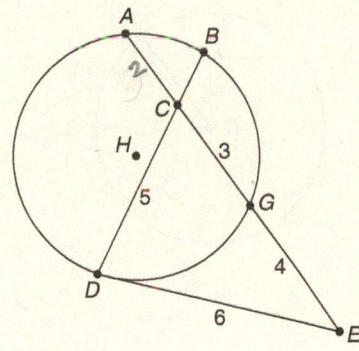

$DE^2 = GE \cdot AE$

$6^2 = 4 \cdot AE$

$36 = 4 \cdot AE$

$9 = AE$

$AC + CG + GE = 9$

$AC + 3 + 4 = 9$

$AC = 2$

$AC \cdot CG = BC \cdot CD$

$2 \cdot 3 = BC \cdot 5$

$6 = BC \cdot 5$

$BC = \dfrac{6}{5}$

SOLUTION

Use the Tangent-Secant Theorem to find AC.

$$DE^2 = GE \cdot AE$$
$$6^2 = 4 \cdot AE$$
$$9 = AE$$
$$AC + CG + GE = AE$$
$$AC + 3 + 4 = 9$$
$$AC = 2$$

Then use the Chord-Chord Theorem to find BC.

$$AC \cdot CG = BC \cdot CD$$
$$2 \cdot 3 = BC \cdot 5$$
$$\frac{6}{5} = BC$$

Circumference

$C = 2\pi r$ or πd

perimeter of circle is circumference

The perimeter of a circle is called its **circumference**. The circumference of a circle with radius r is given by $C = 2\pi r$ or $C = \pi d$ where d is the diameter of the circle. The **length of an arc** of a circle is a fraction of its circumference. Thus, to find the length of an arc, find the fraction of the circle it occupies by dividing its measure by $360°$. Then, multiply the fraction by the circumference of the circle.

$$\text{Length of an arc} = \frac{\text{Measure of arc}}{360°} 2\pi r$$

EXAMPLE 31

Points A and B on circle Q are such that $\triangle AQB$ is equilateral. If the length of side $\overline{AB} = 12$, find the length of arc AB.

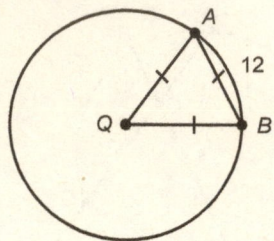

SOLUTION

To find the arc length of arc AB, we must find the measure of $\overarc{AB}$ the central angle $\angle AQB$ and the measure of the radius $\overline{QA}$. $\angle AQB$ is an interior angle of the equilateral triangle $\triangle AQB$. Therefore, $m\angle AQB = 60°$. Similarly, in the equilateral $\triangle AQB$, $AQ = AB = QB = 12$.

Given the radius, r, and the central angle, n, the arc length is given by

$$\frac{n}{360} \times 2\pi r.$$

Therefore, by substitution,

$$\overarc{AB} = \frac{60}{360} \times 2\pi \times 12 = \frac{1}{6} \times 2\pi \times 12 = 4\pi.$$

Therefore, the length of arc $AB = 4\pi$.

Areas of Circles and Sectors

Name and Formula	Diagram
Circle $A = \pi r^2$	
Sector $A = \dfrac{x}{360}\pi r^2$	

Three-Dimensional Figures

Solid figures are three-dimensional. They have length, width and height. We can build solids from two-dimensional patterns called **nets**. Nets consist of the faces that create the solid. Figure 3.37 shows some examples of the net of a cube.

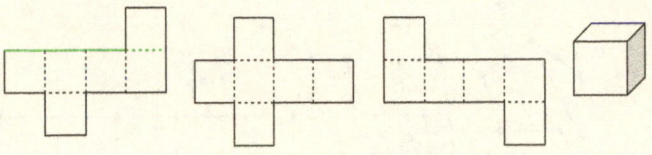

Figure 3.37

Each of the nets for a cube contains six squares since cubes have six square faces. However, not every arrangement of six squares can be folded into a cube. That is, not every arrangement of six squares is a net of a cube. The arrangements in Figure 3.38 are *not* nets of a cube.

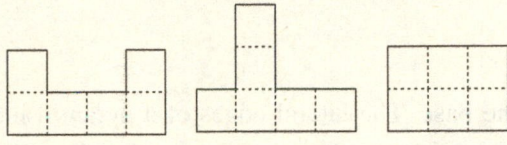

Figure 3.38

A **polyhedron** is a solid with flat faces. The **faces** of a polyhedron are polygons and the lines where they intersect are called **edges**. Edges in three dimensions are equivalent to sides in two dimensions. Prisms, pyramids, cylinders, cones, and spheres are types of polyhedrons.

Prism

A **prism** has congruent parallel faces called **bases**. The faces that are not bases are called **lateral faces**. The lateral faces of a prism are parallelograms. The lateral edges of a prism are parallel. The bases of a **right prism** are aligned one directly above the other. The lateral faces of a right prism are perpendicular to the bases (i.e., the lateral faces are rectangles). Prisms that are not right are called **oblique.** The net of a prism contains two congruent *n*-gons (the bases) and *n* parallelograms. See Figure 3.39.

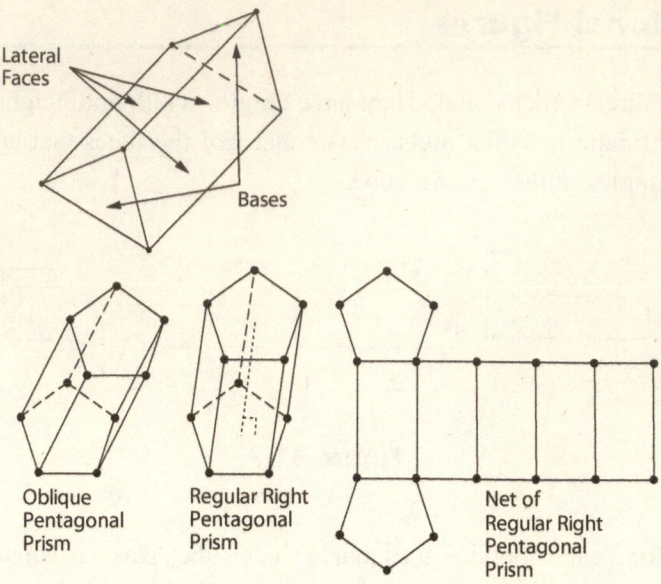

Figure 3.39

Pyramid

A **pyramid** has only one base. The lateral edges of a pyramid intersect in a point called the **vertex** of the pyramid. The lateral faces of a pyramid are triangles. In a **right pyramid**, the vertex is directly above the center of the base. A **regular pyramid** is a right pyramid that has a regular polygon as its base. The faces of a regular pyramid are congruent isosceles triangles. The **altitude** of a pyramid is the perpendicular segment from the vertex to the base. The foot of the altitude is the center of the base of a regular pyramid. The **slant height** is the distance from the vertex to the base along the center of a face. In a pyramid, the slant height is the altitude of the triangular lateral face. The net of a pyramid contains one *n*-gon and *n* triangles. See Figure 3.40.

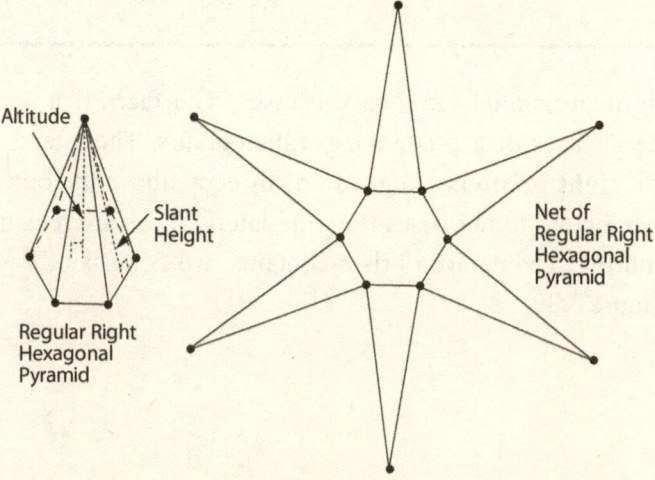

Figure 3.40

Cylinder

Cylinders are similar to prisms. However, the bases of a cylinder are congruent parallel circles. The line connecting the bases of a **right cylinder** is perpendicular to each base. The net of a right cylinder whose base has circumference $2\pi r$ and has height h contains two congruent circles with radii r and a rectangle with dimensions $2\pi r$ by h. See Figure 3.41.

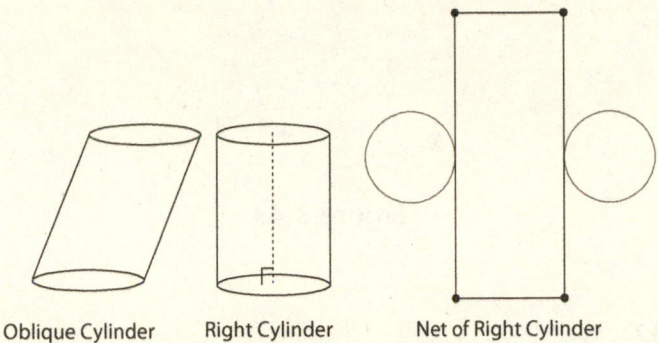

Oblique Cylinder   Right Cylinder   Net of Right Cylinder

Figure 3.41

Cone

Cones resemble pyramids. However, the base of a cone is a circle. In a **right cone**, the line connecting the vertex with the center of the base is perpendicular to the base. The **slant height** of a right cone is the distance from any point on the base to the vertex of the cone. The slant height forms a right triangle with the radius and the altitude. The net of a right cylinder whose base has circumference $2\pi r$ and has slant height s contains one circle and a sector of a circle with radius s whose length is $2\pi r$. See Figure 3.42.

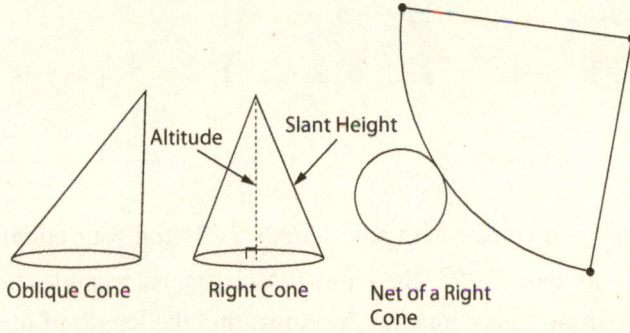

Oblique Cone   Right Cone   Net of a Right Cone

Figure 3.42

Sphere

A **sphere** is the three-dimensional set of points that are a given distance (the radius) from a point (the center). It is generated by rotating a circle 360° around its diameter. Spheres do not have exact two-dimensional nets because they consist of one rounded surface. See Figure 3.43.

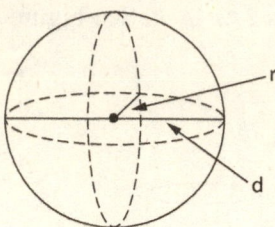

Figure 3.43

EXAMPLE 32

Draw an accurate net of the regular pyramid shown below. Include the lengths of each of the sides.

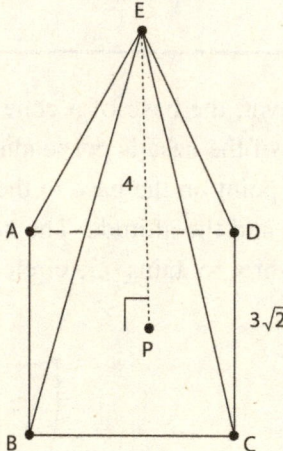

SOLUTION

The net contains one square with side length $3\sqrt{2}$ and four congruent isosceles triangles each with base $3\sqrt{2}$. The legs of the isosceles triangles are the edges of the pyramid. To draw an accurate net, we must find the length of the edges.

The base of the pyramid is a square whose diagonal has length $\sqrt{\left(3\sqrt{2}\right)^2 + \left(3\sqrt{2}\right)^2} = \sqrt{18+18} = \sqrt{36} = 6$.

Since the foot of the altitude is the center of the square base, create a triangle by drawing a segment from the center to one of the vertices of the base. The base of this triangle is half of the diagonal $\left(\frac{1}{2}(6) = 3\right)$ and its height is 4.

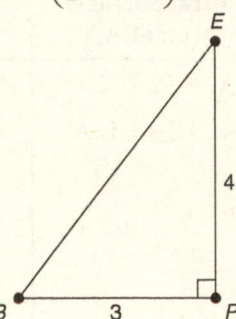

Notice that a 3-4-5 triangle is formed (or use the Pythagorean Theorem to find the length of the hypotenuse). Therefore, each of the edges has length 5.

So the net contains four isosceles triangles whose legs have length 5. One possible configuration of the net is given below.

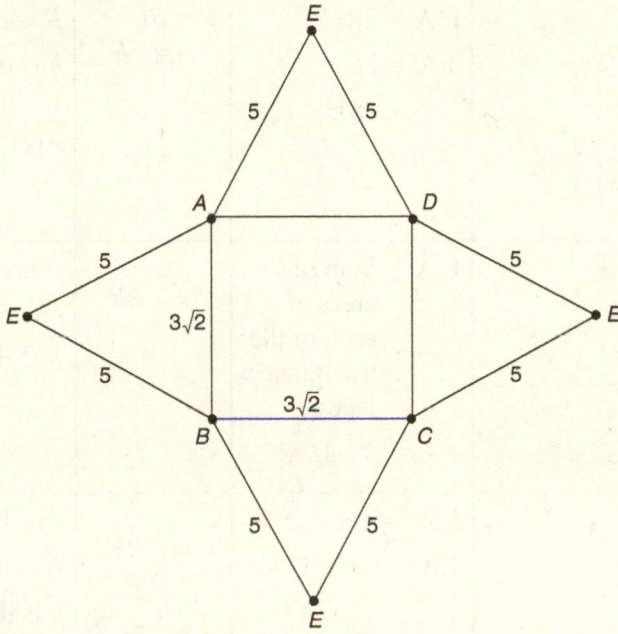

Surface Area and Volume of Three-Dimensional Figures

The total area of the exposed surfaces of a solid is called its **surface area.** The sum of the areas of each lateral face is called the **lateral surface area.** Surface area is measured in square units. The amount of space occupied by a solid is called its **volume.** Volume is measured in cubic units. You can think of surface area as the amount of paint you'd need to cover the solid and volume as the amount of liquid you'd need to fill the solid.

The formulas below describe how to find the surface area and volume of various polyhedrons.

Name	Example	Lateral Surface Area (L.A.) Total Surface Area (T.A.)	Volume	Where
Right Prism	area B h	L.A. $= Ph$ T.A. $= 2B + $ L.A.	$V = Bh$	B is the area of the base. P is the perimeter of the base. h is the distance between the bases.
Right Cylinder	area B r h	L.A. $= 2\pi rh$ T.A. $= 2B + $ L.A. $= 2\pi r^2 + $ L.A.	$V = Bh$ $= \pi r^2 h$	B is the area of the base. h is the distance between the bases. r is the radius of the base.
Right Pyramid	h s_1 s_2 area B	L.A. = Sum of areas of each of the triangular faces T.A. $= B + $ L.A.	$V = \frac{1}{3}Bh$	B is the area of the base. h is the distance from the vertex to the base.
Right Cone	h s r area B	L.A. $= \pi rs$ T.A. $= \pi r^2 + $ L.A.	$V = \frac{1}{3}Bh$ $= \frac{1}{3}\pi r^2 h$	s is the slant height. B is the area of the base. h is the distance from the vertex to the base. r is the radius of the base.
Sphere	r	T.A. $= 4\pi r^2$	$V = \frac{4}{3}\pi r^3$	r is the radius of the sphere.

EXAMPLE 33

Find the surface area of the right pyramid shown below.

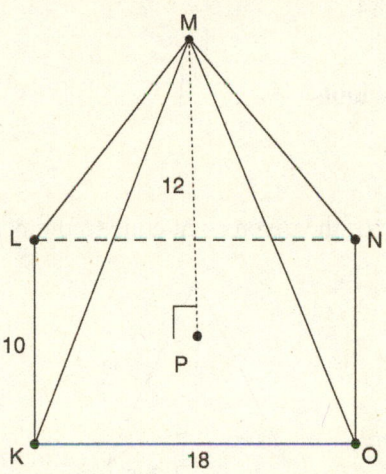

SOLUTION

The lateral area of the pyramid contains two pairs of congruent isosceles triangles. To find the area of these triangles, we must find the slant height of each of the pairs. To do so, create triangles with the altitude by drawing a segment from the center to one of the sides with length 10 and one of the sides with length 18. Since the foot of the altitude is the center of the base, we know the lengths of these segments are 9 (half of 18) and 5 (half of 10), respectively.

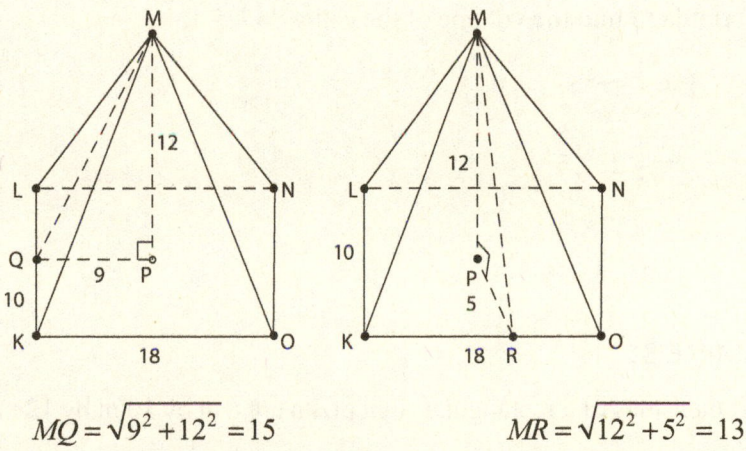

$$MQ = \sqrt{9^2 + 12^2} = 15 \qquad\qquad MR = \sqrt{12^2 + 5^2} = 13$$

Therefore, the lateral area of the pyramid is:

$$\text{L.A.} = 2A_{\,with\,base\,10} + 2A_{\,with\,base\,18}$$

$$= 2\left(\frac{1}{2}(10)(15)\right) + 2\left(\frac{1}{2}(18)(13)\right)$$

$$= 150 + 234$$

$$= 384 \text{ square units}$$

Add the area of the base to find the total surface area of the pyramid:

$$\text{T.A.} = B + \text{L.A.}$$
$$= 10(18) + 384$$
$$= 180 + 384$$
$$= 564 \text{ square units}$$

EXAMPLE 34

Approximate the volume of the given right cone to the nearest hundredth.

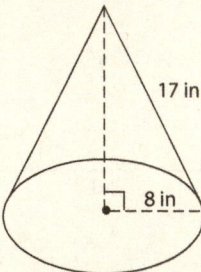

17 in

8 in

SOLUTION

The formula for the volume of a cone is given by $V = \dfrac{1}{3}\pi r^2 h$. First, use the given values to find the value of the altitude (h). The radius, slant height and altitude form a right triangle. You may recognize this as the special right triangle 8-15-17 (if not, use Pythagorean Theorem to find the missing side). Next, substitute the values into the formula to find the volume of the cone. So $h = 15$.

$$V = \frac{1}{3}\pi r^2 h$$
$$= \frac{1}{3}\pi 8^2 15$$
$$= 320\pi$$
$$= 1005.31 \text{ in}^3$$

EXAMPLE 35

The dimensions of a rectangular right prism are 8 m by 10 m by 12 m. A new prism is created by reducing each of the side lengths by $\dfrac{1}{2}$. What is the ratio of the surface area of the new prism to the surface area of the original prism?

SOLUTION

First, sketch a diagram of the two prisms:

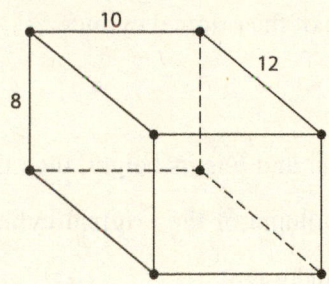 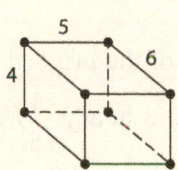

The surface area of a prism is given by T.A. $= 2B + Ph$.

The surface area of the original prism with a 10 by 12 base:

$$T.A. = 2B + Ph$$
$$= 2(10)(12) + (2(10) + 2(12))(8)$$
$$= 240 + 160 + 192$$
$$= 592 \, m^2$$

The surface area of the new prism with a 5 by 6 base:

$$T.A. = 2B + Ph$$
$$= 2(5)(6) + (2(5) + 2(6))(4)$$
$$= 60 + 40 + 48$$
$$= 148 \, m^2$$

Therefore, the ratio of the surface area of the new prism to that of the original prism is

$$\frac{T.A._{\text{new prism}}}{T.A._{\text{original prism}}} = \frac{148}{592} = \frac{1}{4}$$

The results of the previous problem can be generalized. If a figure is dilated (reduced or enlarged) by a factor of $\frac{a}{b}$, then its surface area is dilated by a factor of $\left(\frac{a}{b}\right)^2$.

EXAMPLE 36

The radius and height of a cylinder are reduced by $\frac{1}{5}$. What is the ratio of the volume of the new cylinder to the volume of the original cylinder?

SOLUTION

If r is the radius of the original cylinder and h is its height, then the new cylinder has radius $\frac{1}{5}r$ and height $\frac{1}{5}h$. The volume of the original cylinder is given by $V = \pi r^2 h$. The volume of the new cylinder is

$$V = \pi \left(\frac{1}{5}r\right)^2 \left(\frac{1}{5}h\right)$$
$$= \pi \left(\frac{1}{25}r^2\right)\left(\frac{1}{5}h\right)$$
$$= \frac{1}{125}\pi r^2 h$$

Therefore, the ratio of the volume of the new cylinder to the original cylinder is

$$\frac{V_{\text{new cylinder}}}{V_{\text{original cylinder}}} = \frac{\frac{1}{125}\pi r^2 h}{\pi r^2 h} = \frac{1}{125}$$

In general, if a figure is dilated (reduced or enlarged) by a factor of $\frac{a}{b}$, then its volume is dilated by a factor of $\left(\frac{a}{b}\right)^3$.

Similarity for Three-Dimensional Figures

Let's consider the relationship between similarity of three-dimensional figures as compared to surface areas and volumes. For three-dimensional figures, similarity means that pairs of congruent angles and the corresponding linear measurements must be in the same ratio. Many of the linear measurements refer to edges.

Similar Prisms

Now, let's consider a rectangular prism with length, width and height of 10, 6, and 5, respectively. Its surface area is $(2)(10)(6) + (2)(10)(5) + (2)(6)(5) = 280$, and its volume is $(10)(6)(5) = 300$. Suppose a second rectangular prism has length, width, and height of 30, 18, and 15, respectively.

We note that these rectangular prisms are similar. For this second rectangular prism, the surface area is $(2)(30)(18) + (2)(30)(15) + (2)(18)(15) = 2520$. Its volume is $(30)(18)(15) = 8100$.

The ratio of the corresponding edges is $\frac{1}{3}$. We note that the ratio of the surface areas is $\frac{280}{2520} = \frac{1}{9}$ and the ratio of the volumes is $\frac{300}{8100} = \frac{1}{27}$. We also note that $\frac{1}{9} = \left(\frac{1}{3}\right)^2$ and $\frac{1}{27} = \left(\frac{1}{3}\right)^3$. It appears that the ratio of the surface areas is the square of the ratio of the linear dimensions, and the ratio of the volumes is the cube of the ratio of the linear dimensions.

Similar Cones

Let's consider two similar cones and explore whether we arrive at the same conclusions. The first cone has a radius of 3 and a (perpendicular) height of 4. This means that its lateral height is $\sqrt{3^2 + 4^2} = 5$. The surface area of this cone is $(\pi)(3^2) + (\pi)(3)(5) = 24\pi$, and its volume is $\left(\frac{1}{3}\right)(\pi)(3^2)(4) = 12\pi$.

Suppose a second cone has a radius of 15 and a height of 20. The lateral height is $\sqrt{15^2 + 20^2} = 25$, and the two cones must be similar, since each linear dimension has been multiplied by 5.

For this second cone, the surface area is $(\pi)(15^2) + (\pi)(15)(25) = 600\pi$ and its volume is $\left(\frac{1}{3}\right)(\pi)(15^2)(20) = 1500\pi$. We note that the ratio of the surface areas is $\frac{24\pi}{600\pi} = \frac{1}{25}$ and the ratio of the volumes is $\frac{12\pi}{1500\pi} = \frac{1}{125}$. Noting that $\frac{1}{25} = \left(\frac{1}{5}\right)^2$ and $\frac{1}{125} = \left(\frac{1}{5}\right)^3$, the ratio of the surface areas is the square of the ratio of the linear dimensions, and the ratio of the volumes is the cube of the ratio of the linear dimensions.

Without a formal proof, we declare that given two similar three-dimensional figures, the ratio of their surface areas will be the square of the ratio of their linear dimensions. Also, the ratio of their volumes will be the cube of the ratio of their linear dimensions.

EXAMPLE 37

The ratio of the volumes of two similar rectangular prisms is $\frac{8}{27}$. If the surface area of the smaller figure is 48 square inches, what is the surface area of the larger figure?

SOLUTION

The ratio of the linear dimensions is $\sqrt[3]{\dfrac{8}{27}} = \dfrac{2}{3}$, so the ratio of their surface areas

is $\left(\dfrac{2}{3}\right)^2 = \dfrac{4}{9}$. Let x represent the surface area of the larger figure. Then $\dfrac{4}{9} = \dfrac{48}{x}$, so

$x = 108$ square inches.

Similar Spheres

EXAMPLE 38

The ratio of the radii of two similar spheres is $\dfrac{6}{1}$. If the volume of the larger sphere

is 1620, what is the volume of the smaller sphere?

SOLUTION

The ratio of their volumes is $\left(\dfrac{6}{1}\right)^3 = \dfrac{216}{1}$. Using x to represent the volume of the

smaller sphere, we can write $\dfrac{216}{1} = \dfrac{1620}{x}$. Thus, $x = 7.5$.

Similar Cylinders

EXAMPLE 39

The height of the larger of two similar cylinders is 20 inches more than the height

of the smaller cylinder. If the ratio of their surface areas is $\dfrac{9}{49}$, what is the height

of the larger cylinder?

SOLUTION

The ratio of their heights is $\sqrt{\dfrac{9}{49}} = \dfrac{3}{7}$. Let x and $x + 20$ represent the heights of

the two cylinders. Then $\dfrac{3}{7} = \dfrac{x}{x + 20}$, which simplifies to $7x = 3x + 60$. So $x = 15$,

which means that the height of the larger cylinder is 35 inches.

Transformations in the Coordinate Plane

A geometric **transformation** is a mapping of a figure, called the **pre-image**, to its corresponding figure, called the **image.** Translations, rotations, reflections and dilations are types of transformations.

Translations

A **translation** is a type of transformation that moves an object a fixed distance in a given direction. Under a translation, the image and the pre-image are congruent and have the same orientation. The image and the pre-image of a figure are congruent under a translation.

The image of $P(x, y)$ under a translation a units horizontally and b units vertically is given by:

$$P(x, y) \rightarrow P'(x+a, y+b)$$

EXAMPLE 40

Describe the transformation that maps ABC to $A'B'C'$ in Figure 3.44.

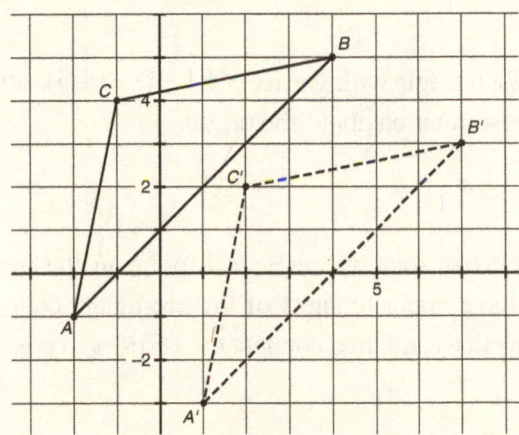

Figure 3.44

SOLUTION

Each point on the pre-image is mapped to an image point that is 2 units below it and 3 units to the right of it.

$$A(-2, -1) \rightarrow A'(-2+3, -1-2) \rightarrow A'(1, -3)$$
$$B(4, 5) \quad \rightarrow B'(4+3, 5-2) \quad \rightarrow B'(7, 3)$$
$$C(-1, 4) \rightarrow C'(-1+3, 4-2) \quad \rightarrow C'(2, 2)$$

Therefore, the transformation is a translation to the right 3 units and down 2 units.

Rotations

A **rotation** is a transformation that turns an object about a fixed point. The fixed point is called the **center of rotation**. Rays drawn from the center of rotation to the pre-image and image form an angle called the **angle of rotation.** The pre-image and image of a figure are congruent under a rotation. Rotations can be clockwise or counterclockwise and the angle of rotation can be any real number. However, the most common rotations are multiples of 90° in the counterclockwise direction about the origin.

The image of $P(x, y)$ rotated 90° counterclockwise about the origin is given by:

$$P(x, y) \rightarrow P'(-y, x).$$ *changes y*

The image of $P(x, y)$ rotated 180° counterclockwise about the origin is given by:

$$P(x, y) \rightarrow P'(-x, -y).$$ *changes both*

The image of $P(x, y)$ rotated 270° counterclockwise about the origin is given by:

$$P(x, y) \rightarrow P'(y, -x).$$ *changes x*

EXAMPLE 41

Sketch the image of a triangle with vertices $A(1, -1)$, $B(4, 5)$, and $C(-1, 4)$ under a 180° counterclockwise rotation about the origin.

SOLUTION

A 180° counterclockwise rotation maps each point in the pre-image to a point whose coordinates have opposite signs of the pre-image coordinates. Apply this rule to each of the vertices and then connect the vertices to create the image on the next pages.

$$P(x, y) \rightarrow P'(-x, -y)$$
$$A(1, -1) \rightarrow A'(-1, 1)$$
$$B(4, 5) \rightarrow B'(-4, -5)$$
$$C(-1, 4) \rightarrow C'(1, -4)$$

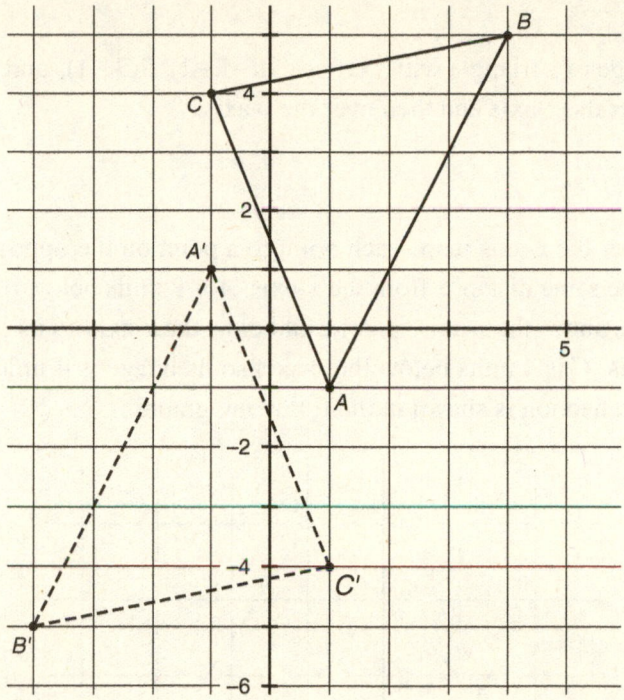

Reflections

A **reflection** over a line l is a transformation in which each point on the pre-image is mapped to a point that is the same distance from the reflection line as the pre-image point but is on the opposite side of the line. The lines joining each pre-image point to its image are perpendicular to the reflection line. The image and the pre-image of a figure are congruent under a reflection. Any line can be a line of reflection. However, the most common are the x-axis, the y-axis and the line $y = x$.

The image of $P(x, y)$ reflected over the x-axis is given by:

$$P(x, y) \rightarrow P'(x, -y).$$

The image of $P(x, y)$ reflected over the y-axis is given by:

$$P(x, y) \rightarrow P'(-x, y).$$

The image of $P(x, y)$ reflected over the $y = x$ is given by:

$$P(x, y) \rightarrow P'(y, x).$$

EXAMPLE 42

Sketch the image of a triangle with vertices $A(-1,-2), B(3,-1)$, and $C(1,-4)$ after a reflection over the x-axis and then over the y-axis.

SOLUTION

A reflection over the x-axis maps each point to a point on the opposite side of the x-axis that is the same distance from the x-axis. A is 2 units below the x-axis so its image is 2 units above the x-axis. B is 1 unit below the x-axis so its image is 1 unit above the x-axis. C is 4 units below the x-axis so its image is 4 units above the x-axis. The first reflection is shown in the following graph.

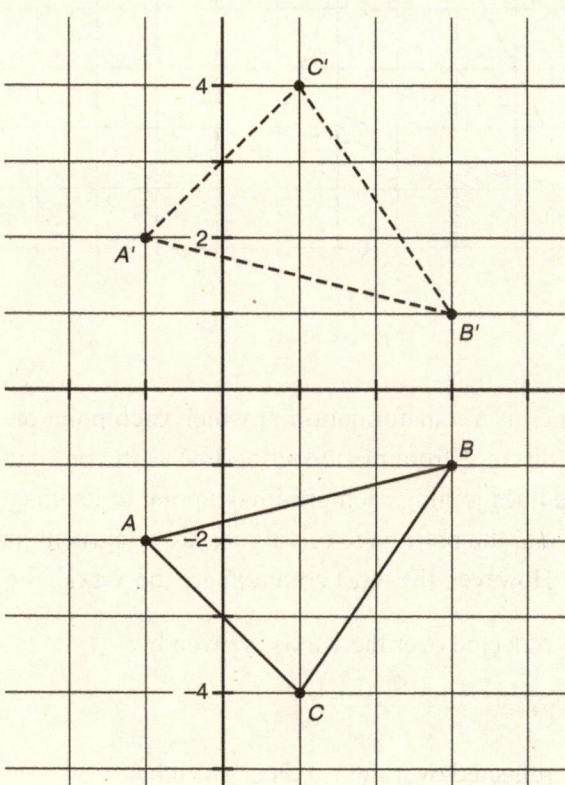

A reflection over the y-axis maps each point to a point on the opposite side of the y-axis that is the same distance from the y-axis. A' is 1 unit to the left of the y-axis so its image is 1 unit to the right of the y-axis. B' is 3 units to the right of the y-axis so its image is 3 units to the left of the y-axis. C' is 1 unit to the right of the y-axis so its image is 1 unit to the left of the y-axis. So final reflection is $\Delta A''B''C''$, as shown below.

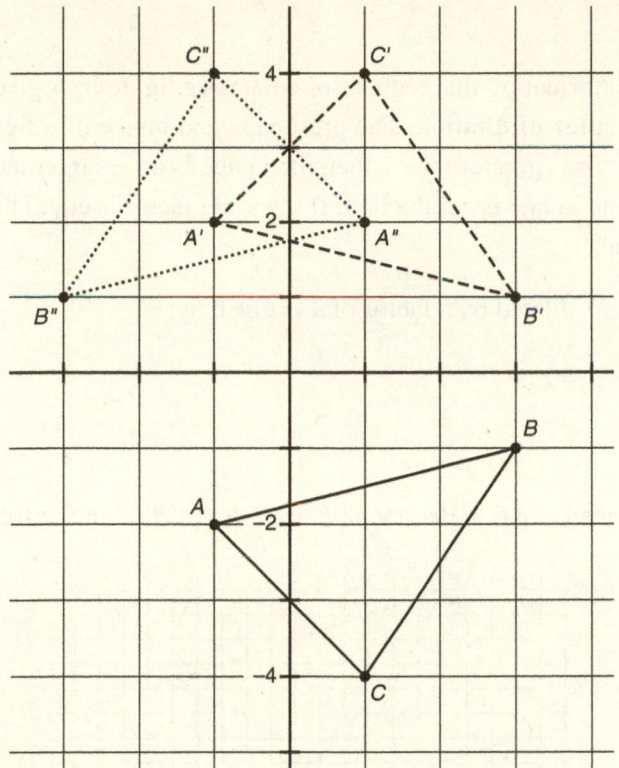

Alternatively, you can apply the rule for reflection over the x-axis, $P(x,y) \rightarrow P'(x,-y)$, followed by the rule for reflection over the y-axis, $P(x,y) \rightarrow P'(x,-y)$ to find each of the coordinates.

$$P'(x,y) \rightarrow P''(-x,y)$$
$$A'(-1,2) \rightarrow A''(1,2)$$
$$B'(3,1) \rightarrow B''(-3,1)$$
$$C'(1,4) \rightarrow C''(-1,4)$$

When two or more transformations are performed in order, the result is called a **composition of transformations**. The previous example found the result of composing a reflection over the x-axis, r_x, with a reflection over the y-axis, r_y. This is written $r_x \circ r_y$. Notice that $r_x \circ r_y$ is the same transformation as a counterclockwise rotation of 180° about the origin.

Dilations

A **dilation** is a transformation that reduces or enlarges a figure by a given **scale factor** about a fixed point called the **center of dilation**. The pre-image and image of a figure are similar under a dilation. If the scale factor is greater than 1 then the image is an enlargement. If the scale factor is between 0 and 1, then the image is a reduction. If the scale factor is equal to 1, then the image and pre-image are congruent.

The image of $P(x, y)$ dilated by a factor of a is given by:

$$P(x, y) \rightarrow P'(ax, ay).$$

EXAMPLE 43

Describe the transformation that maps $\triangle ABC$ to $\triangle A'B'C'$ in the following graph.

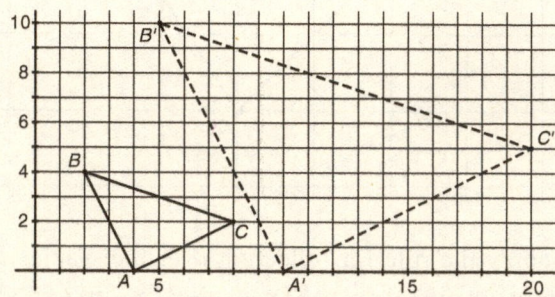

SOLUTION

The image appears to be a dilation of the pre-image. Verify this by analyzing the relationship between the vertices of the pre-image and the vertices of the image.

$$A(4, 0) \rightarrow A'(10, 0)$$

$$B(2, 4) \rightarrow B'(5, 10)$$

$$C(8, 2) \rightarrow C'(20, 5)$$

The x- and y-coordinates of the image points are $\dfrac{5}{2}$ times the x- and y-coordinates of the pre-image. Therefore, the transformation is a dilation with the origin as the center of dilation and a scale factor of $\dfrac{5}{2}$.

TRIGONOMETRY

Right Triangle Trigonometry   SOH-CAH-TOA

Basic Trigonometric Functions

Any two right triangles with one congruent acute angle (Figure 3.44) are similar by the AA Theorem.

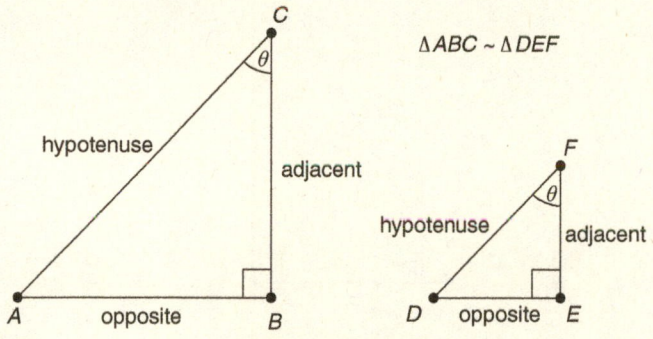

$\triangle ABC \sim \triangle DEF$

Figure 3.44

Therefore, the ratios of their corresponding sides are equal. These ratios are called the trigonometric ratios. For all right triangles, the following trigonometric ratios will result in the same value for a given acute angle.

$$\frac{\text{opposite}}{\text{hypotenuse}} = \text{sine } \theta \text{—abbreviated sin } \theta$$

$$\frac{\text{adjacent}}{\text{hypotenuse}} = \text{cosine } \theta \text{—abbreviated cos } \theta$$

$$\frac{\text{opposite}}{\text{adjacent}} = \text{tangent } \theta \text{—abbreviated tan } \theta$$

Often, the acronym SOH-CAH-TOA (Sine, Opposite, Hypotenuse–Cosine, Adjacent, Hypotenuse–Tangent, Opposite, Adjacent) is used to remember these ratios.

The trigonometric ratios are considered functions of the acute angle because every angle is associated with a unique ratio value.

EXAMPLE 44

Find the exact value of the sine, cosine and tangent of 30°.

SOLUTION

The ratio of the sides of any 30°-60°-90° triangle is $x : x\sqrt{3} : 2x$.

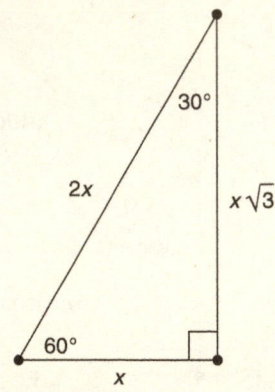

$$\sin 30° = \frac{\text{opposite}}{\text{hypotenuse}} = \frac{x}{2x} = \frac{1}{2}$$

$$\cos 30° = \frac{\text{adjacent}}{\text{hypotenuse}} = \frac{x\sqrt{3}}{2x} = \frac{\sqrt{3}}{2}$$

$$\frac{\sin}{\cos} \Rightarrow \tan 30° = \frac{\text{opposite}}{\text{adjacent}} = \frac{x}{x\sqrt{3}} = \frac{1}{\sqrt{3}} = \frac{\sqrt{3}}{3}$$

The 30°-60°-90° and 45°-45°-90° triangles are unique because the ratio of their sides is known. This allows you to calculate the exact values of the trigonometric functions of 30°, 60°, and 45° without being given side lengths. For other angles, make use of your calculator; it stores the values of the trigonometric functions for every angle.

The trigonometric functions enable us to find a missing side of a triangle if only one side and an angle are known.

EXAMPLE 45

Determine the length of $\overline{AB}$ in the figure below to the nearest tenth.

$$\sin 64 = \frac{x}{8}$$

$$x = 8\sin 64$$

$$x = 7.2$$

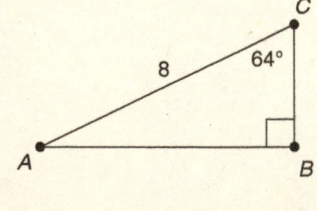

SOLUTION

First, determine if sine, cosine, or tangent is needed. Since the angle and hypotenuse are known, and the opposite side is to be determined, use sine. Write the ratio, substituting the given length and angle. Solve the equation for AB.

$$\sin 64° = \frac{AB}{8}$$
$$AB = 8 \sin 64°$$

Type this expression into your calculator and round your solution to the appropriate place value:

$$AB = 8 \sin 64° \approx 7.2$$

EXAMPLE 46

From the top of a lighthouse 205 feet tall, the keeper spots a boat at a 32° angle of depression. How far is the boat from the foot of the lighthouse (to the nearest foot)?

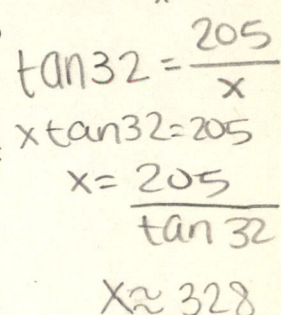

SOLUTION

Let x = the distance from the boat to the foot of the lighthouse. Draw a diagram to represent the information given. The angle of depression lies outside the triangle. It is the angle the keeper's eyes are lowered from the horizontal to view the boat. Since alternate interior angles are congruent, the angle of elevation from the boat to the keeper is 32°.

$$\tan 32 = \frac{205}{x}$$
$$x \tan 32 = 205$$
$$x = \frac{205}{\tan 32}$$
$$x \approx 328$$

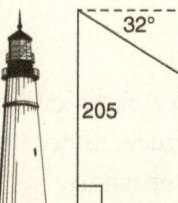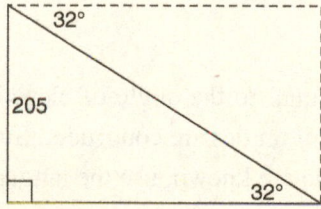

Since the angle and its opposite side are known, and the adjacent side needs to be determined, use tangent. Write the ratio, substituting the given length and angle. Solve the equation for x.

$$\tan 32° = \frac{205}{x}$$
$$x \tan 32° = 205$$
$$x = \frac{205}{\tan 32°} \approx 328 \text{ feet}$$

The boat is approximately 328 feet from the foot of the lighthouse.

Inverse Trigonometric Relations

The trigonometric functions associate a ratio with a given angle. Their inverses associate an angle with a given ratio. That, is, they allow you to find the missing angles of a right triangle when two side lengths are known. Two equivalent notations are used for inverses.

$$\sin^{-1}(x) = \arcsin(x) = \theta \text{ means that } \sin \theta = x.$$

$$\cos^{-1}(x) = \arccos(x) = \theta \text{ means that } \cos \theta = x.$$

$$\tan^{-1}(x) = \arctan(x) = \theta \text{ means that } \tan \theta = x.$$

EXAMPLE 47

An airplane is flying at an altitude of 5,000 ft when the pilot spots a control tower. The horizontal difference (the distance along the ground) between the current position of the plane and the tower is 28,000. Find the angle of depression, θ, of the plane to the nearest hundredth of a degree.

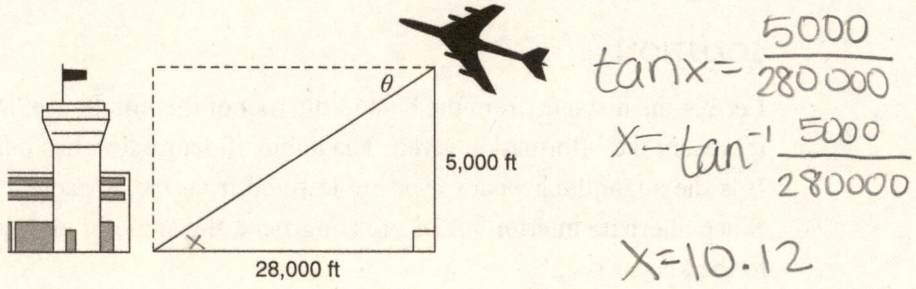

5,000 ft

28,000 ft

$$tan x = \frac{5000}{280\,000}$$

$$x = tan^{-1} \frac{5000}{280000}$$

$$x = 10.12$$

SOLUTION

The angle of depression is equal to the angle of elevation from the tower to the plane because alternate interior angles are congruent. Since the opposite and adjacent sides to the missing angle are known, use the tangent.

$$\tan \theta = \frac{5,000}{28,000}$$

The inverse tangent function provides the angle for the given ratio. Type this expression into your calculator and round the solution to the nearest hundredth.

$$\theta = \tan^{-1}\left(\frac{5,000}{28,000}\right) = \tan^{-1}\left(\frac{5}{28}\right) \approx 10.12°$$

The angle of depression of the plane is approximately 10.12°.

Defining Trigonometric Functions

Trigonometric Functions Related to any Angle

Previously, we defined the trigonometric functions in terms of an acute angle of a right triangle. However, the domain of these functions can be extended to cover any angle.

An angle whose vertex is at the origin of a rectangular coordinate system and whose initial side coincides with the positive x-axis is said to be in standard position with respect to the coordinate system (Figure 3.45).

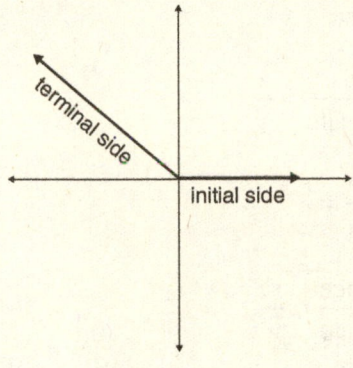

Figure 3.45

Consider rotating the terminal side of an angle through the coordinate plane about the origin (Figure 3.46). The path of a point that is r units from the origin on the terminal side traces a circle of radius r. The coordinates of the point $P(x,y)$ vary but r remains constant.

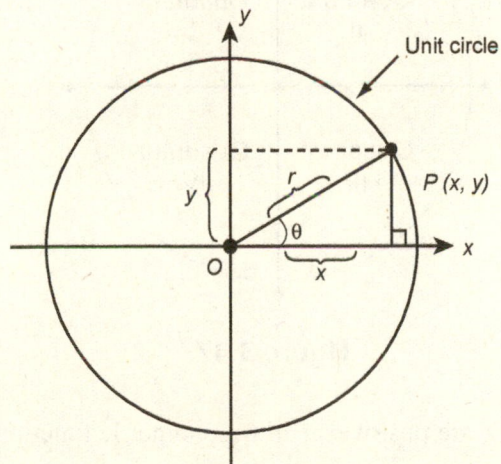

Figure 3.46

If θ is an angle in standard position, $P(x,y)$ is any point (distinct from the origin) on the terminal side of θ and $r = \sqrt{x^2 + y^2}$, then the six trigonometric functions of θ are defined in terms of the abscissa (x-coordinate), the ordinate (y-coordinate), and the length of the radius (r) as follows:

$$\text{sine } \theta = \sin\theta = \frac{\text{ordinate}}{\text{distance}} = \frac{y}{r}$$

$$\text{cosine } \theta = \cos\theta = \frac{\text{abscissa}}{\text{distance}} = \frac{x}{r}$$

$$\text{tangent } \theta = \tan\theta = \frac{\text{ordinate}}{\text{abscissa}} = \frac{y}{x}$$

[handwritten: $\frac{\cos}{\sin}$] $\quad \text{cotangent } \theta = \cot\theta = \frac{\text{abscissa}}{\text{ordinate}} = \frac{x}{y}$

[handwritten: $\frac{1}{\cos}$] $\quad \text{secant } \theta = \sec\theta = \frac{\text{distance}}{\text{abscissa}} = \frac{r}{x}$

[handwritten: $\frac{1}{\sin}$] $\quad \text{cosecant } \theta = \csc\theta = \frac{\text{distance}}{\text{ordinate}} = \frac{r}{y}$

The signs of the functions in the quadrants (Figure 3.47) depend on whether the ordinate or abscissa is positive or negative in that quadrant (the distance is always taken as positive).

[handwritten notes:
Q1 Q2 Q3 Q4
ASTC
All Students take calculus

A - All trig functions positive in Q1
S - sin & csc pos in Q2
T - tan & cot pos in Q3
C - cos & sec positive in Q4]

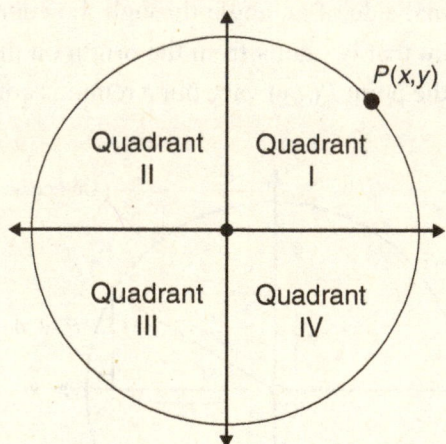

Figure 3.47

Quadrant I: x and y are positive so all trigonometric functions are positive.

Quadrant II: x is negative and y is positive so sine and cosecant are positive. All others are negative.

Quadrant III: x and y are negative so tangent and cotangent are positive. All others are negative.

Quadrant IV: x is positive and y is negative so cosine and secant are positive. All others are negative.

EXAMPLE 48

Given $\tan \theta = -\dfrac{2}{3}$ and $\sin \theta > 0$, find $\cos \theta$ and $\csc \theta$.

SOLUTION

Angle θ lies in Quadrant II because that is the only quadrant in which the tangent is negative and the sine is positive. Since $\tan \theta = \dfrac{y}{x} = -\dfrac{2}{3}$ and x is negative in Quadrant II, let $x = -3$ and $y = 2$. Find r by substituting these values into the equation $r = \sqrt{x^2 + y^2}$:

$$r = \sqrt{(-3)^2 + 2^2} = \sqrt{9+4} = \sqrt{13}$$

Use the definitions of $\cos \theta$ and $\csc \theta$ to find their values:

$$\cos \theta = \frac{x}{r} = \frac{-3}{\sqrt{13}} = \frac{-3\sqrt{13}}{13}$$

$$\csc \theta = \frac{r}{y} = \frac{\sqrt{13}}{2}$$

The basic trigonometric values of some common angles are given below. The angles are given in radians and in degrees. A **radian** is a measure of the central angle in a circle and is usually expressed in terms of θ. A full circle has $360°$, or 2π radians.

θ (degrees)	θ (radians)	$\sin \theta$	$\cos \theta$	$\tan \theta$
$0°$	0	0	1	0
$30°$	$\dfrac{\pi}{6}$	$\dfrac{1}{2}$	$\dfrac{\sqrt{3}}{2}$	$\dfrac{\sqrt{3}}{3}$
$45°$	$\dfrac{\pi}{4}$	$\dfrac{\sqrt{2}}{2}$	$\dfrac{\sqrt{2}}{2}$	1
$60°$	$\dfrac{\pi}{3}$	$\dfrac{\sqrt{3}}{2}$	$\dfrac{1}{2}$	$\sqrt{3}$
$90°$	$\dfrac{\pi}{2}$	1	0	Undefined
$180°$	π	0	-1	0
$270°$	$\dfrac{3\pi}{2}$	-1	0	Undefined

The value of a trigonometric function of an angle greater than 90° (or less than 0°) can be found by using the value of its associated **reference angle**. A reference angle is the acute angle formed by the terminal side of the given angle and the horizontal axis (Figure 3.48).

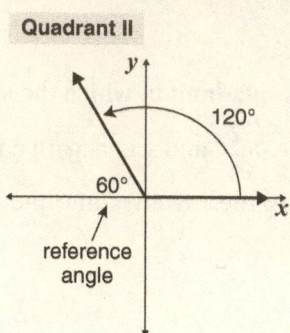

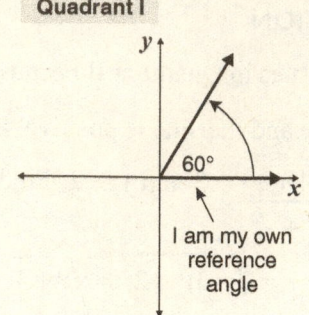

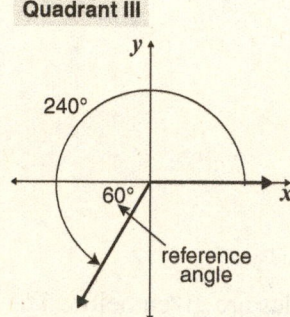

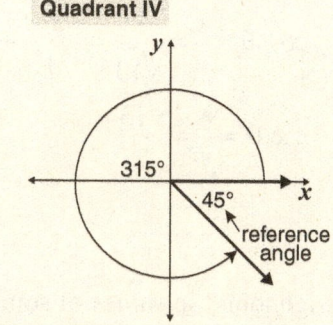

Figure 3.48

EXAMPLE 49

Evaluate cos 240°.

SOLUTION

An angle of 240° lies in Quadrant III, so the reference angle is 240° − 180° = 60°.

$$240 - 180 = 60°$$

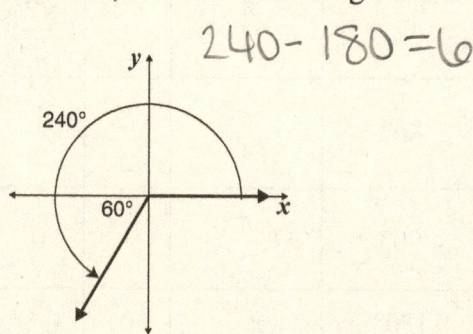

The cosine is negative in Quadrant III, so cos 240° = −cos 60° = −$\frac{1}{2}$.

$$\cos 240 = -\cos 60°$$
$$= -\frac{1}{2}$$

Graphing the Trigonometric Functions

The Six Basic Trigonometric Graphs

The trigonometric functions are examples of **periodic functions** because they repeat their output values at regular intervals, or periods. Periodic functions are used to model periodic phenomena such as ocean waves, sound waves, population change and changes in temperature. One complete repetition of the output values of a periodic function is called a **cycle**. The **period** is the horizontal length of one cycle. The six basic trigonometric functions are shown in Figures 3.49–3.54. The plotted points represent the evaluation of the function at

$$x = 0, \frac{\pi}{6}, \frac{\pi}{3}, \frac{\pi}{4}, \pi, \frac{3\pi}{2}, \text{ and } 2\pi.$$

y = sin x

sin is y value

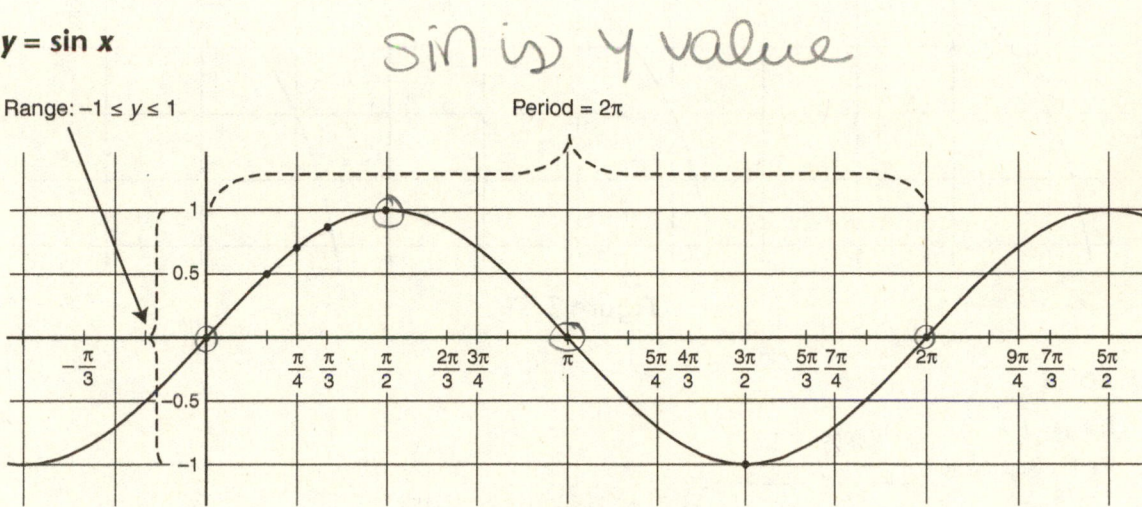

Figure 3.49

y = cos x

cos is x value

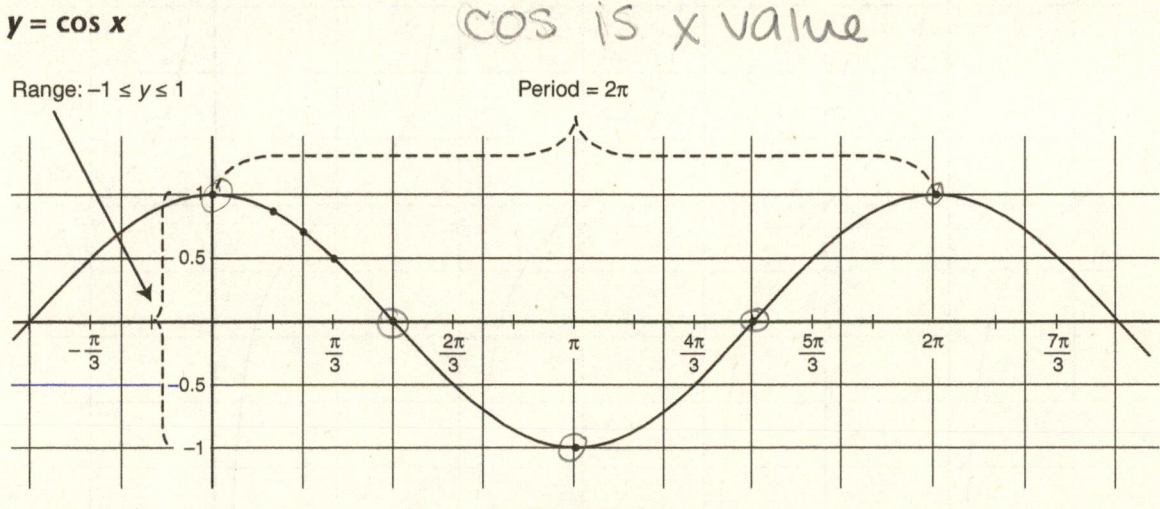

Figure 3.50

$y = \tan x$

Range $= (-\infty, \infty)$

Vertical Asymptotes:

$y = \frac{\pi}{2} + n\pi$

Period $= \pi$

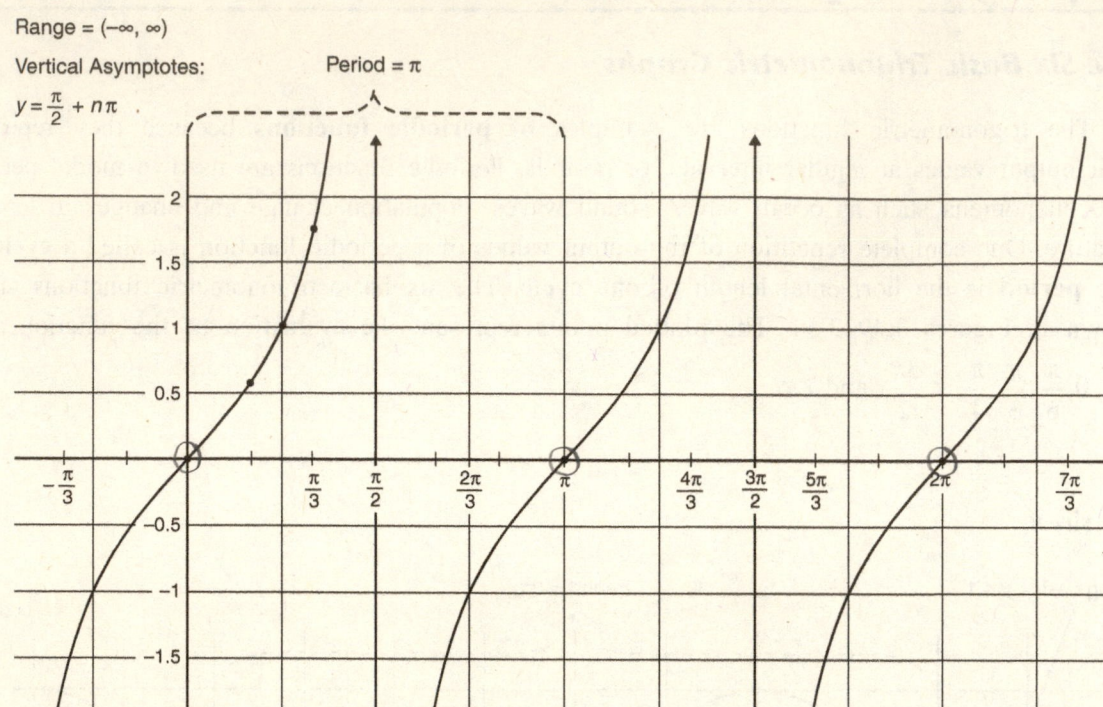

Figure 3.51

$y = \cot x$

Range $= (-\infty, \infty)$

Period $= \pi$

Vertical Asymptotes:

$y = n\pi$

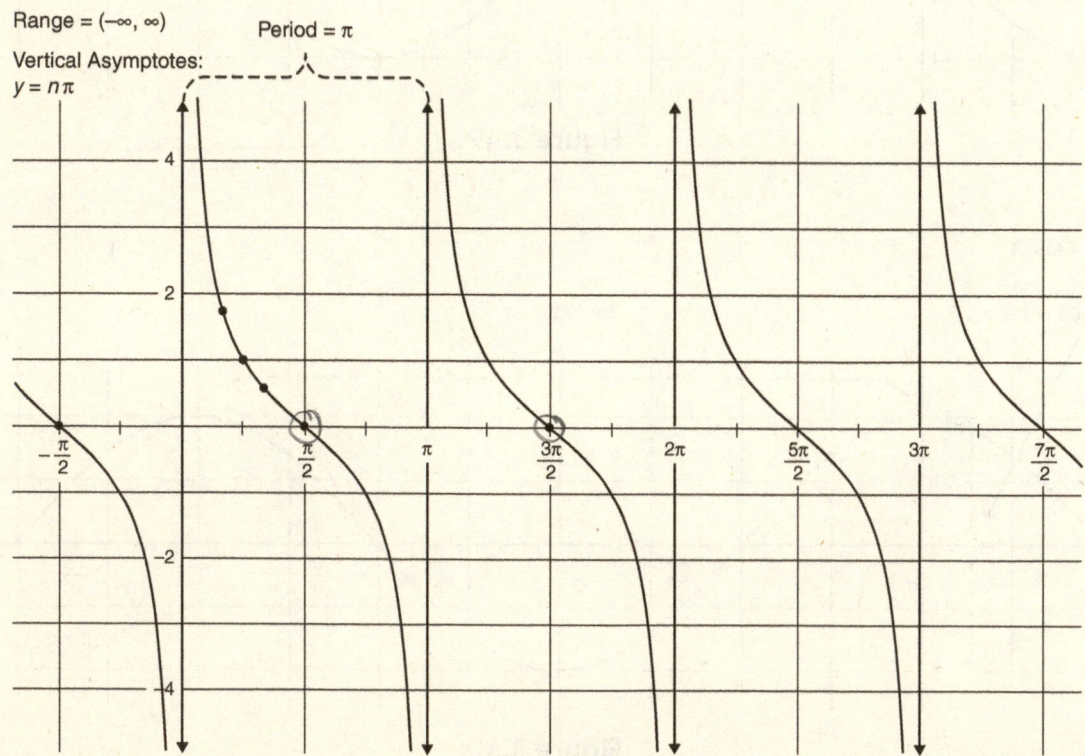

Figure 3.52

y = sec x

Range = $(-\infty, \infty)$

Vertical Asymptotes:

$y = \frac{\pi}{2} + n\pi$

Period = 2π

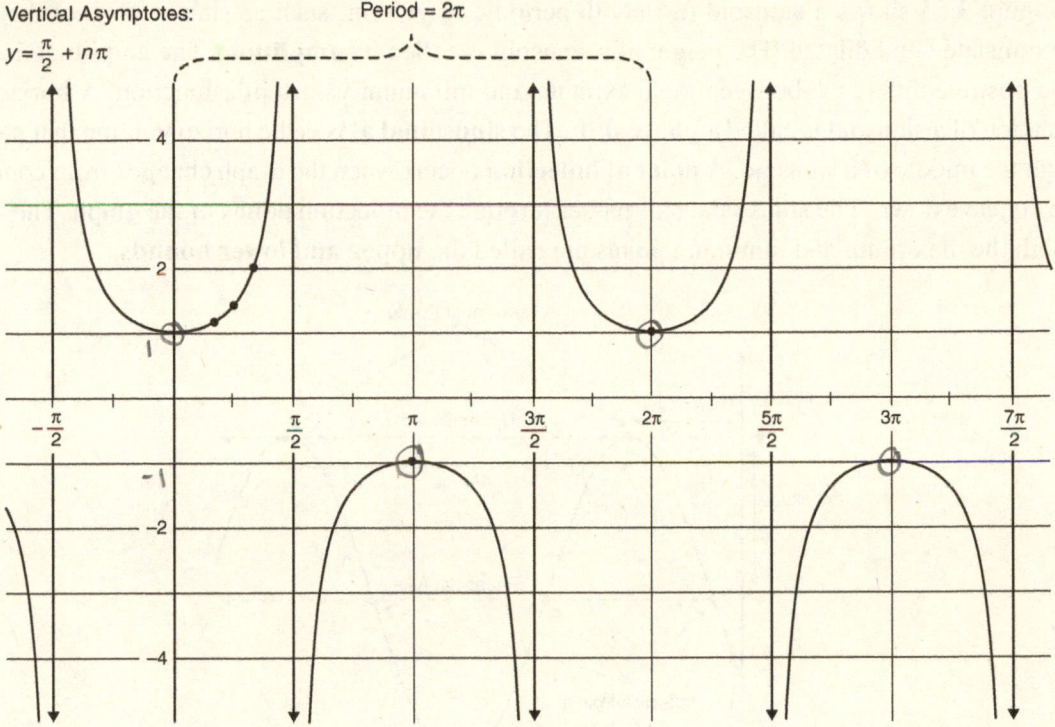

Figure 3.53

y = csc x

Range = $(-\infty, \infty)$

Vertical Asymptotes:

$y = n\pi$

Period = 2π

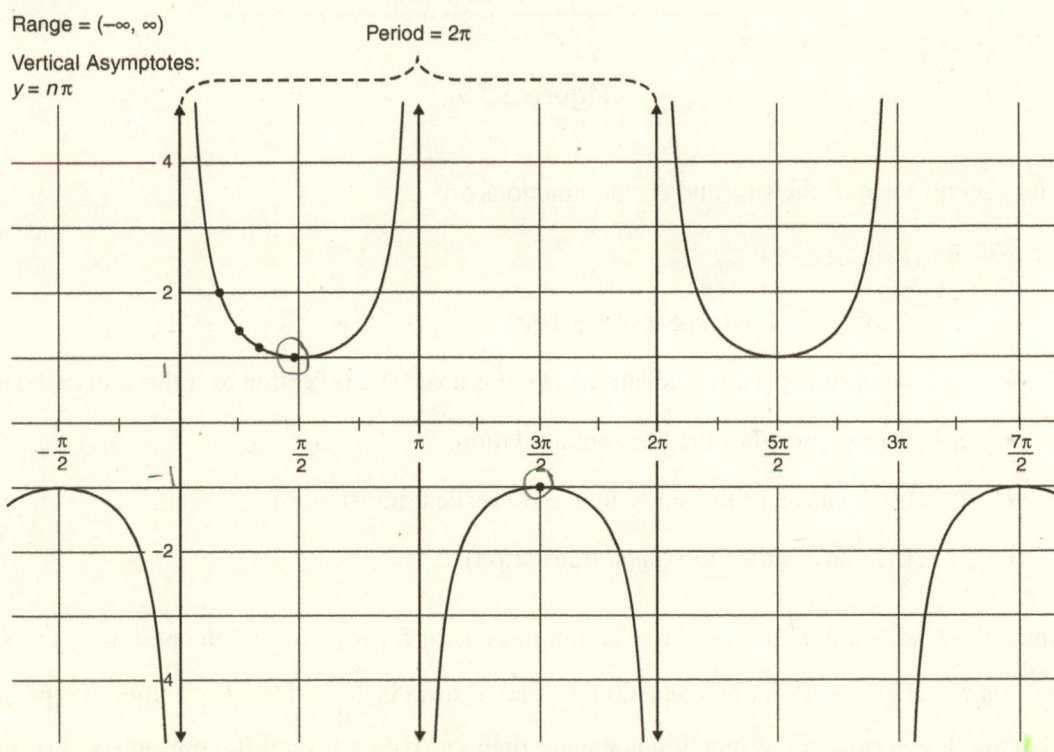

Figure 3.54

Transformations on the Trigonometric Functions

Figure 3.55 shows a sinusoid (a smooth periodic waveform, such as sine or cosine) that has been translated and dilated. The height of a sinusoid is called its **amplitude**. The amplitude is half of the positive difference between the maximum and minimum values of a function. A horizontal translation of a sinusoid is called a **phase shift**. The **sinusoidal axis** is the horizontal line that passes though the middle of a sinusoid. A **point of inflection** occurs when the graph changes from concave up to concave down. The sinusoidal axis passes through the inflection points of the graph. The lines through the maximum and minimum points are called the **upper and lower bounds**.

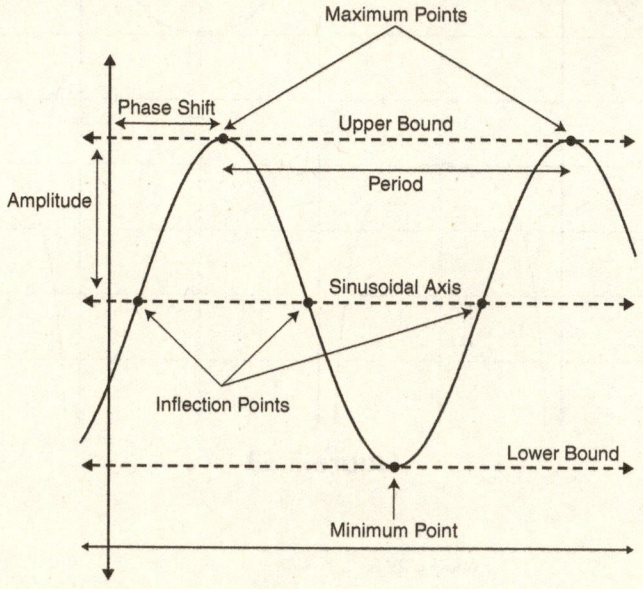

Figure 3.55

The general form of the sine and cosine functions are:

$y = C + A \sin B(x - D)$

$y = C + A \cos B(x - D)$, respectively, where

- $|A|$ is amplitude (vertical dilation). $A < 0$ is a vertical reflection over the sinusoidal axis.

- B is the reciprocal of the horizontal dilation.

- C is the location of the sinusoidal axis (vertical translation).

- D is the phase shift (horizontal translation).

Since the horizontal dilation of an equation in general form is $\frac{1}{B}$ and the period of $y = \sin x$ and $y = \cos x$ is 2π, the period of an equation in general form is $\frac{2\pi}{B}$. If $0 < B < 1$, then B represents a stretch and the period of the function is greater than 2π. If $B > 1$, then B represents a shrink and the period of the function is less than 2π. If B is negative, the general form is written so that B is positive by using $\sin(-x) = -\sin(x)$ and $\cos(-x) = \cos x$.

EXAMPLE 50

Find the amplitude, period, phase shift and sinusoidal axis location of *(vertical)*
$y = -5 + 4\sin\frac{1}{2}\left(x - \frac{\pi}{6}\right).$

vertical   *horizontal*

Amplitude = 4   *(vertical) sinusoidal axis = -5*
Period = $\frac{2\pi}{\frac{1}{2}}$ = 4π
(horizontal) phase shift = $\frac{\pi}{6}$

SOLUTION

The equation is of the form $y = C + A \sin B(x - D)$ with $C = -5$, $A = 4$, $B = \frac{1}{2}$, and $D = \frac{\pi}{6}$. The value of C provides the location of the sinusoidal axis. Therefore, the sinusoidal axis is at $y = -5$. A represents the amplitude of the function. Since $A = 4$, the amplitude of the function is 4. The period of the function is $\frac{2\pi}{B} = \frac{2\pi}{\frac{1}{2}} = 4\pi$.

The phase shift is $\frac{\pi}{6}$ because $D = \frac{\pi}{6}$.

EXAMPLE 51

Graph $y = 1 + \frac{1}{2}\cos 2\left(x - \frac{\pi}{3}\right).$

Amplitude = $\frac{1}{2}$
period = $\frac{2\pi}{2}$ = π
phase shift = $\frac{\pi}{3}$
Sinusoidal axis = 1

SOLUTION

The equation is of the form $y = C + A \cos B(x - D)$ with $C = 1$, $A = \frac{1}{2}$, $B = 2$, and $D = \frac{\pi}{3}$.

The value of C provides the location of the sinusoidal axis. Sketch the sinusoidal axis at $y = 1$. The amplitude ($A = \frac{1}{2}$) indicates the location of the upper and lower bounds. Sketch the upper and lower bounds with a dashed line $\frac{1}{2}$ unit above and $\frac{1}{2}$ unit below the sinusoidal axis:

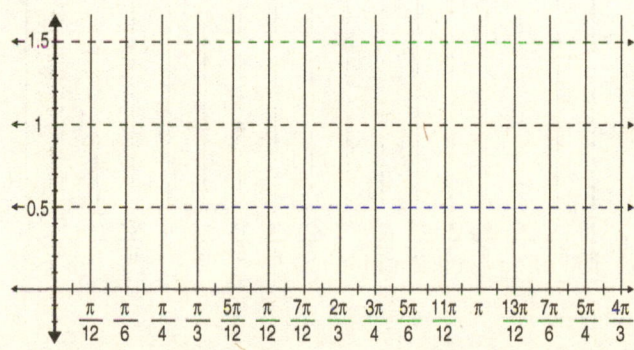

Next, locate the maximum points on the graph. The parent cosine function starts a cycle at the maximum point on the y-axis ($\cos(0) = 1$). $D = \dfrac{\pi}{3}$ is the phase shift. Therefore, the first maximum point is shifted $\dfrac{\pi}{3}$ from the y-axis on the upper bound. It is located at $\left(\dfrac{\pi}{3}, \dfrac{3}{2} \right)$. The period of this function is $\dfrac{2\pi}{2} = \pi$. So, plot the next maximum point at $\dfrac{\pi}{3} + \pi = \dfrac{4\pi}{3}$:

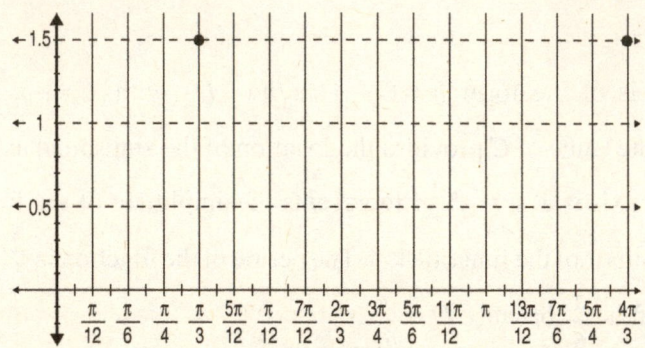

Plot the minimum point halfway between the consecutive maximum points.

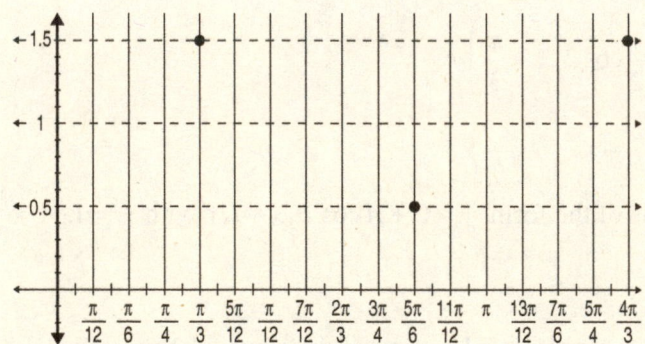

Plot the inflection points halfway between consecutive maximum and minimum points.

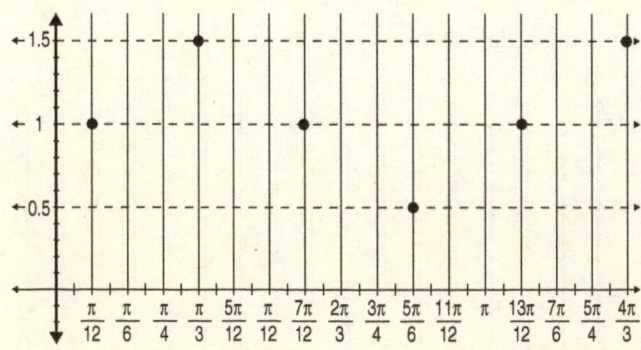

Finally, sketch the graph by connecting the points with a smooth curve.

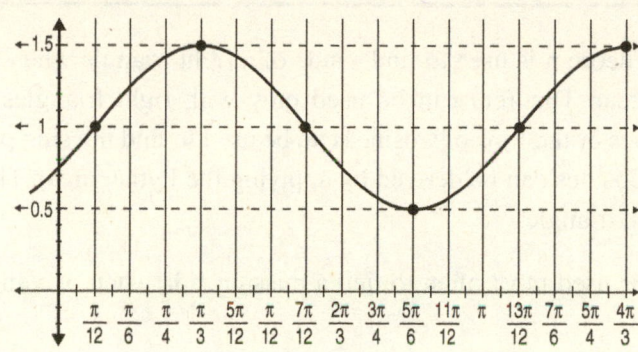

EXAMPLE 52

Find the equation for the following graph:

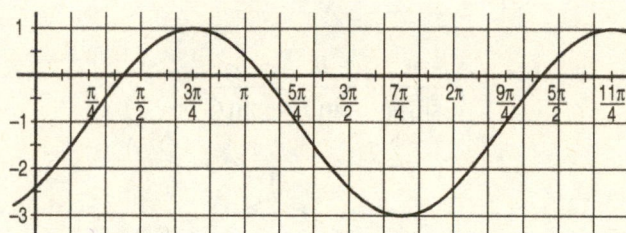

SOLUTION

Finding the equation requires finding the values of A, B, C, and D and substituting them into the general form of the equation. Either the general form of the sine function or the general form of the cosine function can be used since $\sin x = \cos\left(x - \dfrac{\pi}{2}\right)$ (the difference is only in phase shift).

The amplitude is half the difference of the maximum and minimum values, $A = \dfrac{1-(-3)}{2} = 2$. The sinusoidal axis passes through the middle of the curve at $y = -1$, so $C = -1$. The parent sine function starts a cycle at an inflection point ($\sin(0) = 0$). Since the first inflection point has been translated $\dfrac{\pi}{4}$ from the y-axis, $D = \dfrac{\pi}{4}$. The period of the graph is the difference of the x-coordinates of consecutive maximum points, $\dfrac{11\pi}{4} - \dfrac{3\pi}{4} = \dfrac{8\pi}{4} = 2\pi$. Since the period is equal to $\dfrac{2\pi}{B}$, $B = 1$.

Substitute the values of A, B, C, and D into $y = C + A \sin B(x - D)$ to find the equation: $y = -1 + 2\sin\left(x - \dfrac{\pi}{4}\right)$.

Equivalently, this equation can be expressed using cosine as $y = -1 + 2\cos\left(x - \dfrac{3\pi}{4}\right)$.

Law of Sines and Law of Cosines

The Pythagorean Theorem is used to find a side of a right triangle when two sides are known. However, the Pythagorean Theorem can be used only with right triangles. When a triangle is oblique, the Law of Sines or the Law of Cosines can be used to find missing parts. Both the Law of Sines and the Law of Cosines can be derived by applying the Pythagorean Theorem after drawing an altitude in an oblique triangle.

The Law of Sines is used most often to find a missing side when two angles and any side are known.

Law of Sines

The ratios of each side of a triangle to the sine of the angle opposite that side are equal. That is, for Figure 3.56,

$$\frac{a}{\sin A} = \frac{b}{\sin B} = \frac{c}{\sin C}$$

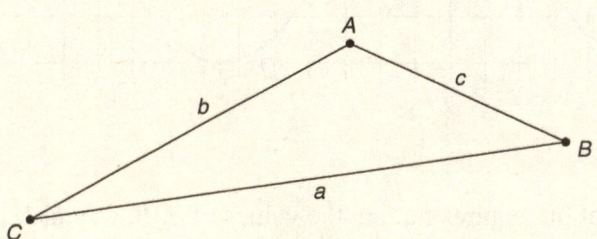

Figure 3.56

The Law of Sines can also be written in reciprocal form: $\frac{\sin A}{a} = \frac{\sin B}{b} = \frac{\sin C}{c}$.

EXAMPLE 53

Luke and Jack are 400 meters apart on a lakefront. They both want to swim to a dock in the middle of the lake. From Luke, an angle of 42° is measured to the dock; from Jack, an angle of 58° is measured to the dock as shown in the following figure. How much farther is Luke from the dock than Jack is?

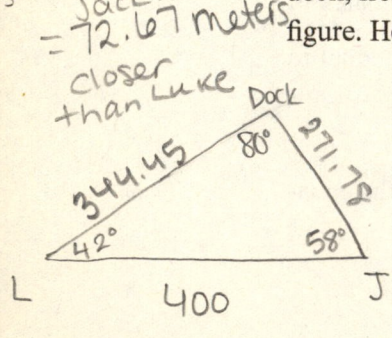

Handwritten work:

344.45 − 271.78
Jack is
= 72.67 meters
closer
than Luke

$$\frac{LJ}{\sin d} = \frac{DL}{\sin j}$$

$$\frac{400}{\sin 80} = \frac{DL}{\sin 58}$$

400 sin58 = DL sin80

$$\frac{400 \sin 58}{\sin 80} = DL$$

DL = 344.45

$$\frac{LJ}{\sin d} = \frac{DJ}{\sin l}$$

$$\frac{400}{\sin 80} = \frac{DJ}{\sin 42}$$

400 sin42 = DJ sin80

$$\frac{400 \sin 42}{\sin 80} = DJ$$

DJ = 271.78

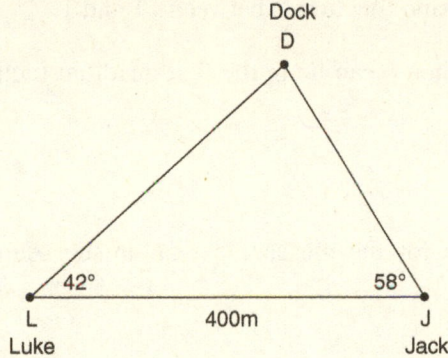

SOLUTION

The missing angle of the triangle is $180° - 42° - 58° = 80°$. Apply the Law of Sines to find DL and DJ.

$$\frac{LJ}{\sin D} = \frac{DL}{\sin J}$$

$$\frac{400}{\sin 80°} = \frac{DL}{\sin 58°}$$

$$DL = \frac{400 \sin 58°}{\sin 80°} \approx 344.45 \text{ meters}$$

$$\frac{LJ}{\sin D} = \frac{DJ}{\sin L}$$

$$\frac{400}{\sin 80°} = \frac{DJ}{\sin 42°}$$

$$DJ = \frac{400 \sin 42°}{\sin 80°} \approx 271.78 \text{ meters}$$

Jack is approximately $344.45 - 271.78 = 72.67$ meters closer to the dock than Luke.

The Law of Sines can also be used to find a missing angle in a triangle. However, when two sides and a non-included angle (SSA) are known, the Law of Sines can provide one solution, two solutions or no solutions to the problem. This is called the ambiguous case. When solving problems of this type it is important to remember:

1.   The sum of the angles of a triangle is 180°.

2.   No triangle can have more than one obtuse angle.

3.   The range of the sine function is between –1 and 1.

4.   If $0 \le \sin \theta < 1$ then θ can lie in the first quadrant (acute angle) or second quadrant (obtuse angle).

EXAMPLE 54

Find the correct value for the measure of $\angle F$ in the triangle below, in which $\angle F > 90°$.

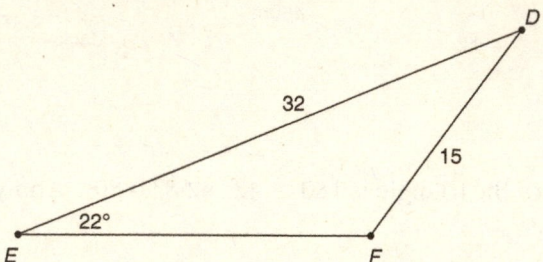

SOLUTION

By the Law of Sines, we have

$$\frac{DF}{\sin E} = \frac{ED}{\sin F}$$

$$\frac{15}{\sin 22°} = \frac{32}{\sin F}$$

$$\sin F = \frac{32 \sin 22°}{15} \approx .799161$$

But, there are two angles between 0° and 180° whose sine is .799161. In the first quadrant lies 53.05°, and 126.95° lies in the second quadrant.

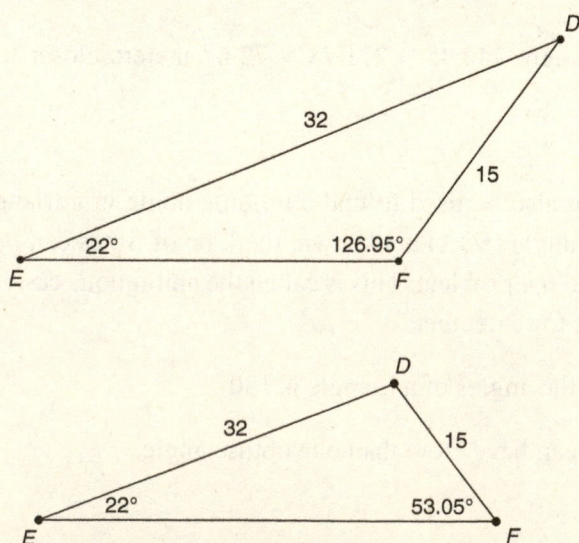

Since $\angle F > 90°$, the correct answer is 126.95°.

Law of Cosines

If you are given three sides or two sides and their included angle, none of the ratios in the Law of Sines would be complete. In these cases, the Law of Cosines can be used. That is, for Figure 3.57,

$$a^2 = b^2 + c^2 - 2bc \cos A$$

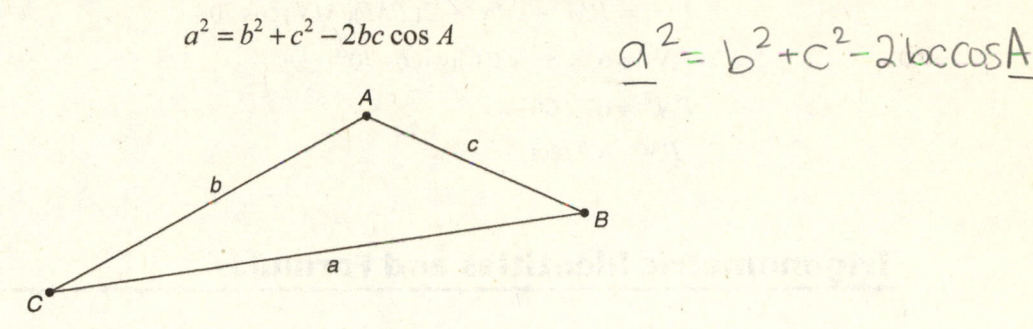

$a^2 = b^2 + c^2 - 2bc\cos A$

Figure 3.57

If $m\angle A = 90°$, then the $\cos A = 0$, and the Law of Cosines becomes the Pythagorean Theorem. Therefore, the Pythagorean Theorem is simply a special case of the more general Law of Cosines. If $m\angle A > 90°$, then the $\cos A$ is negative so you are subtracting a negative number from $b^2 + c^2$, giving a larger value for a^2. This is expected because the longest side of a triangle must be opposite its largest angle.

EXAMPLE 55

Curran is enclosing a garden on the corner of her property with a small fence. The corner of her property intersects at a 70° angle. Two pieces of fence (6 feet and 8 feet long) have already been built on her property lines. How long must the remaining piece of fence be to enclose the garden?

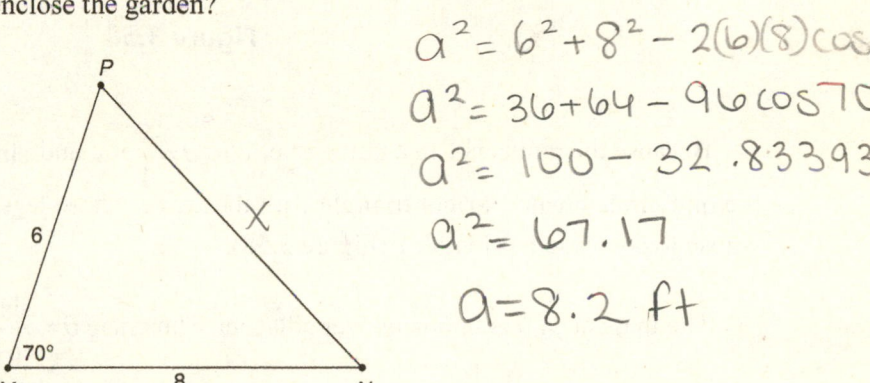

$a^2 = 6^2 + 8^2 - 2(6)(8)\cos 70$

$a^2 = 36 + 64 - 96\cos 70$

$a^2 = 100 - 32.83393376$

$a^2 = 67.17$

$a = 8.2 \text{ ft}$

SOLUTION

Two sides and an included angle are given. Therefore, the Law of Cosines can be used to find the solution.

$$PN^2 = PM^2 + MN^2 - 2(PM)(MN)\cos 70°$$
$$PN^2 = 6^2 + 8^2 - 2(6)(8)\cos 70°$$
$$PN^2 \approx 67.1661$$
$$PN \approx 8.2 \text{ feet}$$

Trigonometric Identities and Formulas

Quotient and Pythagorean Identities

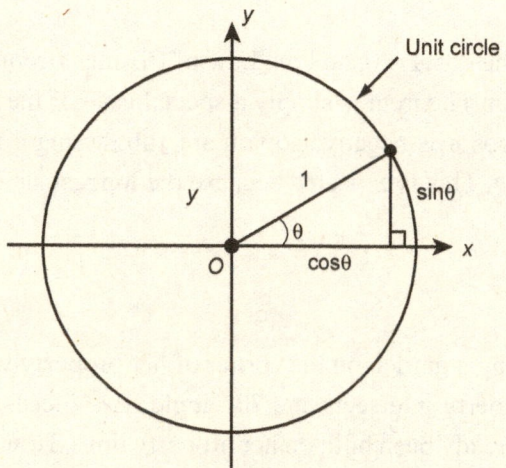

Figure 3.58

Because the radius is 1 in a unit circle, $\cos \theta = \dfrac{x}{1} = x$ and $\sin \theta = \dfrac{y}{1} = y$. Therefore, a point on the unit circle creates a right triangle with the x-axis whose legs have lengths $\sin \theta$ and $\cos \theta$ and whose hypotenuse has length 1 (Figure 3.58).

The tangent of θ is opposite over adjacent. Thus, $\tan \theta = \dfrac{\sin \theta}{\cos \theta}$. Since the cotangent function is defined as the reciprocal of the tangent function, $\cot \theta = \dfrac{\cos \theta}{\sin \theta}$. These two equations are called the **Quotient Identities**.

EXAMPLE 56

Simplify $\tan \theta \csc \theta$ in terms of $\cos \theta$.

$$\tan\theta\csc\theta$$
$$\frac{\sin\theta}{\cos\theta}\cdot\frac{1}{\sin\theta}=\frac{1}{\cos\theta}$$

SOLUTION

Substitute $\tan \theta = \dfrac{\sin \theta}{\cos \theta}$ and $\csc \theta = \dfrac{1}{\sin \theta}$ into the expression and simplify:

$$\tan \theta \csc \theta = \frac{\sin \theta}{\cos \theta} \cdot \frac{1}{\sin \theta} = \frac{1}{\cos \theta}$$

The Pythagorean Theorem can be used on the right triangle to obtain the Pythagorean Identity: $\sin^2 \theta + \cos^2 \theta = 1$. Two additional Pythagorean Identities can be derived from this equation. They are:

$$1 + \tan^2 \theta = \sec^2 \theta$$

$$1 + \cot^2 \theta = \csc^2 \theta$$

These identities can be used to simplify trigonometric expressions and to find missing trigonometric values.

EXAMPLE 57

Simplify $\cos x \sin^2 x - \cos x$.

$$\cos x \sin^2 x - \cos x$$
$$\cos x (\sin^2 x - 1)$$
$$\cos x (-\cos^2 x)$$
$$= -\cos^3 x$$

SOLUTION

The common factor of the terms is $\cos x$. Begin by factoring it out:

$$\cos x \sin^2 x - \cos x = \cos x(\sin^2 x - 1)$$

But $\sin^2 x - 1 = -\cos^2 x$ since $\sin^2 x + \cos^2 x = 1$. Substitute $-\cos^2 x$ into the factored expression to find the solution:

$$\cos x \sin^2 x - \cos x = \cos x(\sin^2 x - 1)$$

$$= \cos x(-\cos^2 x) = -\cos^3 x.$$

EXAMPLE 58

If α is an angle such that $\csc \alpha = 2$ and $\cos \alpha > 0$, find $\sin \alpha$, $\cos \alpha$, $\tan \alpha$, $\sec \alpha$, and $\cot \alpha$.

$$\sin \alpha = \frac{1}{\csc \alpha} = \frac{1}{2}$$

SOLUTION

$$\sin \alpha = \frac{1}{\csc \alpha} = \frac{1}{2}$$

$$\sin^2 \alpha + \cos^2 \alpha = 1$$

$$\cos \alpha = \pm\sqrt{1 - \sin^2 \alpha}$$

$$= \pm\sqrt{1 - \left(\frac{1}{2}\right)^2}$$

$$= \pm\sqrt{\frac{3}{4}}$$

$$= \pm\frac{\sqrt{3}}{2}$$

But $\cos \alpha > 0$ so $\cos \alpha = \dfrac{\sqrt{3}}{2}$.

$$\tan \alpha = \frac{\sin \alpha}{\cos \alpha} = \frac{\frac{1}{2}}{\frac{\sqrt{3}}{2}} = \frac{1}{\sqrt{3}} = \frac{\sqrt{3}}{3}$$

$$\cot \alpha = \frac{1}{\tan \alpha} = \sqrt{3}$$

$$\sec \alpha = \frac{1}{\cos \alpha} = \frac{1}{\frac{\sqrt{3}}{2}} = \frac{2}{\sqrt{3}} = \frac{2\sqrt{3}}{3}$$

The additional trigonometric identities listed below are also valuable in problem solving and simplifications.

Addition and Subtraction Formulas

$$\sin(A \pm B) = \sin A \cos B \pm \cos A \sin B$$

$$\cos(A \pm B) = \cos A \cos B \mp \sin A \sin B$$

$$\tan(A \pm B) = \frac{\tan A \pm \tan B}{1 \mp \tan A \tan B}$$

$$\cot(A \pm B) = \frac{\cot A \cot B \mp 1}{\cot B \pm \cot A}$$

Double-Angle Formulas

$$\sin 2A = 2 \sin A \cos A$$
$$\cos 2A = 2 \cos^2 A - 1$$
$$= 1 - 2 \sin^2 A$$
$$= \cos^2 A - \sin^2 A$$
$$\tan 2A = \frac{2 \tan A}{1 - \tan^2 A}$$

Half-Angle Formulas

On formula sheet

$$\sin \frac{A}{2} = \pm \sqrt{\frac{1 - \cos A}{2}}$$

$$\cos \frac{A}{2} = \pm \sqrt{\frac{1 + \cos A}{2}}$$

$$\tan \frac{A}{2} = \pm \sqrt{\frac{1 - \cos A}{1 + \cos A}}$$

$$= \frac{1 - \cos A}{\sin A}$$

$$= \frac{\sin A}{1 + \cos A}$$

$$\cot \frac{A}{2} = \pm \sqrt{\frac{1 + \cos A}{1 - \cos A}} = \frac{1 + \cos A}{\sin A} = \frac{\sin A}{1 - \cos A}$$

Sum and Difference Formulas

On formula sheet

$$\sin \alpha + \sin \beta = 2 \sin\left(\frac{\alpha + \beta}{2}\right) \cos\left(\frac{\alpha - \beta}{2}\right)$$

$$\sin \alpha - \sin \beta = 2 \cos\left(\frac{\alpha + \beta}{2}\right) \sin\left(\frac{\alpha - \beta}{2}\right)$$

$$\cos \alpha + \cos \beta = 2 \cos\left(\frac{\alpha + \beta}{2}\right) \cos\left(\frac{\alpha - \beta}{2}\right)$$

$$\cos \alpha - \cos \beta = -2 \sin\left(\frac{\alpha + \beta}{2}\right) \sin\left(\frac{\alpha - \beta}{2}\right)$$

$$\tan \alpha + \tan \beta = \frac{\sin(\alpha + \beta)}{\cos \alpha \cos \beta}$$

$$\tan \alpha - \tan \beta = \frac{\sin(\alpha - \beta)}{\cos \alpha \cos \beta}$$

Product Formulas of Sines and Cosines

$$\sin A \sin B = \frac{1}{2}[\cos(A-B) - \cos(A+B)]$$

$$\cos A \cos B = \frac{1}{2}[\cos(A+B) + \cos(A-B)]$$

$$\sin A \cos B = \frac{1}{2}[\sin(A+B) + \sin(A-B)]$$

$$\cos A \sin B = \frac{1}{2}[\sin(A+B) + \sin(B-A)]$$

EXAMPLE 59

Find the exact value of $\sin 75°$.

SOLUTION

$75° = 30° + 45°$. Therefore,

$$\sin 75° = \sin(30° + 45°)$$
$$= \sin 30° \cos 45° + \cos 30° \sin 45°$$
$$= \left(\frac{1}{2}\right)\left(\frac{\sqrt{2}}{2}\right) + \left(\frac{\sqrt{3}}{2}\right)\left(\frac{\sqrt{2}}{2}\right)$$
$$= \frac{\sqrt{2}}{4} + \frac{\sqrt{6}}{4}$$
$$= \frac{\sqrt{2} + \sqrt{6}}{4}$$

Handwritten:

$\sin 75 = \sin(30 + 45)$

$\sin 30 \cos 45 + \cos 30 \sin 45$

$\left(\frac{1}{2}\right)\left(\frac{\sqrt{2}}{2}\right) + \left(\frac{\sqrt{3}}{2}\right)\left(\frac{\sqrt{2}}{2}\right)$

$\frac{\sqrt{2}}{4} + \frac{\sqrt{6}}{4}$

$\boxed{\frac{\sqrt{2} + \sqrt{6}}{4}}$

EXAMPLE 60

Use the following to find $\sin 2\theta$, $\cos 2\theta$, and $\tan 2\theta$.

$$\cos \theta = \frac{8}{17}, \quad \frac{3\pi}{2} < \theta < 2\pi$$

Handwritten:

$17^2 = 8^2 + c^2$

$289 = 64 + c^2$

$225 = c^2$

$c = 15$

$\sin 2\theta = 2 \sin \theta \cos \theta$
$= 2\left(\frac{-15}{17}\right)\left(\frac{8}{17}\right)$
$= \frac{-240}{289}$

$\cos 2\theta = 2\cos^2 \theta - 1$
$= 2\left(\frac{8}{17}\right) - 1$
$= \frac{-161}{289}$

$\tan 2\theta = \frac{\sin 2\theta}{\cos 2\theta} = \frac{-240}{289} \cdot \frac{-289}{161}$
$= \frac{240}{161}$

SOLUTION

Draw a graph to represent the given information:

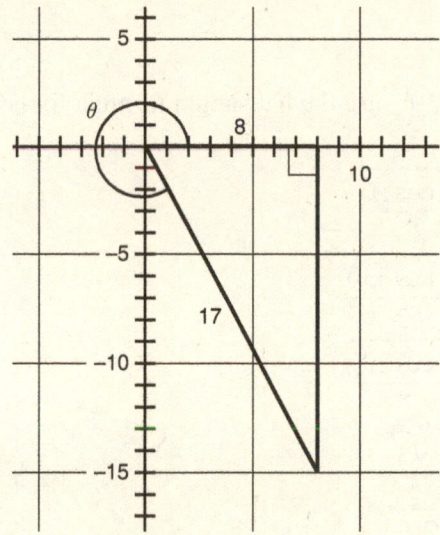

The missing side length is 15 (the triangle is an 8-15-17 triangle). Therefore, the triangle has a vertex at (8,–15), and $\sin\theta = \dfrac{y}{r} = -\dfrac{15}{17}$. Substituting these values into the double-angle formulas, we find

$$\sin 2\theta = 2\sin\theta\cos\theta = 2\left(\frac{-15}{17}\right)\left(\frac{8}{17}\right) = \frac{-240}{289}$$

$$\cos 2\theta = 2\cos^2\theta - 1 = 2\left(\frac{8}{17}\right)^2 - 1 = \frac{-161}{289}$$

$$\tan 2\theta = \frac{\sin 2\theta}{\cos 2\theta} = \frac{-240}{289} \cdot \frac{-289}{161} = \frac{240}{161}$$

EXAMPLE 61

Find the exact value of cos 165°.

SOLUTION

Since 165° is half of 330°, use the half-angle formula for $\cos\dfrac{A}{2}$ with $A = 330°$:

$$\cos\frac{A}{2} = \pm\sqrt{\frac{1+\cos A}{2}}$$

$$= \pm\sqrt{\frac{1+\cos 330°}{2}}$$

$$= \pm\sqrt{\frac{1+\cos 30°}{2}}$$

$$= \pm\sqrt{\frac{1+\dfrac{\sqrt{3}}{2}}{2}}$$

$$= \pm\sqrt{\frac{2+\sqrt{3}}{4}}$$

$$= \pm\frac{\sqrt{2+\sqrt{3}}}{2}$$

Since 165° lies in Quadrant II and cosine is negative in Quadrant II, the negative square root is chosen.

$$\cos 165° = -\frac{\sqrt{2+\sqrt{3}}}{2}$$

EXAMPLE 62

Find the exact value of sin 465° − sin 195°.

SOLUTION

The associated sum formula is $\sin\alpha - \sin\beta = 2\cos\left(\dfrac{\alpha+\beta}{2}\right)\sin\left(\dfrac{\alpha-\beta}{2}\right)$. Substitute $\alpha = 465°$ and $\beta = 195°$ into the formula.

$$\sin\alpha - \sin\beta = 2\cos\left(\frac{\alpha+\beta}{2}\right)\sin\left(\frac{\alpha-\beta}{2}\right)$$

$$= 2\cos\left(\frac{465°+195°}{2}\right)\sin\left(\frac{465°-195°}{2}\right)$$

$$= 2\cos\left(\frac{660°}{2}\right)\sin\left(\frac{270°}{2}\right)$$

$$= 2\cos 330°\sin 135°$$

$$= 2\cos 30°\sin 45°$$

$$= 2\left(\frac{\sqrt{3}}{2}\right)\left(\frac{\sqrt{2}}{2}\right)$$

$$= \frac{\sqrt{6}}{2}$$

EXAMPLE 63

Rewrite $\sin 4x \cos 3x$ using a product formula.

SOLUTION

The associated product formula is $\sin A \cos B = \frac{1}{2}[\sin(A+B)+\sin(A-B)]$. Substitute $A = 4x$ and $B = 3x$ into the formula:

$$\sin A \cos B = \frac{1}{2}[\sin(A+B)+\sin(A-B)]$$

$$= \frac{1}{2}[\sin(4x+3x)+\sin(4x-3x)]$$

$$= \frac{1}{2}[\sin 7x + \sin x]$$

$$= \frac{1}{2}\sin 7x + \frac{1}{2}\sin x$$

EXAMPLE 64

Simplify completely: $\dfrac{1-\cos^2\theta}{\sin^2\theta}$. $\dfrac{\sin^2\theta}{\sin^2\theta} = 1$

SOLUTION

$$\frac{1-\cos^2\theta}{\sin^2\theta} = \frac{\sin^2\theta}{\sin^2\theta} = 1$$

EXAMPLE 65

Using the angle addition and subtraction formulas, find the value of cos 15°.

SOLUTION

Note $(45 - 30) = 15$, and that cos 45° and cos 30° are exact values. Use the cosine angle subtraction identity to find cos 15°.

$$\cos (A - B) = \cos A \cos B + \sin A \sin B$$

$$\cos (45° - 30°) = \cos 45° \cos 30° + \sin 45° \sin 30° = \frac{\sqrt{2}}{2} \cdot \frac{\sqrt{3}}{2} + \frac{\sqrt{2}}{2} \cdot \frac{1}{2}$$

$$= \frac{\sqrt{6}}{4} + \frac{\sqrt{2}}{4} = \frac{\sqrt{6} + \sqrt{2}}{4}.$$

[handwritten:]
$$\cos(45-30)$$
$$\cos 45 \cos 30 + \sin 45 \sin 30$$
$$\left(\frac{\sqrt{2}}{2}\right)\left(\frac{\sqrt{3}}{2}\right) + \left(\frac{\sqrt{2}}{2}\right)\left(\frac{1}{2}\right)$$
$$\frac{\sqrt{6}}{4} + \frac{\sqrt{2}}{4} = \boxed{\frac{\sqrt{6} + \sqrt{2}}{4}}$$

For each of the following examples, round off all answers to the nearest degree. These examples combine algebra and trigonometry.

EXAMPLE 66

What are the values of x in the equation $3 \tan x - 0.56 = 1.25$?

SOLUTION

Adding 0.56 to each side yields $3 \tan x = 1.81$. Then $\tan x \approx 0.6033$, so $x \approx 31°$ or 211°. (The answer is found by finding $\tan^{-1}(0.6033)$.)

EXAMPLE 67

What are the values of x in the equation $6(\csc x - 2) = 13 \csc x$?

SOLUTION

Simplifying, this equation becomes $6 \csc x - 12 = 13 \csc x$. Then $-12 = 7 \csc x$.

Thus, $x = \csc^{-1}\left(-\frac{12}{7}\right) \approx 216°$ or 324°.

[handwritten:]
$$\frac{-12}{7} = \csc x$$
$$\csc^{-1}\left(\frac{-12}{7}\right)$$

EXAMPLE 68

What are the values of x in the equation $5 \cot^2 x - 0.75 = 2 \cot^2 x - 0.5$?

SOLUTION

By rearranging the terms, we get $3\cot^2 x = 0.25$. Then we can write $\cot x = \pm\sqrt{\dfrac{0.25}{3}} \approx \pm 0.2887$. The four possible values for x are $74°$, $106°$, $254°$ and $286°$.

EXAMPLE 69

What are the values of x in the equation $2\cos^2 x - 5\cos x = 0$?

SOLUTION

We can factor the left side so that the equation reads as $(\cos x)(2\cos x - 5) = 0$.

If $\cos x = 0$, $x = 90°$ or $270°$. If $2\cos x - 5 = 0$, $x = \cos^{-1}\left(\dfrac{5}{2}\right)$, which does not

exist. The only answers are $90°$ or $270°$.

EXAMPLE 70

What are the values of x in the equation $3\sec^2 x + 2\sec x - 5 = 0$?

SOLUTION

Factoring the left side, we get $(3\sec x + 5)(\sec x - 1) = 0$. If $3\sec x + 5 = 0$, then

$x = \sec^{-1}\left(-\dfrac{5}{3}\right) \approx 127°$ or $233°$. If $\sec x - 1 = 0$, then $x = \sec^{-1}(1) = 0°$.

EXAMPLE 71

What are the values of x in the equation $\sin x - 2\tan x = 0$?

SOLUTION

Use the identity $\tan x = \dfrac{\sin x}{\cos x}$ to rewrite the equation as $\sin x - \dfrac{2\sin x}{\cos x} = 0$. Multiply by $\cos x$ to get $(\sin x)(\cos x) - 2\sin x = 0$, which factors as $(\sin x)(\cos x - 2) = 0$. The solutions to $\sin x = 0$ are $0°$ or $180°$. The equation $\cos x - 2 = 0$ has no solution. Thus, the answers are $0°$ or $180°$.

EXAMPLE 72

What are the values of x in the equation $\cos^2 x + 8\cos x + \sin^2 x = 0$?

SOLUTION

Use the identity $\sin^2 x + \cos^2 x = 1$. The equation can then be written as $1 + 8\cos x = 0$. Then $\cos x = -\frac{1}{8}$, so $x = \cos^{-1}\left(-\frac{1}{8}\right) \approx 97°$ or $263°$.

EXAMPLE 73

What are the values of x in the equation $5\sec^2 x + 2\tan x - 21 = 0$?

SOLUTION

The key is to use the identity $\tan^2 x + 1 = \sec^2 x$. Then we get $5(\tan^2 x + 1) + 2\tan x - 21 = 0$, which simplifies to $5\tan^2 x + 2\tan x - 16 = 0$. Factoring leads to $(5\tan x - 8)(\tan x + 2) = 0$. If $5\tan x - 8 = 0$, then $x = \tan^{-1}\left(\frac{8}{5}\right) \approx 58°$ or $238°$. If $\tan x + 2 = 0$, then $x = \tan^{-1}(-2) \approx 117°$ or $297°$.

EXAMPLE 74

What are the values of x in the equation $3\cos 2x + 11\cos x + 6 = 0$?

SOLUTION

Use the identity $\cos 2x = 2\cos^2 x - 1$. Then the original equation becomes $3(2\cos^2 x - 1) + 11\cos x + 6 = 0$. Upon simplification, we get $6\cos^2 x + 11\cos x + 3 = 0$. Factoring leads to $(3\cos x + 1)(2\cos x + 3) = 0$. If the first factor is zero, then $x = \cos^{-1}\left(-\frac{1}{3}\right) \approx 109°$ or $251°$. If the second factor is zero, there is no further answer since $\cos^{-1}\left(-\frac{3}{2}\right)$ does not exist.

EXAMPLE 75

What are the values of x in the equation $5\cos x - 4\sin 2x = 0$?

SOLUTION

We need to use the identity $\sin 2x = 2\sin x\cos x$ so that the equation becomes $5\cos x - (4)(2\sin x)(\cos x) = 0$. Factoring leads to $(\cos x)(5 - 8\sin x) = 0$. If $\cos x = 0$, then $x = 90°$ or $270°$. If $5 - 8\sin x = 0$, then $x = \sin^{-1}\left(\frac{5}{8}\right) \approx 39°$ or $141°$.

EXAMPLE 76

What are the values of x in the equation $\cos 2x + \sin^2 x = 0.5$?

SOLUTION

Using the identity $\cos 2x = \cos^2 x - \sin^2 x$, the equation simplifies to $\cos^2 x = 0.5$.
Then, $\cos x = \pm\sqrt{0.5}$. Thus, $x = 45°, 135°, 225°,$ or $315°$.

Rectangular and Polar Coordinates

Rectangular Coordinates

Complex numbers can be illustrated using the xy-coordinate plane. In this setting, the x-axis represents the real part of the complex number, while the y-axis represents the imaginary part. Let A, B, C, D, E, and F represent the following complex numbers: $A = 3 + 0i = 3$, $B = 4 + 2i$, $C = -2 + 5i$, $D = -3 - i$, $E = 0 - 4i = -4i$, and $F = 5 - 6i$.

Figure 3.59 shows how these complex numbers are plotted in the xy-coordinate plane. (This is called the complex plane when complex numbers are used.)

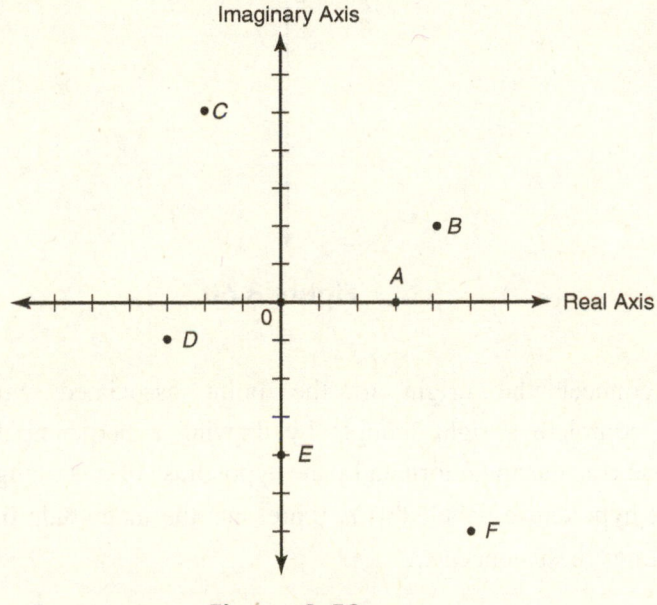

Figure 3.59

Similar to the plotting of points in the real xy-coordinate plane, we can also write the coordinates of points in the complex plane. This is accomplished by just writing the ordered pair using only the real number values of the complex number. For example, since $A = 3 + 0i$, we can write the coordinates of A as $(3, 0)$. Likewise, since $C = -2 + 5i$, we can write the coordinates of C as $(-2, 5)$.

The **magnitude of a complex number** is defined as the distance between its corresponding point on the complex plane and (0, 0), which is the origin. For any complex number $a + bi$, its magnitude is calculated as $\sqrt{a^2 + b^2}$. Symbolically, the magnitude of $a + bi$ is represented as $|a + bi|$. For example, the magnitude of $5 - 6i$ is $\sqrt{5^2 + (-6)^2} = \sqrt{61}$. Likewise, the magnitude of $-3 - i$, represented as $|-3 - i|$, is $\sqrt{(-3)^2 + (-1)^2} = \sqrt{10}$. As a special case, note that the magnitude of $0 + 9i$ is $\sqrt{0^2 + 9^2} = 9$. This is certainly no surprise!

Any complex number written as $a + bi$ is considered to be in rectangular form. (Another name for rectangular is *Cartesian*.) Another popular form for expressing a complex number is called its *polar form*. Suppose the complex number $Z = a + bi$ is graphed, as shown in Figure 3.60.

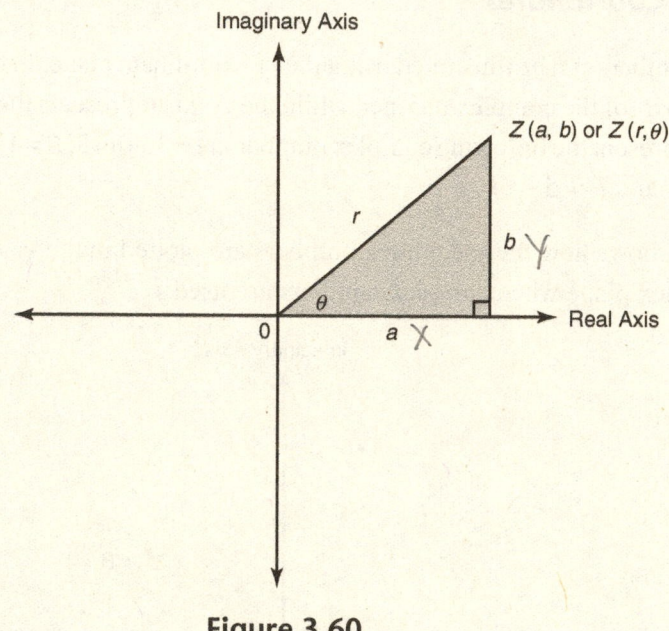

Figure 3.60

Let's now connect the origin to the point associated with the complex number Z. Then we complete a right triangle by drawing a perpendicular segment from (a, b) to the real axis. Use θ as the angle formed by the hypotenuse of this triangle and the segment along the real axis. The hypotenuse, labeled as r, represents the magnitude of Z, since $r = \sqrt{a^2 + b^2}$. Figure 3.60 illustrates these concepts.

Then a represents the horizontal segment, and b represents the vertical segment. Since $\cos \theta = \dfrac{a}{r}$ and $\sin \theta = \dfrac{b}{r}$, $a = r \cos \theta$ and $b = r \sin \theta$.

Polar Coordinates

We can now write $Z = r \cos \theta + (r \sin \theta)i = r(\cos \theta + i \sin \theta)$. This is called the **polar form** of the complex number Z. Also, the angle represented by θ is called the **argument**.

Notice that the point associated with the complex number Z can be labeled using its rectangular coordinates (a, b) or its polar coordinates (r, θ).

Polar coordinates are simply defined as the magnitude of the complex number (hypotenuse) and the angle associated with the right triangle formed by the real axis and the perpendicular segment from the point affiliated with the complex number. Let's discuss the situations in which $\theta > 90°$.

If $90° < \theta < 180°$, then $\sin\theta$ is positive and $\cos\theta$ is negative.

If $180° < \theta < 270°$, then $\sin\theta$ and $\cos\theta$ are both negative.

If $270° < \theta < 360°$, then $\sin\theta$ is negative and $\cos\theta$ is positive.

EXAMPLE 77

What is the polar form of the complex number $Z = -2 + 4i$?

SOLUTION

The diagram below is a graph of $Z = -2 + 4i$. Note that for brevity, we have labeled the imaginary and real axes as simply yi and x. Henceforth, we will use these abbreviations.

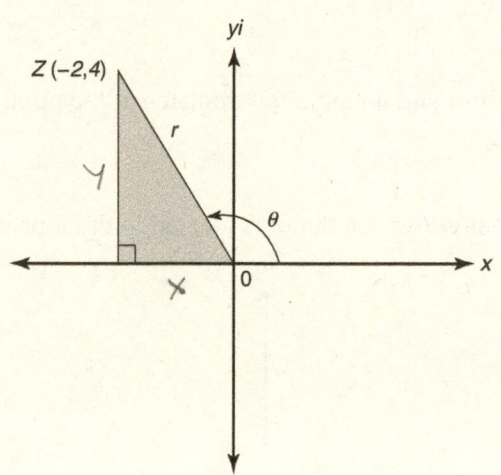

$$r = \sqrt{(-2)^2 + 4^2} = \sqrt{20} = 2\sqrt{5}$$

We calculate r (the hypotenuse) using $r = \sqrt{(-2)^2 + 4^2} = \sqrt{20} = 2\sqrt{5}$. Also,

$\theta = \tan^{-1}\left(\dfrac{4}{-2}\right) \approx 117°$. Note that another value for $\tan^{-1}\left(\dfrac{4}{-2}\right)$ is approximately

297°: however, since our answer is confined to the second quadrant, we can only use the value of 117°. The final answer is $Z = 2\sqrt{5}(\cos 117° + i\sin 117°)$.

EXAMPLE 78

Referring back to Example 74, what are the polar coordinates for Z?

SOLUTION

The polar coordinates are in the form (r, θ), which is $(2\sqrt{5}, 117°)$.

Two comments are needed at this point. First, the value of θ may also be expressed in radians. To convert to radian measure, multiply the number of degrees by $\dfrac{\pi}{180°}$. For example, $60° = (60°)\left(\dfrac{\pi}{180°}\right) = \dfrac{\pi}{3}$ radians.

Second, in Example 74, we found the value of θ by using the inverse tangent function. The value of θ can also be determined by using either the inverse cosine function or the inverse sine function. In Example 74, $\cos\theta = \dfrac{-2}{2\sqrt{5}} = -\dfrac{1}{\sqrt{5}}$ and $\sin\theta = \dfrac{4}{2\sqrt{5}} = \dfrac{2}{\sqrt{5}}$. Then $\theta = \cos^{-1}\left(-\dfrac{1}{\sqrt{5}}\right) = \sin^{-1}\left(\dfrac{2}{\sqrt{5}}\right) \approx 117°$.

EXAMPLE 79

What are the polar form and the polar coordinates of the number $Z = \sqrt{3} - 3i$?

SOLUTION

Using the diagram below, we see that Z is located in the fourth quadrant.

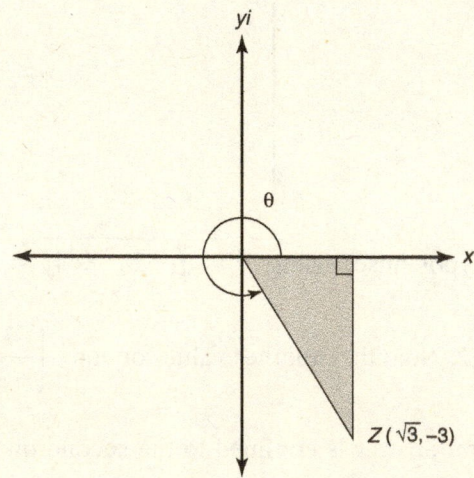

$Z(\sqrt{3}, -3)$

First we determine r, which is $\sqrt{(\sqrt{3})^2 + (3)^2} = \sqrt{12} = 2\sqrt{3}$. Using the cosine ratio, $\theta = \cos^{-1}\left(\dfrac{\sqrt{3}}{2\sqrt{3}}\right) = \cos^{-1}\left(\dfrac{1}{2}\right) = 300°$. The answer becomes $Z = 2\sqrt{3}$ $(\cos 300° + i \sin 300°)$. We must be careful to only use the fourth quadrant angle when finding the value of $\cos^{-1}\left(\dfrac{1}{2}\right)$. The polar coordinates are $(2\sqrt{3}, 300°)$.

EXAMPLE 80

What is the polar form of the number $Z = -1 - 2.5i$?

SOLUTION

In this example, Z is located in the third quadrant, as illustrated in the following diagram.

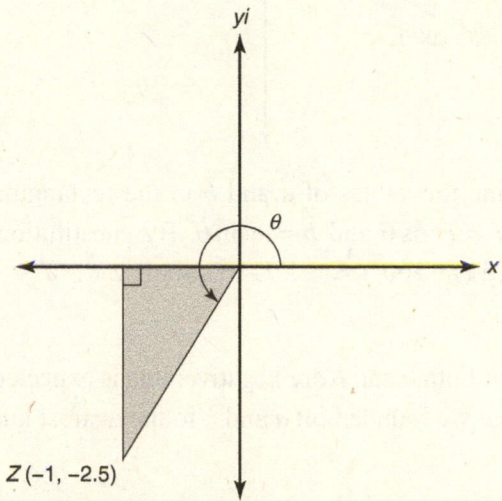

We determine that $r = \sqrt{(-1)^2 + (-2.5)^2} = \sqrt{7.25}$. Using the tangent ratio, $\theta = \tan^{-1}\left(\dfrac{-2.5}{-1}\right) \approx 248°$. The answer is $\sqrt{7.25}(\cos 248° + i \sin 248°)$.

EXAMPLE 81

What is the rectangular form of the complex number whose polar form is given as $Z = 5(\cos 200° + i \sin 200°)$?

SOLUTION

For this example, Z is located in the third quadrant, as shown below.

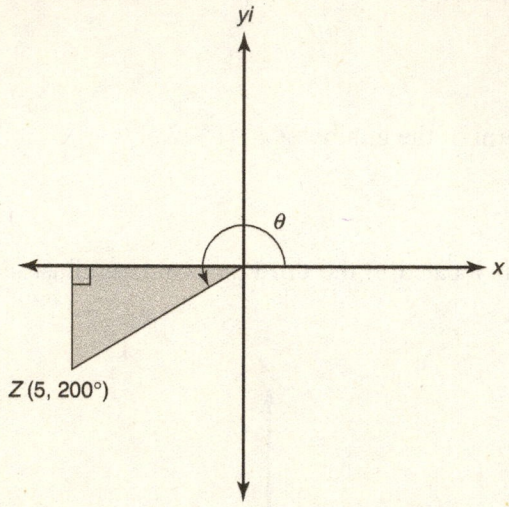

Z (5, 200°)

We need to determine the values of a and b in the rectangular form of $Z = a + bi$. We know that $a = r \cos \theta$ and $b = r \sin \theta$. By substitution, $a = (5)(\cos 200°) \approx -4.70$ and $b = (5)(\sin 200°) \approx -1.71$. Our answer is $Z = -4.70 - 1.71i$.

Notice that in Example 7, both a and b are negative; this is expected because Z is located in the third quadrant. Also, note that we rounded off a and b to the nearest hundredth.

EXAMPLE 82

What is the rectangular form for the complex number $Z = \sqrt{10}(\cos 35° + i \sin 35°)$?

SOLUTION

Let's do this example without a diagram. The value of a is given by $\sqrt{10} \cos 35° \approx 2.59$ and the value of b is given by $\sqrt{10} \sin 35° \approx 1.81$. The answer is $Z = 2.59 + 1.81$.

Of course, we could have also solved Example 78 without a diagram. Whenever we are converting from polar form to rectangular form, we just perform the required arithmetic steps. However, a diagram is recommended when converting from rectangular form to polar form. The only exception to this last statement would be if the rectangular form contained a zero value for either a or b, as explained in the next two examples.

EXAMPLE 83

What is the polar form of the number $Z = 0 + 12i$?

SOLUTION

The point associated with this Z value lies on the positive yi axis. This means that $\theta = 90°$. Instantly, we know that $r = 12$, since $\sqrt{0^2 + 12^2} = 12$. The answer is $Z = 12(\cos 90° + i \sin 90°)$.

EXAMPLE 84

What is the polar form of the number $Z = -5 + 0i$?

SOLUTION

The corresponding point for Z lies on the negative x axis, so $\theta = 180°$. Also, $r = \sqrt{(-5)^2 + 0^2} = 5$. The answer is $Z = 5(\cos 180° + i \sin 180°)$.

FUNCTIONS

Relations

A **relation** is a set (collection) of members that are ordered pairs. Each ordered pair is called an **element**. The set is indicated by braces and is normally assigned a capital letter.

Here are a few examples of relations:

$A = \{(5, 7), (9, 1)\}$. The two elements of set A are $(5, 7)$ and $(9, 1)$.

$B = \{(\text{tree, w}), (6, 6), (\text{math, tree}), \left(-3, \frac{1}{2}\right)\}$. Set B has four elements.

The number 6 appears in both the first and second parts of element $(6, 6)$; also, the word "tree" appears as the first part of (tree, w) but as the second part of (math, tree).

$C = \{(\text{a}, 10), (\text{b}, 10), (\text{c}, 10), (\text{d}, 10), (\text{e}, 10), (\text{f}, 10)\}$. Set C has six elements.

The number 10 appears as the second part of each element.

$D = \{(\text{shoe}, 3), (-2, 5), (\text{shoe}, 7), (\text{c}, 0), (\text{b}, 10)\}$. Set D has five elements.

The word "shoe" appears as the first part of two different elements.

Also, we have used the element (b, 10) in both set D and set C.

In any relation, some elements may have shared "parts," but there is no repetition of elements. Thus, if a set contained the element $(-3, 4)$, it could also include the element $(-3, 5)$ or even $(4, -3)$, but we would not repeat $(-3, 4)$ as an additional element.

For each ordered pair of a relation, the set of all first parts is called the **domain**; the set of all second parts is called the **range**. For set A, the domain is $\{5, 9\}$ and the range is $\{7, 1\}$. For set B, the domain is $\{$tree, 6, math, $-3\}$ and the range is $\{$w, 6, tree, $\frac{1}{2}\}$.

For set C, the domain is $\{a, b, c, d, e, f\}$ and the range is $\{10\}$. Finally, for set D, the domain is $\{$shoe, -2, c, b$\}$ and the range is $\{3, 5, 7, 0, 10\}$.

Recall that the members of a set may be listed in any order. Thus, we could have stated the domain of set B as $\{6, -3$, math, tree$\}$.

Introduction to Functions

A **function** is a special type of relation in which for each different element in the domain, exactly one element in the range is assigned to it. Sets A, B, and C shown above are all functions, since this rule is followed. Notice that there is repetition of the range element in set C. This does not violate the definition of functions, because each of the six elements of the domain (namely a, b, c, d, e, f) is assigned to exactly one range element (namely, 10).

For a relation to not qualify as a function, at least two elements have the same domain value but different range values. Set D shown above is such an example. There are two elements, (shoe, 3) and (shoe, 7), in which the domain value "shoe" is paired with both 3 and 7. This means that D is not a function.

EXAMPLE 1

Given the set $E = \{(-5, 4), (b, 2), (\_, 6)\}$, fill in the blank so that E is not a function.

SOLUTION

The two possibilities are -5 and b. If the third element of E were either $(-5, 6)$ or $(b, 6)$, set E would not be a function.

EXAMPLE 2

Given the set $F = \{(4, \text{hat}), (\text{hat}, -8), (9, z), (\_, z)\}$. If F is a function with four elements, what are the restrictions in filling in the blank?

SOLUTION

The blank may not be filled in with any of 4, hat, or 9. Each of 4 and hat is already paired with a range value. The reason that 9 cannot be used is that (9, z) is already an element of F. If this same element were to be repeated, then F would really have only three elements, not four elements.

Some functions may be described with *equations*. For example, suppose the domain of a function is {0, 2, 4, 6} and the range is described by $f(x) = x - 5$. This means that for each x value in the domain, the range value is found by the expression $x - 5$. Thus, $f(0) = 0 - 5 = -5$, $f(2) = 2 - 5 = -3$, $f(4) = 4 - 5 = -1$, and $f(6) = 6 - 5 = 1$. This function can now be written as {(0, –5), (2, –3), (4, –1), (6, 1)}.

Another example of a function that is described by an equation is $\{(x,y) \mid y = 3x^2$, for $x = -1$, 3, 5\}. When $x = -1$, $y = 3(-1)^2 = 3$; when $x = 3$, $y = 3(3)^2 = 27$; when $x = 5$, $y = 3(5)^2 = 75$. This function may be written as {(–1, 3), (3, 27), (5, 75)}.

A vertical line test can be used to check if a given relation is a function. Any vertical line may intersect the graph of a function *at most once*. In Figure 4.1, $f(x)$ is a function, but $g(x)$ is not a function.

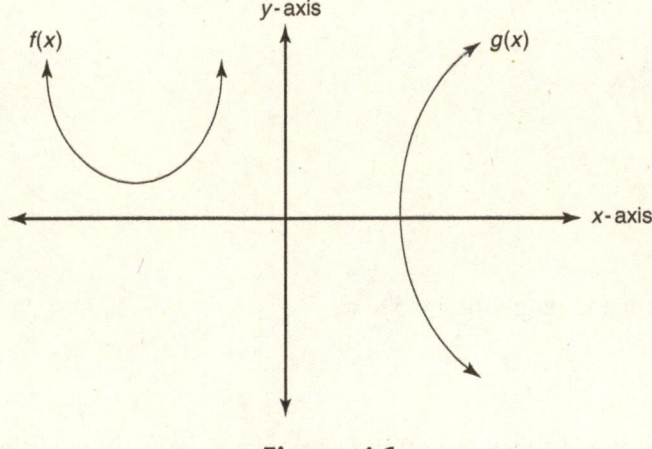

Figure 4.1

Function Notation

Although a function with dependent variable x is usually referred to as $f(x)$, any letter can be used to denote a function. For example, $A(s) = s^2$ can be used to represent the area of a square with side length s. There are two other notations commonly used for functions. Mapping notation uses a colon and an arrow. Set notation uses brackets and a vertical bar. The following notations are all equivalent:

$$y = x^2$$
$$f(x) = x^2$$
$$f : x \rightarrow x^2$$
$$f = \{(x, y) \mid y = x^2\}$$

Domain and Range

To find the specific value of a given function, replace the variable with the given value. The set of all input values by which the function is defined is called the **domain** of the function. The set of corresponding output values is called the **range** of the function. For a function $f(x)$, the domain is the set of all real-number values of x such that the expression defining the function is real. The domain of a function can also be given explicitly. When it is not, it is determined by excluding the values that cause the function to be undefined (division by zero) or complex (negative values under a square root). Determining the range of a function is more complex. The graph of the function is often helpful in identifying the set of output values used (the range).

EXAMPLE 3

Evaluate $f(1)$ for $y = f(x) = 5x + 2$.

SOLUTION

$f(x) = 5x + 2$

$f(1) = 5(1) + 2$

$\quad\quad = 5 + 2$

$\quad\quad = 7$

EXAMPLE 4

Find the domain and range for $y = 5 - x^2$.

SOLUTION

This is not a rational function with a denominator, so there is no need to check for division by zero. This is not a radical function so there is no need to check for negative values under the radical symbol. Thus, the domain is all real numbers. As can be seen in the figure below, every y-value less than or equal to 5 is an output of the function. Therefore, the range is $\{y \mid y \leq 5\}$, the set of real numbers less than or equal to 5.

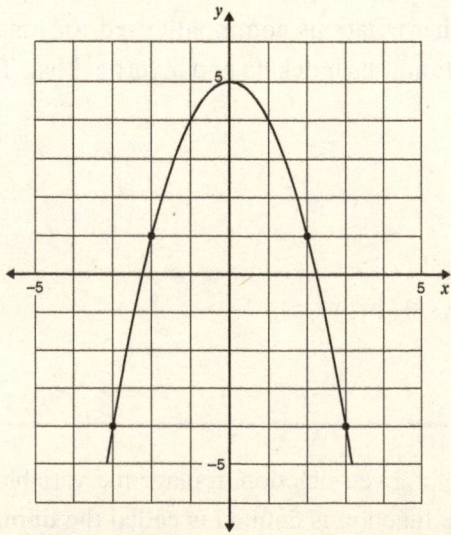

EXAMPLE 5

Find the domain D and range R of the function $\left(x, \dfrac{x}{|x|}\right)$.

SOLUTION

Note that the y-value of any coordinate pair (x,y) is $\dfrac{x}{|x|}$. We can replace x in the formula $\dfrac{x}{|x|}$ with any number except 0, since the denominator, $|x|$, cannot equal 0. This is because division by 0 is undefined. Therefore, the domain D is the set of all real numbers except 0. If x is negative, i.e., $x < 0$, then $|x| = -x$ by definition. Hence, if x is negative, then $\dfrac{x}{|x|} = \dfrac{x}{-x} = -1$. If x is positive, then $|x| = x$ by definition. Hence, if x is positive, then $\dfrac{x}{|x|} = \dfrac{x}{x} = 1$. (The case where $x = 0$ has already been found to be undefined.) Thus, there are only two numbers -1 and 1 in the range R of the function; that is, $R = \{-1, 1\}$.

The graph of the function $y = \dfrac{x}{|x|}$ below confirms that the range is $\{-1, 1\}$.

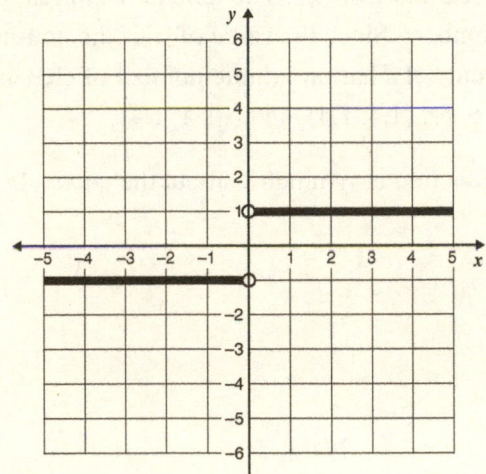

EXAMPLE 6

If $f(x) = 3x + 4$ and $D = \{x \mid -1 \le x \le 3\}$, find the range of $f(x)$.

SOLUTION

This function is a line with positive slope, so we know that the function is increasing on the given domain. Hence, if x belongs to D, the function value $f(x) = 3x + 4$ is least when $x = -1$ and greatest when $x = 3$. Consequently, since $f(-1) = -3 + 4 = 1$ and $f(3) = 9 + 4 = 13$, the range is all y from 1 to 13; that is, $R = \{y \mid 1 \le y \le 13\}$.

Categories of Functions

Two special categories of functions are called *even functions* and *odd functions*, but there are many functions that don't fit into either of these two categories. Another classification involves one-to-one functions.

Even Functions

A function $f(x)$ is called **even** if for each x in the domain, $f(x) = f(-x)$. In this notation, each element of the function is in the form $(x, f(x))$. As ordered pairs, for a specific x (domain) value, each of x and $-x$ must be paired with the same range value.

Here are some examples:

$G = \{(-5, 1), (7, 9), (5, 1), (-7, 9)\}$. Notice that if the domain value is 5 or -5, the range value is 1. Similarly, when the domain value is 7 or -7, the range value is 9.

$H = \{(x, f(x))\mid f(x) = -x^2$, for $x = 0, -1, 1\ -4, 4, -10, 10\}$. The range values are given by $f(0) = 0$, $f(-1) = -1$, $f(1) = -1$, $f(-4) = -16$, $f(4) = -16$, $f(-10) = -100$, and $f(10) = -100$.

$J = \{(x, |x|)\}$, for all real numbers $x\}$. The domain is all real numbers and the range is all non-negative numbers. Since the value of $|x|$ is the non-negative value of x, this function must be even. Set J has an infinite number of elements; some of its elements are $(0, 0)$, $(6, 6)$, $(-6, 6)$, $(1.4, 1.4)$, and $(-1.4, 1.4)$.

Graphically, every even function is symmetric about the y-axis. In Figure 4.2, each of $h(x)$ and $k(x)$ is an even function.

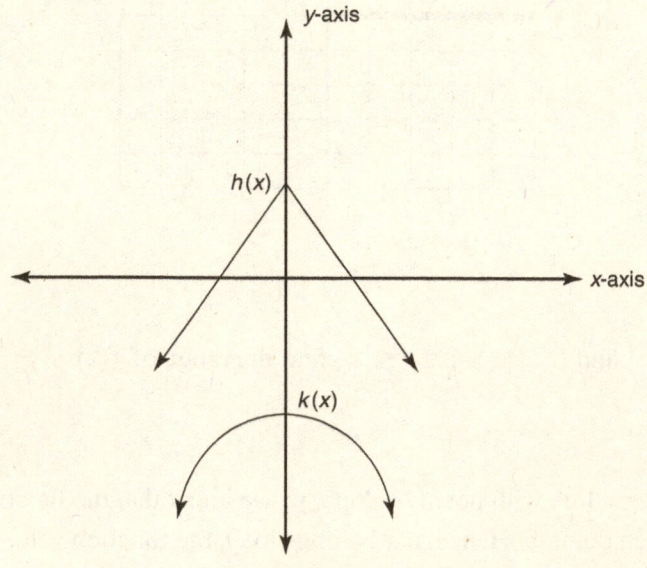

Figure 4.2

Odd Functions

A function $f(x)$ is called **odd** if for each x in the domain, $f(x) = -f(-x)$. In notation form, each element of the function is still shown as $(x, f(x))$. For a specific x value, the range values of x and $-x$ must be additive inverses. Here are two examples:

$K = \{(3, 7), (-3, -7), (0, 0), (8, -1), (-8, 1)\}$. Notice that $f(3) = -f(-3)$ and $f(8) = -f(-8)$. Of course $0 = -0$, so $f(0) = -f(-0) = 0$.

$L = \{(x,y)|\ y = x^3,$ for all real values of $x\}$. The domain is all real numbers and the range is also all real numbers. As examples of elements of L, if $x = 2$, $y = 2^3 = 8$; if $x = -2$, then $y = (-2)^3 = -8$; if $x = 0.3$, then $y = (0.3)^3 = 0.027$; and if $x = -0.3$, $y = (-0.3)^3 = -0.027$.

Graphically, every odd function is symmetric about the origin. In Figures 4.3 and 4.4 shown below, each of $m(x)$ and $n(x)$ is an odd function.

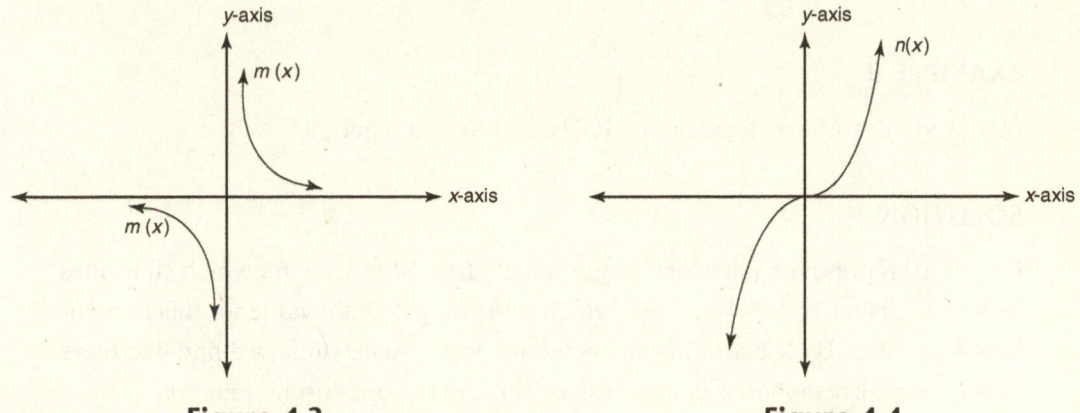

Figure 4.3   **Figure 4.4**

Neither Odd nor Even Functions

There are many functions that are neither odd nor even. Three such examples are $f(x) = 9 - 4x$, $f(x) = x^2 - x + 3$, and $f(x) = |x| + x$. Letting $x = 2$, the three corresponding $f(x)$ values are 1, 5, and 4. Letting $x = -2$, the three corresponding $f(x)$ values are 17, 9, and 0. Note that $f(x) \neq f(-x)$ and $f(x) \neq -f(-x)$.

One-to-One Functions

A one-to-one function satisfies the condition that for each range value, there is exactly one domain value. Mathematically, if $f(x_1) = f(x_2)$, then $x_1 = x_2$. Let's look at a few examples of functions to see if they are one-to-one.

EXAMPLE 7

$N = \{(x,y)|\ y = 4x^2$ for all real values of $x\}$. Is N a one-to-one function?

SOLUTION

Let $y = 16$. Then $16 = 4x^2$, from which $x = \pm\sqrt{4} = \pm 2$. Thus, N is not a one-to-one function. Both $(2, 4)$ and $(-2, 4)$ are elements of N.

EXAMPLE 8

$P = \{(0, 5), (-2, 9), (10, -1)\}$. Is P a one-to-one function?

SOLUTION

For each of the different range values of P, namely 5, 9, and -1, there is exactly one domain value. Thus, P is a one-to-one function.

EXAMPLE 9

$Q = \{x,y)|\ y = 6 + x^3$ for $x \geq 0\}$. Is Q a one-to-one function?

SOLUTION

Let $y = 10$ represent a particular range value. Then $10 = x^3 + 6$, which simplifies to $4 = x^3$. Thus, $x = \sqrt[3]{4} \approx 1.59$, which is the only domain value for this particular range value. By substituting any other allowable range value, we find that there is only one corresponding domain value. Thus, Q is a one-to-one function.

EXAMPLE 10

$R = \{(8, 6), (2, 5), (-2, -4), (5, 1), (3, 6)\}$. Is R a one-to-one function?

SOLUTION

Looking at the two elements, $(8, 6)$ and $(3, 6)$, we can conclude that R is not a one-to-one function. For the given range value of 6, there are two different corresponding domain values, namely 8 and 3.

Graphically, a one-to-one function must obey both the *vertical line* test and the *horizontal line* test. As mentioned earlier, a vertical line may intersect the graph of a function at most once. Additionally, if a horizontal line intersects the graph of a function at most once, then that function is one-to-one. In Figure 4.5, $p(x)$ is a one-to-one function. Notice that $q(x)$ is a function, but it is not one-to-one.

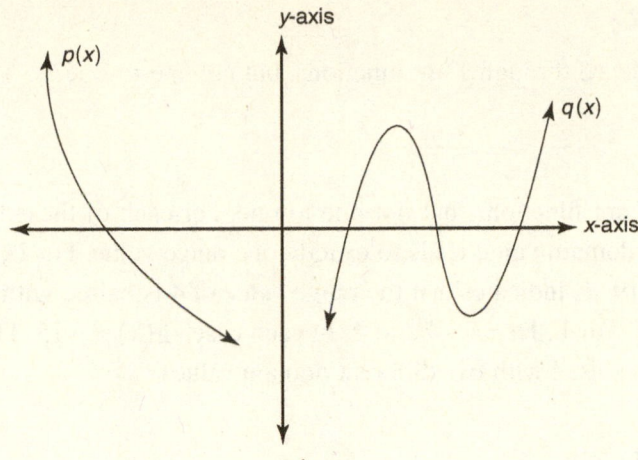

Figure 4.5

Remember that many different small letters may precede (x) to indicate a function. We are not required to always use $f(x)$ or $g(x)$. These other notations are particularly useful when dealing with two or more functions in the same problem.

For Examples 11, 12, and 13, we'll use the following information:

$S = \{(0, 4), (3, 7), (6, -2), (3, -1), (10, -5)\}$

$T = \{(x, y) | \, y = 3x - 9 \,$, for all non-positive values of $x\}$

$U = \{(1, 3), (-2, 4), (3, -3), (9, 4)\}$

$V = \{(x, g(x)) | \, g(x) = 1 - x^2 \,$, for all real values of $x\}$

$W = \{(x,y) | \, x^2 + y^2 = 9 \,$, for all x values between -3 and 3, inclusive$\}$

$X = \{(x, h(x)) | \, h(x) = 5x^3 \,$, for $x = 1, 2, 3, 4, 5\}$

$Y = \{(1, 2), (2, 1), (3, 4), (4, 3), (5, 6), (6, 5) \}$

EXAMPLE 11

Which of the sets S through Y are not functions? S & W

SOLUTION

Both S and W are not functions. For S, the presence of $(3, 7)$ and $(3, -1)$ means that the same domain value is matched up with two different range values. For W, let $x = 1$. Then $1^2 + y^2 = 9$, which simplifies to $y^2 = 8$. Thus, $y = \pm\sqrt{8}$, which again matches up two range values for the same domain value.

EXAMPLE 12

Which of the sets S through Y are functions, but not one-to-one?

SOLUTION

Both U and V are functions, but not one-to-one. For each of these two relations, any allowable domain value leads to exactly one range value. For U, the presence of $(-2, 4)$ and $(9, 4)$ indicates that the range value of 4 is paired with two different domain values. For V, let $x = -4$ and 4. In each case, $g(x) = -15$. Thus the range value of -15 is paired with two different domain values.

EXAMPLE 13

Which one is a one-to-one function in which the domain values are the same as the range values? Y

SOLUTION

Set Y is a one-to-one function for which the $\{1, 2, 3, 4, 5, 6\}$ represents the range and the domain. The graph of this function is just six points, through which any vertical or horizontal line passes at most once.

Note that T and X are also one-to-one functions, but their domains and ranges are different. For T, the domain is non-negative numbers and the range is all numbers less than or equal to -9. For X, the domain is 1, 2, 3, 4, and 5; the range is 5, 40, 135, 320, and 625. The domains and ranges of any of these relations can be verified by their graphs.

Sometimes, we are interested in determining the domain of a function in a strictly algebraic manner. In these instances, the dependent variable (y or $f(x)$) is given explicitly in terms of the independent variable (x). One common type is a rational function that contains a denominator that contains the independent variable.

A second common type is a function involving a square root that contains the independent variable.

EXAMPLE 14

What is the domain of the function $f(x) = \dfrac{3}{x + 7}$? $x \neq -7$

SOLUTION

When dealing with a fraction, the denominator cannot be zero. This means that $x + 7 \neq 0$, which becomes $x \neq -7$. The domain is all numbers except –7.

Composition and Inverse

Composition

The **composition** of functions is the process by which one function is performed and then its result is used as the input for the other function. The composition of functions f and g is written $f \circ g$.

$$(f \circ g) = f(g(x))$$

EXAMPLE 15

Find $(f \circ g)(2)$ if $f(x) = x^2 - 3$ and $g(x) = 3x + 1$

$$3(2)+1 \qquad 7^2-3$$
$$= 6+1 \qquad 49-3$$
$$= 7 \qquad \boxed{46}$$

SOLUTION

$(f \circ g)(2) = f(g(2))$

$g(x) = 3x + 1$

Substitute the value of x.

$g(2) = 3(2) + 1$

$\quad = 7$

$f(x) = x^2 - 3$

Substitute the value of $g(2)$ in $f(x)$.

$f(7) = (7)^2 - 3$

$\quad = 49 - 3$

$\quad = 46$

We can also find the function associated with the composition of two functions. To evaluate functions symbolically, replace the variable of the "outside" function with the "inside" function.

EXAMPLE 16

If $f(x) = x^2 - 3$ and $g(x) = 3x + 1$, find $(g \circ f)(x)$, $(f \circ g)(x)$ and $(f \circ g)(2)$.

$(g \circ f)(x)$

$3(x^2-3)+1$

$3x^2-9+1$

$\boxed{3x^2-8}$

$(f \circ g)(x)$

$(3x+1)^2-3$

$9x^2+3x+3x+1-3$

$\boxed{9x^2+6x-2}$

$(f \circ g)(2)$

$3(2)+1 \qquad (7)^2-3$

$=7 \qquad \boxed{46}$

SOLUTION

$$(g \circ f)(x) = g(f(x)) = 3(x^2 - 3) + 1$$
$$= 3x^2 - 9 + 1$$
$$= 3x^2 - 8$$
$$(f \circ g)(x) = f(g(x)) = (3x + 1)^2 - 3$$
$$= 9x^2 + 6x + 1 - 3$$
$$= 9x^2 + 6x - 2$$
$$(f \circ g)(2) = 9(2)^2 + 6(2) - 2 = 36 + 12 - 2 = 46$$

Notice that although the method for finding $(f \circ g)(2)$ differed from the previous problem, the results are the same. Also, note $(f \circ g)(x) \neq (g \circ f)(x)$. That is, function composition is not commutative.

Inverse

The **inverse of a relation** is the relation found by switching the coordinates of each ordered pair in the relation. For example, the inverse of the relation $\{(1,2),(-5,3),(9,0)\}$ is $\{(2,1),(3,-5),(0,9)\}$. The domain of a relation is the range of its inverse and the range of a relation is the domain of its inverse. The graph of the inverse of a relation is the reflection image of the graph of the relation over the line $y = x$. If an equation for a relation exists, the equation of its inverse can be found by exchanging the x- and y-variables and solving for y.

EXAMPLE 17

Find the inverse of the functions:

(A) $f(x) = 3x + 2$

(B) $k(x) = x^2 - 3$

SOLUTION

(A) $f(x) = y = 3x + 2$

To find the inverse, interchange x and y and solve for y.

$$x = 3y + 2$$
$$3y = x - 2$$
$$y = \frac{x - 2}{3}$$
$$y = \frac{1}{3}x - \frac{2}{3}$$

(A) $f(x) = 3x + 2$

$x = 3y + 2$

$\dfrac{x-2}{3} = y$

$\dfrac{1}{3}x - \dfrac{2}{3} = y$

(B) $k(x) = x^2 - 3$

$x = y^2 - 3$

$x + 3 = y^2$

$\pm\sqrt{x+3} = y$

(B) $k(x) = y = x^2 - 3$.

To find the inverse, interchange x and y and solve for y.

$$x = y^2 - 3$$

$$y^2 = x + 3$$

$$y = \pm\sqrt{x+3}$$

The inverse of a relation is a relation. However, the inverse of a function is not always a function. In Example 17, the inverse of $f(x)$ is a function but the inverse of $k(x)$ is not a function. In a function, no two ordered pairs have the same first coordinate. Therefore, the inverse of a function is a function if no two ordered pairs of the function have the same second coordinate. Whereas the vertical line test is used to determine if a relation is a function, the horizontal line test is used to check if the inverse of a function is a function. That is, any horizontal line will pass through a function only once if its inverse is a function. When a function f has an inverse, the notation f^{-1} is used to represent its inverse and the composite of the function and its inverse (in either order) is the identity function $(f(f^{-1}(x)) = x$ and $f^{-1}(f(x)) = x)$. Figure 4.6 shows the case in which $f^{-1}(x)$ is a function, and Figure 4.7 shows the case in which $f^{-1}(x)$ is not a function. Note that in both figures, the original functions are reflected over the line $y = x$.

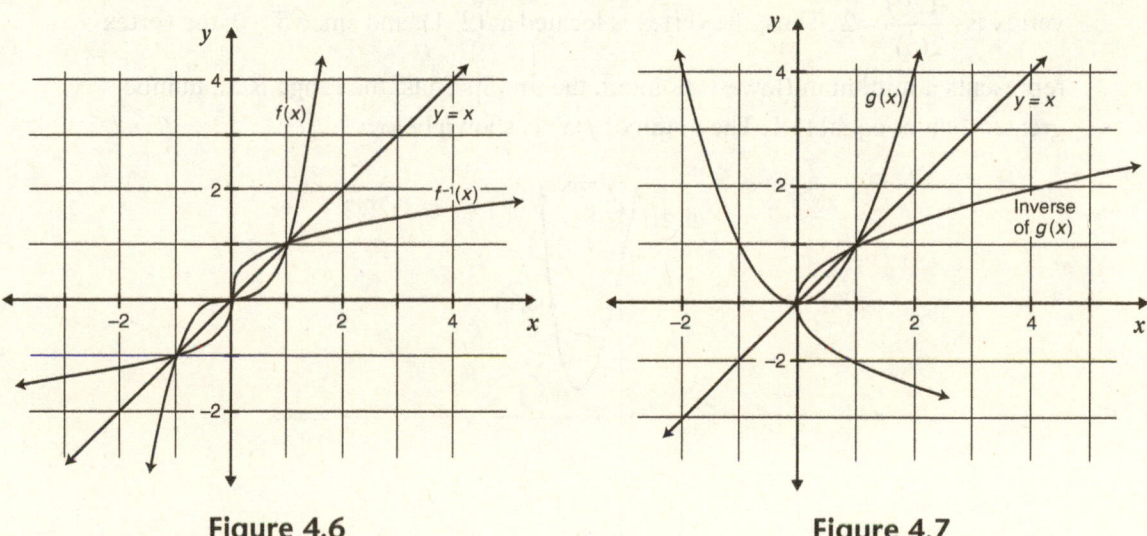

Figure 4.6   Figure 4.7

Quadratic Functions

Parabolas

Second-degree functions, or **quadratic functions**, namely $f(x) = a_2x^2 + a_1x + a_0$, are commonly written in the general form $ax^2 + bx + c$. The graphs of quadratic functions are called **parabolas**. All parabolas are basically U-shaped, opening up or down, and have one lowest (or highest) point called the **vertex**. Parabolas may or mat not have x-intercepts, but they will always have a single y-intercept, which determines the range. The domain is all real numbers.

The general form of a parabola, $f(x) = ax^2 + bx + c$, gives information about the shape of the parabola. The sign of a determines whether the parabola opens up (positive a) or down (negative a). The vertex is given by

$$\text{vertex} \left(-\frac{b}{2a}, f\left(-\frac{b}{2a} \right) \right)$$

So to get the vertex, just compute the x-coordinate from the values of a and b and put this into the function to get the y-coordinate. The y-intercept is always $(0, c)$ since $f(0) = a(0)^2 + b(0) + c = c$.

EXAMPLE 18

What is the range of the function $f(x) = 5(x - 2)^2 + 1$?

vertex
(2, 1)

SOLUTION

y ≥ 1

Rewrite this in general form as $f(x) = 5x^2 - 20x + 21$, and the x-coordinate of the vertex is $\dfrac{-(20)}{2(5)} = 2$. Thus, the vertex is located at $(2, 1)$, and since $5 > 0$, the vertex represents a minimum (lowest) point on the graph. Thus, the range is all numbers greater than or equal to 1. The graph of $f(x)$ is shown below.

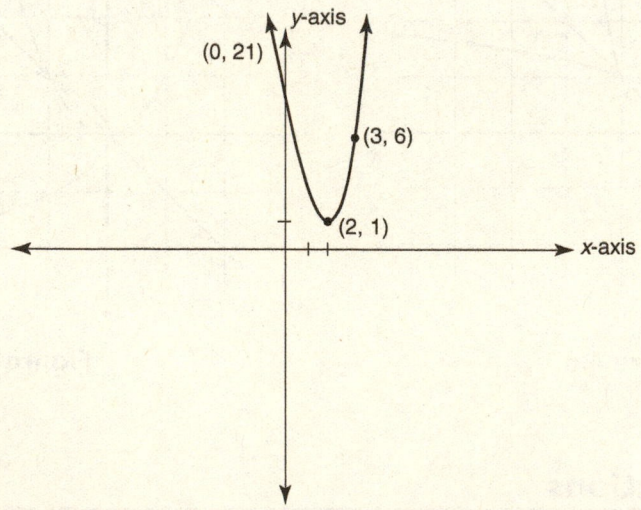

EXAMPLE 19

What is the range of the function $g(x) = -(x + 4)^2 + 10$?

(−4, 10)

y ≤ 10

SOLUTION

The vertex is located at (−4, 10), and since −1 < 0, this vertex is the highest point of the graph. Thus, the range is all numbers less than or equal to 10. The graph of $g(x)$ is shown below.

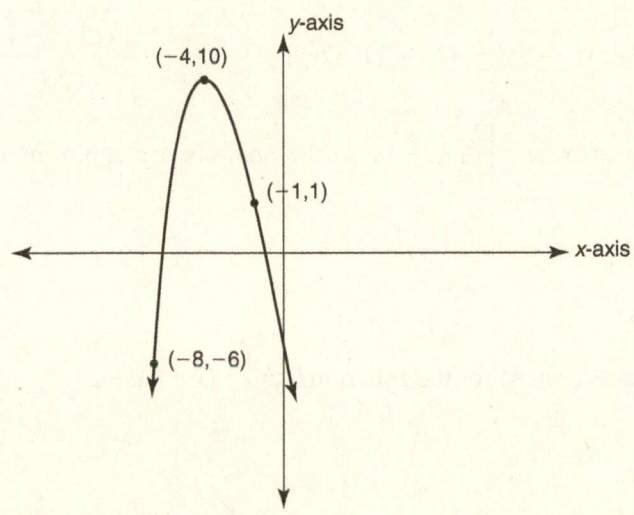

Zeros of a Quadratic Function

If $y = f(x)$ is any function, then the **zeros**, or **roots**, of this function are the values of x for which $y = 0$. When graphing this function, the **zeros** represent the intersection points of the x-axis and the function. In the case of a quadratic function, the number of zeros is either 0, 1, or 2.

The quadratic formula is used to find the actual values of the zeros. For the quadratic function $y = ax^2 + bx + c$, we replace y by 0. The solution(s) to this equation are given by

$$x = \frac{-b \pm \sqrt{b^2 - 4ac}}{2a}.$$

The expression $b^2 - 4ac$ is called the **discriminant**. If $b^2 - 4ac > 0$, then there are two real zeros. If $b^2 - 4ac = 0$, then there is one real zero. If $b^2 - 4ac < 0$, then there are two complex zeros.

EXAMPLE 20

What are the zeros for the function $f(x) = 2x^2 - 4x - 3$ to the nearest hundredth?

$$\frac{-(-4) \pm \sqrt{(-4)^2 - 4(2)(-3)}}{2(2)}$$

$$\frac{4 \pm \sqrt{16 + 24}}{4}$$

SOLUTION

We need to solve $0 = 2x^2 - 4x - 3$. Then $x = \dfrac{-(-4) \pm \sqrt{(-4)^2 - (4)(2)(-3)}}{(2)(2)}$

$$\frac{4 \pm \sqrt{40}}{4}$$

This simplifies to $x = \dfrac{4 \pm \sqrt{40}}{4}$, so the answers are approximately −0.58 and 2.58.

$$\frac{4 - \sqrt{40}}{4}, \frac{4 + \sqrt{40}}{4}$$

EXAMPLE 21

What are the zeros for the function $y = 3x^2 + 12x - 11$ to the nearest hundredth?

SOLUTION

We need to solve $0 = -3x^2 + 12x - 11$. Then $x = \dfrac{-12 \pm \sqrt{(12)^2 - (4)(-3)(-11)}}{(2)(-3)}$.

This simplifies to $x = \dfrac{-12 \pm \sqrt{12}}{-6}$, so the answers are approximately 1.42 and 2.58.

EXAMPLE 22

What are the roots (zeros) for the function $f(x) = -(x + 4)^2 - 2$?

SOLUTION

The equation to solve is $0 = -x^2 - 8x - 18$. In order to avoid an unnecessary number of negative signs, we can rewrite the equation as $0 = x^2 + 8x + 18$. Then $x = \dfrac{-8 \pm \sqrt{(8)^2 - (4)(1)(18)}}{2}$. This simplifies to $x = \dfrac{-8 \pm \sqrt{-8}}{2}$, so the two answers are complex numbers, and there are no real answers.

EXAMPLE 23

What are the roots of $y = x^2 + 3$?

SOLUTION

It is clear that there are no real roots for this equation. The appropriate equation to solve would be $0 = x^2 + 3$. We could use the quadratic formula, but this equation is equivalent to $-3 = x^2$, which has only complex roots.

The use of the quadratic formula is not necessary in solving all second-degree equations; some equations may be solved by factoring.

EXAMPLE 24

What are the zeros of the graph for the function $y = 2x^2 + 9x$?

SOLUTION

In solving $0 = 2x^2 + 9x$, it is much quicker to use factoring than to use the quadratic formula. Then $0 = x(2x + 9)$, which means that $x = 0$ or $2x + 9 = 0$. The two zeros are 0 and $-\dfrac{9}{2}$.

[handwritten: $0 = x(2x+9)$ $x=0$ or $x=\dfrac{-9}{2}$]

EXAMPLE 25

What are the zeros of the graph for the function $y = 3x^2 - x - 2$?

[handwritten: $(3x+2)(x-1)$ $x=\dfrac{-2}{3}$ $x=1$]

SOLUTION

In solving $0 = 3x^2 - x - 2$, we factor the right side so that it reads as $0 = (3x + 2)(x - 1)$. Then $3x + 2 = 0$ or $x - 1 = 0$. The two zeros are $-\dfrac{2}{3}$ and 1.

Another interesting feature of the quadratic function $y = ax^2 + bx + c$ is that when there are real zeros, their **sum equals** $-\dfrac{b}{a}$ and their **product equals** $\dfrac{c}{a}$. In checking Examples 24 and 25, we can verify this information. For Example 24, the sum of the zeros is $-\dfrac{9}{2}$, which is the same as $-\dfrac{b}{a}$.

The product of the zeros is 0, and since $c = 0$, $\dfrac{c}{a} = 0$. Likewise, in Example 25, the sum of the zeros is $\dfrac{1}{3}$, and this matches $-\dfrac{b}{a}$. The product of the zeros is $-\dfrac{2}{3}$, and this equals $\dfrac{c}{a}$.

When the zeros are approximate answers, this check still applies, but a small error may appear. In Example 21, the sum of the zeros should be $-\dfrac{12}{-3} = 4$, and this answer matches exactly the sum of 1.42 and 2.58. The product of the zeros should be $\dfrac{11}{3}$, which is very close to $(1.42)(2.58)$.

EXAMPLE 26

The zeros of $y = 4x^2 + bx + c$ are $\dfrac{1}{2}$ and -4. What are the values of b and c, and what is the equation?

[handwritten: sum zeros for b $-\dfrac{b}{4} = \dfrac{-7}{2}$ $-\dfrac{b}{a}$ $-2b = -28$ $b = 14$]

SOLUTION

The sum of these zeros is $-\dfrac{7}{2}$, so $-\dfrac{b}{4} = -\dfrac{7}{2}$. Then $b = 14$. Likewise, the product of the zeros is -2, so $\dfrac{c}{4} = -2$. Then $c = -8$. The equation is $y = 4x^2 + 14x - 8$.

[handwritten: $\dfrac{c}{a}$ product of zeros for c $\dfrac{c}{4} = -2$ $c = -8$ $y = 4x^2 + 14x + 8$]

EXAMPLE 27

[handwritten: $a \to$ sum zeros (given b)]

The zeros of $y = ax^2 - 16x + c$ are $\dfrac{6}{5}$ and 2. What are the values of a and c, and what is the equation?

[handwritten: $\dfrac{16}{a} = \dfrac{16}{5}$]

[handwritten: $c \to$ product of 0's]

SOLUTION

[handwritten: $16a = 80$, $a = 5$]

[handwritten: $\dfrac{12}{5} = \dfrac{c}{5}$, $5c = 60$, $c = 12$]

Since the sum of the zeros is $\dfrac{16}{5}$, we can write $\dfrac{16}{a} = \dfrac{16}{5}$, so $a = 5$. The product of the zeros is $\dfrac{12}{5}$, so $\dfrac{c}{a} = \dfrac{c}{5} = \dfrac{12}{5}$, and $c = 12$. The equation is $y = 5x^2 - 16x + 12$.

[handwritten: $5x^2 - 16x + 12$]

Polynomial Functions

A **polynomial function** of degree n is an expression of the form $a_n x^n + a_{n-1}x^{n-1} + a_{n-2}x^{n-2} + \ldots + a_{n-2}x^{n-2} + \ldots + a_1 x + a_0$. The stipulations are that all a_i are real numbers and that $a_n \neq 0$. The associated polynomial function, $f(x)$, is normally expressed as $f(x) = a_n x^n + a_{n-1}x^{n-1} + a_{n-2}x^{n-2} + \ldots + a_1 x + a_0$.

Graphs of Polynomial Functions

In general, for any function $f(x) = a_n x^n + a_{n-1}x^{n-1} + a_{n-2}x^{n-2} + \ldots + a_1 x + a_0$, the graph will appear as one of the following four prototypes:

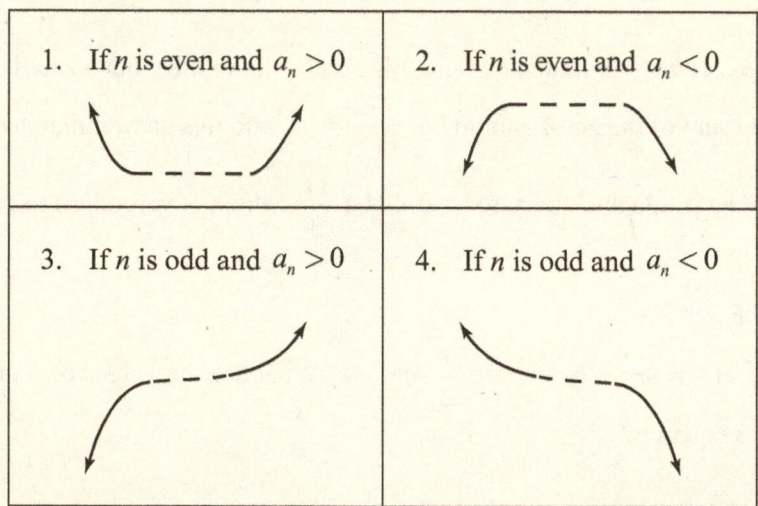

1. If n is even and $a_n > 0$
2. If n is even and $a_n < 0$
3. If n is odd and $a_n > 0$
4. If n is odd and $a_n < 0$

In each instance, the dotted line portion of the graph is not determined by the prototype shown. Thus, within the dotted line portion, the graph may increase, decrease, or both. The conclusions that we can draw are as follows:

For Prototype 1: As $x \to \infty$ or as $x \to -\infty$, the function value approaches ∞.

For Prototype 2: As $x \to \infty$ or as $x \to -\infty$, the function value approaches $-\infty$.

For Prototype 3: As $x \to \infty$, the function value approaches ∞; as $x \to -\infty$, the function value approaches $-\infty$.

For Prototype 4: As $x \to \infty$, the function value approaches $-\infty$; as $x \to -\infty$, the function approaches ∞.

Thus, for the graph of $f(x) = 3x^3 + x^2 - 2$, as x approaches negative infinity, $f(x)$ approaches negative infinity. As another example, for the graph of the quadratic $g(x) = -4x^2 + 5x + 9$, as x approaches infinity, $g(x)$ approaches negative infinity.

Roots of Polynomial Functions

where y = 0

As mentioned previously, the real roots (zeros) of any function are the x values of the points where the function intersects the x-axis, or for which $f(x) = 0$. A polynomial function of degree n has at most n distinct zeros. *Descartes' Rule of Signs* indicates the maximum number of real roots for a polynomial $f(x)$ of any degree. It states that if $f(x)$ is written in descending order for the powers of x, the number of sign changes between terms of $f(x)$ gives the maximum number of positive real roots; likewise, if the number of sign changes between terms of $f(-x)$ gives the maximum number of negative real roots. The number of either positive or negative real roots is either the maximum number (as determined above) or a multiple of two less than the maximum number. Thus, $f(x) = x^5 - 3x^4 - 3x^3 + 3x^2 + x - 3$ has three or one positive real roots and two or zero negative real roots. Note that if this equation had, for example, one real positive root and two real negative roots, the remaining two roots must be complex. Remember that complex roots always come in pairs.

f(x) → max # of positive roots

$-x^5 - 3x^4 + 3x^3 + 3x^2 - x - 3$ *f(-x) → max # of neg roots*

Suppose that a, b, c, and d are the (distinct) zeros of a fourth-degree function $f(x)$. Then we can write an example of the actual function as $f(x) = k[(x - a)(x - b)(x - c)(x - d)]$, where k is a constant. (Usually, we will let $k = 1$.) Likewise, if a fifth-degree function $g(x)$ has only distinct zeros m, n, and p, one possible function is $g(x) = (x - m)^2(x - n)^2(x - p)$. In some textbooks, each of m and n is called a double *zero* or a double root. However, note that when the right side of this function is expanded, the highest exponent of x will be 5. Another equally correct answer for $g(x)$ would be $g(x) = (x - m)(x - n)(x - p)^3$. Here, p would be called a triple zero.

EXAMPLE 28

A polynomial function of degree 5 has at least one complex zero. What is the maximum number of distinct real zeros for this function?

SOLUTION

Complex zeros come in pairs, so there are really at least two complex zeros. Then the maximum number of distinct real zeros must be three.

EXAMPLE 29

A polynomial function of sixth-degree has five distinct real zeros. What is the maximum number of complex zeros for this function?

SOLUTION

The answer is none! It would be impossible for there to exist only one complex zero. One of these five distinct zeros must be a double zero.

EXAMPLE 30

The function $h(x)$ is a fourth-degree polynomial with distinct zeros q and r. If each of these is a double zero, write an expression for $h(x)$.

SOLUTION

One possible answer is $h(x) = (x - q)^2(x - r)^2$. Any multiple of the right side, such as $5(x - q)^2(x - r)^2$, would also be a correct answer.

EXAMPLE 31

Function $f(x)$ is a third-degree polynomial with a real zero of t and a complex zero of $a + bi$. Write an expression for $f(x)$.

SOLUTION

$$\left(x-[a+bi]\right)\left(x-[a-bi]\right),(x-t)$$

It should be noted that if the given zeros include complex numbers, an appropriate polynomial function can still be written using the factored form shown in Example 30. Noting that $a - bi$ must also be a zero, one acceptable answer is $f(x) = (x - [a + bi])(x - [a - bi])(x - t)$.

Rational Functions

A **rational function** is the quotient of two polynomials, in which the denominator is not the zero polynomial. The functions $f(x) = \dfrac{2x^2 - 1}{x}$, $g(x) = \dfrac{-3}{x^4 + x}$, and $h(x) = \dfrac{x^5 + 4x^2 - 7}{6x^3 + 8}$ are all rational function.

Technically, an example such as $p(x) = \dfrac{9x^3 - 6x + 10}{2}$ can be considered a rational function, but this expression can be written as the simpler polynomial function $p(x) = \dfrac{9}{2}x^3 - 3x + 5$. In fact, since each polynomial function can be written as itself divided by 1, all polynomial functions are rational functions.

Asymptotes

An **asymptote** is a line that a graph of a function approaches but does not intersect. The distance between the graph and the asymptote approaches zero as the graph tends to infinity.

Vertical Asymptote

In graphing rational functions, there may be one or more vertical lines that the function approaches but does not intersect. These are called **vertical asymptotes**. In Figure 4.8, $f(x)$ has one vertical asymptote and $g(x)$ has two vertical asymptotes.

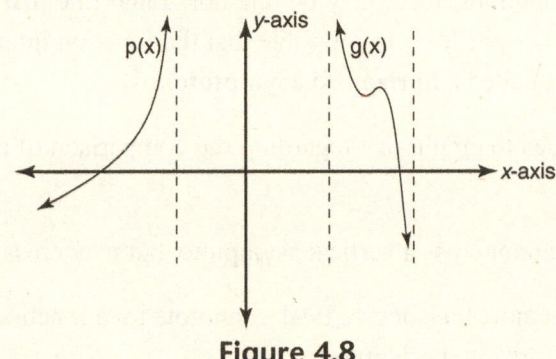

Figure 4.8

In order to locate the vertical asymptote(s) for a rational function, given by $f(x) = \dfrac{p(x)}{q(x)}$, we find all real zeros for $q(x)$. If c is a zero for $q(x)$, then $x = c$ is the equation of the vertical asymptote. If $q(x)$ has no real zeros, even though it may have complex zeros, then there are no vertical asymptotes. We are actually looking for the values of $f(x)$ that are *not* in its domain.

EXAMPLE 32

What are the vertical asymptotes of $f(x) = \dfrac{x^2 + 6x + 5}{3x - 2}$?

To find vertical asymptotes:
set denominator
equal to zero
and solve

SOLUTION

The zero of the denominator is $\dfrac{2}{3}$. Thus, the vertical asymptote is $x = \dfrac{2}{3}$.

$3x - 2 = 0$
$3x = 2$
$x = 2/3$

EXAMPLE 33

What are the vertical asymptotes of $g(x) = \dfrac{x^2 - 4}{(5x)(x^2 + 4)(3x + 7)}$?

$5x = 0$
$x = 0$

$x^2 + 4 = 0$
$x^2 = -4$
$x = \pm 2i$

$3x + 7 = 0$
$3x = -7$
$x = -7/3$

can not be asymptote because imaginary

199

SOLUTION

If $5x = 0$, then $x = 0$. If $3x + 7 = 0$, then $x = -\dfrac{7}{3}$. We need not be concerned about the middle factor of the denominator because the solutions to $x^2 + 4 = 0$ are two complex numbers, which *cannot* be asymptotes. Thus, the two vertical asymptotes are $x = 0$ (y-axis) and $x = -\dfrac{7}{3}$.

Horizontal Asymptote

In graphing rational functions, there may be one horizontal line that the function approaches either as $x \to \infty$ or as $x \to -\infty$. It is also possible that the function intersects this horizontal line for some x value(s). This is called a **horizontal asymptote**.

There are two key issues to emphasize regarding the comparison of a vertical asymptote with a horizontal asymptote.

1.   A function cannot cross a vertical asymptote, but may cross a horizontal asymptote.

2.   There may be more than one vertical asymptote for a function, but there can only exist at most one horizontal asymptote.

In Figure 4.9, $f(x)$ has a horizontal asymptote, but $f(x)$ does not intersect it. The function $g(x)$ also has a horizontal asymptote, but does intersect it once.

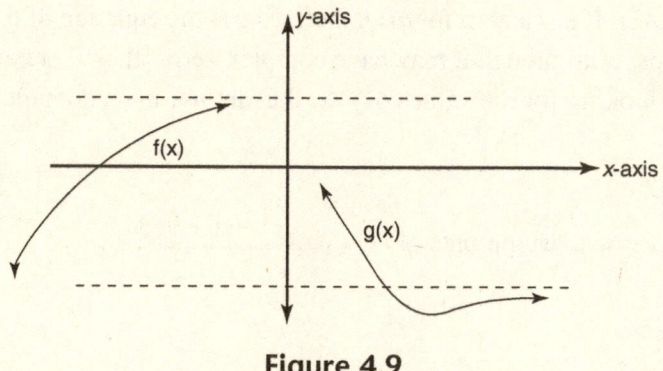

Figure 4.9

As with the situation for vertical asymptotes, there is a direct method for finding the horizontal asymptote, if it exists, of a rational function $f(x) = \dfrac{p(x)}{q(x)}$. For any polynomial function in the form $a_n x^n + a_{n-1} x^{n-1} + \cdot a_{n-2} x^{n-2} + \ldots + a_1 x + a_0$, as x approaches either infinity or negative infinity, the value of the function is most influenced by the leading term $a_n x^n$. There are three different cases to consider to determine the equation of the horizontal asymptote for

$f(x) = \dfrac{p(x)}{q(x)}$. Suppose that $p(x) = a_n x^n + a_{n-1}x^{n-1} + a_{n-2}x^{n-2} + ... + a_1 x + a_0$ and that $q(x) = b_m x^m + b_{m-1}x^{m-1} + b_{m-2}x^{m-2} + ... + b_1 x + b_0$. Of course, $a_n \neq 0$ and $b_m \neq 0$.

first in alphabet
$\dfrac{p(x)}{q(x)}$

1. If p(x) and q(x) have the same degree, (m = n), then the equation of the horizontal asymptote is given by $y = \dfrac{a_n}{b_m}$. This is simply the ratio of the leading coefficients of p(x) and q(x).

$\dfrac{3x^2}{2x^2} \Rightarrow \dfrac{3}{2}$

2. If the degree of p(x) is less than the degree of q(x), or (n < m), then the equation of the horizontal asymptote is given by y = 0 (x-axis). This is really a special instance of case 1. We can always add the term $0x^m$ to the function p(x) without changing its degree. Notice that the ratio of the terms $0x^m$ to $b_m x^m$ is zero. $\dfrac{x^2}{x^3}$

think improper fraction

3. If the degree of p(x) is greater than the degree of q(x), or (n > m), then there is no horizontal asymptote. Even this is a special instance of case 1. We simply add the term $0x^n$ to the function q(x), without changing its degree. Notice that the ratio of the terms $a_n x^n$ to $0x^n$ is undefined. $\dfrac{x^3}{x^2} \Rightarrow$ *no horizontal asymptote*

EXAMPLE 34

What is the horizontal asymptote of $h(x) = \dfrac{x^2 + 11x - 7}{3x^2 - 2x - 8}$? $y = \dfrac{1}{3}$

Same degree rule 1

SOLUTION

The numerator and denominator are each of degree 2. Then just using the ratio of the leading coefficients, the horizontal asymptote is $y = \dfrac{1}{3}$.

EXAMPLE 35

What is the horizontal asymptote of $g(x) = \dfrac{2x^4 - x^3 + 1}{x^5 + 7x^3 + 10x + 5}$? *Rule 2 y=0*

SOLUTION

We only need to compare the leading coefficients. However, since the degree of the numerator is less than the degree of the denominator, the horizontal asymptote is $y = 0$.

EXAMPLE 36

What is the horizontal asymptote of $r(x) = \dfrac{x^6 + x^2 - 3x - 5}{4x^3 - 9x}$. *Rule 3 no horizontal asymptote*

SOLUTION

The degree of the numerator is higher than the degree of the denominator. Our conclusion is that there is no horizontal asymptote.

EXAMPLE 37

What is the horizontal asymptote of $f(x) = \dfrac{(2x-3)(x+7)(3x+2)}{(x^2+8)(2x+11)}$?

[handwritten: $2x^2 + 11x - 21 (3x^2 + 2)$ Leading coefficient on top $= 6x^3$]

SOLUTION *[handwritten: Rule 1 same degree]*

[handwritten: Leading coefficient on bottom $= 2x^3$]   *[handwritten: $y = \dfrac{6}{2}$]*

By inspection, we can determine that the leading term of the numerator is $6x^3$ and the leading term of the denominator is $2x^3$. Since the top and bottom of this fraction have the same degree, the horizontal asymptote is $y = \dfrac{6}{2}$, which simplifies to $y = 3$.

> The existence (or non-existence) of a horizontal asymptote has no bearing on the existence (or non-existence) of a vertical asymptote for a given function. It is important to remember that the existence of either of these asymptotes means that the function must get closer to the asymptote as $x \to \infty$ or as $x \to -\infty$. The function may cross only the horizontal asymptote.

Slant Asymptote

The last type of asymptote to consider is the slant asymptote, also called the oblique asymptote. This represents any linear asymptote that is neither vertical nor horizontal. As with a horizontal asymptote, the function may intersect a slant asymptote. For any function, there is a maximum of one slant asymptote.

[handwritten: One or the other]

CAUTION   There cannot exist both a horizontal and slant asymptote for a given function.

In Figure 4.10, each of *f(x)* and *g(x)* has a slant asymptote. Notice that *f(x)* does not intersect its slant asymptote, but *g(x)* does intersect its slant asymptote.

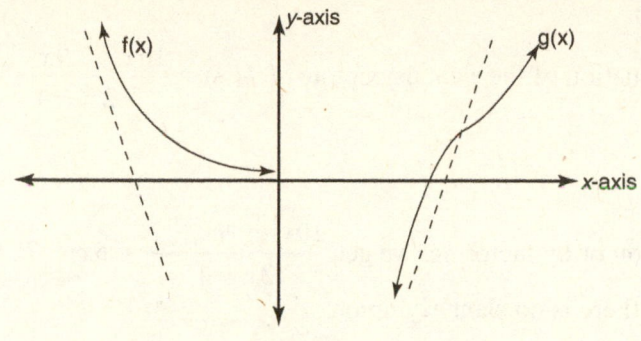

Figure 4.10

In order to find the slant asymptote, if it exists, of the rational function $r(x) = \dfrac{p(x)}{q(x)}$, two conditions must be met.

1. The degree of the numerator must be 1 greater than the degree of the denominator.

2. When $p(x)$ is divided by $q(x)$, there must be a nonzero remainder.

The quotient becomes the equation of the slant asymptote.

EXAMPLE 38

What is the equation of the slant asymptote of $f(x) = \dfrac{4x^2 + x - 4}{x - 1}$?

*numerator
1 degree greater
than degree of
denominator*

SOLUTION

Using the technique of either long division or <u>synthetic</u> division, $\dfrac{4x^2 + x - 4}{x - 1} =$
$4x + 5 + \dfrac{1}{x - 1}$. Thus, the slant asymptote is $y = 4x + 5$.

*slant
$y = 4x + 5$*

$$\begin{array}{r} {-1\rceil}\ 4\quad 1\ -4 \\ -4\quad 5 \\ \hline 4\ -5\quad 1 \end{array}$$

✓ 1 degree greater

EXAMPLE 39

What is the equation of the slant asymptote of $g(x) = \dfrac{-3x^3 + 2x^2 + x - 6}{x^2 - 2}$?

SOLUTION

By long division, we find that $\dfrac{-3x^3 + 2x^2 + x - 6}{x^2 - 2} = -3x + 2 + \dfrac{-5x - 2}{x^2 - 2}$.

slant

Thus, the slant asymptote is $y = -3x + 2$.

$$\begin{array}{r} -3x + 2 \\ x^2-2\ \overline{\smash{\big)}\ -3x^3 + 2x^2 + x - 6} \\ \ominus\ -3x^3 + 6x \\ \hline 2x^2 - 5x - 6 \\ \ominus\ 2x^2 \qquad -4 \\ \hline -5x - 2 \end{array}$$

$-3x + 2 + \dfrac{-5x - 2}{x^2 - 2}$

$y = -3x + 2$

EXAMPLE 40

What is the equation of the slant asymptote of $h(x) = \dfrac{10x^2 + 9x - 7}{2x - 1}$?

$$\begin{array}{r} 5x+7 \\ 2x-1 \overline{\smash{\big)}\,10x^2+9x-7} \\ \ominus\ \underline{10x^2-5x} \\ 14x-7 \\ \ominus\ \underline{14x-7} \\ 0 \end{array}$$

$$y = 5x + 7$$

SOLUTION

By long division or by factoring, we get $\dfrac{10x^2 + 9x - 7}{2x - 1} = 5x + 7$. Since there is no remainder, there is no slant asymptote.

Referring to this last example, the graph of $h(x) = \dfrac{10x^2 + 9x - 7}{2x - 1}$ would be identical to the graph of $y = 5x + 7$, except for the point $\left(\dfrac{1}{2}, \dfrac{19}{2}\right)$. This point does not exist on the graph of $h(x)$ because the domain excludes the number $\dfrac{1}{2}$.

Exponential Functions

Chapter 2 discussed functions of the form $f(x) = x^n$, where the independent variable x was a *base* raised to some power. In summary, the exponent rules are the following.

$$x^n x^m = x^{n+m}$$

$$\frac{x^n}{x^m} = x^{n-m}$$

$$(x^n)^m = x^{nm}$$

$$x^0 = 1$$

$$x^{-n} = \left(\frac{1}{x^n}\right)$$

In contrast, in **exponential functions** the independent variable x is in the *exponent*, so the form is $f(x) = b^x$, where b is a fixed base, which could be any positive real number. If $b > 1$, the function exhibits exponential growth; if $b < 1$, the function exhibits exponential decay.

The rate of growth of the **natural** exponential function e^x is exactly equal to the value of the function at x. The natural exponent e has properties similar to the regular exponents outlined above:

$$e^{x+c} = e^x e^c$$

$$e^{bx} = (e^b)^x = (e^x)^b$$

$$e^0 = 1$$

$$e^{-bx} = \frac{1}{e^{bx}}$$

Exponential Growth

Population growth, whether it deals with people, animals, or even bacteria can be modeled with the function $P(t) = P_0 e^{rt}$, where P_0 = initial population, r = exponential rate of growth, t = time (usually in years), and $P(t)$ = population after a period of t.

EXAMPLE 41

Currently, the population of the town of Fineville is 5,400. If this population grows at the exponential rate of 2.5%, what will be the population in seven years to the nearest integer?

SOLUTION

$P(7) = (5,400)(e^{(0.025)(7)}) \approx 6433$

(handwritten:) $P(t) = 5400\, e^{(.025)(7)}$

$P(t) = 6433$

EXAMPLE 42

Using the information given in Example 13, in how many years will the current population triple to the nearest hundredth?

(handwritten:) $5400(3) = 16,200$
$16,200 = 5400\, e^{(.025)(t)}$
$3 = e^{(.025)(t)}$
$\ln 3 = .025t \cdot \ln e$
$\dfrac{\ln 3}{.025} = t$

SOLUTION

The new population, $P(t)$, will be $(5,400)(3) = 16,200$. Then $16,200 = (5,400)$ $(e^{(0.025)(t)})$. After simplifying this equation to $3 = e^{(0.025)(t)}$, we can write $\ln 3 = 0.025t(\ln e) = 0.025t$. Thus, $t = \dfrac{\ln 3}{0.025} \approx 43.9$ years.

(handwritten:) $t = 43.9$ years

Another application of exponential equations, radioactive decay, is the spontaneous change of one element into another element. Radioactive substances are useful in the field of medicine. Most problems involving radioactive decay are connected to the half-life of the substance. Half-life refers to the time required for half of the substance to decay. The formula to be used is $A(t) = (A_0)\left(\dfrac{1}{2}\right)^{t/h}$, where $A(t)$ = amount left after time t, A_0 = initial amount, t = time, and h = half-life.

(handwritten:) $A(15) = 50\left(\dfrac{1}{2}\right)^{15/10}$
$= 17.68$ grams
how much left

EXAMPLE 43

A radioactive substance has a half-life of 10 hours. Initially, there are 50 grams of this substance. How many grams remain after 15 hours?

SOLUTION

By substitution, $A(15) = (50)\left(\dfrac{1}{2}\right)^{15/10} \approx 17.68$ grams.

(Note that if the problem had asked for the number of grams that had *decayed*, our answer would have been approximately 32.32 grams.)

(handwritten:) how much has decayed $\;\;50 - 17.68 = 32.32$ grams has already decayed

205

EXAMPLE 44

The half-life of an active ingredient in a certain chemical is six hours. What percent of this ingredient <u>has decayed</u> after two hours to the nearest tenth of a percent?

half life

$$A(2) = A_0 \left(\frac{1}{2}\right)^{2/6}$$
$$= A_0 (0.794)$$

SOLUTION

For this example, $A(2) = (A_0)\left(\dfrac{1}{2}\right)^{2/6} \approx 0.794(A_0)$. This means that approximately 79.4% of this ingredient remains after two hours. Thus, $100\% - 79.4\% = 20.6\%$ of this ingredient has decayed. (It is not necessary to know the initial amount of this ingredient.)

$$100 - 79.4 = 20.6\%$$
remaining amount   *how much has decayed*

Logarithmic Functions

<mark>Logarithms are the inverse of exponents</mark>. The relation can be stated as $= n$ is the inverse of $n^a = m$, where $a > 0$, $a \neq 1$, and n and m are real numbers.

So we can express the rules for logarithms directly from the rules for exponents. In summary, the logarithm rules are the following.

$$\log_a(uv) = \log_a u + \log_a v \quad \text{multiplication} \Rightarrow \text{addition}$$

$$\log_a\left(\frac{u}{v}\right) = \log_a u - \log_a v \quad \text{division} \Rightarrow \text{subtraction}$$

$$\log_a u^n = n \log_a u$$

Natural Logarithms

The **natural logarithm**, $\ln(x) = \log_e(x)$, is the inverse of natural exponentiation, e^x, where e is known as Euler's number, $e \approx 2.718$. The relation between e and $\ln$ is: if $e^x = y$, then $\ln(y) = x$. This leads to the following identities:

$$\ln(e^x) = x$$

$$e^{\ln(x)} = x, \text{ if } x > 0$$

The properties of natural logarithms follow from these facts and the properties of logarithms listed above.

$$\ln(ax) = \ln(a) + \ln(x)$$

$$\ln(a^x) = x \ln(a)$$

$$\ln(1) = 0$$

$$\ln\left(\frac{1}{x}\right) = -\ln x$$

EXAMPLE 45

What is the value of x in the equation $\log (x + 6) = (3)(\log 2)$?

$\log(x+6) = \log(2^3)$
$\log(x+6) = \log 8$
$x+6 = 8$
$x = 2$

SOLUTION

Rewrite as $\log (x + 6) = \log(2^3) = \log 8$. Then $x + 6 = 8$, so $x = 2$.

EXAMPLE 46

What is the value of x in the equation $(2)(\log x) = \log 4 + \log (x + 3)$?

$\log x^2 = \log(4x+12)$
$x^2 = 4x+12$
$x^2-4x-12=0$
$(x-6)(x+2)=0$
$x-6=0 \quad x+2=0$
$\boxed{x=6} \quad x=-2$

SOLUTION

Rewrite as $\log(x^2) = \log[(4)(x + 3)] = \log(4x + 12)$. Then $x^2 - 4x - 12 = 0$. So, $(x - 6)(x + 2) = 0$. The possible answers are 6 and –2. However, if we substitute $x = -2$, we recognize that $\log (-2)$ has no meaning. Thus, $x = 6$ is the only answer.

EXAMPLE 47

What is the value of x in the equation $\log x + \log(x - 15) = 2$?

$\log(x^2-15x)=2$
$x^2-15x = 10^2$
$x^2-15x-100$
$(x-20)(x+5)$
$\boxed{x=20} \quad x=-5$

SOLUTION

Rewrite just the left side as $\log(x^2 - 15x)$. Inserting the "invisible" base 10, the equation now appears as $\log_{10}(x^2 - 15x) = 2$. The simplest way to complete this example is to use the exponential form of this last equation, namely $x^2 - 15x = 10^2 = 100$. Then $(x - 20)(x + 5) = 0$. Of the two potential answers, only $x = 20$ is an actual solution.

In Example 47, if you were able to spot that since $10^2 = 100$, then you could have written the right side as $\log 100$. At this point, your equation would still be $x^2 - 15x = 100$.

EXAMPLE 48

What is the value of x in the equation $6^x = 3$?

$\log 6^x = \log 3$
$x(\log 6)=\log 3$
$x = \dfrac{\log 3}{\log 6} \approx 0.613$

SOLUTION

Take the logarithm of each side so that $\log 6^x = \log 3$, which becomes $(x)(\log 6) = \log 3$. Thus, $x = \dfrac{\log 3}{\log 6} \approx 0.6131$.

EXAMPLE 49

What is the value of x in the equation $7^{x+2} = 0.5$?

$\log 7^{x+2} = \log 0.5$
$(x+2)(\log 7)= \log 0.5$
$x+2 = \dfrac{\log.5}{\log 7} \quad x=-2.356$
$x = \dfrac{\log.5}{\log 7} -2$

SOLUTION

Rewrite as $\log(7^{x+2}) = (x + 2)(\log 7) = \log 0.5$. Then $x + 2 = \dfrac{\log 0.5}{\log 7} \approx -0.3562$.

Thus, $x \approx -2.3562$.

EXAMPLE 50

What is the value of x in the equation $e^{3x+1} = 10$?

[handwritten: $\ln e^{3x+1} = \ln 10$; $3x+1 = \ln 10$; $3x = \ln 10 - 1$; $x = \dfrac{\ln 10 - 1}{3}$; $x \approx 0.434$]

SOLUTION

Take the logarithm of each side, but use a base of e instead of a base of 10.

Then $\ln e^{3x+1} = 3x + 1 = \ln 10$. Thus, $x = \dfrac{\ln 10 - 1}{3} \approx 0.4342$.

We used the fact that for any exponent p, $\ln e^p = p$. The justification for this statement is as follows: By Rule 4, $\ln e^p = p \ln e$. Furthermore, $\ln e = 1$.

EXAMPLE 51

What is the value of x in the equation $6^{8-x} = \dfrac{1}{216}$?

[handwritten: $\log 6^{8-x} = \log \dfrac{1}{216} = \dfrac{1}{6^3} = 6^{-3}$; $\log 6^{8-x} = \log 6^{-3}$; $8-x = -3$; $-x = -11$; $x = 11$]

SOLUTION

Instead of taking logarithms of both sides, note that $\dfrac{1}{216} = \dfrac{1}{6^3} = 6^{-3}$. Then $8 - x = -3$. Thus, $x = 11$.

Inverse Logarithmic Functions

Let $f(x) = 3^x$. To write $g(x)$ in an explicit fashion, start with $y = 3^x$ and interchange the variables. This leads to $x = 3^y$, which is equivalent to $y = \log_3 x$. This means that $g(x) = \log_3 x$ is the explicit representation of the inverse function of $f(x)$. We can draw the graph of $g(x)$ by selecting some (positive) values of x. Any decimal values will be rounded off to the nearest hundredth.

In order to use our calculator for values of $\log_3 x$, we will use the formula $\log_3 x = \dfrac{\log_{10} x}{\log_{10} 3}$. For example, $\log_3 20 = \dfrac{\log_{10} 20}{\log_{10} 3} \approx 2.73$.

Using x values of 1, 3, 9, 18, and 30, the points are (1, 0), (3, 1), (9, 2), (18, 2.63), and (30, 3.10). If you check the points we used for $f(x)$, you will notice that $g(x)$ shows the switch in the numbers used in some of the points. For examples (1, 3) and (2, 9) belong to the graph of $f(x)$.

Sure enough, the points $(3, 1)$ and $(9, 2)$ belong to the graph of $g(x)$. This is not a shocking surprise, since we expect the domain of either function to match the range of its inverse function. The graphs of $f(x) = 3^x$ and $g(x) = \log_3 x$ are shown in Figure 4.11. Note that inverse functions represent reflections across the line $y = x$. Also, note that for $f(x)$, the horizontal asymptote is the x-axis. For $g(x)$, the vertical asymptote is the y-axis.

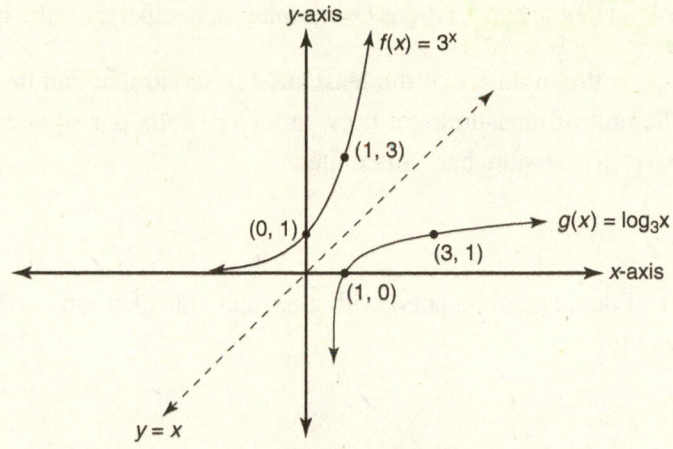

Figure 4.11

For completeness in our discussion, let's also do a similar comparison with $h(x) = \left(\dfrac{1}{2}\right)^x$. To find the inverse function, call it $k(x)$, start with $y = \left(\dfrac{1}{2}\right)^x$ and interchange the variables. Then $x = \left(\dfrac{1}{2}\right)^y$, which is equivalent to $y = \log_{\frac{1}{2}} x$. So, $k(x) = \log_{\frac{1}{2}} x$ is the inverse function. We'll use the formula $\log_{\frac{1}{2}} x = \dfrac{\log_{10} x}{\log_{10} \frac{1}{2}}$ in determining $k(x)$ values. Let's use x values of 0.5, 1, 2, 6, and 10.

Then these x values lead to the following five points on the graph of $k(x)$: $(0.5, 1)$, $(1, 0)$, $(2, -1)$, $(6, -2.58)$, and $(10, -3.32)$. The graphs of $h(x)$ and $k(x)$ are shown in Figure 4.12. As expected, the domain of one function matches the range of its inverse. Note that each function is a reflection of the other across the line $y = x$.

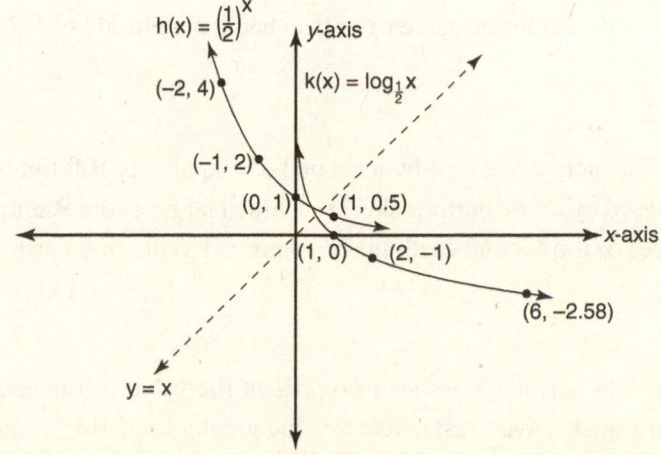

Figure 4.12

Applications in Real-Life Situations

Sound

In the field of science that deals with sound, the level of sound is measured in units called decibels. The formula is $D = (10)\left(\log \dfrac{I}{I_0}\right)$, where D = number of decibels, I = the intensity of the sound being measured, and I_0 = the intensity of the least audible sound that can be heard by an average healthy individual. The unit of measurement for I and I_0 is watts per square meter. The standard acceptable value of I_0 is 10^{-12} watts per square meter.

EXAMPLE 52

If the number of decibels associated with a normal conversation is 65.05, what is its sound intensity?

$$65.05 = (10)\left(\log \dfrac{I}{10^{-12}}\right)$$
$$6.505 = \left(\log \dfrac{I}{10^{-12}}\right) \qquad 10^{6.505} = \dfrac{I}{10^{-12}}$$

SOLUTION

By substitution, $65.05 = (10)\left(\log \dfrac{I}{10^{-12}}\right)$. Then $6.505 = \log \dfrac{I}{10^{-12}}$, which leads to $\dfrac{I}{10^{-12}} = 10^{6.505}$. Thus, $I = 10^{-5.495} \approx 3.20 \times 10^{-6}$ watts per square meter.

$$\dfrac{10^{6.505}}{10^{-12}} = I$$
$$I = 10^{-5.495}$$
$$\approx 3.2 \times 10^{-6}$$

Seismology

The **Richter scale** is used to measure the magnitude of earthquakes. The formula is $M = \left(\dfrac{2}{3}\right)\left(\log \dfrac{E}{E_0}\right)$, where M = magnitude, E = amount of energy released by the actual earthquake, and E_0 = amount of energy released by a small reference earthquake. The values of E and E_0 are measured in joules. The standard acceptable value of E_0 is $10^{4.40}$ joules. Small earthquakes have a magnitude of less than 4.5 on the Richter scale, whereas a very large earthquake has a magnitude of more than 7.5. The 1906 San Francisco earthquake had a magnitude of 8.25.

EXAMPLE 53

Suppose that the energy released by a second earthquake is 100 times the amount of energy released by a first earthquake. How much larger is the Richter scale reading (magnitude) of the second earthquake compared to the first earthquake?

SOLUTION

For simplicity, let's select 10^5 joules to represent the value of the energy released by the first earthquake. We must select a value greater than $10^{4.40}$, since $10^{4.40}$ represents the lowest acceptable reading. So, the magnitude of the first earthquake is

$$\left(\frac{2}{3}\right)\left(\log\frac{10^5}{10^{4.40}}\right) = \left(\frac{2}{3}\right)(\log 10^{0.6}) = 0.4 \text{ . Now, the second earthquake has an energy}$$

value of $(10^5)(100) = 10^7$ joules. So, the magnitude of the second earthquake is

$$\left(\frac{2}{3}\right)\left(\log\frac{10^7}{10^{4.40}}\right) = \left(\frac{2}{3}\right)(\log 10^{2.6}) = 1.7\overline{3} \text{ . Thus, the second earthquake's magnitude}$$

is $1.\overline{3}$ larger than that of the first earthquake.

Radioactivity

EXAMPLE 16

Initially, there are 180 milligrams of a radioactive isotope. After four days, 30% of this isotope has decayed. What is its half-life to the nearest hundredth?

SOLUTION

First, we must remember that $A(t)$ is always the amount *remaining* after a time

period of t. For this example, $A(4) = (180)(0.70) = 126$. Then $126 = (180)\left(\frac{1}{2}\right)^{4/h}$.

After dividing 126 by 180 to get 0.70, take the common logarithm of each side to

get $\log 0.70 = \left(\frac{4}{h}\right)\left(\log\frac{1}{2}\right)$. Thus, $h = \dfrac{(4)\left(\log\dfrac{1}{2}\right)}{\log 0.70} \approx 7.77$ days.

Biology

Biologists use exponential growth models to predict future results.

EXAMPLE 55

A bacterial culture doubles in size every 24 minutes. How many minutes are needed for a culture of 4.8×10^5 bacteria to grow to 7.2×10^5 ?

SOLUTION

Use the formula $N = N_0 b^{\frac{t}{k}}$ where N_0 is the original amount, N is the amount at time t and b is a growth (or decay) factor. Let k equal a predetermined period for

growth (or decay) to occur. Then $7.2 \times 10^5 = 4.8 \times 10^5 (2)^{\frac{t}{24}}$, which simplifies to

$1.5 = 2^{\frac{t}{24}}$. Taking logarithms of both sides leads to $\log 1.5 = \dfrac{t}{24}\log 2$. Then 0.585

$= \dfrac{t}{24}$, so $14.03 \approx t$. The culture will take approximately 14.03 minutes to grow

to 7.2×10^5.

Business and Finance

Mathematical models are useful for making sound business decisions. In Example 56, we use the well-known formula $A = Pe^{rt}$ for amount accrued (A) on principal P, for t years and rate r.

EXAMPLE 56

Jake's software firm is being purchased by a larger company. The buyer has offered Jake $50,000 per year for 20 years or a lump sum of $400,000. Jake makes the following assumptions:

a) He can invest the lump sum offer in a risk-free certificate growing 4.6% per year.

b) The compounding will be continuous.

Excluding tax considerations, should Jake accept the lump sum offer?

SOLUTION

The growth of 4.6% is continuous; using the formula $A = Pe^{rt}$, where:

A is the dollar amount accrued after 20 years

P is the principal, $400,000

r is the rate of growth, .046 (4.6 %)

t is time in years, 20

e is a constant, (approximately 2.718)

$$400,000 \, e^{(.046)(20)} = 1,003,716.2$$
$$50,000 \times 2 = 1,000,000$$

We get $A = 400,000e^{(.046 \times 20)}$, so $A \approx 1,003,716.2$. If Jake takes $50,000 for 20 years, he will have $1,000,000. The lump sum is a more profitable deal, since Jake will earn $1,003,716.20 - 1,000,000 = \$3,716.20$ more money.

CALCULUS

Limits of Functions

We begin by exploring the concept of a limit of a function, both algebraically and graphically. Consider the function $f(x) = x^2 + x - 1$. Let's construct a table of x values near 2, but not equal to 2.

x	1.96	1.97	1.98	1.99	2.01	2.02	2.03	2.04
f(x)	4.8016	4.8509	4.9004	4.9501	5.0501	5.1004	5.1509	5.2016

Notice that as the x value gets closer to 2, in either direction, the value of $f(x)$ gets closer to 5. In fact, $f(2) = 2^2 + 2 - 1 = 5$.

Figure 4.13 is a graph of $f(x) = x^2 + x - 1$. For easy reading, only points with integral values of x and $f(x)$ are shown.

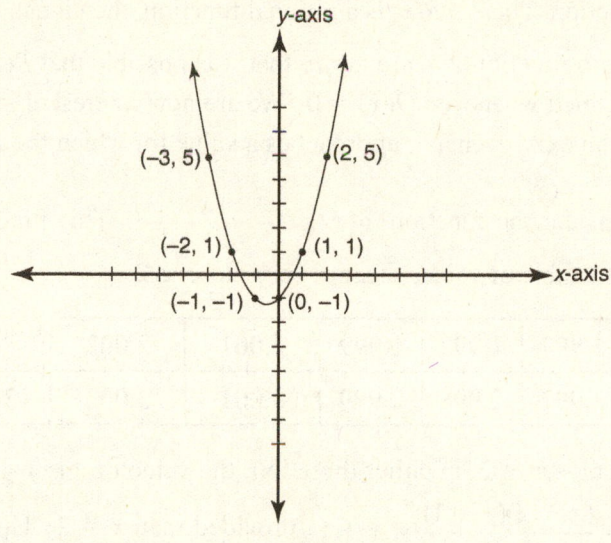

Figure 4.13

In general, for any polynomial function of the form $P(x) = a_0 + a_1x + a_2x^2 + ... + a_nx^n$, the limit of the function as x approaches a particular value c is $P(c)$. This statement also applies to other functions (such as trigonometric, exponential, and logarithmic) whose graphs can be drawn without any "gaps."

EXAMPLE 57

What is the limit of $k(x) = 9x - x^3$ as x approaches -1?

SOLUTION

Since $k(x)$ is a polynomial function, the limit is $k(-1) = 9(-1) - (-1)^3 = -8$.

EXAMPLE 58

What is the limit of $h(x) = 3\sin 2x$ as x approaches $\dfrac{\pi}{4}$, where x is given in radians?

SOLUTION

Simply substitute $\dfrac{\pi}{4}$ for x in the equation of the function. Then $h\left(\dfrac{\pi}{4}\right)$

$= 3\sin\left|(2)\left(\dfrac{\pi}{4}\right)\right| = 3\sin\dfrac{\pi}{2} = 3.$

Limits of Rational Functions

Recall that a **rational function** is a quotient of two polynomial functions in which the denominator is not the zero function. Thus, if $R(x)$ is a rational function, then it can be expressed as $\dfrac{P(x)}{Q(x)}$, where $Q(x)$ is not the zero function. We are aware that it is possible that $R(x)$ is not defined for all x. In fact, $R(x)$ is not defined whenever $Q(x) = 0$. We are now interested in determining if a limit for a rational function can exist even as x approaches a value for which the function is not defined.

As an example, consider the function $g(x) = \dfrac{x^2 - x - 2}{x - 2}$. This function is not defined for $x = 2$, but let's construct a table of values that are very close to 2.

x	1.996	1.997	1.998	1.999	2.001	2.002	2.003	2.004
$g(x)$	2.996	2.997	2.998	2.999	3.001	3.002	3.003	3.004

As the x value gets closer to 2, in either direction, the value of $g(x)$ gets closer to 3. We can simplify $\dfrac{x^2 - x - 2}{x - 2} = \dfrac{(x - 2)(x + 1)}{x - 2} = x + 1$, provided that $x \neq 2$. Thus, the function $g(x)$ is identical to the line $y = x + 1$, except where $x = 2$. Even though $g(x)$ is not defined for $x = 2$, we can still claim that as x approaches 2, the limit of $g(x)$ is 3. Figure 4.14 is a graph of $g(x) = \dfrac{x^2 - x - 2}{x - 2}$. Only points with integral values of x and $g(x)$ are shown. The point $(2, 3)$ is shown with an open circle because it does not belong to the graph of $g(x)$.

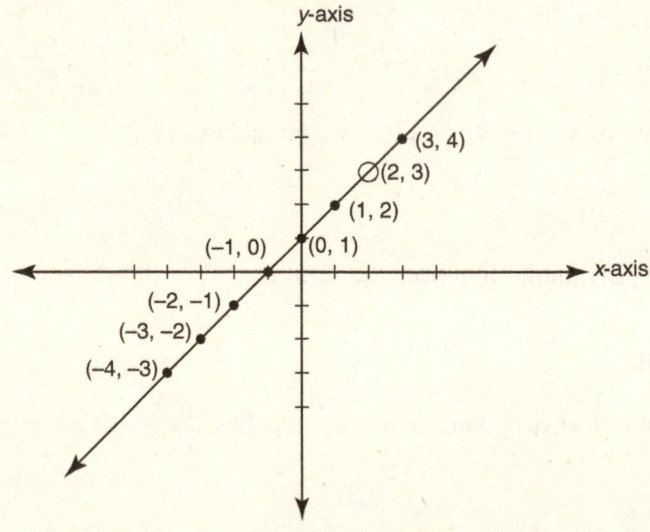

Figure 4.14

Let's check the procedure for finding a limit for this function when $x \neq 2$. If we wanted the limit of $g(x)$ as x approaches 4, for example, we simply substitute into the given equation for $g(x)$. Since $g(4) = \dfrac{4^2 - 4 - 2}{4 - 2} = 5$, as x approaches 4, the limit of $g(x)$ is 5.

EXAMPLE 59

If $m(x) = \dfrac{x-1}{x^2 + x + 3}$, what is the limit of $m(x)$ as x approaches 3?

SOLUTION

The answer is found by determining the value of $m(3)$, which is $\dfrac{3-1}{3^2 + 3 + 3} = \dfrac{2}{15}$.

EXAMPLE 60

If $n(x) = \dfrac{-3x - 6}{x^3 + 8}$, what is the limit of $n(x)$ as x approaches -2?

SOLUTION

We cannot simply calculate $n(-2)$, since the denominator would equal zero. The correct procedure is to reduce the fraction for $x \neq -2$. Rewrite

the function as $n(x) = \dfrac{-3(x+2)}{(x+2)(x^2 - 2x + 4)} = \dfrac{-3}{x^2 - 2x + 4}$. By substitution,

$n(-2) = \dfrac{-3}{(-2)^2 - 2(-2) + 4} = -\dfrac{1}{4}$. Thus, the limit is $-\dfrac{1}{4}$.

Rules for Limits

If $f(x)$ is a rational function in the form $\dfrac{p(x)}{q(x)}$, there are three basic rules to follow:

Rule 1: If the degree of $p(x)$ is less than that of $q(x)$, then $\lim_{x\to\infty} f(x) = 0$.

Rule 2: If the degree of $p(x)$ is equal to that of $q(x)$, then $\lim_{x\to\infty} f(x) = k$, where k is the ratio of the leading coefficients of $p(x)$ and $q(x)$.

Rule 3: If the degree of $p(x)$ is greater than that of $q(x)$, then $\lim_{x\to\infty} f(x) = \infty$. This is equivalent to stating that $\lim_{x\to\infty} f(x)$ does not exist.

EXAMPLE 61

What is the value of $\lim_{x\to\infty}(3x^5 - 10x^3 + 40)$?

SOLUTION

The leading term is $3x^5$. As x increases without bound, the value of $3x^5$ also increases without bound.

EXAMPLE 62

What is the value of $\lim_{x \to -\infty} \dfrac{-3x^4 + 7x - 4}{6x^4 + 91}$?

SOLUTION

Since the degrees of the numerator and denominator are equal, the limit is the ratio of the leading coefficients, which is $-\dfrac{1}{2}$. $= -\dfrac{3}{6}$

EXAMPLE 63

What is the value of $\lim_{x \to -\infty} \dfrac{10x^3 + 5}{8x^5 + x + 9}$?

SOLUTION

The same rules apply whether x approaches ∞ or $-\infty$. Since the degree of the numerator is smaller than that of the denominator, the answer is 0.

EXAMPLE 64

What is the value of $\lim_{x \to \infty} \dfrac{-9x^6 + 5x + 2}{10x^4 - 3x}$? DNE

SOLUTION

The degree of the numerator is larger than that of the denominator. Thus, the limit does not exist.

There is one additional important instance in which a limit does not exist for a rational function. If $f(x) = \dfrac{p(x)}{q(x)}$ is in reduced form and $q(c) = 0$ but $p(c) \neq 0$, then $\lim_{x \to c} f(x)$ does not exist. An example of this phenomenon is $\lim_{x \to 4} \dfrac{5x - 2}{3x - 12}$. By substituting the value of 4 for x, this fraction appears as $\dfrac{18}{0}$, which has no value. The limit does not exist.

Left-Sided and Right-Sided Limits

A specific notation is used when a limit exists for a function. Let $f(x)$ represent a function for which c is a point in the interior of its domain, and let L and M represent real numbers.

If x approaches the value of c from the left, this means that x is increasing from values slightly less than c up to (but possibly not including) c. Suppose that as x approaches this value of c from the left, $f(x)$ approaches a value of L. Then the notation we use is $\lim_{x \to c^-} f(x) = L$. Note the superscript minus sign on c^-.

If x approaches the value of c from the right, this means that x is decreasing from values slightly greater than c down to (but possibly not including) c. Suppose that as x approaches this value of c from the right, $f(x)$ approaches a value of M. Then the notation we use is $\lim_{x \to c^+} f(x) = M$. Note the suerscript plus sign on c^+.

If $L = M$, then we can state that the function has a limit at the point $x = c$. This is true even if $f(c)$ does not exist. The notation becomes $\lim_{x \to c} f(x) = L$. (Of course M could be substituted for L.) However, if $L \neq M$, then $\lim_{x \to c} f(x)$ does not exist. Each of $\lim_{x \to c^-} f(x) = L$ and $\lim_{x \to c^+} f(x) = M$ is called a **one-sided** limit, whether or not $\lim_{x \to c} f(x)$ actually exists. Thus, $\lim_{x \to c^-} f(x) = L$ is a one-sided limit as x approaches c from the left, while $\lim_{x \to c^+} f(x) = M$ is a one-sided limit as x approaches c from the right.

In each of Examples 57 through 60, the limit as x approaches the specific number from the left is equal to the limit as x approaches that same number from the right. Thus, for Example 57, we can write $\lim_{x \to -1}(9x - x^3) = -8$. Likewise, for Example 59, we can write $\lim_{x \to 3} \dfrac{x-1}{x^2 + x + 3} = \dfrac{2}{15}$. Remember that a limit can exist at a point even when the function is not defined at that point. In the graph of $g(x) = \dfrac{x^2 - x - 2}{x - 2}$ (Figure 4.14), even though $g(x)$ is not defined at $x = 2$, we can still write $\lim_{x \to 2} \dfrac{x^2 - x - 2}{x - 2} = 3$.

Let's look at some functions for which the left-sided limit at a specific point does not equal the right-sided limit.

Consider $f(x) = \begin{cases} x - 1, x \leq 0 \\ x^2 + 1, x > 0 \end{cases}$ and its graph shown in Figure 4.15.

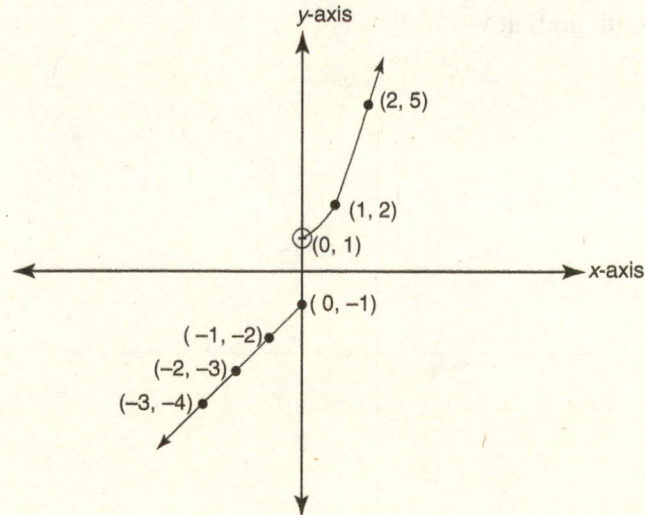

Figure 4.15

From the graph, we can determine that $\lim_{x \to 0^-} f(x) = -1$ and $\lim_{x \to 0^+} f(x) = 1$. Therefore, $\lim_{x \to 0} f(x)$ does not exist.

Now consider $g(x) = \begin{cases} \dfrac{1}{x-3}, & x > 3 \\ 5, & x \le 3 \end{cases}$, and its graph shown in Figure 4.16.

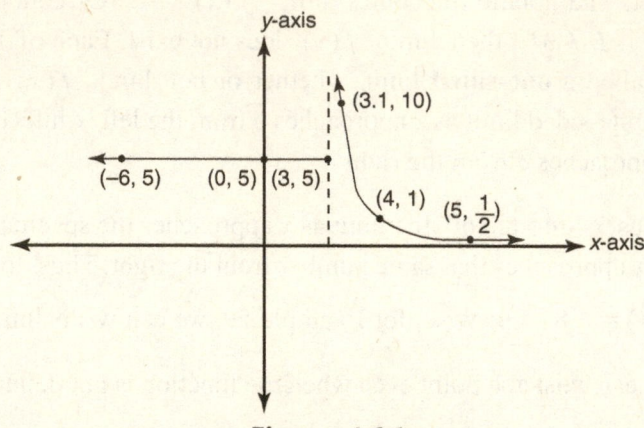

Figure 4.16

From the graph, we can determine that $\lim_{x \to 3^-} g(x) = 5$, but $\lim_{x \to 3^+} g(x)$ does not even exist. Therefore $\lim_{x \to 3} g(x)$ does not exist. Be aware that some books will use the notation $\lim_{x \to 3^+} g(x) = \infty$ to show that $\lim_{x \to 3^+} g(x)$ does not exist.

The concept of continuity for functions is very closely related to that of limits. In a visual sense, continuity of a function at a point means that its graph contains that point and all points within a fixed distance from it. Figures 4.17 and 4.18 illustrate functions that are continuous at $x = 2$. The function $g(x)$ in Figure 4.18 is not continuous at $x = -1$. Also, since the domain of $g(x)$ does not exceed 5, $g(x)$ is not continuous at $x = 5$.

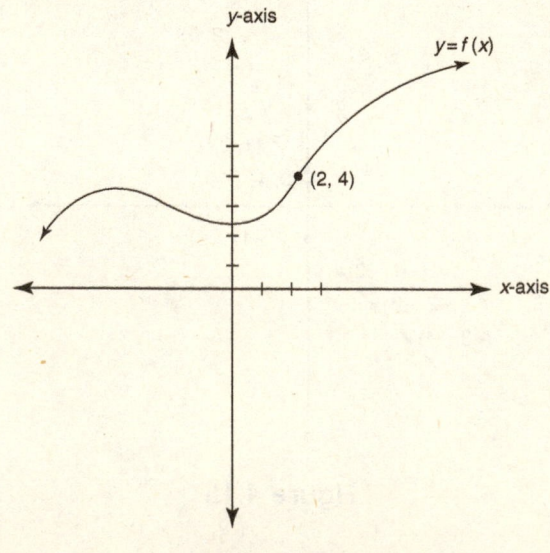

Figure 4.17

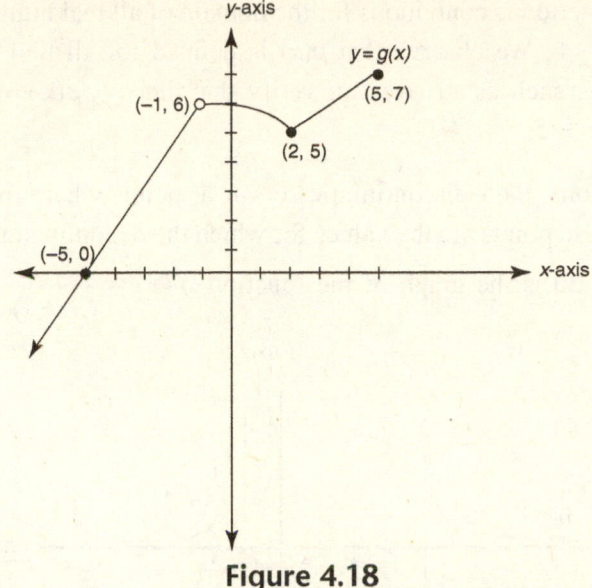

Figure 4.18

The formal definition of **continuity** is: A function $f(x)$ is continuous at a point $x = c$ if, and only if $\lim_{x \to c} f(x) = c$. This definition is really a combination of three distinct sub-statements, namely:

1. $\lim_{x \to c} f(x)$ exists.

2. $f(c)$ exists

3. $\lim_{x \to c} f(x) = f(c)$

If any of these conditions are not met, $f(x)$ is discontinuous at point c. Remember that $x = c$ *cannot* represent an endpoint of an interval on which $f(x)$ is defined. The reason is that $\lim_{x \to c} f(x)$ would not exist.

Figure 4.19 is an example of a function $t(x)$ for which the first two conditions of continuity are met, but the third condition is not met.

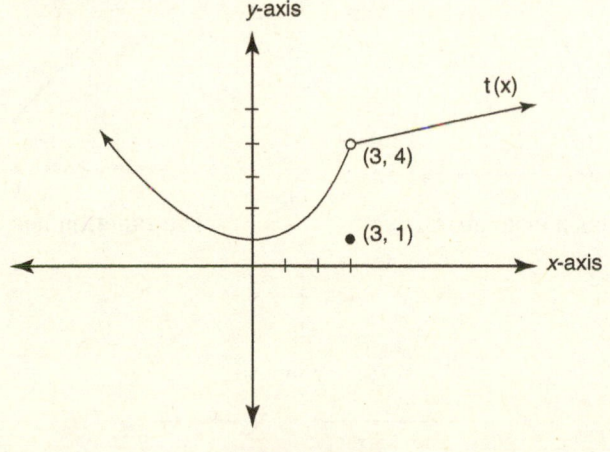

Figure 4.19

Notice that $\lim_{x \to 3} t(x) = 4$, but that $t(3) = 1$. Thus, $t(x)$ is discontinuous at $x = 3$.

Each polynomial function is continuous for the domain of all real numbers. One such example is $p(x) = -2x^5 + 3x - 4$. We observe that $p(x)$ is defined for all real numbers. If we choose a specific domain value, such as −1, we can verify that $\lim_{x \to -1} p(x)$ exists, $p(-1)$ exists, and $\lim_{x \to -1} p(x) = p(-1) = -5$.

With rational functions, their discontinuities occur at points where there are vertical asymptotes. The x values of these points are the values for which the denominator of the rational function is not defined. Figure 4.20 is the graph of the function $f(x) = \dfrac{2}{(x-1)(x+4)}$, showing a few selected points.

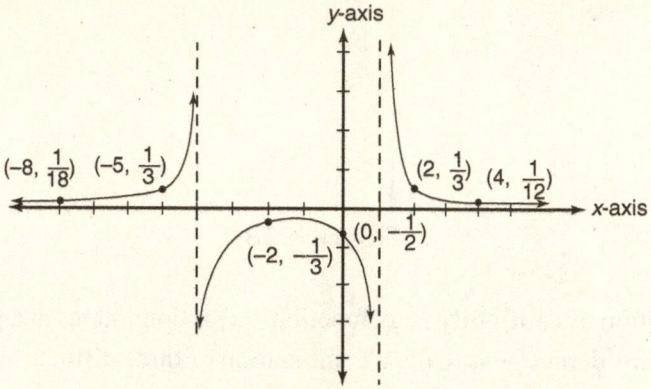

Figure 4.20

Notice that $f(1)$ and $f(-4)$ are not defined, so $f(x)$ cannot be continuous at either $x = 1$ or $x = -4$.

A function does not have a derivative at $x = c$ if:

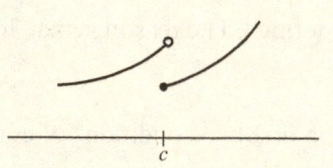

The function is discontinuous at $x=c$

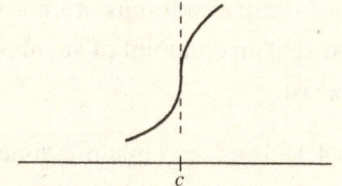

The function has a vertical tangent at $x=c$

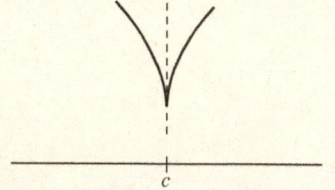

The function has a cusp at $x=c$

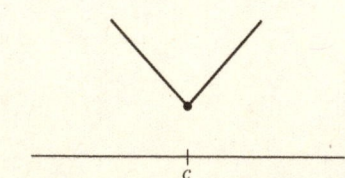

The function has a corner at $x=c$

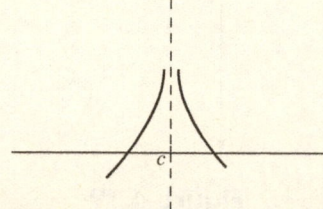

The function has a vertical asymptote at $x=c$

Note: The function is undefined at $x=c$.

The Intermediate Value Theorem

One very important consequence of continuity for a function is the **Intermediate Value Theorem**. First, we must state that a function $f(x)$ is continuous on a closed interval [a, b] if it is continuous at each point of the open interval (a, b). Also, $\lim_{x \to a^+} f(x) = f(a)$ and $\lim_{x \to b^-} f(x) = f(b)$. (A closed interval contains the endpoints, but an open interval does not.)

Now, let $f(x)$ represent a function that is continuous on a closed interval [a,b]. Let N represent any value between $f(a)$ and $f(b)$. The Intermediate Value Theorem states that there exists at least one value c, where $a < c < b$, such that $f(c) = N$. In other words, this theorem is claiming that if a function is continuous between any two x values a and b, then the function must assume all y values between $f(a)$ and $f(b)$. Figure 4.21 shows a general continuous function with the points stated above for the Intermediate Value Theorem.

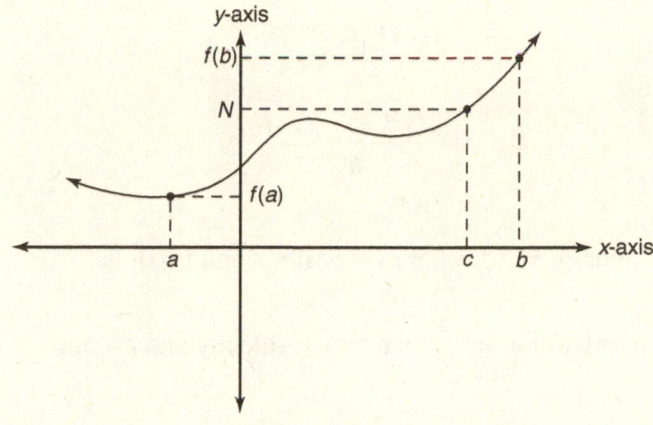

Figure 4.21

As a specific example, consider $g(x) = -x^2 + 6x + 1$, which is continuous for all x values. On the closed interval [–1,4], $g(-1) = -6$ and $g(4) = 9$. Next, any number between –6 and 9 is selected. If we select 6, the Intermediate Value Theorem states that there is at least one x value between –1 and 4 for which $g(x) = 6$. In fact, we are looking for the solution(s) to $6 = -x^2 + 6x + 1$. This equation can be written as $x^2 - 6x + 5 = 0$, which is factored as $(x - 5)(x - 1) = 0$. The two solutions are 5 and 1, and note that 1 does lie in the interval [–1,4].

Rate of Change

Average Rate of Change

Consider the function $f(x)$ that is continuous in the interval [a, b].

The **average rate of change** is defined as the slope of the line segment, with endpoints $(a, f(a))$ and $(b, f(b))$. Its value is calculated as $\dfrac{f(b) - f(a)}{b - a}$. This line segment is part of the secant line through $(a, f(a))$ and $(b, f(b))$, as shown in Figure 4.22.

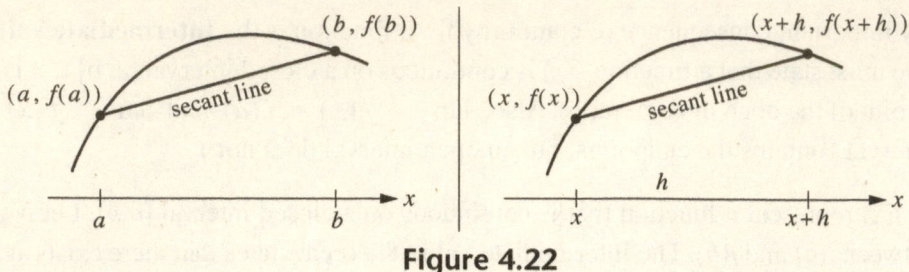

Figure 4.22

Average rate of change = slope of the secant line $\Rightarrow m_{sec}$

$$= \frac{\Delta y}{\Delta x}$$

$$= \frac{f(b) - f(a)}{b - a}$$

$$= \frac{f(x + h) - f(x)}{h}$$

Average velocity = $\frac{\Delta s}{\Delta t}$, where s = position and t = time.

Average acceleration = $\frac{\Delta v}{\Delta t}$, where v = velocity and t = time.

EXAMPLE 65

What is the average rate of change for $g(x) = -x^3 + 4$ over the interval $[1, 6]$?

SOLUTION

$g(1) = 3$ and $g(6) = -212$. Thus, the average rate of change is $\frac{-212 - 3}{6 - 1} = -43$.

EXAMPLE 66

What is the average rate of change for $f(x) = 2x^2 + 5$ over the interval $[2, 5]$?

SOLUTION

$f(2) = 13$ and $f(5) = 55$. Thus, the average rate of change is $\frac{55 - 13}{5 - 2} = 14$.

Similar to a slope, the average rate of change can be positive, negative, or zero. It may also be a non-integer.

Returning to the function in Example 68, let's change the interval to [2, 3].

EXAMPLE 67

What is the average rate of change for $f(x) = 2x^2 + 5$ over the interval [2, 3]?

SOLUTION

$f(2) = 13$ and $f(3) = 23$. This time, the average rate of change is $\dfrac{23 - 13}{3 - 2} = 10$.

EXAMPLE 68

What is the average rate of change for $f(x) = 2x^2 + 5$ over the interval [2, 2.1]?

SOLUTION

$f(2) = 13$ and $f(2.1) = 13.82$. Thus, the average rate of change is $\dfrac{13.82 - 13}{2.1 - 2} = 8.2$.

Notice that in Example 68, the interval was very small, compared to the intervals used for Examples 66 and 67. Figure 4.23 illustrates a magnified version of the secant line for each of Examples 68 and 69.

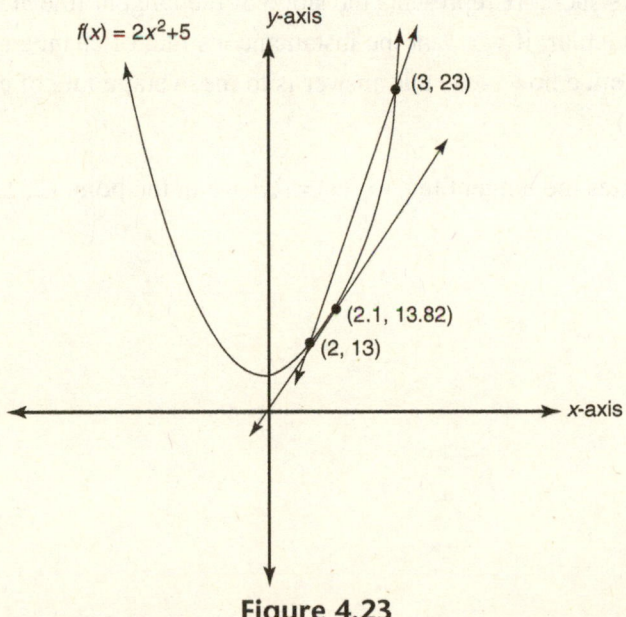

Figure 4.23

Instantaneous Rate of Change

This leads us to the concept of **instantaneous rate change**. For a specific point P of a function, this is defined as the slope of the tangent line at point P. It represents the limit of the average rate of change between P and a second point Q that belongs to the function as $Q - P$ becomes increasingly smaller.

In general, let $f(x)$ be defined and continuous at point P with coordinates $(x, f(x))$. Let point Q belong to $f(x)$ such that its coordinates are $(x + \Delta x, f(x + \Delta x))$, where Δx is a very small number. (Use your own perception of "very small.") Then the instantaneous rate of change of $f(x)$ at point P is given by $\lim_{\Delta x \to 0} \dfrac{f(x + \Delta x) - f(x)}{\Delta x}$.

Let's return to the function $f(x) = 2x^2 + 5$ given in Examples 67, 68, and 69, and calculate the average rate of change by using the interval $[2, 2.001]$. Since $f(2) = 13$ and $f(2.001) = 13.008002$, the average rate of change is $\dfrac{13.008002 - 13}{2.001 - 2} = 8.002$.

Let's now calculate the instantaneous rate at $(x, f(x))$ by using the limit formula shown above. Since $f(x) = 2x^2 + 5$, $f(x + \Delta x) = 2(x + \Delta x)^2 + 5 = 2x^2 + 4x\Delta x + 2(\Delta x)^2 + 5$. Then

$$\lim_{\Delta x \to 0} \frac{f(x + \Delta x) - f(x)}{\Delta x} = \lim_{\Delta x \to 0} \frac{2x^2 + 4x\Delta x + 2(\Delta x)^2 + 5 - (2x^2 + 5)}{\Delta x} = \lim_{\Delta x \to 0} \frac{4x\Delta x + 2(\Delta x)^2}{\Delta x} =$$

$\lim_{\Delta x \to 0} 4x + 2(\Delta x) = 4x.$

The expression $4x$ represents the instantaneous rate of change for the function $f(x) = 2x^2 + 5$ at *any* point $(x, f(x))$. As such, $4x$ represents the slope of the tangent line at any point on the graph of this function. In particular, if we want the instantaneous rate of change at the point $(2, 13)$, the answer is $(4)(2) = 8$. Notice how close this answer is to the average rate of change between $(2, 13)$ and $(2.001, 13.008002)$.

Figure 4.24 illustrates the tangent line to $f(x) = 2x^2 + 5$ at the point $(2, 13)$.

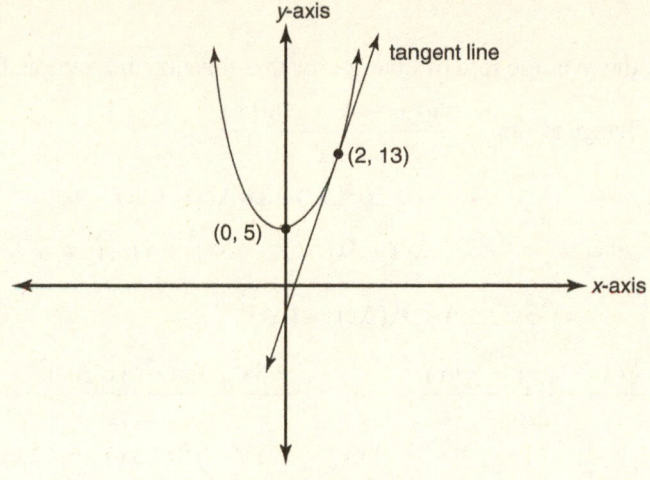

Figure 4.24

EXAMPLE 69

For the function $f(x) = 2x^2 + 5$, what is the instantaneous rate of change at the point $(-4, 37)$?

SOLUTION

Using the expression $4x$, the answer is $(4)(-4) = -16$.

EXAMPLE 70

For the function $f(x) = 2x^2 + 5$, what is the equation of the tangent line at $x = 2$?

SOLUTION

We already know that the slope of the tangent line is $(4)(2) = 8$. Since the tangent line contains the point $(2, 13)$, we can use the following equation for a line: $y - y_1 = m(x - x_1)$. In this equation, m represents the slope and (x_1, y_1) represents a point on the line. By substitution, $y - 13 = 8(x - 2)$, which simplifies to $y = 8x - 3$.

EXAMPLE 71

What is the instantaneous rate of change at the point $(x, g(x))$ for the function $g(x) = -x^3 + 4$?

SOLUTION

We calculated the average rate of change for this function in Example 65. The instantaneous rate of change is $\lim_{\Delta x \to 0} \dfrac{g(x + \Delta x) - g(x)}{\Delta x}$.

Then $g(x + \Delta x) = -(x + \Delta x)^3 + 4 = -x^3 - 3x^2(\Delta x) - 3x(\Delta x)^2 - (\Delta x)^3 + 4$.

So $g(x + \Delta x) - g(x) = (-x^3 - 3x^2(\Delta x) - 3x(\Delta x)^2 - (\Delta x)^3 + 4) - (-x^3 + 4)$

$$= -3x^2(\Delta x) - 3x(\Delta x)^2 - (\Delta x)^3.$$

Now, $\lim_{\Delta x \to 0} \dfrac{g(x + \Delta x) - g(x)}{\Delta x} = \lim_{\Delta x \to 0} \dfrac{-3x^2(\Delta x) - 3x(\Delta x)^2 - (\Delta x)^3}{\Delta x}$

$$= \lim_{\Delta x \to 0} -3x^2 - 3x(\Delta x) - (\Delta x)^2 = -3x^2.$$

This method of finding the instantaneous rate of change is called the "Δ-method" ("Δ" is pronounced "delta"). You can see that the algebraic steps require a great deal of attention to accuracy! We will develop a shortcut later in this chapter.

In summary:

1.   The instantaneous rate of change is always calculated at a single point.

2.   It is the slope of the tangent line at the point (Figure 4.25).

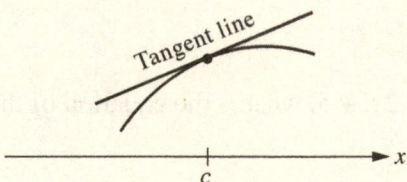

Figure 4.25

First Derivatives

The first derivative of $y = f(x)$ is defined as the instantaneous rate of change $= \lim_{h \to 0} \dfrac{f(x + h) - f(x)}{h}$, which is written as $\dfrac{dy}{dx}$ or $f'(x)$.

Likewise, instantaneous velocity is $\dfrac{ds}{dt}$, where $s =$ position and $t =$ time, and instantaneous acceleration $= \dfrac{dv}{dt}$, where $v =$ velocity and $t =$ time.

Fortunately, there are rules that govern the derivatives for many types of functions.

Rational Functions

Rule	Function	First Derivative
1.	$y = k$, k a constant	$\dfrac{dy}{dx} = 0$
2.	$y = kx$, k a constant	$\dfrac{dy}{dx} = k$
3.	$y = x^k$, k a constant	$\dfrac{dy}{dx} = kx^{k-1}$
4.	$y = a_n x^n + a_{n-1}x^{n-1} + a_{n-2}x^{n-2}$ $+ ... + a_1 x + a_0$	$\dfrac{dy}{dx} = na_n x^{n-1} + (n-1)a_{n-1}x^{n-2} +$ $(n-2)a_{n-2}x^{n-3} + ...a_1$
5.	$y = k f(x)$, k a constant	$\dfrac{dy}{dx} = (k)(f'(x))$
6.	$y = f(x) \pm g(x)$	$\dfrac{dy}{dx} = f'(x) \pm g'(x)$
7.	*Product rule* $y = f(x) \times g(x)$	$\dfrac{dy}{dx} = f(x) \times g'(x) + g(x) \times f'(x)$ *(handwritten: F×S' +S×f')*
8.	*Quotient Rule* $y = \dfrac{f(x)}{g(x)}$	$\dfrac{dy}{dx} = \dfrac{g(x) \times f'(x) - f(x) \times g'(x)}{[g(x)]^2}$ *(handwritten: $\dfrac{B \times T' - T \times B'}{B^2}$)*

EXAMPLE 72

If $y = 7x - 12$, what is the simplified expression for $\dfrac{dy}{dx}$?

SOLUTION

We can use the rules 1 and 2 to get $\dfrac{dy}{dx} = 7 + 0 = 7$.

EXAMPLE 73

If $y = -x^4 + 5x^3 + x$, what is the simplified expression for $\dfrac{dy}{dx}$?

(handwritten: $-4x^3 + 15x^2 + 1$)

SOLUTION

We can just use rule 4, which is really a combination of the first three rules. Then
$\dfrac{dy}{dx} = (4)(-1)x^3 + (3)(5)x^2 + 1 = -4x^3 + 15x^2 + 1$.

[handwritten margin note: $f \times s' + s \times f'$]

EXAMPLE 74

If $y = (x^2 - 2x + 9)(6x + 3)$, what is the value of $\frac{dy}{dx}$ at $x = 2$?

[handwritten annotation: plug in $x=2$ after finding first derivative]

[handwritten work:]
$$(x^2 - 2x + 9)(6) + (6x + 3)(2x - 2)$$
$$= 6x^2 - 12x + 54 + 12x^2 - 12x + 6x - 6$$
$$= 18x^2 - 18x + 48$$

SOLUTION

We have two choices here. Let's use rule 7, with $f(x) = x^2 - 2x + 9$ and $g(x) = 6x + 3$. So, $f'(x) = 2x - 2$ and $g'(x) = 6$. Thus, $\frac{dy}{dx} = (x^2 - 2x + 9)(6) + (6x + 3)(2x - 2) = 6x^2 - 12x + 54 + 12x^2 - 6x - 6 = 18x^2 - 18x + 48$. Finally, when $x = 2$, $\frac{dy}{dx} = (18)(2^2) - (18)(2) + 48 = 84$.

For the second choice, we could have multiplied and simplified the original expression for y to get $6x^3 - 9x^2 + 48x + 27$. Then, $\frac{dy}{dx} = (3)(6)x^2 - (2)(9)x + 48 = 18x^2 - 18x + 48$, which matches the expression for $\frac{dy}{dx}$ we already obtained.

[handwritten margin note: $\dfrac{B \times T' - T \times B'}{B^2}$]

EXAMPLE 75

If $y = \dfrac{x - 3}{x^2 + x - 2}$, what is the simplified expression for $\frac{dy}{dx}$?

[handwritten work:]
$$= \frac{(x^2 + x - 2)(1) - (x - 3)(2x + 1)}{[x^2 + x - 2]^2} = \frac{x^2 + x - 2 - (2x^2 - 5x - 3)}{(x^2 + x - 2)^2}$$

SOLUTION

Rule 8 should be used. Let $f(x) = x - 3$ and let $g(x) = x^2 + x - 2$. Then $f'(x) = 1$ and $g'(x) = 2x + 1$. So, $\frac{dy}{dx} = \dfrac{(x^2 + x - 2)(1) - (x - 3)(2x + 1)}{(x^2 + x - 2)^2} = $

$\dfrac{x^2 + x - 2 - (2x^2 - 5x - 3)}{(x^2 + x - 2)^2} = \dfrac{-x^2 + 6x + 1}{(x^2 + x - 2)^2}$.

We didn't take the extra step to expand the denominator. The answer we have shown is generally accepted as the final answer. However, you should always completely simplify the numerator of a fraction. Also, if there were a common factor in both the numerator and denominator of the final answer, that factor would be divided out.

EXAMPLE 76

If $y = \dfrac{7}{x^2} - \dfrac{5}{2x^6}$, what is the value of $\frac{dy}{dx}$ at $x = -1$?

SOLUTION

We could combine the terms on the right side by using a common denominator, but it is just as easy to rewrite this example using negative exponents. Then $y = 7x^{-2} - $

$\dfrac{5}{2}x^{-6}$, so $\dfrac{dy}{dx} = (-2)(7)x^{-3} + (-6)\left(-\dfrac{5}{2}\right)x^{-7} = -\dfrac{14}{x^3} + \dfrac{15}{x^7} = \dfrac{-14x^4 + 15}{x^7}$. At

$x = -1$, $\dfrac{dy}{dx} = \dfrac{(-14)(-1)^4 + 15}{(-1)^7} = -1$.

An alternative way to answer Example 76 is to rewrite the equation as y $\dfrac{14x^4 - 5}{2x^6}$, then use Rule 8.

Trigonometric, Logarithmic, and Power Functions

Rules 9 through 16 pertain to derivatives applied to trigonometric, logarithmic, and power functions.

Rule	Function	First Derivative
9.	$y = \sin x$	$\dfrac{dy}{dx} = \cos x$
10.	$y = \cos x$	$\dfrac{dy}{dx} = -\sin x$
11.	$y = \tan x$	$\dfrac{dy}{dx} = \sec^2 x$
12.	$y = \cot x$	$\dfrac{dy}{dx} = -\csc^2 x$
13.	$y = \sec x$	$\dfrac{dy}{dx} = \sec x \ \tan x$
14.	$y = \csc x$	$\dfrac{dy}{dx} = -(\csc x)(\cot x)$
15.	$y = a^x$, where $a > 0$	$\dfrac{dy}{dx} = (a^x)(\ln a)$
16.	$y = \log_a x$, where $a > 0$, $a \neq 1$	$\dfrac{dy}{dx} = \left(\dfrac{1}{\ln a}\right)\left(\dfrac{1}{x}\right)$

As special cases, if $y = e^x$, then $\dfrac{dy}{dx} = (e^x)(\ln e) = e^x$.

Also, if $y = \log_e x = \ln x$, then $\dfrac{dy}{dx} = \left(\dfrac{1}{\ln e}\right)\left(\dfrac{1}{x}\right) = \dfrac{1}{x}$.

EXAMPLE 77

quotient Rule

f'(cos)=-sinx

$\dfrac{B \times T' - T \times B'}{B^2}$

If $y = \dfrac{\cos x}{3x^2}$, what is the simplified expression for $\dfrac{dy}{dx}$?

SOLUTION

We'll use rules 8 and 10. Then:

$$\frac{dy}{dx} = \frac{(3x^2)(-\sin x) - (\cos x)(6x)}{(3x^2)^2} = \frac{-3x^2 \sin x - 6x \cos x}{9x^4} = \frac{-x \sin x - 2 \cos x}{3x^3}.$$

EXAMPLE 78

f'(secx)=secx tanx

If $y = 4x^3 \sec x$, what is the simplified expression for $\dfrac{dy}{dx}$?

SOLUTION

fxg'+gxf'

Be careful that you do *not* interpret this as $y = \sec(4x^4)$!

We'll use rules 7 and 13.

Then $\dfrac{dy}{dx} = (\sec x)(12x^2) + (4x^3)(\sec x)(\tan x)$ or $(4x^2 \sec x)(3 + x \tan x)$.

$12x^2(\sec x) + (4x^3)(\sec x \tan x)$

EXAMPLE 79

f'(cscx)=-(cscx)(cotx)

If $y = 3\csc x - 5^x$, what is the simplified expression for $\dfrac{dy}{dx}$?

SOLUTION

We'll use rules 6, 14, and 15. Then $\dfrac{dy}{dx} = -3(\csc x)(\cot x) - (5^x)(\ln 5)$.

EXAMPLE 80

Product Rule

If $y = x(\ln x)$, what is the simplified expression for $\dfrac{dy}{dx}$?

$x\left(\dfrac{1}{x}\right) + \ln x(1)$

SOLUTION

Using rule 7 and the special case that applies to rule 16, $\dfrac{dy}{dx} = (x)\left(\dfrac{1}{x}\right) +$ $(\ln x)(1) = 1 + \ln x$.

1(lnx)

EXAMPLE 81

For a given exponential function $f(x) = a^x$, its derivative is directly proportional to $f(x)$. If $f(x) = 12$, write an explicit expression for $f(x)$.

[handwritten: k = constant of proportionality]
[handwritten: directly proportional: $y = kx$]

SOLUTION

Since $f(x) = a^x$, we can write $f(4) = 12 = a^4$. Then $a = \sqrt[4]{12} \approx 1.86$. Thus, $f(x) = 1.86^x$.

[handwritten: inversely proportional: $y = \dfrac{k}{x}$]

EXAMPLE 82

Given exponential function $g(x) = a^x$ such that $g'(x) = (3)(g(x))$, write an explicit expression for $g(x)$.

SOLUTION

We know that $g(x) = a^x$ and that $g'(x) = (a^x)(\ln a)$. By substitution, we can write $g'(x) = (3)(g(x)) = (3)(a^x) = (a^x)(\ln a)$. Then $3 = \ln a$, so $a \approx 20.09$. Thus, $g(x) = 20.09^x$.

Chain Rule

We now consider the **Chain Rule** as it applies to derivatives. The Chain Rule is a method by which we can take the derivative of a composite function. Suppose $y = g(h(x))$. The function y is considered a composite function of $g(x)$ and $h(x)$. Another way to state this relationship is: $y = g(u)$ and $u = h(x)$. Then

Rule	Function	First Derivative
17.	$y = g(h(x))$, where $y = g(u)$ and $u = h(x)$,	$\dfrac{dy}{dx} = \left(\dfrac{dy}{du}\right)\left(\dfrac{du}{dx}\right)$.

A second way to determine $\dfrac{dy}{dx}$ is to use the formula $\dfrac{dy}{dx} = g'(h(x)) \times (h'(x))$. Either method should work when determining $\dfrac{dy}{dx}$.

EXAMPLE 83

Find the first derivative $\dfrac{dy}{dx}$ for $x^2 + y^2 = 9$.

SOLUTION

Differentiate each term with respect to x:

$$2x + 2y\frac{dy}{dx} = 0$$

Thus, $\dfrac{dy}{dx} = -\dfrac{2x}{2y} = -\dfrac{x}{y}$.

(handwritten annotations):
Find the first derivative of $x^2 + y^2 = 9$

$2x + 2y\frac{dy}{dx} = 0$

$2y\frac{dy}{dx} = -2x$

$\frac{dy}{dx} = \frac{-2x}{2y}$

EXAMPLE 84

Find $\dfrac{dy}{dx}$ for the equation $xy = x^2y^2 + \cos(y)$.

SOLUTION

The solution uses both the <u>product rule</u> and the <u>Chain Rule</u>.

By the Chain Rule,

$$y + x\frac{dy}{dx} = \left(\frac{d(x^2y^2)}{dx}\right) + \frac{d(\cos y)}{dy} \times \frac{dy}{dx}$$

Then, using the product rule,

$$= 2xy^2 + 2x^2y\frac{dy}{dx} - \sin(y)\frac{dy}{dx}$$

So

$$x\frac{dy}{dx} - 2x^2y\frac{dy}{dx} + \sin(y)\frac{dy}{dx} = 2xy^2 - y$$

which becomes

$$\frac{dy}{dx} = \frac{2xy^2 - y}{x - 2x^2y + \sin(y)}$$

Related Rates

The rules for finding derivatives for **related rates** are:

1. Draw and label a good sketch, if applicable.

2. Develop an equation that relates the relevant variables.

3. Differentiate each side of the equation with respect to time t to create a rate equation. Use the Chain Rule if necessary.

4. Substitute the given data into the rate equation and calculate the required unknown.

EXAMPLE 85

A 17-foot ladder is leaning against a brick wall at a height greater than 8 ft. The bottom of the ladder is slipping away from the wall at a constant rate of 1 ft/sec. At what speed is the top of the ladder sliding down the wall when the top is 8 ft above the ground?

SOLUTION

- Draw a diagram

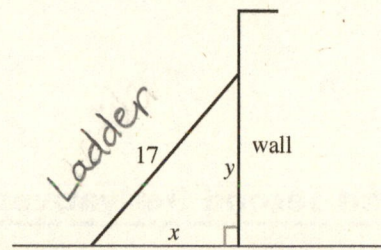

- Establish an equation

$$x^2 + y^2 = 17^2$$

- Create a rate equation by differentiating with respect to t

$$2x\frac{dx}{dt} + 2y\frac{dy}{dt} = 0$$

- Given $\dfrac{dx}{dt} = 1$, $y = 8$, and by the Pythagorean Theorem, $x = 15$

The problem is asking to determine $\dfrac{dy}{dt}$:

$$2(15)(1) + 2(8)\frac{dy}{dt} = 0$$

$$\frac{dy}{dt} = \frac{-15}{8}\,\text{ft/sec} = -1.875\,\text{ft/sec}$$

Answer: $\dfrac{15}{8}$ or 1.875 ft/sec

Note: The minus sign indicates the downward motion.

Second Derivative

The second derivative of a function $f(x)$ is denoted by $f''(x)$. It has a double-prime notation because it is the derivative of the first derivative, $f'(x)$, if it is differentiable.

The second derivative is very useful in determining the <u>concavity</u> of a curve. Also, whereas the first derivative of a position function s of a particle with respect to time t yields the particle's velocity at time t, the second derivative denotes the particle's acceleration at time t.

EXAMPLE 86

If $f(x) = 2x3 + x2 - 4x + 2$, find $f'(x)$ and $f''(x)$.

SOLUTION

$f(x) = 2x^3 + x^2 - 4x + 2$

$f'(x) = 6x^2 + 2x - 4$

$f''(x) = 12x + 2$

Applications of First and Second Derivatives to a Graph

Let's consider $f(x) = 3x$, which is simply the graph of a line with a slope of 3. We find that $f'(x) = 3$, which just confirms that the instantaneous rate of change at any point is 3. Now $f''(x) = 0$, which means that there is no change in the first derivative. This is no surprise because the slope of any line is constant.

Now suppose that $g(x) = x^2 - x$. If we want to determine the values of x for which the tangent line has a positive slope, we only need to solve $g'(x) = 2x - 1 > 0$. This leads to $x > \dfrac{1}{2}$, which means that the tangent line has a positive slope for all x values greater than $\dfrac{1}{2}$. With a similar argument, we can show that the tangent line has a negative slope for $x < \dfrac{1}{2}$. Also, since $g'\left(\dfrac{1}{2}\right) = 2\left(\dfrac{1}{2}\right) - 1 = 0$, we know that the slope changes at $x = \dfrac{1}{2}$.

Figure 4.26 shown below is the graph of $g(x) = x^2 - x$.

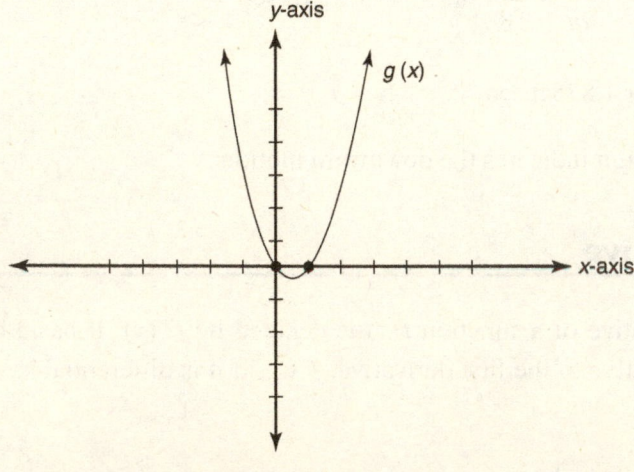

Figure 4.26

The graph immediately tells us that if we were to choose a point whose x value is less than $\frac{1}{2}$, the slope of the tangent line would be negative. By choosing a value of x greater than $\frac{1}{2}$, the tangent line has a positive slope.

To understand the second derivative, $g''(x)$, let's consider any two values of x. For $x = -3$, $g'(-3) = (2)(-3)-1 = -7$; for $x = 0$, $g'(0) = -1$. Bearing in mind that the second derivative measures the *change* in the first derivative, we can see that $g'(0)$ is actually greater than $g'(-3)$. So, as x increases by three units, from -3 to 0, $g'(x)$ increases six units, from -7 to -1. This implies that for $x = -3$, $g'(x)$ is actually positive. In fact, since $g'(x) = 2x - 1$, it follows that $g''(x) = 2$. This statement tells us that for $g(x) = x^2 - x$, the second derivative is always the positive number 2.

Our next objective is to analyze the graphs of continuous functions, as well as their first and second derivatives. All our functions will also be continuous for all values in the domain of x.

Figure 4.27 illustrates a general continuous function $y = k(x)$ over the closed interval $[a, f]$. Note that $k'(x)$ exists at every point in the open interval (a, f) except at $(d, k(d))$, since we cannot draw a single tangent line to the curve at this point. Remember, *only a one-sided limit is possible at an endpoint.*

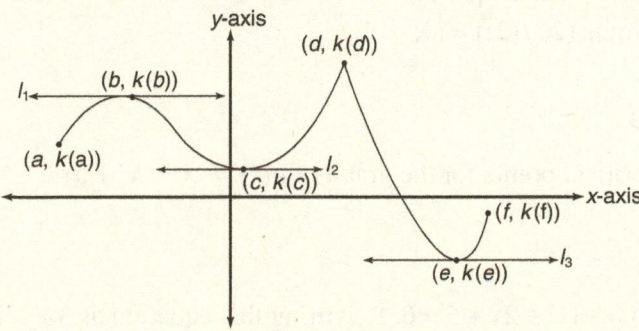

Figure 4.27

Critical Points on a Graph

We need some definitions for the six points of the graph that have been identified with co-ordinates, and some observations about the three horizontal lines.

The function has an **absolute maximum** value of $k(d)$, which occurs when $x = d$. The function has an **absolute minimum** value of $k(e)$, which occurs when $x = e$. The function has a **local maximum** value of $k(b)$, which occurs when $x = b$. A local maximum value means that the point has the largest function value, but only within a specific neighborhood of this point.

The function has a **local minimum** value of $k(c)$, which occurs when $x = c$. A local minimum value means that the point has the smallest function value, but only within a specific neighborhood of this point.

A **critical point** on the graph is one that lies in the open interval (a, f) for which its derivative is either zero or undefined. Each of the four points $(b, k(b))$, $(c, k(c))$, $(d, k(d))$, and $(e, k(e))$ are critical points for this function.

The lines l_1, l_2, and l_3, each of which has **a slope of zero**, are tangent to $(b, k(b))$, $(c, k(c))$, and $(e, k(e))$, respectively. *This implies that given a point on the graph of a continuous function for which the first derivative is zero, this point represents either a **maximum** or **minimum** point.* Be careful that you do *not* accept the converse of this statement as being always true! The point $(d, k(d))$ is an absolute maximum point, but $k'(d)$ does not exist. The reason is that more than one tangent line can be drawn at $(d, k(d))$.

EXAMPLE 87

What are the critical points for the graph of $f(x) = 4x^2 - 16x + 1$?

SOLUTION

We need to find $f'(x)$ and equate it to zero. So $f'(x) = 8x - 16 = 0$. Then, $x = 2$. Thus, the critical point is $(2, f(2)) = (2, -15)$.

$8x = 16$
$x = 2$

EXAMPLE 88

What are the critical points for the graph of $g(x) = -x^3 + x^2 + 5x$?

SOLUTION

We write $g'(x) = -3x^2 + 2x + 5 = 0$. Rewriting this equation as $3x^2 - 2x - 5 = 0$, we can factor to get $(3x - 5)(x + 1) = 0$. Then $x = \dfrac{5}{3}$ or $x = -1$. Thus, the critical points are $\left(\dfrac{5}{3}, g\left(\dfrac{5}{3}\right)\right) = \left(\dfrac{5}{3}, \dfrac{175}{27}\right)$ and $(-1, g(-1)) = (-1, -3)$.

This procedure does not reveal whether the critical points are maximum or minimum. The physical graph of each function will definitely reveal this information. However, we will develop an algebraic method for determining whether a given critical point represents a maximum or minimum function value.

Let's redraw Figure 4.27, calling it Figure 4.28, and replace the lines l_1, l_2, and l_3, with lines, l_4, l_5, and l_6. (Some points are not identified in order to avoid congestion in the figure.)

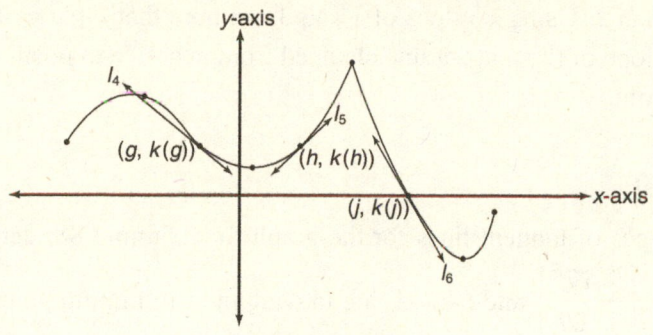

Figure 4.28

Line l_4 is tangent to the graph at $x = g$, line l_5 is tangent to the graph at $x = h$, and line l_6 is tangent to the graph at $x = j$.

We note that the point $(g, k(g))$ lies on a portion of the graph where the value of $k(x)$ is decreasing from $k(b)$ to $k(c)$. Also, the slope of l_4 is negative.

Likewise, the point $(h, k(h))$ lies on a portion of the graph where the value of $k(x)$ is increasing from $k(c)$ to $k(d)$. Thus, the slope of l_5 is positive.

In a similar fashion, $(j, k(j))$ lies on a portion of the graph where the value of $k(x)$ is decreasing from $k(d)$ to $k(e)$. Thus, the slope of l_6 is negative.

We can draw some conclusions from these observations about any continuous function $f(x)$ for which $(x_1, f(x_1))$ and $(x_2, f(x_2))$ are any two consecutive critical values in the domain, with $x_1 < x_2$.

1. If $f(x_1) < f(x_2)$ then the slope of the tangent line is positive for any point $(p, f(p))$, where $x_1 < p < x_2$. Also, $f(x_1) < f(p) < f(x_2)$.

2. If $f(x_1) > f(x_2)$, then the slope of the tangent line is negative for any point $(q, f(q))$, where $x_1 < q < x_2$. Also, $f(x_1) > f(q) > f(x_2)$.

3. As the x value increases, if the slope of the tangent line changes from positive to zero to negative, the point at which the slope is zero is an absolute (or local) maximum point.

4. As the x value increases, if the slope of the tangent line changes from negative to zero to positive, the point at which the slope is zero is an absolute (or local) minimum point.

EXAMPLE 89

Using the slopes of tangent lines for the graph for Example 87, determine if the critical point $(2, -15)$ is a maximum or minimum point.

SOLUTION

Since $(2, -15)$ is the only critical point, let's select two x values, one less than 2 and one greater than 2. Using x values of 1 and 3, we note that $f'(1) = -8$ and $f'(3) = 8$. Since the slope of the tangent line changed from negative to positive, $(2, -15)$ is a minimum point.

EXAMPLE 90 $g'(x) = -3x^2 + 2x + 5$

Using the slopes of tangent lines for the graph for Example 88, determine if the critical points $\left(\dfrac{5}{3}, \dfrac{175}{27}\right)$ and $(-1, -3)$ are maximum or minimum points.

$(-2, -11)$ & $(0, 5)$ minimum

SOLUTION

We start with the point $\left(\dfrac{5}{3}, \dfrac{175}{27}\right)$. We select two x values, one less than $\dfrac{5}{3}$ and one greater than $\dfrac{5}{3}$. Using the values of 1 and 2, we note that $g'(1) = 4$ and $g'(2) = -3$. Since the slope of the tangent line changed from positive to negative, $\left(\dfrac{5}{3}, \dfrac{175}{27}\right)$ is a maximum point. Now for the point $(-1, -3)$, we can use x values of -2 and 0. We find that $g'(-2) = -11$ and $g'(0) = 5$. The slope of the tangent line changed from negative to positive, so $(-1, -3)$ is a minimum point.

As a quick review, the average rate of change is the slope of the line segment that connects endpoints $(a, f(a))$ and $(b, f(b))$ for a continuous function $f(x)$ on the closed interval $[a, b]$. Its value is $\dfrac{f(b) - f(a)}{b - a}$.

Concavity of a Function

We know that the first derivative measures the slope of a function. The second derivative measures the change in the slope, which is also known as the **concavity** of the function.

If $g''(x) > 0$ on an interval, then $g(x)$ is said to be **concave upward**.

If $g''(x) < 0$ on an interval, then $g(x)$ is said to be **concave downward**.

Graphically, Figures 4.29 through 4.32 show four different cases that highlight the appearance of a function when the first derivative is positive or negative, along with the second derivative being positive or negative.

In Figure 4.29, the function is increasing and is <mark>concave upward.</mark>

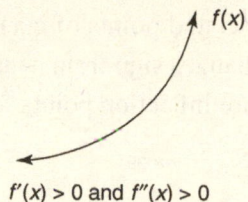

$f(x)$

$f'(x) > 0$ and $f''(x) > 0$

Figure 4.29

In Figure 4.30, the function is increasing and is <mark>concave downward.</mark>

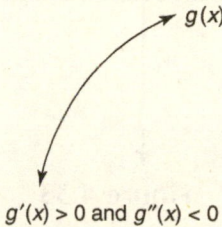

$g(x)$

$g'(x) > 0$ and $g''(x) < 0$

Figure 4.30

In Figure 4.31, the function is decreasing and is <mark>concave upward</mark>.

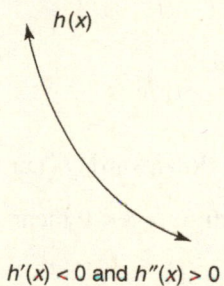

$h(x)$

$h'(x) < 0$ and $h''(x) > 0$

Figure 4.31

In Figure 4.32, the function is decreasing and is <mark>concave downward.</mark>

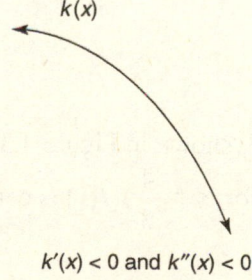

$k(x)$

$k'(x) < 0$ and $k''(x) < 0$

Figure 4.32

These four cases are not dependent on whether the function itself is positive or negative. For that reason, the coordinate axes were not drawn.

Points of Inflection

If $g''(x) = 0$ on an interval, the associated points of $g(x)$ are called **points of inflection.** These are points at which the first derivative changes sign from negative to positive or positive to negative. In Figure 4.33 each of points P and Q are inflection points for the graph of $g(x)$.

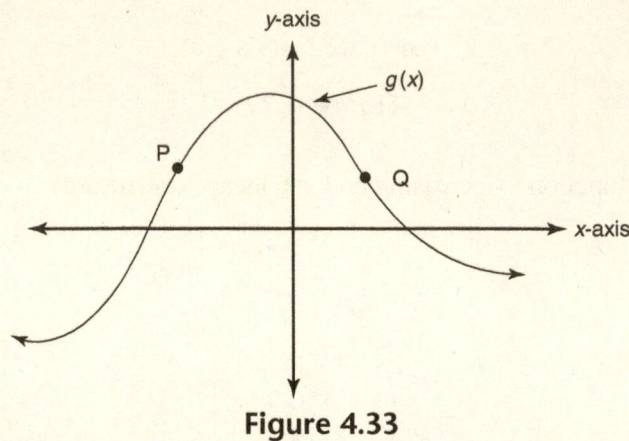

Figure 4.33

EXAMPLE 91

to find concave downward must set second derivative <0 and solve

Given the function $f(x) = x^3 - 4x^2 + 5$, on which interval(s) is $f(x)$ concave downward?

SOLUTION

In order for $f(x)$ to be concave downward, $f''(x)$ must be negative. Now $f'(x) = 3x^2 - 8x$ and $f''(x) = 6x - 8$. Then $6x - 8 < 0$ means that $x < \dfrac{4}{3}$. Thus, the desired interval is the open interval $\left(-\infty, \dfrac{4}{3}\right)$.

By determining $f\left(\dfrac{4}{3}\right) = \left(\dfrac{4}{3}\right)^3 - 4\left(\dfrac{4}{3}\right)^2 + 5 = \dfrac{7}{27}$, we find the actual point of inflection is $\left(\dfrac{4}{3}, \dfrac{7}{27}\right)$.

The graph of $f(x) = x^3 - 4x^2 + 5$, shown in Figure 4.34, will further clarify the concept of concavity. (Notice that for $x > \dfrac{4}{3}$, $f(x)$ is concave upward.)

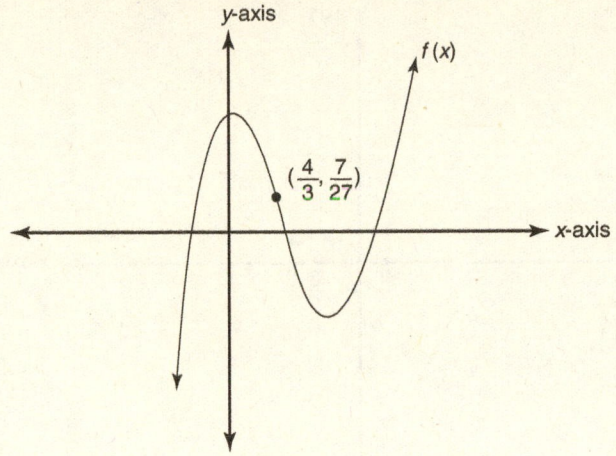

Figure 4.34

EXAMPLE 92

Given the function $g(x) = 2x^3 - 9x^2 + 12x - 3$, on which interval(s) is $g(x)$ both decreasing and concave upward?

SOLUTION

We are looking for values of x for which $g'(x) < 0$ and $g''(x) > 0$. We find that $g'(x) = 6x^2 - 18x + 12$ and $g''(x) = 12x - 18$. To solve $6x^2 - 18x + 12 < 0$, divide by 6 and factor the left side to yield $(x - 2)(x - 1) < 0$. The solution for this inequality is $1 < x < 2$. Now we solve $12x - 18 > 0$ to get $x > \dfrac{3}{2}$. The solution to the two inequalities $1 < x < 2$ and $x > \dfrac{3}{2}$ is the single inequality $\dfrac{3}{2} < x < 2$. Thus, the desired interval is the open interval $\left(\dfrac{3}{2}, 2\right)$.

The graph of $g(x) = 2x^3 - 9x^2 + 12x - 3$ is shown in Figure 4.35.

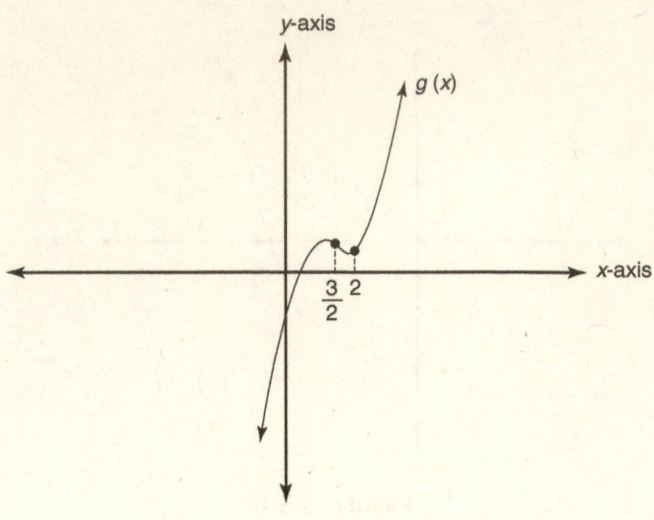

Figure 4.35

Earlier in this chapter, we learned that by solving $f'(x) = 0$, we could find the critical values of $f(x)$. To determine if a given critical value was a minimum or maximum, our best available method was to check $f'(x)$ near these critical values. The good news is that we can use the first and second derivatives to find out if a critical value represents a minimum or maximum point on the graph.

The Second Derivative Test

The **Second Derivative Test** for minimum and maximum values of a function is as follows. Suppose the domain of $f(x)$ is the closed interval $[a, b]$. Let $x = c$ represent a point on the open interval (a, b). These are the guidelines to follow:

If $f'(c) = 0$ and $f''(c) > 0$, then $f(c)$ represents a local minimum value.

If $f'(c) = 0$ and $f''(c) < 0$, then $f(c)$ represents a local maximum value.

If both $f'(c) = 0$ and $f''(c) = 0$, then no conclusion can be drawn.

EXAMPLE 93

If $f(x) = x^3 - 4x^2 + 5$, what are the x-coordinates of the maximum and/or minimum points?

SOLUTION

You have already seen this function in Example 92. We set $f'(x) = 3x^2 - 8x = 0$. Then $(x)(3x - 8) = 0$, so the critical points have x-coordinates of 0 and $\frac{8}{3}$. The next step is $f''(x) = 6x - 8$. Then $f''(0) = -8$, so $x = 0$ must represent a local maximum value.

Also, $f''\left(\dfrac{8}{3}\right) = 8$, so $x = \dfrac{8}{3}$ must be represent a local minimum value. (Figure 4.34 verifies these conclusions.)

EXAMPLE 94

If $g(x) = 2x^3 - 9x^2 + 12x - 3$, what are the x-coordinates of the maximum and/or minimum points?

SOLUTION

You are not imagining things! This function was presented in Example 93. We have already determined that $g'(x) = 6x^2 - 18x + 12$ and $g''(x) = 12x - 18$. To solve $6x^2 - 18x + 12 = 0$, we factor to get $(6)(x - 2)(x - 1) = 0$. Then $x = 2$ or $x = 1$. Now, $f''(2) = 6$, which means that $x = 2$ must represent a local minimum point. Similarly, $f''(1) = -6$, which means that $x = 1$ must represent a local maximum point. (Figure 4.35 verifies these conclusions.)

Applications

Linear Motion

Linear motion is motion in a straight line. Let $x(t)$ represent the position of a particle that moves along the x-axis at a given time t. The particle is moving from time $t = a$ to time $t = b$, which may be represented as the time interval $[a, b]$. The **displacement** is then given by $\Delta x = x(b) - x(a)$. For this same time interval, the **average velocity** is given by $\dfrac{\Delta x}{\Delta t} = \dfrac{x(b) - x(a)}{b - a}$. The **instantaneous velocity** is the limit of the average velocity. As such, the instantaneous velocity is given by $\lim_{\Delta t \to 0} \dfrac{\Delta x}{\Delta t} = \dfrac{dx}{dt}$. Furthermore, if we let $v(t)$ represent the velocity of this particle at any time t in the interval $[a, b]$, and let $\Delta v = v(b) - v(a)$ represent the corresponding change in velocity, the **average acceleration** is given by $\dfrac{\Delta v}{\Delta t} = \dfrac{v(b) - v(a)}{b - a}$. Then the **acceleration** at time t is given by $\lim_{b \to a} \dfrac{v(b) - v(a)}{b - a} = \lim_{\Delta t \to 0} \dfrac{\Delta v}{\Delta t} = \dfrac{dv}{dt}$.

The analogy between the concepts presented here and those for the derivatives should seem very logical. Let $v(t)$ represent the velocity of a particle at any time t and let $a(t)$ represent the acceleration of this particle at any time t. Then if $x(t)$ represents a function $f(x)$, then $v(t)$ would represent $f'(x)$ and $a(t)$ would represent $f''(x)$.

Suppose the position of a particle moving along the x-axis is $x(t) = \frac{1}{3}t^3 + 7t^2 - 3t$ for $3 \leq t \leq 9$, where t represents time. If necessary, use the graphing feature on your calculator in which y represents $x(t)$ and x represents t for Examples 95 to 98.

EXAMPLE 95

What is the average velocity over the time period from $t = 3$ to $t = 9$?

SOLUTION

Since $x(3) = 63$ and $x(9) = 783$, the average velocity is $\frac{783 - 63}{9 - 3} = 120$.

EXAMPLE 96

What is the instantaneous velocity at $t = 5$?

SOLUTION

The instantaneous velocity is $v(t) = \frac{dx}{dt} = t^2 + 14t - 3$, so $v(5) = 92$.

EXAMPLE 97

What is the average acceleration between $t = 2$ and $t = 6$?

SOLUTION

Since $v(2) = 29$ and $v(6) = 117$, the average acceleration is $\frac{117 - 29}{6 - 2} = 22$.

EXAMPLE 98

What is the acceleration at $t = 3$?

SOLUTION

The acceleration is given by $a(t) = \frac{dv}{dt} = 2t + 14$. Thus, $a(3) = 20$.

EXAMPLE 99

Let $s = t^3 - 6t^2$ be the position function of a particle, where t is in seconds and s is in feet. What are the particle's velocity and acceleration at 1 second?

SOLUTION

$$v(t) = \frac{ds}{dt} = 3t^2 - 12t \text{ and } a(t) = \frac{dv}{dt} = 6t - 12$$

At $t = 1$, $v(t) = -9$ ft/sec and $a(t) = -6$ ft/sec², which means the particle is moving in the opposite direction (negative velocity, with "opposite" not necessarily down—it could be a car backing up) but speeding up since the signs of the velocity and acceleration are the same. Indeed, we see in the next second ($t = 2$), the velocity is −12 ft/sec.

Optimization *given so much fence & Barn wall find max area*

Optimization focuses on maximizing or minimizing a particular quantity, so we will use the first derivative of an appropriate function. In doing this type of problem, sometimes a diagram is needed as an aid.

EXAMPLE 100

Consider the triangular region bounded by the positive x-axis, the positive y-axis and the line whose equation is $y = 5 - 2x$. A rectangle will be placed inside this region so that one vertex lies at the origin and its opposite vertex lies on the line. What is the largest possible area for this rectangle?

SOLUTION

Below is a diagram, which is absolutely imperative to the solution.

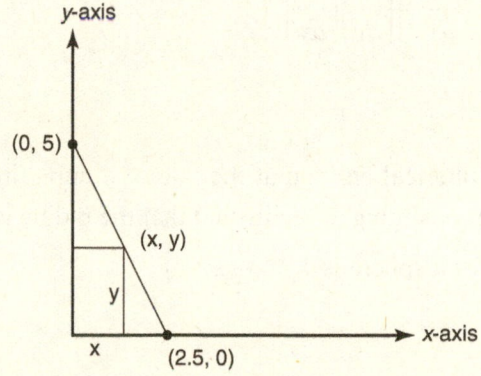

Using x as the width, y as the height, and A as the area, the formula to use is $A = xy$. Since $y = 5 - 2x$, we can write the area formula as $A = x(5 - 2x) = 5x - 2x^2$.

The maximum value of A can be found by using the equation $\frac{dA}{dx} = 0$. So, $5 - 4x = 0$,

which leads to $x = \frac{5}{4}$. Then $y = 5 - (2)\left(\frac{5}{4}\right) = \frac{5}{2}$. Thus, the required area is

$\left(\frac{5}{4}\right)\left(\frac{5}{2}\right) = \frac{25}{8}$.

EXAMPLE 101

In the ABC company, the cost (C) to manufacture x file cabinets each day is given by the equation $C = x^3 - 33x^2 + 336x + 100$. How many file cabinets per day should the ABC company manufacture in order to minimize its cost?

SOLUTION

We need to find the first derivative $\dfrac{dC}{dx}$, which is $3x^2 - 66x + 336$. We can solve $3x^2 - 66x + 336 = 0$ by dividing each side by 3 and factoring. The equation becomes $(x - 14)(x - 8) = 0$. Then $x = 14$ and 8, but we need to check if these answers represent maximum or minimum values. Using the second derivative method to identify critical points, we look at $\dfrac{d^2C}{dx^2} = 6x - 66$. When $x = 14, \dfrac{d^2C}{dx^2} = 18$. Since $\dfrac{d^2C}{dx^2} > 0$, the value of 14 represents a minimum cost. However, when $x = 8, \dfrac{d^2C}{dx^2} = -18$. Since $\dfrac{d^2C}{dx^2} < 0$, the value of 8 would represent a maximum cost. Thus, the only answer is $x = 14$.

Related Rates

Related rates utilize the Chain Rule as applied to three different variables. As a general example, if z is related to y and y is related to x, then z is related to x by the following, using first derivatives:

$$\frac{dz}{dx} = \left(\frac{dz}{dy}\right)\left(\frac{dy}{dx}\right).$$

EXAMPLE 102

Air is blown into a spherical balloon at the rate of 4 cubic inches per minute. At what rate is the radius changing at the instant that the radius is 3 inches? (The formula for the volume of a sphere is $V = \dfrac{4}{3}\pi r^3$.)

SOLUTION

The Chain Rule allows us to use $\dfrac{dV}{dt} = \left(\dfrac{dV}{dr}\right)\left(\dfrac{dr}{dt}\right)$. Now $\dfrac{dV}{dr} = 4\pi r^2$. So, when $r = 3, \dfrac{dV}{dr} = 4\pi(3)^2 = 36\pi$. Since $\dfrac{dV}{dt} = 4$, we have $4 = (36\pi)\left[\dfrac{dr}{dt}\right]$. Thus, $\dfrac{dr}{dt} = \dfrac{4}{36\pi} = \dfrac{1}{9\pi}$ inches per minute.

Mean Value Theorem

Closely related to the average rate of change is the **Mean Value Theorem**. For a continuous function $f(x)$ on a closed interval $[a,b]$, this theorem states that there is at least one value c, where $a < c < b$, such that $f'(c) = \dfrac{f(b) - f(a)}{b - a}$. This means that there is at least one point in the open interval (a, b) for which the instantaneous rate of change (slope of the tangent line) equals the average rate of change of $f(x)$ over $[a, b]$. Figure 4.36 illustrates the Mean Value Theorem.

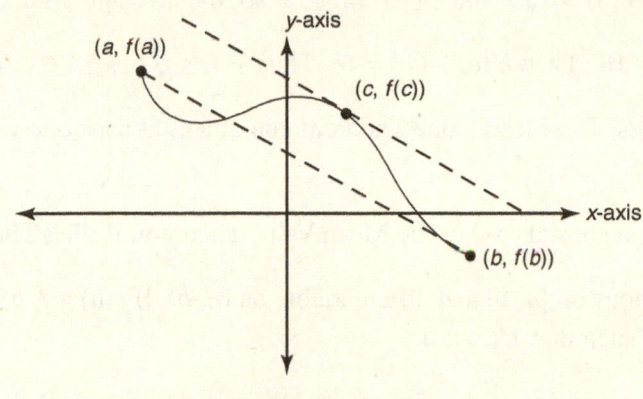

Figure 4.36

EXAMPLE 103

Determine a value of c in the open interval $(1, 6)$ for which $g'(c)$ equals the average rate of change for $g(x) = -x^3 + 4$ over the closed interval $[1, 6]$.

SOLUTION

The average rate of change is $\dfrac{g(6) - g(1)}{6 - 1} = -43$. Since $g'(x) = -3x^2$, $g'(c) = -3c^2 = -43$. Thus, $c = \pm\sqrt{\dfrac{43}{3}} \approx \pm 3.79$, but the only answer in $(1, 6)$ is $+3.79$.

EXAMPLE 104

Determine a value of c in the open interval $(2, 2.1)$ for which $f'(c)$ equals the average rate of change for $f(x) = 2x^2 + 5$ over the closed interval $[2, 2.1]$.

SOLUTION

We found the average rate of change is $\dfrac{f(2.1) - f(2)}{2.1 - 2} = 8.2$. Since $f'(x) = 4x$, we can write $f'(c) = 4c = 8.2$. Thus, $c = 2.05$.

EXAMPLE 105

Given $h(x) = 2x^3 + 1$ over the closed interval $[-3, 3]$, find a value of c in the open interval $(-3, 3)$ such that the slope of the tangent line at c equals the average rate of change of $h(x)$ over $[-3, 3]$.

SOLUTION

We calculate $h(3) = 55$ and $h(-3) = -53$ so the average rate of change is $\frac{55 - (-53)}{3 - (-3)} = 18$. Then $h'(c) = 6c^2 = 18$. Thus $c = \pm\sqrt{3} \approx \pm 1.73$. This example has two c values. The Mean Value Theorem guarantees at least one value of c.

Rolle's Theorem is a special case of the Mean Value Theorem. Rolle's Theorem states:

Let $f(x)$ be continuous on $[a, b]$ and differentiable on (a, b). If $f(a) = f(b)$, then there is at least one number c in (a, b) such that $f'(c) = 0$.

What this theorem is saying is that for any continuous function $f(x)$ that crossed the x-axis, there is at least one place where the tangent line to the curve is horizontal (Figure 4.37).

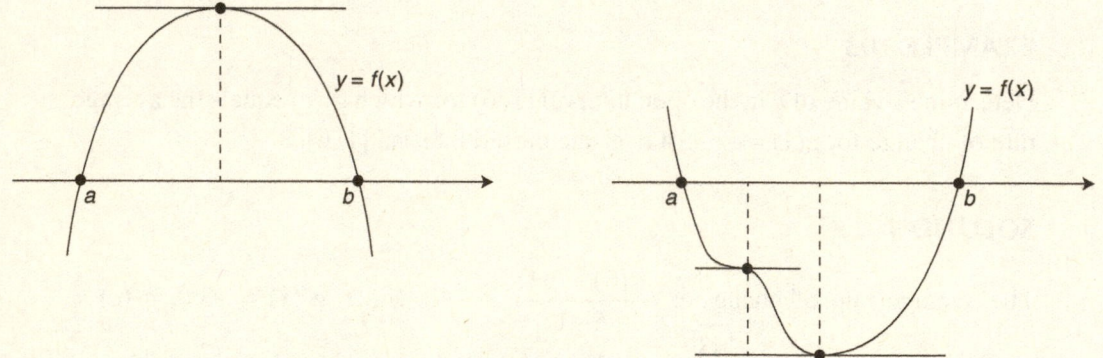

Figure 4.37

Antiderivatives: Integrals

Consider the following three statements:

1.   If $f(x) = 3x^2$, then $f'(x) = 6x$.

2.   If $g(x) = 3x^2 - 10$, then $g'(x) = 6x$

3.   If $h(x) = 3x^2 + 4$, then $h'(x) = 6x$.

Each of the given functions differs only by a constant and their derivatives are identical. Let $k(x) = 6x$. Then each of $f(x)$, $g(x)$, and $h(x)$ is called an **antiderivative** of $k(x)$. Thus, a general function $F(x)$ is an antiderivative of $f(x)$ if $\dfrac{dF}{dx} = f(x)$. As hinted in the three numbered statements above, all antiderivatives of any function can differ only by a constant. Another word for antiderivative is **integral**.

As the name implies, determining an antiderivative is the reverse process of finding a derivative. The symbol for finding an antiderivative is the integral symbol $\int$ with the symbol dx following the function. Thus, using statements 1, 2, and 3 above, we could write $\int 6x\,dx = 3x^2 + C$, where C is a constant.

the most popular rules for finding the antiderivatives of specific types of rational and trigonometric functions follows. For each rule, C and K are constants.

Rational Functions

Rule 1: $\displaystyle\int k\,dx = kx + C$

Rule 2: $\displaystyle\int kx^n\,dx = \frac{k}{n+1}x^{n+1} + C$, provided that $n \neq -1$.

Rule 3: $\displaystyle\int kx^{-1}\,dx = k\ln x + C$

Rule 4: $\displaystyle\int ke^x\,dx = ke^x + C$

Rule 5: $\displaystyle\int ka^x\,dx = \frac{ka^x}{\ln a} + C$

Rule 6: $\displaystyle\int [f(x) \pm g(x)]\,dx = \int f(x)\,dx \pm \int g(x)\,dx + C$

EXAMPLE 106

$\displaystyle\int (5x + 3x^2)\,dx$ is equivalent to which function?   *add 1 to power & divide by new power*

SOLUTION

Writing $5x$ as $5x^1$ and using antiderivative rules 2 and 6, the answer is $\dfrac{5}{2}x^2 + x^3$ + C. Note that "C" is needed only once.

EXAMPLE 107

$\displaystyle\int \left[9 - \frac{7}{x}\right]dx$ is equivalent to which function?

SOLUTION

Writing $\dfrac{7}{x}$ as $7x^{-1}$ and using rules 1, 3, and 6, the answer is $9x - 7\ln x + C$.

EXAMPLE 108

$\int \left[8^x + \dfrac{3}{4} x^4 \right] dx$ is equivalent to which function?

SOLUTION

Using rules 2, 5, and 6, the answer is $\dfrac{8^x}{\ln 8} + \dfrac{3}{20} x^5 + C$. If you are a little confused about the number $\dfrac{3}{20}$, it was obtained by dividing $\dfrac{3}{4}$ by 5, which becomes $\left(\dfrac{3}{4} \right) \left(\dfrac{1}{5} \right)$.

Trigonometric Functions

Since we learned the derivatives of the six trigonometric formulas, it would be worthwhile to recognize the following antiderivatives:

Rule 7: $\quad \int (k \sin x) dx = -k \cos x + C$

Rule 8: $\quad \int (k \cos x) dx = k \sin x + C$

Rule 9: $\quad \int (k \tan x) dx = -k \ln(\cos x) + C$

Rule 10: $\quad \int (k \cot x) dx = k \ln(\sin x) + C$

There are other antiderivative formulas, both for algebraic functions and trigonometric functions, but they are beyond the scope of this book.

EXAMPLE 109

$\int \dfrac{1}{2} \cos x \, dx$ is equivalent to which function?

SOLUTION

By using antiderivative rule 8, the answer is $\dfrac{1}{2} \sin x + C$.

EXAMPLE 110

$\int (4 \cot x + \tan x) dx$ is equivalent to which function?

SOLUTION

By using antiderivative rules 6, 9, and 10, the answer is $4 \ln(\sin x) - \ln(\cos x) + C$.

Fundamental Theorem of Calculus

One part of the **Fundamental Theorem of Calculus** states that if $F(x)$ is any antiderivative of $f(x)$, where $f(x)$ is continuous on the closed interval $[a, b]$, then $\displaystyle\int_a^b f(x)dx = F(b) - F(a)$.

Definite Integrals

To use the Fundamental Theorem of Calculus, it is essential that we can find the antiderivative of the function f(x), designated as F(x), and that the curve of the function be continuous between the two points of interest. These two points are the limits of the integral, which is called a **definite integral**. The notation used is commonly to denote the limits of the integral $[a, b]$ as

$$\int_a^b f(x)\,dx = \left[\int_a^b f(x)\,dx \right]_a^b = \left[F(x) \right]_a^b = F(a) - F(b)$$

Note that the constant, C, which was part of indefinite integrals, is not present in definite integrals because it cancels out in the subtraction.

Definite Integrals as Accumulations

The area under a curve can be thought of as an **accumulation** of rectangles of varying heights between two values, each with a width dx, as shown in Figure 4.38. As that width gets smaller and smaller (approaches 0), the sum of the areas of the rectangles gets closer and closer to the area under the curve as a limit. This concept of accumulation is a basic tool in calculus. It comes into play when we consider integrals in finding areas under the curve, as well as when we use integrals to find the volume of a solid.

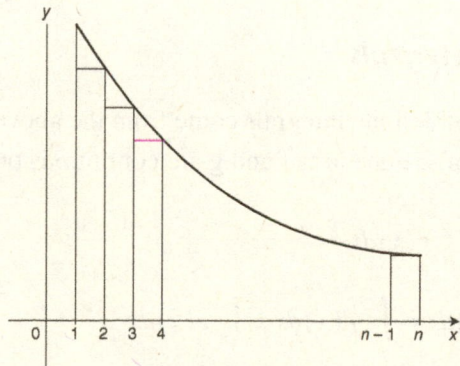

Figure 4.38

$-\frac{1}{3}x^3+4x$

EXAMPLE 111

Integrate $f(x) = -x^2 + 4$ from $x = -2$ to $x = 2$.

plug in

SOLUTION

$$\int_{-2}^{2}(-x^2+4)\,dx = \left(-\frac{1}{3}x^3+4x\right)\Big|_{-2}^{2}\left[-\frac{8}{3}+8\right]-\left[-\frac{8}{3}-8\right]=\frac{32}{3}=10\frac{2}{3}$$

EXAMPLE 112

What is the value of $\int_{0}^{4}(x^2+3)\,dx$?

SOLUTION

Below is the associated diagram:

x value

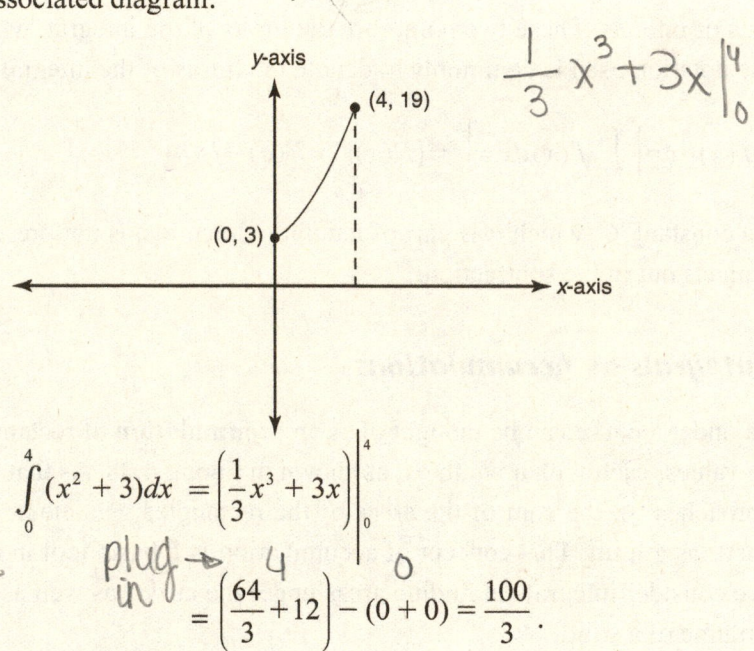

$$\frac{1}{3}x^3+3x\Big|_{0}^{4}$$

$$\int_{0}^{4}(x^2+3)\,dx = \left(\frac{1}{3}x^3+3x\right)\Big|_{0}^{4}$$

plug in bigger number first

plug in   4   0

$$= \left(\frac{64}{3}+12\right)-(0+0) = \frac{100}{3}.$$

Properties of Definite Integrals

The following properties of definite integrals come from the above equation and corresponding properties for indefinite integrals. Functions f and g are continuous on [a, b] and c is a constant.

1. $\int_{a}^{b}cf(x)\,dx = c\int_{a}^{b}f(x)\,dx$

2. $\int_{a}^{b}[f(x)\pm g(x)]\,dx = \int_{a}^{b}f(x)\,dx \pm \int_{a}^{b}g(x)\,dx$

3. $\int_{a}^{a}f(x)\,dx = 0$

4. $\int_a^b f(x)\,dx = -\int_b^a f(x)\,dx$

5. $\int_a^c f(x)\,dx = \int_a^b f(x)\,dx + \int_a^c f(x)\,dx$ (the points can be in any order)

The Definite Integral as the Area under a Curve

If $f(x)$ is continuous on $[a, b]$, then the definite integral gives the area between the curve $f(x)$ and the x-axis between a and b. In Example 112, the area bounded by $f(x) = x^2 + 3$, the x-axis, the y-axis, and $x = 4$ is thus $\dfrac{100}{3}$.

EXAMPLE 113

What is the area of the region bounded by the function $f(x) = \dfrac{5}{x}$, the x-axis, the line $x = 1$, and the line $x = 6$?

[handwritten: integral of $5\ln x$ $\frac{5}{x}$]

SOLUTION

Below is the associated diagram, with the region shaded:

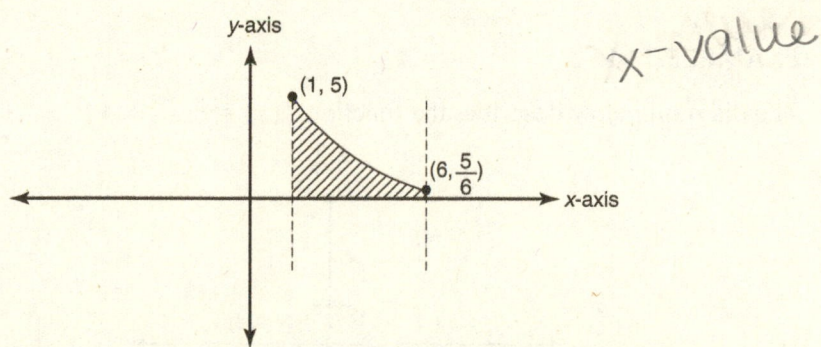

[handwritten: x-value]

We see that $f(x) > 0$ for the interval $[1, 6]$. So, we are looking for the value of $\int_1^6 \dfrac{5}{x}\,dx$, which becomes $(5)(\ln x) = (5)(\ln 6) - 5(\ln 1) \approx 8.96$.

Positive and Negative Areas

The value of the ==definite integral is positive if the curve is above the x-axis== (for positive values of $f(x)$, or y), and the ==value of the definite integral is negative if the curve is below the x-axis== (for negative values of $f(x)$, or y). The absolute (total) area, however, is not the value of the definite integral because it is the sum of the absolute values of the area(s) above the x-axis and the area(s) below the x-axis. In this case, we must find the value at which the function $f(x) = 0$, which determines the

x value at which $f(x)$ changes sign. Then add the absolute values of the definite integrals for each part of the curve as shown in Figure 4.39, for which the total area is

$$A = \left| \int_a^b f(x)\,dx \right| + \left| \int_b^c f(x)\,dx \right|$$

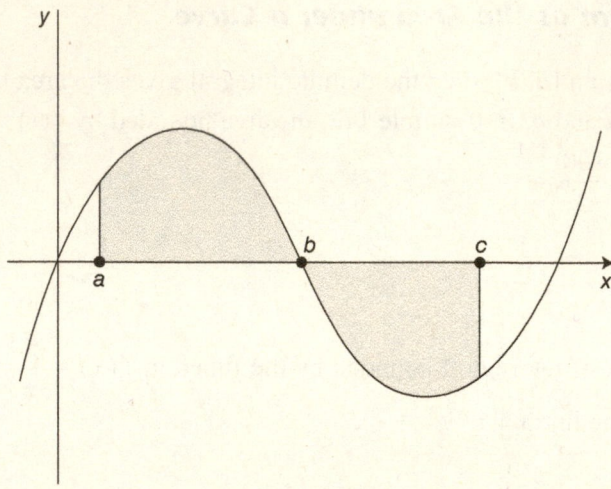

Figure 4.39

EXAMPLE 114

The diagram below describes the function $f(x) = -x^2 + 4$.

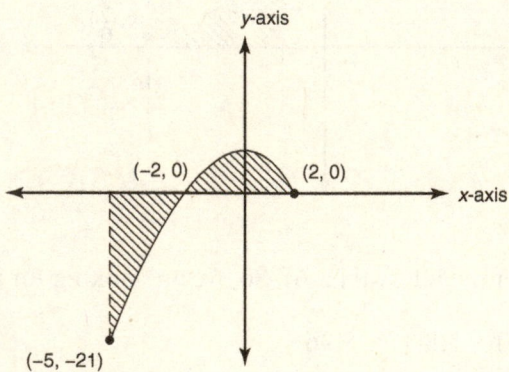

What is the combined area of the shaded regions?

SOLUTION

Set the function equal to 0. Then the critical values of $-x^2 + 4 = 0$ are $x \pm 2$. The region bounded by the function, the x-axis, $x = -2$, and the line $x = -5$ lies below the x-axis, so its area is

[handwritten note:] 1) Set function equal to zero to find region bounded

below x-axis

$$-\int_{-5}^{-2}(-x^2+4)dx = -\left(-\frac{1}{3}x^3+4x\right)\Bigg|_{-5}^{-2} = -\left[\left(\frac{8}{3}-8\right)-\left(\frac{125}{3}-20\right)\right]=27.$$

The area of the region bounded by the function and the x-axis that lies between $x=-2$ and $x=2$ was found in Example 112 to be $10\frac{2}{3}$. Thus, the final answer is the sum of the areas, or $37\frac{2}{3}$. $\rightarrow 27+10\frac{2}{3}$

If the problem had simply asked for the value of the definite integral $\int_{-5}^{2}(-x^2+4)dx$, our answer would have been quite different. The computation would appear as

$$\left[-\frac{1}{3}x^3+4x\right]\Bigg|_{-5}^{2} = \left[-\frac{8}{3}+8\right]-\left[\frac{125}{3}-20\right]=-16\frac{1}{3}.$$

EXAMPLE 115

What is the area of $\int_{\pi/2}^{2\pi}\sin x\,dx$?

SOLUTION

The associated diagram is shown below:

COS = y value
SIN = x value

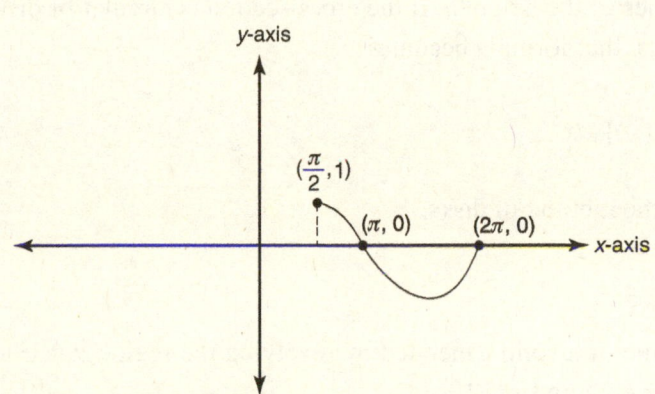

$$\text{Area} = \left|\int_{\pi/2}^{\pi}f(x)\sin x\,dx\right| + \left|\int_{\pi}^{2\pi}f(x)\sin x\,dx\right|$$

$$= \left|\left(\cos\pi-\cos\frac{\pi}{2}\right)\right| + |(\cos 2\pi-\cos\pi)|$$

$$= |-1-0|+|1-(-1)|=1+2=3$$

Note that this is different from the "value" of $\int_{\pi/2}^{\pi}$, which is

$$\int_{\pi/2}^{2\pi} \sin x\, dx = -\cos x \Big|_{\frac{\pi}{2}}^{2\pi}$$

$$= -\cos(2\pi) - (-\cos\frac{\pi}{2}) = -1.$$

The Definite Integral as Volume

Similar to how we defined area as the *accumulation* of rectangles of infinitesimal width, we can think of a geometric solid as a rotation of curves with thickness around an axis of rotation. Here we will consider only solids that are symmetric around some axis of rotation, so we will call them surfaces of revolution. Think of the rotation of curves as "disks" of the solid. As the thickness of the disks tends to 0 as a limit, the figure becomes a geometric solid. This leads to the concept of integration to determine the volume of a solid.

We know that the volume of a solid that is symmetric about the x-axis of rotation is given by $V = Ah$, where V is the volume, A is the cross-sectional area of the surface perpendicular to the x-axis, and h is the height. (Thus, the area of a circular cylinder is $V = \pi r^2 h$.) So the integration that will yield volume is essentially

$$V = \int_{x=a}^{x=b} A\, dx$$

where the limits of integration, $x = a$ and $x = b$, where the planes at the ends of the solid cross the x-axis are the end values of the height h. If the cross-section is circular or disk-shaped rotated perpendicular to the x-axis, that formula becomes

$$V = \int_{x=a}^{x=b} \pi\, [f(x)]^2\, dx$$

This is known as the method of disks.

EXAMPLE 116

Find the volume of a solid generated by revolving the region $y = x^2$ around the x-axis between $x = -1$ and $x = 2$.

SOLUTION

The graph for this region is shown below.

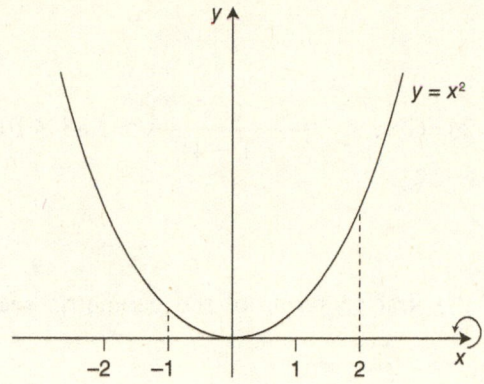

Then the volume is found by

$$V = \int_{-1}^{2} \pi [x^2]^2 \, dx$$

$$= \pi \int_{-1}^{2} x^4 \, dx$$

$$= \pi \left[\frac{1}{5} x^5 \right]_{-1}^{2}$$

$$= \pi \left(\frac{32}{5} - \frac{-1}{5} \right) = \frac{33}{5} \pi$$

Since we have already shown that integration represents area under a curve, it is easy to see that volume could also be a double integral, an integral of the integral representing area, given the equation of the curve, or $\int \int f(x) \, dx \, dh$. Double integration is beyond the scope of this book, however.

Geometric Series

A **geometric series** is a list of numbers that represents the partial sums of a geometric sequence. If $a_1, a_2, a_3, \ldots, a_n$ represents a finite geometric sequence, let $s_1 = a_1$, $s_2 = a_1 + a_2$, $s_3 = a_1 + a_2 + a_3$. This pattern continues up through $s_n = a_1 + a_2 + a_3 + \ldots + a_n$. Then each of $s_1, s_2, s_3, \ldots, s_n$ is a finite geometric series.

The formula for finding the nth term of a geometric series is given by $s_n = \dfrac{a_1 - (a_1)(r^n)}{1 - r}$ *with* ~~finite~~

$r \neq 1$. (If $r = 1$, then $s_n = (n)(a_1)$ because all terms of the corresponding sequence are the same.)

(handwritten notes:)
$a_1 = 1^{st}$ term
$r =$ common ratio
$n = \#$ of terms

EXAMPLE 117

What is the sum of the first 24 terms of the geometric sequence 2, 8, 32, 128,....? (Leave your answer in scientific notation.)

SOLUTION

$a_1 = 2$, $r = 4$, and $n = 24$. Then $s_{24} = \dfrac{2 - (2)(4^{24})}{1 - 4} \approx 1.88 \times 10^{14}$.

EXAMPLE 118

What is the sum of the first 15 terms of the geometric sequence 90, −30, 10, $-\dfrac{10}{3}$, ...?

SOLUTION

$a_1 = 90$, $r = -\dfrac{1}{3}$, and $n = 15$.

Then $s_{15} = \dfrac{90 - (90)\left(-\dfrac{1}{3}\right)^{15}}{1 - \left(-\dfrac{1}{3}\right)} \approx 67.5$.

Consider the following infinite geometric sequence: 3, 6, 12, 24, ... The value of $r = 2$ and each term of the sequence increases in size. There would be no numerical value for the sum of this sequence. Thus, there is no value for s_∞.

However, if $|r| < 1$ for a geometric sequence, then the infinite geometric series has a numerical value, given by the formula $s_\infty = \dfrac{a_1}{1 - r}$. infinite

EXAMPLE 119

What is the sum of all the terms of the infinite sequence 60, 15, $\dfrac{15}{4}$, $\dfrac{15}{16}$, ...?

SOLUTION

$a_1 = 60$ and $r = \dfrac{1}{4}$. Then $s_\infty = \dfrac{60}{1 - \dfrac{1}{4}} = 80$.

EXAMPLE 120

The sum of all the terms of an infinite geometric sequence is $-\dfrac{4}{9}$. If the common ratio is $-\dfrac{1}{2}$, what is the value of the first term?

SOLUTION

$$s_{\infty} = -\frac{4}{9} \text{ and } r = -\frac{1}{2}.$$

Then $-\dfrac{4}{9} = \dfrac{a_1}{1-\left(-\dfrac{1}{2}\right)} = \dfrac{a_1}{\dfrac{3}{2}}.$

Thus, $a_1 = \left(-\dfrac{4}{9}\right)\left(\dfrac{3}{2}\right) = -\dfrac{2}{3}.$

An infinite arithmetic series cannot have a sum, regardless of the values of a_1 or d.

Data Analysis, Statistics, and Probability

DATA ANALYSIS

Sampling and Experimentation

Data are just information, and they don't have to be numerical. Yes/no answers or eye color are data.

There are two types of variables:

1. **Categorical:** Examples of categorical variables (also called nominal variables) are "yes/no"; "freshman/sophomore/junior/senior"; basically qualifiers that don't overlap. Categorical data can be numerical, where the number is an identifier rather than a value, such as invoice numbers, or opinions on a scale of 1 to 5, where, for example, 1 means "totally agree" and 5 means "totally disagree."

2. **Quantitative:** These are counting numbers.

A combination of these two can occur.

Overview of Methods of Data Collection

There are four methods of data collection with which you should be familiar: census, sample survey, experiment, and observational study.

A **census** is a study that observes, or attempts to observe, every individual in a population. The **population** is the collection of all individuals under consideration in the study.

A **sample survey** is a study that collects information from a sample of a population in order to determine one or more characteristics of the population. A **sample** is a selected subset of a population from which data are gathered.

An **experiment** is a study where the researcher deliberately influences individuals by imposing conditions and determining the individuals' responses to those conditions.

An **observational study** attempts to determine relationships between variables, but the researcher imposes no conditions such as those in an experiment. Surveys are a form of observational study.

EXAMPLE 1

The principal of a new school wants to know what mascot the incoming students would prefer. He summons each student into his office and asks what the new mascot should be. What type of data and what type of study is this?

SOLUTION

This is a census of categorial data. The principal has collected data on mascot choice from every individual in the population, in this case, the population of all school students.

EXAMPLE 2

The principal of the new school is also interested in what type of dress code the school should have. He telephones the parents of every tenth student summoned to his office and asks their opinions about school dress codes. What type of data and what type of study is this?

SOLUTION

This is a sample survey of categorial data. The principal has collected data on type of dress code from only a subset of the population, in this case, the population of all school parents.

EXAMPLE 3

A pharmaceutical company wishes to test a new medication it thinks will reduce cholesterol. A group of 20 volunteers is formed and each has his or her cholesterol level measured. Half are randomly assigned to take the new drug and the other half are given a placebo, a pill with no active ingredients. After 6 months the volunteers' cholesterol is measured again and any change from the beginning of the study is recorded. What type of data and what type of study is this?

SOLUTION

This is an experiment with quantitative data (cholesterol levels). The company is imposing conditions (new drug, placebo) on the participants in the study to determine their response (change in cholesterol) to the conditions.

EXAMPLE 4

A health studies research lab is interested in the effect of certain vegetables on cholesterol level. A group of 20 volunteers is formed and each keeps a diary of his or her food consumption for the next 6 months, after which time the diaries are collected and the cholesterol level is measured. The researchers then examine the relationship between the rate of consumption of certain vegetables and cholesterol level. What type of data and what type of study is this?

SOLUTION

This is an observational study with a combination of categorical data (types of vegetable) and quantitative data (cholesterol levels). The researchers are imposing no conditions on the participants in the study.

If we want information about a particular population, we could check every unit (or person) in the population, but this is often cumbersome, effort-intensive, and costly in time and money. (The U.S. Census is an example of polling (or surveying) every unit in a population.) It is better to take a *representative, unbiased* **sample** from the population, get information from it, and assume the whole population would have yielded the same information. **Statistics** is the information we get from a sample; **the population parameter** is what we assume for the whole population, based on our statistics.

Planning and Conducting Surveys

So the purpose of a sample survey is to determine one or more characteristics about a population of interest from the results of the sample. The characteristic of the population is a **population parameter**. The result of the sample survey used to estimate the parameter is a **sample statistic**. There are many methods to obtain a sample from a population.

The most important thing about sampling is that it has to be random and unbiased.

Types of Sampling Methods

Important considerations in sampling: Avoid biases (even inadvertent), unclear question phrasing, ambiguous answers. It's a good idea to have a pilot test of a survey before the sample is chosen, so that any problems can be fixed.

Non-Random Sampling

A **voluntary response sample** is composed of individuals who choose to respond to a survey because of interest in the subject, particularly those with strong opinions or attraction. Voluntary response samples are almost always biased and therefore useless. Examples are surveys of customer satisfaction given at the end of a telephone call made by a consumer to a customer service department. These people are not representative of all shoppers (usually they are only the unhappy ones).

A **convenience** sample is composed of individuals who are easily accessed or contacted. Convenience sampling (such as stopping people as they exit Target) also may not be representative of the entire population. (If the survey is taken in the middle of the day, students and the working population are usually not included; if the survey is taken too late at night, however, the older population may not be included.)

A **convenience sample** is composed of individuals who are easily accessed or contacted.

EXAMPLE 5

A journalism class prints a survey in the school newspaper. Readers are asked to clip the survey from the paper, complete it, and return it to a drop box in the school cafeteria. What type of sample is this?

SOLUTION

This is a voluntary response sample. It is likely that only students interested in the survey's subject matter will take the time to respond.

EXAMPLE 6

A journalism class stations pollsters in front of the stadium during a football game. They ask each student who enters the stadium his or her opinion of the quality of the school's athletics program. What type of sample is this?

SOLUTION

This is a convenience sample. The site was likely chosen because of the ease of gathering data there.

The advantage of convenience samples and voluntary response samples is that gathering data is easy. Respondents are either close at hand, in the case of a convenience sample, or a portion of the initiative in data collection is up to the respondent, in the case of a voluntary response sample. Both of these can be poor designs, as they are subject to bias.

Categorical data samples are counts or percentages of individuals in categories. Categorical data are more descriptive (narrative) than quantitative data, but quantitative data give much more information about a population (and involve a lot more math).

Random Sampling

A **random sample (or probability sample)** is composed of individuals selected by chance. There are several types of random samples.

A **simple random sample (SRS)** is a sample in which *n* individuals are selected from a population in a way that every possible combination of *n* individuals is equally likely. In general, we may think of an SRS as having all the names of all individuals of the population in a hat and selecting *n* names, without replacement, from the hat.

> Not only is it required of a simple random sample that each *individual* has an equally likely chance of being chosen, but also each possible group must be equally likely. That is, if an SRS is to have a size of *n* = 5, no possible group of five individuals can be any more or less likely to be selected than any other group.

A **stratified random sample** is a sample in which sample proportion of subgroups (called **strata**) are chosen to be close to the population proportions. For example, if a population is 30% female and 70% male, we would want to have a sample that is close to this proportion. However, when the sample is taken from within the females and the males (each used as a kind of subpopulation), we still have to choose randomly from within that group to avoid bias.

The advantage of stratified random sampling is that it reduces sampling variability if there are differences between the strata in how they respond. It takes away the chance that one may get a disproportionate number of individuals from a stratum in the sample than exist in the population.

> In a stratified random sample, every individual in each subgroup has an equally likely chance of being chosen, but not every individual in the whole population. Additionally, each possible group of individuals from the population will not have the same chance of being chosen.

A **cluster sample** is a sample in which a simple random sample of heterogeneous subgroups of the population is selected. The subgroups are known as **clusters**. The selected clusters may also themselves be subject to random sampling, or a census done for each.

Although cluster sampling takes "chunks" of a population, it differs from stratified random sampling. Instead, the chunks are taken to avoid bias. An example is taking a sample of a mixture of something to test its pH. If the samples are taken only from the top of the vials, the mixture may not reflect the mixture, so we take some from the top, some from the middle, and some from the bottom. But within each cluster, we must be random regarding which vials are chosen.

A **multistage sample** is a sample resulting from multiple applications of cluster and/or stratified, and/or simple random sampling.

A **systematic random sample** is a sample where every kth individual is selected from a list or queue. The first selection is randomly chosen from the first k individuals.

EXAMPLE 7

A media research firm is conducting a poll on an upcoming election for city council. The firm obtains a list of all 15,000 registered voters in the council ward under consideration. The voters' ID numbers are entered into a computer, and 500 are chosen at random, without replacement, to constitute the sample. What type of sampling design is this?

SOLUTION

This is a simple random sample. Individuals are chosen at random, without replacement, from a list of the entire population. This is a "select n from a hat"-type of sampling.

Note: In this scenario, every possible group of 500 individuals has an equally likely chance of being selected, as does every individual.

EXAMPLE 8

A media research firm is conducting a poll on an upcoming election for city council. The firm obtains a list of all 15,000 registered voters in the council ward under consideration. The voters' ID numbers and party affiliations (Democrat, Republican, Independent) are entered into a computer. The firm randomly selects, without replacement, 200 Democrats, 200 Republicans, and 100 Independents to comprise the sample. What type of sampling design is this?

SOLUTION

This is a stratified random sample. Individuals were first placed in strata—in this case, party affiliation. Then, simple random samples from each stratum were selected to make up the final sample.

In this scenario, all individuals within their respective strata have an equally likely chance of being chosen, but not all individuals in the population. For example, if there are more Democrats than Republicans, it is more likely that a particular Republican voter will be in the sample than a particular Democrat voter. Additionally, every possible group of 500 individuals from the population does not have an equally likely chance of being chosen, since samples of 500 Democrats, or 250 Democrats and 250 Republicans, for example, are not possible.

EXAMPLE 9

A media research firm is conducting a poll on an upcoming election for city council. The firm obtains a list of all 15,000 registered voters in the council ward under consideration. The voters' ID numbers and voting precinct numbers (01–75) are entered into a computer. The firm first randomly selects 20 of the voting precincts. Then, from each of the chosen precincts, 25 voters are chosen with simple random samples. What type of sampling design is this?

SOLUTION

This is a cluster sample. Individuals were first grouped into clusters by voting precinct, of which several were selected. Then, simple random samples from each cluster were selected to make up the final sample.

Note: An additional step could have been added to this scenario. If voters in the selected precincts were then grouped by party affiliation, and an SRS was taken from each group, the result would have been a multistage sample.

EXAMPLE 10

A media research firm is conducting a poll on an upcoming election for city council. The firm obtains a list of all 15,000 registered voters in the council ward under consideration. The list is sorted by voter ID number. The firm randomly selects one person from the first 100 on the list; then it selects every 100th person after that. The sample size is 150. What type of sampling design is this?

SOLUTION

This is a systematic random sample. One of the first k individuals on the list is randomly selected—in this case $k = 100$—and every kth individual on the list is selected after that.

Note that even though each individual has an equally likely chance of being selected in the systematic random sample, it is *not* equivalent to a simple random sample.

Bias and Sampling Error

Bias is the term for purposeful deviation from the truth to influence the results of a study so it is not characteristic of the population (parameter) one wishes to estimate from the sample (statistic). A sampling method is biased if it tends to produce samples that do not represent the population. There are several terms used to describe bias.

Voluntary response bias is present in voluntary response samples. It occurs because people with strong opinions or interest in the survey topics tend to respond more frequently. Voluntary response bias is a form of undercoverage.

Another type of bias, **undercoverage**, occurs when some individuals of a population are somehow excluded from the sampling process. Random sampling, when done properly, tends to reduce the effects of undercoverage by giving each individual in the population a chance to be selected for the survey. This is the greatest advantage of random sampling—it helps produce samples that resemble the population. *Random sampling is a necessary part of a well-designed survey or sampling procedure.*

But even surveys conducted by using properly executed random sampling techniques are still subject to bias. **Nonresponse bias** is the situation in which an individual selected to be in the sample is unwilling, or unable, to provide data. **Response bias** occurs when because of the manner in which an interview is conducted, because of the phrasing of questions, or because of the attitude of the respondent, inaccurate data are collected.

Simple random samples are, in practice, very difficult to produce. The advantage of cluster sampling and multistage sampling is that, when using these methods, it can be easier to obtain a sample than using a simple random sample. For example, if surveys are being conducted door to door, it would be easier to go to several houses in a few randomly selected neighborhoods than to many houses scattered about an entire city. This saves resources in both time and potentially money.

Another problem with random samples is variability. Each possible SRS from a population will generate a different sample statistic. The differences among these statistics are called **sampling variability** or **sampling error**. Sampling variability is a natural part of the random sampling process and should not be confused with bias. It is not the result of a poorly designed study.

EXAMPLE 11

A journalism class prints a survey in the school newspaper about the school charging students for parking. Readers are asked to clip the survey from the paper, complete it, and return it to a drop box in the school cafeteria. What type of sample is this? Is this sample biased? Why or why not?

SOLUTION

This is a voluntary response sample, subject to voluntary response bias. It is likely that only students who drive to school now, or will drive soon, will take the time to respond. Nondrivers will tend to leave themselves out. Even if the population of interest were only driving students, those opposed to parking fees would be more likely to respond.

EXAMPLE 12

A journalism class stations pollsters in front of the stadium during a football game. They ask each student who enters the stadium his or her opinion of the quality of the school's athletics program. What type of sample is this? Is it biased? Why or why not?

SOLUTION

This is a convenience sample. It is subject to undercoverage. The site was likely chosen because of the ease of gathering data there. However, only those students attending the football game will be able to register their opinions, potentially leaving out a large portion of the population.

EXAMPLE 13

A media research firm is conducting a poll on an upcoming election for city council. The firm obtains a list of all 15,000 registered voters in the council ward under consideration and a simple random sample of 500 voters is chosen. Over a 24-hour period, telephone calls are placed to the voters, with follow-up calls made to those voters who do not answer the phone on the first attempt. Pollsters could not reach 37 of the 500 voters selected. What sources of bias could exist in this survey?

SOLUTION

This survey could be subject to nonresponse bias. Thirty-seven voters could not be reached. Their opinions could affect the results of the survey, and the data gathered may not accurately represent the views of the population.

EXAMPLE 14

A journalism class conducts a simple random sample of students at their school. Class members ask each student, "Given the fact that our school has won seven championships in the last five years, do you favor or oppose reducing funding for athletic programs?" What sources of bias could exist in this survey?

SOLUTION

The question is clearly leading the respondent to answer in opposition to reducing funding because of its mention of the school's recent athletic prowess. This is a form of response bias. A better way to phrase the question would be to ask, "Do you favor or oppose reducing funding for the school's athletic programs?"

Frequency Distributions

A **frequency distribution** is a method by which the given data are classified by a type or label. For each label, its frequency in the distribution is recorded.

EXAMPLE 15

At a gathering of 30 people, each person was asked to write his/her eye color. Here are the data:

brown	amber	amber	blue	blue
hazel	hazel	blue	amber	hazel
brown	blue	amber	brown	amber
hazel	brown	hazel	amber	amber
hazel	amber	blue	blue	blue
amber	blue	amber	hazel	amber

Write a frequency distribution for these four eye colors.

SOLUTION

We need to count how many people are counted in each of the four possible eye colors. Since there are only 30 results to tally, we can do this by hand by using tick marks in each frequency cell. The two-column table with the corresponding frequencies is as shown below.

Eye Color	Frequency
Amber	11
Blue	8
Brown	4
Hazel	7

EXAMPLE 16

On a four-question quiz given to her class of 20 students, a student's possible grade is 0, 25, 50, 75, or 100. The results of this quiz for the whole class were as follows: 50, 0, 100, 25, 75, 75, 100, 50, 75, 0, 75, 75, 100, 100, 75, 75, 75, 50, 100, and 50. Create a vertical table of the five possible grades and show their respective frequencies.

SOLUTION

We need to count how many scores are in each of the five possible grades. Since there are only 20 results to tally, we can do this by hand by using tick marks in each frequency cell. Or, using the sorting feature of a calculator, this list can be sorted from lowest to highest, and the number of results that belong to each cell can be counted. Either way, the table showing the corresponding frequencies is as shown below.

Grade	Frequency
0	2
25	1
50	4
75	8
100	5

Bar Graph or Chart

Bar graphs, or charts, come from frequency distributions. The data in bar graphs are discrete, which distinguishes them from histograms, which are for continuous data (see the "Displays to Represent Quantitative Data" section). Note that the bars are distinct from one another and that the vertical axis is appropriate for the data.

EXAMPLE 17

Construct a bar graph for the data from Example 15.

SOLUTION

First, we must make a frequency table, as was done in the solution to Example 15. Then that data can be put into a bar graph.

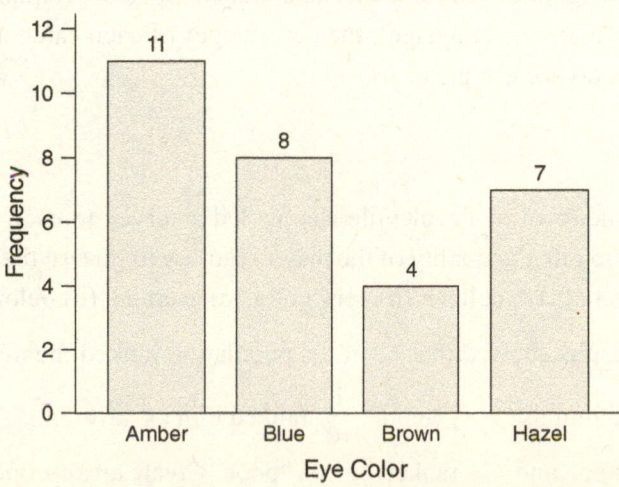

EXAMPLE 18

Construct a bar graph for the data from Example 16.

SOLUTION

First, we must make a frequency table, as was done in the solution to Example 16. Then that data can be put into a bar graph.

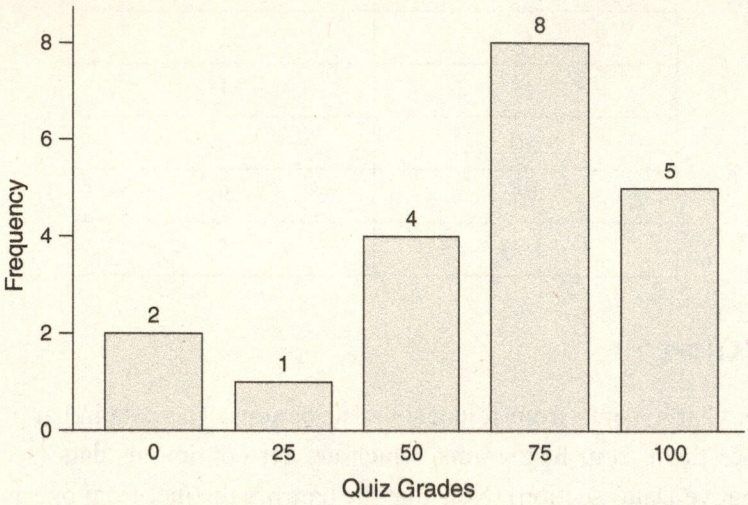

Pie Graphs

Another popular pictorial method for showing data is a **pie graph**. This type of graph is best used to show the percentage (or fractional) contribution of the component parts of one category. In a pie graph, each component is assigned to a percent, which then becomes a sector of the circle containing all the component parts. The sum of all of the sectors must total 100% (in the case of percentages) or 1 (in the case of fractions). This may involve computing percentages by dividing the value of the data in each sector by the total value of the data in all sectors. If categories overlap (for example, when tallying how many students take French, Spanish, Italian, German, where some students may take more than one language), the percentages of each category may add up to more than 100%. In this case, do *not* use pie charts.

EXAMPLE 19

The mayor of the town of Peopleville has mailed a survey to each adult resident, who was asked to rate the quality of the mayor's ability to govern the town. The five ratings given were (a) excellent, (b) very good, (c) average, (d) below average, and (e) poor. The results showed that $\frac{2}{5}$ of the population ranked the mayor as "excellent," $\frac{1}{3}$ ranked him as "very good," $\frac{1}{10}$ ranked him as "average," $\frac{1}{12}$ ranked him as "below average," and $\frac{1}{12}$ ranked him as "poor." Create an appropriate pie graph.

SOLUTION

You recall that a circle contains 360°, so we need to convert each fraction into degrees. For example, $\frac{2}{5}$ corresponds to $\left(\frac{2}{5}\right)(360°) = 144°$. Following this procedure, here are the conversions for the other given fractions: $\frac{1}{3}$ corresponds to 120°, $\frac{1}{10}$ corresponds to 36°, and $\frac{1}{12}$ corresponds to 30°. The last step is to partition a circle into sectors with the appropriate central angles. Each sector is labeled with a category. Here is the completed pie graph.

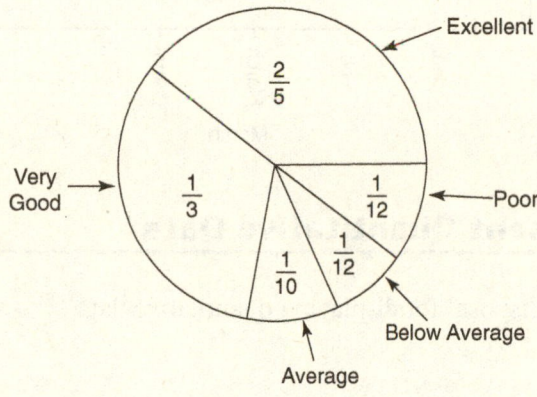

Time Series Line Graphs

Our final pictorial method for showing data will be a **time series line graph**. This type of graph is extremely useful when we wish to show trends of a single quantity over a period of time.

EXAMPLE 20

During the first six months of this year, Amanda kept track of how many different projects to which she was assigned at work. Here are her results: January, 28; February, 22; March, 52; April, 8; May, 12; June, 40. Construct a time series graph.

SOLUTION

The months are placed on the horizontal axis, in order from January through June. Dots are placed that correspond to the respective values for each month. Finally, line segments are drawn to connect the monthly values. We will use a scaling unit of 4. Notice that all but one of the numbers divides evenly by 4. The number 22 will be measured by approximating one-half the distance between 20 and 24. Here is how the time series graph should appear:

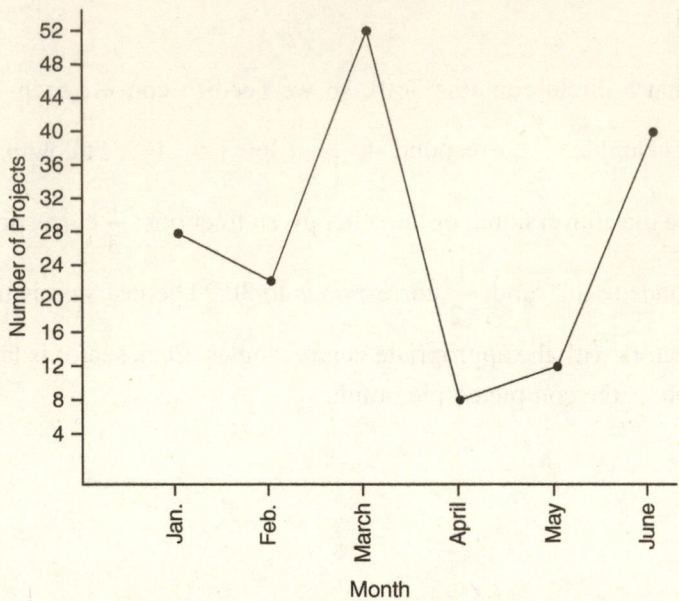

Displays to Represent Quantitative Data

Many tools are at our disposal for displaying quantitative data.

Scatter Plots

A **scatter plot** is a method of showing the relationship of two different numerical quantities by using an xy-coordinate plane, where one quantity is the x value and the other is the y value. This type of plot allows us to visualize the strength and form of any relationship between the quantities by how closely the plot approximates a straight (or curved) line, the direction of the relationship (direct or inverse), and any unusual features in the relationship, such as obvious points that do not fall within the general pattern of the data. The mathematical formulas related to these correlations are discussed later in this chapter, in the Statistics section under "Regression Analysis."

EXAMPLE 21

In a small class of 9 students, the teacher was interested in comparing the number of absences during the school year with each student's final numerical grade. Here are the results in tabular form:

Number of Absences	0	5	3	9	1	7	3	2	6
Final Grade:	98	80	90	60	93	55	85	90	75

Draw a scatter plot of these results.

SOLUTION

The positive x-axis will be labeled "Number of Absences" and the positive y-axis will be labeled "Final Grade."

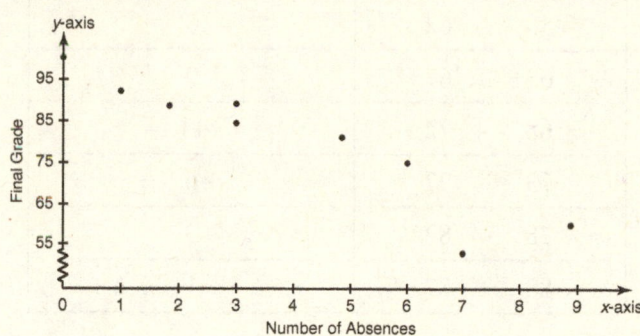

Since the grades range from 55 to 98, a squiggle line is shown on the vertical axis between 0 and 55. This indicates that there are no values between 0 and 55. From this scatter plot, the teacher could draw the conclusion that absences negatively affect students' final grade.

Frequency Tables

In the next example, we group numerical data into classes. Each class of numbers contains a minimum and a maximum value. With this method, two or more numbers may be placed into the same class. For example if a class is listed as 73–77, then each of 73 and 76 would be placed into this class. No two classes may overlap.

EXAMPLE 22

Employees at the XYZ watch company were requested to state their heights, to the nearest inch. The shortest person listed her height as 58 inches, and the tallest person listed his height as 86 inches. Here is the list of the heights, in inches, of all 36 employees: 73, 86, 66, 82, 73, 66, 80, 76, 75, 70, 79, 69, 62, 68, 63, 77, 76, 64, 68, 71, 71, 60, 68, 71, 58, 72, 59, 65, 59, 71, 68, 65, 64, 65, 59, and 64. Construct a grouped frequency distribution, using the following six classes of data:

$$58 - 62, 63 - 67, 68 - 72, 73 - 77, 78 - 82, \text{ and } 83 - 87.$$

SOLUTION

You can count tick marks for each class as we did in Examples 15 and 16. Or you can use your TI-83 calculator to sort the list of 36 numbers in ascending order. The list of numbers reads as follows: 58, 59, 59, 59, 60, 62, 63, 64, 64, 64, 65, 65, 65, 66, 66, 68, 68, 68, 68, 69, 70, 71, 71, 71, 71, 72, 73, 73, 75, 76, 76, 77, 79, 80, 82, and 86. Now we list each class and count its corresponding frequency. The grouped frequency distribution appears as follows:

Class	Frequency
58 – 62	6
63 – 67	9
68 – 72	11
73 – 77	6
78 – 82	3
83 – 87	1

Each class identifies the same number of potential entries; that is, the first class contains the five entries 58, 59, 60, 61, 62; the second class contains the five entries 63, 64, 65, 66, 67, and so on. This pattern of five entries per class is used for each class. The frequency column corresponds to the actual number of data that belong to the entries of the particular class. For a class such as 58 – 62, the number 58 is called the **lower limit** and the number 62 is called the **upper limit**. For each class, the difference between the upper and lower limits *must* be the same. Furthermore, there is no overlap of assigned entry numbers from one class to the next.

Stem-and-Leaf Plots

Another method in which individual data may be displayed is called a **stem-and-leaf plot.** This method requires that the data be arranged in ascending order. It should be used only when all the data are integers that contain the same number of placeholders. The data are arranged into two groups in which a vertical bar is used. The stem consists of all digits, except the units digit. The leaf contains the units digit of each number that is associated with that stem. Thus, if each of the data are between 100 and 999, the stem would consist of the hundreds digit and the tens digit; the leaf would consist of the units digit of each of the data points. For example, the number 235 would appear as 23 | 5. The stems are shown in ascending order in a vertical column and the leaves for each stem are written horizontally in ascending order.

EXAMPLE 23

Using the individual data in Example 3, create a stem-and-leaf plot.

SOLUTION

Using the solution to Example 22, which contains the data sorted in ascending order, the stem-and-leaf plot would be as follows:

```
5 | 8 9 9 9
6 | 0 2 3 4 4 4 5 5 5 6 6 8 8 8 8 9
7 | 0 1 1 1 1 2 3 3 5 6 6 7 9
8 | 0 2 6
```

EXAMPLE 24

Ken is an avid bowler. He has kept track of his bowling scores for the 30 most recent games. As a tribute to his consistency, his lowest score was 160 and his highest score was 219. (He hopes to bowl 300 someday!) His results are as follows: 189, 209, 195, 162, 175, 189, 202, 218, 213, 210, 192, 178, 176, 163, 196, 160, 188, 182, 195, 212, 168, 197, 219, 210, 210, 184, 198, 161, 169, and 192. Construct a stem-and-leaf plot.

SOLUTION

Since each number has three digits, the first two digits appear on the left side of the vertical bar. The right side of the vertical bar (i.e., the "leaf" part) must only contain every single digits.

Arranged in ascending order, the data appear as follows: 160, 161, 162, 163, 168, 169, 175, 176, 178, 182, 184, 188, 189, 189, 192, 192, 195, 195, 196, 197, 198, 202, 209, 210, 210, 210, 212, 213, 218, and 219. The completed stem-and-leaf plot is as follows:

```
16 | 0 1 2 3 8 9
17 | 5 6 8
18 | 2 4 8 9 9
19 | 2 2 5 5 6 7 8
20 | 2 9
21 | 0 0 0 2 3 8 9
```

Histograms

In addition to the preceding examples of organizing and interpreting data, there are several pictorial methods that are available. One of these is called a **histogram,** which is a graph that contains vertical connected rectangular bars in the first quadrant of the *xy*-coordinate plane. The given data is grouped into classes and each bar shows the frequency of a class. Histograms differ from the bar graphs of quantitative data because the data are continuous quantities.

EXAMPLE 25

The record low temperatures of last year for twenty-five cities were collected. The results were displayed in a grouped frequency distribution, which appeared as follows:

Class	Frequency
3° – 9°	3
10° – 16°	5
17° – 23°	9
24° – 30°	6
31° – 37°	2

Construct an appropriate histogram.

SOLUTION

Following Example 22, we use the words **lower limit** and **upper limit** in referring to the two extreme numbers of each class. Thus, for the first class, 3° represents the lower limit and 9° represents the upper limit. In order to create connected rectangular bars, we use lower and upper boundaries for each class. Each temperature represents a continuous number. For example, 3° could represent any number between 2.5° and 3.5°, not including 3.5°. Similarly, 9° could represent any number between 8.5° and 9.5°, not including 9.5°. The numbers 2.5 and 3.5 are called the **lower** and **upper boundaries** for 3. In creating the connected bars for each class, we use the lower boundary of the lower limit and the upper boundary of the upper limit. The classes would then appear as 2.5° – 9.5°, 9.5° – 16.5°, 16.5° – 23.5°, 23.5° – 30.5°, and 30.5° – 37.5°. They will be shown on the x-axis. The frequencies will be listed on the y-axis. The completed histogram appears below.

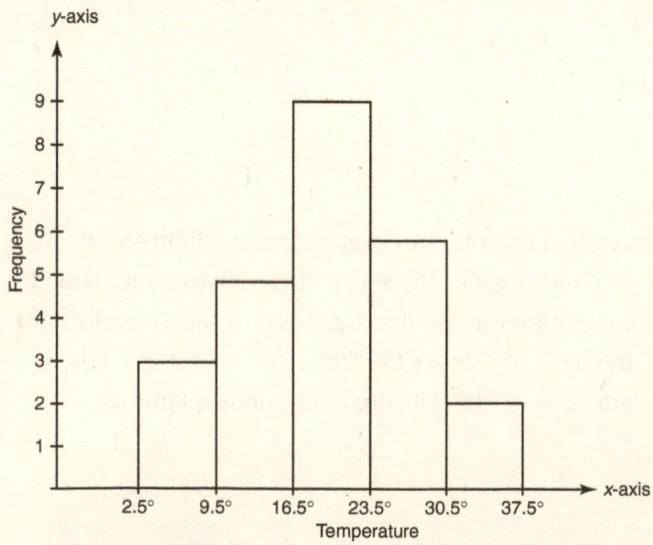

STATISTICS

Qualitative Data Descriptors

Due to the nature of qualitative data, as we have seen, they can be presented in a table, but are best represented as a pie chart or bar graph. Tables are usually presented as tables with one column for the category and another column with the count (frequency tables) or percentage of the whole (relative frequency tables).

To make categorical data more understandable, it is best to use fewer than 12 categories. This may involve grouping some categories together. These groups must be identical in structure (e.g., if we lump together four years of data in a group on a table or a bar graph, each group must be data for four years).

Qualitative data can be described in terms of the **mode** of the data, which is the most common value (not the frequency, but the actual data point). It is possible to have more than one mode in a data set. If there are two modes, the data are described as being bimodal. The only time when a mode does not exist is when each of the given data points has a frequency of 1. (No number occurs more than once.) Thus, the set of data 3, 8, 19, 20, and 90 has no mode.

Here are three sets of data that have a single mode:

Group A: 15, 16, 18, 5, 5, 12

Group B: 1, 5, 1, 3, 5, 1, 4, 9

Group C: 7, 7, 7, 7, 2, 2, 2, 10, 10, 10

In group A, the mode is 5; in group B, the mode is 1; and in group C, the mode is 7.

Here are three sets of data that have two modes:

Group D: 2, 4, 2, 4, 2, 4

Group E: 14, 30, 30, 25, 19, 14, 11, 20, 40

Group F: 1, 1, 1, 1, 5, 5, 3, 8, 8, 8, 8

In group D, the modes are 2 and 4; in group E, the modes are 14 and 30; and in group F, the modes are 1 and 8.

EXAMPLE 26

In which one of the following groups of data is the mode?

    (A) 6, 9, 10, 10, 11, 19, 20

    (B) 6, 9, 9, 9, 12, 12, 16, 21

    (C) 6, 10, 11, 13, 13, 13

    (D) 6, 6, 11, 14, 17, 17, 17

SOLUTION

For answer choice (A), the mode is 10; for answer choice (B), the mode is 9; for answer choice (C), the mode is 13; and for answer choice (D), the mode is 17.

Other descriptors, which are used for quantitative data, are meaningless for qualitative data. For example, consider data collected in which 660 respondents state their political party affiliations as follows:

Democrat	268
Republican	190
Other/None	202

We can state that the mode of the data is Democrat, and if we put the data into a pie graph or a bar chart, we would see that Democrat has a bigger piece of the pie or a higher bar, respectively. But to state the mean (average) voter is meaningless because the classifications are exclusive; there is no such thing as a registered Democrat-Republican. Likewise, there is no representative data point that is in the middle of the responses, as a median would be.

Quantitative Data Descriptors

A quantitative data set can be described by measurements of its center (mean or median) and the spread of the data (variance, standard deviation, or interquartile range). The range of a data set, which is the difference between the maximum value and the minimum value, simply measures dispersion and is rarely a good choice to describe a data set, especially because it is affected by outliers.

Measuring Center: Mean and Median

The mean and median are measures of center. They locate the middle or the center of a distribution.

The **mean** is the average of a data set. The mean is calculated by the formula, $\bar{x} = \dfrac{\sum x_i}{n}$, where n is the number of observations in the data set, and x_i represents individual observations counting from 1 to n. The summation symbol, Σ, is the command to add up the expression following it.

EXAMPLE 27

The weights (in pounds) of 10 jockeys who are going to race at Arlington Park are 113, 117, 112, 113.5, 115.8, 114, 114.6, 113.5, 112.4, and 113. Calculate the mean weight of the jockeys.

SOLUTION

The sum of the weights is 1,138.8. Thus, the mean weight is $\dfrac{1{,}138.8}{10} = 113.88$ pounds.

A variation of the word *mean* is a weighted mean. A **weighted mean** occurs when some data values contribute more to the average than other data values, due to their frequency. Mathematically, a weighted mean $\bar{x}_w = \dfrac{\displaystyle\sum_{i=1}^{n} w_i x_i}{\displaystyle\sum_{i=1}^{n} w_i} = \dfrac{w_1 x_1 + w_2 x_2 + \ldots + w_n x_n}{w_1 + w_2 + \ldots + w_n}$, where n is the number of data, x_i is the value of each different data value, and w_i is the associated frequency or "weight." In some cases, the weights are assigned "percents."

EXAMPLE 28

A college professor's syllabus states that exams are worth 70% of a student's final grade, while the final exam is worth 30%. Suppose that a student's exam scores are 95, 91, 85, and 91. If his final exam score is 80, what is the student's final grade?

SOLUTION

This is a weighted average problem. The average of the exams is $\dfrac{95 + 91 + 85 + 91}{4}$

$= \dfrac{362}{4} = 90.5$. Then the final grade is calculated as $\dfrac{(0.7)(90.5) + (0.3)(80)}{(0.3) + (0.7)} =$

$\dfrac{63.35 + 24}{1} = 87.35$. The student's final grade is 87.

The **median** is the middle number of a data set that has been arranged from the smallest to largest value or vice versa. If there is an even number of values in the data set, the median is the mean of the two in the middle.

EXAMPLE 29

What is the median of the data set 4, 5, 5, 6, 6, 7, 7, 7, 9?

SOLUTION

The median is 6 since it is the middle value.

EXAMPLE 30

What are the mean and median of the set 4, 5, 5, 6, 6, 7, 7, 7, 9, 10?

SOLUTION

The median is 6.5 since the mean of the middle two numbers, 6 and 7, is 6.5. Note that the median does not have to be one of the data points. The mean is the sum of the data divided by the number of data, or $\frac{66}{10} = 6.6$.

The median is a better measure of center if the data set has outliers or is skewed in any way. The maximum value in Example 30 was 10. If it were larger, the median would not be affected, but the mean would, since the mean is computed using the actual values of the data, as Example 31 shows.

EXAMPLE 31

What are the mean and median of the set 4, 5, 5, 6, 6, 7, 7, 7, 9, 30?

SOLUTION

The median is still 6.5, as it was in the previous question. The median is not affected by extreme values or outliers. The mean for the data set is 8.6.

The shape of a distribution can tell us about the relationship between the mean and median. In symmetric distributions, the mean and median are close to the same. In skewed distributions, the mean is "pulled" away from the median toward the tail. Since the mean is based on the values of the data, it tends to go toward more extreme values, which in skewed distributions are located in the tail.

EXAMPLE 32

What is the median for the following set of data? 132, 153, 186, 105, 103, 142, 191, 118, 188, and 186?

SOLUTION

When arranged in ascending order, the data set appears as follows: 103, 105, 118, 132, **142**, **153**, 186, 186, 188, and 191. Since $n = 10$, the position of the median is $(n + 1) \div 2 = (10 + 1) \div 2 = 5.5$. This implies that we must calculate the mean of the fifth and sixth numbers. Thus, the median is $(142 + 153) \div 2 = 147.5$.

EXAMPLE 33

The median of a set of numbers arranged in order occurs midway between the 29th and 30th numbers. How many data are there in the set?

SOLUTION

In this case, the median is in the 29.5th position. We need to solve the equation $(n + 1) \div 2 = 29.5$, where n is the number of data. Multiplying both sides by 2, we get $n + 1 = 59$. Thus, $n = 58$.

EXAMPLE 34

Estimate the median of each distribution shown in the histograms below and describe how the mean compares to the median.

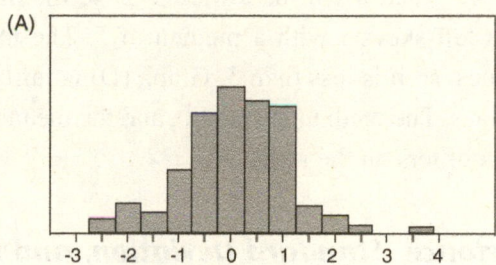

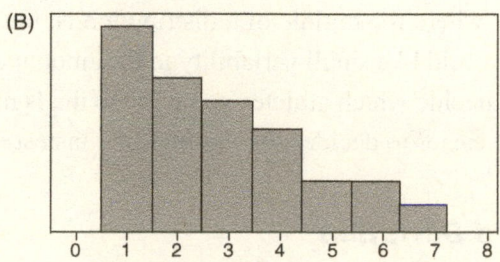

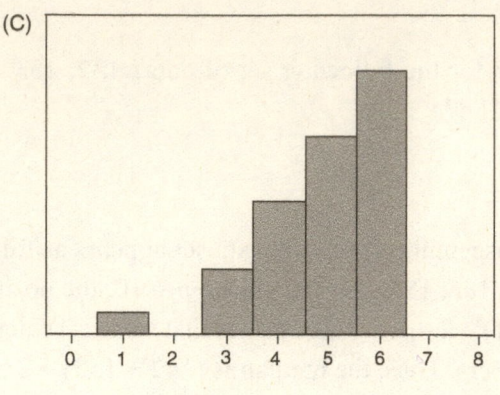

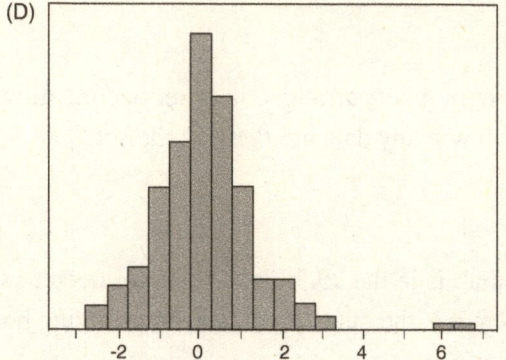

SOLUTION

Graph (A) is symmetric with a median at about 0. The mean will also be about 0. Graph (B) is right-skewed with a median of about 3. The mean will be pulled more toward the values of 4–7 than it will be toward 1–2, so the mean will be greater than 3. Graph (C) is left-skewed with a median of 5. The mean will be pulled toward the lower values, so it is less than 5. Graph (D) is fairly symmetric with a few extreme high values. The median is about 0, and the mean will be just slightly larger because of the outliers on the right.

Measuring Spread: Variance, Standard Deviation, and Interquartile Range

In addition to measures of center, distributions need to be described with measures of variability. It is not enough to know where the middle of a distribution is, but also how spread out it is. A manufacturer of light bulbs would like small variability in the amount of hours the bulbs will likely burn. A coach who needs to decide which athletes go on to the finals may want larger variability in heat times because it will be easier to decide who are truly the fastest runners.

Variance and Standard Deviation

For data that are fairly symmetric and not affected by outliers, variance and standard deviation are useful measures of variability.

The **variance** tells us how much variability exists in a distribution. It is the "average" of the squared differences between the data values and the mean.

The variance is calculated with the formula $s^2 = \frac{1}{n-1}\sum(x_1 - \bar{x})^2$. The **standard deviation** is the square root of the variance. The formula for the standard deviation is therefore $s^2 = \sqrt{\frac{1}{n-1}\sum(x_i - \bar{x})^2}$. The standard deviation is used for most applications in statistics. It can be thought of as the typical distance an observation lies from the mean.

EXAMPLE 35

The average monthly rainfall in inches in Birmingham, England, is shown in the table below.

Jan	Feb	Mar	Apr	May	Jun
2.3	1.9	2.1	1.8	2.2	2.2
Jul	Aug	Sep	Oct	Nov	Dec
2.0	2.8	2.2	2.1	2.5	2.6

Compute the variance and standard deviation of the monthly rainfall.

SOLUTION

To compute the variance and standard deviation, the mean must first be computed. In this data set, $\bar{x} = \frac{26.7}{12} = 2.225$. The variance is computed as follows:

$$s^2 = \frac{1}{n-1}\sum(x_1 - x)^2$$

$$= \frac{1}{12-1}(2.3 - 2.225)^2 + (1.9 - 2.225)^2$$

$$+ (2.1 - 2.225)^2 + \ldots + (2.6 - 2.225)^2$$

$$= \frac{1}{11}(0.9225)$$

$$\approx 0.084.$$

The standard deviation is the square root of the variance, or $\sqrt{0.084} \approx 0.290$. The monthly mean rainfall in Birmingham is 2.225 inches, and it varies by about 0.290 inches from that each month, sometimes more, sometimes less.

Interquartile Range

For data sets that have extreme values or skewness, the interquartile range would be a better measure of variability. This is because standard deviation and variance are computed with the actual values of the data, like the mean. Interquartile range, like the median, is not.

The **interquartile range** is a five-number summary is composed of the minimum, maximum, median, first quartile (Q_1), and third quartile (Q_3) of a data set. The quartiles and the median (which is the second quartile or Q_2) break the data into four equally sized groups. However, these groups may not have the same spreads.

To find Q_1, determine the middle value of all observations below the median in an ordered data set. The value of Q_3 is found at the middle value of all observations above the median of a data set.

The interquartile range (IQR) is a measure of variability that works well for data that are skewed or have outliers. The IQR is the spread of the middle 50% of the data and not affected by extreme values. The IQR is calculated by $Q_3 - Q_1$. The interquartile range is a single value, like the range.

EXAMPLE 36

Find the five-number summary and interquartile range of the data set 4, 5, 5, 6, 6, 7, 7, 7, 9, 30.

SOLUTION

The minimum value is 4, the maximum is 30, and the median is 6.5. The first quartile is the middle of the five values below the median, or 5. The third quartile is the middle of the five values above the median, or 7. The five-number summary is min = 4, $Q_1 = 5$, median = 6.5, $Q_3 = 7$, max = 30.

The interquartile range is $Q_3 - Q_1 = 7 - 5 = 2$.

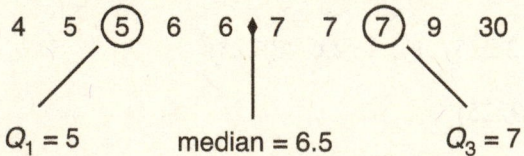

A common rule for determining **outliers**, or extreme values that do not fall within the general pattern of the data, is the 1.5 *IQR* rule. If an observation is farther than 1.5*IQR* above the third quartile, or farther than 1.5 *IQR* below the first quartile, it is considered an outlier. Those boundaries at $Q_1 - 1.5\ IQR$ and $Q_3 + 1.5\ IQR$ are called "fences." Outliers are points lying outside the fences.

For Example 36, 1.5 *IQR* = 1.5(2) = 3, so 30 is an outlier because it is outside the upper fence of $Q_3 + 1.5\ IQR = 7 + 3 = 10$.

Normal Distributions

To understand normal distributions, you must understand the Law of Large Numbers and how it related to frequency distributions (or histograms). The **Law of Large Numbers** theorem states that as the number of trials of a probability experiment increases, the observed number of "successful" outcomes will get increasingly closer to the theoretical number "successful" outcomes. For example, if a fair coin is flipped, let's identify the number of tails as the number of "successful" outcomes. On any one flip, the theoretical probability of getting tails is 0.5. If this coin is flipped 10,000 times, the expected number of tails is $(0.5)(10,000) = 5,000$. The Law of Large Numbers states that we should observe that the actual number of tails is very close to 5,000. If we decide to flip this coin 100,000 times, we should observe that the number of tails is extremely close to 50,000.

The most widely used distribution of data is the **normal distribution**. Some examples of this type of distribution are (a) heights of all adult women, (b) weights of all adult men, (c) highest daily temperatures in a given city over a period of time, and (d) the diameters of cylinders manufactured in a factory in which the machines produce them. So the Law of Large Numbers implies that the more data points, the closer the histogram of those points comes to look like a normal distribution, also known as a bell curve due to its shape.

The normal curve has these properties.

a) The mean, median, and mode are equal.

b) The curve is symmetric about the mean.

c) The y-coordinate of the mean is the maximum point on the curve.

d) Approximately 68.3% of the data are within one standard deviation of the mean ($\mu \pm \sigma$)

e) Approximately 95.5% of the data are within two standard deviations of the mean ($\mu \pm 2\sigma$)

f) Approximately 99.7% of the data are within three standard deviations of the mean ($\mu \pm 3\sigma$)

g) The curve never touches the x-axis and all y-values are positive.

h) The curve is continuous and assumes all values of x.

Figure 5.1 illustrates these properties.

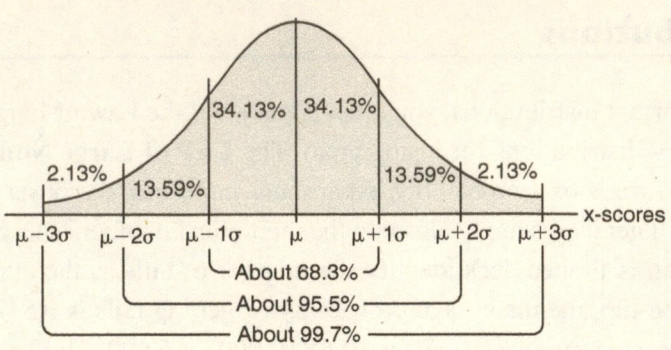

Figure 5.1

EXAMPLE 37

Referring to the table and results of Example 35, what can be said about the data, assuming they are normally distributed?

SOLUTION

About 68.3% of the time, the average monthly rainfall in Birmingham, England, is 2.225 ± 0.290, or between 1.935 and 2.515 inches. About 95.5% of the time, it is $2.225 \pm 2(0.290)$, or between 1.645 and 2.805 inches, and 99.7% of the time, it is $2.225 \pm 3(0.290)$, or between 1.355 and 3.095 inches.

Standard Normal Distribution

A **standard normal distribution** is a special case of the normal distribution, in which the mean is standardized to 0, and the standard deviation is 1, and the area under the curve above the x-axis is standardized to 1. Figure 6.18 illustrates the standard normal distribution.

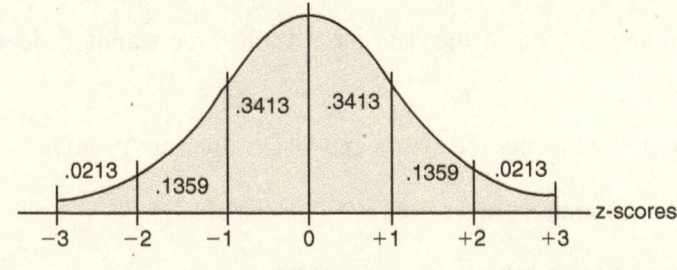

Figure 5.2

The values of x of a normal distribution (x-scores) are called **raw scores**. For a standard normal distribution, the independent values become **z-scores**, which are also called **standard scores**. Z-scores are used to determine how many standard deviations from the mean a data value lies. Just as *x* scores can assume any value, *z*-scores can also assume any value. But from Figure 5.2 we can see that a negligible amount of the area of the curve lies in the regions greater than 3 or less than −3. (In fact, it is $1 - .997 = .003$, or 3% of the data.) For this reason, our *z* values will be confined to the closed interval [−3, 3]. The actual normalizing formula for converting *x*-scores to *z*-scores is $z = \dfrac{x - \mu}{\sigma}$, where *x* is the raw score, μ is the mean, and σ is the standard deviation. Incidentally, this formula applies to *any* distribution of data, not just those that belong to a normal distribution.

Applications of the Standard Normal Distribution

One of the main advantages of using *z*-scores rather than raw scores is that the normalization allows comparison of two sets of data, as shown in Example 38.

EXAMPLE 38

A mathematics test was given to both a class that met in the morning and a class that met in the afternoon. For the morning class, the mean was 84 and the standard deviation was 3.4. For the afternoon class, the mean was 82 and the standard deviation was 3.6. For which class would a raw score of 90 correspond to a higher *z*-score, and thus better performance compared to the class?

SOLUTION

We calculate the *z*-scores separately.

$$\text{Morning class: } z = \frac{x - \mu}{\sigma} = \frac{90 - 84}{3.4} = \frac{6}{3.4} \approx 1.76.$$

$$\text{Afternoon class: } z = \frac{x - \mu}{\sigma} = \frac{90 - 82}{3.6} \approx 2.22.$$

Thus, the grade of 90 corresponded to a higher *z*-score in the afternoon class, so getting a 90 in the afternoon class was "better" than getting a 90 in the morning class.

A negative *z* score corresponds to a raw (*x*) score that lies below the mean. In Example 52, if a person received a raw score of 80 in the morning class, the corresponding *z* score would be $\dfrac{80 - 84}{3.4} \approx -1.18$, indicating a score less than the mean of 84, as we would expect. Also, note that a *z*-score of zero corresponds to a raw score that equals the mean.

Statistics textbooks list a table of *z*-scores and the probabilities for a standard normal curve, such as the one shown below in Figure 5.3.

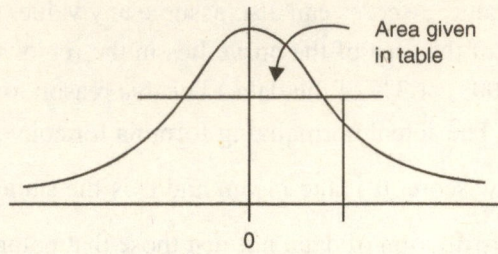

Area given
in table

Figure 5.3

The table entries indicate the area of the curve between $z = 0$ and any other z score. We can also determine the area between two given z-scores, as well as the area that lies completely to the right (or to the left) of any z-score. The z-scores are found by using the left column for the first two digits of the number and using the top row for the hundredths place digit. Due to the symmetry of the standard normal distribution, the area between $z = 0$ a given positive z value is equivalent to the area between $z = 0$ and the opposite of this positive z value.

EXAMPLE 39

What is the area between $z = 0$ and $z = 1$?

SOLUTION

We find the number 1.00 by first locating the row with 1.0. Now go to the column indicated by .00. The corresponding table entry is 0.3413, which is the area shown in Figure 5.2.

EXAMPLE 40

What is the area between $z = 0$ and $z = -2.25$?

SOLUTION

This question is equivalent to finding the area between $z = 0$ and $z = 2.25$.

Locate the row marked 2.2. Now find the column marked .05 and you should see the table entry of 0.4878, which is the answer. Looking at Figure 5.2, we see this makes sense since it is to the right of -2, which would have a value of .0213.

Although the z-score table will *not* be distributed when you sit for the PRAXIS Mathematics Content Knowledge Test, it is still important to understand how the table works. The good news is that a calculator such as the TI-83 can perform any necessary calculations involving the area between any two z-scores. If we want the area to the left of a specific z value, we can use -1×10^{99} as the lower bound. Likewise, if we want any area to the right of a specific z value, we can use

1×10^{99} as the upper bound. The calculator interprets -1×10^{99} as $-\infty$ and interprets 1×10^{99} as $+\infty$. The next few examples show diagrams of the areas; each of these examples refers to a standard normal distribution.

EXAMPLE 41

What is the area between $z = -1$ and $z = 1$?

SOLUTION

The following figure illustrates the desired area of the curve.

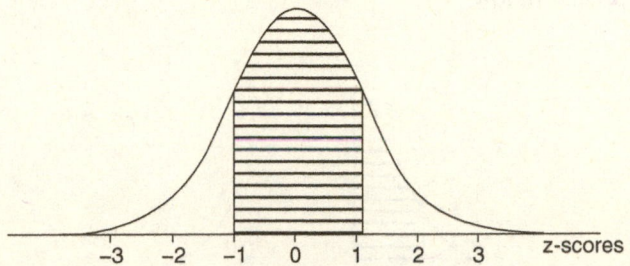

z-scores

Since we know that the area of the mean ± 1 standard deviation $= .683$, that is the desired area. If using a calculator, first, press in sequence: "2nd," "DISTR," and the number 2. At this point, your TI-83 reads as "normalcdf(". Now press in sequence the numbers -1, 1, 0, 1, followed by a right parenthesis. (Be sure that you have placed commas between these numbers.) Finally, press "Enter," and your answer should be approximately 0.6827.

The sequence of numbers -1, 1, 0, and 1, refers to the lower bound of z, the upper bound of z, the mean of a standard normal distribution, and the standard deviation of a standard normal distribution, respectively.

EXAMPLE 42

What percent of the area lies to the right of $z = 0.8$?

SOLUTION

The diagram appears below.

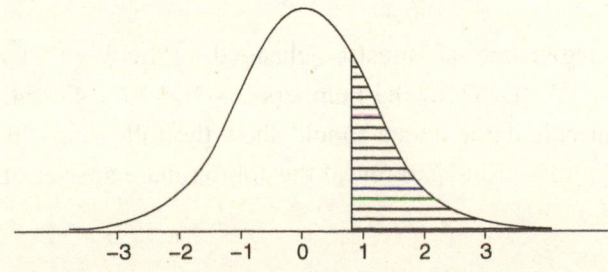

As in Example 41, first, press in sequence: "2nd," "DISTR," and the number 2 on the calculator. Now press in sequence the numbers 0.8, 1×10^{99}, 0, 1, followed by a right parenthesis. Press "Enter" and your result is approximately 0.2119, which is slightly more than 21%.

EXAMPLE 43

What is the area between $z = -1.5$ and $z = -0.5$?

SOLUTION

The diagram appears below.

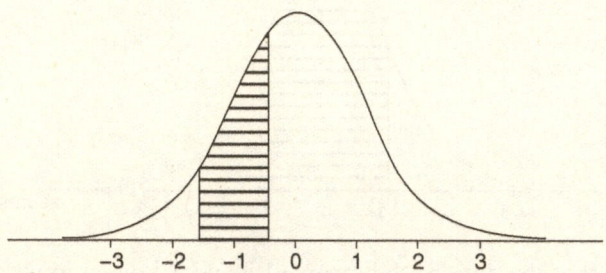

Follow the steps in Example 41 up to the point where the calculator reads as "normalcdft." Now press in sequence -1.5, -0.5, 0, 1, then a right parenthesis. Finally, press "Enter" to get the answer of approximately 0.2417.

Applications of the Normal Distribution

The steps we followed to solve Examples 41–43 can be applied to any normal distributions, provided that we know the mean and standard deviation. In some cases, the word "probability" will be used in place of "area" or "percent." The procedure for finding a probability is identical to that of finding a percent or area. We assume a normal distribution for each of Examples 44–46.

EXAMPLE 44

The mean age of the chief operating officers (COOs) in the United States is 54 years old, with a standard deviation of 5 years. What percent of these COOs are younger than 47 years old?

SOLUTION

The phrase "younger than 47" must be changed to "between -1×10^{99} and 47." After pressing "2nd," "DISTR," the numbers 2, -1×10^{99}, 47, 54, 5, and a right parenthesis, your calculator screen should show the following: "normalcdf (-1×10^{99}, 47, 54, 5)." Press "Enter" to reveal the approximate answer of 0.0808, which is 8.08%.

The mean and standard deviation appear as the third and fourth numbers respectively following the left parenthesis after "normalcdf."

EXAMPLE 45

The Time is Tight company makes watches. The mean lifetime of these watches is 38 months, with a standard deviation of 4 months. What percent of this company's watches will last longer than 35 months?

SOLUTION

In order to use the TI-83 calculator, the phrase "longer than 35" must be changed to "between 35 and 1×10^{99}." After pressing "2nd," "DISTR," the numbers 2, 35, 1×10^{99}, 38," and 4, a right parenthesis, and "Enter," your answer should be approximately 0.7734, which is 77.34%.

EXAMPLE 46

The amount of coffee dispensed in the paper cups of an automatic machine has a mean of 5.5 ounces and a standard deviation of 0.3 ounces. A paper cup is randomly selected. What is the probability that it will contain between 5.2 and 5.6 ounces of coffee?

SOLUTION

Use the same sequence of steps as in the other examples. When the calculator screen shows "normalcdf (5.2, 5.6, 5.5, 0.3)," press "Enter" to display approximately 0.4719, which expresses the required probability of 47.2%.

Using Samples to Estimate Populations

In many statistical instances, we are interested in drawing conclusions concerning a sample taken from a population of normally distributed data. Let's return to Example 59, which involves the Time is Tight company. Suppose this company made 100,000 watches in a year. If you were to consider all samples of 20 watches each, there would be a total of $_{100,000}C_{20} \approx 4.10 \times 10^{81}$ different samples! Each one of these 4.10×10^{81} samples would have a sample mean. This group of 4.10×10^{81} means is called the **distribution of sample means**. If you could then determine the mean of this distribution of sample means, you would find that it equals 38 months. This number matches exactly the mean of all watches made by this company. (Please do not try to perform this experiment, for it would take more years than a lifetime!)

The Central Limit Theorem states that as the sample size n increases, the distribution of sample means taken from <u>any</u> population with mean μ and standard deviation σ will approach a normal distribution. Furthermore, this distribution will have a mean of μ and a standard deviation of $\dfrac{\sigma}{\sqrt{n}}$.

So, for the watch company, this huge distribution of 4.10×10^{81} sample means would have a standard deviation equal to $\dfrac{4}{\sqrt{20}} \approx 0.89$ months. (Recall that 4 months is the standard deviation of the population of all the watches this company makes, and the sample size is 20.)

Note that each of the samples *must* be the same size. The notation for the mean and standard deviation of this distribution of sample means is denoted as $\mu_{\bar{X}}$ and $\sigma_{\bar{X}}$, respectively. Thus, we can write $u_{\bar{X}} = \mu$ and $\sigma_{\bar{X}} = \dfrac{\sigma}{\sqrt{n}}$.

To summarize, given a population that is normally distributed, with a mean of μ and a standard deviation of σ, consider the set of sample means of all samples of size n. This distribution of sample means is itself a normal distribution, whose mean equals the mean of the population. In addition, the standard deviation of this distribution is equal to the standard deviation of the population divided by the square root of the size of each sample.

Obviously, there will be some variability among samples from the same population. These are what is called **sampling error**, but unlike the name, these are *not* errors. They just reflect the variability in the data. The standard deviation of the distribution of sample means is commonly called the **standard error of the mean**.

Note that the original population need not be normally distributed. Statisticians have agreed that to apply the Central Limit Theorem, the minimum size of n should be 30. Also, we generally assume that the population size is considerably larger than 30.

EXAMPLE 47

A random sample of 300 students was found to have a mean height of 64 inches and standard deviation of 2.3 inches. What is the standard error of the mean?

(Assume that the population from which the 300 students are drawn is much larger than 300.)

SOLUTION

$\sigma_{\bar{x}} = \dfrac{\sigma}{\sqrt{n}} = \dfrac{2.3}{\sqrt{300}} \approx 0.13.$

EXAMPLE 48

The town of Whisper Pines has been keeping statistics on its highest temperature each day for more than 200 years. For that period of time, its mean high temperature has been 47.3 degrees with a standard deviation of 3.6 degrees. A random sample of 64 days is chosen. What is the probability that the sample mean will exceed 48 degrees?

SOLUTION

We are not told whether the population of temperatures is normally distributed. But the value of n is greater than 30, so the distribution of sample means can be treated as a normal distribution. We first determine that $\mu = \mu_{\bar{X}} = 47.3$ and $\sigma_{\bar{X}} = \dfrac{\sigma}{\sqrt{n}} = \dfrac{3.6}{\sqrt{64}} = 0.45$. Following the procedure shown in Examples 47–48, the calculator should display normalcdf $(48, 1 \times 10^{99}, 47.3, 0.45) \approx 0.0599$, or 6.0%.

Confidence Intervals

Two-Sided Confidence Intervals

In Examples 47 and 48, we assumed knowledge of the population, and then determined the value of statistics related to samples. More often, we have better information about the sample data and wish to extend this information to draw conclusions about the population data.

For example, we can usually determine the value of a sample mean, $\bar{x}$. Based on this value, we would like to project a good estimate of the mean of the population, μ, from which this sample was extracted. For the following discussion, we assume that at least one of the following two conditions holds.

(a)   The sample size n is at least 30.

(b)   The population standard deviation, σ, is known and the population is normally distributed. If we do not know that value of σ but condition (a) is met, then we may substitute the sample standard deviation, s.

A **confidence interval** for the mean of a population indicates the accuracy of estimating the population mean, μ, from the sample mean $\bar{x}$. It is a two-sided open interval that corresponds to the percent of samples whose mean satisfies $\bar{x} \pm (z_c)(\dfrac{\sigma}{\sqrt{n}})$, when σ is known. This expression changes to $\bar{x} \pm (z_c)(\dfrac{s}{\sqrt{n}})$, when σ is not known and the sample size is at least 30.

The term z_c refers to a **critical z value** of the standard normal distribution. We already know the confidence intervals of ±1, ±2, and ±3 standard deviations from the percentages in the normal distribution (Figure 5.1):

±1 standard deviation (when $z_c = 1$) contains 68.3% of the data

±2 standard deviations (when $z_c = 2$) contain 95.5% of the data

±3 standard deviations (when $z_c = 3$) contain 99.7% of the data

However, confidence intervals are usually stated in terms of 90%, 95%, or 99% confidence. The z_c values for these percentages, which are obtained from the z table, but repeated here because they are used so frequently, are:

For 90% confidence, z_c is 1.645

For 95% confidence, z_c is 1.960

For 99% confidence, z_c is 2.576

These are the values for z_c that allow us to say, "Based on the sample mean, we are X% confident that the population mean lies in the interval $\bar{x} \pm (z_c)\left(\dfrac{\sigma}{\sqrt{n}}\right)$, with the z_c value corresponding to the percentage of confidence.

Figure 5.4 graphically shows what this means for a 95% confidence interval. Notice that this is a two-tailed test, since both "tails" of the normal curve are outside of the interval. That is why each tail has a probability of 2.5%, rather than the entire 5%.

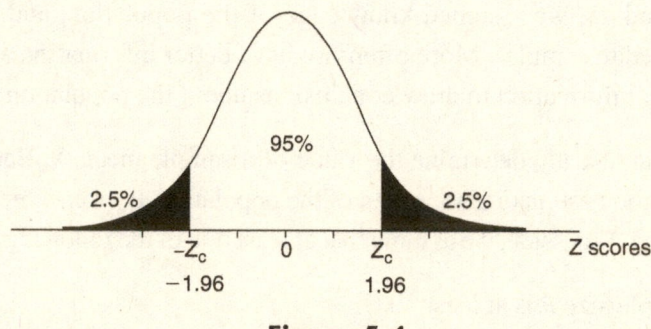

Figure 5.4

Some examples will help in understanding this basic use of statistics.

EXAMPLE 49

A survey of 60 homeowners in Maryland was conducted, during which time it was discovered that the average age of their homes was 25 years, with a sample standard deviation of 4 years. What is the 95% confidence interval for the age of all homes in Maryland?

SOLUTION

Our aim is to create an open interval for which the probability is 95% that this range of values includes the true mean of the population (μ). Since $n = 60$, we know that the distribution of all samples of size 60, from the population of Maryland homes, is normally distributed. For 95% confidence, $z_c = 1.96$, as shown in Figure 5.4.

The TI-83 calculator has the feature of finding as follows.. Press "2nd", "DISTR," then press 3. The screen will display "invNorm(." At this point, you want to enter the decimal equivalent of the percent of the area under the normal curve that lies to the left of z_c. This decimal value is $1 - 0.025 = 0.975$. Now insert a right parenthesis and press "Enter." The screen will show a value which is approximately 1.96. This implies that 2.5% of the area lies to the right of $z_c = 1.96$ and 2.5% of the area lies to the left of $-z_c$, which is $- 1.96$.

Thus, the required interval for the population mean becomes $25 \pm (1.96)(\dfrac{4}{\sqrt{60}}) \approx 25 \pm 1.01$. The more common way to write this interval is $23.99 < \mu < 26.01$.

In general, the value $(z_c)(\dfrac{s}{\sqrt{n}})$ or $(z_c)(\dfrac{\sigma}{\sqrt{n}})$ is known as the **maximum error of estimate** when determining a confidence interval for the population mean, given a particular sample mean. For Example 49, it is 1.01.

EXAMPLE 50

The heights of a particular type of plant are normally distributed. The heights of 400 plants were measured with a mean of 26 inches and a standard deviation of 4.8 inches. To the nearest hundredth, what is the 90% confidence interval for the mean height of all these plants?

SOLUTION

For a 90% confidence level, the value of z_c is 1.645. If you don't remember this value from the list above, you can use a calculator as outlined in the solution to Example 49. Remember that the calculator uses the area that is strictly to the left of z_c, so for a 90% confidence level, that would be 95%, as shown by the graph below.

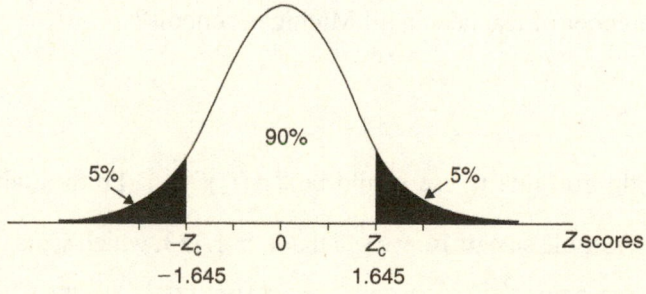

Using the values $\bar{x} = 26$, $s = 4.8$, and $n = 400$, the required interval for the population mean is $26 \pm (1.645)(\dfrac{4.8}{\sqrt{400}}) \approx 26 \pm 0.39$. The interval may also be written as $25.61 < \mu < 26.39$.

The TI-83 calculator is programmed to provide confidence intervals for the population mean, even without the calculation of the critical z values. All that is needed is the sample mean, standard deviation, number of data in the sample, and the desired percent confidence interval. We'll show this process for Example 51.

Press "STAT," scroll to "TESTS," and press 7. At this point, your screen will display "ZInterval" at the top. On the second line, highlight "Stats." Now follow these steps:

For σ, fill in the value of s, which is 4.8. For $\bar{x}$, fill in 26. For n, fill in 400. For "C-Level," fill in 0.90. Scroll to "Calculate" and press "Enter." On the second line, your screen will show (25.605, 26.395), which is equivalent to $25.605 < \mu < 26.395$.

t-Scores

Suppose that we are given a sample size that is less than 30 from a normally distributed population, but we do <u>not</u> know the value of σ. In this scenario, we cannot use the formulas in Examples 64 and 65 to create a confidence interval for μ. However, we can use t-scores in place of z-scores. A t-distribution is a family of curves that approaches the curve of the standard normal distribution, as n approaches 30. Critical t values will replace critical z values, so that the confidence interval becomes $\bar{x} \pm (t_c)(\frac{s}{\sqrt{n}})$. Statistics textbooks do contain tables of critical t values, but since they depend on the sample size, no one t_c value represents, for example, a 90% confidence interval for all samples, as was the case for z_c. The TI-83 is already programmed to do the necessary calculations, though. We'll show the steps for both using a t_c table and using a calculator in the next two examples.

EXAMPLE 51

In a small city in Michigan, a survey of 16 schools was conducted to determine the number of teachers in each school. The results showed a mean of 35 with a sample standard deviation of 5. Assuming that the population of the number of teachers in each Michigan school is normally distributed, what is the 90% confidence interval for the mean number of teachers in all Michigan schools?

SOLUTION

Since $n < 30$, the formula to use would be $\bar{x} \pm (t_c)(\frac{s}{\sqrt{n}})$. From a table of critical values of t for a sample size of 16, we see that t_c is 1.753, which yields a confidence interval of $35 \pm (1.753)\left(\frac{5}{4}\right)$, or $32.809 < < 37.191$. Using the TI-83, follow these steps: Press "STAT," scroll to "TESTS," and press 8. At this point, your screen will display "Tinterval" at the top. On the second line, highlight "Stats." For $\bar{x}$, fill in 35.

For s_x, fill in 5. For n, fill in 16. For "C-Level," fill in 0.90. Now scroll to "Calculate" and press "Enter." On the second line, your screen will show (32.809, 37.191), which is equivalent to $32.809 < \mu < 37.191$.

EXAMPLE 52

The Texas State Police recorded the speed for each of 24 randomly selected vehicles on a busy road. Their mean speed was 43 miles per hour, with a standard deviation of 5.5 miles per hour. Assuming that the speeds of all vehicles on this road are normally distributed, what is the 99% confidence interval for the mean speed of all vehicles on this road?

SOLUTION

Again, with a sample size less than 30, and a fairly normal population, we use t values. If we have a t_c table, we see that $t_c = 2.797$, which yields a confidence interval of $43 \pm (2.797)\left(\dfrac{5.5}{5}\right)$, or $39.923 < < 46.077$.

As in Example 51, using the TI-83, press "STATS," scroll to "TESTS," then press "8." Now enter 43, 5.5, 25, and .99 for $\bar{x}$, s_x, n, and C-Level, respectively. By scrolling to "Calculate" and pressing "Enter," your answer should be (39.923, 46.077). This is equivalent to $39.923 < \mu < 46.077$.

The "Tinterval" feature was necessary in Examples 51 and 52 because even though the population was normal, the sample size was less than 30 and the value of σ was not known. Figure 5.5 provides a helpful flow chart to assist you in deciding which of Tinterval or Zinterval to use when calculating a confidence interval.

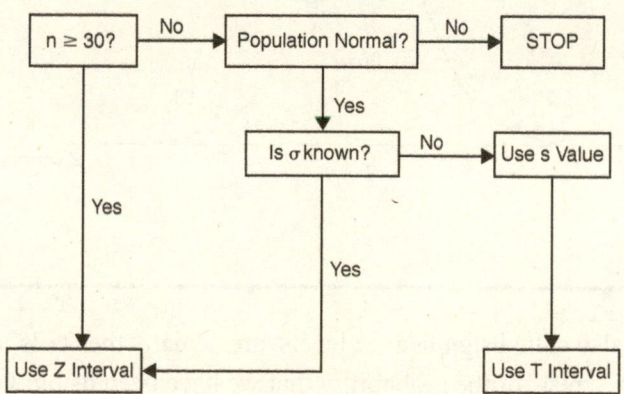

If $n \geq 30$ and σ is not known, use the value of s.

Figure 5.5

One-Tailed Tests

Sometimes data that is only greater than or less than a certain value is of interest. In that case, it is important to remember that the probability represented by the "tail" at the other end of the normal curve has to be included. Example 53 shows one scenario in which this is the case.

EXAMPLE 53

The mean score of the first two tests in a math class is 80, and the standard deviation is 10.5. Assume a normal distribution and that the score on the third test will have the same distribution. What is the probability that the mean score for today's test will be higher than 59 (passing)?

SOLUTION

Let's see what z-score is represented by a score of 59: $z = \dfrac{x - \bar{x}}{s} = \dfrac{59 - 80}{10.5} = -2$. So a score of 59 is 2 standard deviations below the mean (below because it is negative), and we know that ± 2 standard deviations represents 95.5% of the data. But this question asks the probability that the score is higher than the mean. So we must add in also the probability that the score is more than +2 standard deviations from the mean. So we have for our total probability: Probability of scoring from 59 to 80 plus the probability of scoring >80. The probability of scoring from 59 to 80 is half of 95.5%, or 47.75%. The probability of scoring above 80 is 50% (it is the whole right side of the graph). So the total probability of scoring more than 59 is 47.75% + 50% = 97.75%.

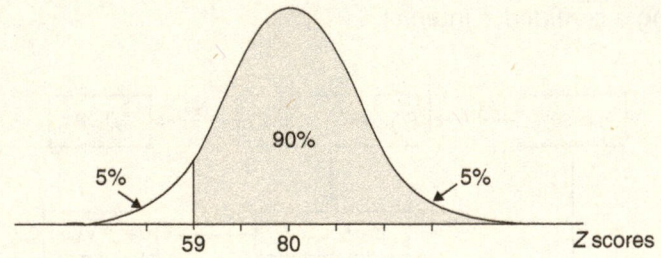

Alpha Values

Alpha (α) values, also called significance levels, are actually the "tails" of the normal distribution. So α is actually the "rest" of the probability that we have been using. For example,

90% confidence corresponds to = .10

95% confidence corresponds to = .05

99% confidence corresponds to = .010

Note that on a two-sided curve, each "tail" has a probability of $\frac{\alpha}{2}$, but on a one-sided curve, is all on one side.

Results are stated as "The test results are statistically significant at the ___ level," where the blank is the value.

Statistical Significance

A value is termed "statistically significant" if it would not occur due to chance. What this means in a normal distribution is that the value lies outside the confidence interval (higher or lower). The value (significance level) is another way to state the chance, or probability, that a value is determined to be statistically significant when, in fact, it is not. For example, stating that "we are 95% confident of our conclusion that result A is statistically significant" is equivalent to saying "There is a 5% chance ($\alpha = .05$) that a value we determined to be statistically significant really is not."

Correlation of Bivariate Data

Scatter Plots

As discussed previously, a scatter plot shows the relationship between two variables. Scatter plots are created by plotting points using (x, y) coordinates where x represents the data of the independent variable and y represents the data of the dependent variable.

In using a scatter plot, we may be interested in determining the best linear relationship between two given quantities. The corresponding mathematical relationship is called a **correlation**. The term **correlation coefficient,** denoted as r, is used to describe mathematically the strength of the relationship between the variables. The value of r lies between -1 and 1, inclusive. When two variables both increase or both decrease at the same time, the value of r will be positive. When one variable increases as the other variable decreases, the value of r will be negative. The closer to -1 or to 1 the value of r lies, the stronger the relationship between the variables. Perfect correlation exists when $r = 1$ or $r = -1$. If $r = 0$, then there is no relationship between the changes in the variables. As an example in which $r = 0$, let the number of people in a household represent one variable and the number of pets in the household represent the second variable.

Figures 5.6, 5.7, and 5.8 illustrate the three categories of r values.

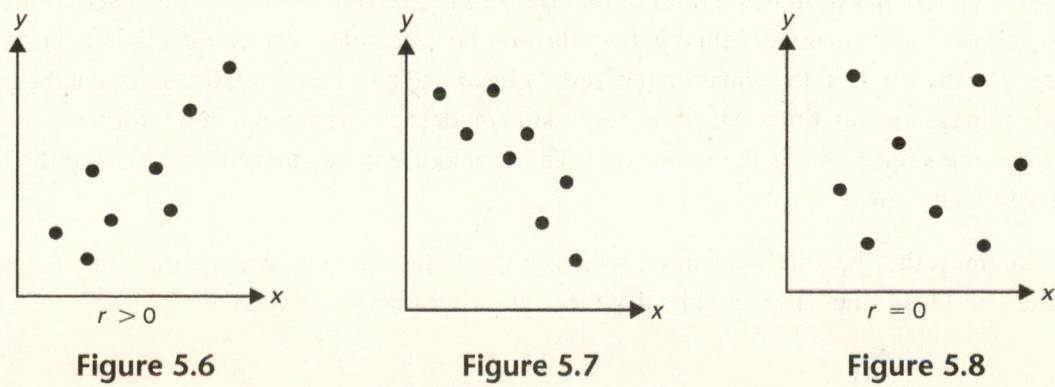

Figure 5.6   **Figure 5.7**   **Figure 5.8**

The actual value of r is given by the following formula:

$$r = \frac{n\left(\sum xy\right) - \left(\sum x\right)\left(\sum y\right)}{\sqrt{\left[n\left(\sum x^2\right) - \left(\sum x\right)^2\right]\left[n\left(\sum y^2\right) - \left(\sum y\right)^2\right]}},$$

where n represents the number of ordered pairs of values. The TI-83 calculator has a program to do this intense computation. This procedure is shown in Example 54.

EXAMPLE 54

Ms. Jones was interested in trying to determine whether a correlation existed between students' final exam grade and the number of hours they claimed they studied for this exam. Her class consisted of eight students, for which the results are shown below. The independent variable x represents the number of hours of study, and the dependent variable y represents the exam grade. For ease of reading, Ms. Jones arranged the number of hours of study in ascending order:

x	1	1.5	2	2.5	3.5	4	5	6.5
y	70	78	75	82	80	85	83	90

What is the value of r?

SOLUTION

Using the TI-83, press "STAT," then highlight "EDIT" and press "1." You will see three columns, labeled L_1, L_2, and L_3. Next, fill in the column L_1 with x values and the column L_2 with the corresponding y values. After all data has been entered, press "STAT," scroll to "CALC," then press "4" (Linear Regression). Your screen will show "LinReg(ax+b)." Press "Enter" and one of the entries on the screen will show that r is approximately 0.895. This number indicates a strong positive correlation, since this value is close to +1.

Regression Analysis

Regression is the process of determining a mathematical equation that models the relationship between two variables. The higher the correlation between the two variables the better the regression equation will model values in the data set. Regression lines are often used to predict future values. This process is called **extrapolation**. For example, perfect correlations mean the data set variables will fit the equation perfectly. Linear and non-linear relationships can be modeled via regression equations. All linear regression models can be written in the form $y = ax + b$, where a is the slope and b is the y-intercept. This equation can be determined by using the **line-of-best fit** technique.

Sometimes the "best fit" is a curve, such as a quadratic equation, exponential function, even a circle. The TI-83 calculator can identify these non-linear curves of best fit.

The equation $y = ax + b$ applies to the line of best fit, which is known as the **least squares line**. This line is determined by minimizing the sum of the squares of the vertical distances (y values) from each point to the line. The values of a and b are found as follows: $a = \dfrac{n(\sum xy) - (\sum x)(\sum y)}{n(\sum x^2) - (\sum x)^2}$ and $b = \dfrac{\sum y - a(\sum x)}{n}$.

Fortunately, the TI-83 calculator provides the least squares line. Return to Example 54. After you pressed "STAT" and scrolled to "CALC," you pressed "4", then "Enter." In addition to revealing the value of r (and of r^2), the screen will show that for the least squares line, $a \approx 2.95$ and $b \approx 70.8$.

Thus, the equation for the least squares line is $y = 2.95x + 70.79$.

Figure 5.9 shows both the scatter plot and the least squares line for Example 54.

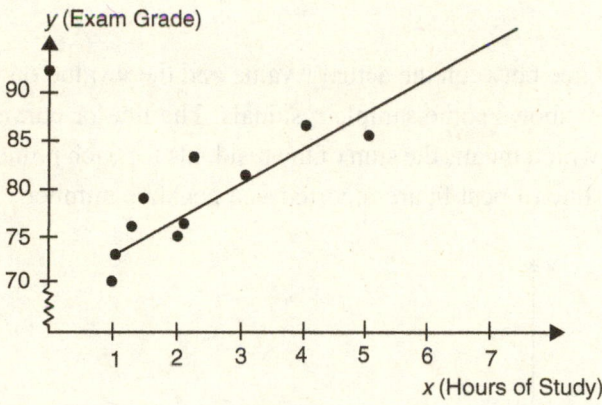

Figure 5.9

EXAMPLE 55

Find the least squares line for the following data. Also, determine the value for 200 roundtrip miles using that equation.

Roundtrip Distance Flown	Price Paid ($)
200	100
640	178
1000	310
150	88
420	150

SOLUTION

Using the TI-83 calculator, after pressing "STAT" and scrolling to "EDIT," remove all current entries for lists L_1 and L_2. Enter the distances flown in L_1 and the prices paid in L_2. The results are as follows: The equation of the least squares line is $y = 0.25x + 44.43$.

We already know that when $x = 200$, $y = 100$. Let's use these two equations to "predict" the y value for $x = 200$. For the least squares line, $y = (0.25)(200) + 44.43 = 94.43$.

Had we chosen to "predict" the y value for $x = 1000$, the least squares line equation produces a value of 294.43, which would be a better approximation to the actual value of 310.

Residuals

For any x, the difference between the actual y value and the y value on the best fit line is called the **residual**. Figure 5.10 shows some sample residuals. The line or curve of best fit should have well-behaved residuals, which means the sum of the residuals for each point should be close to zero. The residuals below the line of best fit are reported as a negative number.

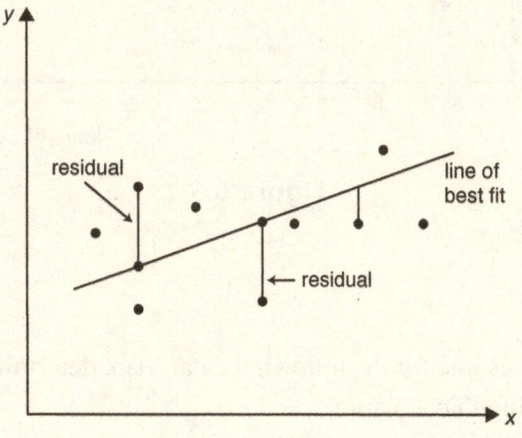

Figure 5.10

PROBABILITY

Probability is the likelihood that a specific event will occur. It is often defined as the ratio of the number of successes to the number of trials, which means how many times a specific event will occur in a number of trials. The larger the number of trials, the more accurate the value for the probability is. One note of caution is needed here. When probability is defined in terms of the number of successes, "success" merely means the specific event of interest. It is possible to find the probability of a student failing an exam, or the probability that an organism in biology lab will die, and in each of these cases, "success" would be failure or death—hardly what we usually think of as success.

Probabilities can be expressed in fractions, or decimals, and always have a value between 0 and 1, or equivalently, when converted to percentages, between 0% and 100%. The probability of an event that cannot occur is 0 (for example, the probability that the sum of two dice is 1), and the probability of an event that *must* occur is 1 (for example, the probability that the sum of two dice is 12 or less). Obviously, the probability of something happening is equal to 1 minus the probability of it not happening.

When working with the normal curves, we used percentages of the area under the curve to determine probabilities of certain values occurring. Probability also is used in many other situations.

Sample Spaces

A **probability experiment** is simply a series of actions from which we can ascertain the likelihood of a particular action to occur. For example, when we toss a penny twice, there are four different results, known formally as **outcomes**, that may occur. Letting H = heads and T = tails, the four outcomes are HH, HT, TH, and TT. There are two parts to each outcome. Also, the outcome HT is different from the outcome TH.

A **sample space,** usually denoted as *S,* is the set of all possible outcomes of a probability experiment. In the example mentioned above, we can write $S = \{HH, HT, TH, TT\}$.

EXAMPLE 56

A probability experiment consists of rolling an ordinary die once. What is the complete sample space?

SOLUTION

Since the only possible outcomes are 1, 2, 3, 4, 5, and 6, the sample space is {1, 2, 3, 4, 5, 6}.

EXAMPLE 57

A five-sided solid figure is numbered 1, 2, 3, 4, and 5 on each of its faces. If this solid is rolled twice, how many outcomes are in its sample space?

SOLUTION

Any of the numbers 1, 2, 3, 4, or 5 may appear on either the first roll or the second roll. Thus, there are (5)(5) = 25 different outcomes that can occur. As examples,

(2,4), (5,5), and (3,2) are three of these outcomes. In this example, (2,4) means "2" is the number on the first roll and "4" is the number on the second roll.

The outcome (2,4) is *not* equivalent to the outcome (4,2), since (4,2) means "4" is the result of the first roll and "2" is the result of the second roll.

EXAMPLE 58

An experiment consists of drawing three cards in succession from a deck of 52 playing cards. Each of the second and third cards are drawn without replacement. How many outcomes are there in the sample space?

SOLUTION

Each outcome consists of three parts. For the first draw, there are 52 possibilities; however, since each of the remaining two cards are drawn without any replacement, there are 51 and 50 possibilities, respectively, for these two draws. Thus, there are $(52)(51)(50) = 132,600$ outcomes.

In Example 58, *if* the selections were made *with* replacement, then we could have the same card appear twice or even three times. For this experiment, there would be $(52)(52)(52) = 140,608$ outcomes.

Any collection of outcomes is called an event, usually denoted by a capital letter. However, an event may consist of just one outcome. In Example 1, if event A consists of outcomes that are even numbers, then $A = \{2, 4, 6\}$. In Example 2, if event B consists of outcomes in which the same number appears twice, then $B = \{(1,1), (2,2), (3,3), (4,4), (5,5)\}$. In Example 3, if event C consists of outcomes in which the first draw is the jack of diamonds, the second draw is the ace of clubs, and the third draw is the 5 of hearts, then $C = \{(J_D, A_C, 5_H)\}$. In this example, the subscripts represent the suits of the cards (D = diamonds, C = clubs, H = hearts).

Leisure time activities can have connections to probability, as shown in Example 59, which relies on some geometry knowledge as well.

EXAMPLE 59

In the diagram of a target shown below, each of the concentric rings numbered 10, 20, 30 or 40 has a radius that is 1′ larger than the next smallest ring. The bull's eye, worth 50 points, has a 1′ radius.

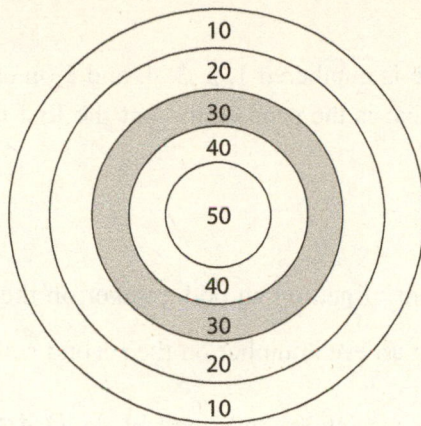

Marcia is a skillful dart player. What is the probability that her dart will land in the 30-ring?

SOLUTION

First, we'll find the area of the 30-ring. The radius of the circle, from the center of the bull's-eye to the edge of the 30 ring, is 3 inches. Therefore, its area is 9π. The inner circle containing the bull's eye and the 40 ring has a radius of 2 inches. So, its area is 4π. Then the area of the 30-ring is $9\pi - 4\pi = 5\pi$. The target has a radius of 5", so its area is 25π. Thus, the required probability is $\dfrac{5\pi}{25\pi} = \dfrac{1}{5}$ or 0.20.

Compound Events

An event that consists of two or more "actions" is called a **compound event**. Examples are (a) rolling a die twice, (b) tossing a coin three times, (c) drawing two cards from a deck of cards, one at a time, with replacement, and (d) selecting two different people from a group of 20 people. Most of the examples presented thus far in this chapter are compound events.

Independent Events

Two events are **independent** if the probability for one event to occur has no effect on the probability of the other event to occur. Further, the probability that both occur is the product of the probability for each event to occur. In symbols, the probability for both events A and B to occur is denoted as $P(A \cap B)$. So, if A and B are independent events, we can write $P(A \cap B) = P(A) \bullet P(B)$.

EXAMPLE 60

A five-sided solid figure is numbered 1, 2, 3, 4, and 5 on each of its faces. If this solid is rolled twice, what is the probability that the first number is odd and the second number is even?

SOLUTION

Let A represent the event of getting an odd number on the first roll and B represent the event of getting an even number on the second roll. Then $P(A) = \dfrac{3}{5}$ and $P(B) = \dfrac{2}{5}$. Clearly, these events are independent, so $P(A \cap B) = \left(\dfrac{3}{5}\right)\left(\dfrac{2}{5}\right) = \dfrac{6}{25}$.

EXAMPLE 61

An ordinary die is rolled twice. What is the probability that the first roll will land on an even number and the second roll will land on a number greater than 4?

SOLUTION

Let A represent the event of getting an even number on the first roll and let B represent the event of getting a number greater than 4 on the second roll. By just using the sample space for a single roll of the die, we can see that $P(A) = \dfrac{3}{6} = \dfrac{1}{2}$ and $P(B) = \dfrac{2}{6} = \dfrac{1}{3}$. These events are independent, so $P(A \cap B) = \left(\dfrac{1}{2}\right)\left(\dfrac{1}{3}\right) = \dfrac{1}{6}$. (This matches our answer in Example 10.)

EXAMPLE 62

In drawing two cards from a deck of playing cards, one card at a time, with replacement of the first card prior to drawing the second card, what is the probability that the first card is an ace and the second card is a black picture card?

SOLUTION

The sample space is 52 outcomes that represent the 52 cards. Let A represent the event of getting an ace on the first draw and let B represent the event of getting a black picture card on the second draw. Since the first card is replaced before the second one is drawn, these events are independent. $P(A) = \dfrac{4}{52} = \dfrac{1}{13}$ and $P(B) = \dfrac{6}{52} = \dfrac{3}{26}$. Thus, $P(A \cap B) = \left(\dfrac{1}{13}\right)\left(\dfrac{3}{26}\right) = \dfrac{3}{338}$.

Dependent Events

Events A and B are called **dependent** if the occurrence of one event will affect the probability of the occurrence of another event. There are many examples in real life that illustrate dependence of events. As an example, leaving on time for work will affect the probability that you will arrive at work on time.

We now introduce the symbol $P(A \mid B)$. This notation means the probability that event A occurs, given that event B has occurred. This is generally *not* equivalent in meaning to $P(B \mid A)$, which means the probability that event B occurs, given that event A has occurred. Note that if $P(A \mid B) = 0$, then event A *cannot* occur if event B has already occurred. Similarly, if $P(A \mid B) = 1$, then event A *must* occur if event B has occurred. Based on the examples we have shown thus far, when two (or more) cards are drawn from a deck *without* replacement, the events are dependent. When A and B are dependent events, the formula to use for $P(A \cap B)$ is as follows: $P(A \cap B) = P(A) \bullet P(B \mid A)$.

EXAMPLE 63

In drawing two cards from a deck of playing cards, one at a time, with no replacement, what is the probability that the first card is red and the second card is a black 10?

SOLUTION

Let A represent the event of drawing a red card. Let $B \mid A$ represent the event of drawing a black 10, given that a red card has already been drawn. Then

$$P(A \cap B) = \left(\frac{26}{52}\right)\left(\frac{2}{51}\right) = \left(\frac{1}{2}\right)\left(\frac{2}{51}\right) = \frac{1}{51}.$$

EXAMPLE 64

A bag of jellybeans contains 6 red, 8 yellow, 4 black, and 7 green ones. Two jellybeans will be randomly selected, one at a time, with no replacement. What is the probability of drawing a red jellybean followed by a green jellybean?

SOLUTION

We need not always use the letters A and B to represent events. Let R represent the event of selecting a red jellybean. Let G represent the event of selecting a green jellybean. Then $P(R) = \dfrac{6}{25}$, and since then only 24 jellybeans remain,

$P(G \mid R) = \dfrac{7}{24}$. Thus, $P(R \cap G) = \left(\dfrac{6}{25}\right)\left(\dfrac{7}{24}\right) = \dfrac{7}{100}.$

EXAMPLE 65

The probability that it will rain today is 0.24. The probability that it will rain today and rain tomorrow is 0.15. What is the probability that it will rain tomorrow, given that it rains today? (Assume that these events are dependent.)

SOLUTION

Let T represent the event that it rains today, and let M represent the event that it rains tomorrow. Then $P(T \cap M)$ represents the event that it rains today and tomorrow, and $P(M \mid T)$ represents the event that it will rain tomorrow, given that it rains today. Substituting into the formula, $P(T \cap M) = P(T) \cdot P(M \mid T)$, we get,

$0.15 = [0.24][P(M \mid T)]$. Thus, $P(M \mid T) = \dfrac{0.15}{0.24} = 0.625$.

In Example 65 we used decimals to solve for the conditional probability value. We don't have enough information to calculate $P(M)$, which is just the probability that it will rain tomorrow. Fortunately, that value is not needed to complete the solution.

EXAMPLE 66

The probability that Laura will go to work today is 0.85. The probability that she will go to work today and finish all her projects is 0.68. What is the probability that she will finish all her projects, given that she goes to work today?

SOLUTION

Let C represent the event that Laura will go to work today, and let $(C \cap D)$ represent the event that Laura will go to work today and finish all her projects. Then $(D \mid C)$ represents the event that she will finish all her projects, given that she goes to work today. Substituting into the formula $P(C \cap D) = P(C) \cdot P(D \mid C)$, we get $0.68 = 0.85 \cdot P(D \mid C)$. Thus, $P(D \mid C) = 0.80$.

Addition Rule of Probability

Suppose we have *any* two events M and N. The symbol $P(M \cup N)$ means the probability that event M occurs, *or* event N occurs, *or* both M and N occur. Another interpretation for $P(M \cup N)$ is the probability that at least one of M and N occurs. The general formula for calculating the value of $P(M \cup N)$ is as follows: $P(M \cup N) = P(M) + P(N) - P(M \cap N)$.

The justification for this formula is more readily understood with the use of a Venn diagram. Consider Figure 5.11, shown below.

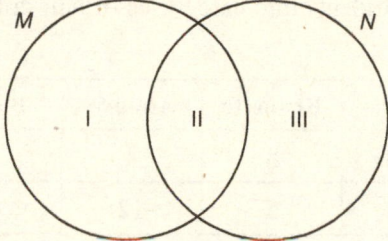

Figure 5.11

In this diagram, M and N represent subsets that overlap. Each Roman numeral indicates elements that belong to that region. So, set M consists of regions I and II; set N consists of regions II and III; set $M \cap N$ consists of region II. By substitution, Regions (I + II + III) = Regions (I + II) + Regions (II + III) – Region II, since we can't count Region II twice.

Non-Mutually Exclusive Events

The term **mutually exclusive** means that both events *cannot* occur together. Let's look first at the general case of **non-mutually exclusive events**, events that may *both* occur together, so $P(X \cap Y) \neq 0$. As we have seen, the calculation of $P(X \cap Y)$ is either $P(X) \cdot P(Y)$ or $P(X) \cdot P(Y | X)$, based on whether X and Y are independent or dependent events, respectively.

EXAMPLE 67

A nickel is tossed 3 times. What is the probability of getting exactly 2 tails or getting a heads on the third toss?

SOLUTION

Let K represent the event of getting exactly 2 tails, and let L represent the event of getting a heads on the third toss. There are a total of 8 outcomes in the sample space. $K = \{TTH, THT, HTT\}$, so $P(K) = \frac{3}{8}$. $L = \{HHH, HTH, THH, TTH\}$, so $P(L) = \frac{4}{8} = \frac{1}{2}$. The only outcome that belongs to the event $K \cap L$ is TTH, so $P(K \cap L) = \frac{1}{8}$. Thus, $P(K \cup L) = \frac{3}{8} + \frac{1}{2} - \frac{1}{8} = \frac{6}{8} = \frac{3}{4}$.

EXAMPLE 68

In Ms. Green's class, there are 36 students. One day, Ms. Green decided to create a chart that divides the students into categories of hair color and gender. Here are the results:

	Brunette	Auburn	Blond
Female	8	4	3
Male	5	12	4

Ms. Green selects a student from her class and tosses an ordinary dime twice. What is the probability that she selects a student with auburn hair or gets tails both times when tossing the dime twice?

SOLUTION

Let C represent the event of selecting a student with auburn hair, and let D represent getting two tails when tossing the dime twice. Since there are 16 students with auburn hair, $P(C) = \dfrac{16}{36} = \dfrac{4}{9}$. In tossing the dime twice, only one of the four possible outcomes shows TT, so $P(D) = \dfrac{1}{4}$. Then $P(C \cap D) = \dfrac{4}{9} \times \dfrac{1}{4} = \dfrac{1}{9}$. Thus,

$$P(C \cup D) = \frac{4}{9} + \frac{1}{4} - \frac{1}{9} = \frac{21}{36} = \frac{7}{12}.$$

EXAMPLE 69

In a bag of 40 marbles, 15 are white, 20 are yellow, and the rest are purple. Two marbles will be randomly drawn, one at a time, with replacement. What is the probability that at least one of these is white?

SOLUTION

Let V represent the event that the first marble is white, and let W represent the event that the second marble is white. Then $P(V) = P(W) = \dfrac{15}{40} = \dfrac{3}{8}$. Even though these events are independent, it is possible for both events to occur, so they are not mutually exclusive, and $P(V \cap W) = \left(\dfrac{3}{8}\right)\left(\dfrac{3}{8}\right) = \dfrac{9}{64}$. Thus, $P(V \cup W) = \dfrac{3}{8} + \dfrac{3}{8} - \dfrac{9}{64} = \dfrac{39}{64}.$

EXAMPLE 70

Two cards will be randomly drawn from a deck of playing cards, one at a time, without replacement. What is the probability that at least one of them is a picture card?

SOLUTION

Let X represent the event that the first card drawn is a picture card and let Y represent the event that the second card drawn is a picture card. Since these events are without replacement, they are dependent, and $P(X \cap Y) = P(X) \bullet P(Y \mid X) = \left(\dfrac{12}{52} \right)\left(\dfrac{11}{51} \right)$

$= \dfrac{11}{221}$, $P(X) = P(Y) = \dfrac{12}{52} = \dfrac{3}{13}$, so $P(X \cup Y) = \dfrac{3}{13} + \dfrac{3}{13} - \dfrac{11}{221} = \dfrac{91}{221} = \dfrac{7}{17}$.

Example 70 had two *dependent* events. Be careful that you understood the difference between the meaning of $P(Y)$ and $P(Y \mid X)$. Another (longer) approach to the solution would be to note that the sample space for drawing two cards, without replacement consists of $(52)(51) = 2652$ elements. Of these, the number of elements that do *not* contain at least one picture card is $(40)(39) = 1560$. So, there are $2652 - 1560 = 1092$ elements that do contain at least one picture card. Thus the required probability is $\dfrac{1092}{2652} = \dfrac{7}{17}$.

By the way, if these two cards had been drawn *with* replacement, the answer would have been $\dfrac{69}{169}$.

Mutually Exclusive Events

As stated previously, two events A and B are called **mutually exclusive** if they cannot both occur at the same time. Here are a few examples of mutually exclusive events.

(a) In drawing one playing card from a deck, event C represents getting an ace, and event D represents getting a queen.

(b)   In rolling a die once, event E represents getting an even number, and event F represents getting a 3.

(c) In tossing a penny twice, event G represents getting two tails, and event H represents getting two heads.

If A and B are any two mutually exclusive events, then $P(A \cap B) = 0$. This is a natural conclusion because the two events cannot both occur at the same time. But it is possible that *neither* event actually occurs. Using example (a) shown above, it is possible to draw a card that is neither an ace nor a queen.

Furthermore, each of $P(A|B)$ and $P(B|A)$ must equal zero, because the occurrence of one of these events automatically prevents the occurrence of the other event. For this reason, mutually exclusive events must also be dependent events.

EXAMPLE 71

A die is rolled twice. What is the probability of getting a sum of 3 or a sum of 8?

SOLUTION

Let C represent the event of getting a sum of 3, and let D represent the event of getting a sum of 8. There are a total of 36 outcomes. When a die is rolled twice the only outcomes for which a sum of 3 is possible are $(1,2)$ and $(2,1)$, so $P(C) = \dfrac{2}{36} = \dfrac{1}{18}$. The outcomes for which a sum of 8 is possible are $(2,6)$, $(3,5)$, $(4,4)$, $(5,3)$, and $(6,2)$. So $P(D) = \dfrac{5}{36}$. Thus, $P(C \cup D) = \dfrac{1}{18} + \dfrac{5}{36} = \dfrac{7}{36}$.

EXAMPLE 72

One card is drawn from a deck of playing cards. What is the probability of drawing a picture card or a 2?

SOLUTION

Let G represent the event of drawing a picture card, and let H represent the event of drawing a 2. There are 12 picture cards and four 2s, so $P(G) = \dfrac{12}{52} = \dfrac{3}{13}$ and $P(H) = \dfrac{4}{52} = \dfrac{1}{13}$. Thus, $P(G \cup H) = \dfrac{4}{13}$.

Expected Value

The **expected value** of any quantity is the theoretical average value after performing the probability experiment an infinite number of times. Mathematically, it is calculated as follows. Let X represent the given quantity and let $E(X)$ represent its expected value. Then $E(X) = \sum_{1}^{n} (X_i) \times P(X_i)]$, where n represents the number of different values of X. If we are talking about a game of chance, the expected value of the game is the expected winnings minus the cost of the game.

EXAMPLE 73

Based on previous experience, a public speaker has developed a probability distribution for the number of speeches that she makes in one week. Each week, she made at least one speech, but never more than five speeches.

X	1	2	3	4	5
P(X)	0.3	0.1	0.2	0.2	0.2

What is the value of $E(X)$?

SOLUTION

$E(X) = (1)(0.3) + (2)(0.1) + (3)(0.2) + (4)(0.2) + (5)(0.2) = 2.9$. This means that 2.9 is the expected (or average) number of speeches that she will make per week.

EXAMPLE 74

A game consists of spinning a 4-color spinner (red, blue, green, and yellow). The probability that the spinner will stop at any one color is 0.25. The game costs $5 to play. A player wins $8 if the spinner stops on red or blue. A player wins $1 if the spinner stops on green or yellow. What is the expected value of the game?

SOLUTION

As stated above,

Expected value of the game = Expected winnings – Cost of the game.

Let X represent the expected winnings. X can assume the values of 1 and 8. Then $E(X) = 8(\frac{1}{4}) + 8(\frac{1}{4}) + 1(\frac{1}{4}) + 1(\frac{1}{4}) = \$4.50$. Thus, the expected value of the game is $\$4.50 - \$5.00 = -\$0.50$. This means that the player should expect to lose an average of 50 cents per game when playing this game over time.

An easy way to check this answer is to assume that the player plays this game four times. Suppose that the spinner stops at each of the four colors in the following order: red, blue, green, yellow. Then the player would collect $8 + $8 + $1 + $1 = $18.
However, the cost for playing the four games is (4)($5) = $20. So, the player actually lost $2. If we divide the loss of $2 by the four games, we arrive at an average loss of $0.50 per game.

Games of chance are designed so that the customer can win money over a short period of time, but the probability is high that he or she will lose money over a long period of time.

Empirical Probability

Empirical probability refers to the determination of probability values based on observations or historical data. If A represents an event, its empirical probability is simply the ratio of its frequency to the total frequency of all observations (or data).

EXAMPLE 75

A particular die is rolled 1,800 times and the results of the frequency of each outcome are as follows:

Outcome	Frequency
1	120
2	140
3	250
4	450
5	300
6	540

Based on this chart, what is the probability that in rolling this die, it will land on a 3 or a 4?

SOLUTION

The number of times in which this die has landed on 3 or 4 is $250 + 450 = 700$.

Since this die was rolled 1,800 times, the required probability is $\frac{700}{1,800} = \frac{7}{18}$.

EXAMPLE 76

A particular dime is tossed 3 times, and the experiment is repeated 4,000 times. Here are the results:

Outcome	Frequency
HHH	2,050
HHT	510
HTH	430
HTT	240
THH	500
THT	100
TTH	120
TTT	50

Based on this chart, what is the probability that when this dime is tossed three times, the result will be all exactly two tails?

SOLUTION

The "successful" outcomes are HTT, THT, and TTH, for which the combined frequency is $240 + 100 + 120 = 460$. Thus, the required probability is $\dfrac{460}{4,000}$, which reduces to $\dfrac{23}{200}$.

EXAMPLE 77

A random group of 90 people was asked to select their favorite ice cream flavor. The choice of flavors was limited to vanilla, chocolate, strawberry, butter pecan, and cherry. Here are the results:

Flavor	Frequency
Vanilla	32
Chocolate	24
Strawberry	16
Butter Pecan	10
Cherry	8

Based on this chart, what is the probability that a person selected from this group had chosen either vanilla or chocolate as his/her favorite flavor?

SOLUTION

A total of $32 + 24 = 56$ people chose one of these two flavors. Thus, the required probability is $\dfrac{56}{90}$, which reduces to $\dfrac{28}{45}$.

Matrix Algebra and Discrete Mathematics

MATRIX ALGEBRA

Four Basic Number Properties

For the real number system, as we saw in Chapter 2, four basic properties exist for the addition and multiplication operations, namely:

(a) Associative

(b) Commutative

(c) Distributive

(d) Inverse

Let's show examples of each.

(a) Associative for addition: $3 + (7 + 6) = (3 + 7) + 6$; Associative for multiplication: $(3)[(7)(6)] = [(3)(7)](6)$

(b) Commutative for addition: $2 + 8 = 8 + 2$; Commutative for multiplication: $(2)(8) = (8)(2)$

(c) Distributive for multiplication over addition: $(4)(9 + 5) = (4)(9) + (4)(5)$

(d) Additive inverse: $(5) + (-5) = 0$; Multiplicative inverse: $(5)\left(\dfrac{1}{5}\right) = 1$

Vectors

We have been working mainly with scalar quantities, which have only magnitude. Quantities that have both magnitude and *direction* are called **vectors**. There are several notations for vectors. Here, we will use the notation $\overrightarrow{AB} = a\mathbf{i} + b\mathbf{j}$, where a and b indicate the components of the vector in the *x* and *y* directions, respectively. Other notations for vectors include $\overrightarrow{AB} = <a, b>$, $\mathbf{AB} = (a, b)$, $\mathbf{v} = v_x + v_y$, $\mathbf{v} = v_1, v_2$, or $\mathbf{v} = \begin{bmatrix} v_1 \\ v_2 \end{bmatrix}$. Of course, vectors can have more than two components. Two components indicate a planar vector.

Thus, vector $\overrightarrow{AB} = 3\mathbf{i} + 4\mathbf{j}$ has an *x*-component of 3 and a *y*-component of 4, and from the Pythagorean Theorem, we can determine that it has magnitude 5 and direction as shown in Figure 6.1. However, it can appear anywhere on the *xy*-plane, just as long as it has magnitude 5 and the direction shown. Vectors with the same magnitude and direction are considered to be **equivalent vectors**, even if they appear in different places on the *xy*-plane, as shown by vectors $\overrightarrow{AB}$ and $\overrightarrow{CD}$ in Figure 6.1.

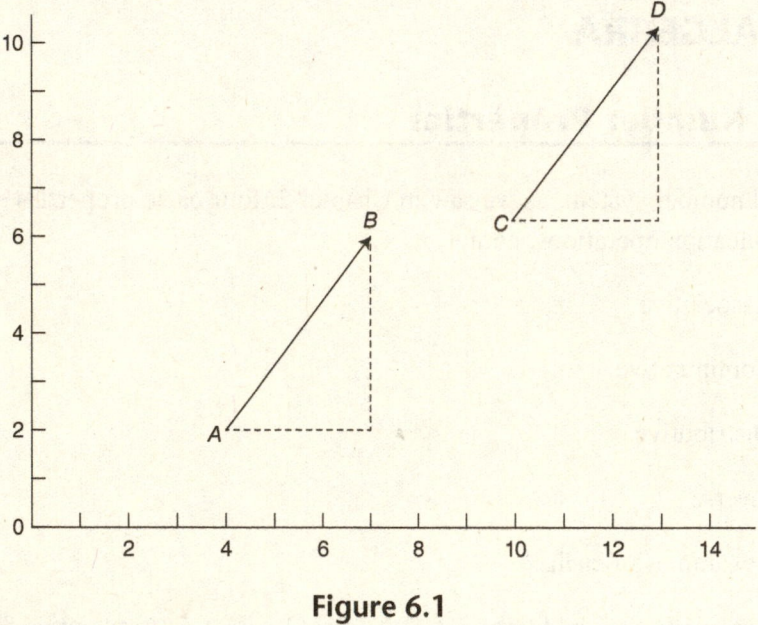

Figure 6.1

Vector Addition and Subtraction

For the addition of two vectors, the result is a vector called the **resultant**, which is formed when two vectors are placed with the initial vector. If the vectors are in the same direction, it is easy to see that the resultant would just be a vector in the same direction but with length equal to the sum of the lengths of the vectors. If two two-dimensional vectors have different directions, their sum is a vector that completes the triangle when the vectors are placed head to tail, as shown in Figure 6.2. These resultants can be calculated as follows: $[(a\mathbf{i} + b\mathbf{j}) + (c\mathbf{i} + d\mathbf{j})] = (a+c)\mathbf{i} + (b+d)\mathbf{j}$. Subtraction of two vectors is similar, $[(a\mathbf{i} + b\mathbf{j}) - (c\mathbf{i} + d\mathbf{j})] = (a + c)\mathbf{i} - (b + d)\mathbf{j}$, but graphically it looks like Figure 6.3.

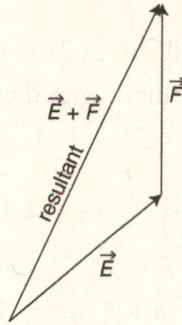

Figure 6.2

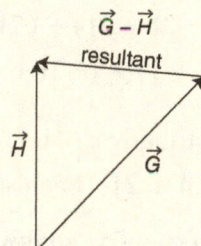

Figure 6.3

Vector Multiplication

We consider two types of vector multiplication. The first is a vector multiplied by a scalar, in which each component is multiplied by the scalar, $k(a\mathbf{i} + b\mathbf{j}) = ka\mathbf{i} + kb\mathbf{j}$, and the result is a vector k times as long as the original vector and in the same direction.

The second type of multiplication is multiplying a vector by a vector, called the **dot product**, and the result is not a vector (as perhaps expected); instead, it is a real number, or a scalar. The dot product of two vectors is calculated as $(a\mathbf{i} + b\mathbf{j}) \bullet (c\mathbf{i} + d\mathbf{j}) = ac + bd$.

EXAMPLE 1

Find the sum, difference, and dot product of vectors $2\mathbf{i} - 5\mathbf{j}$ and $-3\mathbf{i} + \mathbf{j}$.

SOLUTION

$(2\mathbf{i} - 5\mathbf{j}) + (-3\mathbf{i} + \mathbf{j}) = -\mathbf{i} - 2\mathbf{j}$

$(2\mathbf{i} - 5\mathbf{j}) - (-3\mathbf{i} + \mathbf{j}) = 5\mathbf{i} - 6\mathbf{j}$

$(2\mathbf{i} - 5\mathbf{j}) \bullet (-3\mathbf{i} + \mathbf{j}) = -6 + (-5) = -11$

[Handwritten annotations:]
Sum: $-i - 2j$
diff: $5i - 6j$
dot product: $-6 + (-5) = -11$

Properties of Vectors

We now investigate whether the basic number properties exist for vectors.

To check out the four properties, let's use $\overrightarrow{AB} = 4\mathbf{i} - \mathbf{j}$, $\overline{CD} = 2\mathbf{i} + \mathbf{j}$, and $\overline{EF} = -3\mathbf{i} + 2\mathbf{j}$.

(a) Associative: For addition, $[(4\mathbf{i} - \mathbf{j}) + (2\mathbf{i} + \mathbf{j})] + (-3\mathbf{i} + 2\mathbf{j}) = 3\mathbf{i} + 2\mathbf{j}$. However, for multiplication, we have $(4\mathbf{i} - \mathbf{j}) \bullet [(2\mathbf{i} + \mathbf{j}) \bullet (-3\mathbf{i} + 2\mathbf{j})] \neq [(4\mathbf{i} - \mathbf{j}) \bullet (2\mathbf{i} + \mathbf{j})] \bullet$

$(-3\mathbf{i} + 2\mathbf{j})$. The left side of this inequality simplifies to $-16\mathbf{i} + 4\mathbf{j}$, whereas the right side simplifies to $-21\mathbf{i} + 14\mathbf{j}$.

(b) Communicative: For addition, using vectors $\overrightarrow{CD}$ and $\overrightarrow{EF}$, $(2\mathbf{i} + \mathbf{j}) + (-3\mathbf{i} + 2\mathbf{j})$ $= (-3\mathbf{i} + 2\mathbf{j}) + (2\mathbf{i} + \mathbf{j}) = -\mathbf{i} + 3\mathbf{j}$. For multiplication, using these same vectors, $(2\mathbf{i} + \mathbf{j}) \bullet (-3\mathbf{i} + 2\mathbf{j}) = (-3\mathbf{i} + 2\mathbf{j}) \bullet (2\mathbf{i} + \mathbf{j}) = -4$.

(c) Distributive: $(4\mathbf{i} - \mathbf{j}) \bullet [(2\mathbf{i} + \mathbf{j}) + (-3\mathbf{i} + 2\mathbf{j})] = (4\mathbf{i} - \mathbf{j}) \bullet (2\mathbf{i} + \mathbf{j}) + (4\mathbf{i} - \mathbf{j}) \bullet$ $(-3\mathbf{i} + 2\mathbf{j})$. Each side of this equation has a value of -7.

(d) Inverse: For additive inverses, for example, using vector $\overrightarrow{AB} = 4\mathbf{i} - \mathbf{j}$, there is a unique vector $-4\mathbf{i} + \mathbf{j}$ such that $(4\mathbf{i} - \mathbf{j}) + -4\mathbf{i} + \mathbf{j} = 0\mathbf{i} + 0\mathbf{j}$, called the zero vector; however, multiplicative inverses for vectors do not exist.

In summary, the following are the number properties that exist among vectors.

For **addition of vectors**, the properties of *Associativity, Commutativity*, and *Inverses* apply.

For the **multiplication of vectors**, the property of *Commutativity* applies. However, the property of *Associativity* does *not* apply, and there does *not* exist a multiplicative inverse. The *Distributive property involving multiplication over addition* applies.

Matrices

A matrix is a rectangular array of numbers, called entries. The number of rows and columns of a matrix are called its **dimensions.** The number of rows is the first dimension and the number of columns is the second dimension.

$$\begin{bmatrix} 6 & 2 \\ 3 & 1 \\ 0 & 0 \end{bmatrix}$$ is a matrix with dimensions 3×2.

row ↓

↳ column

$[1\ 7\ 2\ 1]$ is a matrix with dimensions 1×4.

Entries starting at the top left and proceeding to the bottom right of a square matrix are said to be on the main diagonal of that matrix.

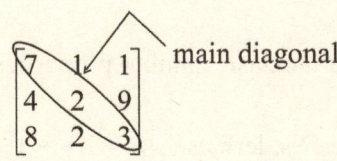

main diagonal

Matrix Addition and Subtraction

Suppose there are two $m \times n$ matrices, A and B. Then the sum of the two matrices, $A + B$, is obtained by adding corresponding entries of A and B. The difference, $A - B$, is obtained by subtracting the entries of B from the corresponding entries of A. Both $A + B$ and $A - B$ have dimensions of $m \times n$.

EXAMPLE 2

If $A = \begin{bmatrix} 2 & 3 & 4 \\ 1 & 2 & 1 \end{bmatrix}$ and $B = \begin{bmatrix} 0 & 2 & 7 \\ 1 & -3 & 5 \end{bmatrix}$, find $A - B$.

SOLUTION

$A - B$ is obtained by subtracting the entries of B from the corresponding entries of A.

$$A - B = \begin{bmatrix} 2 & 3 & 4 \\ 1 & 2 & 1 \end{bmatrix} - \begin{bmatrix} 0 & 2 & 7 \\ 1 & -3 & 5 \end{bmatrix}$$

$$= \begin{bmatrix} 2-0 & 3-2 & 4-7 \\ 1-1 & 2-(-3) & 1-5 \end{bmatrix}$$

$$= \begin{bmatrix} 2 & 1 & -3 \\ 0 & 5 & -4 \end{bmatrix}$$

Scalar Multiplication

The product of a matrix A by a scalar k is obtained by multiplying each entry of A by k.

EXAMPLE 3

What is the product $5 \times \begin{bmatrix} 3 & 7 \\ -\dfrac{1}{3} & -2 \end{bmatrix}$?

SOLUTION

Just multiply 5 by each element. The answer is $\begin{bmatrix} 15 & 35 \\ -\dfrac{5}{3} & -10 \end{bmatrix}$

EXAMPLE 4

If $A = \begin{bmatrix} 2 & -2 & 4 \\ -1 & 1 & 1 \end{bmatrix}$ and $B = \begin{bmatrix} 0 & 1 & -3 \\ 1 & 3 & 1 \end{bmatrix}$, find $2A + B$.

SOLUTION

$$2A = 2\begin{bmatrix} 2 & -2 & 4 \\ -1 & 1 & 1 \end{bmatrix}$$

$$= \begin{bmatrix} 2 \times 2 & 2 \times (-2) & 2 \times 4 \\ 2 \times (-1) & 2 \times 1 & 2 \times 1 \end{bmatrix}$$

$$= \begin{bmatrix} 4 & -4 & 8 \\ -2 & 2 & 2 \end{bmatrix}$$

Then,

$$2A + B = \begin{bmatrix} 4 & -4 & 8 \\ -2 & 2 & 2 \end{bmatrix} + \begin{bmatrix} 0 & 1 & -3 \\ 1 & 3 & 1 \end{bmatrix}$$

$$= \begin{bmatrix} 4+0 & -4+1 & 8-3 \\ -2+1 & 2+3 & 2+1 \end{bmatrix}$$

$$2A + B = \begin{bmatrix} 4 & -3 & 5 \\ -1 & 5 & 3 \end{bmatrix}$$

Matrix Multiplication

Multiplying two matrices, A and B, requires multiplying each entry of a row of A by the corresponding entries in the columns of B and adding the resulting products. That is, to obtain the *(ij)* entry of AB, multiply the entries of row i of A by the corresponding entries of column j of B and add the products.

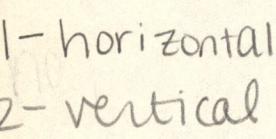

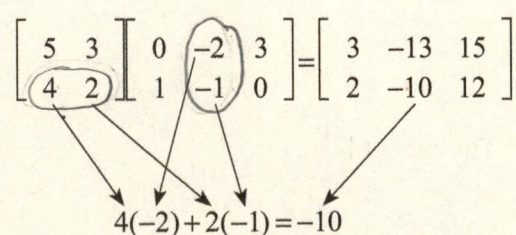

$$4(-2) + 2(-1) = -10$$

The number of entries in a row of matrix A must equal the number of entries in each column of B for the multiplication of the matrices to be defined. The solution matrix will have the same number of rows as A and the same number of columns as B. That is, if A is $m \times n$ and B is $n \times p$ then AB is $m \times p$.

EXAMPLE 5

If $A = \begin{bmatrix} 1 & 2 & 4 \\ 2 & 6 & 0 \end{bmatrix}$ and $B = \begin{bmatrix} 4 & 1 & 4 & 3 \\ 0 & -1 & 3 & 1 \\ 2 & 7 & 5 & 2 \end{bmatrix}$, find AB.

SOLUTION

Since A is a 2×3 matrix and B is a 3×4 matrix, the product AB is a 2×4 matrix.

$$AB = \begin{bmatrix} 1 & 2 & 4 \\ 2 & 6 & 0 \end{bmatrix} \begin{bmatrix} 4 & 1 & 4 & 3 \\ 0 & -1 & 3 & 1 \\ 2 & 7 & 5 & 2 \end{bmatrix}$$

$$= \begin{bmatrix} 1 \cdot 4 + 2 \cdot 0 + 4 \cdot 2 & 1 \cdot 1 + 2 \cdot (-1) + 4 \cdot 7 & 1 \cdot 4 + 2 \cdot 3 + 4 \cdot 5 & 1 \cdot 3 + 2 \cdot 1 + 4 \cdot 2 \\ 2 \cdot 4 + 6 \cdot 0 + 0 \cdot 2 & 2 \cdot 1 + 6 \cdot (-1) + 0 \cdot 7 & 2 \cdot 4 + 6 \cdot 3 + 0 \cdot 5 & 2 \cdot 3 + 6 \cdot 1 + 0 \cdot 2 \end{bmatrix}$$

$$= \begin{bmatrix} 4 + 0 + 8 & 1 - 2 + 28 & 4 + 6 + 20 & 3 + 2 + 8 \\ 8 + 0 + 0 & 2 - 6 + 0 & 8 + 18 + 0 & 6 + 6 + 0 \end{bmatrix}$$

$$AB = \begin{bmatrix} 12 & 27 & 30 & 13 \\ 8 & -4 & 26 & 12 \end{bmatrix}$$

EXAMPLE 6

A restaurant has three specials. The number of calories, the number of grams of fat and the number of grams of protein for each special are listed below.

	Calories	Fat	Protein
Salmon	375	20	30
Steak	650	20	45
Chicken	275	5	30

One table of patrons places the following order: 2 salmon specials, 2 steak specials and 1 chicken special. What is the total number of calories, grams of fat, and grams of protein consumed at the table?

SOLUTION

Create a row matrix to represent the order: $\begin{bmatrix} 2 & 2 & 1 \end{bmatrix}$. Multiplying the order matrix by the given matrix will result in a 1×3 matrix containing the total number of calories, total number of grams of fat, and total number of grams of protein consumed at the table.

$$\begin{bmatrix} 2 & 2 & 1 \end{bmatrix} \begin{bmatrix} 375 & 20 & 30 \\ 650 & 20 & 45 \\ 275 & 5 & 30 \end{bmatrix}$$

$$= \begin{bmatrix} 2(375) + 2(650) + 275 & 2(20) + 2(20) + 5 & 2(30) + 2(45) + 30 \end{bmatrix}$$

$$= \begin{bmatrix} 2,325 & 85 & 180 \end{bmatrix}$$

A total of 2,325 calories, 85 grams of fat and 180 grams of protein were consumed by the table during the meal.

Inverse of a Matrix

With respect to inverses, we first consider the **additive inverse** of a matrix under addition. The *identity matrix for addition* is any matrix with all zeros. Given any matrix A, its additive inverse is represented as $-A$. The actual numbers (elements) in $-A$ are simply the additive inverses of the elements in A. For example, if $A = \begin{bmatrix} 2 & 3 \\ -1 & 5 \\ 7 & -4 \end{bmatrix}$, then $-A = \begin{bmatrix} -2 & -3 \\ 1 & -5 \\ -7 & 4 \end{bmatrix}$, and $A + -A) = \begin{bmatrix} 1 & 0 & 0 \\ 0 & 1 & 0 \\ 0 & 0 & 1 \end{bmatrix}$, the identity matrix.

Before we explore **multiplicative inverses** for matrices, we need to define the *identity matrix for multiplication*. This matrix must be square and consists of all 1s on its main diagonal and 0s everywhere else. As examples, each of $\begin{bmatrix} 1 & 0 \\ 0 & 1 \end{bmatrix}$ and $\begin{bmatrix} 1 & 0 & 0 \\ 0 & 1 & 0 \\ 0 & 0 & 1 \end{bmatrix}$ is an identity matrix. Identity matrices are denoted as I.

If B is any square matrix with m rows and m columns, its multiplicative inverse, if it exists, is denoted as B^{-1} and will also contain m rows and m columns.

Then $B \times B^{-1} = B^{-1} \times B = I$. For example if $B = \begin{bmatrix} 3 & 5 \\ 1 & 2 \end{bmatrix}$, then $B^{-1} = \begin{bmatrix} 2 & -5 \\ -1 & 3 \end{bmatrix}$.

In fact, $B \times B^{-1} = \begin{bmatrix} 3 & 5 \\ 1 & 2 \end{bmatrix} \times \begin{bmatrix} 2 & -5 \\ -1 & 3 \end{bmatrix} = \begin{bmatrix} 1 & 0 \\ 0 & 1 \end{bmatrix}$.

The actual technique for finding B^{-1} will be shown in Example 9. First, we must define the determinant of a matrix. Given the matrix $X = \begin{bmatrix} a & b \\ c & d \end{bmatrix}$, the **determinant** of X, written as det X is defined as the value of $ad - bc$. Note that the determinant of a matrix is a scalar, not a matrix. The requirement for the existence of a multiplicative inverse is that the determinant of the given matrix is not zero.

The Commutative property of multiplication does apply to a matrix and its multiplicative inverse. Non-square matrices do not have multiplicative inverses. Furthermore, not every square matrix has a multiplicative inverse.

The multiplicative inverse X^{-1} is given by the matrix that results from the product $\left(\dfrac{1}{ad-bc}\right) \times \begin{bmatrix} d & -b \\ -c & a \end{bmatrix}$, provided $ad - bc \neq 0$.

EXAMPLE 7

What is the determinant of the matrix $Y = \begin{bmatrix} -2 & 6 \\ 4 & 1 \end{bmatrix}$?

SOLUTION

The determinant equals $(-2)(1) - (6)(4) = -26$.

EXAMPLE 8

If the matrix $\begin{bmatrix} 5 & x \\ -2 & 3 \end{bmatrix}$ does *not* have a multiplicative inverse, what is the value of x?

SOLUTION

In order that the multiplicative inverse does not exist, the determinant must equal 0. So $(5)(3) - (-2)(x) = 0$. Then $x = -7\frac{1}{2}$. (Elements of matrices need not be integers.)

EXAMPLE 9

What is the multiplicative inverse matrix for $A = \begin{bmatrix} -3 & 2 \\ 4 & -6 \end{bmatrix}$?

SOLUTION

First calculate $(-3)(-6) - (4)(2) = 10$.

The multiplicative inverse is given by $\left(\dfrac{1}{10}\right) \times \begin{bmatrix} -6 & -2 \\ -4 & -3 \end{bmatrix} = \begin{bmatrix} -\dfrac{3}{5} & -\dfrac{1}{5} \\ -\dfrac{2}{5} & -\dfrac{3}{10} \end{bmatrix}$

To check this answer, $\begin{bmatrix} -3 & 2 \\ 4 & -6 \end{bmatrix} \times \begin{bmatrix} -\dfrac{3}{5} & -\dfrac{1}{5} \\ -\dfrac{2}{5} & -\dfrac{3}{10} \end{bmatrix}$ must equal $\begin{bmatrix} 1 & 0 \\ 0 & 1 \end{bmatrix}$, and it does!

The procedure for finding the multiplicative inverse of a matrix with 3 rows and 3 columns is beyond the scope of this book. However, for further practice in matrix multiplication, if $M = \begin{bmatrix} 3 & 3 & -1 \\ -2 & -2 & 1 \\ -4 & -5 & 2 \end{bmatrix}$, then $M^{-1} = \begin{bmatrix} 1 & -1 & 1 \\ 0 & 2 & -1 \\ 2 & 3 & 0 \end{bmatrix}$, and the product of these two matrices is the identity matrix for 3 rows and 3 columns.

Properties of Matrices

We will now investigate whether the four basic properties of numbers apply to matrices.

In order to check the properties as they apply to addition, we must select two matrices that have an equal number of rows and an equal number of columns.

Let $A = \begin{bmatrix} 3 & -1 & 2 \\ 4 & 1 & 0 \end{bmatrix}$ $B = \begin{bmatrix} 5 & -2 & 3 \\ -4 & 2 & 1 \end{bmatrix}$ and $C = \begin{bmatrix} -3 & 1 & -5 \\ 2 & 0 & 4 \end{bmatrix}$

We will now check the basic properties of numbers that involve only addition.

(a)   Associative:

$A + (B + C)$

$$= \begin{bmatrix} 3 & -1 & 2 \\ 4 & 1 & 0 \end{bmatrix} + \left\{ \begin{bmatrix} 5 & -2 & 3 \\ -4 & 2 & 1 \end{bmatrix} + \begin{bmatrix} -3 & 1 & -5 \\ 2 & 0 & 4 \end{bmatrix} \right\}$$

$$= \begin{bmatrix} 3 & -1 & 2 \\ 4 & 1 & 0 \end{bmatrix} + \begin{bmatrix} 2 & -1 & -2 \\ -2 & 2 & 5 \end{bmatrix} = \begin{bmatrix} 5 & -2 & 0 \\ 2 & 3 & 5 \end{bmatrix}$$

$(A + B) + C$

$$= \left\{ \begin{bmatrix} 3 & -1 & 2 \\ 4 & 1 & 0 \end{bmatrix} + \begin{bmatrix} 5 & -2 & 3 \\ -4 & 2 & 1 \end{bmatrix} \right\} + \begin{bmatrix} -3 & 1 & -5 \\ 2 & 0 & 4 \end{bmatrix}$$

$$= \begin{bmatrix} 8 & -3 & 5 \\ 0 & 3 & 1 \end{bmatrix} + \begin{bmatrix} -3 & 1 & -5 \\ 2 & 0 & 4 \end{bmatrix} = \begin{bmatrix} 5 & -2 & 0 \\ 2 & 3 & 5 \end{bmatrix}$$

==*Thus, the Associativity property of addition does apply to matrices.*==

(b)   Commutative:

Using matrices A and B,

$$\begin{bmatrix} 3 & -1 & 2 \\ 4 & 1 & 0 \end{bmatrix} + \begin{bmatrix} 5 & -2 & 3 \\ -4 & 2 & 1 \end{bmatrix} = \begin{bmatrix} 8 & -3 & 5 \\ 0 & 3 & 1 \end{bmatrix}$$

and this matrix sum is exactly the sum of $B + A$.

==*Thus, the Commutative property of addition does apply to matrices.*==

For the operation of multiplication to apply to two matrices, the number of columns of the first matrix must match the number of rows of the second matrix. As a review, suppose $W = \begin{bmatrix} -1 & 0 & 7 \\ 5 & 2 & 6 \end{bmatrix}$, $Y = \begin{bmatrix} -4 & -2 \\ -1 & 2 \\ 3 & 1 \end{bmatrix}$ and $Z = W \times Y$.

Then $Z = \begin{bmatrix} (-1)(-4)+(0)(-1)+(7)(3) & (-1)(-2)+(0)(2)+(7)(1) \\ (5)(-4)+(2)(-1)+(6)(3) & (5)(-2)+(2)(2)+(6)(1) \end{bmatrix} = \begin{bmatrix} 25 & 9 \\ -4 & 0 \end{bmatrix}$

The conventional symbol for multiplication with matrices is $\times$ in place of $\bullet$.

Returning to our original discussion of the multiplication properties of numbers as they apply to matrices, let

$$A = \begin{bmatrix} 3 & -1 & 2 \\ 4 & 1 & 0 \end{bmatrix} \quad D = \begin{bmatrix} -2 & 1 \\ 3 & -3 \\ 2 & 3 \end{bmatrix} \quad \text{and } E = \begin{bmatrix} -4 \\ 1 \end{bmatrix}$$

(a) Associative:

$$A \times (D \times E) = \begin{bmatrix} 3 & -1 & 2 \\ 4 & 1 & 0 \end{bmatrix} \times \left\{ \begin{bmatrix} -2 & 1 \\ 3 & -3 \\ 2 & 3 \end{bmatrix} \times \begin{bmatrix} -4 \\ 1 \end{bmatrix} \right\}$$

$$= \begin{bmatrix} 3 & -1 & 2 \\ 4 & 1 & 0 \end{bmatrix} \times \begin{bmatrix} 9 \\ -15 \\ -5 \end{bmatrix} = \begin{bmatrix} 32 \\ 21 \end{bmatrix}$$

$$(A \times D) \times E = \left\{ \begin{bmatrix} 3 & -1 & 2 \\ 4 & 1 & 0 \end{bmatrix} \times \begin{bmatrix} -2 & 1 \\ 3 & -3 \\ 2 & 3 \end{bmatrix} \right\} \times \begin{bmatrix} -4 \\ 1 \end{bmatrix}$$

$$= \begin{bmatrix} -5 & 12 \\ -5 & 1 \end{bmatrix} \times \begin{bmatrix} -4 \\ 1 \end{bmatrix} = \begin{bmatrix} 32 \\ 21 \end{bmatrix}$$

Thus, the *Associative property of multiplication applies to matrices, provided that the given matrices can be multiplied.* The number of columns of the first matrix must match the number of rows of the second matrix; furthermore, the number of columns of the second matrix must match the number of rows of the third matrix.

In order to check the Commutative property of multiplication, we need either two square matrices or a situation in which the number of rows and columns of one matrix is the reverse of the number of rows and columns of the second matrix.

Let $F = \begin{bmatrix} 1 & 3 \\ -4 & 2 \end{bmatrix}$ and $G = \begin{bmatrix} -2 & -1 \\ 5 & 4 \end{bmatrix}$

(b) Commutative: NO!

Then $F \times G = \begin{bmatrix} 1 & 3 \\ -4 & 2 \end{bmatrix} \times \begin{bmatrix} -2 & -1 \\ 5 & 4 \end{bmatrix} = \begin{bmatrix} 13 & 11 \\ 18 & 12 \end{bmatrix}$

However,

$$G \times F = \begin{bmatrix} -2 & -1 \\ 5 & 4 \end{bmatrix} \times \begin{bmatrix} 1 & 3 \\ -4 & 2 \end{bmatrix} = \begin{bmatrix} 2 & -8 \\ -11 & 23 \end{bmatrix}$$

It is evident that $F \times G \neq G \times F$ for two square matrices. Let's now consider two non-square matrices. Suppose matrix H has m rows and n columns, and matrix J has n rows and m columns. Then $H \times J$ is a square matrix with m rows and m columns; however, $J \times H$ is a square matrix with n rows and n columns. *This implies that $H \times J \neq J \times H$, so the* ==*Commutative property of multiplication does not apply to matrices.*==

Let's check for the Distributive property of multiplication over addition, using new matrices K, L, and M. We want to know if $K \times (L + M) = K \times L + K \times M$. In order to use a numerical example, matrices L and M must match in rows and columns. In addition, the number of columns in K must match the number of rows in L (which matches the number of rows in M).

$$\text{Let } K = \begin{bmatrix} 2 & 0 & 5 \\ -1 & 4 & 3 \end{bmatrix}, \quad L = \begin{bmatrix} -2 \\ 1 \\ -3 \end{bmatrix} \text{ and } M = \begin{bmatrix} 3 \\ -5 \\ 2 \end{bmatrix}$$

$$\text{(c) \quad Then } K \times (L + M) = \begin{bmatrix} 2 & 0 & 5 \\ -1 & 4 & 3 \end{bmatrix} \times \left\{ \begin{bmatrix} -2 \\ 1 \\ -3 \end{bmatrix} + \begin{bmatrix} 3 \\ -5 \\ 2 \end{bmatrix} \right\}$$

$$= \begin{bmatrix} 2 & 0 & 5 \\ -1 & 4 & 3 \end{bmatrix} \times \begin{bmatrix} 1 \\ -4 \\ -1 \end{bmatrix} = \begin{bmatrix} -3 \\ -20 \end{bmatrix}$$

$$K \times L + K \times M = \begin{bmatrix} 2 & 0 & 5 \\ -1 & 4 & 3 \end{bmatrix} \times \begin{bmatrix} -2 \\ 1 \\ -3 \end{bmatrix} + \begin{bmatrix} 2 & 0 & 5 \\ -1 & 4 & 3 \end{bmatrix} \times \begin{bmatrix} 3 \\ -5 \\ 2 \end{bmatrix}$$

$$= \begin{bmatrix} -19 \\ -3 \end{bmatrix} + \begin{bmatrix} 16 \\ -17 \end{bmatrix} = \begin{bmatrix} -3 \\ -20 \end{bmatrix}$$

==*This implies that the Distributive property of multiplication over addition applies to matrices.*== The only provision is that the operations of multiplication and addition can actually be performed.

Any square matrix A has an inverse A^{-1} if and only if the determinant of matrix $A \neq 0$. If matrix A has an inverse A^{-1} then $A \bullet A^{-1} = A^{-1} \bullet A = I$.

$$\text{For a } 2 \times 2 \text{ matrix } A = \begin{bmatrix} a & b \\ c & d \end{bmatrix}, A^{-1} = \frac{1}{ad - bc} \begin{bmatrix} d & -b \\ -c & a \end{bmatrix}.$$

EXAMPLE 10

Find A^{-1} if $A = \begin{bmatrix} 2 & 3 \\ 4 & 5 \end{bmatrix}$.

SOLUTION

First, find the determinant of A, which is $\begin{vmatrix} 2 & 3 \\ 4 & 5 \end{vmatrix} = 10 - 12 = -2$. Since the determinant of matrix $A \neq 0$, A^{-1} exists.

$$A^{-1} = \frac{1}{(2)(5)-(3)(4)} \begin{bmatrix} 5 & -3 \\ -4 & 2 \end{bmatrix} = -\frac{1}{2} \begin{bmatrix} 5 & -3 \\ -4 & 2 \end{bmatrix} = \begin{bmatrix} -\frac{5}{2} & \frac{3}{2} \\ 2 & -1 \end{bmatrix}.$$

Thus, *matrices do not always have inverses*. To have an inverse, a matrix must be a square matrix with a non-zero determinant.

Solving Systems of Two Equations in Two Unknowns

Inverse matrices are often used to solve systems of linear equations. A matrix equation, consisting of a coefficient matrix, variable matrix, and constant matrix, is used to solve the system of linear equations. For two linear equations in two unknowns,

$$ax + by = e$$

$$cx + dy = f$$

the coefficient matrix is $\begin{bmatrix} a & b \\ c & d \end{bmatrix}$, the variable matrix is $\begin{bmatrix} x \\ y \end{bmatrix}$, and the constant matrix is $\begin{bmatrix} e \\ f \end{bmatrix}$.

The matrix equation is then $\begin{bmatrix} a & b \\ c & d \end{bmatrix} \times \begin{bmatrix} x \\ y \end{bmatrix} = \begin{bmatrix} e \\ f \end{bmatrix}$. To find $\begin{bmatrix} x \\ y \end{bmatrix}$, we multiply both sides of

the equation by the inverse of the coefficient matrix to get $\begin{bmatrix} x \\ y \end{bmatrix} = \begin{bmatrix} a & b \\ c & d \end{bmatrix} \times \begin{bmatrix} e \\ f \end{bmatrix}$.

EXAMPLE 11

Using matrices, solve the following system of equations:

$$x + 4y = 6$$
$$2x + 6y = 4$$

SOLUTION

First, we write the matrix equation $\begin{bmatrix} 1 & 4 \\ 2 & 6 \end{bmatrix} \cdot \begin{bmatrix} x \\ y \end{bmatrix} = \begin{bmatrix} 6 \\ 4 \end{bmatrix}$, or $\begin{bmatrix} x \\ y \end{bmatrix} = \begin{bmatrix} 1 & 4 \\ 2 & 6 \end{bmatrix}^{-1} \begin{bmatrix} 6 \\ 4 \end{bmatrix}$.

Second, to find $\begin{bmatrix} 1 & 4 \\ 2 & 6 \end{bmatrix}^{-1}$ we need to find the determinant of $\begin{bmatrix} 1 & 4 \\ 2 & 6 \end{bmatrix}$, which

is $(1)(6) - (4)(2) = 6 - 8 = -2$. Third, we identify the inverse of $\begin{bmatrix} 1 & 4 \\ 2 & 6 \end{bmatrix}$ as $-\dfrac{1}{2}$

$\begin{bmatrix} 6 & -4 \\ -2 & 1 \end{bmatrix}$. Fourth, we solve $\begin{bmatrix} x \\ y \end{bmatrix} = -\dfrac{1}{2} \begin{bmatrix} 6 & -4 \\ -2 & 1 \end{bmatrix} \times \begin{bmatrix} 6 \\ 4 \end{bmatrix}$.

The right side of this equation simplifies to $\begin{bmatrix} -3 & 2 \\ 1 & -\dfrac{1}{2} \end{bmatrix} \times \begin{bmatrix} 6 \\ 4 \end{bmatrix} =$

$\begin{bmatrix} (-3)(6) + (2)(4) \\ (1)(6) + (-\dfrac{1}{2})(4) \end{bmatrix} = \begin{bmatrix} -10 \\ 4 \end{bmatrix}$. Thus, $x = -10$ and $y = 4$.

> The inverse matrix times the coefficient matrix must always equal the identity matrix. That is,
>
> $\begin{bmatrix} 1 & 4 \\ 2 & 6 \end{bmatrix} \times \begin{bmatrix} -3 & 2 \\ 1 & -\dfrac{1}{2} \end{bmatrix}$ *must* equal $\begin{bmatrix} 1 & 0 \\ 0 & 1 \end{bmatrix}$. If not, the calculated identity matrix is incorrect
>
> and must be recalculated before completing the solution.

Augmented Matrix

A matrix can be used to represent a system of equations. An **augmented matrix** contains a column for the coefficients of each variable and a final column (separated by a vertical bar) for the constant terms, and can be used to solve a system of three or more linear equations.

System of Equations	Associated Augmented Matrix
$\begin{bmatrix} x + 6y - 2z = 4 \\ 3x \qquad + z = 7 \\ 5x - 3y + z = 0 \end{bmatrix}$	$\begin{bmatrix} 1 & 6 & -2 & \vert & 4 \\ 3 & 0 & 1 & \vert & 7 \\ 5 & -3 & 1 & \vert & 0 \end{bmatrix}$

Elementary row operations are used on rows of the augmented matrix to solve for the solutions of the system of linear equations. Valid operations stem from the fact that each row represents an equation.

a. Since an equation is still true if both sides are multiplied by a constant, we can multiply a row by a non-zero constant.

b. Since the order of the equations makes no difference in a system of equations, we can interchange two rows.

c. Using (a), and since equals added to equals are still equal, we can add a multiple of one row to another row.

Our objective is to transform the given augmented matrix into the following form: $\begin{bmatrix} 1 & 0 & 0 & a \\ 0 & 1 & 0 & b \\ 0 & 0 & 1 & c \end{bmatrix}$,

so that the solution will be $x = a$, $y = b$, and $z = c$. As an alternative, we can look for a single row that matches any of the three rows of this augmented matrix. For example, if we get the first row, then we conclude that $x = a$. In similar fashion, the middle row implies that $y = b$, and the last row implies that $z = c$.

When solving a system of equations through elimination, multiples of equations are combined with other equations until an equation with one variable is reached. Similarly, row operations combine multiples of rows with other rows until a solution matrix is found. The goal of the row operations is to reduce the coefficient matrix to one that has all 1s along the main diagonal and 0s above and below the main diagonal. Zeros represent variables that have been eliminated. The last column of the solution matrix is the solution to the system of equations.

Although the order in which the row operations is performed can vary, it is often easiest to perform them in such a way that a 1 is obtained on a diagonal entry, followed by 0s underneath that entry. When there are 1s on the main diagonal and 0s below it, use each entry on the main diagonal to obtain 0s above it. This procedure is best understood by example.

EXAMPLE 12

Solve the following system:

$$x + y + 2z = 9$$
$$2x + 4y - 3z = 1$$
$$3x + 6y - 5z = 0$$

SOLUTION

The augmented matrix for the system is:

$$\begin{bmatrix} 1 & 1 & 2 & 9 \\ 2 & 4 & -3 & 1 \\ 3 & 6 & -5 & 0 \end{bmatrix}.$$

It can be reduced by elementary row operations. Remeber to do the operations on both the left and right sides of the matrix.

Add –2 times the first row to the second row to get a new second row, and –3 times the first row to the third row to get a new third row.

$$\begin{bmatrix} 1 & 1 & 2 & | & 9 \\ 0 & 2 & -7 & | & -17 \\ 0 & 3 & -11 & | & -27 \end{bmatrix}$$

Multiply the second row by $\frac{1}{2}$.

$$\begin{bmatrix} 1 & 1 & 2 & | & 9 \\ 0 & 1 & -\frac{7}{2} & | & -\frac{17}{2} \\ 0 & 3 & -11 & | & -27 \end{bmatrix}$$

Add –3 times the second row to the third row.

$$\begin{bmatrix} 1 & 1 & 2 & | & 9 \\ 0 & 1 & -\frac{7}{2} & | & -\frac{17}{2} \\ 0 & 0 & -\frac{1}{2} & | & -\frac{3}{2} \end{bmatrix}$$

Multiply the third row by –2 to obtain

$$\begin{bmatrix} 1 & 1 & 2 & | & 9 \\ 0 & 1 & -\frac{7}{2} & | & -\frac{17}{2} \\ 0 & 0 & 1 & | & 3 \end{bmatrix}$$

Add $\frac{7}{2}$ times the third row to the second row and –2 times the third row to the first row.

$$\begin{bmatrix} 1 & 1 & 0 & | & 3 \\ 0 & 1 & 0 & | & 2 \\ 0 & 0 & 1 & | & 3 \end{bmatrix}$$

Add –1 times the second row to the first row.

$$\begin{bmatrix} 1 & 0 & 0 & | & 1 \\ 0 & 1 & 0 & | & 2 \\ 0 & 0 & 1 & | & 3 \end{bmatrix}$$

The solution is $x = 1$, $y = 2$ and $z = 3$.

EXAMPLE 13

In a recent basketball game, Courtney, Kayla and Madelaine scored a combined 53 points. Courtney scored 10 less than twice the points Madelaine did and Kayla scored three more points than Madelaine. Use an augmented matrix and row operations to determine the number of points that each girl scored.

SOLUTION

Define your variables and write equations to model the scenario:

Let c = the number of points Courtney scores

Let m = the number of points Madelaine scored

Let k = the number of points Kayla scored

The girls scored a combined 53 points: $c + m + k = 53$.

Courtney scored 10 less than twice the points Madelaine scored: $c = 2m - 10$ or $c - 2m = -10$.

Kayla scored 3 more points than Madelaine: $k = m + 3$ or $m - k = -3$.

The system of equations $\begin{cases} c+m+k=53 \\ c-2m=-10 \\ m-k=-3 \end{cases}$ can be written in augmented matrix form

as $\left[\begin{array}{ccc|c} 1 & 1 & 1 & 53 \\ 1 & -2 & 0 & -10 \\ 0 & 1 & -1 & -3 \end{array}\right]$. Use the following elementary row operations to reduce

the matrix:

Add -1 times the first row to the second row.

$$\left[\begin{array}{ccc|c} 1 & 1 & 1 & 53 \\ 0 & -3 & -1 & -63 \\ 0 & 1 & -1 & -3 \end{array}\right]$$

Divide the second row by -3.

$$\left[\begin{array}{ccc|c} 1 & 1 & 1 & 53 \\ 0 & 1 & \frac{1}{3} & 21 \\ 0 & 1 & -1 & -3 \end{array}\right]$$

Add -1 times the second row to the third row.

$$\left[\begin{array}{ccc|c} 1 & 1 & 1 & 53 \\ 0 & 1 & \frac{1}{3} & 21 \\ 0 & 0 & -\frac{4}{3} & -24 \end{array}\right]$$

Multiply the third row by $\dfrac{-3}{4}$.

$$\begin{bmatrix} 1 & 1 & 1 & | & 53 \\ 0 & 1 & \frac{1}{3} & | & 21 \\ 0 & 0 & 1 & | & 18 \end{bmatrix}$$

Add $\dfrac{-1}{3}$ times the third row to the second row and -1 times the third row to the first row.

$$\begin{bmatrix} 1 & 1 & 0 & | & 35 \\ 0 & 1 & 0 & | & 15 \\ 0 & 0 & 1 & | & 18 \end{bmatrix}$$

Add -1 times the second row to the first row.

$$\begin{bmatrix} 1 & 0 & 0 & | & 20 \\ 0 & 1 & 0 & | & 15 \\ 0 & 0 & 1 & | & 18 \end{bmatrix}$$

The solution is $c = 20$, $m = 15$ and $k = 18$.

Therefore, Courtney scored 20 points, Madelaine scored 15 points and Kayla scored 18 points in the game.

EXAMPLE 14

Using an augmented matrix, solve the following system of linear equations.

$$2x - y + 3z = 4$$

$$3x + 2z = 5$$

$$-2x + y + 4z = 6$$

SOLUTION

We start with the augmented matrix $\begin{bmatrix} 2 & -1 & 3 & 4 \\ 3 & 0 & 2 & 5 \\ -2 & 1 & 4 & 6 \end{bmatrix}$.

Change the third row to the sum of the first and third rows to get $\begin{bmatrix} 2 & -1 & 3 & 4 \\ 3 & 0 & 2 & 5 \\ 0 & 0 & 7 & 10 \end{bmatrix}$.

Next, divide the third row by 7 to get $\begin{bmatrix} 2 & -1 & 3 & 4 \\ 3 & 0 & 2 & 5 \\ 0 & 0 & 1 & \frac{10}{7} \end{bmatrix}$.

From the last equation $z = \dfrac{10}{7}$. Substituting $z = \dfrac{10}{7}$ into the second equation and solving for x gives $x = \dfrac{5}{7}$. Substituting $z = \dfrac{10}{7}$ and $x = \dfrac{5}{7}$ into the first equation and solving for y gives $y = \dfrac{12}{7}$. The solution to the system is $x = \dfrac{5}{7}$, $y = \dfrac{12}{7}$, and $z = \dfrac{10}{7}$.

Transformations

A **transformation** is motion applied to a geometric figure that causes it to change size, location, or orientation. Theoretically, it is possible to apply more than one transformation to a given figure; however, our discussion will be limited to just one transformation per figure. All transformations will take place in a *plane*. Transformations of geometric figures involve translation, reflection, glide reflection, rotation, and dilation.

Translation

Our first transformation is called a translation. A **translation** is a motion in which the figure changes its location, but not its size or orientation. This motion is accomplished by sliding the figure along a stationary vector. Each point of the figure will move the same distance and in the same direction. Figures 6.4 and 6.5 show a translation of a triangle and a circle. In each case, the vector that determines the translation is shown.

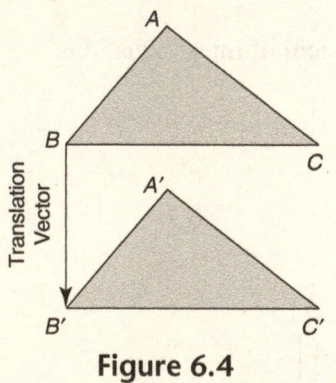

Figure 6.4

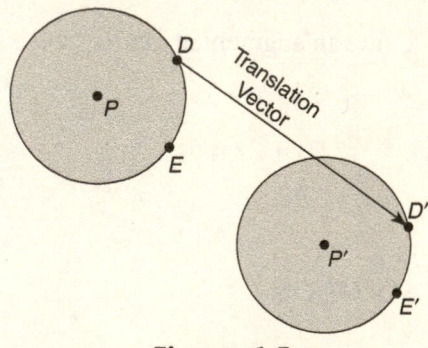

Figure 6.5

Each point of the new location of the figure is called an **image**. Thus, in Figure 6.4, the image of point B is point B'. In Figure 6.5, the image of point D is point D'. Also, in Figure 6.5, point E is called the **pre-image** of point E'.

Earlier in this chapter (Figure 6.1), we saw0 that equivalent vectors have the same magnitude and the same direction. This means that for Figure 6.1, we could have used the translation vector $\overrightarrow{AA'}$. Likewise, for Figure 6.5, we could have used the translation vector $\overrightarrow{EE'}$.

In the xy-coordinate plane, a translation can be shown by the change in x-coordinates, y-coordinates, or both. Let's consider a line segment $\overline{AB}$, for which the coordinates of A and B are $(-2, 4)$ and $(3, 1)$, respectively (Figure 6.6). If the translation vector $\overrightarrow{AA'}$ is $3\mathbf{i} - \mathbf{j}$, then we will move each point of $\overline{AB}$ 3 units to the right and 1 unit down. Then the location of A' must be $(1, 3)$ and the location of B' becomes $(6, 0)$. Each point of $\overline{AB}$ will be translated in exactly the same way, so that this segment does not change size or orientation.

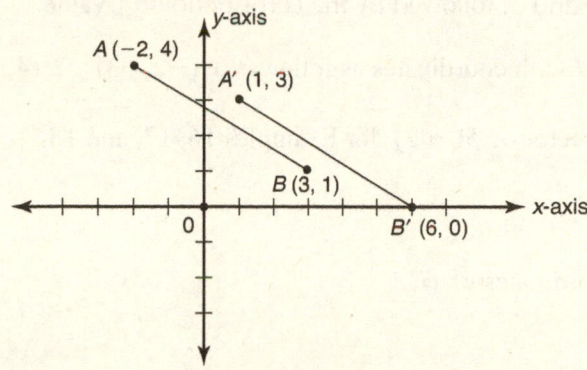

Figure 6.6

EXAMPLE 15

Using the translation vector $3\mathbf{i} - \mathbf{j}$, if point C lies on $\overline{AB}$ and the coordinates of C are $\left(0, \dfrac{14}{5}\right)$ what is the location of point C'?

SOLUTION

We just add 3 units to the x-coordinate of C and subtract 1 unit from the y coordinate of C. The coordinates of C' are $\left(3, \dfrac{9}{5}\right)$.

EXAMPLE 16

Point D also lies on $\overline{AB}$, and the coordinates of its image D' are $\left(2, \dfrac{12}{5}\right)$. Using the same translation vector in Example 15, what are the coordinates of D?

SOLUTION

In a sense, we are going "backwards," since we have the image point D' and we need to find D. The procedure to follow will be to subtract 3 units from the x coordinate and add 1 unit to the y coordinate. Thus, the coordinates of D are $\left(-1, \dfrac{17}{5}\right)$.

The translation vector has been omitted in Figure 6.6 solely for the reason that it would clutter the diagram. This is a common practice when using the *xy*-coordinate plane, since one can see the change in coordinates from the original figure to the image figure.

Notice that the points chosen for Examples 15 and 16 are not completely random. The points must actually lie on $\overline{AB}$, since the translation applies to this entire segment. One way in which these points can be found is to first establish the equation of the line segment, and then assign any *x* value between −2 and 3, followed by the corresponding *y* value.

Now consider $\triangle GHJ$ with coordinates as follows: $G\colon(-2,-3)$, $H\colon(4,-3)$, and $J\colon(6,5)$.

Use the translation vector of $5\mathbf{i} + 2\mathbf{j}$ for Examples 16, 17, and 18.

EXAMPLE 17

What are the coordinates of G'?

SOLUTION

The translation vector is telling us to move each point 5 units to the right and 2 units up. Thus, the coordinates of G' are $(3,-1)$.

EXAMPLE 18

What are the coordinates of the image of the midpoint of $\overline{HJ}$?

SOLUTION

Let K represent the midpoint of $\overline{HJ}$. The coordinates of K are $\left(\dfrac{4+6}{2},\dfrac{-3+5}{2}\right) =$
$(5,1)$. Then the coordinates of K' are $(10, 3)$.

EXAMPLE 19

Point L' is the image of point L, which lies on $\triangle GHJ$. If the coordinates of L' are $\left(5\dfrac{1}{2}, 1\dfrac{1}{2}\right)$, what are the coordinates of L?

SOLUTION

In order to *reverse* the translation vector, subtract 5 units from the *x*-coordinate and subtract 2 units from the *y*-coordinate. Thus, the coordinates of L are $\left(\dfrac{1}{2}, -\dfrac{1}{2}\right)$.

Figure 6.7, though not required to find the solutions to Examples 16, 17, and 18, shows the actual translation.

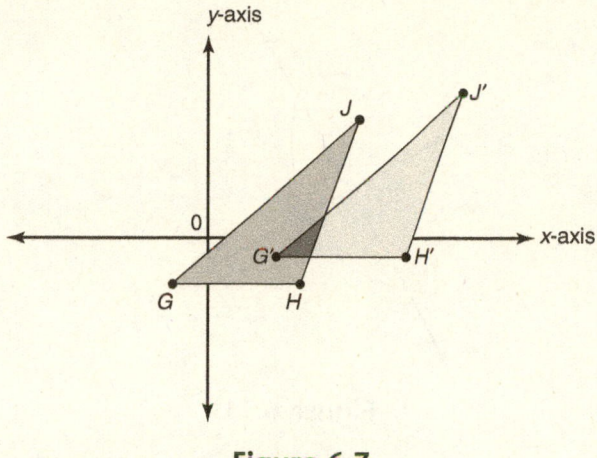

Figure 6.7

To avoid any congestion on the graph for Figure 6.7, the coordinate values were omitted. Note that $\Delta G'H'J'$ overlaps ΔGHJ.

Reflection

The transformation called **reflection** is a motion in which a figure is presented as a mirror image about a given line, which is called the **axis of reflection**. Figures 6.8, 6.9, and 6.10 illustrate a reflection of a line, a triangle, and a quadrilateral, respectively. The individual axis of reflection is shown for each figure as l_1, l_2, or l_3, respectively.

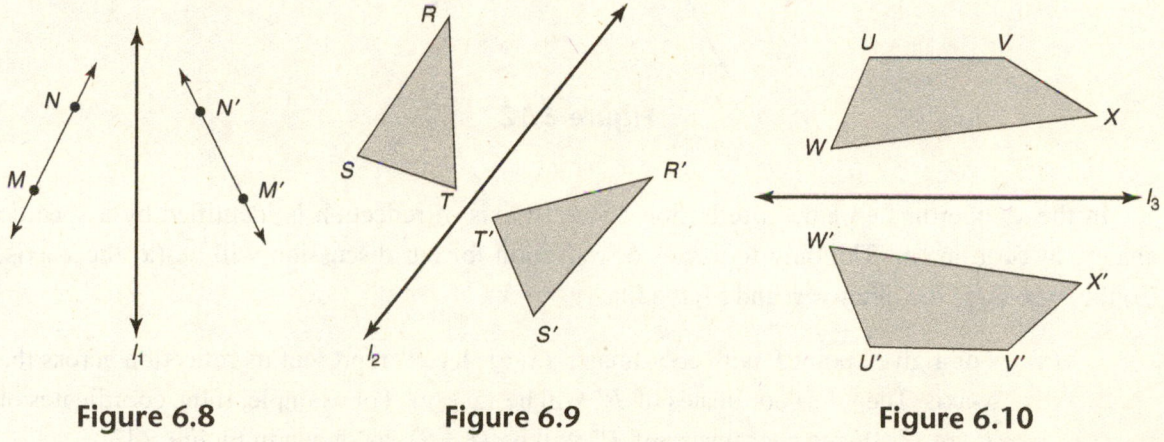

Figure 6.8   **Figure 6.9**   **Figure 6.10**

As with translations, each point of the new location of the figure is called an *image*. The mathematical procedure used to find any image point P' for a given point P and a given axis of reflection l is as follows:

1. Construct the ray $\overrightarrow{PQ}$ that is perpendicular to l at point Q. This is shown in Figure 6.11.

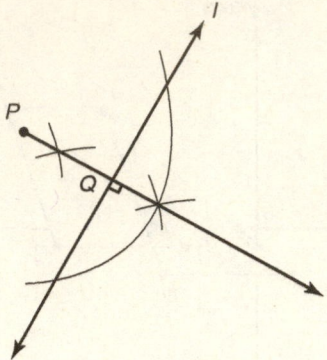

Figure 6.11

2. Using your compass, determine point P' on $\overrightarrow{PQ}$ such that $PQ = QP'$. Point P' is the location of the image of P, with l as the axis of reflection. This step is shown in Figure 6.12.

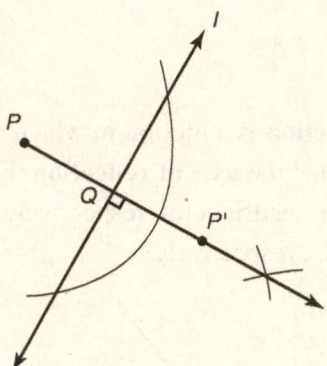

Figure 6.12

In the xy-coordinate plane, a reflection about an axis of reflection is identified by a specific change in coordinates. The only four axes of reflection for our discussion will be (a) the x-axis, (b) the y-axis, (c) the line $y = x$, and (d) the line $y = -x$.

(a) For a given point P with coordinates (x, y), let P' represent its reflection across the x-axis. Then the coordinates of P' will be $(x, -y)$. For example, if the coordinates of P are $(8, 3)$, the coordinates of P' will be $(8, -3)$, as shown in Figure 6.13.

(b) For a given point Q with coordinates (x, y), let Q' represent its reflection across the y-axis. Then the coordinates of Q' will be $(-x, y)$. For example, if the coordinates of Q are $(9, -4)$, the coordinates of Q' will be $(-9, -4)$, as shown in Figure 6.14.

(c)   For a given point R with coordinates (x, y), let R' represent its reflection across the line $y = x$. Then the coordinates of R' will be (y, x). For example, if the coordinates of R are $(-7, 5)$, the coordinates of R' will be $(5, -7)$, as shown in Figure 6.15.

(d)   For a given point S with coordinates (x, y), let S' represent its reflection across the line $y = -x$. Then the coordinates of S' will be $(-y, -x)$. For example, if the coordinates of S are $(-4, 6)$, the coordinates of S' will be $(-6, 4)$, as shown in Figure 6.16.

The first two reflections are normally easy to remember because the graphing aspect will practically reveal the correct answer. The last reflection is usually the most difficult to remember. A suggestion would be to think of a reflection across $y = x$ as a "switch" and a reflection across $y = -x$ as a "switch with a twist."

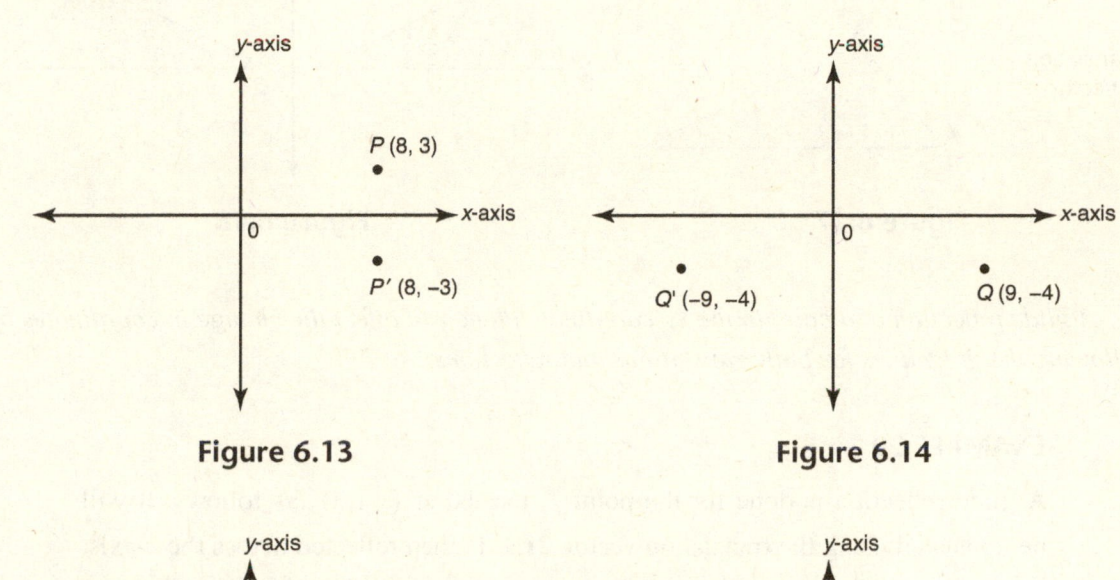

Figure 6.13   Figure 6.14

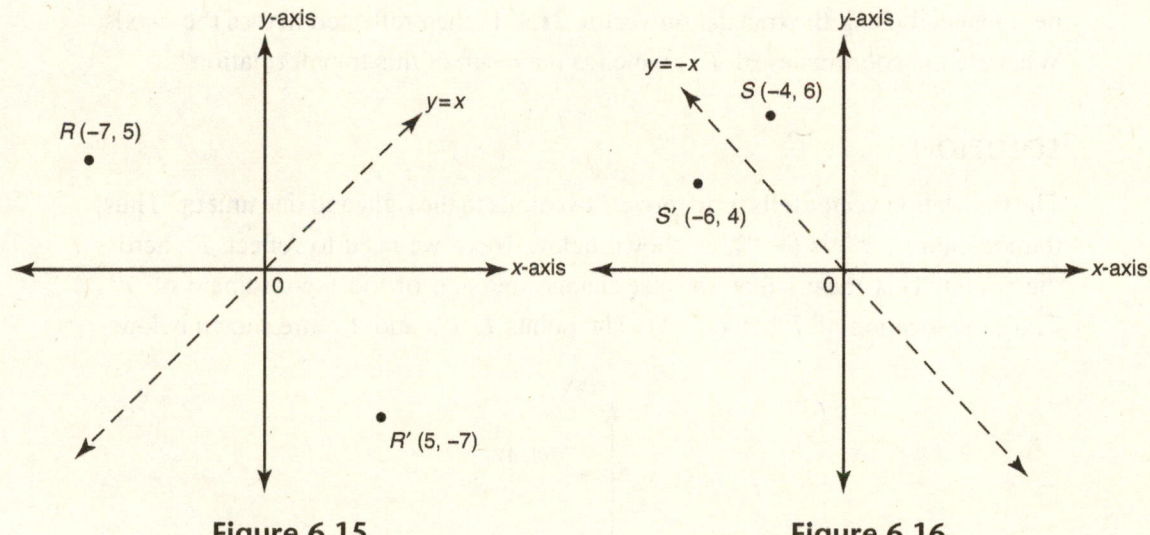

Figure 6.15   Figure 6.16

Glide Reflections

A **glide reflection** is a combination of a translation and a reflection. A clever way to remember this type of transformation is to imagine a dancer gliding across the dance floor, then changing positions with his/her partner. Since this requires two separate steps, a point A will be labeled as A' following the translation. Then the point will be labeled as A'' following the reflection. Figures 6.17 and 6.18 combined show a glide reflection of $\triangle ABC$.

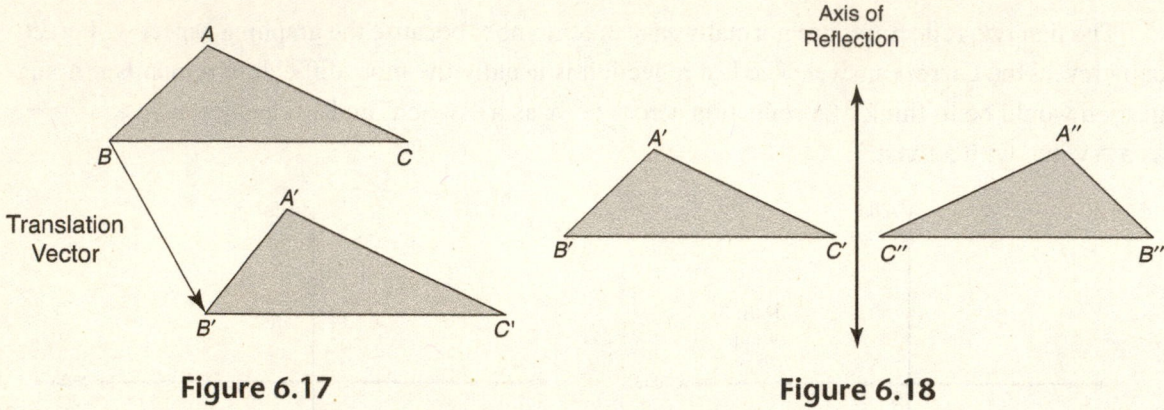

Figure 6.17   Figure 6.18

A glide reflection of a point in the xy-coordinate plane will affect the change in coordinates by following the guidelines for both translations and reflections.

EXAMPLE 20

A glide reflection is done for the point T, located at $(-1, 3)$, as follows: It will be translated using the translation vector $2\mathbf{i} + \mathbf{j}$, then reflected across the x-axis. What are the coordinates of T'', which is the result of this transformation?

SOLUTION

The translation vector tells us to move T two units to the right and one unit up. Thus, the location of T' is $(1, 4)$, as shown below. Next, we need to reflect T' across the x-axis. This means that we just change the sign of the y-coordinate of T'. Thus, the location of T'' is $(1, -4)$. The points T, T', and T'' are shown below.

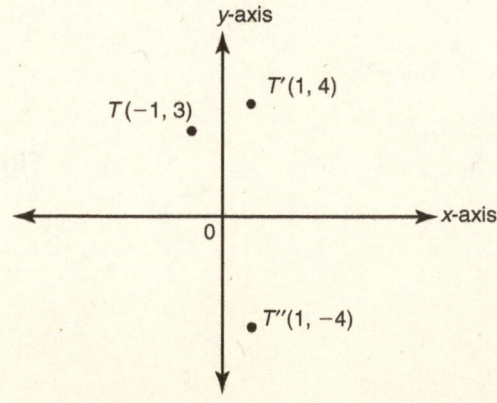

EXAMPLE 21

A glide reflection for the point V, located at $(-3, -4)$, is done as follows: It will be translated using the translation vector $-2\mathbf{i} + 3\mathbf{j}$, then reflected across the line $y = x$. What are the coordinates of V'', which is the result of this transformation?

SOLUTION

First, move V two units to the left and three units up. Thus, the location of V' is $(-5, -1)$. Next, by reflecting V' across the line $y = x$, we simply interchange the x and y coordinates of V'. Thus, the coordinates of V'' are $(-1, -5)$. The points V, V', and V'' are shown below.

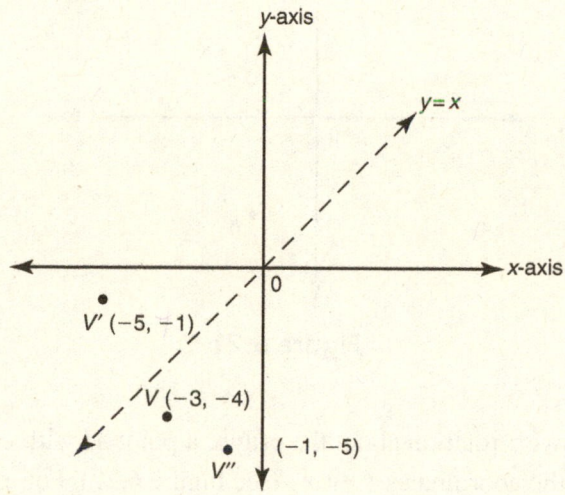

Rotation

Given two rays $\overrightarrow{PQ}$ and $\overrightarrow{PR}$, a rotation about P is a motion created as follows: We start with a point W on $\overrightarrow{PQ}$. Then the point W' on $\overrightarrow{PR}$ is the result of a rotation corresponding to the measure of $\angle QPR$ if $PW = PW'$. Figures 6.19 and 6.20 illustrate this concept of rotation. Notice that the rotation in Figure 6.19 is clockwise, whereas the rotation in Figure 6.20 is counterclockwise.

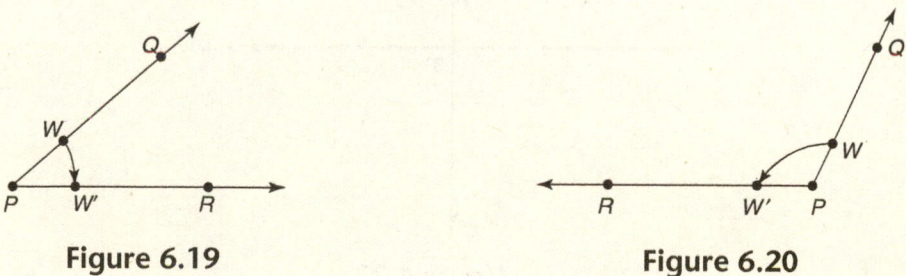

| Figure 6.19 | Figure 6.20 |

The concept of rotation could be extended to other fixed points, and other geometric figures can be used for rotation. In the xy-coordinate plane, we will be concerned with just three different rotations of points, each of which will be about the origin. They are (a) 90°-clockwise, (b) 90°-counterclockwise, and (c) 180°.

In a 90° clockwise rotation about the origin, a point K with coordinates (x, y) will become the point K' with the coordinates $(y, -x)$ (see Figure 6.21). For example, if K is located at (3, 2), then K' is located at (2, –3). The slope of $\overline{OK}$ is $\dfrac{2}{3}$ and the slope of $\overline{OK'}$ is $-\dfrac{3}{2}$. This result is what we expect because the slopes of two perpendicular lines (or line segments) must be negative reciprocals of each other.

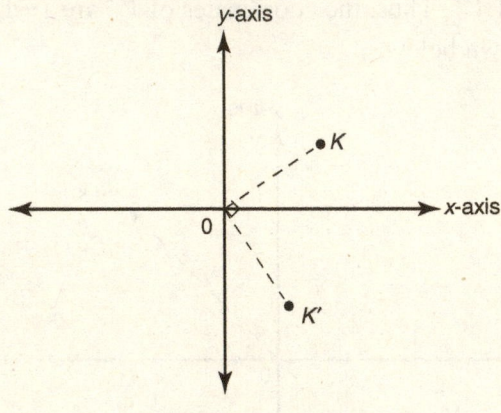

Figure 6.21

In a 90° counterclockwise rotation about the origin, a point M with coordinates (x, y) will become the point M' with the coordinates $(-y, x)$ (see Figure 6.22). For example, if M is located at $(-1, 3)$, then M' is located at $(-3, -1)$. Just as with a clockwise rotation, the slope of $\overline{OM}$ is -3 and the slope of $\overline{OM'}$ is $\dfrac{1}{3}$. This means that $\overline{OM}$ must be perpendicular to $\overline{OM'}$.

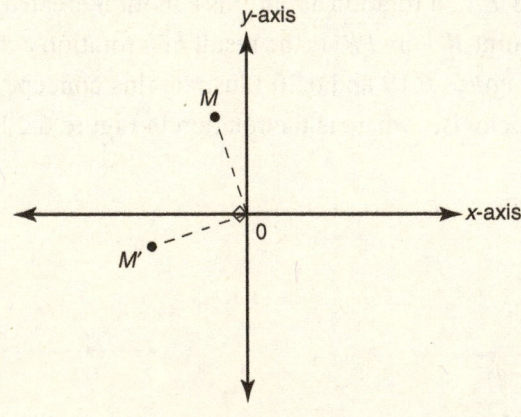

Figure 6.22

The last of our rotations for consideration is the 180° rotation. In this case, it is not important whether the rotation is clockwise or counterclockwise; the result is the same. Imagine that initially you are facing east. Whether you turn 180° clockwise or counterclockwise, the result is that you are then facing west.

In a 180° rotation about the origin, a point N with the coordinates (x, y) will become the point N' with the coordinates $(-x, -y)$. For example, if N is located at $(6, -2)$, then N' is located at $(-6, 2)$. Note that the points $(6, -2)$, $(0, 0)$, and $(-6, 2)$ are collinear and that $ON = ON'$. Figure 6.23 shows this 180°-rotation.

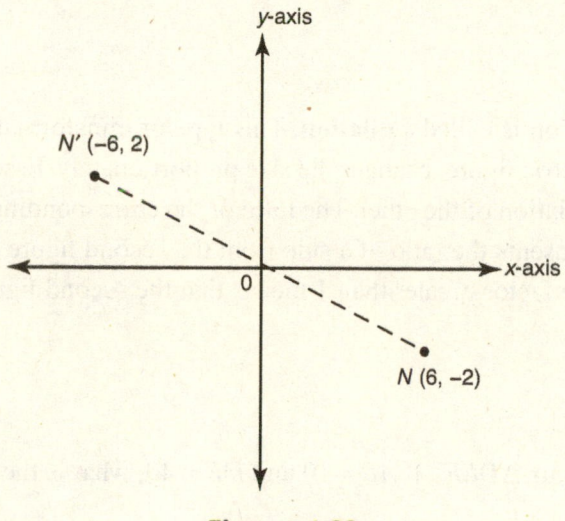

Figure 6.23

EXAMPLE 22

If the point W is located at $(5, -9)$ and is rotated 90° counterclockwise about the origin to the point W', what are the coordinates of W'?

SOLUTION

Switch the original x and y values and change the sign of the new x value. The coordinates of W' are $(9, 5)$.

EXAMPLE 23

If the point V is located at $(-8, 10)$ and is rotated 180° about the origin to the point V', what are the coordinates of V'?

SOLUTION

Change the signs of the original x and y values. The coordinates of V' are $(8, -10)$.

EXAMPLE 24

The point Z', which is located at $(-5, -7)$, is the result of a 90° clockwise rotation of point Z about the origin. What are the coordinates of Z?

SOLUTION

Caution, this is a curve ball! In order to find the coordinates of Z, we are looking for a 90°-*counter*clockwise rotation of Z'. Following the procedure used in Example 8, the answer is $(7, -5)$.

Dilations

Our fifth transformation is called a **dilation**. This type of transformation, which is most often applied to a closed geometric figure, changes the size proportionately. Essentially, if two figures are similar, then either is a dilation of the other. The ratio of the corresponding sides is called the **scale factor**. This number represents the ratio of a side from the second figure to its corresponding side of the first figure. A scale factor greater than 1 means that the second figure is larger than the first figure.

EXAMPLE 25

$\triangle ABC$ is similar to $\triangle DEF$. If $AB = 10$ and $DE = 40$, what is the scale factor.

SOLUTION

The scale factor is $\dfrac{40}{10} = 4$. Here is a quick diagram (although it is not needed):

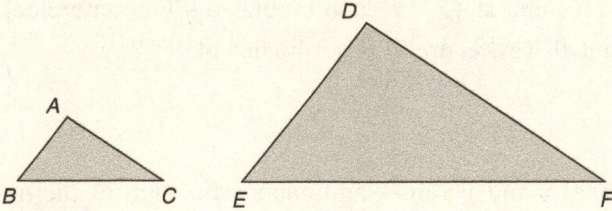

EXAMPLE 26

Quadrilateral $GHJK$ is similar to quadrilateral $LMNP$. The perimeter of $GHJK$ is 36 and the scale factor is 5:6. What is the perimeter of quadrilateral $LMNP$?

SOLUTION

Here is another quick diagram, but it is not needed either. Let x represent the perimeter of $LMNP$. The ratio of the perimeters equals the ratio of the corresponding sides. Then $\dfrac{5}{6} = \dfrac{x}{36}$, so $x = 30$.

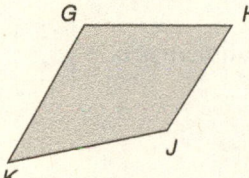

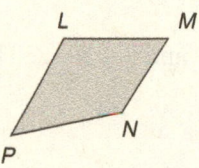

Geometric Properties of Matrices and Vectors

The first part of this chapter discussed the basic rules for arithmetic operations on matrices and vectors. In addition, we investigated the properties of associativity, commutativity, and distributivity for matrices and vectors. Furthermore, we identified the existence of an inverse for certain matrices.

Earlier in this chapter, we also explored the geometric and algebraic meanings of several different types of transformations. These included translations, reflections, glide reflections, rotations, and dilations. Now we want to show a connection between each of the transformations and both matrices and vectors.

Translation Matrices

Consider the point $(7, -1)$ in the xy-coordinate plane. We could express this point in matrix form as $\begin{bmatrix} 7 \\ -1 \end{bmatrix}$. Next, suppose that we are to perform the following matrix addition: $\begin{bmatrix} 7 \\ -1 \end{bmatrix} + \begin{bmatrix} 20 \\ 3 \end{bmatrix} = \begin{bmatrix} 27 \\ 2 \end{bmatrix}$. We can interpret the matrix $\begin{bmatrix} 20 \\ 3 \end{bmatrix}$ as a translation of the point $(7, -1)$ to the point $(27, 2)$ using the translation vector $20\mathbf{i} + 3\mathbf{j}$. In words, we have moved the point $(7, -1)$ 20 units to the right and 3 units up in the xy-coordinate plane.

We can also represent this transformation algebraically for any point (x, y). If this point is moved a units horizontally and b units vertically (where a, b may be positive, negative, or zero), then the point's new location (x', y') can be expressed as $\begin{bmatrix} x \\ y \end{bmatrix} + \begin{bmatrix} a \\ b \end{bmatrix}$.

The matrix $\begin{bmatrix} a \\ b \end{bmatrix}$ is called the **translation matrix**. The translation vector is $a\mathbf{i} + b\mathbf{j}$.

EXAMPLE 27

If the point $\begin{bmatrix} -3 \\ 5 \end{bmatrix}$ is translated to the point $\begin{bmatrix} -8 \\ 7 \end{bmatrix}$, what is the translation matrix?

SOLUTION

$-8 - (-3) = -5$ and $7 - 5 = 2$. The translation matrix is $\begin{bmatrix} -5 \\ 2 \end{bmatrix}$

Reflection Matrices

Another transformation that we had previously considered is a reflection. Our reflections involved four possibilities, namely (a) over the x-axis, (b) over the y-axis, (c) over the line $y = x$, and (d) over the line $y = -x$. Suppose that P is the original point that is located at (x,y). (In terms of vectors, this is the vector $x\mathbf{i} + y\mathbf{j}$.) For the reflections mentioned in (a), (b), (c), and (d), the coordinates of P' are $(x, -y)$, $(-x, y)$, (y, x), and $(-y, -x)$, respectively. Let (x', y') represent the reflection of (x, y) for these four different types of reflections.

Without a formal proof, we claim that $\begin{bmatrix} x' \\ y' \end{bmatrix} = \begin{bmatrix} \cos 2\theta & \sin 2\theta \\ \sin 2\theta & -\cos 2\theta \end{bmatrix} \times \begin{bmatrix} x \\ y \end{bmatrix}$.

This is called the **reflection matrix**. In equation form, we have $x' = x\cos 2\theta + y\sin 2\theta$ and $y' = x\sin 2\theta - y\cos 2\theta$. As you would guess, θ is the angle between the axis of reflection and positive position of the x-axis. For our four different reflections, the only values of θ we are using are 0°, 45°, 90°, and 135°.

EXAMPLE 28

If the point $(8, 2)$ is reflected across the y-axis, what is the reflection matrix?

SOLUTION

Since $\theta = 90°$, the reflection matrix is $\begin{bmatrix} \cos 180° & \sin 180° \\ \sin 180° & -\cos 180° \end{bmatrix} = \begin{bmatrix} -1 & 0 \\ 0 & 1 \end{bmatrix}$.

The solution is quite easy to check, since $\begin{bmatrix} -1 & 0 \\ 0 & 1 \end{bmatrix} \times \begin{bmatrix} 8 \\ 2 \end{bmatrix} = \begin{bmatrix} -8 \\ 2 \end{bmatrix}$.

EXAMPLE 29

If the point $(-3, -6)$ is reflected across the line $y = -x$, what is the reflection matrix?

SOLUTION

The line $y = -x$ forms an angle of $135°$ with the positive x-axis. Since $\theta = 135°$,

the reflection matrix is $\begin{bmatrix} \cos 270° & \sin 270° \\ \sin 270° & -\cos 270° \end{bmatrix} = \begin{bmatrix} 0 & -1 \\ -1 & 0 \end{bmatrix}.$

Glide Reflection Matrices

Recall that a glide reflection is simply a combination of a translation and a reflection. We use the information given in Example 20 for the translation and we then seek the reflection matrix.

EXAMPLE 30

What is the glide reflection matrix of the point $(-1, 3)$ that is translated by the vector $2\mathbf{i} + \mathbf{j}$, then reflected across the x-axis?

SOLUTION

In matrix form, following the given translation, the point becomes $\begin{bmatrix} 1 \\ 4 \end{bmatrix}$. For the re-

flection, $\theta = 0°$. Thus, the reflection matrix is $\begin{bmatrix} \cos 0° & \sin 0° \\ \sin 0° & -\cos 0° \end{bmatrix} = \begin{bmatrix} 1 & 0 \\ 0 & -1 \end{bmatrix}.$

Rotation Matrices

The three rotations that we have studied in this chapter are (a) $90°$ clockwise, (b) $90°$ counterclockwise, and (c) $180°$ rotation.

Remember that we are considering rotations only about the origin.

Let (x', y') represent a clockwise rotation of θ degrees about the origin for the point (x, y).

Without a formal proof, we claim that $\begin{bmatrix} x' \\ y' \end{bmatrix} = \begin{bmatrix} \cos \theta & \sin \theta \\ -\sin \theta & \cos \theta \end{bmatrix} \times \begin{bmatrix} x \\ y \end{bmatrix}.$

This is called a **rotation matrix**. We really do not need a separate formula for a counterclockwise rotation, since a counterclockwise rotation of θ degrees leads to the same point as a clockwise rotation of $(360° - \theta)$ degrees. Furthermore, a 180-degree rotation is also included in the above-mentioned formula.

EXAMPLE 31

If a point is rotated 90° clockwise about the origin, what is the rotation matrix?

SOLUTION

By substituting $(\theta = 90°)$, the matrix becomes $\begin{bmatrix} \cos 90° & \sin 90° \\ -\sin 90° & \cos 90° \end{bmatrix} = \begin{bmatrix} 0 & 1 \\ -1 & 0 \end{bmatrix}$.

EXAMPLE 32

If the point $(7, -5)$ is rotated 90° counterclockwise about the origin, what is the rotation matrix?

SOLUTION

To change this to a clockwise rotation, we substitute $\theta = 270°$ in the rotation matrix. Thus, the answer is $\begin{bmatrix} \cos 270° & \sin 270° \\ -\sin 270° & \cos 270° \end{bmatrix} = \begin{bmatrix} 0 & -1 \\ 1 & 0 \end{bmatrix}$.

To ensure that our matrix is correct, let's check it for the point $(7, -5)$. Note that $\begin{bmatrix} 0 & -1 \\ 1 & 0 \end{bmatrix} \times \begin{bmatrix} 7 \\ -5 \end{bmatrix} = \begin{bmatrix} 5 \\ 7 \end{bmatrix}$, which corresponds to the point $(5, 7)$.

DISCRETE MATHEMATICS

Permutations and Combinations

The distinction between continuous and discrete mathematics is very important. Continuous mathematics is based on the continuous number line, or the real numbers, so that for any two numbers, there is *always* another number between them. A graph of a function in continuous math can be a perfectly smooth curve without any gaps or breaks.

Discrete mathematics, in contrast, deals with distinct numbers. There *aren't* an infinite number of points between them. Discrete numbers, or variables, differ by some finite amount. The numbers do not have to be whole numbers or positive numbers, they just have to be "separate" numbers. A graph of discrete numbers would consist of separate points.

To understand permutations and combinations, we first must recall the fundamental counting principle (sometimes called the basic counting rule).

Fundamental Counting Principle

When dealing with the occurrence of more than one event, the **Fundamental Counting Principle** can be used to determine the total number of possible outcomes. It states that if there are m ways for an event to happen and n ways to second event to happen, then there are mn ways for both to occur.

This is the principle used in Chapter 5 to find the numerator for many probability problems, for example, the number of ways two dice can land, which is $6 \cdot 6 = 36$ ways.

EXAMPLE 33

A deli offers 6 sandwiches and 12 drinks. How many different combinations of sandwiches and drinks are possible?

SOLUTION

There are 6 possible sandwiches and 12 possible drinks. Applying the Fundamental Counting Principle, there are $6(12) = 72$ possible combinations of sandwiches and drinks.

EXAMPLE 34

One dime, one penny, and one six-sided die are tossed. How many results are possible?

SOLUTION

It makes no difference whether the coin tossed is a dime or a penny. There are only two possibilities for the result of tossing a coin: heads or tails. There are six possibilities for the roll of a die. According to the fundamental counting principle, then, there are $2 \cdot 2 \cdot 6 = 24$ results possible.

A **tree diagram**, such as that shown in Figure 6.24 will help in visualizing the possible results in Example 34.

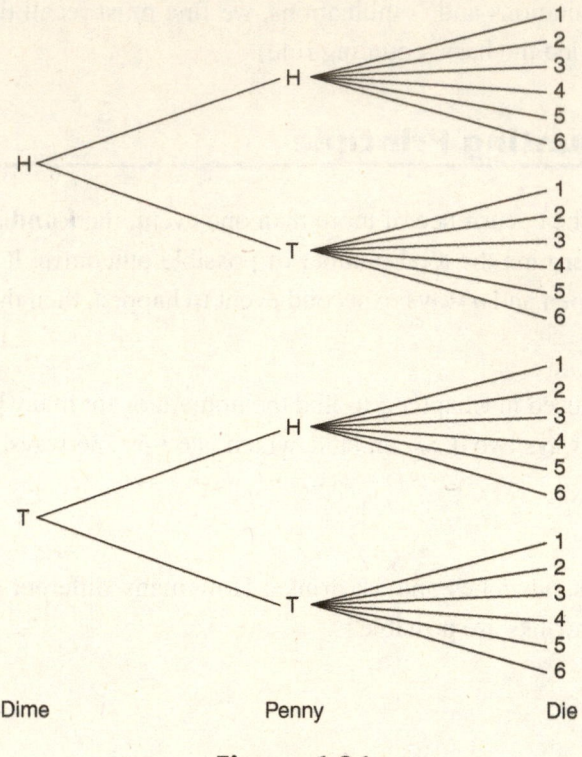

Figure 6.24

EXAMPLE 35

How many four-letter groupings can the letters of the word DESK form (repeat letters allowed)?

SOLUTION

There are four ways to choose each of the letter positions of each four-letter group, so the answer is $4 \cdot 4 \cdot 4 \cdot 4 = 256$

For the rest of the discussion in this section, we need to know about factorials.

FACTORIALS

The symbol $n!$ is read as "n factorial", where $n! = n \times (n-1) \times (n-2) \times (\cdots) \times 1$. This definition only applies to nonnegative integers. Thus, $(\frac{1}{3})!$ and $(-2)!$ have no meaning.

By definition, $0! = 1$.

The TI-83 calculator has a factorial button, which is especially useful for large numbers. In order to calculate 19!, do the following steps: press 19, press "MATH," scroll to "PRB, press 4, press "Enter." The result will be 1.216...E 17. This is interpreted as the number 1.216×10^{17}.

EXAMPLE 36

What is the value of 6!?

SOLUTION

$6! = 6 \times 5 \times 4 \times 3 \times 2 \times 1 = 720$

Permutations order does matter

Let's take Example 35 one step further: suppose we don't allow letters to repeat. Then combinations such as DDDD, DESS, or SSKK aren't allowed.

EXAMPLE 37

How many four-letter groupings can the letters of the word DESK form if repetition is not allowed?

SOLUTION

We can see that the number of groups now is only $4 \cdot 3 \cdot 2 \cdot 1 = 24$. In other words, once one of the four letters is chosen for the first position, it is no longer available for any other position, so the number of choices for the second position is 3, and the number of choices for the third position is 2, and that leaves only one letter to fill the last position.

The definition of **permutation** is the number of ways r out of n objects can be arranged, where order matters. The formula for permutations of n things taken r at a time is

$$_nP_r = \frac{n!}{(n-r)!}$$

In Example 37, where $r = n = 4$, this reduces to $_4P_4 = \frac{4!}{(4-4)!} = \frac{4!}{0!} = 4! = 4 \cdot 3 \cdot 2 \cdot 1$, which is the same answer we obtained by analyzing the situation above.

Now, what if we had asked how many ways two letters could be chosen in this manner from the same group of four? In that case, answers would include DE, SK, DS, and so on. This is also a permutation, as long as order is included in the arrangement of the letters.

EXAMPLE 38

How many two-letter groupings can the letters of the word DESK form if repetition of a letter is not allowed and order makes a difference?

SOLUTION

Once a letter is chosen for the first position, it is eliminated from being chosen for the second position. The number of two-letter groupings in this permutation is $_nP_r = {_4}P_2 = \dfrac{4!}{(4-2)!} = \dfrac{4!}{2!} = \dfrac{4 \cdot 3 \cdot 2 \cdot 1}{2 \cdot 1} = 4 \cdot 3 = 12$. These are DE, DS, DK, ED, ES, EK, SD, SE, SK, KD, KE, KS.

Combinations   Order does NOT matter

Notice that DE and ED are counted as two different answers in Example 38. That is because order made a difference in Example 38. What if order didn't make a difference, though? In that case, we would be talking about **combinations**, not permutations. Obviously, if DE and ED are counted as only one response, the number of arrangements would change, as shown in Example 39. The formula for combinations is

$$_nC_r = \frac{n!}{r!(n-r)!}$$

The difference between the formula for permutations and the formula for combinations is the factor $r!$ in the denominator, which takes care of eliminating duplicates, such as DE and ED, which are the same if order is not important. There are $r!$ of these instances, which is why we divide the number of permutations in Example 38 by $r!$ in Example 39.

EXAMPLE 39

How many two-letter groupings can the letters of the word DESK form if repetition is not allowed and order doesn't make a difference?

SOLUTION

The number of two-letter groupings in this combination is $_nC_r = {_4}C_2 = \dfrac{4!}{2!(4-2)!} = \dfrac{4!}{2!2!} = \dfrac{4 \cdot 3 \cdot 2 \cdot 1}{2 \cdot 1 \cdot 2 \cdot 1} = \dfrac{4 \cdot 3}{2 \cdot 1} = 6$. These are DE, DS, DK, ES, EK, and SK.

EXAMPLE 40

Draw tree diagrams for the situations in Examples 38 and 39 to show the number of choices, and then check the answers from the appropriate formulas (permutation or combination) to calculate the number of choices. The two numbers should match.

SOLUTION

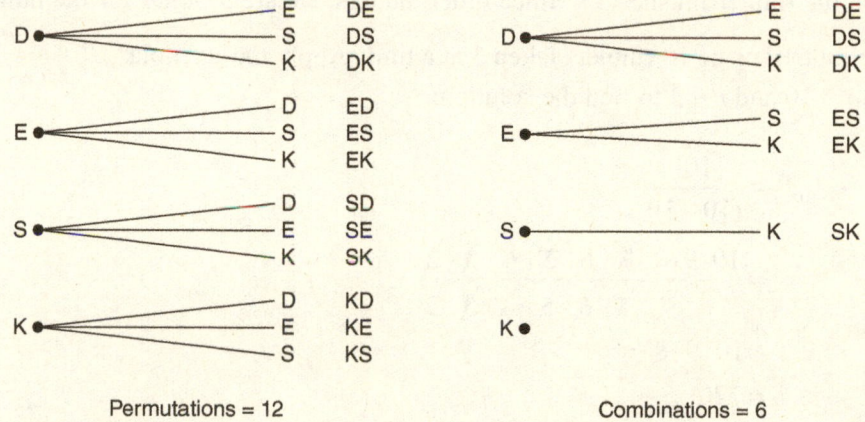

Permutations = 12   Combinations = 6

EXAMPLE 41

Ms. Petunia would like to bring her mother 5 plants from her garden. Her garden consists of 20 plants. How many different groups of plants are possible?

$_{20}C_5$
order doesn't matter

SOLUTION

The order of the plants does not matter, so we are interested in the number of combinations of 20 plants taken 5 at a time. Apply the formula $_nC_r = \dfrac{n!}{r!(n-r)!}$ with $n = 20$ and $r = 5$ to find the solution:

$$_{20}C_5 = \frac{20!}{5!(20-5)!}$$

$$= \frac{20 \cdot 19 \cdot 18 \cdot 17 \cdot 16 \cdot 15 \cdot 14 \cdot 13 \cdot 12 \cdot 11 \cdot 10 \cdot 9 \cdot 8 \cdot 7 \cdot 6 \cdot 5 \cdot 4 \cdot 3 \cdot 2}{(5 \cdot 4 \cdot 3 \cdot 2)(15 \cdot 14 \cdot 13 \cdot 12 \cdot 11 \cdot 10 \cdot 9 \cdot 8 \cdot 7 \cdot 6 \cdot 5 \cdot 4 \cdot 3 \cdot 2)}$$

$$= \frac{20 \cdot 19 \cdot 18 \cdot 17 \cdot 16}{5 \cdot 4 \cdot 3 \cdot 2}$$

$$= 15{,}504$$

There are 15,504 different combinations of plants possible when choosing 5 from a garden of 20.

EXAMPLE 42

Ten runners take part in a race. The first, second and third place finishers stand on the winner's podium. How many different ways can runners appear on the podium?

order does matter $10 \cdot 9 \cdot 8$

SOLUTION

A list containing a runner finishing 1st is different from a list of the same people in which the runner finishes 3rd. Since order matters, we are looking for the number of permutations of 10 runners taken 3 at a time. Apply the formula $_nP_r = \dfrac{n!}{(n-r)!}$ with $n = 10$ and $r = 3$ to find the solution:

$$_{10}P_3 = \frac{10!}{(10-3)!}$$

$$= \frac{10 \cdot 9 \cdot 8 \cdot 7 \cdot 6 \cdot 5 \cdot 4 \cdot 3 \cdot 2}{7 \cdot 6 \cdot 5 \cdot 4 \cdot 3 \cdot 2}$$

$$= 10 \cdot 9 \cdot 8$$

$$= 720$$

There are 720 different ways that the runners can appear on the podium.

EXAMPLE 43

There are 12 girls and 8 boys in the school chorus. Find the number of ways the conductor can select a group of 5 singers to debut in an upcoming concert if the group must consist of 3 girls and 2 boys.

$$_{12}C_3 \cdot {}_8C_2$$

SOLUTION

Order is not important when choosing the group. The number of combinations of 3 girls chosen from 12 is

$$_{12}C_3 = \frac{12!}{3!(12-3)!}$$

$$= \frac{12 \cdot 11 \cdot 10 \cdot 9 \cdot 8 \cdot 7 \cdot 6 \cdot 5 \cdot 4 \cdot 3 \cdot 2}{(3 \cdot 2)(9 \cdot 8 \cdot 7 \cdot 6 \cdot 5 \cdot 4 \cdot 3 \cdot 2)}$$

$$= \frac{12 \cdot 11 \cdot 10}{3 \cdot 2}$$

$$= 220$$

The number of combinations of 2 boys chosen from 8 is

$$_8C_2 = \frac{8!}{2!(8-2)!}$$

$$= \frac{8 \cdot 7 \cdot \cancel{6} \cdot \cancel{5} \cdot \cancel{4} \cdot \cancel{3} \cdot \cancel{2}}{2(\cancel{6} \cdot \cancel{5} \cdot \cancel{4} \cdot \cancel{3} \cdot \cancel{2})}$$

$$= \frac{8 \cdot 7}{2}$$

$$= 28$$

Finally, use the multiplication counting principle to find the solution:

$$_{12}C_3 \cdot {}_8C_2 = 220 \cdot 28 = 6,160 \,.$$

There are 6,160 ways to choose a group of 3 girls and 2 boys from the chorus.

Recursive Sequence *On 3rd Praxis test*

A **recursive sequence** is a list of numbers in which each number depends on the values of previous numbers. In this type of sequence, the value of the first term (and sometimes also the second term) is given. For each successive term, a formula is given that depends on the value of one or more previous terms. These sequences may also be infinite and can be labeled as $a_1, a_2, a_3, \ldots a_n, \ldots$. The term *difference equation* sometimes is used to refer to *any* recursive relation.

Examples of recursive functions are *factorials* and the *Fibonacci sequence*. The Fibonacci sequence is named for a 13th-century mathematician, and the appearance of this sequence in nature has held the interest of students for centuries, even to today. For the Fibonacci sequence, $a_1 = 1$, $a_2 = 1$, and $a_n = a_{n1} + a_{n-2}$. The first ten terms of this sequence are 1, 1, 2, 3, 5, 8, 13, 21, 34, and 55. Sometimes the first two terms are stated as 0 and 1, but this makes little difference in the sequence (it just starts with 0 instead of 1). Fibonacci numbers are found in the structure of crystals, the spiral of galaxies, a nautilus shell, the branching of trees, the arrangement of leaves on a stem, and the arrangement of a *pine cone*, among many others.

EXAMPLE 44

Given a sequence in which $a_1 = 5$ and $a_n = 4a_{n-1} + 7$ for $n > 1$, what are the values of the second, third, and fourth terms?

SOLUTION

$a_2 = 4a_1 + 7 = (4)(5) + 7 = 27$;

$a_3 = 4a_2 + 7 = (4)(27) + 7 = 115$;

$a_4 = 4a_3 + 7 = (4)(115) + 7 = 467$.

a_1

$a_2 = 4(5) + 7 = 27$

$a_3 = 4(27) + 7 = 115$

$a_4 = 4(115) + 7 = 467$

EXAMPLE 45

Given a sequence in which $a_1 = -12$ and $a_n = \frac{1}{2}a_{n-1} + 1$ for $n > 1$, what are the values of the second, third, and fourth terms?

SOLUTION

$a_2 = \frac{1}{2}a_1 + 1 = \left(\frac{1}{2}\right)(-12) + 1 = -5;$

$a_3 = \frac{1}{2}a_2 + 1 = \left(\frac{1}{2}\right)(-5) + 1 = -\frac{3}{2};$

$a_4 = \frac{1}{2}a_3 + 1 = \left(\frac{1}{2}\right)\left(-\frac{3}{2}\right) + 1 = \frac{1}{4}.$

[handwritten:]
$a_2 = \frac{1}{2}(-12) + 1 = -5$

$a_3 = \frac{1}{2}(-5) + 1 = -\frac{3}{2}$

$a_4 = \frac{1}{2}\left(-\frac{3}{2}\right) + = \frac{1}{4}$

EXAMPLE 46

Given a sequence in which $a_1 = 0.6$, $a_2 = 2$, and $a_n = 3a_{n-1} - 5a_{n-2}$ for $n > 2$, what are the values of the third and fourth terms?

SOLUTION

$a_3 = 3a_2 - 5a_1 = (3)(2) - (5)(0.6) = 3;$

$a_4 = 3a_3 - 5a_2 = (3)(3) - (5)(2) = -1$

[handwritten:]
$a_3 = 3(2) - 5(.6) = 3$

$a_4 = 3(3) - 5(2) = -1$

Arithmetic Sequences and Series

[handwritten:] $a_n = a_1 + (n-1)d$

An arithmetic sequence is a sequence of numbers in which a fixed number is added from each term to the next. The following sequences are arithmetic sequences:

2, 4, 6, 8, 10, . . . (add 2 to each term to get the next term)

21, 18, 15, 12, 9, . . . (add –3 to each term to get the next term; note that the fixed number is a negative number and that this sequence will eventually have negative numbers as elements)

The fixed number in an arithmetic sequence is often called the *common difference, d*. Likewise, it is common practice to use $a_1, a_2, a_3, a_4, \ldots$ to denote the first, second, third, fourth . . . terms of an arithmetic sequence. Thus, a_{20} is the twentieth term of a sequence. Then *d* can be calculated from $d = a_n - a_{n-1}$, where *n* is any positive integer greater than 1.

Finding the nth Term

Thus, the *n*th term in an arithmetic sequence is calculated by $a_n = dn + c$, where c is a constant that can be determined. For example, for the sequence 2, 4, 6, 8, 10, we have $d = 2$. So we have, for the first few terms,

$2 = (2)(1) + c = 2 + c$

$4 = (2)(2) + c = 4 + c$

$6 = (2)(3) + c = 6 + c$

[handwritten: $a_{207} = 2 + (206)(2) = 414$]

and $c = 0$ for this sequence. Thus, for example, the 207th term would be $a_{207} = (2)(207) = 414$.

Finding the Number of Terms

If there are a finite number of terms in a sequence (usually indicated by beginning and *ending* terms such as in 2, 4, 6, . . ., 48), we are able to find how many terms are in the sequence. To find the number of terms, use the formula for the *n*th term, $a_n = dn + c$, and equate it to the last term and solve for *n*. So in this series, we have $48 = (2)n$, or $n = 24$.

EXAMPLE 47

Find how many terms are in the sequence 5, 8, 11, 14, ..., 47.

SOLUTION

First we must find d and c for this series. By subtracting two adjacent terms, we see that $d = 3$. Then, referring to the first two terms in the sequence, $a_n = dn + c$ gives us the equation $8 = (3)(2) + c$, or $c = 2$. Thus, the formula for the nth term is $a_n = (3)n + 2$. So the position of 47 is found by solving the equation $47 = 3n + 2$, or $n = 15$. This means that there are 15 terms in the sequence and that the 15th term, a_{15}, is equal to 47.

EXAMPLE 48

How many terms are in the sequence 20, 18, 16, 14, 12, . . . , –26?

[handwritten: $a_n = 20 + (n-1) \cdot 2$ $a_n = 20 - 2n + 2$ $a_n = -2n + 22$]

SOLUTION

The formula for the general term is $a_n = -2n + 22$, which we set equal to the last term, –26. So $-26 = -2n + 22$ yields $n = 24$. This means that there are 24 terms in the sequence and that $a_{24} = -26$.

[handwritten: $-26 = -2n + 22$ $-48 = -2n$ $n = 24$ terms]

Arithmetic Series

The sum of the finite arithmetic sequence $a_1, a_2, a_3, a_4, \ldots, a_n$ is called an **arithmetic series**, and it has the form $a_1 + a_2 + a_3 + a_4 + \ldots + a_n$. To find the value of this series, S_n, we use the formula

$$S_n = \frac{1}{2}n(a_1 + a_n)$$

Note that the sum of an infinite sequence or series is meaningless since the term $(a_1 + a_n)$ would be $(a_1 +)$ or $(a_1 -)$.

We usually know either the first number in the sequence and the number of terms, or the first number and the last number of the sequence, so we can use that information to find the values for n, a_1, and a_n. For example, for the sequence 2, 4, 6, $\ldots$ 48, the series is $2 + 4 + 6 + \ldots + 48$. Here we know a_1, and a_n, and we can calculate n by using $a_n = dn + c$, as we did above, to find $n = 24$. Thus, $S_n = \frac{1}{2}(24)(2 + 48) = 600$. Similarly, if we knew only n and a_1, we would use the same formula to get $a_n = 48$, and again $S_n = \frac{1}{2}(24)(2 + 48) = 600$.

EXAMPLE 49

For the sequence 5, 8, 11, 14, $\ldots$, 47 from Example 47, find the value of the corresponding series.

[handwritten: $\frac{1}{2}(15)(5+47) = \frac{1}{2}(15)(52)$
$= (15)(26) = 390$ # of terms]

SOLUTION

Example 47 gave us $n = 15$, so $S_n = \frac{1}{2}n(a_1 + a_n) = \frac{1}{2}(15)(5 + 47) = \frac{1}{2}(15)(52) = (15)(26) = 390$. Note that we used the Associative property to multiply $\frac{1}{2}$ times the even number 52 to make calculation easier than $\left(72\frac{1}{2}\right)(52)$ would have been.

EXAMPLE 50

For the sequence 20, 18, 16, 14, 12, $\ldots$, –26 from Example 48, find the value of the corresponding series.

SOLUTION

[handwritten: total # of terms]

Example 48 gave us $n = 24$, so $S_n = \frac{1}{2}n(a_1 + a_n) = \frac{1}{2}(24)(20 - 26) = \frac{1}{2}(24)(-6) = -72$. Note that in this series, the terms from 20 to –20 cancel each other out, so the sum would simply be the sum of $(-22) + (-24) + (-26) = -72$.

Application of Arithmetic Sequence

An application of an arithmetic sequence in the world of finance is *simple interest*. Suppose $P =$ the original principal, $r =$ annual interest rate, $t =$ time in years, and $A =$ amount. Then $A = P + Prt$. The corresponding values of the amount for 1 year, 2 years, 3 years, 4 years, …. are given by $P + Pr$, $P + 2Pr$, $P + 3Pr$, $P + 4Pr$, ….. This is an arithmetic sequence in which the first term is $P + Pr$ and the common difference is Pr.

EXAMPLE 51

If $200 is deposited into a bank in which the annual simple interest rate is 4.5%, what is the amount after 9 years?

SOLUTION *starting money* — *interest*

$A = \$200 + (\$200)(0.045)(9) = \$281.$

time

EXAMPLE 52

If $350 is deposited into a bank in which that amount becomes $402.50 after 2.5 years, what is the annual simple interest rate?

$402.50 = 350 + (350)(2.5)(i)$

SOLUTION

$\$402.50 = \$350 + (\$350)(r)(2.5) = \$350 + \$875r.$ Then $r = \dfrac{\$52.50}{\$875} = 0.06$, which is 6%.

Geometric Sequences and Series

$a_n = a_1 (r)^{n-1}$

A **geometric sequence** is a sequence of numbers in which each term is multiplied by a fixed number to get the next term. The following sequences are geometric sequences:

2, 4, 8, 16, . . . (multiply each term by 2 to get the next term)

256, –64, 16, –4, . . . (multiply each term by to get the next term; note that the fixed number is a negative number and so the signs of the terms alternate)

.001, .003, .009, . . . (multiply each term by 3 to get the next term; note that terms can be fractions of whole numbers)

Like its arithmetic counterpart, it is common practice to use a_1, a_2, a_3, a_4, . . . to denote the first, second, third, fourth . . . terms of a geometric sequence. Thus, a_{20} is the twentieth term of a sequence. A geometric sequence is also known as a **geometric progression**.

Common Ratio

A geometric sequence has the general form $a, ar, ar^2, ar^3, \ldots$ The fixed number r in a geometric sequence is often called the **common ratio**. It should be obvious that if $r = 0$, we get the sequence $a, 0, 0, 0, \ldots$; if $r = 1$, the sequence is constant ($a, a, a, a, \ldots$); and if $r = -1$, the sequence is an alternating sequence ($a, -a, a, -a, \ldots$).

So we limit our discussion of geometric sequences to values of r that are not equal to $-1, 0, 1$. Then the common ratio has the following properties:

- If $r > 0$, the signs of the terms are all the same as the initial term.

- If $r < 0$, the signs of the terms alternate between positive and negative.

- If $r > 1$, the terms have *exponential growth* toward .

- If $|r| < 1$ but $r \neq 0$, the terms have *exponential decay* toward 0.

- If $r < -1$, the terms have *exponential growth* toward $\pm$ (due to their alternating signs).

An interesting result of the definition of a geometric sequence is that for any value of r, any three consecutive terms b, c, and d satisfy the equation $c^2 = bd$.

Finding the nth Term

The common ratio r can be calculated as the ratio between any term and the previous term, or $r =$, where n is any positive integer greater than 1. Thus, the nth term in a geometric sequence is calculated by $a_n = a_1 r^{n-1}$. So, for the sequence 2, 4, 8, 16, . . ., where $r = 2$, we have, for example, $a_6 = (2)(2)^5 = 2(32) = 64$, or the 6th term is 64, and $a_{10} = (2)(2)^9 = 2048$, or the 10th term is 2048.

Finding the Number of Terms

If there are a finite number of terms in a geometric sequence (usually indicated by beginning and *ending* terms such as in 2, 4, 8, . . . , 128), we are able to find how many terms are in the sequence. Similar to the method for arithmetic sequences, to find the number of terms, use the formula for the nth term, $a_n = a_1 r^{n-1}$, equate it to the last term in the sequence, and solve for n. So in the given sequence, we have $128 = (2)(2)^{n-1}$, or $64 = 2^{n-1}$. Usually, this type of equation needs logarithms to solve for n, but since this involves powers of 2, we know that $n-1 = 6$, or $n = 7$. This means there are 7 terms in the given sequence 2, 4, 8, . . . , 128.

EXAMPLE 53

Find how many terms are in the sequence $256, -64, 16, -4, \ldots, -\dfrac{1}{64}$.

SOLUTION

First we must find r for this series. By dividing two adjacent terms, we see that $r = -\dfrac{1}{4}$. Thus, the formula for the nth term is $a_n = a_1 r^{n-1}$, or $-\dfrac{1}{64} = 256\left(-\dfrac{1}{4}\right)^{n-1}$.
Again, equations of this type usually are solved by using logarithms, but since we can easily determine the first several powers of 4, we can convert these to powers of $\left(-\dfrac{1}{4}\right)$ in the following way: $-\dfrac{1}{64} = 256\left(-\dfrac{1}{4}\right)^{n-1}$ becomes $\left(-\dfrac{1}{4}\right)^{3} = \left(-\dfrac{1}{4}\right)^{-4}\left(-\dfrac{1}{4}\right)^{n-1}$.
Since these terms are all powers of $\left(-\dfrac{1}{4}\right)$, we can use the laws of exponents to get $3 = -4 + (n-1)$, or $n = 8$. So there are 8 terms in the given sequence.

EXAMPLE 54

How many terms are in the sequence $.001, .003, .009, \ldots, .243$?

$$\times 3 \quad \times 3 \qquad .001(3)^{n-1} = 243$$

SOLUTION

We can see that $r = 3$. Thus, the formula for the nth term is $a_n = a_1 r^{n-1}$, or $.243 = .001(3)^{n-1}$. Thus $(3)^{n-1} = 243$. Once again, logarithms would be used to solve for n, but since we can figure out that $243 = 3^5$, exponent properties give $n - 1 = 5$, or $n = 6$. Thus this sequence has 6 terms.

Geometric Series

The sum of the geometric sequence $a_1, a_2, a_3, a_4, \ldots, a_n$ is called a **geometric series**, and it has the form $a_1 + a_2 + a_3 + a_4 + \ldots + a_n$. To find the value of this series, S_n, we use formulas based on the formula for the nth term of a geometric sequence.

$$S_n = \frac{a_1(1-r^n)}{(1-r)}$$ for a finite geometric series, and $$\frac{a_1(1-r^n)}{(1-r)}$$

$$S_\infty = \frac{a_1}{1-r}$$ for an infinite series. $$\left(\frac{a_1}{1-r}\right)$$

The infinite formula is equivalent to the finite formula when $n \to \infty$.

Finite Geometric Series

We usually know either the first number in the sequence and the number of terms, or the first number and the last number of the sequence, so we can use that information to find the values for r, a_1, and a_n. For example, for the sequence 2, 4, 8, . . . , 128, the series is $2 + 4 + 8 + \ldots + 128$. Here we know a_1, and a_n, and we can calculate r by using $r = \dfrac{a_n}{a_{n-1}}$, as we did above, to find $r = 2$. Thus, $S_n = \dfrac{a_1(1-r^n)}{(1-r)} = \dfrac{2(1-2^7)}{1-2} = \dfrac{2(-127)}{-1} = 254$. Note that we found n by using the formula for the nth term, as we did previously. Similarly, if we knew only n and a_1, we would use the same formula to get $a_n = 48$, and again $S_n = 254$.

EXAMPLE 55

For the sequence 256, –64, 16, –4, . . . $-\dfrac{1}{64}$, from Example 53, find the value of the corresponding series.

SOLUTION

Example 53 gave us $n = 8$, so $S_n = \dfrac{a_1(1-r^n)}{(1-r)} = \dfrac{256\left(1-\left(-\frac{1}{4}\right)^8\right)}{1-\left(-\frac{1}{4}\right)} = \dfrac{256 - \frac{1}{256}}{\frac{5}{4}} = \dfrac{13107}{64} = $

$204\dfrac{51}{64}$.

EXAMPLE 56

For the sequence .001, .003, .009, . . . , .243 from Example 54, find the value of the corresponding series.

SOLUTION

Example 54 gave us $n = 6$, so $S_n = \dfrac{a_1(1-r^n)}{(1-r)} = \dfrac{.001(1-(3)^6)}{(1-3)} = \dfrac{-.728}{-2} = .364$.

Infinite Geometric Series

Since geometric sequences (with $r \neq -1, 0, 1$) show either *exponential growth* or *exponential decay*, infinite geometric series diverge except when $|r| < 1$, $r \neq 0$. Let's look at two convergent series:

- If $a = \dfrac{1}{2}$, and $r = \dfrac{1}{2}$, then the series is $\dfrac{1}{2} + \dfrac{1}{4} + \dfrac{1}{8} + \dfrac{1}{16} + \ldots$, and it converges absolutely to 1.

- If $a = \dfrac{1}{2}$, and $r = -\dfrac{1}{2}$, then the series is $\dfrac{1}{2} - \dfrac{1}{4} + \dfrac{1}{8} - \dfrac{1}{16} + \ldots$, and it converges absolutely to $\dfrac{1}{3}$.

EXAMPLE 57

Show that the series is $\frac{1}{2} + \frac{1}{4} + \frac{1}{8} + \frac{1}{16} + \ldots$ converges absolutely to 1.

SOLUTION

For an infinite series, $S = \frac{a_1}{1-r}$, so for this series, $S = \frac{\frac{1}{2}}{1-\frac{1}{2}} = \frac{\frac{1}{2}}{\frac{1}{2}} = 1.$

EXAMPLE 58

Show that the series is $\frac{1}{2} - \frac{1}{4} + \frac{1}{8} - \frac{1}{16} + \ldots$ converges absolutely to $\frac{1}{3}$.

SOLUTION

For an infinite series, $S = \frac{a_1}{1-r}$, so for this series, $S = \frac{\frac{1}{2}}{1+\frac{1}{2}} = \frac{\frac{1}{2}}{\frac{3}{2}} = \frac{1}{3}.$

Application of Geometric Sequence

Now let's look at an application of a geometric sequence as it relates to the mathematics of finance. In particular, consider the topic of *compound interest*. Suppose that P_0 = original principal, r = annual interest rate, n = number of compounding periods per year, t = total number of years, and $P(t)$ = amount after t years. Then $P(t) = P_0\left(1 + \frac{r}{n}\right)^{nt}$. The corresponding values of the amount for 1 year, 2 years, 3 years, 4 years, ... are given by $P_0\left(1 + \frac{r}{n}\right)^{n}$, $P_0\left(1 + \frac{r}{n}\right)^{2n}$,

$P_0\left(1 + \frac{r}{n}\right)^{3n}$, $P_0\left(1 + \frac{r}{n}\right)^{4n}$, ,....

This is a geometric sequence in which the first term is $P_0\left(1 + \frac{r}{n}\right)^{n}$ and the common ratio is $\left(1 + \frac{r}{n}\right)^{n}$.

EXAMPLE 59

4 times per year ↓

If $600 is deposited into a bank in which the interest rate is 8% compounded quarterly, what is the amount after five years?

SOLUTION

There are four compounding periods per year, so there is a total of $(5)(4) = 20$ compounding periods in five years, and we have

$$P(5) = (\$600)\left(1 + \frac{0.08}{4}\right)^{20} \approx \$891.57 \,.$$

EXAMPLE 60

A person will need $5000 in 3 years to help pay off a car loan. To the nearest dollar, how much money should be deposited into a bank in which the interest rate is 10% compounded monthly?

$12 \times 3 = 36$

SOLUTION

There are twelve compounding periods per year, so there is a total of $(12)(3) = 36$ compounding periods in three years. Then $\$5000 = P_0\left(1 + \frac{0.10}{12}\right)^{36} \approx 1.3482 P_0$, and thus, $P_0 \approx \$3709$.

If the number of compounding periods per year gets increasingly larger, the value of n approaches infinity. This concept is called *continuous* compounding and would be appropriate in examples dealing with inflation. *The formula for continuous compounding is* $P(t) = P_0 e^{rt}$, *where* $e = \lim\limits_{n \to \infty}\left(1 + \frac{1}{n}\right)^n \approx 2.7183$. See Chapter 4 for a discussion of the natural logarithm and e.

EXAMPLE 61

If the annual rate of inflation is 4.4 %, and the annual rate of interest is compounded continuously, to the nearest dollar, what will be the value of $2000 in 12 years?

SOLUTION:

$P(12) = (\$2000)(e^{(0.044)(12)}) = (\$2000)(e^{0.528}) \approx \$3391$.

EXAMPLE 62

If the annual rate of inflation is 3%, and the annual rate of interest is compounded continuously, to the nearest tenth, in how many years will $1500 grow to $4500?

SOLUTION

We have $4500 = ($1500)(e^{0.03t})$, which simplifies to $3 = e^{0.03t}$. Taking the natural logarithm of each side, $\ln 3 = (0.03t)(\ln e) = 0.03t$. Thus, $t = \dfrac{\ln 3}{0.03} \approx 36.6$ years.

EXAMPLE 63

Assuming that the annual rate of interest is compounded continuously, to the nearest tenth, at what interest rate will $900 grow to $3800 in a period of 20 years?

SOLUTION

We have $3800 = ($900)(e^{20r})$, which simplifies to $-1\dfrac{1}{3}$ $4.\overline{2} = e^{20r}$. Then

$\ln 4.\overline{2} = (20r)(\ln e) = 20r$. Thus, $r = \dfrac{\ln 4.\overline{2}}{20} \approx 0.072 = 7.2\%$.

Binary Relations

As the name implies, binary relations are relations between two objects. These "objects" may be sets, geometric figures, points on a graph, even people. Examples of some relations are "A is a subset of B," "10 is greater than 5," "2 divides 8," "$\triangle ABC$ is congruent to $\triangle DEF$," "Mona is a daughter of Pamela," "$\angle 1$ is adjacent to $\angle 2$," and "line l is perpendicular to line m."

Binary relations are often used in set theory. If set $A = \{2, 4, 6\}$ and set $B = \{1, 2, 3, 4, 5, 6\}$, then the set $\{(2, 1), (4, 2), (6, 3)\}$ is a binary relation from A to B, but $\{(2, 2), (4, 8)\}$ is not a binary relation because set B does not contain 8. For these two sets, we can also state the binary relation that A is a subset of B.

If we use R to mean "binary relation" for elements a in set A and b in set B, we have the following properties of binary relations for sets:

- Reflexive: a R a.

  o Equality is reflexive, since $a = a$ is true.

  o "Less than" is not reflexive, since $a < a$ is not true.

  o However, "less than or equal to" is reflexive, since is true.

- Symmetric: if $a \, R \, b$, then $b \, R \, a$.

    o Equality is symmetric, since if $a = b$, then $b = a$.

    o "Less than" is not symmetric, since if $a < b$, then $b < a$ is not true.

    o "Less than or equal to" is symmetric, since if is true, is true (thanks to the "equal" part of "less than or equal to").

- Transitive: if $a \, R \, b$ and $b \, R \, c$, then $a \, R \, c$

    o Equality is transitive, since if $a = b$ and $b = c$, then $a = c$

    o "Less than" is transitive, since if $a < b$ and $b < c$, then $a < c$

    o "Less than or equal to" is transitive, since if a b and b c, then a c

- Equivalent: if and only if it is reflexive, symmetric, and transitive

EXAMPLE 64

Is "is a brother of" reflexive, symmetric, or transitive in the set of all males? In the set of all people? What about "is a father of"? What about "is a friend of"?

SOLUTION

In the set of all males, "is a brother of" is symmetric and transitive.

In the set of all people, "is a brother of" is not symmetric but is transitive.

In the set of all males, "is a father of" is not symmetric and not transitive.

In the set of all people, "is a father of" is not symmetric and not transitive.

In the set of all males, "is a friend of" is symmetric but not transitive.

In the set of all people, "is a friend of" is symmetric but not transitive.

Networks

A **network** is a diagram of points (vertices or nodes) and edges (line segments or arcs) that join various points to one another.

Vertex-Edge Graphs

A **vertex-edge graph** is a diagram consisting of a set of points (called vertices) along with segments or arcs (called edges) joining some or all of the points. In *graph theory*, we assign labels to elements of a *graph* (such as vertices) subject to certain constraints. In its simplest form, it is a way of coloring the vertices of a graph such that no two adjacent *vertices* share the same color.

By converting mapping problems, for example, to vertex-edge graphs, we can visualize solutions easier. Two famous mapping problems are the Knigsburg bridge problem and the four-color conjecture.

Knigsburg Bridge Problem

The study of networks, or graph theory, began as a way to answer a question about traveling in the town of Königsburg in the eighteenth century. The river that ran through the town had an island at its center. After passing the island, the river split into two parts. Seven bridges were built to allow the people of the town to travel from one part to another (see Figure 6.25). People wondered if it was possible to walk through the town crossing every bridge once and only once.

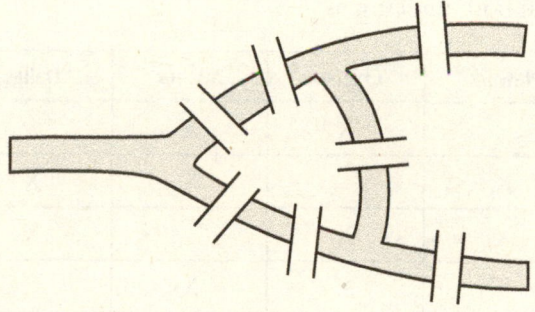

Figure 6.25

The Swiss mathematician Euler approached this problem by modeling the map as a network with a diagram in which the land masses were represented with points (vertices A, B, C, D) and the bridges were represented with arcs (edges a, b, c, d, e, f). See Figure 6.26.

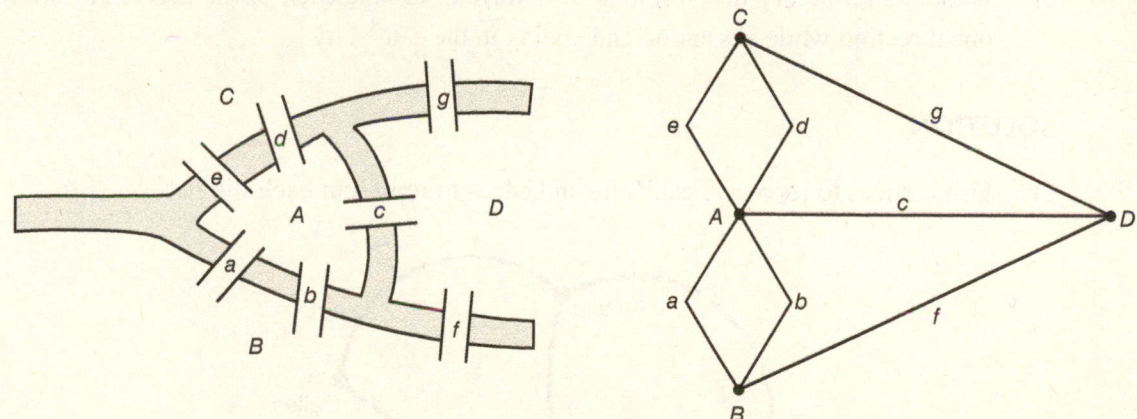

Figure 6.26

Euler discovered that the ability to traverse a network (or pass through every edge once and only once) was based on analyzing the number of edges going to each vertex. A vertex is considered odd if there is an odd number of edges going to it. Otherwise, it is considered even. Euler found that a network is traversable if all its vertices are even or exactly two vertices are odd. Since the network modeling the bridges in Königsburg has all odd vertices, it is impossible to travel over each bridge exactly once. A continuous path that passes through every edge exactly once is now known as an **Euler path**. Euler paths start at one vertex and end on another. An **Euler circuit** is an Euler path that starts and stops on the same vertex. A network is an Euler circuit if all vertices are even.

EXAMPLE 65

The following chart represents the flights available on a new airline. Every flight listed is available in both directions.

	Newark	Chicago	Atlanta	Dallas	San Francisco
Newark		X	X		X
Chicago	X		X	X	X
Atlanta	X	X		X	
Dallas		X	X		
San Francisco	X	X			

a) Create a network to model this data set.

b) Provide an itinerary that would allow a traveler to take each of the flights in exactly one direction.

c) Is there an itinerary that would allow a traveler to take each of the flights in exactly one direction while beginning and ending in the same city?

SOLUTION

a) Use vertices to represent each city and edges to represent each flight.

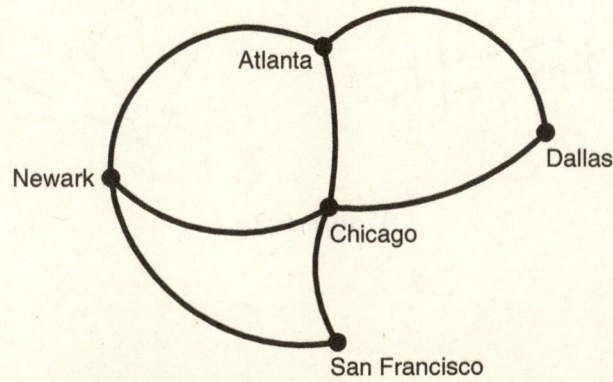

b) This network has three even vertices and two odd ones. Since it has exactly two odd vertices, it has an Euler path which means there exists an itinerary that would allow a traveler to take each of the flights in exactly one direction. For example: Newark to San Francisco to Chicago to Dallas to Atlanta to Chicago to Newark to Atlanta.

c) Since there are odd vertices in this network, the network is not an Euler circuit. Therefore, there is no itinerary that would allow a traveler to take each of the flights in one direction and begin and end in the same city.

The Four-Color Conjecture

The four-color conjecture dates back to the 1850s, when an English mapmaker made a map of all the counties in England. He noticed that it took only four colors to ensure that no two counties sharing a border were the same color. He found maps of other regions where three colors were not enough, but he could not find a map requiring five colors. Proof of this four-color conjecture, that any map in a *plane* can be colored using only four colors in such a way that regions sharing a common boundary (other than a single point) do not share the same color, became a popular math "puzzle" until it was proven with the help of computer techniques in 1976. It is now known as the four-color theorem.

Think about a map of the continental United States in which states are colored with different colors. It is customary to color such a map so that no two states sharing a border are the same color. However, you need only four colors to color the U.S. map this way.

EXAMPLE 66

Consider a smaller "map," such as the one shown below.

a) How many colors will it take to color this figure so that no two adjacent regions have the same color?

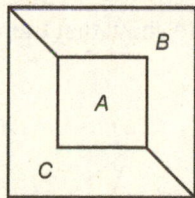

b) Now add an edge in region *B* that ends at region *A* so that there are four distinct regions, as shown below. How many colors will it take to color this figure so that no two adjacent regions have the same color?

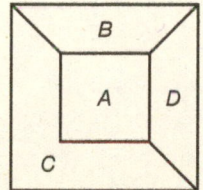

c) Now add an edge in region *C* that ends at region *A* so that there are five distinct regions, as shown below. How many colors will it take to color this figure so that no two adjacent regions have the same color?

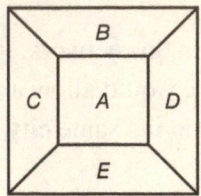

d) What happens when you add more edges? How many colors will it take?

SOLUTION

a) It will take only three colors.

b) Now it will take four colors, since each region touches every other region. If this map is converted to a vertex-edge graph, we can see that each vertex must be a different color so that no two adjacent vertices have the same color.

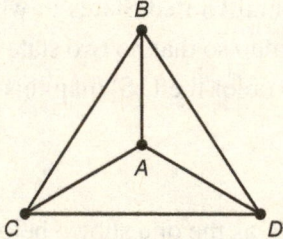

c) Surprisingly, it will take only three colors. Regions *B* and *E* can now have the same color, as can regions *C* and *D*. The vertex-edge graph of this map shows that vertices *B* and *E* are not adjacent, nor are vertices *C* and *D*. We draw vertex *A* offset a bit to show that there are no edges connecting *B* and *E* or *C* and *D*.

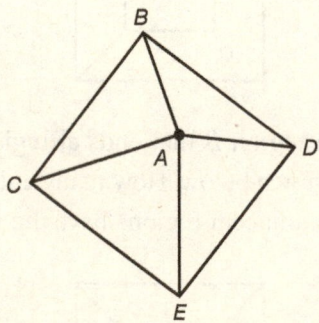

d) When you add another region, say F, to make six regions, you end up with four colors again, and this remains the number no matter how many other regions are added. Note that in the vertex-edge graph, vertices B and E, vertices F and E are not adjacent; however, vertices B and F now are, so E cannot be the same color as B nor as F, adding back the need for another color. A similar situation holds for the vertex pairs C and F, C and D, and D and F. Possible colors are: A = blue, E = green, and F = red.

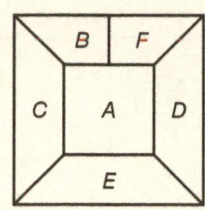 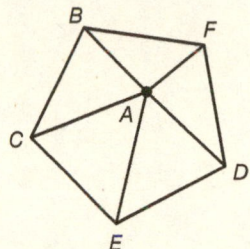

Trees

In *graph theory*, a **tree** is a set of straight line segments (edges) in which any two endpoints (*vertices)* are connected by *exactly one simple path*. A tree contains no closed loops (cycles). Every tree has exactly one more vertex than it has edges, as can be seen in Figure 6.27, in which vertices A, D, E, and H are terminal vertices, and there are 8 vertices and (8 − 1 =) 7 edges. The unique simple path connecting vertices D and G is D–C–F–G.

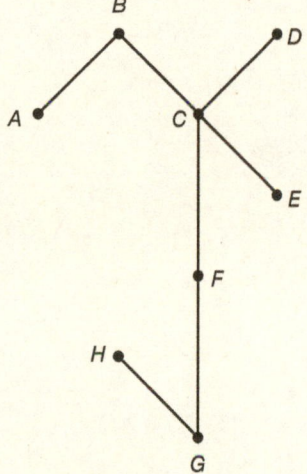

Figure 6.27

Applications of trees are found in many diverse fields, including, among others, computer science, probability (see Figure 6.24), chemistry (e.g., enumeration of saturated hydrocarbons), genealogy (family trees), and electrical circuits.

PRACTICE TEST 1

PRAXIS II Mathematics Content Knowledge (0061/5061)

Also available at the REA Study Center (*www.rea.com/studycenter*)

This practice test is also offered online at the REA Study Center. Although the PRAXIS II Mathematics Content Knowledge (0061/5061) exam is offered in both paper- and computer-based formats, we recommend that you take the online version of the test to receive these added benefits:

- **Timed testing conditions** – help you gauge how much time you can spend on each question

- **Automatic scoring** – find out how you did on the test, instantly

- **On-screen detailed explanations of answers** – give you the correct answer and explain why the other answer choices are wrong

- **Diagnostic score reports** – pinpoint where you're strongest and where you need to focus your study

NOTE: Many graphing calculators, such as the TI-83, can readily perform computations on normal distributions, approximate areas under a curve, intersections of lines, and so forth. Different calculators have different keystrokes necessary to perform these functions, however, so it is important that you know how to use your chosen calculator before you take the exam. Check the documentation with your calculator or the manufacturer's website.

PRAXIS II Mathematics Content Knowledge Practice Test 1

TIME: 150 minutes (2 hours and 30 minutes)
50 questions

Directions: Read each item and select the best response.

---

1. A discussion group is composed of six randomly chosen students. Which of the following approximately represents the probability that two or more of these students have birthdays in the same month (but perhaps different years)? You may assume that each month is equally likely to be a birthday month.

   (A) $\dfrac{10}{12}$

   (B) 0.67

   (C) $\dfrac{2}{12}$

   (D) 0.78

2. Eighty students respond to a survey about their favorite color. Their responses are summarized in the table below. What is the probability that a girl chosen randomly from the sample will like blue?

	Boys	Girls
Red	25	20
Blue	18	?

   (A) $\dfrac{18}{43}$

   (B) $\dfrac{17}{37}$

   (C) $\dfrac{17}{80}$

   (D) $\dfrac{17}{37}$

3. A scale consists of a nonlinear spring upon which a mass is loaded so that the spring compresses. The spring produces a force, f, in response to its compression, x, given by the expression $f(x) = 10x + x^2$. When the scale is loaded, the weight of the object is equal to the force produced by the spring. If a mass placed on the scale produces a force of 5.7 lb, which of the following best represents the compression of the spring?

   (A) 0.71

   (B) −0.81

   (C) 10.5

   (D) 0.54

4. Which of the following approximates the area of the largest equilateral triangle that can fit in a circle of radius R?

   (A) 1.3 R^2

   (B) 2 R^2

   (C) 2.6 R^2

   (D) 3.14 R^2

5. In the figure below, what is the area of the shaded region if each of the circles in the figure has a radius of 1?

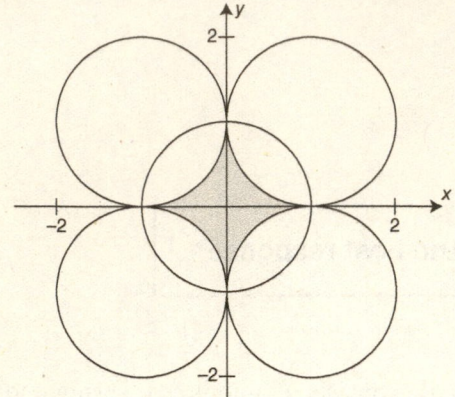

(A) $1\dfrac{1}{4} - \pi$

(B) $2\pi - 4$

(C) $4 - \pi$

(D) $4 - 2\pi$

6. The fuel economy of a heavy vehicle per unit time is represented by $f(s) = a + bs + cs^2$, where a, b, and c are constants and s is the speed of the vehicle. The fuel consumed, F, for a trip of length D may be computed using the formula: $F(s) = f(s) \cdot \dfrac{D}{s}$.

Which of the following expresses the optimum speed for traveling a given distance in order to minimize the fuel consumed?

(A) $\sqrt{\dfrac{c}{a}}$

(B) $\sqrt{\dfrac{a}{c}}$

(C) $\sqrt{\dfrac{a}{bc}}$

(D) $\sqrt{\dfrac{a}{(bc)}}$

7. The roots of the polynomial $x^3 + 3x^2 - 10x - 24$ are

(A) $-2, 3, -4$

(B) $-3, 3, -4$

(C) $-2, 3, 4$

(D) $2, -3, 4$

8. Given the functions $f(x) = 4\sin(8x)$ and $g(x) = \dfrac{2x}{4+x}$, which of the following represents $f(g(x))$?

(A) $\dfrac{2\sin(8x)}{4+x}$

(B) $4\sin\left(\dfrac{16x}{4+x}\right)$

(C) $\dfrac{8\sin(8x)}{4+x}$

(D) $2(4+x)\sin(4x)$

9. Consider the following set of equations:

$y_1 = 5x_1 + 3x_2 + 7x_3 + 4$

$y_2 = 4x_3 + 9x_2 + 5x_1 + 8$

$y_3 = 2x_1 + 2x_3 + 6x_2 + 3$

They can be rewritten as a single matrix equation:

$y = Sx + M$ with $y = \begin{bmatrix} y_1 \\ y_2 \\ y_3 \end{bmatrix}$, $x = \begin{bmatrix} x_1 \\ x_2 \\ x_3 \end{bmatrix}$,

$M = \begin{bmatrix} 4 \\ 8 \\ 3 \end{bmatrix}$, and S represented by

(A) $\begin{bmatrix} 5 & 3 & 7 \\ 4 & 9 & 5 \\ 2 & 2 & 2 \end{bmatrix}$

(B) $\begin{bmatrix} 5 & 3 & 7 \\ 5 & 9 & 4 \\ 2 & 6 & 2 \end{bmatrix}$

(C) $\begin{bmatrix} 5 & 3 & 7 \\ 5 & 9 & 4 \\ 2 & 2 & 6 \end{bmatrix}$

(D) $\begin{bmatrix} 5 & 4 & 2 \\ 3 & 9 & 2 \\ 7 & 5 & 6 \end{bmatrix}$

10. The inverse function of $f(x) = y = \dfrac{2x}{5x+1}$ is

   (A) $f^{-1}(x) = \dfrac{5x+1}{2x}$

   (B) $f^{-1}(x) = \dfrac{-2x}{5x+1}$

   (C) $f^{-1}(x) = \dfrac{-x}{5x-2}$

   (D) $f^{-1}(x) = \dfrac{5x+1}{5x+23}$

11. Given the point $(-2, 2)$ in the rectangular coordinate system, choose the correct representation of the point in polar coordinates.

   (A) $\left(8, \dfrac{3\pi}{4}\right)$

   (B) $\left(\sqrt{8}, \dfrac{5\pi}{4}\right)$

   (C) $\left(2\sqrt{2}, -\dfrac{5\pi}{4}\right)$

   (D) $\left(2\sqrt{2}, -\dfrac{3\pi}{4}\right)$

12. Which of the following correctly represents $\lim\limits_{x \to 0} \dfrac{\sin(x)+4x}{x}$?

   (A) 0

   (B) 1

   (C) 5

   (D) 4

13. Which of the following correctly represents $\int 4x^2 e^{2x}\,dx$?

   (A) $2x^2 e^{2x} - 2xe^{2x} + 4e^{2x} + C$

   (B) $2x^2 e^{2x} + 2xe^{2x} + e^{2x} + C$

   (C) $x^2 e^{2x} - 2xe^{2x} + e^{2x} + C$

   (D) $2x^2 e^{2x} - 2xe^{2x} + e^{2x} + C$

14. The number of bacteria in a certain sample doubles in 1 hour. The bacterium grows according to $N = N_o e^{\frac{t}{k}}$, where N is the number of bacteria of that type in the sample at time t in hours, N_0 is the initial number of bacteria, and k is a constant. If the initial number of bacteria is 1000, which of the following approximates the time required for that number to reach 50,000?

   (A) 2.3 hours

   (B) 5.6 hours

   (C) 0.7 hours

   (D) 9.2 hours

15. A cylindrical tank 50 centimeters in diameter is being filled with water at a rate of 0.2 m³/min. Which of the following approximates the rate at which the level of water increases in the tank?

   (A) 10.2 m/min.

   (B) 0.31 m/min.

   (C) 1.02 m/min.

   (D) 3.1 m/min.

16. Jim is practicing for a track meet. Each day he runs a quarter-mile track two and a half times. How many miles does he run in five days?

   (A) $\dfrac{5}{8}$ miles

   (B) $12\dfrac{1}{2}$ miles

   (C) $3\dfrac{1}{8}$ miles

   (D) $1\dfrac{1}{4}$ miles

17. At a movie theater, 1664 tickets were sold in a day, for $25,000 in revenue. Kids' tickets are sold at $8.00 and adult and senior citizens tickets are sold at $20.00. On this day, the sum of the kids' tickets and three times the senior citizens tickets sold equal the amount of adult tickets sold. How many of each ticket was sold?

    (A) 71 kids, 903 adult, 609 senior citizen

    (B) 903 kids, 609 adult, 71 senior citizen

    (C) 690 kids, 903 adult, 71 senior citizen

    (D) 71 kids, 609 adult, 903 senior citizen

18. Determine the number and types of solutions for the equation $2x^2 = -13x - 15$.

    (A) One real rational solution

    (B) Two real rational solutions

    (C) Two real irrational solutions

    (D) Two imaginary solutions

19. Which of the following conic section equations best represents the graph below?

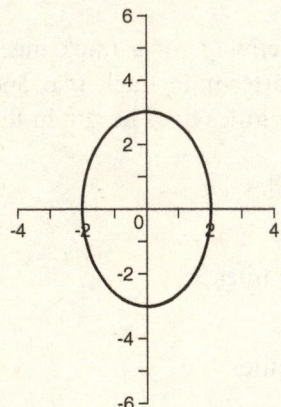

    (A) $\dfrac{x^2}{9} - \dfrac{y^2}{4} = 1$

    (B) $\dfrac{x^2}{4} - \dfrac{y^2}{9} = 1$

    (C) $\dfrac{x^2}{9} + \dfrac{y^2}{4} = 1$

    (D) $\dfrac{x^2}{4} + \dfrac{y^2}{9} = 1$

20. The interior of a circular pool has a radius of 10 meters and has a uniform circular sidewalk along the outside of the pool as shown in the diagram. If the area of the pool and sidewalk is 452.16 square meters, what is the total radius of the pool and the sidewalk in meters? (Use $\pi = 3.14$ for this problem.)

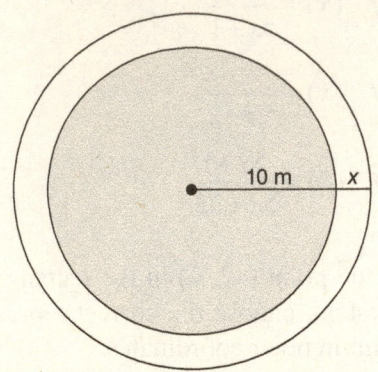

    (A) 2

    (B) 12

    (C) 22

    (D) 32

21.

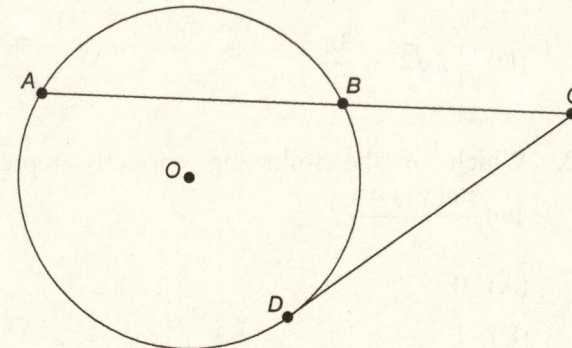

    Note: Figure not drawn to scale.

    In the circle above with center O, segment AC is secant and segment DC is tangent to circle O. The measure of arc minor AB is 60°, the measure of minor arc AD is $(4y + 15)°$, and the measure of minor arc DB is $(3y - 2)°$. What is the measure of $\angle ACD$?

    (A) 29°

    (B) 41°

    (C) 121°

    (D) 150°

22. Determine the period and phase shift of $y = 4\cos(2x - 4)$.

    (A) Period $= \dfrac{\pi}{2}$, phase shift $= -2$

    (B) Period $= \dfrac{\pi}{2}$, phase shift $= 2$

    (C) Period $= \pi$, phase shift $= -2$

    (D) Period $= \pi$, phase shift $= 2$

23. The set of values that do NOT satisfy $2y - 3 \le 5y + 6 < 2(y + 9)$ are

    (A) $(-4, \infty)$

    (B) $(-\infty, -3] \cup (4, \infty)$

    (C) $(-3, 4]$

    (D) $(-\infty, 3] \cup (4, \infty)$

24. Which of the following correctly represents the distance traveled by a person whose velocity is given by $\dfrac{dx}{dt} = v(t) = 5.0 + 4.9t^2$ meters/second over the time interval $t = 1$ second to $t = 2$ seconds?

    (A) 16.43 meters

    (B) 5 meters

    (C) 9.9 meters

    (D) 22.15 meters/second

25. The function $f(t) = -16t^2 + 874t + 250$ models the height of a rocket shot vertically into the air, where t is time since launch in seconds and $f(t)$ is height in feet. Find the velocity (in feet per second) of the rocket after 3 seconds.

    (A) 2647

    (B) 2397

    (C) 826

    (D) 778

26. A student has scored 79, 86, 100, 83, and 94 on five tests so far in the math course. What does the student need to score on the next test for the final average on tests to be 90 percent?

    (A) 98

    (B) 94

    (C) 90

    (D) 86

27. Identify the type of correlation that would best fit the scatter plot below.

    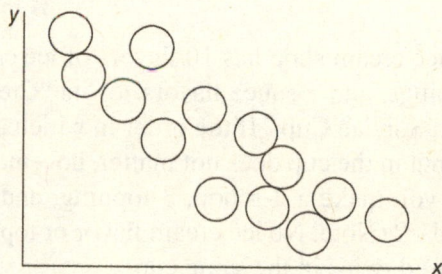

    (A) Positive linear correlation

    (B) Negative linear correlation

    (C) Non-linear correlation

    (D) No correlation

28. What is the probability of getting doubles (1 and 1, 2 and 2, etc.) three consecutive times when rolling a standard pair of 6-sided dice?

    (A) $\dfrac{1}{2}$

    (B) $\dfrac{1}{36}$

    (C) $\dfrac{1}{216}$

    (D) $\dfrac{1}{532}$

29. Which of the following matrices is NOT its own inverse?

(A) $\begin{bmatrix} 1 & 0 \\ 0 & 1 \end{bmatrix}$

(B) $\begin{bmatrix} 0 & -1 \\ -1 & 0 \end{bmatrix}$

(C) $\begin{bmatrix} 0 & -1 \\ 1 & 0 \end{bmatrix}$

(D) $\begin{bmatrix} -1 & 0 \\ 0 & -1 \end{bmatrix}$

30. An ice cream shop has 10 flavors of ice cream, 20 toppings, and 5 sauce flavors for its "Create Your Own Sundae Cup." If the order in which the items are put in the cup does not matter, how many ways can you make a 2-scoop, 3-topping, and 1-sauce sundae? (Note: No ice cream flavor or topping can be used twice in the same cup.)

(A) 256,500

(B) 171,000

(C) 85,000

(D) 51,300

31. What is the coefficient of the term containing x^3 in the expansion of $(x + 4)^8$?

(A) 0

(B) 57344

(C) 3584

(D) 1024

32. A recipe for a dessert pudding consists of seven different ingredients. Each ingredient is added one at a time to a mixing bowl. In how many different orders may the seven ingredients be added?

(A) 7

(B) 49

(C) 7^7

(D) 7!

33. Which of the following is the ratio of surface area to volume for a sphere of radius R and a cube of side $2R$, respectively?

(A) $\dfrac{3}{R}, \dfrac{3}{R}$

(B) $\dfrac{R}{\pi}, \dfrac{R}{3}$

(C) $\dfrac{\pi}{R}, \dfrac{3}{2R}$

(D) $\dfrac{3}{R}, \dfrac{3}{2R}$

34. Michelle has a length of rope. When cut into seven equal parts, Michelle finds that five of the parts together equal three-fifths of a meter. What is the original length of Michelle's rope?

(A) $\dfrac{3}{7}$ meters

(B) $\dfrac{3}{25}$ meters

(C) $\dfrac{3}{35}$ meters

(D) $\dfrac{21}{25}$ meters

35. What is the probability that a six-sided die never comes up an odd number when it is rolled four times?

(A) $\dfrac{3}{64}$

(B) $\dfrac{12}{24}$

(C) $\dfrac{6}{24}$

(D) $\dfrac{1}{16}$

36. For which values of x and y is the matrix $\begin{bmatrix} x & 2 \\ y & 3 \end{bmatrix}$ invertible?

    I. $x = \dfrac{2}{3}$, $y = \dfrac{3}{2}$

    II. $x = \dfrac{1}{3}$, $y = \dfrac{1}{2}$

    III. $x = 2, y = 3$

(A) I only

(B) I and II

(C) III and II

(D) III only

37. The histogram below displays frequency of heights for students in a class. For example, there are six students in the class who are greater than or equal to 5′3″ tall and less than 5′6″ tall. If a student is chosen at random from this class, what is the probability that the student will be at least 6′ tall?

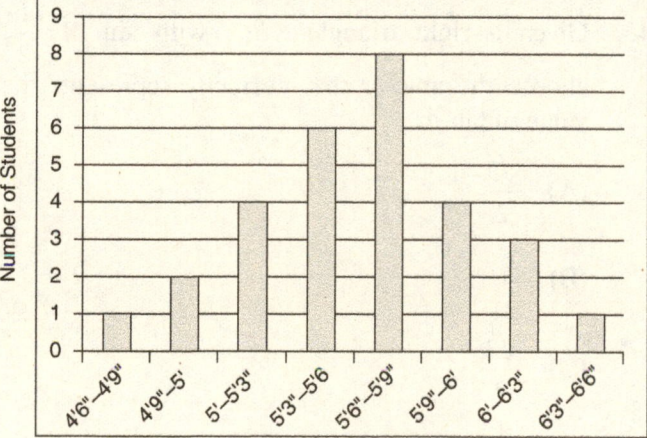

(A) $\dfrac{1}{30}$

(B) $\dfrac{1}{10}$

(C) $\dfrac{4}{29}$

(D) $\dfrac{8}{29}$

38. The diameter of hailstones resulting from a particular thunderstorm is found to be normally distributed with a mean of 5.2 millimeters and a standard deviation of 0.8 millimeters. Approximately what percentage of hailstones has a diameter greater than 6.0 millimeters?

(A) 50%

(B) 16%

(C) 67%

(D) 34%

39. The function $f(x,y)$ is defined by $f(x,y) = \dfrac{x}{x^2 + y^2}$. The value of y is in turn given by $y(z) = \cos(2z)$. For $x = 0.5$ and $z = 1$ radian, which of the following most nearly approximates the value of $f(x,y)$?

(A) 1.18

(B) 0.40

(C) −0.40

(D) 0.01

40. The function $f(x) = \dfrac{2\pi}{x^5}$ is

    I.   Antisymmetric or odd

    II. Symmetric or even

    III. Continuous over the real numbers

(A) II only

(B) II and III only

(C) I and III only

(D) I only

41. The half-life of an unknown radioactive substance is found to be 8 years. How many years must pass before only 30% of the initial quantity remains? Round your answer to the nearest integer.

(A) 13

(B) 14

(C) 10

(D) 15

42. Global Phone is a long-distance telephone company. Customers of Global Phone pay a monthly fee for Global Phone's services in addition to a small fee for each minute used. Last month, Tom's Global Phone bill was $25. His friend Larry had a Global Phone bill of $45. During this month, Tom used 300 minutes and Larry used 700. How much money can Larry save if can limit his minutes used to only 550?

(A) $9.64

(B) $12.50

(C) $7.50

(D) $17.50

43. Two flagpoles are positioned next to each other in front of a school. At 3:00 p.m., the taller flagpole, which is 18 feet tall, casts a shadow that is 6 feet long. At the same time, the shorter flagpole casts a shadow that is only 4 feet long. How tall is the shorter flagpole?

(A) 16 feet

(B) 12 feet

(C) 27 feet

(D) 10 feet

44. In the figure below, *AC* has a length of 4 meters and *BD* is a diameter of the circle with center *C*. The length of *BD* is 6 meters. Determine the length of *BA*. Note: The image is NOT drawn to scale.

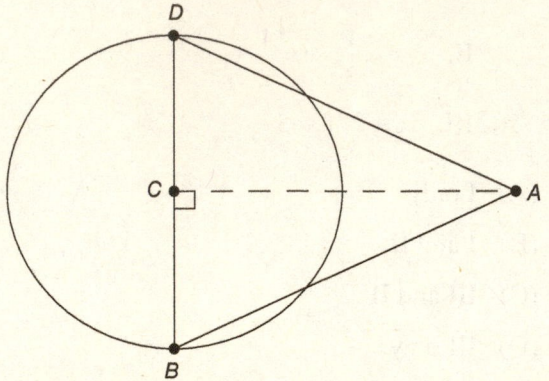

(A) 3 meters

(B) 5 meters

(C) 6 meters

(D) 8 meters

45. Given a right triangle *ABC*, with $\sin A = \frac{1}{2}$, choose the answer that correctly represents the value of tan *A*.

(A) $\dfrac{\sqrt{3}}{2}$

(B) $\dfrac{2}{3}$

(C) $\dfrac{\sqrt{2}}{2}$

(D) $\dfrac{\sqrt{3}}{3}$

46. Given the table below, find the value of $(f \circ g)(3)$.

x	0	1	2	3	4	5	6
$f(x)$	3	4	5	6	7	8	9
$g(x)$	0	1	2	2	2	3	3

(A) 3

(B) 12

(C) 5

(D) 8

47. For which values of a and b is the equation

$$\begin{bmatrix} 1 & -4 \\ 2 & 9 \end{bmatrix} \begin{bmatrix} a \\ 3 \end{bmatrix} = \begin{bmatrix} -1 \\ b \end{bmatrix} \text{ satisfied?}$$

(A) $a = -7, b = 55$

(B) $a = 11, b = 49$

(C) $a = \dfrac{1}{4}, b = 54$

(D) $a = 11, b = 45$

48. Choose the sequence below that has the first five

terms: $1, \dfrac{1}{2}, \dfrac{1}{4}, \dfrac{1}{8}, \dfrac{1}{16}$

(A) $a_n = \dfrac{1}{2}n$, where $n = 1, 2, 3, \ldots$

(B) $a_n = \left(\dfrac{1}{2}\right)^n$, where $n = 0, 1, 2, \ldots$

(C) $a_n = \dfrac{1}{2} + a_{n-1}$, where $n = 0, 1, 2, \ldots$ and $a_0 = 1$

(D) $a_n = 1 - \dfrac{1}{2}n$, where $n = 0, 1, 2, \ldots$

49. Which of the following functions could be given by the following graph?

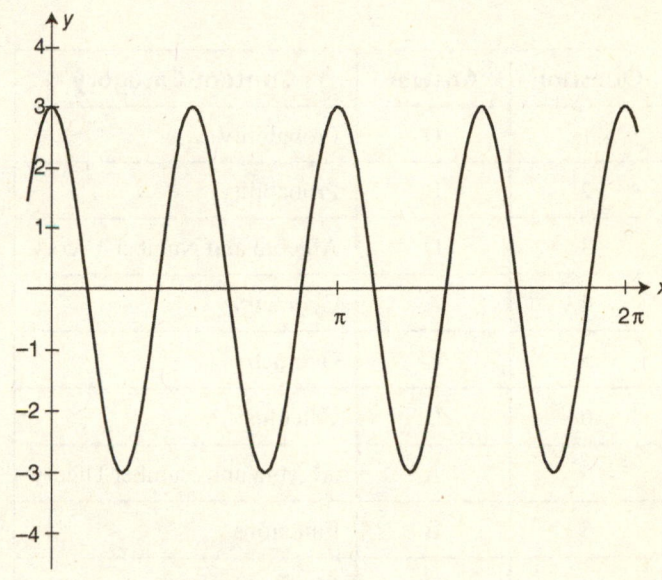

(A) $4 \cos(3\theta)$

(B) $4 \sin(3\theta)$

(C) $3 \sin(4\theta)$

(D) $3 \cos(4\theta)$

50. The matrix M is given by $\begin{bmatrix} -3 & 2 \\ -6 & d \end{bmatrix}$. For all of

the following values of d, M is invertible EXCEPT for

(A) 4

(B) -9

(C) 1

(D) -4

Answer Key—Practice Test 1

Question	Answer	Content Category	Question	Answer	Content Category
1	D	Probability	26	A	Data Analysis and Statistics
2	B	Probability	27	B	Data Analysis and Statistics
3	D	Algebra and Number Theory	28	C	Probability
4	A	Geometry	29	C	Matrix Algebra
5	C	Geometry	30	A	Discrete Mathematics
6	B	Calculus	31	B	Algebra and Number Theory
7	A	Algebra and Number Theory	32	D	Discrete Mathematics
8	B	Functions	33	A	Geometry
9	B	Matrix Algebra	34	D	Algebra and Number Theory
10	C	Functions	35	D	Probability
11	C	Trigonometry	36	A	Matrix Algebra
12	C	Calculus	37	C	Data Analysis and Statistics
13	D	Calculus	38	B	Data Analysis and Statistics
14	B	Functions	39	A	Functions
15	C	Calculus	40	D	Functions
16	C	Measurement	41	B	Functions
17	C	Algebra and Number Theory	42	C	Algebra and Number Theory
18	B	Algebra and Number Theory	43	B	Measurement
19	D	Algebra and Number Theory	44	B	Geometry
20	B	Measurement	45	D	Trigonometry
21	A	Geometry	46	C	Functions
22	D	Trignonometry	47	B	Matrix Algebra
23	B	Functions	48	B	Discrete Mathematics
24	A	Calculus	49	D	Trigonometry
25	D	Calculus	50	A	Matrix Algebra

Detailed Explanations for Practice Test 1

1. (D)

The correct answer is (D). Instead of calculating the probability directly, we can calculate the probability that all of the students were born in unique months. P(all unique months) $= \left(\frac{12}{12}\right) \cdot \left(\frac{11}{12}\right) \cdot \left(\frac{10}{12}\right) \cdot \left(\frac{9}{12}\right) \cdot \left(\frac{8}{12}\right) \cdot \left(\frac{7}{12}\right) \approx 0.22$. Having all students have birthdays in unique months is the complement of having two or more students have birthdays in the same month, so P(two or more in the same month) $= 1 - P$(all unique months) $\approx 1 - 0.22 = 0.78$.

2. (B)

The correct answer is (B). This question is asking us about a conditional probability. To begin with, we are told there are 80 respondents to the survey. We know the entries for all the boys and for those girls who like red account for $25 + 18 + 20 = 63$ individuals. Therefore, the remaining cell, girls who like blue, must contain 17 individuals. The question is asking us *if a girl chosen at random will like blue*. There are only $17 + 20 = 37$ females who responded to the survey. Of them, only 17 like blue. Therefore, the correct probability is $\frac{17}{37}$.

3. (D)

The correct answer is (D). Rewrite the quadratic equation in the form $0 = -5.7 + 10x + x^2$. Solve the equation using the quadratic formula, $x = \frac{-b \pm \sqrt{b^2 - 4ac}}{2a} = \frac{-10 \pm \sqrt{100 - 4 \cdot 1 \cdot (-5.7)}}{2 \cdot 1} \approx 0.54$ *or* -10.54. We are interested in the positive root only since this number represents the compression of the spring; therefore, the answer is 0.54.

4. (A)

The correct answer is (A). The largest equilateral triangle can be decomposed into six 30-60-90 degree triangles of hypotenuse R. To see this, inscribe a circle with an equilateral triangle with each of the vertices lying on the circle. Then draw radii to the vertices of the triangle and draw three line segments from the center of the circle to the midpoints of the sides of the triangle. This process produces the six 30-60-90 right triangles shown in the accompanying figure with $\beta = 30°$ and $\alpha = 60°$. The length of the hypotenuse of each of these triangles is R. Using the relationships of a 30-60-90 right triangle, the length of the base b is $\frac{\sqrt{3}}{2}R$ and the heights h are $\frac{R}{2}$. The area of each of these triangles is $\frac{1}{2} \cdot \frac{\sqrt{3}}{2}R \cdot \frac{R}{2} = \frac{\sqrt{3}}{8}R^2$; hence the total area of the equilateral triangle is $6 \cdot \frac{\sqrt{3}}{8}R^2 = \frac{3\sqrt{3}}{4}R^2$, which is approximately $1.3\,R^2$.

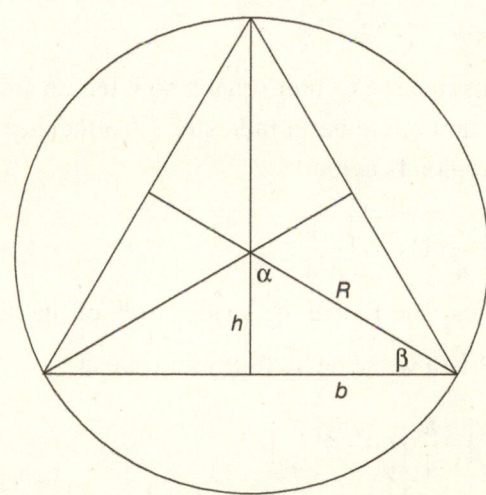

Equilateral triangle inscribed in a circle of radius R.

5.   (C)

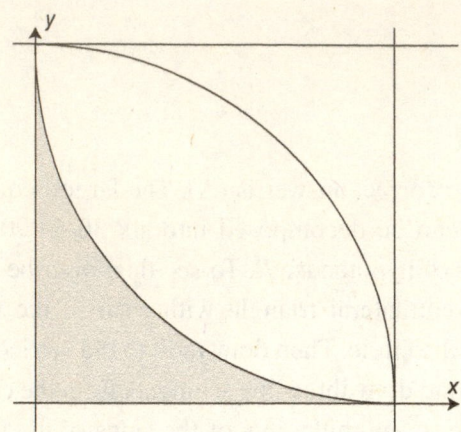

The correct answer is (C). The image is symmetrical. If we can figure out the area shaded in the first quadrant, we can scale it by 4 to get the area of the entire shaded figure. We can thus draw a unit square that encloses the intersection of these two circles, like our diagram (the additional guide lines have been added to highlight the unit square). Notice that the shaded area here is actually equal to the area of the square minus one fourth the area of a circle. Furthermore, we know from the problem that all circles have a radius of 1. Therefore, the shaded region is

$$A_{\text{square}} - \frac{1}{4} A_{\text{circle}} \,.$$

Our square is a unit square, so it has an area of 1, and our unit circle has a radius of 1, so the area of the shaded region becomes

$$1 - \frac{1}{4}\pi(1)^2 = 1 - \frac{\pi}{4} \,.$$

Thus, one fourth the shaded area of the figure is $1 - \frac{\pi}{4}$. When we scale by four we arrive at

$$4\left(1 - \frac{\pi}{4}\right) = 4 - 4\left(\frac{\pi}{4}\right)$$
$$= 4 - \pi$$

6.   (B)

The correct answer is (B). The fuel consumed for a trip is $F = \left(\frac{D}{s}\right) \cdot f(s) = \frac{Da}{s} + Db + Dcs$, and is

equal to the duration of the trip times the rate of fuel consumption. Differentiate the fuel consumption for a trip with respect to speed to obtain $\frac{df}{ds} = D(-as^{-2} + c)$. Set this derivative to zero and solve for the speed at an extremum, so $s = \sqrt{\frac{a}{c}}$. Note that the second derivative of the fuel consumed with respect to speed is positive, $\frac{d^2F}{ds^2} = \frac{2a}{s^2}$. Therefore, the extremum is a minimum.

7.   (A)

The correct answer is (A). There are several ways to approach this problem. Designate the three roots by $r_1, r_2,$ and r_3. Because there are four choices to consider, one approach to the problem is to assume each answer is correct and multiply $(x - r_1)(x - r_2)(x - r_3)$ to see if the result agrees with the cubic given. However, (C) and (D) can be ruled out immediately by realizing that the product of $r_1, r_2,$ and r_3 must be positive, as the constant term of the original polynomial is –24. Then you need only test (A) and (B). If you multiply $(x + 2)(x - 3)(x + 4)$, which corresponds to (A), you see that it is correct. Also, the function could be graphed with a graphing calculator to see that the roots of the polynomial are –2, 3, and –4. (The Rational Root Test or synthetic division could also be used here.)

8.   (B)

The correct answer is (B). Replace x with $g(x)$ in the definition of $f(x)$ to obtain $f(g(x)) = 4\sin\left(8\left(\frac{2x}{4+x}\right)\right) = 4\sin\left(\frac{16x}{4+x}\right)$.

9.   (B)

The correct answer is (B). You can show this by taking the dot product of each row of the matrix S with the vector $\boldsymbol{x}$ and adding the corresponding element of the vector M. For example, we may eliminate answer D by performing this process and obtaining $y_1 = 5x_1 + 4x_2 + 2x_3 + 4$; $y_2 = 2x_3 + 9x_2 + 3x_1 + 8$; $y_3 = 7x_1 + 6x_3 + 5x_2 + 3$, which do not agree with the equations given in the problem statement. We may likewise eliminate all answers except (B). It is also instructive to write the matrix S from inspection of the original equations; note that each row of the matrix S corresponds to an equation and each column of the matrix corresponds to an element of the vector x. Also note that order is important.

10. (C)

The correct answer is (C). To demonstrate this answer, rearrange the definition of the function $f(x)$ to solve for x in terms of y. In steps:

$$f(x) = y = \frac{2x}{5x+1}$$

$$y(5x + 1) = 2x$$

$$5xy + y = 2x$$

$$5xy - 2x = -y$$

$$x(5y - 2) = -y$$

$$x = -\frac{y}{5y-2}$$

To obtain the inverse from this, we switch x and y, so $f^{-1}(x) = \frac{-x}{5x-2}$.

11. (C)

The correct answer is (C). A point in the rectangular plane (x, y) can be represented in polar coordinates by the point (r, θ) where $r = \sqrt{x^2 + y^2}$ and $\theta = \tan^{-1}\left(\frac{y}{x}\right)$. Substituting $(-2, 2)$, we find $r = \sqrt{(-2)^2 + (2)^2} = \sqrt{8} = 2\sqrt{2}$ and $\theta = \tan^{-1}\left(\frac{2}{-2}\right) = \frac{3\pi}{4}$, where θ is measured from the positive x-axis with a counterclockwise orientation. Subtracting 2π from θ has no effect on the location of the point. This subtraction yields $\frac{3\pi}{4} - 2\pi = -\frac{5\pi}{4}$ and so the correct answer is $\left(2\sqrt{2}, \frac{5\pi}{4}\right)$. None of the other points will satisfy both of the equations $r = \sqrt{x^2 + y^2}$ and $\theta = \tan^{-1}\left(\frac{y}{x}\right)$.

12. (C)

The correct answer is (C). You may demonstrate this with numerical approximations or by using L'Hopital's rule for which the expression can be rewritten as $\lim_{x \to 0} \frac{\cos(x)+4}{1} = \cos(0) + 4 = 1 + 4 = 5$.

13. (D)

The correct answer is (D). It may be obtained by repeated integration by parts. In the standard nomenclature, for the first integration $u = 4x^2$ and $dv = e^{2x}dx$. Therefore, $du = 8xdx$ and $v = \frac{1}{2}e^{2x}$. The original integral can be rewritten as $2x^2e^{2x} - \int 4xe^{2x}dx$. In order to evaluate the resulting integral we must use integration by parts again. This time $u = 4x$ and $dv = e^{2x}dx$, so $du = 4dx$ and $v = \frac{1}{2}e^{2x}$. The integral can be rewritten again as $2x^2e^{2x} - (2xe^{2x} - \int 2e^{2x}dx) = 2x^2e^{2x} - (2xe^{2x} - e^{2x}) + C = 2x^2e^{2x} - 2xe^{2x} + e^{2x} + C$.

14. (B)

The correct answer is (B). The first step is to solve for the constant k. We may use the information about the time it takes for the population of bacteria to double in order to do that. From that information, we can generate the following equation: $2000 = 1000e^{\frac{1}{k}}$. Solving for k yields $k = \frac{1}{\ln 2} \approx 1.44$. Using this value of k, we can now solve the problem: $50000 = 1000e^{\frac{t}{1.44}}$. Solving for t gives us $t = 1.44 \cdot \ln 50 \approx 5.6$ hours.

15. (C)

The correct answer is (C). The cross-sectional area of the tank is constant: $A = \pi (25 \text{ cm})^2 = .1963 \text{ m}^2$. The volume of water in the tank is $V = Ah$, where h is the height of water in the tank. Both V and h are changing, and the problem is asking us to find the rate of change of h, $\dfrac{dh}{dt}$. Differentiating both sides of the volume equation with respect to t yields $\dfrac{dV}{dt} = A \cdot \dfrac{dh}{dt}$. The volume of water in the tank increases at a rate of 0.2 m³/min, so $\dfrac{dV}{dt} = \dfrac{0.2 \text{ m}^3}{\text{min}}$. So by substituting the known quantities into the differential equation, we get $0.2 = 0.1963 \cdot \dfrac{dh}{dt}$. Solving the equation yields, $\dfrac{dh}{dt} = \dfrac{0.2}{0.1963} \approx 1.02 \text{ m/min}$.

16. (C)

The correct answer is (C). Every day, Jim runs $\left(\dfrac{1}{4}\right)\left(2\dfrac{1}{2}\right) = \dfrac{5}{8}$ mile. In five days, that would be $(5)\left(\dfrac{5}{8}\right) = \dfrac{25}{8} = 3\dfrac{1}{8}$ miles.

17. (C)

The correct answer is (C). The tickets in this problem can be expressed in three equations with k representing the kids' tickets, a representing adult tickets, and s representing the senior tickets. The three equations for this problem are:

$$k + a + s = 1664$$
$$8k + 20a + 20s = 25000$$
$$k + 3s = a$$

There are various ways to solve this system; the following demonstrates one method. Start by substituting $k + 3s$ for a in the other two equations. The resulting equations are:

$$k + k + 3s + s = 1664 \quad \rightarrow$$
$$2k + 4s = 1664$$

$$8k + 20(k + 3s) + 20s = 25000 \quad \rightarrow$$
$$28k + 80s = 25000$$

Multiply the first equation by –20 to get

$$-40k - 80s = -33280$$

Then add the two equations, so the s terms disappear, and you are left with $-12k = -8280$. The result for k, the number of kids' tickets, is 690. Then, substitute k into one equation and solve: $2(690) + 4s = 1664$; $1380 + 4s = 1664$; $4s = 284$. So, the number of senior tickets is 71. Finally, solve for a by substituting into the third equation $690 + 3 \cdot 71 = 903 = a$. So, 903 adult tickets were sold.

18. (B)

The correct answer is (B). To start solving this quadratic equation, put the equation into standard form $(Ax^2 + Bx + C = 0)$: $2x^2 + 13x + 15 = 0$. To find the types of solutions for this equation, you need to find the discriminant $(b^2 - 4ac)$, $13^2 - 4 \cdot 2 \cdot 15 = 49$, which is a perfect square. Because the discriminant is a perfect square, the solutions to the equation are two real rational solutions.

19. (D)

The correct answer is (D). This question asks you to determine which conic section best represents the given graph. You should recall the conic section equations for a hyperbola and an ellipse. You can see that answers (A) and (B) are hyperbolas since the two terms are subtracted; therefore, (A) and (B) are incorrect for this problem. The graph in this problem has y as the major axis (length of 6) and x as the minor axis (length of 4). So $2a = 6$ and $2b = 4$ which means $a = 3$ and $b = 2$ in the standard form of an ellipse centered at the origin with a vertical major axis: $\dfrac{x^2}{b^2} + \dfrac{y^2}{a^2} = 1$. Thus, the correct equation is $\dfrac{x^2}{4} + \dfrac{y^2}{9} = 1$.

20. (B)

The correct answer is (B). This question requires your knowledge of the area of a circle in order to find the radius of the circular sidewalk and pool $(10 + x)$. Recall that the formula for the area of the circle is πr^2. The area of the pool with the circular sidewalk is 452.16 square meters and this area can be represented as $\pi(10 + x)^2 = 452.16$. Solving this equation for x yields

$$\pi(10 + x)^2 = 452.16$$
$$3.14(100 + 20x + x^2) = 452.16$$
$$314 + 62.8x + 3.14x^2 = 452.16$$
$$3.14x^2 + 62.8x - 138.16 = 0$$
$$x^2 + 20x - 44 = 0$$
$$(x + 22)(x - 2) = 0$$
$$x = -22 \text{ or } x = 2$$

Since x represents a length, cannot be negative, so only $x = 2$ makes sense in the context of the question; therefore, the radius of the pool with the sidewalk is $10 + x = 10 + 2 = 12$.

21. (A)

The correct answer is (A). The measure of $\angle ACD$ is half of the difference of the intercepted arcs. First, we need to find the measurement of each arc. Because a circle has $360°$, measure of arc AB + measure of arc AD + measure of arc $BD = 360°$. The equation that results is $60 + 4y + 15 + 3y - 2 = 360$. Solving this equation for y results in

$$60 + 4y + 15 + 3y - 2 = 360$$
$$7y + 73 = 360$$
$$7y = 287$$

So, $y = 41$, which makes the measure of arc $AD = (4y + 15)° = (4 \cdot 41 + 15)° = 179°$ and the measure of arc $BD = (3y - 2)° = (3 \cdot 41 - 2)° = 121°$. Then to find the measure of $\angle ACD$, we take half of the difference of the intercepted arcs. Therefore, $m\angle ACD = \dfrac{179° - 121°}{2} = 29°$.

22. (D)

The correct answer is (D). There are two ways to answer this question. The first solution is based on the function $y = a \cos b(x - c)$. First, you will need to factor the expression such that $y = 4 \cos 2(x - 2)$. Recall the period of the cosine function is $\dfrac{2\pi}{b}$, so here it is $\dfrac{2\pi}{2} = \pi$. The phase shift is the c value so the phase shift would be 2. Another option is to graph $y = 4 \cos(2x - 4)$ and find the period and phase shift from the graph.

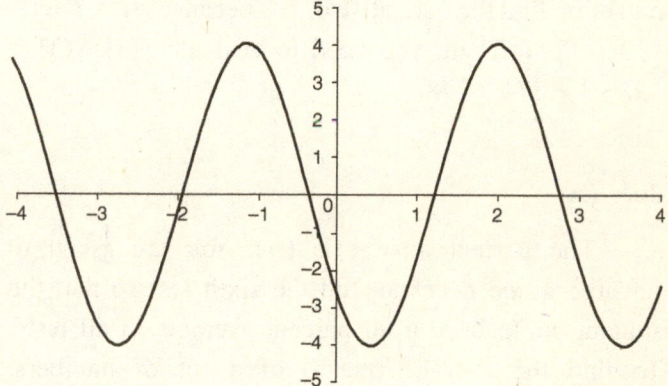

The period is π and the phase shift is 2.

23. (B)

The correct answer is (B). Recall that in order to find the set of values that do not satisfy the inequality, we will need to find the set of values that do and then take their complement. Thus, we first must isolate y.

$$2y - 3 \leq 5y + 6 < 2(y + 9)$$
$$2y - 3 \leq 5y + 6 < 2y + 18$$
$$-3 \leq 3y + 6 < 18$$
$$-9 \leq 3y < 12$$
$$-\frac{9}{3} \leq y < \frac{12}{3}$$
$$-3 \leq y < 4$$

Thus the set of values which satisfy the inequality is $[-3, 4)$. When we take the complement of this set, we get everything NOT part of the set, which is

$$(-\infty, -3] \cup (4, \infty)$$

24. (A)

The correct answer is (A). The distance travelled is found by using the definite integral of velocity over the time period. In this case, it is given by $\int_{t=1}^{t=2} 5.0 + 4.9t^2 \, dt = 16.43$ meters.

25. (D)

The correct answer is (D). In this problem, you are asked to find the velocity at a specific time. You must first find the derivative of $f(t)$ because $v(t) = f'(t) = -32t + 874$. Then, you need to evaluate $v(3)$. $v(3) = -32 \cdot 3 + 874 = 778$.

26. (A)

The correct answer is (A). You are asked to find the grade necessary on the sixth test so that the student could have a 90 percent average on all tests. To find the average (mean) of a set of numbers, you can find the sum of the elements and divide by the number of elements: $\text{mean} = \frac{\text{sum of scores}}{\text{number of scores}}$. If x represents the score necessary on the sixth test, $90 = \frac{79 + 86 + 100 + 83 + 94 + x}{6} = \frac{442 + x}{6}$. Solving this equation yields $x = 98$, so that is the necessary score.

27. (B)

The correct answer is (B). To determine if a model has relationship, a best-fit line has to be placed within the data. In this problem, the best-fit line would be

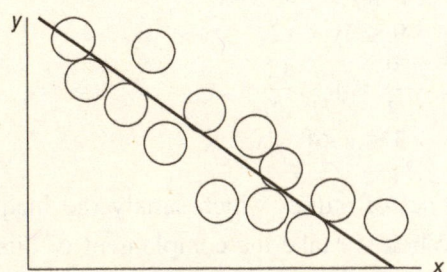

This line has a negative slope, so the regression is negative and linear.

28. (C)

The answer is (C). You are asked to apply the knowledge of independent events to find the probability of rolling doubles three consecutive times when using a pair of dice. Because each roll is independent, the probability of rolling doubles three consecutive times $P(\text{doubles, doubles, doubles}) = P(\text{doubles}) \cdot P(\text{doubles}) \cdot P(\text{doubles})$, where $P(\text{doubles})$ is the probability of rolling doubles. $P(\text{doubles}) = \frac{6}{36} = \frac{1}{6}$ since of the 36 ways to roll two dice, only 6 produce doubles. Therefore, $P(\text{doubles, doubles, doubles}) = \frac{1}{6} \cdot \frac{1}{6} \cdot \frac{1}{6} = \frac{1}{216}$.

29. (C)

The answer is (C). You must determine in this problem the inverse of each matrix. The formula for finding the inverse of a 2×2 matrix $A = \begin{bmatrix} a & b \\ c & d \end{bmatrix}$ is $A^{-1} = \frac{1}{\det A} \cdot \begin{bmatrix} d & -b \\ -c & a \end{bmatrix}$.

For answer (A), the determinant is 1. Then, the inverse is $1 \cdot \begin{bmatrix} 1 & 0 \\ 0 & 1 \end{bmatrix} = \begin{bmatrix} 1 & 0 \\ 0 & 1 \end{bmatrix}$. So, answer (A) is the inverse of itself. For answer (B), the determinant is -1. Then, to find the inverse is $-1 \cdot \begin{bmatrix} 0 & 1 \\ 1 & 0 \end{bmatrix} = \begin{bmatrix} 0 & -1 \\ -1 & 0 \end{bmatrix}$. So, answer B is the inverse of itself. For (C), the determinant is 1. Then, the inverse is $1 \cdot \begin{bmatrix} 0 & 1 \\ -1 & 0 \end{bmatrix} = \begin{bmatrix} 0 & 1 \\ -1 & 0 \end{bmatrix}$. So, (C) is NOT the inverse of itself. For (D), the determinant is 1. Then, the inverse is $1 \cdot \begin{bmatrix} -1 & 0 \\ 0 & -1 \end{bmatrix} = \begin{bmatrix} -1 & 0 \\ 0 & -1 \end{bmatrix}$, and answer (D) is the inverse of itself.

30. (A)

The answer is (A). You are asked in the problem to determine the number of combinations for a 2-scoop,

3-topping, and 1-sauce sundae. To solve, you would need to find the combination ($_nC_r$) for each part of the ice cream sundae:

$$\text{Ice cream} = {}_{10}C_2 = \frac{10!}{2!(10-2)!} = 45$$

$$\text{Topping} = {}_{20}C_3 = \frac{20!}{3!(20-3)!} = 1140$$

$$\text{Sauce} = {}_5C_1 = \frac{5!}{1!(5-1)!} = 5$$

Then, to find the total number of combinations, you would multiply the ice cream, topping, and sundae combinations. There are $45 \cdot 1140 \cdot 5 = 256,500$ combinations.

31. (B)

The correct answer is (B). The formula for binomial expansion is $(x+y)^n = \sum_{i=0}^{\infty} \binom{n}{i} x^{n-i} y^i$. Thus, $(x+y)^8 = \sum_{i=0}^{8} \binom{8}{i} x^{8-i} 4^i$. Therefore, the coefficient of the x^3 term ($i = 3$) is $\binom{8}{3} 4^5 = \frac{8!}{5!3!} 4^5 = 57344$.

32. (D)

The correct answer is (D). This answer may be calculated from the permutations of 7 items taken 7 at a time is $_7P_7 = \frac{7!}{0!} = 7!$.

33. (A)

The correct answer is (A). The surface area of a sphere is $4\pi R^2$, and the volume of that sphere is $\frac{4}{3}\pi R^3$, so the ratio is $\frac{3}{R}$. The surface area of a cube of side $2R$ is $6 \times 2R \times 2R = 24R^2$, and the volume of the cube is $2R \times 2R \times 2R = 8R^3$, so the ratio is $\frac{3}{R}$.

34. (D)

The correct answer is (D). Let x represent the original length of the rope. Then $\frac{5}{7}x = \frac{3}{5}$. Solving this equation for x yields $x = \frac{7}{5} \cdot \frac{3}{5} = \frac{21}{25}$ meters.

35. (D)

The correct answer is (D). The probability that a single roll is not odd is $\frac{3}{6} = \frac{1}{2}$. Because the following die roll is not influenced by the preceding die roll, the possibility of four rolls not resulting in a single odd number is $\frac{1}{2} \cdot \frac{1}{2} \cdot \frac{1}{2} \cdot \frac{1}{2} = \left(\frac{1}{2}\right)^4 = \frac{1}{16}$.

36. (A)

The correct answer is (A). The matrix $\begin{bmatrix} x & 2 \\ y & 3 \end{bmatrix}$ is invertible as long as its determinant is not equal to zero, or $\begin{vmatrix} x & 2 \\ y & 3 \end{vmatrix} \neq 0 \rightarrow 3x - 2y \neq 0$. This implies that $x \neq \frac{2}{3}y$. Substituting the values given for (I), $\frac{2}{3} \neq \frac{2}{3}\left(\frac{3}{2}\right)$, whereas for (II), $\frac{1}{3} = \frac{2}{3}\left(\frac{1}{2}\right)$, and for (III), $2 = \frac{2}{3}(3)$. Thus, only the values in (I) satisfy the condition that the determinant is not zero.

37. (C)

The correct answer is (C). First find the total number of students in the class by adding $1 + 2 + 4 + 6 + 8 + 4 + 3 + 1 = 29$. The number of students at least 6 feet in height corresponds to the last two bars in the histogram and equals $3 + 1 = 4$. Hence, 4 students out of 29 are at least 6 feet tall.

38. (B)

The correct answer is (B). In order to answer this question, you can use two facts: the normal distribution is symmetric about the mean; approximately 68% of the population falls within plus or minus one standard deviation of the mean. It follows that 32% of the population falls outside of one standard deviation of the mean and that half of that (or 16%) is larger than the mean plus one standard deviation.

39. (A)

The correct answer is (A). First calculate $y = \cos(2 \text{ radians}) \approx -0.416$. Then, $f(0.5, -0.416) = \dfrac{0.5}{0.5 \cdot 0.5 + (-0.416) \cdot (-0.416)} \approx 1.18$.

40. (D)

The correct answer is (D). The function has a discontinuity at $x = 0$ and is antisymmetric, or odd, because $f(x) = -f(-x)$.

41. (B)

The correct answer is (B). The continuous decay of a radioactive substance can be modeled by exponential decay, $A = A_0 e^{kt}$, where A_0 is the initial amount of the substance. Alternatively, $\dfrac{A}{A_0} = e^{kt}$. Using the half-life, $\dfrac{A}{A_0} = 0.50 = e^{k(8)} \rightarrow k \approx -0.0866$. Now assuming 30% remains, $\dfrac{A}{A_0} = 0.30 = e^{-0.0866t} \rightarrow t = \dfrac{\ln 0.30}{-0.0866} \approx 13.9$ years, which is rounded to 14 years as requested in the question.

42. (C)

The correct answer is (C). We can find the charge per minute used by finding the slope of the line that passes through the points (300, 25) and (700, 45). The slope is $\dfrac{45 - 25}{700 - 300} = \$0.05$ per minute. Thus, if Larry can reduce his minutes used by 150, he will save $150(0.05) = \$7.50$.

43. (B)

The correct answer is (B). If the 18-foot tall pole casts a shadow of 6 feet and a pole of height x feet casts a shadow of 4 feet, then $\dfrac{18}{6} = \dfrac{x}{4} \rightarrow 18 \cdot 4 = 6x \rightarrow x = 12$.

44. (B)

The correct answer is (B). We know that the length of BD is 6 meters, and because it is the diameter and C is the center, we know that the length of BC is 3 meters. Now the triangle ABC is a right triangle in which we know the length of both legs of the triangle. We can therefore use the Pythagorean Theorem to compute the length of $AB = \sqrt{3^2 + 4^2} = \sqrt{25} = 5$ meters.

45. (D)

The correct answer is (D). We are given that $\sin A = \dfrac{1}{2}$ in the right triangle ABC. Therefore, we can assume that the length of side BC is 1 and the length of side AB is 2. By the Pythagorean Theorem, we can calculate that the length of CA is $\sqrt{3}$. Now, the value of $\tan A = \dfrac{1}{\sqrt{3}} = \dfrac{\sqrt{3}}{3}$.

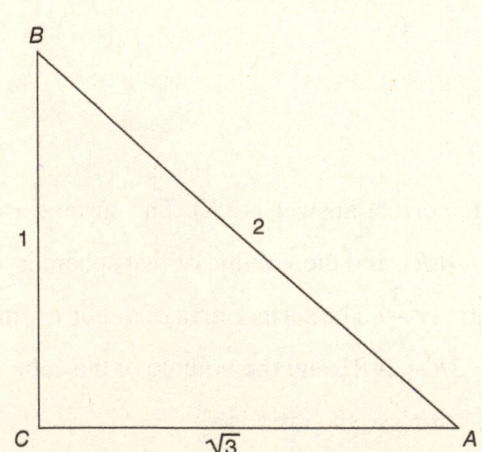

46. (C)

The correct answer is (C). $(f \circ g)(3) = f(g(3))$. From the table, $g(3) = 2$. Therefore, $f(g(3)) = f(2) = 5$, again from the table.

47. (B)

The correct answer is (B). Compute the matrix multiplication on the left-hand side of the equation.

$$\begin{bmatrix} 1 & -4 \\ 2 & 9 \end{bmatrix} \begin{bmatrix} a \\ 3 \end{bmatrix} = \begin{bmatrix} -1 \\ b \end{bmatrix} \quad \begin{bmatrix} 1a - 12 \\ 2a + 27 \end{bmatrix} = \begin{bmatrix} -1 \\ b \end{bmatrix}.$$

This implies that row one in the left matrix is equal to row one in the right matrix, and likewise for row two. $1a - 12 = -1 \rightarrow a \rightarrow 11$ and thus $2(11) + 27 = b \rightarrow b = 49$.

48. (B)

The correct answer is (B). Let us examine each choice. For (A), $a_n = \frac{1}{2}n$, where $n = 1, 2, 3, \ldots$ If we let $n = 1$, then $a_1 = \frac{1}{2}(1) = \frac{1}{2}$ which is not the correct first term. For (C), $a_1 = \frac{1}{2} + a_{n-1}$ where $n = 1, 2, 3, \ldots$ and $a_0 = 1$. The first term is defined to be $a_0 = 1$, the second term is obtained by substituting $n = 1$ into the equation, which yields $a_1 = \frac{1}{2} + a_0 = \frac{1}{2} + 1 = \frac{3}{2}$. This is not the correct second term. For (D), $a_n = 1 - \frac{1}{2}n$, where $n = 0, 1, 2, \ldots$ If $n = 0$, this gives the first term, $a_0 = 1$. If $n = 1$ this gives the second term. However, if $n = 2$, then $a_2 = 1 - \frac{1}{2}(2) = 1 - 1 = 0$, which is correct. The answer is (B), $a_n = \left(\frac{1}{2}\right)^n$, where $n = 0, 1, 2, 3, 4$ generates all first five terms.

49. (D)

The correct answer is (D). This question has a graph of a trigonometric function. It is certainly possible to plug in the respective answers into your graphing calculator and see which graph matches in the interval $[0, 2\pi]$; however, it is swifter to identify the properties of the function. First, note that the graph is stretched vertically, ranging not from -1 to 1 but instead from -3 to 3. Therefore, the amplitude of the wave is 3. This immediately eliminates answers (A) and (B) since it is the constant multiplier on a sine or cosine function that indicates amplitude. It remains only to be determined if the function is either sine or cosine. In this case, given that the wave is scaled by 3, then 3 times the function at 0 gives us 3. Because $\cos(0) = -1$, it follows that the correct answer must be (D).

50. (A)

The correct answer is (A). To answer this question, you should recall that a matrix is invertible if and only if its determinant is non-zero. You should also recall that the determinant of a 2×2 matrix:

$$\det \begin{bmatrix} a & b \\ c & d \end{bmatrix} = ad - bc.$$

Thus, our problem amounts to finding the value of d such that the difference $ad - bc = 0$. Given the values of our matrix, this means

$$-3d - (2)(-6) = 0$$
$$-3d + 12 = 0$$
$$-3d = -12$$

And so

$$d = 4.$$

The correct answer is thus (A). All the other values give a non-zero determinant and therefore are invertible.

PRACTICE TEST 2

PRAXIS II Mathematics Content Knowledge (0061/5061)

Also available at the REA Study Center (www.rea.com/studycenter)

This practice test is also offered online at the REA Study Center. Although the PRAXIS II Mathematics Content Knowledge (0061/5061) exam is offered in both paper- and computer-based formats, we recommend that you take the online version of the test to receive these added benefits:

- **Timed testing conditions** – help you gauge how much time you can spend on each question

- **Automatic scoring** – find out how you did on the test, instantly

- **On-screen detailed explanations of answers** – give you the correct answer and explain why the other answer choices are wrong

- **Diagnostic score reports** – pinpoint where you're strongest and where you need to focus your study

NOTE: Many graphing calculators, such as the TI-83, can readily perform computations on normal distributions, approximate areas under a curve, intersections of lines, and so forth. Different calculators have different keystrokes necessary to perform these functions, however, so it is important that you know how to use your chosen calculator before you take the exam. Check the documentation with your calculator or the manufacturer's website.

PRAXIS II Mathematics Content Knowledge Practice Test 2

TIME: 150 minutes (2 hours and 30 minutes)
50 questions

> **Directions: Read each item and select the best response.**

1. Given the two lines with equations $y = 3x + 1$ and $y + \dfrac{x}{3} = \dfrac{18}{8}$, which of the following statements are true?

    I.   The point $\left(\dfrac{3}{8}, \dfrac{17}{8}\right)$ is on both lines.

    II.   The lines are parallel.

    III.   The lines are perpendicular.

  (A)   I only

  (B)   I and III

  (C)   III only

  (D)   I and II

2. Which of the following is a factor of the expression $x^4 + 3x^3 - \dfrac{7}{4}x^2 - 6x - \dfrac{9}{4}$?

  (A) $x - 1$

  (B) $6x - \dfrac{9}{4}$

  (C) $x - 3$

  (D) $x - \dfrac{3}{2}$

3. Two different cubes have side lengths with a ratio of $3 : 4$ to each other. What is the ratio of their volumes?

  (A) $27 : 64$

  (B) $3 : 4$

  (C) $9 : 16$

  (D) $9 : 12$

4. Given a rectangular piece of cardboard with dimensions 10 inches by 20 inches, what are the dimensions of the squares you should remove from the corners to make a topless box that has a volume of 192 cubic inches? (Image is NOT to scale.)

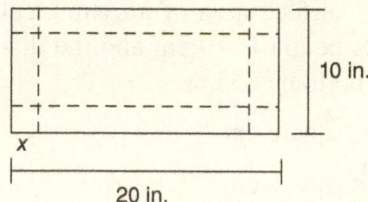

  (A) $\dfrac{1}{2}$ inch by $\dfrac{1}{2}$ inch

  (B)   1 inch by 1 inch

  (C)   3 inches by 3 inches

  (D)   2 inches by 2 inches

5. You wish to build a fence in your backyard using the back of your house as one of the walls to enclose a rectangular plot of land. How many feet of fencing are required to enclose an area of land of 3,000 square feet? (Image is NOT to scale.)

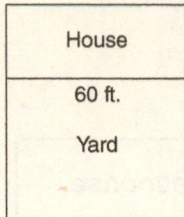

House

60 ft.

Yard

(A) 220 feet

(B) 160 feet

(C) 110 feet

(D) 100 feet

6. When inflated, a basketball is approximately 29 inches in circumference. Which of the following is the most reasonable approximation for the surface area of the basketball?

(A) 89 cubic inches

(B) 268 cubic inches

(C) 268 square inches

(D) 2642 square inches

7. Find the surface area of a cylindrical aluminum can if its height is 10 cm and the diameter of its top and bottom is 6 cm.

(A) 78π square cm

(B) 72π square cm

(C) 90π square cm

(D) 60π square cm

8. A circular swimming pool is surrounded by a sidewalk with a constant width of 4 feet as shown in the image below. The surface of the water has a total area of 64π square feet. What is the area of the sidewalk only?

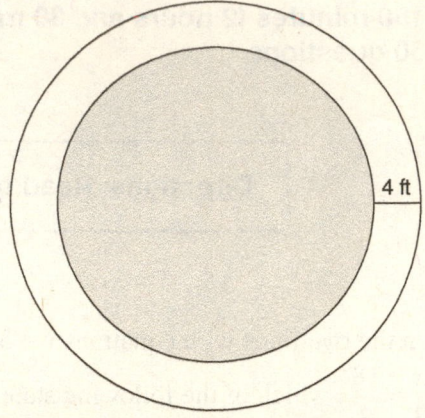

4 ft

(A) 80π square feet

(B) 16π square feet

(C) 144π square feet

(D) 32π square feet

9. A radio tower is 100 feet tall. It is supported by 4 cables that are each 65 feet long and are fastened to the ground 25 feet away from the base of the tower. How far does the tower extend past the point at which the cables are fastened to the tower? (Image is NOT to scale.)

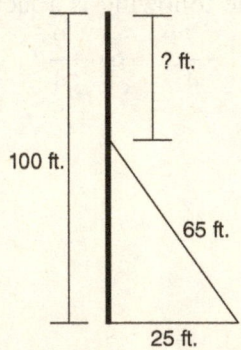

? ft.

100 ft.

65 ft.

25 ft.

(A) 60 feet

(B) 140 feet

(C) 160 feet

(D) 40 feet

10. Solve the following equation:

$$\begin{pmatrix} 1 & 3 \\ 2 & 4 \end{pmatrix}\begin{pmatrix} x \\ y \end{pmatrix} = \begin{pmatrix} 14 \\ 6 \end{pmatrix}$$

(A) $\begin{pmatrix} -19 \\ \frac{1}{5} \end{pmatrix}$

(B) $\begin{pmatrix} -12 \\ 18 \end{pmatrix}$

(C) $\begin{pmatrix} -19 \\ 11 \end{pmatrix}$

(D) $\begin{pmatrix} 14 \\ 11 \end{pmatrix}$

11. The rotation of the coordinate plane by an angle of 90° counterclockwise can be represented by the matrix equation $A\begin{pmatrix} x \\ y \end{pmatrix} = \begin{pmatrix} x' \\ y' \end{pmatrix}$ where A is which of the following matrices?

(A) $\begin{pmatrix} 0 & 1 \\ 1 & 0 \end{pmatrix}$

(B) $\begin{pmatrix} 1 & 0 \\ 0 & 1 \end{pmatrix}$

(C) $\begin{pmatrix} 0 & -1 \\ 1 & 0 \end{pmatrix}$

(D) $\begin{pmatrix} 1 & 0 \\ 0 & -1 \end{pmatrix}$

12. Which of the following does NOT satisfy the following dot product? $\vec{k} \cdot (1,4,2) = 25$

(A) (4,4,5)

(B) (5,4,2)

(C) (1,5,2)

(D) (−3,7,0)

13. Which of the following operations are associative over the real numbers?

  I.   Addition

  II. Subtraction

  III. Multiplication

  IV. Division

(A) IV only

(B) I and II only

(C) I and III only

(D) II, III, and IV

14. Which of the following values of k below gives $f(x) = x^2 - kx + 7$ an absolute minimum at $x = -3$?

(A) $-\dfrac{7}{3}$

(B) 6

(C) −6

(D) 3

15. A triangle has side lengths 5 inches, 11 inches, and 12 inches. Therefore, the triangle must be

(A) acute

(B) right

(C) obtuse

(D) isosceles

16. All of the following matrices M have $M^2 = M$ EXCEPT which of the following?

(A) $M = \begin{pmatrix} 0 & 1 \\ 0 & 1 \end{pmatrix}$

(B) $M = \begin{pmatrix} 1 & 1 \\ 0 & 0 \end{pmatrix}$

(C) $M = \begin{pmatrix} 0 & 1 \\ 1 & 0 \end{pmatrix}$

(D) $M = \begin{pmatrix} 1 & 0 \\ 0 & 1 \end{pmatrix}$

17. You drive 160 miles to your friend's house, and your rate is 50 miles per hour for part of the trip and 55 miles per hour for the other part. The entire trip takes 3 hours. If t represents time, which of the following equations models the amount of time to determine how long you travel at each rate?

(A) $160 = 55t - 50(3 - t)$

(B) $160 = 50t - 55(3 - t)$

(C) $160 = 55t + 50(3 + t)$

(D) $160 = 50t + 55(3 - t)$

18. In $\triangle XYZ$ (not shown), the length of side XY is 13, the length of side YZ is 20, and the measure of angle YZX is 28°. How many distinct triangles can be drawn given these measurements?

(A) No distinct triangle can be formed.

(B) One distinct triangle can be formed.

(C) Two distinct triangles can be formed.

(D) It cannot be determined from the given information.

19. If $f(x) = 3x^2 + 4x - 2$ and $g(x) = 5x^2 - 3x + 1$, find the possible number of positive and negative real roots of $h(x) = f(x) \cdot g(x)$ using Descartes' Rule of Signs.

(A) 3 or 1 positive roots, 1 negative root

(B) 1 positive roots, 3 or 1 negative roots

(C) 2 or 0 positive roots, 2 or 0 negative roots

(D) 4, 2, or 0 positive roots, 0 negative roots

20. For the following series of values of the diameter of an aluminum rod coming off a manufacturing line (0.125 inches, 0.133 inches, 0.129 inches, 0.126 inches, 0.127 inches, 0.130 inches, 0.126 inches), which of the following statements are true?

 I. The mean of the data is approximately 0.128 inches.

 II. The mode of the data is approximately 0.128 inches.

III. The standard deviation of the data is approximately 0.003 inches.

IV. The mode of the data is approximately 0.126 inches.

(A) I and IV only

(B) I, III and IV only

(C) I and IV only

(D) II and III only

21. Given $f(x) = 3x^2 + 1$ and $g(x) = x - 4$, find $f(g(a))$.

(A) $3a^2 - 24a + 49$

(B) $3a^2 - 8a + 17$

(C) $3a^2 + 17$

(D) $3a^2 - 3$

22. What is $\lim\limits_{x \to \infty} \dfrac{20}{x^2 + 4}$?

(A) $-\infty$

(B) 0

(C) 20

(D) ∞

23. The function $P(t) = 1000e^{0.25t}$ can be used to model the approximate population of gentoo penguins on a particular island in Antarctica t years after January 1, 1995, where $0 \le t \le 5$. Estimate the rate, measured in penguins per year, at which the population is increasing on January 1, 1998.

(A) 529

(B) 2117

(C) 412

(D) 250

24. Let $\mathfrak{R}$ be the relation on the set of real numbers, such that $x\mathfrak{R}y$ if and only if $x^2 = y^2$. $\mathfrak{R}$ is

    I.   antisymmetric

    II. symmetric

    III. transitive

    (A) II only

    (B) II and III

    (C) I and III

    (D) I, II, and III

25. Choose the answer that completes the following to form a true statement. If $S \subseteq T$, then

    (A) $S \cap T \neq \varnothing$

    (B) $S \cup T \neq \varnothing$

    (C) $x \in T \rightarrow x \in S$

    (D) $x \notin T \rightarrow x \notin S$

26. Consider the figure below, which has angles of equal measure.

    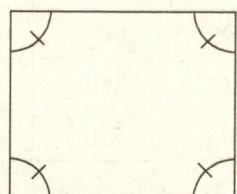

    Which of the following MUST be true?

    (A) The image is a square.

    (B) The image is a trapezoid.

    (C) The image is a rhombus.

    (D) The image is a rectangle.

27. You wish to save \$40,000 for your child's education. How much must you deposit into an account today so that the account will have a balance of \$40,000 in 15 years, if the account earns 7% interest yearly, compounded continuously?

    (A) \$14,498

    (B) \$2,493

    (C) \$19,513

    (D) \$13,998

28. Determine the values of a and b such that $f(x) = 4x^2 - 2ax + b$ has a local minimum at the point $(4, 3)$.

    (A) $a = 16, b = 67$

    (B) $a = 16, b = 3$

    (C) $a = 12, b = 40$

    (D) $a = 12, b = 35$

29. If $\lim\limits_{x \to a} f(x) = 0$ and $\lim\limits_{x \to a} g(x) = \infty$, what is the value of $\lim\limits_{x \to a} f(x)g(x)$?

    (A) 0

    (B) The value is not finite.

    (C) The value is unable to be determined.

    (D) 1

30. A student rolls two six-sided dice. What is the probability that the sum of both dice is exactly nine?

    (A) $\dfrac{2}{9}$

    (B) $\dfrac{1}{3}$

    (C) 30%

    (D) $\dfrac{1}{9}$

31. When drawing two cards at random from a standard deck of 52 cards, what is the probability of drawing a pair of aces?

(A) $\dfrac{2}{663}$

(B) $\dfrac{2}{13}$

(C) $\dfrac{1}{169}$

(D) $\dfrac{1}{221}$

32. Which of the following is the accurate value of $\displaystyle\lim_{k \to 0} \frac{\sin(\pi + k) - \sin(\pi)}{k}$?

(A) 0.998

(B) ∞

(C) 0

(D) –1

33. A calculus textbook is on sale for $83.25. If this is a 16% discount, what was the original price of the textbook?

(A) $96.57

(B) $99.25

(C) $99.11

(D) $98.15

34. The least common multiple of $2^2 3^2$, $5^1 3^2$, $2^2 3^1 5^1$, $7^1 13^1$, and 11^2 is

(A) $2^5 3^5 5^2 7^1 11^3 13$

(B) $2^2 3^2 5^1 7^1 11^2 13^1$

(C) $2^2 3^2 5^1 7^1 11^2$

(D) $2^1 3^1 5^1 7^1 11^2 13^1$

35. In the figure below, triangle I is similar to triangle II. What is the area of triangle II?

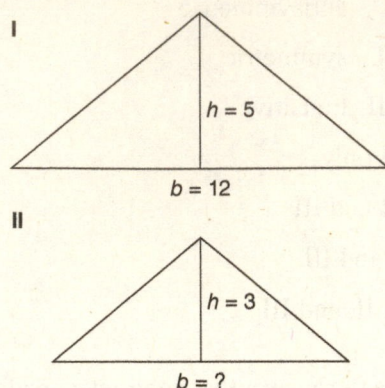

(A) 30

(B) 21.6

(C) 18

(D) 10.8

36.

Name	Score	Max Exam Score	Exam Mean	Exam Std. Dev.
Alice	27	32	24	3
Bill	899	900	600	200
Carey	142	150	125	5
David	505	750	400	25

The students Alice, Bill, Carey, and David each took one of four standardized tests, as the table above shows. The test makers found that their data were roughly normally distributed. The mean and standard deviation of each exam is given along with the students' scores. Which student scored in the highest percentile?

(A) Alice

(B) Bill

(C) Carey

(D) David

37. If $y = 4 \cos x + 2$, what is the maximum value of y on the interval $\left[\pi, \dfrac{3\pi}{2} \right]$?

    (A) –2

    (B) 2

    (C) 4

    (D) 6

38. Consider the triangle ABC (not drawn to scale).

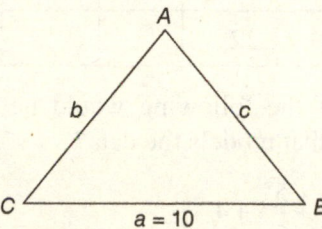

    If angle B is 25° and angle A is 35°, what is the length of side b?

    (A) $\dfrac{\sin(35)}{10 \cdot \sin(25)}$

    (B) $\dfrac{\sin(35)}{\sin(25)}$

    (C) $\dfrac{10 \cdot \sin(25)}{\sin(35)}$

    (D) There is insufficient information given.

39. If the function f takes an input, doubles it, squares the value, and subtracts four, and the function g is a line with –2 slope that intersects the point $(3, 4)$, which of the following is $(f \circ g)(3)$?

    (A) –54

    (B) –18

    (C) 28

    (D) 60

40. If the function f is given by the following graph,

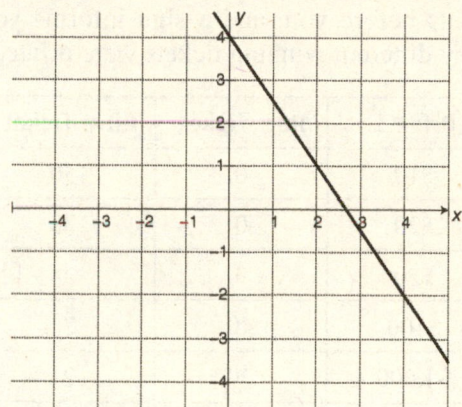

    which of the following is $f^{-1}(x)$?

    (A) $y = \dfrac{1}{-\left(\dfrac{2}{3}\right)x + 4}$

    (B) $y = -\dfrac{2}{3}x + \dfrac{8}{3}$

    (C) $y = \dfrac{2}{3}x - \dfrac{8}{3}$

    (D) $y = -\dfrac{2}{3}x + 4$

41. Given an event that has three possible outcomes, A, B, and C, if the probabilities are as listed below, what value of k will make it a valid distribution?

A	B	C
$\dfrac{1}{2}$	$\dfrac{2}{k}$	$\dfrac{3}{7}$

    (A) $\dfrac{1}{28}$

    (B) 28

    (C) 14

    (D) $\dfrac{1}{14}$

42. A lottery had a drawing. You could buy either a blue ticket or a red ticket. No one else has bought tickets before you, and a sign informs you how many different winning tickets were printed:

Prize $	Red Ticket	Blue Ticket
$10	0	150
$20	0	100
$50	0	50
$100	40	7
$1,000	20	2
$10,000	10	1

If there were 400 red tickets and 600 blue tickets, and assuming that if a ticket is not a winning ticket it loses (and pays $0 in prizes), which of the following is nearest the expected value of buying one red ticket and one blue ticket?

(A) $310

(B) $142

(C) $250

(D) $341

43. The line l passes through the points (2, 4) and (–1, –2). Line r is parallel to line l and contains the point (4, –2). What is the x-intercept of r?

(A) (–4, 0)

(B) (8, 0)

(C) (–10, 0)

(D) (5, 0)

44. Given the discrete data below, let Δx be the first difference defined as $f(x + 1) - f(x)$, and $\Delta^2 x$ be the second difference defined as $\Delta f(x + 1) - \Delta f(x)$. They are presented in the following table:

x	$f(x)$	Δx	$\Delta^2 x$
0	4	3	1
1	7	4	1
2	11	5	1
3	16	6	
4	22		

Which of the following would be a continuous function that models the data?

(A) $\dfrac{1}{2}x^2 + \dfrac{5}{2}x + 4$

(B) $\dfrac{1}{2}x^2 + 2x + 4$

(C) $x^2 + 2x + 4$

(D) $\dfrac{1}{2}x^2 + 2x + \dfrac{5}{2}$

45. Stephen wants to save for his son's education. If he needs to have $40,000 saved in 15 years, and he has a CD account that pays 5% interest compounded yearly, what is the approximate minimum balance he needs to invest as principal?

(A) $42,130

(B) $22,860

(C) $19,240

(D) $15,320

46. The test scores of a mathematics exam are normally distributed. The mean score is 75, and the standard deviation is 8. Which of the following is expected to contain the most students?

(A) between 83 and 99

(B) less than 67 or more than 83

(C) between 67 and 75

(D) fewer than 67

47. A class has 10 students. They line up to walk to recess. Two notable students in the class are Alexa and Billy, a brother and sister pair. Alexa is happy only if she is in line anywhere before Billy. How many ways can the students line up so that Alexa is satisfied?

    (A) 10!

    (B) 8!2!

    (C) $\dfrac{10!}{8!2!}$

    (D) $\dfrac{10!}{2!}$

48. Which of the following have a removable discontinuity?

    I. $\dfrac{2x^2+10x+12}{x^2-2x-3}$

    II. $\dfrac{3x^2+10x-8}{2x^2+9x+4}$

    III. $\dfrac{4x^2+4x-3}{9x^2+16}$

    (A) II only

    (B) I and II only

    (C) III only

    (D) III and II only

49. Which of the following could be the graph of the inverse of $y = 2^x$?

    (A)

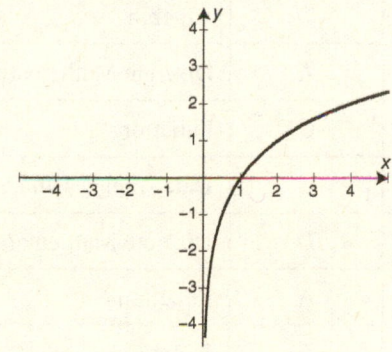

(B)

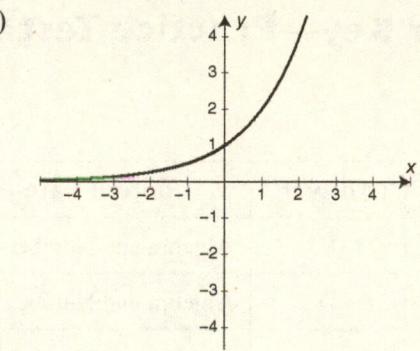

(C)

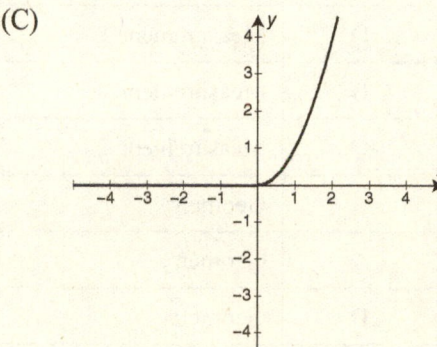

(D)

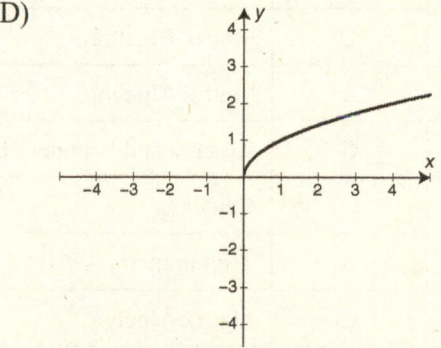

50. The motion of a projectile is monitored by recording its position at specific times. The following time–position pairs are recorded: (10 seconds, 200 meters), (20 seconds, 180 meters), (30 seconds, 165 meters), (40 seconds, 150 meters). Which of the following LEAST describes the process of obtaining a speed from these data?

    (A) integration

    (B) calculation of a slope

    (C) differentiation

    (D) data fitting

Answer Key—Practice Test 2

Question	Answer	Content Category
1	B	Algebra and Number Theory
2	D	Algebra and Number Theory
3	A	Algebra and Number Theory
4	D	Measurement
5	B	Measurement
6	C	Measurement
7	A	Geometry
8	A	Geometry
9	D	Geometry
10	C	Matrix Algebra
11	C	Matrix Algebra
12	A	Matrix Algebra
13	C	Algebra and Number Theory
14	C	Calculus
15	A	Trigonometry
16	C	Matrix Algebra
17	D	Algebra and Number Theory
18	C	Trigonometry
19	A	Functions
20	B	Data Analysis and Statistics
21	A	Functions
22	B	Calculus
23	A	Calculus
24	B	Discrete Mathematics
25	D	Discrete Mathematics

Question	Answer	Content Category
26	D	Geometry
27	D	Functions
28	A	Calculus
29	C	Calculus
30	D	Probability
31	D	Probability
32	D	Calculus
33	C	Algebra and Number Theory
34	B	Algebra and Number Theory
35	D	Geometry
36	D	Data Analysis and Statistics
37	B	Trigonometry
38	C	Trigonometry
39	D	Functions
40	B	Functions
41	B	Probability
42	D	Data Analysis and Statistics
43	D	Algebra
44	A	Discrete Mathematics
45	C	Functions
46	C	Data Analysis and Statistics
47	D	Discrete Mathematics
48	A	Functions
49	A	Functions
50	A	Data Analysis and Statistics

Detailed Explanations for Practice Test 2

1. (B)

The correct answer is (B). Let us first examine the second equation. $y + \dfrac{x}{3} = \dfrac{18}{8}$ can be rewritten as $y = -\dfrac{x}{3} + \dfrac{18}{8}$. Now that the equation is written in slope-intercept form, we can see that the slope of the second line is $-\dfrac{1}{3}$, whereas the slope of the first is 3. Because the slopes are negative reciprocals of each other, the two lines must be perpendicular. If the lines were parallel, they would have the same slope. By plugging in the point $\left(\dfrac{3}{8}, \dfrac{17}{8}\right)$ into both equations, we can see that this point is indeed on both lines. $\dfrac{17}{8} = 3\left(\dfrac{3}{8}\right) + 1 = \dfrac{17}{8} = \dfrac{9}{8} + \dfrac{8}{8}$ and $\dfrac{17}{8} + \dfrac{1}{3}\left(\dfrac{3}{8}\right) = \dfrac{17}{8} + \dfrac{1}{8} = \dfrac{18}{8}$. Thus, I and III are true.

2. (D)

The correct answer is (D). Recall that if $x - c$ is a factor of the function $f(x)$, then $f(c) = 0$. So we may simply plug each c in for x for choices (A), (C), and (D). First, (A): $1^4 + 3(1)^3 - \dfrac{7}{4}(1)^2 - 6(1) - \dfrac{9}{4} = 1 + 3 - \dfrac{7}{4} - 6 - \dfrac{9}{4} = -6 \neq 0$. (C): $3^4 + 3(3)^3 - \dfrac{7}{4}(9) - 6(3) - \dfrac{9}{4} = 81 + 81 - \dfrac{63}{4} - 18 - \dfrac{9}{4} = 126 \neq 0$. (D): $\left(\dfrac{3}{2}\right)^4 + 3\left(\dfrac{3}{2}\right)^3 - \dfrac{7}{4}\left(\dfrac{3}{2}\right)^2 - 6\left(\dfrac{3}{2}\right) - \dfrac{9}{4} = \dfrac{81}{16} + \dfrac{81}{16} - \dfrac{63}{16} - 9 - \dfrac{9}{4} = 0$. Thus, (D) is the correct answer. To verify that (B) is incorrect: if $6x - \dfrac{9}{4}$ were a factor, then $x - \dfrac{3}{8}$ would also be a factor; however, $\left(\dfrac{3}{8}\right)^4 + 3\left(\dfrac{3}{8}\right)^3 - \dfrac{7}{4}\left(\dfrac{3}{8}\right)^2 - 6\left(\dfrac{3}{8}\right) - \dfrac{9}{4} = \dfrac{81}{4096} + \dfrac{81}{512} - \dfrac{63}{256} - \dfrac{18}{8} - \dfrac{9}{4} = -\dfrac{18711}{4096} \neq 0$ and so (B) is incorrect.

3. (A)

The correct answer is (A). Because the two shapes are both cubes, they must be similar, and thus proportional. If the linear ratio is 3 : 4, then the ratio of the volume is the cube of the linear ratio. This yields 27 : 64.

4. (D)

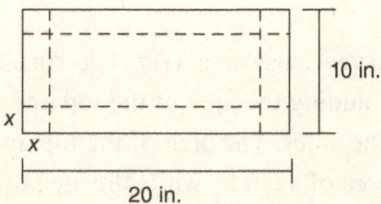

The correct answer is (D). If we cut a square from each corner with edges of x inches, then fold the sides of the box up, the volume of the box is $(10 - 2x)(20 - 2x)x$. We are given that the volume of the box should be 192 cubic inches; therefore, $(10 - 2x)(20 - 2x)x = 192 \rightarrow 4x^3 - 60x^2 + 200x - 192 = 0 \rightarrow 4[x(x^2 - 15x + 26) + 24(x - 2)] = 0 \rightarrow 4(x - 2)[(x - 13)x + 24] = 0$. Thus, $x = 2$ is a solution, and (D) is the correct answer. We could also have approximated the solutions by graphing. Let us check to make sure this is correct. If we let $x = 2$ inches, then the volume of the box is $(10 - 2(2))(20 - 2(2)(2)) = 6 \times 16 \times 2 = 192$

5. (B)

The correct answer is (B). The back of your house is 60 feet. If you want to enclose a total of 3,000 square feet, then your fence must be 50 feet long because $60 \times 50 = 3000$. Because you are using the 60-foot back of the house as one side of the rectangular area, the perimeter, or the length of fencing required, is only $50 + 50 + 60 = 160$ feet.

6. (C)

The correct answer is (C). If the circumference of the basketball is about 29 inches, then $C = 2\pi r = 29 \rightarrow$ $r = \dfrac{29}{2\pi}$ and so the surface area is $4\pi r^2 = 4\pi \left(\dfrac{29}{2\pi}\right)^2 = \dfrac{29^2}{\pi} \approx 267.7$. Depending on your rounding, you might decide the answer is either 267 or 268. However, (B) is incorrect as the units are cubic inches, which are not the correct units for area. Thus the only reasonable answer is (C).

7. (A)

The correct answer is (A). The surface area can be found by adding the area of the top and bottom and the area of the sides. The area of the top and bottom is simply the area of a circle, while the area of the sides is the same as the area of a rectangle in which the length of the rectangle is equal to the circumference of the top and bottom circles. $S.A. = \pi r^2 + \pi r^2 + 2\pi rh = 9\pi + 9\pi + 60\pi = 78\pi$.

8. (A)

The correct answer is (A). If the area of the pool is 64π square feet, then using the formula for area of a circle we find $r = \sqrt{\dfrac{64\pi}{\pi}} = 8$ feet. Therefore the distance from the center of the pool to the outside of the sidewalk is $8 + 4 = 12$ feet, and so the area of the large circle is $\pi(12)^2 \approx 144\pi$ square feet. Subtracting the area of the pool from the area of the large circle, we find the area of the sidewalk to be $144\pi - 64\pi = 80\pi$ square feet.

9. (D)

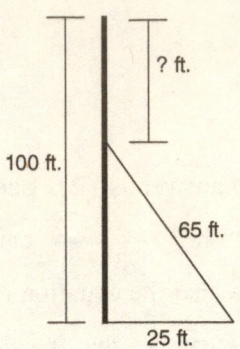

The correct answer is (D). We can start by using the Pythagorean Theorem to calculate the distance from the ground to the point at which the cable is attached. $a^2 = 65^2 - 25^2 = 3600 \rightarrow a = 60$ feet. If the tower is 100 feet, then there is still $100 - 60 = 40$ feet of tower higher than the cable. Therefore the answer is (D).

10. (C)

The correct answer is (C). We can begin by finding the inverse of $\begin{pmatrix} 1 & 3 \\ 2 & 4 \end{pmatrix}$, which is $\dfrac{1}{4-6}\begin{pmatrix} 4 & -3 \\ -2 & 1 \end{pmatrix}$ $= \begin{pmatrix} -2 & \frac{3}{2} \\ 1 & -\frac{1}{2} \end{pmatrix}$. We can then multiply both sides of the equation by the inverse, $\begin{pmatrix} -2 & \frac{3}{2} \\ 1 & -\frac{1}{2} \end{pmatrix}\begin{pmatrix} 1 & 2 \\ 3 & 4 \end{pmatrix}\begin{pmatrix} x \\ y \end{pmatrix}$ $= \begin{pmatrix} -2 & \frac{3}{2} \\ 1 & -\frac{1}{2} \end{pmatrix}\begin{pmatrix} 14 \\ 6 \end{pmatrix}$ $\begin{pmatrix} x \\ y \end{pmatrix} = \begin{pmatrix} -19 \\ 11 \end{pmatrix}$, which is (C).

11. (C)

The correct answer is (C). First, notice that if you rotate an arbitrary vector by 90° about the origin, the new x component is the negative of the y component and the new y component is the x component, as shown in the diagram.

So, $A \begin{pmatrix} x \\ y \end{pmatrix} = \begin{pmatrix} -y \\ x \end{pmatrix}$ for all x and y. Then A must have a negative component, and we can see that $\begin{pmatrix} 0 & -1 \\ 1 & 0 \end{pmatrix} \begin{pmatrix} x \\ y \end{pmatrix} = \begin{pmatrix} -y \\ x \end{pmatrix}$, and so (C) is the correct answer.

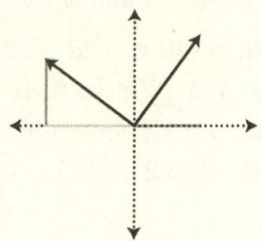

12. (A)

The correct answer is (A). Let us examine each possible answer:

(A) $(4, 4, 5) \cdot (1, 4, 2) = 4 \times 1 + 4 \times 4 + 5 \times 2$
$= 4 + 16 + 10$
$= 30 \neq 25$

(B) $(5, 4, 2) \cdot (1, 4, 2) = 5 \times 1 + 4 \times 4 + 2 \times 2$
$= 5 + 16 + 4$
$= 25$

(C) $(1, 5, 2) \cdot (1, 4, 2) = 1 \times 1 + 5 \times 4 + 2 \times 2$
$= 1 + 20 + 4$
$= 25$

(D) $(-3, 7, 0) \cdot (1, 4, 2) = -3 \times 1 + 7 \times 4 + 0 \times 2$
$= -3 + 28 + 0$
$= 25$

Only (A) does not satisfy the equation.

13. (C)

The correct answer is (C). Both addition and multiplication are associative since $(a + b) + c = a + (b + c)$ and $(a \times b) \times c = a \times (b \times c)$ for all real numbers a, b, c. There are many examples why subtraction and division are not associative, such as $0 = (10 - 5) = 0$, but $-5 \neq 10 - (5 - 5) = 10$, and $(8 \div 4) \div 2 = 1$, but $8 \div (4 \div 2) = 4$.

14. (C)

The correct answer is (C). To find extrema, differentiate with respect to the variable x and set the derivative to zero. Because the leading coefficient of $f(x)$ is positive, the extremum of this quadratic will be an absolute minimum. As for finding such a k, differentiating with respect to x gives $f'(x) = 2x - k$. Substituting in $x = -3$ and $f'(x) = 0$ gives the following:

$$0 = 2(-3) - k$$
$$0 = -6 - k$$
$$k = -6$$

15. (A)

The correct answer is (A). If it were a right triangle, 12^2 would equal $11^2 + 5^2 = 146$, so the triangle is not a right triangle. This shows that the longest side (12) is smaller than the corresponding hypotenuse of the right triangle would be with 5 and 11 as its bases. Thus, the angle is smaller than $90°$, and so it is acute.

Another way would be to use the Law of Cosines. The angle across from the side of length 12 can be solved in the following way:

$$12^2 = 11^2 + 5^2 - 2(11)(5)\cos(\theta)$$
$$144 = 121 + 25 - 110\cos(\theta)$$
$$144 = 146 - 110\cos(\theta)$$
$$-2 = -110\cos(\theta)$$
$$\frac{1}{55} = \cos(\theta)$$
$$\theta \approx 88.96°$$

16. (C)

The correct answer is (C). For (A), multiplication on the right of any matrix by $M = \begin{pmatrix} 0 & 1 \\ 0 & 1 \end{pmatrix}$ adds the columns together and puts it into the right column. Thus $M^2 = M$. For (B), multiplication on the left of any matrix by $M = \begin{pmatrix} 1 & 1 \\ 0 & 0 \end{pmatrix}$ adds the rows together and puts it into the top row. Thus $M^2 = M$. For (D), this is the identity matrix, which always satisfies $M^2 = M$. Option (C) is a matrix that, when multiplied on the left-hand side, reverses rows, thus $M^2 = 1$, the identity matrix.

Another way would be to directly compute the square of each matrix and compare it with the original matrix, by which it can be seen that (C) is the correct answer.

17. (D)

The correct answer is (D). You are given a distance traveled with two rates, and the total trip of 3 hours. Use the formula distance (d) = rate $(r) \bullet$ time (t) with time t for the first part and $3 - t$ for the second. Set up a chart using these values:

	d	r	t
first part	d	50	t
second part	$160 - d$	55	$3 - t$
total	160	—	3

Using $d = rt$, the first equation is $d = 50t$ and the second equation is $160 - d = 55(3 - t)$. Substitute $50t$ in for d in the second equation, and then the final equation is $160 = 50t + 55(3 - t)$.

18. (C)

The correct answer is (C). The angle given is not the one between the two given sides, so the problem is essentially one of finding what the other angles are and whether there are zero, one, or two choices for the shape of $\triangle XYZ$. Use the Law of Sines to find $\angle YXZ$:

$$\frac{\sin(\angle YZX)}{XY} = \frac{\sin(\angle YXZ)}{YZ} \text{ and } \frac{\sin(28)}{13} = \frac{\sin(\angle YXZ)}{20}.$$

So $\sin(\angle YXZ) = \frac{20\sin 28}{13}$, and since $\sin 28$ is positive, $\sin(\angle YXZ)$ is also positive, and $\angle YXZ$ can have two values between $0°$ and $180°$, so there are two possible triangles, one with $\angle YXZ$ acute ($46.2°$) and one with $\angle YXZ$ obtuse ($180° - 46.2° = 133.8°$).

19. (A)

The correct answer is (A). The question asks you to find the possible number of positive and negative real roots of $h(x) = f(x) \bullet g(x)$ using Descartes' Rule of Signs. First, $h(x) = f(x) \bullet g(x) = 15x^4 + 11x^3 - 19x^2 + 10x - 2$. Using Descartes' Rule of Signs, we need to find the number of sign changes for $h(x)$ to determine to number of possible positive real roots. There are three sign changes, so this means there are 3 or 1 possible positive real roots. Using Descartes' Rule of Signs, we need to find the number of sign changes for $h(-x)$ to determine to number of possible negative real roots. $h(-x) = 15x^4 - 11x^3 - 19x^2 - 10x - 2$ there is one sign change so this means there is 1 possible negative real root. You can conclude then that there are 3 or 1 positive roots and 1 negative root. (Note that it is possible that two roots are imaginary.)

20. (B)

The correct answer is (B). The mean is
$$\frac{0.125 + 0.133 + 0.129 + 0.126 + 0.127 + 0.130 + 0.126}{7}$$
$= 0.128$ inches. The mode is the most common result, which is 0.126 inches. Use a calculator to get the standard deviation or hand-calculate by first determining

the deviations of the measured values from the mean for each of the measured values. Then square each of these deviations. Because these measurements are a random sample of a large population, divide the sum of the squared deviations by $N - 1 = 6$ and take the square root to obtain a standard deviation of 0.003 inches.

21. (A)

The correct answer is (A). The question asks you to find the composite of $f(g(a))$. First, you must find $g(a) = a - 4$. Then, $f(a - 4) = 3(a - 4)^2 + 1 = 3(a^2 - 8a + 16) + 1 = 3a^2 - 24a + 49$.

22. (B)

To find the limit, you are determining the limit as x becomes infinite. As x gets larger, because it is in the denominator, y gets very small numbers. The resulting fractions approach 0.

23. (A)

The correct answer is (A). On January 1, 1998, $t = 3$ because t represents the number of years after January 1, 1995. The instantaneous rate of change of any function is given by the derivative. Thus, the rate at which the population is increasing on January 1, 1998 is found by finding $P'(t)$ when $t = 3$. The derivative is $P'(t) = 1000(0.25)e^{0.25t}$, so $P'(3) = 1000(0.25)e^{0.25(3)} \approx 529$.

24. (B)

The correct answer is (B). First, notice that the relation $\mathfrak{R}$ IS symmetric because $x\mathfrak{R}y \to x^2 = y^2 \to y^2 = x^2 \to y\mathfrak{R}x$. Second, the relation $\mathfrak{R}$ IS transitive because if $x\mathfrak{R}y$ and $x\mathfrak{R}z$, then $x^2 = y^2$ and $y^2 = z^2$, thus $x^2 = z^2$, which implies $x\mathfrak{R}z$. The relation $\mathfrak{R}$ is NOT antisymmet-

ric. Consider $x = 1$ and $y = -1$. $x\mathfrak{R}y$ and $y\mathfrak{R}x$ because $(1)^2 = (-1)^2$; however, $x = 1 \neq -1 = y$. Therefore $\mathfrak{R}$ is NOT antisymmetric.

25. (D)

The correct answer is (D). This can be seen by examining the other three choices. First, consider the case when $S = T = \varnothing$; notice that $S \subseteq T$ still holds. However, $S \cap T = S \cup T = \varnothing$; therefore, choices (A) and (B) are incorrect. Choice (C) does not hold, for example, when $S = \{1\}$ and $T = \{1, 2\}$, because $2 \in T$ but $2 \notin S$. Thus, choice (D) must be correct, which can be verified by considering the following: if $S \subseteq T$ then $S' \supseteq T'$, where S' and T' represent the complement of S and T, respectively. Thus, $x \notin T \to x \in T' \to x \in S'$, (by the definition of a subset) and $x \in S' \to x \notin S$, which cannot be true if $S \subseteq T$.

26. (D)

The correct answer is (D). Since all four angles are equal, the measure of each must be 90°. In addition, both pairs of opposite sides must be parallel. All rectangles must have four 90-degree angles and both pairs of opposite sides parallel. Choices (A) and (C) are wrong because we are not guaranteed that all sides are equal. Choice (B) is wrong because if a kite has four equal angles, it must be a square, and again, we do not know that all sides are equal.

27. (D)

The correct answer is (D). If the interest compounds continuously, we can use $B = Pe^{rt}$ to model this situation, where B is the balance in 15 years, r is the interest rate, t is years after initial deposit and P is the principal deposit. Thus, $\$40,000 = Pe^{0.07(15)} \to P \approx \$13,998$.

28. (A)

The correct answer is (A). If $f(x) = 4x^2 - 2ax + b$ has a local minimum at (4, 3) then $f'(4) = 0$, where $f'(x) = 8x - 2a$. Therefore, $f'(4) = 8(4) - 2a = 0 \rightarrow a = 16$. Substituting the value of a into the function, we obtain $f(x) = 4x^2 - 32x + b$. However, we know the point (4, 3) lies on the graph of f and so $f(4) = 4(4)^2 - 32(4) + b = 3 \rightarrow b = 67$.

29. (C)

The correct answer is (C). In this situation, we cannot determine the value of the limit. Let us look at two examples: $\lim_{x \to 0} x^2 = 0$ and $\lim_{x \to 0} \frac{1}{x} = \infty$, and $\lim_{x \to 0} \frac{x^2}{x} = \lim_{x \to 0} x = 0$. However, $\lim_{x \to 0} x^2 = 0$ and $\lim_{x \to 0} \frac{1}{x^3} = \infty$, and $\lim_{x \to 0} \frac{x^2}{x^3} = \lim_{x \to 0} \frac{1}{x} = \infty$. So we can see from just these examples that it depends on the functions f and g.

30. (D)

The correct answer is (D). Each die has six possible outcomes that are independent of the outcomes of the other die. Therefore, there are $6 \times 6 = 36$ total outcomes, counting the dice separately. There are only four possible outcomes that will add to 9. They are (3, 6), (4, 5), (5, 4), and (6, 3). Therefore, the probability is the number of possible ways to sum to 9, divided by the total number of possible rolls, or $\frac{4}{36} = \frac{1}{9}$.

31. (D)

The correct answer is (D). In a standard 52 card deck, there are four of each of the numbers 2–10, four jacks, four queens, four kings, and four aces. The probability of drawing a pair of aces when randomly drawing two cards is the probability of drawing the first ace times the probability of drawing the second. The probability of the first ace is $\frac{4}{52}$, but the probability of drawing the second is now $\frac{3}{51}$ because there is one less ace and one less card in the deck. Thus, the total probability is $\left(\frac{4}{52}\right)\left(\frac{3}{51}\right) = \frac{12}{2652} = \frac{1}{221}$.

32. (D)

The correct answer is (D). It is important to recognize that the limit that you are asked to compute is actually the definition of the derivative of $f(x)$, where $f(x) = \sin(x)$, where $x = \pi$. When you recognize that it is merely a derivative, you can use differentiation to get $\frac{d}{dx}\sin(x) = \cos(x)$, and then from trigonometry we know that $\cos(\pi) = -1$.

33. (C)

The correct answer is (C). It is important to keep in mind how discounts work. Discounts are some percentage off the *original* price. So if the original price is x, and the discount is 16% off the original price, we can model this by $0.16x$. Because original price minus the discount is the sale price, we have

$$x - 0.16x = 83.25$$

$$0.84x = 83.25$$

$$x = \frac{83.25}{0.84} = 99.1071 \approx \$99.11$$

34. (B)

The correct answer is (B). By definition, the least common multiple must contain every prime factor of every integer in the set. This automatically eliminates (C). It must also contain *enough* of the respective prime factors; that is, each prime factor must be raised to the highest exponent to which it occurs in the set. For example, (D) is incorrect because it is not divisible by $2^2 3^2$.

The easiest method to find the LCM is to list each distinct prime factor that occurs in any number in the set and raise each to the *highest* power at which it occurs. This will give $2^2 3^2 5^1 7^1 11^2 13^1$, which is (B). Note that (A) is a *multiple* of every integer in the set, but it is not the *least* such multiple, (C) doesn't include 13, and (D) doesn't include 2^2 or 3^2.

35. (D)

The correct answer is (D). This question is based upon two figures being similar. Because they are similar, their corresponding sides are proportional, so $\frac{\text{height}_2}{\text{height}_1} = \frac{\text{base}_2}{\text{base}_1}$, or $\frac{3}{5} = \frac{\text{base}_2}{12}$, and $\text{base}_2 = \frac{36}{5} = 7.2$.

Now to compute the area of the triangle, use the formula from geometry, $A = \frac{1}{2}bh$, giving $\frac{1}{2}(3)(7.2) = 3(3.6) = 10.8$, the correct answer.

36. (D)

The correct answer is (D). This question is asking us to use the properties of normal distributions. In particular, note that you are *not* trying to find the student who scored the *highest percentage*. Instead you are trying to find which student scored in the highest percentile; that is, which student scored more than the rest of the test takers, for their particular test.

To compare different tests, you need to examine how many standard deviations away from the mean each score is by using the normalized z-score,

$$z = \frac{x_1 - \mu}{\sigma}$$

where x_i corresponds to each individual data point. Thus,

$$z_{\text{Alice}} = \frac{27 - 24}{3} = 1$$

$$z_{\text{Bill}} = \frac{899 - 600}{200} = 1.495$$

$$z_{\text{Carey}} = \frac{142 - 125}{5} = 3.4$$

$$z_{\text{David}} = \frac{505 - 400}{25} = 4.2$$

David has the largest z-score. To interpret this, it means he scored more than four standard deviations above the mean. We don't even need to know the exact percentile (in practice, we would need either a computer program or a table of standard deviations to tell us the exact percentile, which is close to the 99.999[th] percentile); with this score being the largest, the correct answer is David.

37. (B)

The correct answer is (B). The key to the answer is the interval in question. Even though $4\cos x + 2$ has a maximum value of 6, we are interested only in the closed and bounded interval $\left[\pi, \frac{3\pi}{2}\right]$. Given the shape of the cosine function, we know that the maximum value of $\cos(x)$ in the interval occurs at $\frac{3\pi}{2}$. Therefore, $4\cos\left(\frac{3\pi}{2}\right) + 2 = 4(0) + 2 = 2$.

38. (C)

The correct answer is (C). To answer this question, it is necessary to use the Law of Sines. Recall that the Law of Sines states

$$\frac{\sin A}{a} = \frac{\sin B}{b} = \frac{\sin C}{c}.$$

For this question we are given two angles and one side length. Therefore, using the Law of Sines, we have

$$\frac{\sin(35)}{10} = \frac{\sin(25)}{b}$$

which, when we solve for b yields

$$b = \frac{10 \cdot \sin(25)}{\sin(35)}.$$

39. (D)

The correct answer is (D). Note that $(f \cdot g)(x) = f(g(x))$. To solve this problem we can translate both f and g into equations, then compute their composition. However, this approach is considerably longer; we can instead take advantage of the fact that g intersects the point $(3, 4)$. That tells us that $g(3) = 4$. Therefore we can immediately evaluate $f(g(3)) = f(4)$. When we do, we see $f(4) = (2 \times 4)^2 - 4 = (8)^2 - 4 = 64 - 4 = 60$.

40. (B)

The correct answer is (B). You first need an equation to represent f. You are given sufficient information from the picture to do so. The y-intercept is the point $(0, 4)$. Further, from the graph, you can determine that the function descends three units for every two units moved to the right; thus, the slope of this line is $-\frac{3}{2}$. Therefore,

$$y = -\frac{3}{2}x + 4$$

To take the inverse of this function, we need to solve for x. Thus,

$$y - 4 = -\frac{3}{2}x$$

$$-\frac{2}{3}(y - 4) = x.$$

Finally, renaming the variables gives the inverse function as

$$y = -\frac{2}{3}(x - 4)$$

$$y = -\frac{2}{3}x + \frac{8}{3}.$$

41. (B)

The correct answer is (B). For this question, you need to know that a valid distribution must have the total probabilities of the sample space be 1. Therefore, $P(a) + P(b) + P(c) = 1$. This implies

$$\frac{1}{2} + \frac{3}{7} + \frac{2}{k} = 1$$

$$\frac{7}{14} + \frac{6}{14} + \frac{2}{k} = 1$$

$$\frac{13}{14} + \frac{2}{k} = 1$$

$$\frac{2}{k} = \frac{14}{14} - \frac{13}{14}$$

$$2 = \frac{1}{14}k$$

So therefore,

$$k = 28.$$

42. (D)

The correct answer is (D). To answer this question, we need to be able to compute expected value $E(X)$. You are buying one red ticket and one blue ticket, so you need to compute the respective expected values and add them together: $E(\text{red}) + E(\text{blue})$. Using the definition of expected value,

$$E(\text{red}) = 100\left(\frac{40}{400}\right) + 1000\left(\frac{20}{400}\right) + 10000\left(\frac{10}{400}\right)$$

$$E(\text{red}) = 10 + 50 + 250 = 310.$$

Similarly, you can use the definition to directly compute $E(\text{blue})$. Thus,

$$E(\text{blue}) = 10\left(\frac{150}{600}\right) + 20\left(\frac{100}{600}\right) + 50\left(\frac{50}{600}\right)$$

$$+ 100\left(\frac{7}{600}\right) + 1000\left(\frac{2}{600}\right) + 10000\left(\frac{1}{600}\right)$$

which is

$$E(\text{blue}) \approx 31.16666 \approx 31.$$

Therefore, the correct answer is $E(\text{red}) + E(\text{blue}) \approx 310 + 31 = 341$.

43. (D)

The correct answer is (D). There are two main ways to approach this question. One way is to draw a picture. However, trying to draw figures in a hurry on the test leads to the risk of introducing inaccuracies. The algebraic approach is just as effective and more accurate.

Because the lines r and l are parallel, their slopes are the same. We don't need to know an equation for l, just its slope. Therefore

$$m_l = \frac{y_2 - y_1}{x_2 - x_1} = \frac{4 - (-2)}{2 - (-1)} = \frac{6}{3} = 2.$$

Because the lines are parallel, $m_r = m_l = 2$. Because r contains the point $(4, -2)$, we can use point-slope form to get an equation for r. The point-slope form is

$$y - y_0 = m(x - x_0).$$

Therefore, plugging in the point $(4, -2)$ gives

$$y - (-2) = 2(x - 4).$$

To find the x-intercept, you can either graph the above equation on a calculator or set $y = 0$ and solve for x. The latter method yields

$$2 = 2x - 8$$
$$10 = 2x$$
$$5 = x$$

so the x-intercept of r is the point $(5, 0)$.

44. (A)

The correct answer is (A). This is a question about finite differences, a topic for which there are many equivalent ways to arrive at the answer. One perfectly valid way if you don't know anything about finite differences is simply to use the calculator to graph the functions and look at a table of results. This way you can determine which function matches the data.

Alternatively, and more simply, since this is a multiple-choice test, you can just substitute the values into the answers. For $x = 0$, you can eliminate answer (D) because $f(0) \neq 4$. For $x = 1$, you can eliminate (B) because $f(1) \neq 7$, and for $x = 2$, you can eliminate (C) because $f(2) \neq 11$. This leaves (A) as the only potentially correct answer. You should substitute the remaining values, $x = 3$ and $x = 4$, to double-check that (A) is correct.

45. (C)

The correct answer is (C). Recall that in the case of compound interest, the balance of the account is given by

$$B = P(1 + r)^t.$$

where P = principal, r = annual interest rate, and t = time (in years).

We are given most of the values, and want to find P. So, when we plug in our values we have

$$40,000 = P(1.05)^{15} \approx P \cdot 2.0789$$

Thus, solving for P yields

$$\frac{40,000}{2.0789} \approx \$19,240.$$

46. (C)

The correct answer is (C). There are two main ways to arrive at the solution of this problem. One is to use a graphing calculator, such as the TI-83.

Another way is to make use of the 68 – 95 – 99 rule for standard deviations. It is helpful to visualize the regions of the area under the curve, and to know the approximate probabilities of each area.

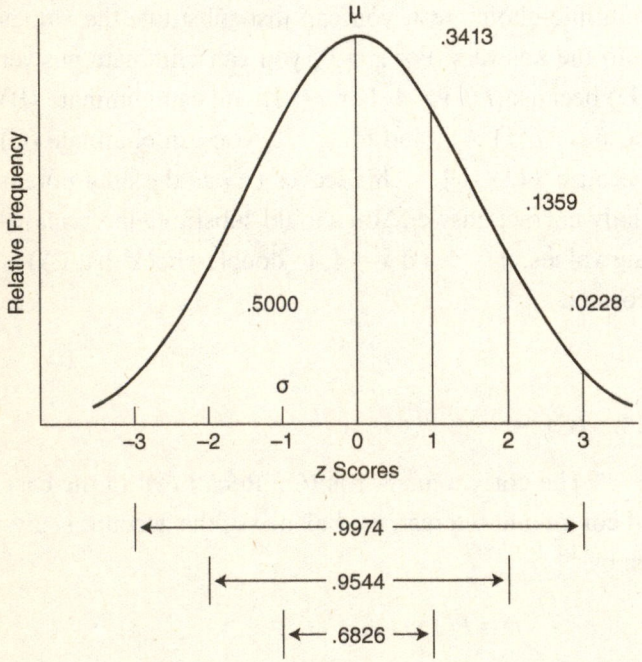

You need to recognize what the answer choices are asking with regard to standard deviations. This could involve transforming the intervals to z-scores to translate these intervals into standard deviations. For example, (A) is asking the probability of scoring between 83 and 99, or between $z = \frac{83 - 75}{8} = \frac{8}{8} = 1$ standard deviation and $z = \frac{99 - 75}{8} = \frac{16}{8} = 2$ standard deviations. Similar computations can be carried out for the other answer choices. From the normal curve, we can determine the probability of (A) (47–34%), or is about 14%. (B) is asking about being less than 67 or more than 83. This is the probability of being below on standard deviation (approx. 16%) or being more than two standard deviations above the mean (approx. 3%). Therefore, the probability of (B) is nearly 16% + 3% = 19%. This also includes (D), so we can now eliminate (D). Answer (C) is equivalent to asking the probability of being within one standard deviation below the mean. This corresponds to roughly 34% and is the correct answer.

47. (D)

The correct answer is (D). Answering this question requires an ability to count permutations. The best way to think of this problem is to consider one arrangement of students that satisfies the conditions:

ABOOOOOOOO.

Here the *O*s represent other students in the class. For this one example, where Alexa is at the very front and Billy is right behind her, there are 8! ways the other students can line up. In fact, for *any* instance that satisfies the problem, you will have to multiply by 8! to account for the eight other students. Therefore, you just have to count the number of ways Alexa and Billy can line up.

If Alexa is at the very front of the line, Billy has a choice of 9 positions. When she moves back one, it follows that there are 8 possibilities for Billy. Similarly, when she steps back to second from the front, there are 7 possibilities. This trend continues, to the very last case where there is only one option for them to line up. Thus, there are 9 + 8 + 7 + 6 + 5 + 4 + 3 + 2 + 1 ways for Alexa and Billy to line up. Use the formula for the sum of n consecutive integers, namely,

$$9 + 8 + 7 + \ldots + 1 = \frac{9(9+1)}{2} = \frac{9(10)}{2}$$

When we multiply this by 8!, we have

$$\frac{10(9)}{2} 8! = \frac{10 \cdot 9 \cdot 8 \cdot \ldots \cdot 1}{2} = \frac{10!}{2}.$$

48. (A)

The correct answer is (A). We need to first factor the rational expressions listed. However, once we factor them we see I is

$$\frac{2x^2+10x+12}{x^2-2x-3}=\frac{2(x^2+5x+6)}{(x-3)(x+1)}=\frac{2(x+2)(x+3)}{(x-3)(x+1)}$$

therefore Option I does not have a removable discontinuity, only asymptotes at $x=3$ and $x=-1$. This eliminates answer (B). Factoring II, we see

$$\frac{3x^2+10x-8}{2x^2+9x+4}=\frac{(x+4)(3x-2)}{(2x+1)(x+4)}=\frac{3x-2}{2x+1}$$

Thus Option II does have a removable discontinuity at $x=-4$. This eliminates (C).

The denominator of III is $9x^2+16$. This is a sum of perfect squares and therefore an irreducible polynomial. We could verify this by computing the discriminate $0^2-4(9)(16)$, which is clearly negative. This implies that the denominator of III is never zero, and so it will be a continuous function. There are no discontinuities of any sort. Therefore, the only option

with a removable discontinuity is II, and the correct answer is (A).

49. (A)

The correct answer is (A). You can rule out all but (A) because it is the only answer with $(1, 0)$ touching the graph. Alternatively, it is important to note that 2^x is an exponential function. Therefore, it has an inverse, and that inverse is a logarithmic function. Graphs (B) and (C) both contain functions that are growing much too rapidly for a logarithmic function. We can rule out (D) because $\log(1)$ is 0. Therefore, all that remains is (A).

50. (A)

The correct answer is (A). The speed is a slope or derivative of position with respect to time. It can be obtained by calculating a slope from two points or by fitting a larger number of points. Integration is not directly involved in that calculation.

PRACTICE TEST 3

PRAXIS II Mathematics Content Knowledge (0061/5061)

Also available at the REA Study Center (*www.rea.com/studycenter*)

This practice test is also offered online at the REA Study Center. Although the PRAXIS II Mathematics Content Knowledge (0061/5061) exam is offered in both paper- and computer-based formats, we recommend that you take the online version of the test to receive these added benefits:

- **Timed testing conditions** – help you gauge how much time you can spend on each question

- **Automatic scoring** – find out how you did on the test, instantly

- **On-screen detailed explanations of answers** – give you the correct answer and explain why the other answer choices are wrong

- **Diagnostic score reports** – pinpoint where you're strongest and where you need to focus your study

NOTE: Many graphing calculators, such as the TI-83, can readily perform computations on normal distributions, approximate areas under a curve, intersections of lines, and so forth. Different calculators have different keystrokes necessary to perform these functions, however, so it is important that you know how to use your chosen calculator before you take the exam. Check the documentation with your calculator or the manufacturer's website.

PRAXIS II Mathematics Content Knowledge Practice Test 3

TIME: 150 minutes (2 hours and 30 minutes)
50 questions

Directions: Read each item and select the best response.

---

1. For which of the following values of k does $f(x) = x^4 - 15x^2 - 10x + k$ have a root at -2?

   (A) $k = -12$

   (B) $k = -23$

   (C) $k = 22$

   (D) $k = 24$

2. Let a_n be the arithmetic sequence generated by $a_0 = 2$ and $a_{n+1} = a_n + 3$. Let b_n be the geometric sequence generated by $b_0 = 200$ and $b_{n+1} = \frac{1}{2} b_n$. At what minimum value of n is $a_n > b_n$?

   (A) 2

   (B) 3

   (C) 4

   (D) 5

3. N is a number such that $N = 1 \bmod 3$, $N = 2 \bmod 5$, and $N = 3 \bmod 7$. What is the least positive such value of N?

   (A) 52

   (B) 37

   (C) 157

   (D) 84

4. What is the coefficient of the x^2 term in the expanded form of $(x + 3)^5$?

   (A) 27

   (B) 108

   (C) 162

   (D) 270

5. Given that $i = \sqrt{-1}$, what is $(2i)^{14}$?

   (A) $16384i$

   (B) 16384

   (C) -16384

   (D) $-16384i$

6. What is

   $$\sum_{k=0}^{\infty} \frac{3}{10^k}$$

   (A) $\frac{1}{3}$

   (B) $\frac{7}{10}$

   (C) $\frac{10}{3}$

   (D) $\frac{4}{3}$

7. Solve the system of linear equations:

$$\frac{5}{3}x + y = 3$$

$$\frac{1}{3}x - \frac{2}{3}y = \frac{7}{3}$$

(A) (–2, 3)

(B) (2, –7)

(C) (3, –2)

(D) (–3, 1)

8. A farmer's field is three times as wide as it is long, and is bounded by a stream on one side. If it takes 1500 yards of fence to enclose the field, find the width of the field in yards.

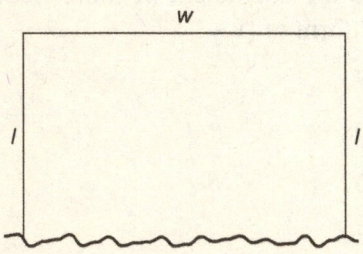

(A) 900

(B) 650

(C) 750

(D) 300

9. In *The Art of War*, Sun Tzu says an army can march 100 *li* per day. If one *li* is about $\frac{1}{8}$ km, about how fast does the army march in km/hr?

(A) 0.52 km/hour

(B) 1.05 km/hour

(C) 4.17 km/hour

(D) 33.33 km/hour

10. A candle is guaranteed to burn for six hours, and another candle of the same length is guaranteed to burn for four hours. If they are lit at the same time, how long will they be burning when one candle is twice as long as the other?

(A) 1 hour

(B) 2 hours

(C) 3 hours

(D) 3.5 hours

11. What is the area of the triangle inscribed in the circle, given $B = 38$ degrees?

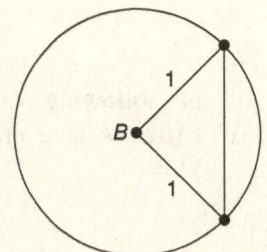

(A) $\frac{1}{2}(\sin 38)$

(B) $\frac{1}{2}(\sin 71)$

(C) $\frac{1}{2}\left(\frac{\sin 71}{\sin^2(38)}\right)$

(D) $\frac{1}{2}\left(\frac{\sin^2(38)}{\sin(71)}\right)$

12. The value of angle $a = 7.5°$; the length of arc $\overset{\frown}{BC}$ is 500 miles. Given that $\overrightarrow{DB}$ and $\overline{OC}$ are parallel, what is the circumference of circle O?

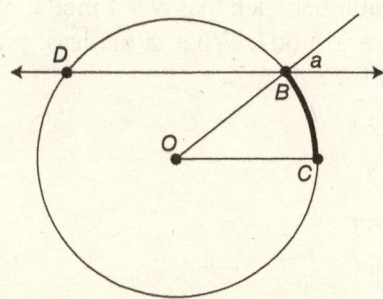

(A) 12,600 miles

(B) 15,700 miles

(C) 22,100 miles

(D) 24,000 miles

13. Find the approximate perimeter of a regular pentagon inscribed in a circle with a radius of 5.

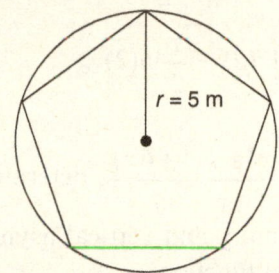

(A) 19.65

(B) 25

(C) 29.4

(D) 49.6

14. A boat is moored to the dock and floats with the
tide. If the height of the boat (above the bottom) is
given by

$$h(t) = 10 \sin\left(\frac{2\pi t}{4}\right) + 15$$

where $t = 0$ corresponds to 8 a.m., and time t is
measured in hours, what is the height of the boat
(above the bottom) at 9 p.m.?

(A) 25

(B) 20

(C) 15

(D) 5

15. A physicist has a wave tank to create controlled
waves. If the waves' lowest point is measured at
6 feet above the floor of the tank, and the highest
point is recorded at 14 feet above the floor of the
tank, and it has a period of 4 minutes, what is the
best model to represent the height of the waves as
a function of time, x (x is measured in minutes)?

(A) $10 + 6\sin\left(\dfrac{4\pi x}{2}\right)$

(B) $6 + 8\sin\left(\dfrac{2\pi x}{4}\right)$

(C) $14 - 4\sin\left(\dfrac{2\pi x}{4}\right)$

(D) $10 + 4\sin\left(\dfrac{2\pi x}{4}\right)$

16. A surveyor on a flat plain records angle $a = 42°$
from his position to the peak of a mountain in one
spot, and then moves back 1600 feet where he
measures his second angle, angle b, which is 38°.
Which of the following is the best approximation
of the height of the mountain?

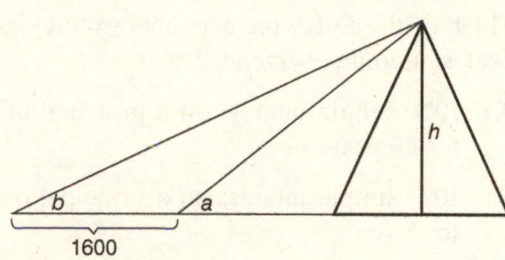

(A) 7300 feet

(B) 9600 feet

(C) 8100 feet

(D) 3700 feet

17. This graph portrays

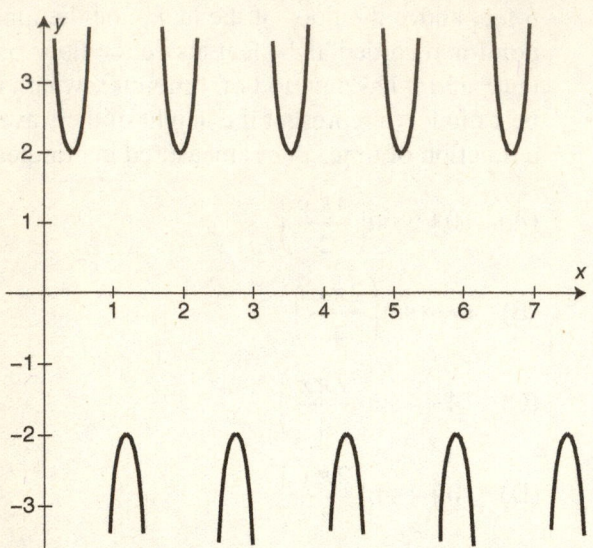

(A) $2\csc(4x)$

(B) $4\csc(2x)$

(C) $2\sec(4x)$

(D) $4\sec(2x)$

18. Which of the following accounts would yield the greatest amount of interest?

(A) 10% simple interest on a principal of $500 for 20 years

(B) 30% simple interest on a principal of $800 for 5 years

(C) 40% simple interest on a principal of $310 for 10 years

(D) 20% simple interest on a principal of $550 for 12 years

19. At how many places do the curves $f(x) = 2x^3 - 3x^2 - 17x + 30$ and $g(x) = -2(x - 2)^2 + 5$ intersect?

(A) one

(B) two

(C) three

(D) four

20. For what value of x is $\dfrac{2}{\sqrt{2}}e^x - 2^4 = -2^3$ a true statement?

(A) $x = 3\ln(2) - \dfrac{1}{2}\ln(2)$

(B) $x = -2.5\ln(2)$

(C) $x = -3\ln(2) - \dfrac{1}{2}\ln(2)$

(D) $x = 3\ln(2) + \dfrac{1}{2}\ln(2)$

21. If $f(x) = \dfrac{(x^3 + 7x^2 + 6x)}{(x^3 - x)}$, determine the point(s) of discontinuity and vertical asymptote(s) of the graph of the function.

(A) Points of discontinuity: $x = 0$ and $x = -1$; Vertical asymptote: $x = 1$

(B) Point of discontinuity: $x = 0$; Vertical asymptotes: $x = 1$ and $x = -1$

(C) Points of discontinuity: $x = 0$ and $x = 1$; Vertical asymptote: $x = -1$

(D) Point of discontinuity: $x = -1$; Vertical asymptotes: $x = 0$ and $x = 1$

22. If $f = g + h \bullet g$, where $f = 2x^3 + 3x^2 + 4x + 6$, and $g = 2x + 3$, what is h?

(A) $x^2 + 3$

(B) $x^2 - 2x - 1$

(C) $x^2 + 1$

(D) $2x^3 + 3x^2 + 2x + 3$

23. Which of the following quadratics have no real roots?

I. $y = 4(x + 3)^2 - 2$

II. $y = [(-5x + 6)x - 2]$

III. $y = x^2 + 3x + 3$

(A) I only

(B) III only

(C) II and III only

(D) I and II only

24. If $f(x) = \sqrt{9 - x^2}$ and $g(x) = \sqrt{x}$, what is the complement of the domain of $f \circ g(x)$?

    (A) $(-\infty, -3) \cup (3, \infty)$

    (B) $(0, 3)$

    (C) $(0, 9)$

    (D) $(-\infty, 0) \cup (3, \infty)$

25. Given the graph of $f(x)$,

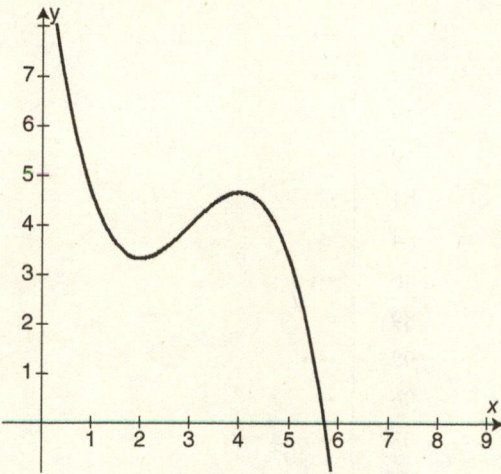

    which of the following values of x has the highest value of $f'(x)$ on the interval $[0, 6]$?

    (A) $x = 1$

    (B) $x = 2$

    (C) $x = 3$

    (D) $x = 4$

26. Consider a right cylinder h inches tall, with a radius of $3''$. What is the smallest integer value of h such that the cylinder will have a volume greater than that of a cube with a side length of $4''$?

    (A) 3

    (B) 7

    (C) 15

    (D) 23

27. If a line l passes through the points $(3, 2)$ and $(5, 3)$, and the line r is perpendicular to line l and intersects the point $(4, 1)$, what is the equation of line l?

    (A) $y - 4 = -2(x - 1)$

    (B) $y - 1 = -2(x - 4)$

    (C) $y - 1 = 2(x - 4)$

    (D) $y - 4 = 2(x - 1)$

28. The stem-and-leaf plot below shows the height of 20 high school students, in inches. What is the mean height of these 20 students?

Stem	Leaf
5	8 9 9
6	1 2 3 3 4 5 6 6 7 8 9 9
7	1 1 3 5 6

    (A) 66.25 inches

    (B) 65.25 inches

    (C) 66 inches

    (D) 64.7 inches

29. The average weight of bloodhounds has a normal distribution, with a mean weight of 120 pounds and a standard deviation of 15 pounds. Approximately what percentage of bloodhounds weighs between 105 and 135 pounds?

    (A) 34%

    (B) 95%

    (C) 68%

    (D) 50%

30. The following table shows the price of seven houses in a small town and the corresponding size of the houses. Which equation represents the line of best fit for the price of a house as a function of its size?

Size of House (S) (Square Feet)	Price (P) (Thousands of Dollars)
1400	90
1800	110
2200	142
2600	145
3000	173
3400	205
3800	248

(A) $P = 0.062S - 2.34$

(B) $P = 15.548S + 127.85$

(C) $P = 14.607S + 277.53$

(D) $P = 0.073S - 23.05$

31. A student is required to complete a simple research project over spring break. He decides to research the typical income of college students attending his university. To gather data, he sits outside of a campus cafeteria asking students their income from 11 a.m. until noon every day for all of spring break. After he turns in his project, his lecturer explains that his study may not be valid due to his sample. Which of the following may contribute to a bad sample?

    I. The limited time period in which he conducted his survey

    II. The limiting of his study to just his university

    III. The manner in which he surveyed fellow students

(A) I only

(B) II only

(C) I, II, and III

(D) I and III

32. The following dot plot shows the grades of each student in a small class on the final exam. Using the data, what is the median score on the final exam?

Grade	Frequency
63	•
64	•
69	••
70	•
73	••
76	•••
77	•••
78	•
79	•
81	••
84	•
86	•••
89	•
92	••••
96	••
98	••
100	•

(A) 76

(B) 81

(C) 84.5

(D) 92

33. In a lottery, five balls are chosen at random from a set of 30 balls numbered 1 through 30. A player must match all five numbers, in any order, to win. What is the probability of winning?

(A) $\dfrac{1}{142,506}$

(B) $\dfrac{1}{17,100,720}$

(C) $\dfrac{1}{3,420,144}$

(D) $\dfrac{1}{24,300,000}$

34. The following data record the height of a plant during the growing season.

DAY	HEIGHT (meters)
14	0.2
21	0.5
30	0.7
38	1.2
45	1.6
60	2.4

Which of the following best estimates the growth rate (meters/day) obtained by linear least-squares regression with equal certainty for each data point?

(A) 0.048 meters/day

(B) 0.050 meters /day

(C) 0.046 meters/day

(D) 0.052 meters/day

35. A roulette wheel has 38 positions on it numbered 0 through 36 plus 00. When it is spun, the probability that it lands on any particular number is $\frac{1}{38}$. What is the probability that the wheel never lands on 0 or 00 in three consecutive spins?

(A) $\frac{5832}{6859}$

(B) $\frac{4896}{5814}$

(C) $\frac{108}{114}$

(D) $\frac{108}{38}$

36. Solve the following system of equations:

$$\begin{cases} 4x+9y+z=12 \\ x-2y+2z=1 \\ y+\dfrac{z}{2}=4 \end{cases}$$

(A) $\begin{cases} x=-\dfrac{97}{15} \\ y=\dfrac{64}{15} \\ z=-\dfrac{8}{15} \end{cases}$

(B) $\begin{cases} x=-\dfrac{81}{31} \\ y=\dfrac{64}{31} \\ z=\dfrac{120}{31} \end{cases}$

(C) $\begin{cases} x=-\dfrac{449}{31} \\ y=\dfrac{168}{31} \\ z=\dfrac{408}{31} \end{cases}$

(D) $\begin{cases} x=\dfrac{64}{9} \\ y=\dfrac{27}{2} \\ z=9 \end{cases}$

37. Which vector satisfies $\langle 4, 6, -2 \rangle - \vec{v} = \langle 8, 4, 10 \rangle$?

(A) $\langle 4, -2, 12 \rangle$

(B) $\langle -4, 2, -8 \rangle$

(C) $\langle -4, 2, -12 \rangle$

(D) $\langle -4, -2, -12 \rangle$

38. A matrix of the form $\begin{pmatrix} a & b \\ b & 1 \end{pmatrix}$ is invertible whenever

    (A) $a \neq 0$

    (B) $a + b \neq 0$

    (C) $\sqrt{a} \neq b$

    (D) $b^2 - a \neq 0$

39. Given two matrices, A and B, if it is known that $AB = \begin{pmatrix} w & x \\ y & z \end{pmatrix}$, what can be known about BA?

    I. It must be a two-by-two matrix

    II. It must be a square matrix

    III. It must be invertible

    (A) I only

    (B) II only

    (C) I and III

    (D) II and III

40. Ten students are chosen to compete for three scholarships: one is for $5,000, the next is for $3,500, and the last is for $2,000. How many different ways can three winners be chosen?

    (A) 120 ways

    (B) 1000 ways

    (C) 720 ways

    (D) 30 ways

41. Consider the recursive sequence given by $a_0 = 4$, and $a_n = \dfrac{1}{2} a_{n-1}$ when $n = 1, 2, 3, \ldots$ Evaluate $\sum_{i=1}^{\infty} a_i$.

    (A) 8

    (B) The sum diverges.

    (C) 4

    (D) 0

42. Consider the three identical circles of radius R in the figure below. Which of the following is the area of the unshaded region that is bounded by the three circles?

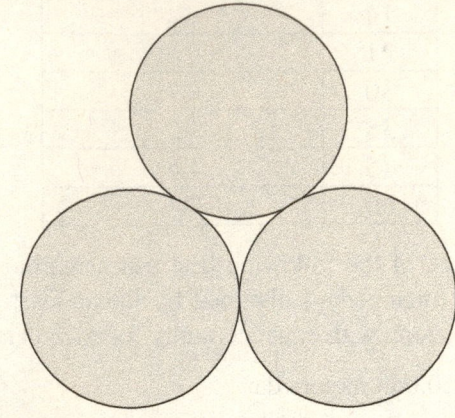

    (A) $\sqrt{3}R^2$

    (B) πR^2

    (C) $\left(\sqrt{3} - \dfrac{\pi}{2} \right) R^2$

    (D) $\left(\sqrt{3} - \dfrac{\pi}{3} \right) R^2$

43. Which of the following is a closed form representation of the recursive sequence given by $a_0 = 3$, and $a_{n+1} = a_n + \dfrac{7}{3}$ when $n = 1, 2, 3, \ldots$.

    (A) $a_n = 3 \left(\dfrac{7}{3} \right)^n$

    (B) $a_n = 3 + \sum_{i=0}^{n} \left(\dfrac{7}{3} \right)^i$

    (C) $a_n = \left(3 + \dfrac{7}{3} \right)^n$

    (D) $a_n = 3 + \dfrac{7}{3} n$

44. For which of the following values of k will $\lim_{x \to -2} f(x)$ exist if this equation is true?

$$f(x) = \begin{cases} -3x^3 + 9x, & x > -2 \\ 10, & x = -2 \\ x^2 + x + k, & x < -2 \end{cases}$$

(A) 4

(B) 8

(C) 10

(D) –44

45. If the graph to the below is a graph of $f'(x)$, which of the following could be a graph of $f(x)$?

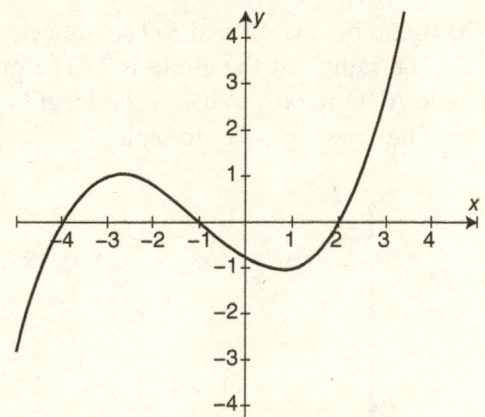

(A)

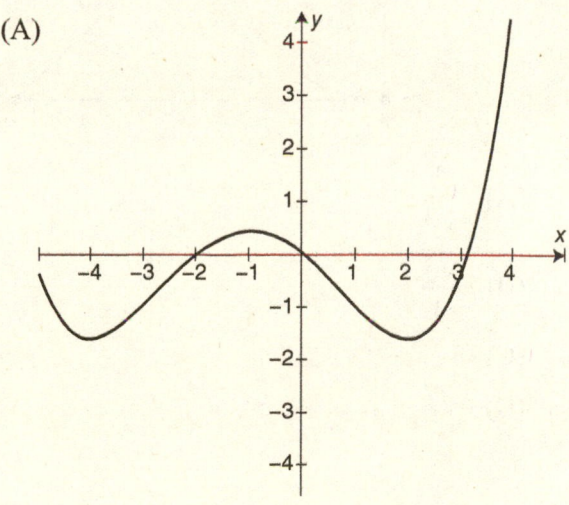

(B)

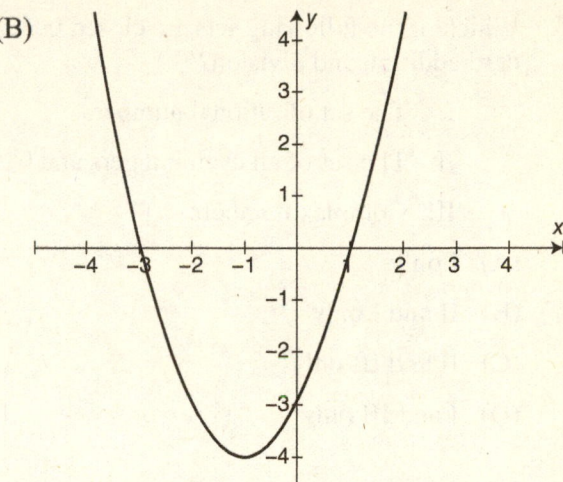

(C)

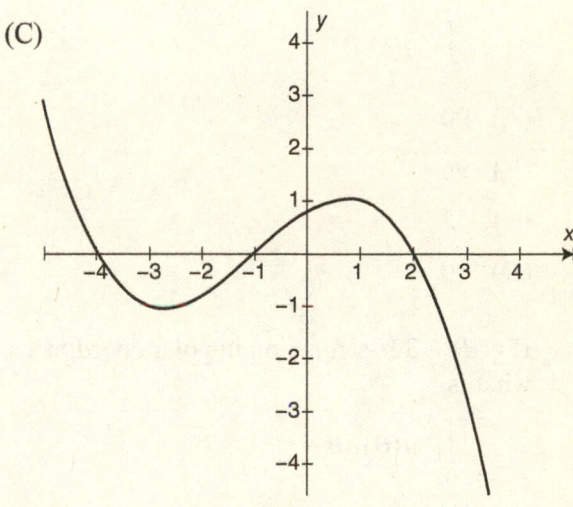

(D)

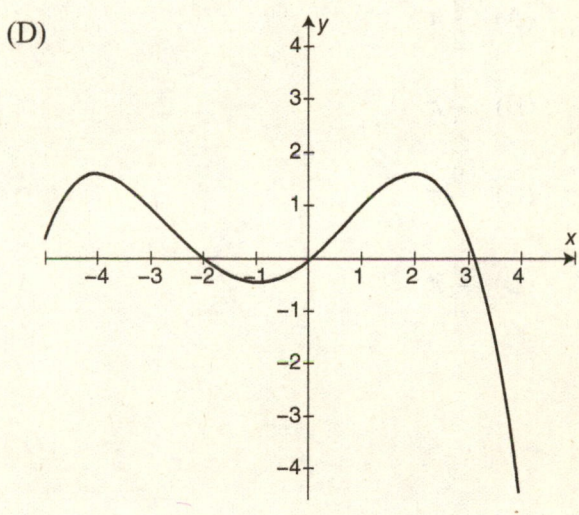

46. Which of the following sets are closed under standard addition and division?

   I.   The set of rational numbers

   II. The set of all even integers and 0

   III. Complex numbers

   (A) I only

   (B) II and I only

   (C) II and III only

   (D) I and III only

47. If $g(x)=$ is given by $g(x) = 3x + 6$, what is

$$\int_{-2}^{6} g(t)\,dt$$

   (A) 90

   (B) 96

   (C) 72

   (D) 102

48. If $g(\theta) = 3$ is a function in polar coordinates, then what is

$$\int_{0}^{\frac{\pi}{2}} g(\theta)\,d\theta$$

   (A) $\dfrac{9}{2}\pi$

   (B) $\dfrac{3}{2}\pi$

   (C) $\dfrac{9}{4}\pi$

   (D) $\dfrac{3}{4}\pi$

49. A chemist is causing a chemical reaction. He starts with 1 gram of sodium; as the chemical reaction progresses, the sodium is consumed. If the rate of change of the sodium reaction is given by

$$f(t) = -\frac{1}{2}e^{-0.5t}$$

where t is measured in minutes, how many minutes until half the sodium is left?

   (A) $2\ln\left(\dfrac{1}{2}\right)$

   (B) $2\ln(2)$

   (C) $-2\ln(2)$

   (D) $-2\ln(-2)$

50. In the figure below, $\overline{AB}$ and $\overline{BD}$ are tangent to circle C. The radius of the circle is 1. The measure of angle ABD is 60°. What is the length of $\overline{AD}$? (Note: The drawing is not to scale.)

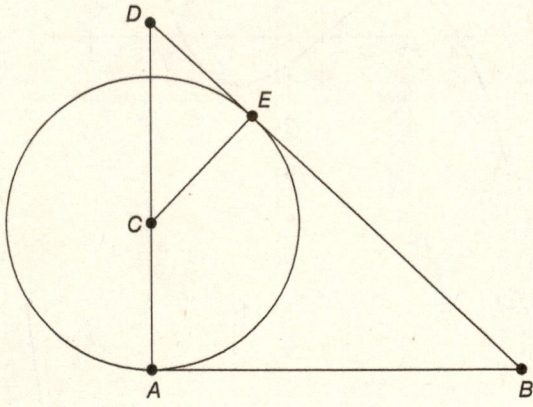

   (A) $\dfrac{3}{\sqrt{3}}$

   (B) $\dfrac{\sqrt{3}}{3}$

   (C) 3

   (D) $\sqrt{3}$

Answer Key—Practice Test 3

Question	Answer	Content Category
1	D	Algebra and Number Theory
2	C	Discrete Mathematics
3	A	Algebra and Number Theory
4	D	Algebra and Number Theory
5	C	Algebra and Number Theory
6	C	Algebra and Number Theory
7	C	Algebra and Number Theory
8	A	Measurement
9	A	Measurement
10	C	Measurement
11	A	Trigonometry
12	D	Geometry
13	C	Geometry
14	A	Algebra and Number Theory
15	D	Trigonometry
16	B	Trigonometry
17	A	Trigonometry
18	D	Functions
19	C	Functions
20	A	Functions
21	A	Functions
22	C	Functions
23	C	Functions
24	D	Functions
25	C	Calculus

Question	Answer	Content Category
26	A	Geometry
27	B	Functions
28	A	Data Analysis and Statistics
29	C	Data Analysis and Statistics
30	A	Data Analysis and Statistics
31	D	Data Analysis and Statistics
32	B	Data Analysis and Statistics
33	A	Probability
34	A	Probability
35	A	Probability
36	B	Matrix Algebra
37	C	Matrix Algebra
38	D	Matrix Algebra
39	B	Matrix Algebra
40	C	Discrete Mathematics
41	A	Discrete Mathematics
42	C	Geometry
43	D	Discrete Mathematics
44	A	Calculus
45	A	Calculus
46	D	Algebra and Number Theory
47	B	Calculus
48	C	Calculus
49	B	Calculus
50	C	Geometry

Detailed Explanations for Practice Test 3

1. (D)

The correct answer is (D). You need to determine for which k values of $f(-2) = 0$. Because k is a constant, you need to evaluate the variable terms only once. Thus,

$$f(-2) = (-2)^4 - 15(-2)^2 - 10(-2) + k$$
$$= 16 - 15(4) + 20 + k$$
$$= -60 + 36 + k$$
$$= -24 + k$$

If $-24 + k = 0$, then $k = 24$.

2. (C)

The correct answer is (C). For this problem, we need only evaluate the terms of the sequences. The sequence a_n simply adds 3 to every term, and the sequence b_n is halving its value every step. Thus, the terms of the sequences are

n	a_n	b_n
0	2	200
1	5	100
2	8	50
3	11	25
4	14	12.5

3. (A)

The correct answer is (A). There are multiple ways to approach this problem. One way is to examine each of the answers and determine whether they fit the criteria. Remember that for this problem, the number must have a remainder of 1 when divided by 3, 2 when divided by 5, and 3 when divided by 7. Since the problem asks for the least positive number for which this is true, start with 37, but 37 is not 3 mod 7. Now try 52. The criteria are all true for 52, so (A) is the correct answer.

A second approach checks the criteria for each answer choice. It is easy to determine what a number is mod 5; we can quickly determine that $52 \equiv 37 \equiv 157 \equiv 2 \bmod 5$, but $84 \equiv 4 \bmod 5$, and so (D) is eliminated. If you use this procedure, start with the lowest numbers first because you are looking for the least such value. So now check the three remaining choices for 1 mod 3: again, $52 \equiv 37 \equiv 157 \equiv 1 \bmod 3$. Check now for 3 mod 7, $52 \equiv 3 \bmod 7$, but 37 is not, so 52 is the value.

4. (D)

The correct answer is (D). This is a straightforward application of the binomial theorem. Recall that the binomial theorem states

$$(a+b)^n = \sum_{k=0}^{n} c_{n,k} a^{n-k} b^k$$

where $c_{n,k} = \binom{n}{k} = \dfrac{n!}{(n-k)!k!}$. In this problem, $a = x$ and $b = 3$, and $n = 5$. Therefore the term with x^2 would mean $k = 3$, and the term is

$$c_{5,3} x^2 b^3 = c_{5,3} \cdot 27x^2$$

To compute $c_{5,3}$ it is rapid to either use the formula above or Pascal's triangle. The formula yields

$$c_{5,3} = \frac{5!}{(5-3)!(3!)} = \frac{5 \cdot 4}{2 \cdot 1} = 10$$

so the term is $10 \cdot 27x^2 = 270x^2$, and the coefficient is 270.

5. (C)

The correct answer is (C). First, break up the exponents to get

$$(2i)^{14} = 2^{14}i^{14}.$$

Since all answer choices have value 16384, the problem reduces to finding the value of i^{14}. Note that $i^1 = i$, $i^2 = -1$, $i^3 = i \cdot i^2 = -i$, and $i^4 = i \cdot i^3 = i \cdot -i = 1$, and $i^5 = i \cdot i^6 = i$. That is, the exponents of i repeat in a cycle of length 4. Therefore we need only examine 14 mod 4, and since $14 \equiv 2 \mod 4$, $i^{14} = i^2 = -1$. Therefore, $(2i)^{14} = -16384$.

6. (C)

The correct answer is (C). The key for this question is to expand the summation. This is

$$\sum_{k=0}^{\infty} \frac{3}{10^k} = \frac{3}{1} + \frac{3}{10} + \frac{3}{100} + \frac{3}{1000} + \dots,$$

But this is just the definition of a decimal expansion. In fact, this is the decimal expansion for 3.3333…, the decimal form of $3\frac{1}{3} = \frac{9+1}{3} = \frac{10}{3}$.

7. (C)

The correct answer is (C). To answer this question, there are two possible approaches. One is to solve each equation for y and then graph them on a calculator. You can then attempt to visually identify the point of intersection. This method can be very quick.

An alternative method is still fairly swift and less prone to error. To derive the algebraic solution, first multiply each equation by the denominator to get integer coefficients. In both cases, multiply by 3 to get

$$5x + 3y = 9$$
$$1x - 2y = 7$$

Now multiply the second equation by −5 to get opposite coefficients on the x terms and add the equations together, which gives

$$
\begin{aligned}
5x + 3y &= 9 \\
-5x + 10y &= -35 \\
\hline
0x + 13y &= -26
\end{aligned}
$$

Therefore $y = -2$. At this point we can actually remove all the answers except one, answer (C), but a good double-check of the algebra done thus far is to follow through on the problem.

Now substituting the value $y = -2$ into any of the two original equations, the first equation becomes

$$\frac{5}{3}x - 2 = 3$$

so

$$\frac{5}{3}x = 5$$
$$5x = 15$$
$$x = 3.$$

Thus the point of intersection of these two lines is $(3, -2)$, which verifies the earlier work.

8. (A)

The correct answer is (A). The tricky part of this problem is recognizing that "the field is three times as wide as it is long" means $w = 3l$, and not $l = 3w$.

We can use this relationship and the perimeter of the field to determine the width. The perimeter of the field is $P = 2l + 2w$, but one width is the stream, so the fence needs to enclose only one width and two lengths, or

$$1500 = 2l + w.$$

However, because $w = 3l$, substitute this value into the above equation to get

$$2l + (3l) = 1500$$
$$5l = 1500$$

Thus $l = 300$. Because the length is 300, and $w = 3l$, $w = 3 \cdot 300 = 900$.

9. (A)

The correct answer is (A). This is a question about unit conversions. Use unit fractions to make this a straightforward conversion. Because they march 100 *li* per day, write this as the ratio

$$\frac{100 \; li}{1 \; \text{day}}$$

Now multiply first by a series of unit fractions to transform the unit of the denominator of the fraction into hours. Note that 1 day has 24 hours, so

$$\frac{100 \; li}{1 \; \text{day}} \left(\frac{1 \; \text{day}}{24 \; \text{hours}} \right)$$

If we computed the above ratio, we would have a unit of *li* per hour. We now need to use the given information. If one *li* is about $\frac{1}{8}$ km, that means 1 km = 8 *li*. Therefore

$$\frac{100 \; li}{1 \; \text{day}} \left(\frac{1 \; \text{day}}{24 \; \text{hours}} \right) \left(\frac{1 \; \text{km}}{8 \; li} \right)$$

The units cancel properly to give only kilometers per hour, and the answer is .5208 km per hour.

10. (C)

After x hours, the first candle will have burned $\frac{x}{6}$ of its length, and have $\frac{6-x}{6}$ left. Similarly, after the same x hours, the second candle will have $\frac{4-x}{4}$ left. The first candle will be twice as long as the second one when $\frac{6-x}{6} = 2\left(\frac{4-x}{4} \right)$, or $x = 3$.

11. (A)

The correct answer is (A). The sum of the interior angles of a triangle is 180 degrees, and because this is an isosceles triangle, the remaining two angles must be the same. Therefore,

$$38 + 2a = 180$$
$$2a = 142$$
$$a = 71$$

The base of the triangle is the chord connecting the edges of the circle. The height of the triangle is the distance from the origin to the base. So use the Law of Sines

$$\frac{\sin A}{a} = \frac{\sin B}{b}$$

where a is the side opposite A and b is the side opposite B, to calculate both the base and height of the triangle. To find the base, b, $\frac{\sin 38}{b} = \frac{\sin 71}{1}$, or $b = \frac{\sin 38}{\sin 71}$. It is unnecessary to compute the actual value for b in this problem.

It remains to find the height. To find the height, make a right triangle by bisecting the angle B. This gives us a new triangle:

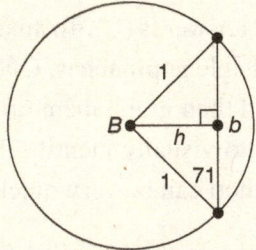

We know that each half of the bisected angle is $\frac{1}{2} B = \frac{1}{2} 38 = 19°$. Now we only need to apply the law of sines to find the height h. So

$$\frac{\sin 90}{1} = \frac{\sin 71}{h}, \text{ or } h = \frac{\sin 71}{\sin 90}.$$

Again, it is unnecessary to calculate the actual value for h in this problem.

Now substitute both h and b into the equation for the area of a triangle to get

$$A = \frac{1}{2} b \cdot h = \frac{1}{2} \cdot \frac{\sin 38}{\sin 71} \cdot \frac{\sin 71}{\sin 90} = \frac{1}{2} \sin 38.$$

12. (D)

The correct answer is (D). Since $\overrightarrow{DB}$ and $\overline{OC}$ are parallel, their corresponding angles are equal, or $\angle\alpha = \angle BOC$. In a circle, the ratio of a central angle to $360°$ equals the ratio of its arc length to the circumference, or $\frac{\theta}{360} = \frac{d}{C}$, where d is the distance of the arc highlighted in the diagram and C is the circumference of the circle. Thus,

$$\frac{7.5}{360} = \frac{500}{C}.$$

Now solve the above equation for C to get

$$7.5C = 360 \cdot 500$$

$$C = \frac{360 \cdot 500}{7.5} = 24,000.$$

13. (C)

The correct answer is (C). The pentagon can be broken up into five identical triangles. The vertex angle for each of the triangles located at the origin of the circle can be deduced by dividing 360 by 5. Then each vertex angle is $\frac{360}{5} = 72°$.

We now have two side lengths (the radii of the circle) and their included angle. To solve for the base, which is a side of the pentagon, use the Law of Cosines to get

$$a = \sqrt{5^2 + 5^2 - 2(5)(5)\cos(72)}$$

$$a = \sqrt{50 - 50\cos(72)}$$

$$a = \sqrt{50 - 15.45} \approx \sqrt{34.55}$$

so $a \approx 5.88$. This is the length of the base of the triangle, or one edge of the pentagon. To find the perimeter of the pentagon, all that remains is to multiply by 5, which yields a perimeter of

$$5 \cdot 5.88 = 29.4.$$

14. (A)

The correct answer is (A). First, note that at 8 a.m. the official time is 0. To figure what value of t corresponds to 9 p.m., from 8 a.m. to 8 p.m. is 12 hours, and then an additional hour makes a total of 13 hours having elapsed. Thus, merely evaluate the model given at $t = 13$, or

$$10\sin\left(\frac{13\pi}{2}\right) + 15 = 10 \cdot 1 + 15 = 25.$$

15. (D)

The correct answer is (D). This question requires us to take the verbal description and represent that as the appropriate mathematical model. Recall that sine is an oscillating function. For the function to match the model, add the sine term to the *midpoint* of the highest and lowest values. Thus, the constant term should be $\frac{14 + 6}{2} = \frac{20}{2} = 10$. This immediately eliminates (B) and (C).

Recall that the extreme values of sine are ± 1; therefore, in (A), $6\sin\left(\frac{4\pi x}{2}\right)$ the range is ± 6. Thus, model (A) has a lowest value of $10 + (-6) = 4$ and a maximum value of $10 + 6 = 16$ feet. These extreme values don't match the verbal model. By the same reasoning, the range is ± 4 for answer (D), and the lowest value is $10 - 4 = 6$ and the highest value is $10 + 4 = 14$, so (D) is the correct answer.

16. (B)

The correct answer is (B). The first thing to notice is that the model really has two distinct triangles. The first triangle (hereafter called triangle 1) consists of where the surveyor got the measurement of 42°. Triangle 2 is from where the surveyor moved back. It has an angle of 38°.

Given these angles and the 90° angle we know from the drawing, first solve for the remaining angle in the respective triangles.

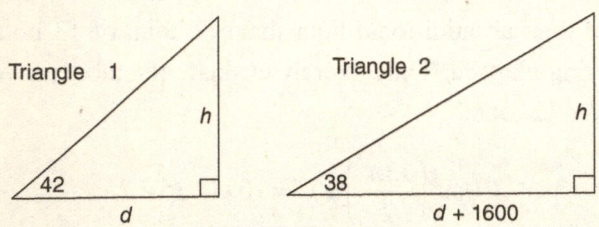

These are both right triangles with a leg of length h, the height of the mountain. Use the cotangent function to avoid fractions when finding h. For triangle 1, $\cot 42° = \dfrac{d}{h}$, and for triangle 2, $\cot 38° = \dfrac{d+1600}{h}$. Solve each of these equations for d and equate them to find an equation for h.

For triangle 1,

$$d = h \cdot \cot 42°$$

For triangle 2,

$$d + 1600 = h \cdot \cot 38°$$

Then

$$h \cdot \cot 42° = h \cdot \cot 38° - 1600$$

$$1600 = h(\cot 38° - \cot 42°)$$

$$h = \frac{1600}{\cot 38° - \cot 42°}$$

The problem asks to approximate the value of h, so even though a calculation at this point is easy, let's do an approximation. The cotangent function is positive and increasing around 38°–42°, so the difference in the cotangent of these two angles is small, probably less than .20, which would give a value of h of more than 9000, and answer (B) would be a good approximation. In fact, cot 38° = 1.28 and cot 42° = 1.11, so the difference is 0.17, and h ≈ 9411.

17. (A)

The correct answer is (A). The easiest way to solve this problem is to graph the answer choices on your calculator and see what matches the listed graph. Barring that, however, we can still deduce the answer based on the information in the graph by eliminating incorrect answers. Notice that the unknown function edges up to $y = \pm 2$, but is never between these values. This automatically rules out the options with a constant of 4; thus it must be either (A) or (C). To choose between these two options, note that for (C),

$$2\sec(0) = \frac{2}{\cos(0)} = 2 .$$

This eliminates (C) because it doesn't match the picture. Therefore, (A) must be the correct answer.

18. (D)

The correct answer is (D). Recall that the formula for simple interest is

$$I = Prt$$

where I is the total interest earned, P is the principal, or intial amount deposited, r is the annual interest rate (written as a decimal), and t is time (in years). For this question, it suffices to compute this for each of the options. Notice that we care only about *interest*, NOT the balance of the bank account.

(A)   yields $I = (500)(0.1)(20) = \$1,000$.

(B)   yields $I = (800)(0.3)(5) = \$1,200$.

(C)   yields $I = (300)(0.4)(10) = \$1,200$.

Finally computing (D), we have $I = (550)(0.2)(12) = \$1,320$.

Thus, of our options, (D) yields the largest amount of interest, and is the correct answer.

19.   (C)

The correct answer is (C). Use your calculator and graph both functions, zooming out so you have a good-sized window. Make sure you zoom out sufficiently far. Doing so, you will see there are three points of intersection; one of them is (1.5, 4.5).

Alternatively, you could set the equations equal and subtract them to see where their difference is equal to zero. This is because the distance between two lines at a point of intersection is zero. Then

$$2x^3 - 3x^2 - 17x + 30 = -2(x-2)^2 + 5$$
$$2x^3 - 3x^2 - 17x + 30 = -2x^2 + 8x - 3$$
$$2x^3 - 3x^2 + 2x^2 - 17x - 8x + 30 + 3 = 0$$
$$2x^3 - x^2 - 25x + 33 = 0$$

Now you merely need to find how many roots this quadratic has. Graph it on your calculator, and you can determine how many roots this cubic has by using Descartes' Rule of Signs, $f(x)$ changes sign twice and $f(-x)$ changes sign once, so there are two positive and one negative real roots, for a total of three real roots.

20.   (A)

The correct answer is (A). To solve, we need first to simplify the equation:

$$\frac{2}{\sqrt{2}}e^x = -2^3 + 2^4$$

$$\frac{2}{\sqrt{2}}e^x = -8 + 16$$

$$\sqrt{2}e^x = 2^3$$

$$e^x = \frac{2^3}{2^{\frac{1}{2}}}$$

$$\ln(e^x) = \ln\left(\frac{2^3}{2^{\frac{1}{2}}}\right)$$

Now we take logarithms, and get

$$\ln(e^x) = \ln(2^3) - \ln\left(2^{\frac{1}{2}}\right)$$

$$x = 3\ln(2) - \frac{1}{2}\ln(2)$$

21.   (A)

The correct answer is (A). In this problem, you must find the values of x that make the denominator zero for this rational function. To start, we need to solve the equation $x^3 - x = 0$.

$$x^3 - x = 0$$
$$x(x^2 - 1) = 0$$

$$x(x + 1)(x - 1) = 0$$

$$x = 0 \text{ or } x = -1 \text{ or } x = 1$$

So, the values of $x = 0$, $x = -1$, $x = 1$ make the denominator zero. Next, determine if these values are removable discontinuities or vertical asymptotes. The numerator needs to be factored to help the points of discontinuity, and $x^3 + 7x^2 + 6x$ factors to $x(x + 1)(x + 6)$. Because the numerator and denominator both have the term x and $x + 1$, the points $x = 0$ and $x = -1$ are points of discontinuity. Since the term $(x - 1)$ is only found in the numerator, $x = 1$ is a vertical asymptote. So, the points of discontinuity are $x = 0$ and $x = -1$ and the vertical asymptote is $x = 1$.

22. (C)

The correct answer is (C). To answer this question, it is necessary to perform some operations on polynomials. Fortunately, the familiar rules of algebra apply. The operations, however, will be different.

The first step is to isolate h. When we do this, we have

$$f = g + h \bullet g$$
$$f - g = h \bullet g$$
$$\frac{f - g}{g} = h.$$

Now we need to compute.

$$f - g = (2x^3 + 3x^2 + 4x + 6) - 2x - 3$$
$$= 2x^3 + 3x^2 + 2x + 3.$$

When we divide that result by $g = 2x + 3$ by, using polynomial long division, we get the final result,

$$h = x^2 + 1.$$

23. (C)

The correct answer is (C). There are two ways to answer this question. The first method is to simply graph all three equations on a calculator. A quadratic has no real roots if and only if it never touches the x-axis.

The second way to solve this problem utilizes algebraic methods. Recall that given a quadratic equation in standard form, $ax^2 + bx + c = 0$.

The *discriminant* of the quadratic is $b^2 - 4ac$.

A quadratic has no real roots if and only if the discriminant is less than zero. We merely need to compute the discriminant of options I, II, and III.

We start with option III (it is already in standard form). Note

$$b^2 - 4ac = 3^2 - 4(1)(3) = 9 - 12 = -3 < 0$$

therefore option III does NOT have real roots. Therefore we can immediately eliminate (A) and (D).

It suffices then for us to check the discriminant of option II only. We need to put this equation in standard form first, however. Clearing parentheses and combining like terms give us

$$y = -5x^2 + 6x - 2$$

which, when we compute the discriminant, yields

$$36 - 4 \bullet (-5) \bullet (-2) = 36 + (20) \bullet (-2)$$
$$= 36 - 40 = -4 < 0.$$

Therefore option II also has no real roots, and so options II and III have no real roots. Note that the discriminant of option I is 32. So, this option has real roots.

24. (D)

The correct answer is (D). For this question, we need to first determine the domain of $f \circ g(x) = f(g(x))$. Note that the domain of $g(x) = [0, \infty)$. So the question is what values of $[0, \infty)$ give us an answer for f. Well, note that the function f is defined only if

$$9 - x^2 \geq 0.$$

Therefore $9 \geq x^2$ implies $3 \geq x \geq -3$. Further, because we are restricting f to valid points of the domain in g, the domain of $f \circ g(x) = [-3, 3] \cap [0, \infty) = [0, 3]$. The complement of $[0, 3] = (-\infty, 0) \cup (3, \infty)$, which is answer (D).

25. (C)

The correct answer is (C). For this problem, we are given a graph of the function and are told to determine the maximum value of that function's derivative. First, note that the graph is smooth, and we are asked about a closed interval. Therefore, we know such a maximum value exists.

This is a question that is easy to answer once we recall the interpretation of the derivative. The derivative is the slope of the line tangent to the curve. The maximum value of the derivative will exist where there is the steepest (*upward*) slope.

Examining the possible answers, the slope at 2 and 4 are both 0, because the function is flat at those points. At point 1, the function is steep but *decreasing*. Whatever the derivative is, it is negative at that point. Finally, at point 3, notice that the function is increasing, so its slope is positive and it is also at a point of inflection, so f' is greatest at $x = 3$.

26. (A)

The correct answer is (A). Recall that the volume of a right cylinder with a radius of r and a h eight of h is

$$\pi r^2 h = V.$$

Thus, the volume of our cylinder in terms of h is $V = 9\pi h$.

We know the volume of a cube is just s^3, so the volume of the cube is $4^3 = 64$. Our goal is to determine the least value such that $V \geq 64$. So solving this inequality for h, we have

$$9\pi h \geq 64$$

which implies

$$h \geq \frac{64}{9\pi} \approx 2.263$$

Therefore the *least* such integer that satisfies this is answer (A).

27. (B)

The correct answer is (B). For this question, we first need to compute the slope of line l. Using our co-ordinates, we get

$$m_l = \frac{3-2}{(5-3)} = \frac{1}{2}.$$

Because line r is perpendicular to line l, we know

$$m_r = -\frac{1}{m_l} = -2.$$

Now that we know the slope of line r, we can now use point slope formula to get an equation for r. Thus, we get

$$y - 1 = -2(x - 4).$$

which is the correct answer, (B).

28. (A)

The correct answer is (A). Use your calculator to find the mean is

$$\frac{58+59+59+61+62+63+63+64+65+66+66+67+68+69+69+71+71+73+75+76}{20}$$

$$= 66.25.$$

29. (C)

The correct answer is (C). First notice that 120 − 15 = 105 while 120 + 15 = 135. Thus, we are looking for the percentage within one standard deviation of the mean. For any normal distribution, the percentage within one standard deviation of the mean is approximately 68%.

30. (A)

The correct answer is (A). Using the calculator's linear regression function, we can see that the line of best fit is $P = 0.062S - 2.34$.

31. (D)

The correct answer is (D). The student chose to do his research in a very limited time frame, 11 a.m. until noon, during spring break when a considerable proportion of the student body may not be present. Thus, statement I may lead to a bad sample. The student chose to collect his data by verbally asking students about their income, which may result in students providing incorrect information. Thus, statement III may lead to a bad sample. However, because the student wished to study the income of students at his university, it is not correct to include students from other universities. Thus, II will not lead to a bad sample, and therefore only I and III are reasons for a possible bad sample.

32. (B)

The correct answer is (B). The median is the middle score. When all of the scores are written out in increasing order, we can see that the middle score is 81. Fifteen scores are above (or equal to) 81, and 15 are below (or equal to) it.

33. (A)

The correct answer is (A). There are $_{30}C_{35} = \dfrac{30!}{25!5!}$ =142,506 different possible combinations of five numbered balls chosen from the initial thirty. However, only one combination is the winning one. Thus the probability of winning is $\dfrac{1}{142,506}$.

34. (A)

The correct answer is (A). This answer is obtained from linear least-squares regression; you may perform this calculation manually or by using the regression function on your calculator. In order to perform the calculation manually, tabulate the following

$$\sum_1^6 x_i = 208, \quad \sum_1^6 y_i = 6.6, \quad \sum_1^6 x_i^2 = 8606,$$
$$\sum_1^6 x_i y_i = 295.9,$$

where the x_i are the days and the y_i are the heights. The least squares slope with equal weighting is then

$$\left(\frac{\sum_1^6 x_i y_i - \frac{1}{6} \sum_1^6 x_i \sum_1^6 y_i}{\sum_1^6 x_i^2 - \frac{1}{6}\left(\sum_1^6 x_i\right)} \right) = 0.0481 \frac{\text{meters}}{\text{day}}.$$

35. (A)

The correct answer is (A). Each spin is mutually exclusive of every other spin, therefore the probability that the wheel does not land on 0 or 00 in three straight spins is the product of the probability that the wheel does not land on 0 or 00 in any single spin.

$$\frac{36}{38} \cdot \frac{36}{38} \cdot \frac{36}{38} = \left(\frac{18}{19}\right)^3 = \frac{5832}{6859}.$$

36. (B)

The correct answer is (B). The system

$$\begin{cases} 4x + 9y + z = 12 \\ x - 2y + 2z = 1 \\ y + \dfrac{z}{2} = 4 \end{cases}$$

can be written as the matrix equation

$$\begin{pmatrix} 4 & 9 & 1 \\ 1 & -2 & 2 \\ 0 & 1 & \frac{1}{2} \end{pmatrix} \begin{pmatrix} x \\ y \\ z \end{pmatrix} = \begin{pmatrix} 12 \\ 1 \\ 4 \end{pmatrix}.$$

We need to find the inverse of the matrix on the left so we can multiply both sides of the equation by it to get values for $\begin{pmatrix} x \\ y \\ z \end{pmatrix}$. Using a graphing calculator we can find that

$$\begin{pmatrix} 4 & 9 & 1 \\ 1 & -2 & 2 \\ 0 & 1 & \frac{1}{2} \end{pmatrix}^{-1} = \begin{pmatrix} \frac{6}{31} & \frac{7}{31} & -\frac{40}{31} \\ \frac{1}{31} & -\frac{4}{31} & \frac{14}{31} \\ -\frac{2}{31} & \frac{8}{31} & \frac{34}{31} \end{pmatrix}.$$

Multiplying both sides of the equation by this inverse results in

$$\begin{pmatrix} x \\ y \\ z \end{pmatrix} = \begin{pmatrix} \frac{6}{31} & \frac{7}{31} & -\frac{40}{31} \\ \frac{1}{31} & -\frac{4}{31} & \frac{14}{31} \\ -\frac{2}{31} & \frac{8}{31} & \frac{34}{31} \end{pmatrix} \begin{pmatrix} 12 \\ 1 \\ 4 \end{pmatrix}.$$

$$= \begin{pmatrix} -\frac{81}{31} \\ \frac{64}{31} \\ \frac{120}{31} \end{pmatrix}$$

Which yields
$$\begin{cases} x = -\dfrac{81}{31} \\ y = \dfrac{64}{31} \\ z = \dfrac{120}{31} \end{cases}.$$

37. (C)

The correct answer is (C). $(4, 6, -2) - \vec{v} = (8, 4, 10)$
$\rightarrow (4, 6, -2) - (8, 4, 10) = \vec{v} = (4 - 8, 6 - 4, -2 - 10) =$
$(-4, 2, -12)$.

38. (D)

The correct answer is (D). A 2×2 matrix is invertible whenever its determinant is not zero. So $\begin{pmatrix} a & b \\ b & 1 \end{pmatrix}$ must be invertible whenever $a - b^2 \neq 0 \rightarrow b^2 - a \neq 0$. Notice that (C) is not the correct answer. This can be seen by letting $a = 4$ and $b = -2$, because even though $\sqrt{4} = -2$, $\begin{pmatrix} 4 & -2 \\ -2 & 1 \end{pmatrix}$ is not invertible because $4 - (-2)(-2) = 0$.

39. (B)

The correct answer is (B). Let us look at a few examples. Let $A = \begin{pmatrix} 2 \\ 1 \end{pmatrix}$ and $B = (1 \quad 1)$, then $AB = \begin{pmatrix} 2 \\ 1 \end{pmatrix}(1 \quad 1) = \begin{pmatrix} 2 & 2 \\ 1 & 1 \end{pmatrix}$ as desired. However, $BA = (1 \quad 1)\begin{pmatrix} 2 \\ 1 \end{pmatrix} = (3)$, therefore I is not a requirement.

Now, let $A = \begin{pmatrix} 2 & 2 \\ 2 & 2 \end{pmatrix}$ and $B = \begin{pmatrix} 1 & 0 \\ 0 & 1 \end{pmatrix}$ then $AB = BA = \begin{pmatrix} 2 & 2 \\ 2 & 2 \end{pmatrix}$. However, this is not invertible, so III is not a requirement. To show that II is required, for example, if AB is a 2×2 square matrix, the number of rows in A is equal to the number of columns in B. In addition, because the product AB exists, the number of columns in A must be equal to the number of rows in B. For this reason, when the order is changed, the final product AB still has the same number of rows as columns and is a square matrix. This is true for all square matrices.

40. (C)

The correct answer is (C). Because the three awards have different values, the order in which winning students are chosen matters, so we should consider the number of different permutations. $P(10,3) = \dfrac{10!}{7!}$

= 10 • 9 • 8 = 720 ways that the three winners may be chosen.

41. (A)

The correct answer is (A). The recursive sequence can be expressed in closed form as $a_n = 4\left(\frac{1}{2}\right)^n$ where $n = 0, 1, 2, \ldots$. Recall that $\sum_{i=0}^{\infty} a(r)^i = \frac{a}{1-r}$ for all $-1 < r < 1$. Therefore, $\sum_{i=0}^{\infty} a_i = \sum_{i=0}^{\infty} 4\left(\frac{1}{2}\right)^i = \frac{4}{1-\frac{1}{2}} = \frac{4}{\frac{1}{2}} = 8$.

42. (C)

The correct answer is (C). First construct an equilateral triangle by connecting the centers of each of the circles as shown below. A side length of this triangle is $2R$. The area can be determined using the formula for equilateral triangles where s is side length: $A = \frac{\sqrt{3}s^2}{4}$. In this case, the area of the triangle is $\frac{\sqrt{3}(2R)^2}{4} = \frac{4\sqrt{3}R^2}{4} = \sqrt{3}R^2$. Then determine the area of the three sectors contained in both a circle and the triangle. Each one has a 60° central angle, so the area comprised by all three is $3 \cdot \frac{60}{360} \cdot \pi R^2 = \frac{\pi R^2}{2}$. Hence the area inside the triangle but not in any circle is given by the difference between those two areas, $\sqrt{3}R^2 - \frac{\pi R^2}{2} = \left(\sqrt{3} - \frac{\pi}{2}\right)R^2$.

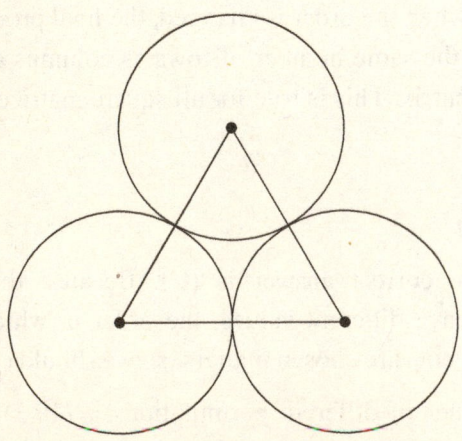

43. (D)

The correct answer is (D), $a_n = 3 + \frac{7}{3}n$. When $n = 0$, $a_0 = 3$. Because the common difference is $\frac{7}{3}$, this closed form sequence will produce all of the same terms as the initial recursive sequence.

44. (A)

The correct answer is (A). A limit of a function exists if the left-hand limit and the right-hand limit both exist and are equal; in notation it exists if and only if

$$\lim_{x \to 2^+} f(x) = \lim_{x \to 2^-} f(x).$$

Notice that we do not actually care about the value of the function at -2.

Our function $f(x)$ is defined piecewise by polynomials. Because polynomials are continuous functions, to determine the limit as $f(x)$ approaches -2 from the left and the right, we may simply evaluate the respective cases for -2. In particular, we want to find the value of k for which

$$-3x^3 + 9x = x^2 + x + k$$

when $x = -2$. Thus, evaluating and solving, we have

$$-3(-2)^3 + 9(-2) = (-2)^2 + (-2) + k$$
$$24 - 18 = 4 - 2 + k$$
$$6 = 2 + k$$
$$4 = k$$

45. (A)

The correct answer is (A). We are given the graph of the derivative. The first thing to take note of is the critical values of the graph, which are points where the *derivative* is zero. The graph shows $f(x) = 0$ at the points -4, -1, and 2. Only (A) and (D) have these three flat spots. Answer (B) has only one inflection point, and it isn't at any of the three critical values. Graph (C) has two, also not at the critical values. Therefore, (B) and (C) are false.

To determine whether the correct answer is (A) or (D), note the sign of the derivative. In the interval $x < -4$, the derivative is negative. The graph in (D) is increasing in that same interval; therefore, it isn't the correct graph, but (A) is.

46. (D)

The correct answer is (D). To understand this question, it is important to know the properties of elementary number systems. First, statement I is true because the rational numbers form a field, so they are closed under all four basic operations. In other words, with common denominators, if you start with a fraction, you get another fraction back, and fraction division is closed because

$$\frac{\frac{p}{q}}{\frac{r}{s}} = \frac{p}{q} \times \frac{s}{r} = \frac{ps}{qr}.$$

Statement II is about a subset of the integers, namely, integers divisible by 2. This set is certainly closed under addition, because an even number plus an even number is still even. However, it is not closed under division because, for example,

$$\frac{10}{8} = \frac{5}{4}$$

a non-integer value. Therefore, statement II is false.

Finally, the complex numbers also fulfill this criterion. They are a field and are also closed under all the basic operations. In fact,

$$\frac{a+bi}{c+di} = \frac{ac+bd}{c^2+d^2} + i\frac{(bc-ad)}{c^2+d^2}$$

which is still a complex number.

Therefore, the correct answer is I and III only.

47. (B)

The correct answer is (B). This is a mundane integral; however, you can save considerable time if you consider the picture of the equation and the interpretation of the integral. The picture is a right triangle, with a base 8 units long and a height 24 units tall. The integral is really asking for the area of this triangle. Therefore, instead of computing the integral and using the fundamental theorem of calculus, use geometry:

$$A = \frac{1}{2}bh = \frac{1}{2}(8)(24) = 96.$$

48. (C)

The correct answer is (C). To properly answer this question, you need to know how to interpret a constant function in polar coordinates. If a function is constant in polar coordinates, the radius from the origin is a constant, meaning it is a circle. When we are being asked to integrate around part of this path, it is easiest to use geometric reasoning. The interval $\left[0, \frac{\pi}{2}\right]$ corresponds to one fourth of a circle with radius 3. Therefore, compute the area of that circle and divide by 4:

$$\frac{\pi r^2}{4} = \frac{\pi(3)^2}{4} = \frac{9}{4}\pi.$$

49. (B)

The correct answer is (B). The given function $f(t)$ is *a rate of change*. Noting that if we let $u = -\frac{1}{2}t$, the function becomes

$$e^u du$$

Therefore,

$$\int e^u du = e^u + c = e^{-\frac{1}{2}t} + c$$

Next, we need to find the constant of integration. This requires the information about the initial value. We are told there is initially 1 gram of sodium, therefore

$$1 = e^{-\frac{1}{2}0} + c = 1 + c$$

Thus, the constant of integration is 0. The payoff of this work is that the amount of sodium after the amount of time t is given by

$$F(t) = e^{-\frac{1}{2}t}$$

Thus, we need to find the value of t such that $F(t) = \frac{1}{2}$. Thus,

$$\frac{1}{2} = e^{-\frac{1}{2}t}$$

Taking logarithms of both sides, we get

$$\ln\left(\frac{1}{2}\right) = -\frac{1}{2}t$$
$$-2\ln(2^{-1}) = t$$
$$(-2)(-1)\ln(2) = t$$
$$2\ln(2) = t.$$

50. (C)

The correct answer is (C). Angles DAB and CED are both right angles because they are formed by a radius to a point of tangency; and, the radius and the tangent are always perpendicular at the point of tangency. Because the measure of angle DAB is 90° and the measure of angle ABE is 60°, the measure of angle ADB must be 30°, and so is angle CDE since it is the same angle. So triangle CDE also is a 30-60-90 right triangle, and triangle CDE is similar to triangle ADB. Thus, we can apply the known proportions among side lengths for such triangles. We know that radius $CE = 1$. The hypotenuse is twice as long as the side opposite the 30° angle, according to 30-60-90 right triangle proportions. So $DC = 2$. Radius $AC = 1$, so $AD = AC + CD = 1 + 2 = 3$.

PRAXIS II Mathematics Content Knowledge
Practice Test 1 Answer Sheet

1. Ⓐ Ⓑ Ⓒ Ⓓ	18. Ⓐ Ⓑ Ⓒ Ⓓ	35. Ⓐ Ⓑ Ⓒ Ⓓ
2. Ⓐ Ⓑ Ⓒ Ⓓ	19. Ⓐ Ⓑ Ⓒ Ⓓ	36. Ⓐ Ⓑ Ⓒ Ⓓ
3. Ⓐ Ⓑ Ⓒ Ⓓ	20. Ⓐ Ⓑ Ⓒ Ⓓ	37. Ⓐ Ⓑ Ⓒ Ⓓ
4. Ⓐ Ⓑ Ⓒ Ⓓ	21. Ⓐ Ⓑ Ⓒ Ⓓ	38. Ⓐ Ⓑ Ⓒ Ⓓ
5. Ⓐ Ⓑ Ⓒ Ⓓ	22. Ⓐ Ⓑ Ⓒ Ⓓ	39. Ⓐ Ⓑ Ⓒ Ⓓ
6. Ⓐ Ⓑ Ⓒ Ⓓ	23. Ⓐ Ⓑ Ⓒ Ⓓ	40. Ⓐ Ⓑ Ⓒ Ⓓ
7. Ⓐ Ⓑ Ⓒ Ⓓ	24. Ⓐ Ⓑ Ⓒ Ⓓ	41. Ⓐ Ⓑ Ⓒ Ⓓ
8. Ⓐ Ⓑ Ⓒ Ⓓ	25. Ⓐ Ⓑ Ⓒ Ⓓ	42. Ⓐ Ⓑ Ⓒ Ⓓ
9. Ⓐ Ⓑ Ⓒ Ⓓ	26. Ⓐ Ⓑ Ⓒ Ⓓ	43. Ⓐ Ⓑ Ⓒ Ⓓ
10. Ⓐ Ⓑ Ⓒ Ⓓ	27. Ⓐ Ⓑ Ⓒ Ⓓ	44. Ⓐ Ⓑ Ⓒ Ⓓ
11. Ⓐ Ⓑ Ⓒ Ⓓ	28. Ⓐ Ⓑ Ⓒ Ⓓ	45. Ⓐ Ⓑ Ⓒ Ⓓ
12. Ⓐ Ⓑ Ⓒ Ⓓ	29. Ⓐ Ⓑ Ⓒ Ⓓ	46. Ⓐ Ⓑ Ⓒ Ⓓ
13. Ⓐ Ⓑ Ⓒ Ⓓ	30. Ⓐ Ⓑ Ⓒ Ⓓ	47. Ⓐ Ⓑ Ⓒ Ⓓ
14. Ⓐ Ⓑ Ⓒ Ⓓ	31. Ⓐ Ⓑ Ⓒ Ⓓ	48. Ⓐ Ⓑ Ⓒ Ⓓ
15. Ⓐ Ⓑ Ⓒ Ⓓ	32. Ⓐ Ⓑ Ⓒ Ⓓ	49. Ⓐ Ⓑ Ⓒ Ⓓ
16. Ⓐ Ⓑ Ⓒ Ⓓ	33. Ⓐ Ⓑ Ⓒ Ⓓ	50. Ⓐ Ⓑ Ⓒ Ⓓ
17. Ⓐ Ⓑ Ⓒ Ⓓ	34. Ⓐ Ⓑ Ⓒ Ⓓ	

PRAXIS II Mathematics Content Knowledge Practice Test 2 Answer Sheet

1. Ⓐ Ⓑ Ⓒ Ⓓ
2. Ⓐ Ⓑ Ⓒ Ⓓ
3. Ⓐ Ⓑ Ⓒ Ⓓ
4. Ⓐ Ⓑ Ⓒ Ⓓ
5. Ⓐ Ⓑ Ⓒ Ⓓ
6. Ⓐ Ⓑ Ⓒ Ⓓ
7. Ⓐ Ⓑ Ⓒ Ⓓ
8. Ⓐ Ⓑ Ⓒ Ⓓ
9. Ⓐ Ⓑ Ⓒ Ⓓ
10. Ⓐ Ⓑ Ⓒ Ⓓ
11. Ⓐ Ⓑ Ⓒ Ⓓ
12. Ⓐ Ⓑ Ⓒ Ⓓ
13. Ⓐ Ⓑ Ⓒ Ⓓ
14. Ⓐ Ⓑ Ⓒ Ⓓ
15. Ⓐ Ⓑ Ⓒ Ⓓ
16. Ⓐ Ⓑ Ⓒ Ⓓ
17. Ⓐ Ⓑ Ⓒ Ⓓ

18. Ⓐ Ⓑ Ⓒ Ⓓ
19. Ⓐ Ⓑ Ⓒ Ⓓ
20. Ⓐ Ⓑ Ⓒ Ⓓ
21. Ⓐ Ⓑ Ⓒ Ⓓ
22. Ⓐ Ⓑ Ⓒ Ⓓ
23. Ⓐ Ⓑ Ⓒ Ⓓ
24. Ⓐ Ⓑ Ⓒ Ⓓ
25. Ⓐ Ⓑ Ⓒ Ⓓ
26. Ⓐ Ⓑ Ⓒ Ⓓ
27. Ⓐ Ⓑ Ⓒ Ⓓ
28. Ⓐ Ⓑ Ⓒ Ⓓ
29. Ⓐ Ⓑ Ⓒ Ⓓ
30. Ⓐ Ⓑ Ⓒ Ⓓ
31. Ⓐ Ⓑ Ⓒ Ⓓ
32. Ⓐ Ⓑ Ⓒ Ⓓ
33. Ⓐ Ⓑ Ⓒ Ⓓ
34. Ⓐ Ⓑ Ⓒ Ⓓ

35. Ⓐ Ⓑ Ⓒ Ⓓ
36. Ⓐ Ⓑ Ⓒ Ⓓ
37. Ⓐ Ⓑ Ⓒ Ⓓ
38. Ⓐ Ⓑ Ⓒ Ⓓ
39. Ⓐ Ⓑ Ⓒ Ⓓ
40. Ⓐ Ⓑ Ⓒ Ⓓ
41. Ⓐ Ⓑ Ⓒ Ⓓ
42. Ⓐ Ⓑ Ⓒ Ⓓ
43. Ⓐ Ⓑ Ⓒ Ⓓ
44. Ⓐ Ⓑ Ⓒ Ⓓ
45. Ⓐ Ⓑ Ⓒ Ⓓ
46. Ⓐ Ⓑ Ⓒ Ⓓ
47. Ⓐ Ⓑ Ⓒ Ⓓ
48. Ⓐ Ⓑ Ⓒ Ⓓ
49. Ⓐ Ⓑ Ⓒ Ⓓ
50. Ⓐ Ⓑ Ⓒ Ⓓ

PRAXIS II Mathematics Content Knowledge
Practice Test 3 Answer Sheet

1. Ⓐ Ⓑ Ⓒ Ⓓ
2. Ⓐ Ⓑ Ⓒ Ⓓ
3. Ⓐ Ⓑ Ⓒ Ⓓ
4. Ⓐ Ⓑ Ⓒ Ⓓ
5. Ⓐ Ⓑ Ⓒ Ⓓ
6. Ⓐ Ⓑ Ⓒ Ⓓ
7. Ⓐ Ⓑ Ⓒ Ⓓ
8. Ⓐ Ⓑ Ⓒ Ⓓ
9. Ⓐ Ⓑ Ⓒ Ⓓ
10. Ⓐ Ⓑ Ⓒ Ⓓ
11. Ⓐ Ⓑ Ⓒ Ⓓ
12. Ⓐ Ⓑ Ⓒ Ⓓ
13. Ⓐ Ⓑ Ⓒ Ⓓ
14. Ⓐ Ⓑ Ⓒ Ⓓ
15. Ⓐ Ⓑ Ⓒ Ⓓ
16. Ⓐ Ⓑ Ⓒ Ⓓ
17. Ⓐ Ⓑ Ⓒ Ⓓ

18. Ⓐ Ⓑ Ⓒ Ⓓ
19. Ⓐ Ⓑ Ⓒ Ⓓ
20. Ⓐ Ⓑ Ⓒ Ⓓ
21. Ⓐ Ⓑ Ⓒ Ⓓ
22. Ⓐ Ⓑ Ⓒ Ⓓ
23. Ⓐ Ⓑ Ⓒ Ⓓ
24. Ⓐ Ⓑ Ⓒ Ⓓ
25. Ⓐ Ⓑ Ⓒ Ⓓ
26. Ⓐ Ⓑ Ⓒ Ⓓ
27. Ⓐ Ⓑ Ⓒ Ⓓ
28. Ⓐ Ⓑ Ⓒ Ⓓ
29. Ⓐ Ⓑ Ⓒ Ⓓ
30. Ⓐ Ⓑ Ⓒ Ⓓ
31. Ⓐ Ⓑ Ⓒ Ⓓ
32. Ⓐ Ⓑ Ⓒ Ⓓ
33. Ⓐ Ⓑ Ⓒ Ⓓ
34. Ⓐ Ⓑ Ⓒ Ⓓ

35. Ⓐ Ⓑ Ⓒ Ⓓ
36. Ⓐ Ⓑ Ⓒ Ⓓ
37. Ⓐ Ⓑ Ⓒ Ⓓ
38. Ⓐ Ⓑ Ⓒ Ⓓ
39. Ⓐ Ⓑ Ⓒ Ⓓ
40. Ⓐ Ⓑ Ⓒ Ⓓ
41. Ⓐ Ⓑ Ⓒ Ⓓ
42. Ⓐ Ⓑ Ⓒ Ⓓ
43. Ⓐ Ⓑ Ⓒ Ⓓ
44. Ⓐ Ⓑ Ⓒ Ⓓ
45. Ⓐ Ⓑ Ⓒ Ⓓ
46. Ⓐ Ⓑ Ⓒ Ⓓ
47. Ⓐ Ⓑ Ⓒ Ⓓ
48. Ⓐ Ⓑ Ⓒ Ⓓ
49. Ⓐ Ⓑ Ⓒ Ⓓ
50. Ⓐ Ⓑ Ⓒ Ⓓ

PRAXIS II Mathematics Content Knowledge
Extra Answer Sheet

1. Ⓐ Ⓑ Ⓒ Ⓓ
2. Ⓐ Ⓑ Ⓒ Ⓓ
3. Ⓐ Ⓑ Ⓒ Ⓓ
4. Ⓐ Ⓑ Ⓒ Ⓓ
5. Ⓐ Ⓑ Ⓒ Ⓓ
6. Ⓐ Ⓑ Ⓒ Ⓓ
7. Ⓐ Ⓑ Ⓒ Ⓓ
8. Ⓐ Ⓑ Ⓒ Ⓓ
9. Ⓐ Ⓑ Ⓒ Ⓓ
10. Ⓐ Ⓑ Ⓒ Ⓓ
11. Ⓐ Ⓑ Ⓒ Ⓓ
12. Ⓐ Ⓑ Ⓒ Ⓓ
13. Ⓐ Ⓑ Ⓒ Ⓓ
14. Ⓐ Ⓑ Ⓒ Ⓓ
15. Ⓐ Ⓑ Ⓒ Ⓓ
16. Ⓐ Ⓑ Ⓒ Ⓓ
17. Ⓐ Ⓑ Ⓒ Ⓓ

18. Ⓐ Ⓑ Ⓒ Ⓓ
19. Ⓐ Ⓑ Ⓒ Ⓓ
20. Ⓐ Ⓑ Ⓒ Ⓓ
21. Ⓐ Ⓑ Ⓒ Ⓓ
22. Ⓐ Ⓑ Ⓒ Ⓓ
23. Ⓐ Ⓑ Ⓒ Ⓓ
24. Ⓐ Ⓑ Ⓒ Ⓓ
25. Ⓐ Ⓑ Ⓒ Ⓓ
26. Ⓐ Ⓑ Ⓒ Ⓓ
27. Ⓐ Ⓑ Ⓒ Ⓓ
28. Ⓐ Ⓑ Ⓒ Ⓓ
29. Ⓐ Ⓑ Ⓒ Ⓓ
30. Ⓐ Ⓑ Ⓒ Ⓓ
31. Ⓐ Ⓑ Ⓒ Ⓓ
32. Ⓐ Ⓑ Ⓒ Ⓓ
33. Ⓐ Ⓑ Ⓒ Ⓓ
34. Ⓐ Ⓑ Ⓒ Ⓓ

35. Ⓐ Ⓑ Ⓒ Ⓓ
36. Ⓐ Ⓑ Ⓒ Ⓓ
37. Ⓐ Ⓑ Ⓒ Ⓓ
38. Ⓐ Ⓑ Ⓒ Ⓓ
39. Ⓐ Ⓑ Ⓒ Ⓓ
40. Ⓐ Ⓑ Ⓒ Ⓓ
41. Ⓐ Ⓑ Ⓒ Ⓓ
42. Ⓐ Ⓑ Ⓒ Ⓓ
43. Ⓐ Ⓑ Ⓒ Ⓓ
44. Ⓐ Ⓑ Ⓒ Ⓓ
45. Ⓐ Ⓑ Ⓒ Ⓓ
46. Ⓐ Ⓑ Ⓒ Ⓓ
47. Ⓐ Ⓑ Ⓒ Ⓓ
48. Ⓐ Ⓑ Ⓒ Ⓓ
49. Ⓐ Ⓑ Ⓒ Ⓓ
50. Ⓐ Ⓑ Ⓒ Ⓓ

NOTES

NOTES

NOTES

NOTES